Cases in Organizational Development

Cases in Organizational Development

Cab Baldwin
Chris Gould
Brad Cloys
Monty Palma
WALTSTER

Alan M. Glassman
California State University, Northridge

Thomas G. Cummings
University of Southern California

CASE ANALYSIS:
ENGINEERED MATERIALS

IRWIN

Homewood, IL 60430
Boston, MA 02116

Sponsoring editor: Craig S. Beytien
Project editor: Paula M. Buschman
Production manager: Diane Palmer
Cover designer: Mike Finkelman
Artist: Jay Benson
Compositor: Precision Typographers
Typeface: 10/12 Century Schoolbook
Printer: R. R. Donnelley & Sons Company

Library of Congress Cataloging-in-Publication Data

Cases in organizational development / [edited by] Alan M. Glassman,
 Thomas G. Cummings.
   p.   cm.
  ISBN 0-256-09937-5
   1. Organizational change—Case studies. I. Glassman, Alan M.
 II. Cummings, Thomas G.
 HD58.8.C373 1991
 658.4′063—dc20   90–33269
                                                     CIP

Printed in the United States of America
1 2 3 4 5 6 7 8 9 0 DO 7 6 5 4 3 2 1 0

Jonathan and Emily
Seth and Sarah
Our children, whose changes challenge us
to learn and develop

Preface

The idea for *Cases in Organizational Development* originated at an academic conference in Big Sky, Montana, in the spring of 1988. One evening while sitting around the fireplace and chatting with colleagues, we lamented the difficulty of teaching students about organization development (OD) without the benefit of case studies describing first hand what practitioners do when intervening in organizations. Case studies can be a powerful teaching method for linking concepts and techniques to practical problems. However, most existing cases describe specific organizational issues from a managerial perspective. We argued that teaching OD required cases describing the realities of organizational change from the vantage of the OD practitioner. This would provide students with concrete descriptions of what the OD process entails and allow them to place themselves into the change agent's role. It would challenge them to think about and describe what they would do if they were the practitioner in the case.

Although the need for practitioner-centered cases in OD was strongly shared by our colleagues around the fireplace, a major question about developing such cases quickly arose: Could we get OD practitioners, who tend to be heavily action oriented, to take the time to write personal accounts of their experiences? Both of us had previously encountered the typical problems in trying to get colleagues to write chapters for an academic book, and we expected the task of soliciting OD cases for a teaching text to be even worse.

Fortunately, our expectations could not have been more inaccurate. We invited a diversity of OD practitioners to contribute cases to this book. The response was overwhelmingly positive; some even asked if they could contribute more than one case. Equally surprising, we had few problems with contributors meeting deadlines and satisfying recommended changes in format. The quality and richness of the cases attest to the expertise and caring shown by the case writers. The cases demonstrate convincingly that OD is far more complex and uncertain than is typically portrayed in current OD texts. It is both art and science.

We would like to express our appreciation to the staff members at Richard D. Irwin, Inc. for their aid and encouragement. Special thanks go to Craig Beytien and Paula Buschman for their help in the development and production of this book.

Alan M. Glassman

Thomas G. Cummings

Contents

Cases in Organizational Development

Introduction: The Evolving Field of Organization Development

Thomas G. Cummings
University of Southern California
Alan M. Glassman
California State University, Northridge

Organization development (OD) is concerned with helping organizations solve problems and improve effectiveness. It involves applying behavioral science knowledge to the planned change of organizational structures and processes aimed at enhancing human resources, productivity, and environmental exchanges.

This introductory chapter describes the evolving nature of organization development, showing how the field has progressed since its beginnings in the late 1940s and where it is likely heading. Against this background, it is argued that practical learning about OD can be facilitated by case studies depicting what OD practitioners actually do in organizations. The cases help to explain the intricacies of OD and enable students to project themselves into the action so they can decide what to do in the situation.

The cases convey that organization development is a blend of scientific discipline and professional practice and that OD includes a diversity of concepts, methods, and applications. It is carried out by a variety of practitioners across a wide spectrum of private- and public-sector organizations. The chapter ends with a summary of the practical learnings that can be derived from studying the cases in this book. This provides a grounded understanding of the practice of OD as both an art and a science.

CURRENT TRENDS

In a little over four decades, organization development has progressed from a limited conceptual and practice base into a comprehensive approach to organizational improvement. The field has grown and ma-

tured, developing new concepts, techniques, and applications at a remarkable rate. Although this proliferation of theory and practice makes
it difficult to keep up with the evolving nature of the field, some discern-
ible trends help to identify how the field is developing.

Broader and Fuzzier Boundaries

During the early stages of OD in the 1950s and 1960s, the field was far
more coherent than it is today. Practitioners attended mainly to the social side of organizations, helping to overcome many of the dysfunctional consequences of rigid bureaucracy. They worked primarily with
managers to improve communications, decision making, and teamwork
and to resolve troublesome conflicts between work groups. OD practice
was heavily guided by concepts and methods from group dynamics and
interpersonal relations and by humanistic values promoting trust,
openness, and collaboration. The change process typically followed
Lewinian action research that emphasized collaboration between practitioners and clients and an evolving cycle of diagnostic, intervention,
and evaluation activities.

By the 1970s, the focus of OD expanded beyond the social side of organizations to include their technological and structural sides. Practitioners increasingly attended to how organizations divided labor into departments and coordinated across them and how work designs linked
people to technology. They helped organizations to structure themselves more productively and to provide employees with improved quality of work life. Concepts from industrial engineering, sociotechnical
systems, and organization theory guided these efforts, and OD's humanistic values were augmented with concerns for productivity and organizational effectiveness.

The 1980s witnessed explosive growth of the OD field. Fueled by stringent competitive pressures, rapid technological and economic change,
and globalization of the economy, organizations increasingly sought to
transform how they operated and related to their environment. OD
practitioners responded by developing a variety of interventions aimed
at redesigning organizations, changing their cultures, and aligning corporate strategy with external demands and opportunities. Concepts and
techniques from strategic management, human resources management, corporate culture, and organization theory became increasingly
relevant to OD. OD values of humanism and organization effectiveness
expanded to include concern for environmental relations and external
stakeholders, such as customers, competitors, owners, and government
regulators.

The expanding boundaries of the OD field over the past 40 years show that OD is robust and growing. Although the field has lost much of its initial coherence, its increasing variety of concepts, methods, and values are responsive to the changing needs of modern organizations. As those needs continue to expand and change in the coming years, OD can be expected to change accordingly, becoming broader yet more diffuse, making it harder to distinguish OD applications from other disciplines.

Greater Contingency Thinking

Historically, organization development has been highly normative, specifying how organizations should be designed and managed. Following humanistic values, practitioners have tended to prescribe organizational conditions promoting open communication and feedback, trust among managers and employees, and collaborative relationships among role holders and departments.

In recent years, the field has moved beyond this normative orientation to encompass a contingency perspective. This approach is based heavily on empirical research and proposes that the positive effects of organization designs and processes are contingent on fitting or aligning with certain contextual factors, such as the organization's environment, technology, and people. There is no one best way to organize or manage for all situations. Consequently, to achieve positive results, OD interventions, such as job enrichment, teambuilding, pay for performance, and strategic change, must be tailored to fit the situation.

So far, researchers have identified several contingencies as affecting the results of OD interventions (e.g., technology, environment, personality). An increasing amount of study is being devoted to uncovering additional limiting factors, and knowledge about the contingent effects of OD interventions should continue to grow. This contingency thinking will continue to move OD beyond its traditional normative stance toward a new science of improving organizations.

Larger-Scale Change Efforts

Organization development has traditionally focused on limited parts and features of organizations and on making them function more smoothly and effectively. In the 1960s, heavy emphasis was placed on management and staff teams and on helping them alleviate dysfunctional conflicts, decision making, and interpersonal relations that often occurred. During the 1970s, considerable attention was paid to work design on the shop floor and to making boring, repetitive jobs more challenging and motivating. In general, these efforts focused on subparts of the total organization and on fine-tuning them so they worked better.

More recently, OD has engaged increasingly in larger-scale change efforts involving most parts and features of organizations. This greater scale of change is more concerned with radically transforming the organization than with fine-tuning it. The need for such radical, large-scale change derives largely from the complexity and rapid change of today's environments. Public and private organizations are finding they cannot compete and be effective by simply doing what they already do better. Rather, they must fundamentally alter their strategies and how they operate, making themselves more streamlined and agile and more responsive to changing conditions.

Many of the newer OD concepts and interventions aim at helping organizations transform themselves. Change programs are increasingly geared to modifying most features of organizations including strategy, structure, work design, human resource practices, and information and control systems. The different features are aligned to support new strategic directions and to foster the kinds of values, beliefs, and norms needed to compete in today's complex and changing environment. Because these external conditions are likely to persist if not intensify, this shift in the perspective of OD to large-scale efforts should continue in the coming years.

Greater Management and Business Focus

Earlier OD efforts tended to focus on professional practitioners as the change agents and on social processes as the major change targets. Practitioners were generally consultants, either internal or external to the organization, and they used behavioral science concepts and jargon that were often foreign to managers and business settings.

The last decade has seen growing attention to general managers and administrators as the key agents of change and to business-related concerns as the primary change targets. This movement is evident in the increasing application of OD to business issues, such as strategic planning, budgeting, succession planning, and mergers and acquisitions. Moreover, greater numbers of managers and administrators are discovering the need to manage change continuously particularly in the face of highly turbulent and competitive conditions.

OD has increasingly become an integral part of the management role as well as a powerful tool to address business matters. Practitioners have adapted to this new focus by becoming more business oriented (i.e., more attentive to bottom-line results) and more involved in management development activities.

CASE STUDIES IN OD

Case studies depicting organizational behavior have long been an effective method of teaching practical applications in such areas as management, public administration, and organizational behavior. Generally, students are presented with a particular organizational problem from the perspective of an administrator or staff specialist, and they are asked to solve the issue from that position. Although OD concepts and methods can be applied to these cases, the case material tends to be heavily slanted to managerial and employee actions and only rarely addresses what OD change agents actually do. For students interested in learning to apply OD, this makes it difficult to understand the intricacies of the OD process and to project themselves into what is often a complex and messy change-agent role.

The cases in this book are an attempt to remedy this problem by providing rich descriptions of OD change efforts from the perspective of the change agent. The cases depict OD in a variety of private and public settings, detailing the kinds of issues and dilemmas that change agents typically encounter and their actual thinking and feelings as they made their choices. Consequently, students are afforded a firsthand account of the complex and evolving nature of the OD process and are able to place themselves in the position of the OD consultant. They are asked to take an active role and to prescribe what they would do in the situation.

PRACTITIONER'S PERSPECTIVE

The cases provide a realistic account of organization development in action; they offer a practitioner's perspective on OD, a view from the firing line that is often missing in texts on the topic. As an introduction, this section describes a number of common threads running through the cases.

OD Is Messy

OD is typically described as a linear process involving such steps as entry/contracting, diagnosis, and intervention. Although this book is organized around these stages, the cases portray a process that is far messier and nonlinear than generally described in the literature. For example, entry and contracting often involve preliminary diagnosis and some initial interventions. The act of entering an organization with the intention of possibly helping it improve itself constitutes an intrusive act no matter how skillfully accomplished.

Moreover, the different stages of OD often overlap, interact, and feed back on themselves. Practitioners, for instance, frequently have to modify initial contracts based on new information gained during diagnosis; they often continue to diagnose during intervention in order to assess how the change process is progressing and whether it needs to be modified.

OD Interventions Evolve

OD interventions have typically been described as discrete sets of activities with names such as teambuilding, conflict resolution, sociotechnical design, and culture change. In practice, however, interventions do not easily fit into such neat categories. Rather, they often evolve as the change process unfolds into a combination of interventions. For example, an organization may initially use a sociotechnical intervention to redesign jobs into self-regulating work teams. This may in turn require additional interventions aimed at reward systems and selection practices that may need to be changed to support the new team work design. Thus, what started as a sociotechnical intervention evolved into something far more complex involving different yet related interventions.

OD Embodies Art

The practice of OD is more art than science. Practitioners must not only know the requirements needed to intervene in an organization, but they must also be able to perform those change tasks personally. This personal competence is evident throughout the cases in this book and attests to the fact that OD is essentially a human practice requiring considerable personal skill and intuition. Practitioners do not simply go about facilitating change in a rote way, but are attuned to the nuances of the situation. They adapt to emerging events and make judgment calls with limited and often ambiguous data. They use experience, judgment, and skill to fill the unique and often changing needs of client organizations and to help them design change programs appropriate to their situations.

OD Requires Leadership

Although the role of organizational leaders has long been seen as a key ingredient of OD success, the cases in this book highlight the relationship between the OD practitioner and the organization leader, strongly suggesting that leaders are even more important than typically imagined. They are essential to initiating, managing, and sustaining organizational change. Organizational members are highly attuned to the behaviors and reinforcements of leaders, particularly when conditions are changing and likely to be ambiguous. Consequently, effective leaders take an active role in getting members to feel a strong need for change. They provide a clear vision of where the organization should be headed and of how it will get there. These leadership behaviors also include modeling the new way of operating and reinforcing others behaving similarly.

OD Involves Power

Power means getting others to do what you want. It has traditionally had a negative connotation in OD because it has been seen as something underhanded and manipulative, thwarting OD values of trust, openness, and collaboration. The cases in this book, however, provide a more positive view of power and show that change agents often use various sources of power to carry out successful organizational change.

Managers and administrators, for example, employ their position and the ability to reward and punish to initiate and reinforce changes. They also take advantage of information and resource networks to gain support for change and, in a few cases, use their charisma to motivate others to change. OD consultants often use their expertise and access to both the leader and information sources to gain the power needed to facilitate change. Although the use of power can be manipulative, it can just as readily be used to facilitate positive change and to empower others.

OD Practitioners Play Varied Roles

The cases in this book show that OD practitioners play a diversity of roles depending on the situation and circumstances. At one moment, they may be process facilitators helping groups manage how they accomplish tasks. At other times, they may provide specific content knowledge about how to do things. Similarly, practitioners may alternate between being analysts of organizational functioning and being active interveners into organization structures and processes. They may listen empathetically to people's problems and at other times confront them about incongruous behaviors. These different roles are all legitimate parts of OD practice, and skillful practitioners know when and how to perform them. They fit these roles to the unfolding change situation and the shifting needs of clients.

OD Generates Ethical Dilemmas

Because OD is a helping profession, practitioners invariably face issues about what behaviors are in the best interest of the client organization. The cases in this book show that practitioners sometimes encounter thorny ethical dilemmas that are not easily resolved.

The issues and their outcomes can be seen from conflicting perspectives, making it difficult to know what is the right or wrong solution. For example, change agents are often privy to information that is highly confidential, yet, if made available, could significantly help some person or group. At other times, OD practitioners find that their values and/or personal desires for an outcome clash with the client's demands, creating internal conflict on appropriate actions. Answers to these kinds of issues are rarely straightforward, and OD practitioners spend considerable time agonizing over what response is right for the client.

## Part I

Entering and Contracting

The cases in this part involve the first stage of organization development, entering and contracting with the client organization. OD consultants, whether internal or external to the client system, establish an initial relationship with potential clients to find out their needs for OD, their readiness for change, and whether the consultant has the skills and experience appropriate to satisfy those needs. This process typically entails scouting the situation to gain preliminary understanding of the client's issues and expectations. In many cases, the scouting reveals that the client's stated problems are symptoms of underlying issues. It may also show that the initial identification of the client may need to be expanded to include other organizational stakeholders and units.

Once scouting determines there is an appropriate match between the client's needs and the consultant's expertise, the two parties establish a relationship. This generally involves both a psychological contract, where the parties develop a personal commitment to working with each other, and a legal contract specifying the terms of the collaborative effort. This latter contract may include the client's expectations and goals for the OD project, the consultant's tasks, time schedules, terms of payment, and other ground rules. The contracting stage of OD is rarely finalized, and consultants and clients often return and modify it as the change process unfolds and unexpected events occur.

In "The Castor Company," Glenn H. Varney and Richard Ward describe the preliminary scouting that occurs before forming an OD contract. Initially contacted to help solve a problem with setting objectives in a wheel caster firm, the two consultants show vividly how different stakeholders' perceptions of the company's problems can diverge. Moreover, observed symptoms can signal a more fundamental problem than originally imagined.

Craig C. Lundberg, in "Kenworth Motors," describes the mental preparation that takes place before entering a client organization for the first time. His assumptions and scenarios about what might happen reveal much about the consultant's biases and values. His account of the initial meeting with the client shows the kinds of questions that consultants typically ask when trying to discover the client's needs.

"State Transportation," by Rupert R. Chisholm and Robert F. Munzenrider, indicates the complexity involved in trying to contract for an evaluation of a productivity improvement program in a government maintenance repair shop. The consultants, members of a state quality-of-work-life center, encounter divergent and ambiguous goals for the evaluation project from politicians, unions, administrators, and employees. They show the difficulty of contracting for OD in the public sector where politics and goal conflicts are more the rule than the exception.

In "Commercial Fertilizer (A)," Achilles A. Armenakis and Henry B. Burdg describe the mutual questioning and feeling out that occur between clients and consultants during the entry process. The authors, representing a university-affiliated consulting center, show how OD consultants often have to explain their services and way of working to clients having only a vague idea of what consultants have to offer.

The Castor Company

Glenn H. Varney
Bowling Green State University
Richard Ward
Bowling Green State University

It was an early spring morning and the phone call was a welcome interruption from several mundane office tasks. The voice at the other end of the line exclaimed, "Glenn, how are you? It's been a long time since I've talked to you!"

The caller was Bill S., an old friend. It had been some 20 years since I last had contact with him. I was delighted to hear his career had progressed smoothly since our last meeting; he was now president of the Castor Company, a profit-center subsidiary of a major corporation.

After we renewed our acquaintance, Bill explained he was prompted to call by an article of mine concerning Management by Objectives (MBO). He had discovered the article while searching for a way to deal with a serious problem, and he wondered if I might be able to help him with it.

He and his staff members had established a set of objectives for his division that had been accepted by the parent company. The problem was that his division was not achieving these objectives. Further, he believed that some of his staff were unclear about the goals they were to achieve, since there appeared to be, at best, a very disjointed effort at goal achievement. Bill, although not desperate, was very anxious about the ability of his division to deliver on the promises he had made to the parent company. He realized I probably was very busy, but could I find the time to help him out?

I was not about to turn down an old friend who had what he described as an MBO problem when I had some expertise in MBO. Because it was difficult to obtain additional insights over the phone, Bill agreed that I, and perhaps an associate, would visit his plant. Once we had obtained a better appreciation of his problem, we could prepare a proposal for how to approach it.

The next day, I asked Dick, an associate, to join me in this visit. I explained that Bill, an old friend, had described his problem as an MBO problem, and that he was asking for help in re-energizing his organization. It was not clear whether we would have a contract with this organization. However, the organization appeared to be open to OD kinds of processes and technology, and we would be expected to prepare a proposal, out of which could come a substantive contract to assist the organization. Dick responded with enthusiasm, so we contacted Bill to set up a time to visit with him and his staff at their location.

BACKGROUND INFORMATION

After establishing a date for our visit, I asked Bill to send us information about the firm and the community. Bill sent a fact sheet about the company, a Chamber of Commerce booklet designed to promote the community, and a two-year old attitude survey of company employees. Included with these items was a note from Bill suggesting that we call him if we needed any additional information.

According to its fact sheet, the Castor Company is about 75 years old. The firm was owned by a prominent local family until three years ago, when it was purchased by a major corporation seeking forward integration. The Castor Company produces 250 types of wheel casters, ranging in size from half inch wheels to units that are as large as eight feet in diameter. These casters are made in a stamping and assembly operation in a 900-employee main plant and in two satellite plants employing about 150 individuals each. Casters are produced to customer order in a batch operation that requires significant setup time for each order.

The Chamber of Commerce booklet summarizes the community as a "pleasant city of 100,000 hard working individuals" located along the Ohio River. The Castor Company is one of several manufacturing organizations in the area that are subsidiaries of major firms. The booklet points out that these subsidiaries are fortunate enough to possess a product mix that is relatively invulnerable to economic changes. Further, the chamber claims the community's cost of living is moderate, when compared with other communities of comparable size.

Despite its size, this community apparently is very close-knit. The chamber's booklet says, "Everyone knows everyone!" According to the booklet, the community is infused by a tremendous local loyalty and civic pride. For example, while the local high school was winning a recent state basketball tournament, the city "turned itself into a giant cheering section." According to the chamber, another source of community athletic pride is the local college, which is "developing a national reputation" among institutions in its class.

Of the three documents, we were the most interested in the attitude survey. Two years ago, about when Bill was being hired, the University of Chicago was completing a previously contracted attitude survey of all unionized employees of the Castor Company. This survey asked how employees felt about their benefits, compensation, working relationships, working conditions, safety, and supervision. Some of the key findings growing out of the study are summarized in Exhibit 1.

BREAKFAST WITH BILL

The visit to the Castor Company's plant was planned as a daylong activity. First, we would spend some time with Bill. Next, we would meet with his team, followed by a tour of the main plant. At the end of the day, we would give Bill our recommendation concerning the next steps to take.

Bill met us at the airport. As he drove us to a restaurant for breakfast, he summarized the current situation at the company with the statement, "Things were moving along nicely." However, he expressed concern about the way in which the plant was falling behind the goals stated in its annual plan. He mentioned he had alerted everybody to our visit. He assured us everything was set for what promised to be a productive day.

At breakfast, Bill again commented on the need to "get the organization moving." As he discussed this point, it became apparent he was concerned about how he could explain the plant's variance in goal achievement to his boss at the next quarterly review meeting to be held in Chicago.

I asked Bill to fill in the gaps left by the firm's fact sheet and the Chamber of Commerce booklet. Bill said area residents describe the Castor Company as a "hire and retire" organization, in which "you could come in right out of school and work till you retired." On the average, the work force is between 45 and 50 years old, although employee ages range widely. The overwhelming majority of employees are white males; the division employs only 100 females and a very small number of minorities.

According to Bill, the plant is unionized, primarily because the community has a strong pro-union orientation. However, he warned us not to think of the employees as "typical union members." Virtually all Castor Company's employees are long-term local residents, and many are related to one another. As Bill explained it, the result is a "family" orientation in the plant culture. In addition, employees have a very traditional way of thinking about how an organization should operate and, according to Bill, a high degree of loyalty and commitment to the Castor Company.

I next asked Bill for his reaction to the University of Chicago attitude survey. In response, Bill asked us for our perceptions of the study find-

EXHIBIT 1   University of Chicago Attitude Survey: Employee Responses to Selected Survey Items (based on 356 responses—39.6% response rate)

To What Extent Do You:	Very Small Extent 1	2	Moderate Extent 3	4	Very Large Extent 5
Feel that you receive a fair wage for the work you do?	0%	5%	25%	60%	10%
Feel that you have a good benefits package?	0	8	32	55	5
Believe that the company is well-managed?	5	30	50	12	3
Feel that your immediate supervisor is helpful to you in doing your work?	0	1	41	30	28
Feel that your own working conditions are healthy & safe?	8	21	70	1	0
Feel that the future of your job is secure?	0	2	41	38	19

ings. Dick commented that the workers appeared to see themselves as well paid, with good fringe benefits, and Bill nodded with satisfaction. I said the employees seem to believe that their jobs are secure, and Bill showed obvious pleasure in his agreement. When I asked for his reaction, Bill indicated that a variety of minor complaints were revealed by the survey. However, he was emphatic in stating that no really significant problems were uncovered.

Before leaving the restaurant, we asked Bill for some background information on the managers we would be meeting. Bill gave us some basic data on each of several managers and apologized for not thinking to send that information to us before our visit. His comments are summa-

EXHIBIT 2   The Castor Company's Management Team

Name	Castor Service (years)	Age	Education	Experience	Title
Bill	2	52	Attorney	Former CEO, small metal distributing company	President
Jack	40	62	Mechanical engineer	Started as a Castor Co. engineer and worked up to present job	Manufacturing vice president; reports to the president
Dennis	8	44	Bachelor of science in liberal arts obtained at the local college	Worked for four local firms; was promoted from plant ER job at Castor Co.	Employee relations manager; staff position; reports to the president
Will	1.5	38	Industrial engineer	Previously employed as industrial engineer at General Motors	Plant manager; reports to the manufacturing vice president

[handwritten margin notes: "potential prob.— bringing in someone from the outside" with arrow to President row; "hard to read"; "tension" with bracket pointing to Dennis and Will rows]

rized in Exhibit 2. Bill summed up his views on his "management team" in the following way:

> I have a cadre of very competent people. I am confident that, once we start pulling together, we can manage this organization in a way that will help us meet the goals to which we have made a commitment. I think there is some tension among the members of my staff, particularly between Dennis and Will. Jack is a little hard to read, but he has been supportive and helpful in all his efforts.

Finally, Bill outlined his intentions for the day. First, he would take us back to his office and spend about an hour reviewing the problem from his perspective. Next, he would bring in his key managers and we could obtain their perspectives. Following this meeting, we would go to lunch at the country club and then tour the plant. If we wished, we then could meet individually with each of the key managers. Finally, we would meet with Bill to present our recommendations before we departed at the end of the day.

We accepted this schedule with only one exception. We asked Bill for what we called "sink" time before the final meeting with him. We explained we would need a chance to organize what we had seen during the day before we could make a useful presentation to Bill. Bill said that this change was no problem.

When we approached the plant, Bill drove his company car into his private garage, one of 10 made available for the cars of company executives. We walked in through a side door and then up to the plant office's second floor. We followed Bill into a corner office, where we were greeted by Bill's secretary. Bill asked us to wait in the reception area while he attended to some details "that couldn't wait." We shed our coats, cheerfully accepted the secretary's offer of coffee, and took advantage of the extra time to quietly chat about the information we had obtained at breakfast.

We were both impressed with Bill's candidness in outlining what was of concern to him. He seemed sincere but not overly concerned. One point we both picked up on was his apparent uncertainty about what he expected us to do for him. He repeatedly stated he "needs help in figuring out what to do next." This surprised us because we shared a stereotype of an attorney as a good fact finder and a logical problem solver. Why was Bill failing to resolve this problem?

When Bill returned, we entered his office. Bill started the discussion by reviewing some basic data and statistics about the main plant's product line. The conversation quickly turned to the goals that Bill was trying to achieve. He estimated the plant was running from 5 to 8 percent behind target on each of a variety of performance measures, including volume and profit. Bill believed the actions of his staff were somehow preventing those at lower levels of the organization from being committed to the plant's goals or appreciating the role they play in achieving the goals.

As an illustration, Bill pointed out that Will and Dennis do not speak to each other unless absolutely necessary. Further, Will has nothing good to say about the employee relations manager, and Dennis has a similar view of the plant manager. The tension between the two appears to arise from a major disagreement about implementing the plant's new time standards. Dennis (according to Will, a member of the old school) wants every change in the plant to be discussed with the union. Will, on the other hand, believes that most changes, and especially the new standards, should be imposed on the plant rather than negotiated.

Mention of the union triggered a recollection from Bill. Several weeks ago, Bill was lunching at the country club when the community's mayor visited his table. The mayor expressed concern about rumors circulating about the Castor Company. He had heard there was going to be a "major revolution" in the plant's union; within the next four to eight weeks, either the union's leadership was going to be changed or the union was going to be decertified.

EXHIBIT 3   Seating Arrangement

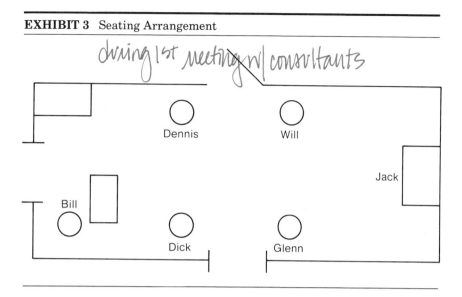

during 1st meeting w/ consultants

Since this rumor caught Bill by surprise, he questioned its accuracy. The mayor said he knew many families who worked at the Castor plant and he was sure what they had told him was accurate. After that meeting, Bill had shared the rumor with both Will and Jack, the vice-president of manufacturing. Both managers agreed the rumor was "utter nonsense." They believed no problems existed in the union and there simply was no possibility of a decertification drive.

Now that he thought about it, Bill was not so sure that a potential union problem should be dismissed so easily. If the union was facing a problem, it might explain part of the plant's inability to reach its goals. Bill wasn't sure how the union situation fit in, but he had a growing feeling that maybe it should be looked into, if for no other reason than the great variation between the mayor's story and the reaction of his managers.

THE STAFF MEETING

At the end of about 45 minutes of discussion, Bill called in Will, Dennis, and Jack. We both stood to Bill's introductions and were asked to sit in the two seats located across from the office door. When everyone was settled in, the seating pattern in the office was arranged as shown in Exhibit 3.

At the time, this arrangement did not seem very important to us. However, as we watched the evolving activity in the office, we began to realize the position of each manager was significant. For example, the plant manager was positioned next to the vice president to whom he reported. The employee relations manager sat adjacent to Bill and at a considerable distance from the plant manager. We weren't sure why we had been asked to move our seats, but it didn't seem likely that the request was without purpose. Interestingly, the seating arrangements evolved before the arrival of Will, who came in about 15 minutes later than the other two. We filled the time with idle chatter.

Bill began by proposing that this meeting should serve two purposes: (1) finding ways to improve the organization's goal-setting process and (2) finding ways to improve communications. Bill added that he had asked Dick and me to join the group because he knew we had worked with similar problems in other firms and he believed we could be of help to the plant. Bill finished his introduction by stating his wish that staff members would welcome and cooperate with us.

Bill asked us to explain our background and our roles and how we thought we could assist the plant. We emphasized ethical considerations of importance to us, such as our belief in confidentiality. We also stressed that we had not yet been hired. We were present to help examine the problem; we would stay only if we thought we could help solve it.

Bill then reviewed the two problems as he saw them. He again mentioned the problem of goal setting, and he reviewed the story of the mayor's rumor as an example of a possible communication problem. He then asked for Jack's opinion concerning the two issues. The vice president responded that he did not share Bill's belief that these are major issues. However, he said that he was willing to look more carefully at the goal-setting issue. It might be a good idea to examine the goal-setting process to see if it could be made better.

At this point, Will interrupted the president with an outburst: "I don't understand why we are here. We are quite capable of running this plant without any outside assistance." This took us by surprise and the look on Jack's face suggested that others did not expect this behavior. Our own reactions were surprise and concern that we had walked into a major conflict between Bill, Jack, and Will. Bill patiently suggested the group should "examine the problem anyway and see if there is any way in which Glenn and Dick can be of assistance to us."

The plant manager then effectively took over the meeting with a steady flow of statements. Will said he thought the plant's goals were perfectly clear. Further, he knew exactly what he was supposed to do and how to do it, and he didn't need any outsiders telling him how to do his job. He pointed to the new time standards he was using and cited several examples of how these had increased productivity. He also pointed out that 50 percent of all the time standards were now installed. Moreover, the union was accepting the time standard process without any questions. Finally Will directly challenged us: "What do you think you can do that we can't do?"

Problems w/Will's behavior

This very challenging question triggered another question in my mind: Why is Will so agitated by our presence? One hypothesis might be that Will is using deflecting behavior in an attempt to head off any investigation of activity in the plant. A second question naturally arises: What is Will trying to hide?

We diverted his challenge with an honest response. We pointed out that we are not industrial engineers and that we know very little about how to establish and instill time standards. However, we stressed that we do know how to help organizations diagnose problems and find ways to solve them.

At this point, Bill intervened. He acknowledged that progress had been made in the plant and he was pleased with the time standards and the way they were being installed. However, Bill then returned to his earlier theme—even though plant productivity had improved, he believed there was less than total commitment to the goal achievement expected by the parent company.

Bill then expressed his concern about how the union might be handling the installation of time standards. He pointed to "rumblings" from the community that suggested many workers were significantly unhappy about the installation process. Will's reaction was sharp: "What're you talking about? I've told you this isn't a problem. Don't you believe me?" Bill responded that the mayor's rumor suggested two sides to the issue and that he simply wanted to get to the bottom of the problem. Will was adamant: "All is well in the union. Just who are you going to believe—the insiders or the outsiders?"

It was interesting to watch Bill and Will's interactions because they helped to sharpen our focus on the underlying issues behind their behavior. It seemed to us that two divergent points of view were emerging from this discussion. The next logical question is which perception more accurately reflects what is actually happening in the plant.

Will's position was abundantly clear, and Bill had clarified his position—his concern was with how the time standards were being implemented rather than whether they were being implemented. Bill appeared to be too much of a gentleman to force his position on Will despite the fact the interaction between the two had taken up about 70 percent of the meeting time to this point. Will seemed very sure of himself, possibly because of his extensive experience in productivity standards. In addition, it was clear that Will has a very strong and dominant personality.

Dennis, in contrast, had no opportunity to speak during the hour and a half we all invested in the meeting. Jack had several opportunities to speak but had not taken advantage of any of them. Our impression of Jack was that he is a considerate and cooperative person who was behaving in a very subdued and shy manner. Dennis also appeared to be a quiet and nonassertive person, but it was our impression that he remained on the verge of an explosion throughout the meeting.

In view of the time, Bill suggested that we break for lunch at the country club. When we stood up to leave, Will stepped over to Dick and me and quietly suggested that we ride out to the country club with him. We agreed and Will escorted us to his car. During the 15-minute ride to the country club, Will kept reiterating his theme that there was no problem in the plant. He had, he said, done an outstanding job of installing the standards; they were now accepted by employees and in fact were causing plant productivity to improve. We should listen to him and not to others in the plant. We especially should not be misled by conversations Bill had with outsiders.

Although all of the group arrived at the country club at the same time, Will entered the facility slightly ahead of the others. He arranged for our table and then positioned himself between Dick and me with Bill across the table from us. Throughout lunch, Will continued to dominate the conversation. Most of his comments concerned steps he had taken to improve plant operations.

After lunch, we returned with Bill, who made no mention of any of the morning's conversations. He spent the 15-minute trip explaining the diversity of the firm's product lines and the problems this diversity created for the plant. When we arrived at the plant, the employee relations manager announced he would join Will, Dick, and me on the plant tour. Dennis explained he wanted to get out into the plant as often as possible and saw our tour as a good excuse to do so.

Although Will started as our tour guide, within a few moments he had disappeared to talk to an individual who appeared to be a supervisor. The three of us paused because Dick and I were unsure about what we were watching and Dennis didn't seem eager to take Will's place. We did ask Dennis what he thought of the plant. His answer was blunt: "It's a mess! It is a depressingly poor place to work, and generally speaking, it's not a very healthy environment."

Will rejoined us and the tour continued, although at a start and stop pace. Will would constantly dash off to talk to someone and then return to point things out to us. We noticed that operators would try to disappear as the plant manager would approach their area and would reappear after he had passed. It became obvious that people in the plant were not interested in communicating with the plant manager or, to our surprise, with us. For example, during one of Will's side trips, we stepped over to one operator and asked how he felt about his job. His exact response was: "Get the hell away from me—I don't want to be seen talking to you!"

Our overall impression of the plant was that it was dark and dirty and in generally poor condition. It was very old, and its equipment was antiquated. In addition, it seemed that the plant was a very unfriendly and uncomfortable place for outsiders to enter. From our perspective, the plant could have only a negative impact on the way people felt about the company and their jobs.

Interviews:

Jack

Will

Dennis

After the plant tour, we had interviews with the vice president, the plant manager, and the employee relations manager. The meeting with the vice president lasted only 30 minutes. The tone of the meeting was very positive; Jack expressed great pleasure about the plant's progress. He stated that this change (involving the time standards) was long overdue and that Will needed everyone's support to make it work. Jack stressed that he would do anything to make the time standards successful, including hiring us if we could be of value to the project!

The meeting with the plant manager lasted an hour. Will continued to present his basic message: The time standards worked and they increased productivity. He repeatedly pointed out how he was using what he had learned at General Motors. In his opinion, the Castor Company had been in dire need of the kinds of talents and experiences he brought to the plant.

Another of Will's themes was the lack of talent shown by the employee relations manager. In his opinion, Dennis was weak, a union sympathizer, and out of touch with what was going on in the plant. Unless he was required to do so by higher authority (Bill or Jack), Will would have nothing to do with Dennis. Will's final point was his belief that no need existed for outside help. However, if we could help the rest of the organization understand what Will was trying to accomplish, then he would be willing to have us work with the company.

Our final interview was with the employee relations manager. Dennis started by expressing warm feelings toward Bill and the vice president. However, the topic quickly shifted to Dennis's growing anger and frustration with the plant manager. In Dennis's opinion, Will was single-handedly destroying the morale and commitment of the plant's work force. Dennis said the plant had an unusual labor relations history. The plant had been unionized for a long time, but the workers were very loyal to the company. The union had never been very strong, but it had earned the full support of the rank and file.

Now, Will's time standards (Dennis hissed this phrase through clenched teeth) threatened to upset the delicate balance of worker loyalties. The union had succumbed to the plant manager's pressure and was not fighting back on some of the less reasonable time standards. As a result, the rank and file now feel the union betrayed them. Dennis described the plant as a time bomb that could blow up at any time.

From Dennis's perspective, the worst aspect of the situation was his inability to do anything to resolve these problems. As an example, Dennis explained that he had been forbidden to enter the production area without the permission of the plant manager or without being escorted by a member of Will's staff. Dennis complained to us that this rule prevented him from gaining any meaningful access to employees and union officials. However, he was still held accountable for union relationships and contract administration processes within the plant.

EXHIBIT 4   Diagram of Consultant's Perceptions

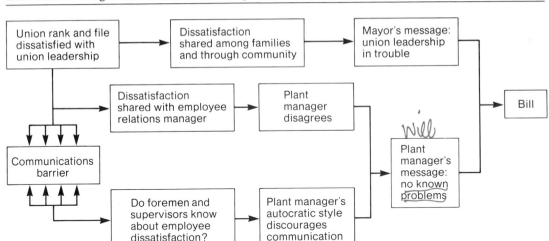

Following these interviews, Dick and I reminded Bill that we wanted to take about 30 minutes of "sink" time to think through a day's worth of observations. Bill provided us with the plant's conference room, and for the next half hour, we discussed what we had seen. Using the conference room's blackboard, we evolved the diagram shown in Exhibit 4 to summarize our perceptions.

The diagram illustrates our belief that there is a major communication break or barrier between the plant's production employees and its management team. We do not believe Will constitutes that barrier; the sincerity he showed during our meetings with him suggests he is simply not receiving information from the employees. In the past, when normal channels failed to operate, the employees had two alternative channels: the union and the employee relations manager. However, now the union appears to be selling out to the plant manager, and Dennis is not seen by the plant manager as a credible source.

We think information Bill received from the community probably is correct and the message he was getting from the plant manager was incorrect, although undoubtedly sincere. This is the basic conclusion we presented to Bill when we returned to his office and showed him our diagram. Bill expressed interest in our perceptions and wondered aloud whether Will's management style was a major factor in the communications problem. He also expressed concern about the poor relationship between Will and Dennis.

As we discussed the situation with Bill, he made no further reference to the goal-setting process. Somehow, that issue had washed out, and Bill was now focusing exclusively on the communications issue. Bill began to wonder about whether he had picked the right man for the plant manager position. He pointed out that Will would undoubtedly resist any attempt to deal with the problem as we had defined it. We acknowledged his concern, but suggested that Will might not be as great a difficulty as Bill thought. We believed Will was as concerned as the rest of the team about a performance problem; he simply didn't agree with the way others had analyzed or diagnosed it. Bill seemed relieved by our reassurances.

In this final meeting with Bill, it became apparent to us that we had initially underestimated the pressure Bill felt from his superiors. Bill apparently had been holding off this pressure in hopes that his team would resolve these issues, but that prospect seemed less likely as time passed. Now, Bill seemed unsure of what to do next. His final question to us was direct and to the point: "What can I do about this situation?"

We requested two weeks to formulate a report that would summarize our observations and hypotheses about the plant's problems and their apparent causes. We would include a contract proposal that explained how we planned to verify our hypotheses and design an intervention to resolve the plant's problems. The proposal would specify the actions we would want the firm to take, the role we would play in these actions, who would be involved and the roles that they should play, and finally how much time and money the proposal would require. Bill agreed to our next step and arranged for out return to the airport. As the plane took off, we had already started on the report outline.

[handwritten margin note: Present a Report]

QUESTIONS FOR DISCUSSION

1. Do you agree with our preliminary hypotheses about the communications problem and its causes? What facts in the case support our perceptions?

2. What other alternative hypotheses fit the case facts and observations? What facts in the case support these alternative hypotheses?

3. What initially led Bill to believe the problem was his management system (MBO) rather than a problem involving a communications breakdown?

ASSIGNMENT

Given either your hypotheses or our hypotheses about conditions at the Castor Company, prepare a contract proposal that explains how the hypotheses will be verified and an appropriate intervention will be designed. Be sure to include all of the information we promised to provide in the proposal.

Kenworth Motors

Craig C. Lundberg

Cornell University

It began with a telephone call, as did so many of my engagements. The person calling identified himself as Robert Denton, the plant manager of Kenworth Motors' Seattle truck manufacturing operations. Denton said he'd gotten my name from Charles Wright, a client of mine in Seattle. Charlie is the OD manager for a major timber products company. I'd been doing several projects with Charlie's group of internal consultants for the past three years and occasionally served as the OD group's consultant. Denton noted that Charlie and he were members of the same sailing club. He went on to say that when, as someone relatively new to Seattle, he'd asked Charlie if he knew any consultants, Charlie had spoken highly of me. I remember thinking that Charlie probably wouldn't have mentioned me unless he thought I could be useful to Denton. My trust in Charlie's competence and judgment was very high.

Denton went on to explain that he'd been the plant manager for only eight months, that things seemed to be going well, but that he had a gnawing sense that things could be better. I must have murmured something appropriate because Denton invited me to visit him and become acquainted with his operation.

I was both flattered by and interested in Denton's invitation. After all, I thought to myself, it's nice to be wanted, a consulting engagement might come out of it, I always wanted to get behind the gate of the Kenworth plant, and Denton sounded like a basically smart guy and nice besides. However, reality intruded into my thoughts, as it often does.

THOUGHTS ON THE ROAD

I reminded Denton that I lived across the state in Spokane and added that I had limited time available in the short run. I noted that I had plans to visit Seattle in three weeks and could see him then, otherwise it might not be for a month. Denton sounded almost eager as he agreed to a 10 A.M. appointment on April 11.

The drive westward from Spokane across the state of Washington on Interstate 90 begins with several hours of boring highway. I had purposely put off thinking about my appointment with Robert Denton until I was on the road. As the interstate stretched out over the rolling sagebrush hills and checkered wheat fields, I turned my thoughts to Kenworth Motors and Denton. Uppermost in my mind was that I was about to talk with a man I knew little about, consult with a firm I knew very little about, and I had no focused agenda. What should I say and do?

As the miles went by, I envisioned several alternative scenarios for my upcoming appointment with Robert Denton, the plant manager of the truck manufacturing division of Kenworth Motors Corporation. I saw his office in several possible ways. It could be spartan and centrally located to the production floor. It could be conventionally furnished but of a fair size. It could be large. It might even be opulent. It could be personalized with mementos of career, hobbies, or family. It might be far from the production floor, or even in a separate building. The more I tried to envision Denton's office, the more alternatives came to mind. So I focused on Denton, trying to imagine him from the voice cues on the telephone—not old, probably fit, probably clean shaven. Again the futility of trying to imagine came home to me.

What did I think I knew? I didn't know much beyond a handful of facts about his title and his job tenure, the fact that he knew Charlie, believed things were generally going OK at the plant, and had some vague notion something wasn't quite right. I also had the distinct impression he had been fairly eager to talk with me—after all, he'd initiated calling me and had quickly settled for an appointment convenient to me.

What did I really want to accomplish when I met with Denton? The more I considered this question, the more I pared down my answers. At minimum, it seemed for me a low-cost situation—a couple of hours of my time, perhaps some impressions of me that would be communicated to Charlie (though I believed Charlie and I had a relationship of mutual respect and trust based on a lot of shared work). On the other hand, there was potentially a lot to gain—perhaps another consulting job, perhaps more visibility and reputation in Seattle, which would be good for my business.

I decided I couldn't plan for our meeting in much detail; about all I could reasonably do was to be true to the posture I found to be useful in situations like this. I had to be myself, be as real as possible. I see myself as a curious, friendly person who basically likes others. I also know I can be bold and thought I might have to be to get the conversation going, to help Denton become clear as to why we were talking together, and to clarify my role.

I also wanted to leave our meeting with a decision to either go forward or not. While I didn't mind investing a little time, my time was valuable.

what to do at the Meeting

I also felt strongly, as I always do, that I didn't want to work with anyone who I didn't basically like as a person or who didn't seem to genuinely want to do some real work. Seeing the Cascade mountains on the horizon, I began to feel easier. I'd be myself, whatever happened. Only one question nagged: Could Denton and I connect swiftly enough so there would be time to push for clarity in our possible work relationship?

MAKING CONTACT

At the Kenworth plant, the uniformed guard at the plant gate checked his clipboard, slipped around my car, and copied down my license plate number. Returning to my open window, he pointed ahead to a one-story brick building attached to the multistoried plant and told me I could park in the space in front and then go inside and identify myself to the receptionist.

The floor of the wide hallway inside the double glass doors of the office building was freshly waxed. Framed photographs of trucks and large buildings lined the walls. A middle-aged woman in a suit looked up from her desk and smiled. After I identified myself, she led me down a side corridor to an alcove and informed the secretary there who I was and that I was there to see Mr. Denton. She then turned to me, smiled again, and wished me a good day. The seated secretary told me Mr. Denton was expecting me, but was on the telephone. She gestured toward a bank of chairs and asked me to wait. As I sat down, I observed the corridor traffic, busy but quiet. I settled back to wait.

About 10 minutes later, a man of medium height and build wearing a sports jacket over an open-collared shirt came through the door behind the secretary and walked directly to me. He extended his hand, smiled, introduced himself as Bob Denton and motioned me into his office.

The office was larger than I expected. It was paneled and a large Persian rug was centered on the floor. At one end were a clean desk with side chairs and a table full of papers behind it. At the other side of the office were a couch and two stuffed chairs around a low coffee table. Drapes framed one large window that looked out on the parking lot. Denton asked if I wanted coffee, and I said I did. He went to the door and asked the secretary to bring us both coffee and added we were not to be disturbed. While waiting for the coffee, we sat on the two stuffed chairs and made small talk. He asked about my drive across the state; I asked about the framed sailing prints on the wall and whether he'd been sailing lately. We chatted about the Sonics, the Kingdome, and the coming World's Fair in Vancouver. After our coffee arrived, I asked him to tell me about his plant and products.

Denton spoke excitedly for 10 or 12 minutes on a wide range of topics—the daily production rate of 23 trucks, the cost of a truck, the sales order backlog, some equipment updating just finished, his coming to this job from a plant in the Midwest, his spending a lot of time lately with the next year's budget, and so forth. My impression of Denton was that he was highly involved in his work. He spoke rapidly but clearly with enthusiasm. Finally, he leaned back, smiled, and said, "Well, I've been going on, haven't I?" I remember thinking I liked Denton's ease and his willingness to talk about his plant and himself. I'd already learned a lot about the plant and his job without more than looking interested. Denton certainly did seem likable, and he was younger and more casual than I expected.

GETTING DOWN TO BUSINESS

I clearly recall my response to Denton's question. "Actually, I've appreciated your sharing all this background with me. I've always been curious about this plant. Years ago, I had a part-time job when I was in college and used to deliver some industrial supplies in this end of town and always wanted to know what happened in this plant. All I could see from the road were those lines of big shiny trucks. It's nice to know they're built with care. But you asked for this meeting, Bob. Remember you told me that while things were going well here you sensed something wasn't quite right. Can you tell me a little more now?"

"Not really. I know the plant is doing fine. I feel pretty much on top of my job. I like what I'm doing here very much. My department heads—all nine of them—are all good people. All but two have been here quite a while. They're dependable, damn good at what they do, get along fine, and basically are good managers," he said.

"I get along good with everyone. I go out in the plant every day and circulate around. Things are moving smoothly. My two newer managers—one runs our purchasing and inventory, the other is in personnel—couldn't be working out better. Yet some things nag at me that I can't put my finger on. I guess it boils down to some crazy notion I have that while we get along fine and work together well, we haven't jelled together as a team quite like I'd hoped."

I bombarded Denton with questions, trying to find something that didn't hang together or might indicate a problem. No matter what I asked about—from union relations to accounts receivable, from engineering-production relations to turnover figures—Denton's responses were consistently factual and full, and everything seemed to be in remarkably good shape.

I caught myself from going on with more questions. Instead I said, "Bob, everything I've been asking about tells me you're OK. Maybe things here really are OK. Maybe you've just got some apprehension that things couldn't be that good. After all, you've been here long enough to really know. While there is some chance that you're not well informed, and some things aren't so hot, the odds are against it. About all I can suggest is whether you might want someone like me to independently confirm how things are going." Denton smiled as if to himself and replied, "Hmm, maybe, what would you suggest?"

"What's usually done in situations like this, if there is the interest and if there is the money to pay for it, is to engage someone like me to spend a few days interviewing a sample of managers and other key staff people to see what might turn up."

"From what you've heard so far, do you think that makes sense here?" Denton asked.

"Frankly, I don't know. It might be worth it to you just to learn things really are OK. What usually happens, however, is that I do find out about something that could be improved. After all that's what I'm supposed to be good at, finding problems. One way or another, Bob, the mere fact I was here would have some impact. The word would spread pretty fast that some outsider was snooping around. What impact that might have I can't say. If things really are OK, my presence might mean little. If there are real problems, my being here would probably create some tensions, it could raise expectations that something would be done about them, and it could even cause problems."

Denton nodded, "I see what you mean. If you came in, it would cost me some bucks, it would have some risks in how my people reacted; one way or another I'd have to do something." He paused and then went on. "Well, to tell the truth, I don't want to upset things if they're OK, but just finding out whether they are or not appeals to me. Isn't there some other way to do this?"

Bob Denton seemed to me to be open to some minimal work by me. He'd responded as I'd hoped to my candidness about the risks of some conventional diagnostic snooping. He'd really seemed to pay attention to what I'd said, and I was beginning to like him and was intrigued with the situation. At times like this, my thought processes seem to jump into high gear. After all, a careful response was called for and there were a number of considerations to factor in. The things I recall noting to myself went like this: apparently some minimal motivation on Bob's part; my real lack of information about the Kenworth situation; my own schedule for the coming months—which was pretty full; my intuition that probably nothing major was wrong with Bob and his managers; and that whatever I proposed had to be of modest cost.

LET'S HAVE A RETREAT

I said to Bob: "Let me sketch out one idea that comes to mind. We could do a modest retreat. You, your department managers, and I could meet away from here for a couple of days, say on a weekend, to jointly explore how things are going. At minimum, I see several probable outcomes from such a meeting: everyone would get somewhat better acquainted with one another; we'd know better if there were serious issues to tackle; we'd have the experience of jointly going through problem identification; and you'd get a sense of whether or not your team was open to working with an outsider like myself."

I paused and went on: "Such a meeting would be relatively efficient. It wouldn't take time away from work, and it wouldn't cost an arm and a leg." Bob nodded, sipped his coffee and looked at me intently. "OK," he said, "I can see your points. Just what would we be doing?"

Seeing Bob's interest as well as warming to the idea myself, I went on to outline a retreat. I suggested doing it at a country club or lodge within a few hours' drive of Seattle. This setting was to provide a symbolic break from the customary business environment, and because it would cost everyone weekend time and the company the expense of travel, food, and lodging, it would show Bob's seriousness about the event. I then suggested we begin with cocktails and dinner on a Friday evening, work all day Saturday with appropriate breaks, and conclude by noon Sunday. Again, Bob nodded. He then asked, "But what would we do? What would you charge?"

I did some quick calculations and responded, "As for my fee, I'd have to bill you for a minimum of three days at my daily rate of \$1500 per day, and travel expenses—assuming Kenworth would provide food and lodging. As for what we'd actually do, that's more difficult to say exactly. Frankly, while I have several ways to get us started, I'd need to play it by ear. In general, it would be my responsibility to see we talked straight and a lot with one another to surface our concerns both big and small. I'm afraid you'd have to trust me on this." I said this last couple of sentences with some trepidation, knowing from my experience that most managers would want much more clarity, but I needed to know how Bob was viewing me.

I was surprised at what happened next. Denton quickly agreed to have a retreat weekend as I'd outlined. We also selected a weekend a month-and-a-half away. He would find a site and let me know. In addition, we agreed he would use the phrase "a communications workshop" when he informed participants. Glancing at my watch as I left Denton's office, I saw it was just 11:30.

QUESTIONS FOR DISCUSSION

1. Consider the consultant's preparation for his meeting with Bob Denton. Was it sufficient? What might you have done differently?

2. In the discussion reported between the consultant and Bob Denton about Denton's situation, what points of the consultant's behavior

seemed to be effective and ineffective? Was he probing too much or too little? Did he learn what he set out to learn? What else might he usefully learn about?

3. Think through the "contracting" process described in the last section of the case. Be able to comment on the scope and clarity of the agreement reached. What are the risks and opportunities of this agreement for the client? For the consultant?

4. The case ends with a retreat scheduled in six weeks. Given what you know about the consultant, predict his design for the retreat (or at least how he will get it started). What design should he utilize?

Case 3

State Transportation

Rupert R. Chisholm
Pennsylvania State University, Harrisburg
Robert F. Munzenrider
Pennsylvania State University, Harrisburg

During a recent gubernatorial campaign in a large Eastern state, one of the leading candidates promised that if he were elected, he would "clean up the mess" in the state's Department of Transportation. Over the years, the department had acquired an increasingly bad reputation because of its political involvement and the poor quality, the high costs, and the slowness of its road work. People joked about cars and trucks being swallowed by bottomless potholes and about seeing six-person repair crews on the roads with five people standing around watching one person work.

The candidate who had promised to revitalize the Department of Transportation won the election, and one of the first appointments he announced was the nomination of a nationally respected transportation engineer with an academic background to be the new secretary of the Department of Transportation. The nominee had agreed to serve only after obtaining a promise from the new governor that he would have a free hand and full support to modernize the department.

Once confirmed by the State Senate, the new secretary set about his modernization program. Throughout the department, including the headquarters staff, the regional offices, and the county road units, he removed incompetent political appointees and replaced them with qualified personnel. He installed new computer systems and procedures to improve administrative, planning, and work routines. In keeping with a general state government program for downsizing the state work force, he cut the size of road maintenance crews about 20 percent. He increased the use of private contractors for new road and bridge building and for major repair projects on the interstate highway network. Under this new system, the county road units' role increasingly emphasized maintenance and repair work. The new secretary also reviewed and revised work productivity standards throughout the department and established or improved training programs and work procedures.

While carrying out all of these administrative and technical changes, the new secretary also sought to develop and build support, both internally and externally, for the changes he was instituting. Internally, he sponsored management training and development programs for both headquarters and field units. To gain employee input, he supported the development of a departmentwide quality circle program.

Externally, he worked hard to foster political and citizen support for his modernization program. One of the mechanisms was development of a productivity council (PC) to which he appointed key representatives from the political, business, financial and academic communities of the state as well as senior executives from the department. Rupert Chisholm was invited to sit on the Council in his capacity as director of the Center for Quality of Work Life at a leading state university. At the Council's quarterly meetings, managers from throughout the department would make presentations about productivity initiatives and results. Council members would comment on these presentations and offer suggestions.

Support for the changes was not universal. State employee unions fought some of the changes, especially the downsizing of the departmental work force. In the early years of the administration, a long and bitter strike by state employees had closed many state government operations, including the Department of Transportation. In addition, the unions opposed the quality circle program, claiming it bypassed union involvement via labor-management committees stipulated in the formal labor agreement.

During the spring meeting of the PC one year, management representatives of the department maintenance garage from one rural county (hereinafter called Rural County) made a presentation on a productivity improvement effort that had occurred the previous year. This attempt to improve productivity had focused on the garage that maintains and repairs equipment used on state highways in the county. The presentation documented numerous improvements in garage operations that resulted both in improved productivity in that setting and, because of decreased downtime for equipment, improved road maintenance and repair operations in the whole county.

Discussion of the findings resulted in a generally good feeling among those present, and PC members generally agreed the project had been successful. However, one council member from a legislative committee observed that all the results dealt with tangible things and used industrial engineering measures almost exclusively. He went on to ask, "How do employees perceive and feel about these changes?" When Rural County managers replied, "Everybody up there liked the changes that had been made," the legislative member replied, "How do you *know* that employees view the changes so positively?" Because no one could answer this question, discussion abruptly halted. After several attempts by department representatives (predominantly engineers and top-level managers with engineering backgrounds) to reach the position that everyone was satisfied with the changes, they finally admitted they could not answer the questions. Some additional discussion ensued. Afterward, a top-level manager addressed Rupe Chisholm:

Manager

Is it possible to design a study to determine employee reactions to the Rural County productivity improvement effort?

R. C.

It seems possible to conduct such a study. . . . Of course, it depends on exactly what the study would attempt to find out and how it's carried out . . . and the availability of adequate resources.

Manager

Could this type of research be done by your QWL Center?

R. C.

Yes, it could.

Manager

Would the Center be interested in doing a study?

R. C.

We definitely would like to explore the possibility. Naturally, we'll need to get more information about the situation in the county, determine goals of the research, design the study, and so forth. This would take further discussion outside the Council meeting.

Manager

Sam (staff person in Operations Review Group), will you please take responsibility for contacting Dr. C. to see if we can work out something here?

Sam

Yes, sir!

Manager

Is that OK, Dr. C.?

R. C.

Yes it is. I look forward to hearing from Sam.

This exchange satisfied the Council member who had raised the question about employee perceptions, and other members agreed that adding employee views and feelings to existing "hard" outcome measures would be desirable. These events triggered the evaluation study described in this case.

R. C. engaged in intense internal dialogue during the preceding exchange. Many thoughts, feelings, and images rushed through him simultaneously, including the following:

Pro

This really sounds interesting . . . some innovative things might be included if an OD approach is used!

Con

Careful, Pollyanna. These guys don't have a clue about the behavioral aspects of productivity . . . they're a bunch of engineers who believe that if you can't count it, it doesn't exist!

Pro

> Still, there is a lot of energy to do something . . . and the council was suffi-ciently interested in QWL to request me to do a presentation on it at the last meeting . . . and they responded with great interest.

Con

> Yeah, but the interest shown now in the study is just to satisfy the legislative representative on the council. They're worried about possibly jeopardizing future funding from the legislature. This is strictly CYA behavior.

Pro

> The people from Rural County seem extremely sincere and interested in the people side of productivity. The equipment manager in particular seems to place great importance on behavioral aspects and how to involve employees. He also comes across as a very savvy manager who is willing to try new things.

Con

> This is just another example of the top-down management style that prevails in the department. Once the authority figure(s) indicates which way to march, people below in the organization close rank and march. They're just being good soldiers.

Pro

> Maybe so . . . and, yet, the secretary of transportation appears genuinely in-terested in the study. And, during his six years as head of the department, he has demonstrated an ability to get things done and to involve employees to an increasing degree over the past couple of years with his strong support of establishing quality circles (QCs) . . . and the recent talk about using partici-pative management.

Con

> That's just it; it's talk without recognizing what would be required to bring about a truly participative organization.

Neutral

> Despite all this, there may be a chance to help the organization take a small step forward and to evolve a different way of doing things. Let's not close off that possibility yet.

ORGANIZATIONAL CONTEXT

Transportation Department

This current case covers aspects of an OD-oriented approach to evaluat-ing the productivity improvement effort in the county organization of the Transportation Department of a large eastern state. The depart-ment employs more than 12,000 employees and has an annual budget that exceeds $3 billion. A primary part of the department's mission is to ensure that the existing highway system receives year-round maintenance and to manage major highway and bridge construction and restoration.

The state highway system, fourth largest in the United States, includes over 40,000 miles of roads and about 25,000 bridges. Total population of the state approximates 12 million. Over 10,000 members of the total department work force work in field operations under the direction of 11 district engineers. Exhibit 1 depicts the formal department organization. The situation described in the case occurred within the Rural County organization of District B. The case covers issues involved in entry and linking up with the organization.

Productivity Improvement in Rural County

Two years before the PC meeting just discussed, a consulting engineer completed a review of several randomly selected county maintenance repair shops. This preliminary assessment indicated that most shops were functioning at 40 to 60 percent of the calculated optimal efficiency level; a few were at approximately 80 percent. These findings suggested the department might reap substantial savings through improving productivity in county maintenance shops. Consequently, the Rural County shop was selected the next year as a pilot site to develop and implement productivity improvement recommendations. Official goals of this effort were:

1. To demonstrate the department commitment to improving shop productivity.
2. To identify and disseminate information on specific productivity improvements throughout the department.
3. To serve as a model for implementing organized shop productivity improvement efforts in other county maintenance shops across the state.

Engineer Study. The consulting engineer who had conducted the statewide review of maintenance organizations made an in-depth study of the Rural County shop operations as a first step toward improving productivity. This step was intended to lend credibility and objectivity to the productivity improvement effort. His study collected data by observation and by comparison of operations to "accepted standards." His findings revealed:

• Mechanics spent approximately 70 percent of their time at their work station. (This was considered a good outcome.)

EXHIBIT 1 Organization Chart: Department of Transportation

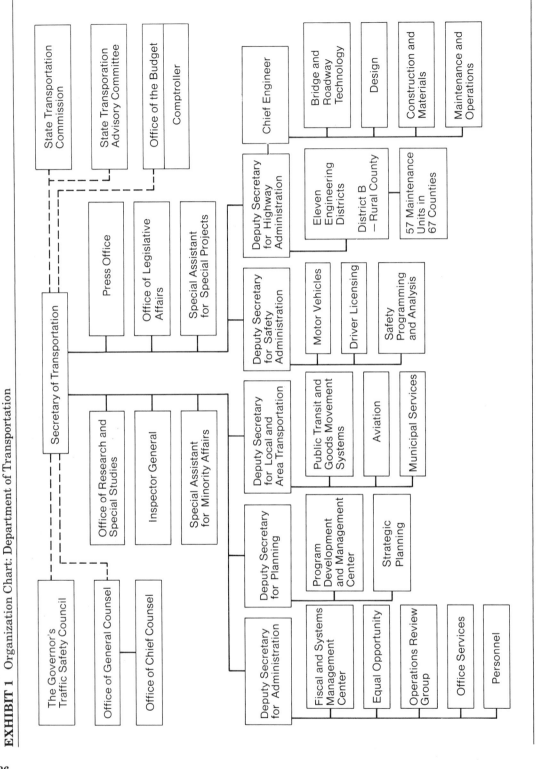

- Individual mechanics were performing at about 50 percent efficiency because of deficient work procedures and lack of the proper tools.
- Several physical conditions detracted further from mechanics' efforts to do their jobs effectively. These included layout of the shop floor, workbench design, lighting, and frequent distractions by nonmechanics.
- Efficiency versus established time standards for specific jobs was 45 percent.
- Overall efficiency of shop operations was rated as 55 percent.

The next step in the improvement effort involved preparing a video of shop operations to document conditions before changes were made. Having employee support for improvements was identified as crucial to success, so district management conducted a closed-door, brainstorming session for shop mechanics to solicit their feedback on the consultant's findings and recommendations. Establishing a quality circle (QC) for mechanics and defining training needs were longer-run outcomes of this meeting.

Action Plans. Action plans to improve the situation were developed for different organizational groups. These plans are summarized in Exhibit 2.

The content of these action plans suggested two things: (1) the productivity improvement effort had dealt with improving basic resources that employees need to do their jobs (tools, lighting, equipment); (2) carrying out many of the action steps required the coordinated effort of several groups at different locations and different organizational echelons. This coordination was very complex and time consuming.

"Hard" Outcome Measures. Department management considered the Rural County productivity improvement effort highly successful. This conclusion was based largely on quantitative measures developed to reveal the effects of the effort to improve productivity. As indicated earlier, the organization emphasized industrial engineering indexes.

Table 1 lists results of key measures used to assess productivity improvement. Performance for virtually all of these criteria showed positive changes from the base period to the period after the changes; only a small increase in equipment downtime defied this pattern. Stated financial savings depended on assumptions about the continuation of initial reduction of personnel, equipment, or parts over a fairly long period. Despite this caveat, the quantitative results attributed to the productivity improvement effort suggested substantial success. Based largely on this experience in Rural County, top management intended to extend similar productivity improvement efforts to several other counties.

EXHIBIT 2   Action Plans Developed for Productivity Improvement in Rural
County

County/District Action Plan

- Conduct shop tool needs survey among the mechanics
- Combine and relocate the parts room into the stockroom
- Purchase and install bulk waste oil tanks
- Purchase and install mirrors in the PM bays
- Paint the ceiling in the shop area white
- Update the shop manager's office to eliminate the congestion
- Install larger air lines for shop tools
- Purchase and install new shop doors
- Implement a complete purging of storage cabinets
- Designate new work bay areas

Architectural Action Plan

- Purchase and install new shop lights
- Install new electrical outlets
- Purchase and install bulk oil tanks for the fuel system
- Purchase and install new telephone/paging system
- Update the existing ventilation system
- Upgrade and relocate the parking area

Equipment Division Action Plan

- Purchase new shop tools
- Purchase electronic testing equipment
- Purchase shop sweeper
- Purchase shop compressor
- Purchase new fast lubricating oil change system

District Action Plan

- Develop requirements for air lines
- Solicit bids at local level for air lines
- Organize brainstorming sessions
- Assist in obtaining shop costs
- Develop sweeper specifications
- Write contract for shop dumpsters
- Review personnel requirements

County Action Plan

- Paint ceiling white
- Relocate parts room
- Identify intercom sytstem needs
- Purchase mirrors for PM bay
- Repair doors and purchase new ones where needed
- Purge obsolete parts from parts inventory

TABLE 1 Effects of Productivity Improvement Effort on Key "Hard"
Outcome Measures

Outcome Measures	*After Changes vs. Base Period*
Amount of repair work performed	+11.9%
Average repair time per unit	−12.8%
Repair work performed by nonmechanics	−48.4%
Repair time per unit	−3.55 hours/month
Unscheduled shop activity	−23.7%
Mechanic trips to field to repair equipment	−19.6%
Equipment downtime	+2.9%
Nonmechanic shop hours	−14.0%
Financial savings:	
Annual savings (estimated)	$85,332/year
Depreciation	$13,297/year
Initial cost	$132,960
Return on investment	54%
Payback period	1.55 years

CONTRACTING AND ENTRY

Following the PC meeting, I contacted Robert Munzenrider, the senior
research associate at the QWL Center, and recounted the events that led
to the study request. Bob also thought the study could be done, and we
agreed to develop an evaluation process that met both client goals and
our own. Goals of the department were unclear and, as we began to discuss the project, a feeling of "What might we be getting ourselves into?"
prevailed. Discussion began to clarify our interests and goals for the
project and to raise other entry issues.

R.M.

What do they really want us to do?

R.C.

What they've said so far indicates that they want to find out the real perceptions and reactions of Rural County employees to the productivity improvement effort. But, this gives us a broad hunting license . . . and, I'm not sure
what the real goals are. Maybe they want us as window dressing—to lend
academic credibility to their project and answer the questions of the legislative representative on the council.

R.M.

That's scary! I certainly don't want to be part of that!

R.C.

Me either! . . . Perhaps we should just tell them we aren't interested.

R.M.

Wait a minute . . . not so fast! . . . Let's see. . . . Why are we even talking about this . . . What are the possibilities here? . . . What would we like to get from the project? Let's see whether we can identify our goals for the project.

R.C.

One thing I'm very clear about: I have zero interest in using a traditional evaluation approach. For me to be interested, the possibility of really engaging county employees to find out how they're experiencing the situation must be present. And, there also must be the likelihood that employees and the organization will learn from the process. In other words, we must follow a developmental approach like OD.

R.M.

That's really important to me too. Do you think the department representatives in the operations review group are thinking this way? . . . Will they support the approach?

R.C.

They definitely don't have this fix on our work right now. Most of them are engineers, and their operating mode is to devise and apply industrial engineering measures. Are they open to a different approach? . . . That remains to be seen.

R.M.

So, let's see. . . . Where are we? Seems that we're saying we may like to do the study as long as the department allows enough leeway to have employee perceptions and feelings emerge from an OD-oriented research process.

R.C.

That's right . . . and, to keep the process honest and try to make sure we don't get out of hand, employees must have a strong role in managing the research process as well.

R.M.

That's a lot to ask! . . . Are we being realistic?

R.C.

Maybe not, but if we can't propose an approach that meets the real needs of the situation and is generally consistent with what we consider important, we shouldn't become involved.

R.M.

OK . . . and, how do we proceed?

R.C.

I'm not sure. Our contact point is Sam in the operations review group. Suppose I give him a call to get additional information and test out our thoughts about the general approach.

R.M.

What are you going to tell him? He'll want to know what we plan to do.

R.C.

I'll say that we need to schedule a meeting with him and other relevant people in the central office. We need to know what he sees as the most important research questions. I'll emphasize the importance of our getting clarity and agreement with him about what we'll do and how we'll do it. This will undoubtedly require several meetings.

R.M.

How about the union?

R.C.

Oh, yeah! We must determine more specifics about the present department-union situation and how to link with and keep union officers informed about what we're doing. Strong opposition here could scotch the whole deal! I'll let you know Sam's reactions after the phone conversation. We also need to meet again ASAP to map further steps and plan our meeting with Sam. What's your schedule like until the end of the week?

R.M.

I'm free almost any time Tuesday morning, all day Thursday, and Friday morning.

R.C.

Let's shoot for Tuesday A.M. or Thursday at the latest.

R.M.

Sounds good! How about covering all of this in one meeting?

R.C.

Agreed—it's unlikely that I can reach Sam on the first try, anyhow . . . he's very busy. Catch you later!

The next day:

R.M.

Well, what did you find out from Sam on the phone? How did it go?

R.C.

It was very interesting. Sam was very open about sharing information on the organization . . . there was no hint of holding back and he gave a lot of information about research questions. The main research interests that emerged from our discussion are:

- To determine garage employees' perceptions of the overall effectiveness of the productivity effort.
- To get the perceptions of equipment operators in the field (truck drivers, grader operators, etc.) who bring equipment into the garage for repairs and maintenance. Of course they are the direct "customers" of the garage. By the way, he verified that productivity improvement so far had focused only on the garage.
- How do foremen and managers feel about the quality and speed of repairs/maintenance now versus before the changes in the garage?

- Fear of losing jobs. Despite management guarantees against job loss due to productivity improvement, some employees and the union appear concerned about this. To what extent does this fear exist?
- How do mechanics view the changes made to improve garage productivity? What do they see as positive and negative aspects? (This is critical because the mechanics and other garage personnel were affected most directly by the changes.)
- What are the relationships between mechanics and field personnel like? Did the emphasis on improving garage conditions drive a wedge between the "privileged" group and "underprivileged" field employees?

R.M.

These are good questions . . . and suggest a desire by the department to find out what really happened because of changes in the garage.

R.C.

Yeah, but what happens if we begin to find out things they don't want to hear? . . . Will they be so open then? . . . Still, Sam's input does suggest a degree of openness about research content and process. He didn't back away when I mentioned that obtaining these types of data would require lots of employee involvement and that we are working on ways of getting it. That's another good sign. . . . However, it's impossible to say until we've gotten more concrete about the "what" and "how" of a proposed process.

R.M.

This is really beginning to get to me! It seems that every time we make progress and begin to clarify an issue or an action step, we end up saying "*Yes, but,* . . . we can't reach a definite conclusion until a discussion with Sam" or "further information on the situation in Rural County is needed" or something like that! Each step seems to depend on the next step!

R.C.

Take it easy! . . . I'm frustrated too and the ambiguity does cause a lot of stress. Any thoughts on how to deal with it?

R.M.

I don't know. . . . I guess our implicit strategy of slowly developing a joint proposal with Sam and remaining open to revising it based on new information and understanding is the way to go . . . but I'd like to know whether we have a project or not . . . and, if so, what we're going to do!

R.C.

I really hear you, and me too! At times, I wonder whether we're wasting time and energy too and want to make a clear-cut go/no-go decision about involvement. However, I'd like to continue at least through our meeting with Sam and then take stock of where things stand.

R.M.

OK . . . I suppose I can live with that. . . . What else do we need to cover today? . . . What did Sam say about relationships between the department and AFSCME (the union that represents bargaining unit employees)?

R.C.

The situation here is cloudy. Here's the deal, based on Sam's comments and information gleaned from the newspapers and informal sources recently. *Union relations* General relations between the state and AFSCME are strained. Since his election, the governor has taken a hard-nosed approach to bargaining with the union, and considerable resentment among union leadership exists because of this. The governor also campaigned on a theme of cutting the size of state government, and reductions in the work force of transportation and other departments resulted. Hence, more strain on department-union relations. In addition, the state is currently negotiating a master labor-management agreement with all employees of the state represented by the union. A strike at the end of the existing labor-management agreement is threatened; the contract would expire at the end of June . . . only two and one half months away! These ongoing negotiations have added more tension to the situation. For all these reasons, it's quite uncertain about whether we can get union understanding and support of the evaluation effort.

R.M.

That's a real bummer! . . . Is the situation so bad that we should consider scuttling the effort entirely before getting more heavily invested in it?

R.C.

It's impossible to tell at this point, but I don't think so. However, it certainly highlights the need to talk with knowledgeable individuals in the department to get more information and thoughts on possible ways of proceeding. It also makes clear the need to consider very carefully the process of linking up with, getting, and maintaining union support at the district and county levels. Oh, he did mention one other thing: The union local in Rural County recently voted to prohibit union officers from being members of QCs.

R.M.

What's that about?

R.C.

Sam didn't know, but it surely indicates some hard feelings between the union and management in the county. Guess we'll find out more about it when we arrive in the field . . . assuming we get that far in the process!

R.M.

What do we need to do to prepare for our meeting with Sam and the operations review group next Tuesday?

R.C.

Let's make sure we've talked about all the issues that concern us at this point. Then, let's map out an agenda and process for the meeting.

We identified the following issues that had emerged so far in working on the project:

1. Was the department genuinely interested in a research process that would determine real employee perceptions and attitudes?

2. Was it possible in a fairly short time to assist the organization in examining critical aspects of its functioning and learn from the process? Would other practical constraints preclude the possibility of conducting a meaningful study? Questions about such constraints included:

- Was enough money available?
- Was the organization willing to make managers and employees available for the study?
- Would we have sufficient time available to conduct the research?
- Would the level of thrust in Rural County permit open discussion and collection of valid data from employees?

3. To what extent would the existing organization structure pose a barrier? The department was structured as a traditional functional organization (see Exhibit 1). District B consists of seven counties, and Rural County had a county manager and four assistant county managers. Each assistant manager covered a particular geographic area within the county. Another key member of the county management team was the equipment manager, who supervised the county garage and the maintenance of equipment. How to intervene in this complex, hierarchical system was unclear.

4. How could we gain the support of employees, management, and union at the district and county levels? Support from the central office was essential to the success of the study. At the same time, having the project initiated from the top ran the danger of having us seen as lackeys of top management. In addition, it ran the risk of having managers and employees "go along for the ride" without taking the effort seriously.

5. How risky would district and county managers perceive the research to be? And, what level of trust did ordinary employees (e.g., mechanics, equipment operators) have in the organization? Would the existing trust levels support the research process?

6. Was it possible to design an evaluation process that would help the organization learn about behavioral aspects of productivity, the importance of work life, and possible connections between the two? The initial request was thought of by the department as a traditional evaluation research project. Ways of designing the entry research processes to broaden and deepen organizational understanding of the behavioral aspects of productivity improvement had to be devised. The degree to which this might be possible under existing conditions was highly uncertain.

QUESTIONS FOR DISCUSSION

Unforeseen events have suddenly emerged that have made it impossible for the two original consultants to continue with the study. You have been selected to replace them. The two consultants have given you an in-depth briefing about the situation and their involvement so far. You have not yet fully agreed to conduct the proposed evaluation research. However, you are interested in the project.

Your task is to define steps for completing the entry and linking up process with the organization to enable an effective OD-oriented evaluation research process to occur. Your action plan should respond to the various questions, issues, and dilemmas described so far. In addition, the following questions occur to you as you reflect on how to continue with the intervention.

1. How do you gain sufficient information about various segments of the organization to allow an effective intervention? Information about organizational functioning, organization climate and management style, relevant information about power and politics, and other aspects are required. The complexity of the existing organizational system and remoteness of Rural County from the state capital pose a serious problem for obtaining firsthand information about the various units and individuals involved. Devising an effective way to obtain the necessary information and assessing it to determine whether to intervene and how to work with the system pose serious challenges.

2. How do you gain understanding of the situation in which participants in the county organization work? And, how do you assure that these employees have a chance to make informed choices about whether to participate and how involved to get? These issues pose a special challenge in a traditional hierarchical structure with a culture that supports unquestioning response to requests from top management.

3. How do you describe the evaluation research process so that relatively unsophisticated audiences can understand it? Gaining understanding of the "process" nature of the activity and the emergent character of the approach seem especially difficult. In addition, a large number of individuals and groups must be involved in understanding/supporting the process. A procedure that is fairly straightforward and relatively easy to describe/understand is required, but oversimplifying the description of the process and action steps may be misleading and may doom the research and organizational learning. Maintaining sufficient flexibility to allow changes to be made as you learn more about the organization also is critical.

4. What part of the organization is the client system—the county organization, the district, the department, or some other entity? How do employee interests fit in? Can the interests of different groups and individuals be integrated?

5. How do you identify and approach the key union officers and leaders? Should entry begin at the top and then work down or is another route more likely to gain union understanding and support? What do existing union-management relations suggest?

Commercial Fertilizer (A)

Achilles A. Armenakis
Auburn University
Henry B. Burdg
Auburn University

Jimmy awoke Sunday morning and went through the normal routines of making coffee and getting prepared to read the newspaper. The past few weeks had been extremely stressful because he had just decided to eliminate the transportation subsidiary of his family-owned fertilizer company. He had added several tractors the last couple of years to combat rising costs of transporters, but now trucking industry deregulation changed the situation. His analysis had revealed his company was losing approximately $250,000 annually by shipping his products exclusively with his own private trucking company. Because the marketing and technological issues in the fertilizer industry were so challenging, he did not think he could devote the necessary time and other resources to make the trucking business profitable.

It was not simply a matter of economics. He was concerned with not having control over delivery of his products to the retailer. He preferred knowing *his* company was also delivering his products. He was truly sympathetic to the plight of those hurt by his decision. He did not like thinking about the disruptions to the families of those mechanics and drivers who would no longer be employed by Commercial Fertilizer Transportation Company.

He turned to the business section of the *News* where, on the front page, he began to read a half-page article describing a nearby university-sponsored center that assisted businesses. As he read the article, he wondered whether the center could help him with the other issue he had been putting off—company growth.

His oldest son, 22-year-old Taylor, had demonstrated a keen interest in the company. Like himself in his younger days, Taylor was enthusiastic, energetic, an excellent salesman, and full of ideas for expanding company operations. However, Mr. Anson, Jimmy's confidant, had a more conservative attitude. He was skeptical of trying to grow too rapidly. Jimmy faced a dilemma. After reading the article, he decided to call the center the next morning and talk with the director.

The phone rang early Monday morning at the center, and Carolyn, the secretary, answered in her polite manner, "Management Assistance Center (MAC), may I help you?"

"Yes," Jimmy replied. "I read an article yesterday in the *News* about your center, so I thought I would call to talk with the director. Is Mr. Armenakis there?"

"Yes he is, may I tell him who is calling?" Carolyn replied.

"Yes, this is Jimmy Parker, with Commercial Fertilizer Company, in Sycamore, Alabama."

"One moment, Mr. Parker," Carolyn answered, then transferred the call to Achilles Armenakis' office, informing him of who was on the line.

"Hello, Mr. Parker. This is Achilles Armenakis. What can I do for you?"

Jimmy began, "Mr. Armenakis, I read the article in the Sunday *News* about the Management Assistance Center and thought I would call you. I didn't realize that the university did this sort of thing. Do you work with all companies? And, what are some of the projects that you all have worked on?"

Achilles was used to these type of calls, so he responded by summarizing a recent organizational diagnostic project in a nearby foundry and by naming some clients MAC had worked with in the past who had agreed to be used as references.

"Well, would you have any interest in visiting my company?" Jimmy asked. "I have been putting off getting some assistance with an issue that we are facing and after reading the article yesterday, and after hearing your description of your work with the foundry, I feel you may be able to help." He continued by giving some basic information about the company—products, when the business was established, number of employees, and so on.

Achilles answered, "Yes, I would like to discuss this with you further. When would you like to meet?"

"At your earliest convenience. . . . How about Friday?" Jimmy responded.

"Sounds OK with me," answered Achilles. "Shall we meet at about 9:30 A.M.?"

"Yes, I would like to show you around our plants and if you have time I would like you to meet some of our managers," Jimmy said.

"That's fine. I'll see you then. I have a package of materials describing the operation of our center that I will send you: I may bring an associate with me also," Achilles said. After hanging up, he composed a short letter to Jimmy and asked Carolyn to prepare the usual package of materials to send him.

THE MANAGEMENT ASSISTANCE CENTER

The MAC had been established by the university five years ago. The primary purpose of the center was to contribute to the university's extension mission by providing management and technical assistance to companies located in the state. Although the concept was patterned after the traditional agricultural extension model (which provides free agricultural assistance to farmers), the companies were required to pay fees for the assistance they received.

In addition to the extension mission, personnel employed by the MAC contributed to the research and instruction missions of the university. The research mission was satisfied by publishing articles in journals. For example, unique approaches devised to solve company problems were described in manuscripts and published in various journals. The instruction mission was satisfied by involving graduate students in projects so they could apply the theory learned in their respective curricula in solving client problems. In some instances, the projects were unique enough to satisfy the requirements of theses and dissertations.

The MAC employed three full-time professionals—the director and two management scientists. In addition, there were three graduate students (one doctoral and two master's level), one administrative secretary, and two clerical personnel.

The MAC was designed to accommodate a variety of client requests. Prospective clients learned about the center from press releases printed in newspapers, speeches by the full-time professionals at civic luncheons, referrals from MAC clients, and letters sent to targeted companies.

The full-time professionals served as project managers for the projects undertaken. As project managers, they were to work with the client in diagnosing problems and then to identify the most technically competent resource to provide the assistance. Frequently, the full-time professional served as the technical resource with the assistance of one or more of the graduate students. However, it was not uncommon for the project manager to contract with faculty in the colleges and schools to assist on projects.

The university permitted faculty to participate in the MAC projects as consultants and receive extra compensation. The limits on the faculty amounted to one day per week. The daily compensation rate was determined by multiplying a factor by the faculty member's salary. Since MAC had been established, projects had involved faculty from numerous departments, including mechanical engineering, industrial engineering, industrial design, fisheries, pharmacy, economics, marketing, and management. The types of projects completed were quite diverse, involving line balancing, product design, market feasibility, and organizational diagnosis.

THE INITIAL VISIT TO COMMERCIAL FERTILIZER

Achilles and Henry Burdg, one of the center's management scientists, were both between projects so they agreed to do a little reading on the fertilizer industry and Commercial Fertilizer. Henry ordered the Dun & Bradstreet Consolidated Report and searched the library for other information on the industry.

The Company

The company was a family-owned fertilizer mixer (SIC number 2875) that was established in the early 1900s. The current chief executive officer purchased the company in the 1960s, having worked in top management for 10 years. The products are mixed in three plants. Total employment is about 125. Company sales grew from about $2 million in 1965 to about $7 million in 1982. However, much of the growth occurred after 1978, when one of the CEO's sons joined the company as a nonresident salesman. After the CEO's oldest son joined the company as vice president for marketing, a new product was introduced and the marketing effort for a specialty brand was increased. The potential for substantial growth was realized.

Although the company was profitable, the profit margin was volatile and much smaller than average. The majority of the company's sales depended on a single large private-label contract the company had secured a few years ago. There was a market-driven desire to move the business from an agricultural focus to a consumer orientation.

The company's relative market share amounted to less than 0.5 percent. The industry growth rate amounted to approximately 12 percent per year.

All managers except the vice president for marketing earned bachelor's degrees in a technical field or in business administration. This vice president was exceptionally capable, having worked in all phases of the business. In order to continue his own development, he read business journals and attended executive development programs regularly.

Meeting the CEO

On arriving at the corporate offices at about 9:30 A.M. Friday, Achilles and Henry were greeted by the receptionist and told Mr. Parker was expecting them. He was in the main plant. "Would you all like to have a seat and wait for a moment while I page him? Can I get you a cup of cof-

fee?'' Both Henry and Achilles took a seat and waited for the receptionist to bring the coffee.

Soon, Jimmy came to the reception area, greeted them, and invited
them into his office. He began talking about the university and how he
was recruited and awarded a scholarship to run the 100 yard dash. ''I
don't get to visit the campus as much as I would like. Seems I am always
working on improving my business. Why this morning, just before you
arrived, I was in the plant with Jim Roberts, the plant superintendent,
discussing a humidity problem that caused the fertilizer to form lumps,
which slows down the production line. Have you ever been through a
fertilizer plant?'' Jimmy asked.

Achilles replied, ''No, neither one of us has. We have worked with
many types of businesses, like apparel, textile, and foundry, but not fertilizer.''

''As you will see, we are a mixer, so the production process is quite simple. However, that doesn't mean we don't have our difficulties. Why
don't we go on through the plant and I'll show you what I am talking
about,'' Jimmy said.

The three spent some time going through the plant getting a feel for
the process and meeting the managers and some of the operative personnel. Jimmy then said, ''Why don't we go get some lunch? Then, at about
1 o'clock I would like for us to meet with my managers.''

During lunch, the discussion touched on the backgrounds of Henry
and Achilles. Henry's father had spent the majority of his career working with a family-owned steel business in Cleveland. Henry had worked
summers for the business. His interest in aviation led him to major in
aviation management. Upon graduation with his B.S. degree, he
worked for an airport engineering consulting firm for two years. He
then decided to enter the M.B.A. program and after graduation began
working with the MAC after graduation. He has been in his current position for three years.

Achilles's father had emigrated to the United States and ultimately
established a restaurant in Louisiana. Achilles grew up in the business, working in every job. While earning his B.S. and M.B.A. degrees
at a college close to his hometown, he would work on weekends and hol-
idays when he returned for visits. However, when he began his doctorate at another university, much farther from his hometown, his father
retired from the business. After completing his D.B.A., Achilles accepted an offer to teach at this university. Four years later, he was
named director of the newly established MAC and has served in this
position since.

Jimmy had used consultants before for various projects, some management related, but most of the consulting he contracted for was product
related. That is, he retained the services of a research firm to conduct
basic research on new products. His current concerns were related to

management. He explained that he expected to retire in about 15 years and wanted to turn over management of the business to his two sons and daughter. He was concerned about the direction of the company, specifically, about whether the company should attempt to expand operations, and if so, how fast.

"My family has had numerous discussions about the future of the company," he said. "My oldest son, Taylor, feels that we should develop an aggressive strategy. He has said, 'There is no reason why we can't have sales of $90 million by 1990!' While I think that is a bit too optimistic, we do need to try to grow. Do you think you are interested in this kind of project? How do you feel you can help?"

Achilles responded by saying he and Henry viewed themselves as being able to facilitate the change process. "What you have described is organizational change that will probably cause you, your managers, and others to begin doing things differently. We can help you determine what your company needs to do in order to prepare itself for growth. We would like to have a positive influence on the direction of your company and be able to assist you in accomplishing your personal goals."

Jimmy responded, "I feel your experience is important to working with us. Why don't we go on back to the office to continue this discussion with the other managers?"

Meeting the Managers

On arriving at the office, Jimmy, Henry, and Achilles entered the conference room. Seated around the table were several of the managers they had already met during the plant tour. After a few preliminary remarks, Jimmy asked Achilles to describe how he and Henry would like to proceed.

Achilles began by saying they appreciated the plant tour, admitting that neither he nor Henry had previously seen the production process of a fertilizer mixer but adding they believed that should not prohibit them from getting involved. Jimmy had expressed the belief that the company should grow and that managing is a fairly generic process. The practices needed to effectively manage a fertilizer mixer are not substantially different now from the practices necessary to effectively manage a foundry. Based on the conversation with Jimmy, Henry and he thought the purpose of the project would be to determine what will be required to develop and implement an aggressive growth strategy. Achilles then asked the group how they felt about the stated purpose of the project.

Daniel, a salesman, indicated he did not think he could work any longer hours. "I am already traveling more than I expected. When I hear you saying *growth,* I think more travel," he replied.

Henry said, "The company must realize that there are limitations to what can be expected of everyone. We hope to find out what those limitations are and determine what changes must be made to develop the growth strategy.''

Richard, an operations manager, asked, ''If you don't have experience in this business, how would you recommend solutions to technically related problems?''

Achilles replied, ''Good point. We have the capability to contract with other faculty within the university, so the limits on our problem solutions are related to the capabilities of the faculty in the university. Therefore, we don't think that will be a major stumbling block. Besides, plant capacity is not fully utilized, so some growth can be handled by just selling and producing more.''

Mr. Anson, another operations manager, said, ''I think there are some things that we could be doing differently that would improve our profitability.'' Daniel asked to what he was referring. ''Well, for one, I think there are some accounts that we could be calling on closer to home rather than trying to sell to companies way up in New Jersey.'' Ogden, a manufacturing manager, reacted by saying, ''But that company is one of our largest accounts!'' Mr. Anson replied, ''But they are too far away!'' ''So what's distance from here got to do with it?'' Ogden asked. Mr. Anson answered, ''Freight charges!''

Achilles said, ''I am glad to see that you are willing to express yourself. The approach that we would like to follow requires a great deal of input from you. We propose a two-phase project. The first phase is the diagnostic part, which consists of individual interviews with each manager. The typical interview will last for at least an hour, and we'll ask questions about the strengths and weaknesses or constructive criticisms of the company.

''The second phase is more difficult to describe at this point because it will depend on the results of the first phase,'' he continued. ''But whatever we do is going to involve this group. The analysis of the diagnostic information will be presented to you and, with us acting as facilitators, we will help you determine what you feel needs to be done. You can elect to keep us involved throughout phase two and beyond.'' Achilles looked at Jimmy, then to Henry as if to invite additional comments.

Mack, the controller, asked Jimmy, ''Is this *really* what you want to do?''

Jimmy responded by saying, ''I think so. Don't you feel we need to try something like this so we can determine whether we should attempt to expand and, if so, to determine how we should go about doing this?''

Mack said, ''Well, I've gone through this type of project before. And I can tell you it is going to be extremely time consuming.''

Jimmy said, ''I realize it will be. But I would like us to agree that we will make time. It is the only way we are going to map out our future.''

The other managers offered encouraging comments. Daniel said he welcomed something like this and was ready to cooperate immediately. Even Mr. Anson seemed to go along with the idea, saying he thought this kind of project should have been completed long ago. Jimmy adjourned the meeting by thanking everyone for their time and support.

Jimmy, Henry, and Achilles walked into Jimmy's office. Jimmy agreed with the plan of action, although he expressed some reservations about the possibility of losing control. Both Achilles and Henry felt positive about what had transpired up to this point and assured Jimmy that these steps would only help him gain more control. The discussion seemed to satisfy Jimmy's expectations. Achilles said he would send Jimmy a letter of engagement that would serve as a proposal, briefly describing the procedure and including the costs of the diagnostic phase.

THE DIAGNOSTIC APPROACH

Soon after returning, Achilles and Henry organized their thoughts about their visit to Commercial Fertilizer. They agreed the most appropriate approach to this project was to get information on current managerial practices. The managers were all technically competent. Furthermore, the production process was simple, consisting of mixing and packaging. The plant was not at full capacity, so there did not seem to be technical limitations on the growth strategy.

The managerial expertise of the managers (most of whom were young) was largely from their limited experience with Commercial Fertilizer. Little, if any, formal management training could be attributable to the managers. Therefore, it seemed appropriate to focus on their current management practices, that is, planning, organizing, staffing, directing, and controlling. However, during the interviews, Achilles and Henry could be aware of the possibility of technical issues being mentioned as problems.

Henry and Achilles were eager to begin. The managers seemed to be ready to cooperate. Furthermore, working with Commercial Fertilizer was consistent with the extension mission of the MAC. This project would be a challenge but they felt confident they could handle virtually any problem they encountered. Not only did they believe they were qualified to identify and solve any management problem, they felt they could identify any technical problem and, if necessary, could subcontract with competent faculty to solve it.

CONTRACT ISSUES

Henry and Achilles were concerned about Jimmy's reaction to a proposed agreement. Was Jimmy going to think the direct cost for the project was too high? The cost of the project was going to consist of travel expenses (per diem and mileage) to Sycamore as well as the professional costs. The professional costs would be estimated to be portal to portal (i.e., travel time plus on-site time) and incubation time (i.e., off-site analytical and report-writing time). Achilles and Henry used a rule of thumb of one day of incubation time for each day on-site. In addition to the direct cost, was Jimmy going to think the lost time for the managers' involvement was worth it?

Achilles and Henry needed to be cautious in developing a plan and corresponding agreement (contract) with Jimmy that would provide the necessary flexibility in addressing the most critical problems. The major issues they wanted to cover in an agreement were flexibility (to bring in technical resources if necessary) and termination points convenient to Achilles and Henry. Similarly, Achilles and Henry thought it important to let Jimmy commit to a multiphased project that could be conveniently terminated. Henry and Achilles agreed on the following plan, which they sent to Jimmy in the engagement letter.

The project would consist of two phases. Phase one comprised two steps: organizational diagnosis and feedback. Phase two was a series of work sessions, resulting in the formulation of plans. The engagement letter dealt only with phase one. Included in it were the following points:

1. What day the confidential interviews should begin; what time they should start and approximately when they would finish.
2. Henry and Achilles would conduct four tandem interviews the first day. Then, on one other day both would conduct solo interviews. Each interview should last for approximately one hour, and some personnel may need to be interviewed more than once.
3. Which day the feedback report would be presented. Jimmy would be presented the information privately. Then, after his approval, the findings would be presented to the managers.
4. A budget providing the total cost of the diagnosis including the presentations.
5. A signature block for Jimmy to acknowledge his acceptance of the proposal.

Achilles called Jimmy to tell him the letter was in the mail, thanked him for the opportunity to visit with them, and hoped that Jimmy would accept the proposal because both Achilles and Henry were interested in working with the Commercial Fertilizer managers on the project. Five weeks later, Jimmy called Achilles and informed him the engagement letter had been signed and returned. "When can you begin the interviewing?" Jimmy asked.

QUESTIONS FOR DISCUSSION

1. Discuss the ethics of the tactics used by the MAC in client development. Were Henry and Achilles ethical in developing Commercial Fertilizer? Should Achilles have discussed prior clients with Jimmy?

2. Entry consists of assessing client readiness. What does this mean? How is readiness determined? What evidence do Henry and Achilles have to assess readiness?
3. Is a contract between the MAC and Commercial Fertilizer necessary? Comment on the precautions taken in developing the terms of the contract. Was anything important omitted?
4. Are Achilles and Henry biased in their approach to the project? That is, is their focus on managerial practices unbiased?

Part II

Diagnosing

Part II consists of cases addressing diagnosing how the client system is functioning. In OD, diagnosis is aimed at discovering the sources of organizational problems and/or opportunities for improvement. It is generally guided by a diagnostic model specifying what to look for in the organization. Practitioners use a variety of methods to collect diagnostic data, including interviews, observations, questionnaires, and unobtrusive measures such as company records. The diagnostic data are typically fed back to client members so they can analyze the information, draw conclusions, and design appropriate interventions to improve the organization.

"Commercial Fertilizer (B)," by Achilles A. Armenakis, Henry B. Burdg, and J. Taylor Pursell, describes the diagnostic stage of the OD process begun in the (A) case in Part I. The consultants use a management practices model to guide the diagnosis, which focuses on activities having to do with planning, organizing, staffing, directing, and controlling. They gather data by interviewing the top 13 managers of the firm, and the case includes the interview responses.

In "Engineered Materials," W. Warner Burke is initially asked to design and conduct an off-site meeting for the firm's top executives to discuss how to implement a new business strategy. The case shows how careful diagnosis led the executives to reconsider the meeting and to focus instead on understanding the underlying causes of current problems.

Joan G. Dahl and Alan M. Glassman describe in the "Legal Defense Corporation" an extensive diagnosis of the problems facing a new firm created to defend indigents in a large, metropolitan county. The company is a national model of privatization of public defense. The consultants use both interviews and questionnaires to uncover the sources of the problems and are asked to design a data feedback process.

In "Informatics Inc. and Framus Computers," Marcia V. Wilkof shows the difficulty of doing diagnosis in an interorganizational context. The consultant is asked by a computer systems company to help improve relations with its hardware supplier. The case describes how she collects and analyzes data to discover the underlying causes of the conflict between the two firms.

"First National Bank," by D. D. Warrick, describes a comprehensive diagnosis of a small bank experiencing a variety of problems. The case shows how a diagnostic model can help consultants gather appropriate data. It also demonstrates how two different data-collection methods, interviews and questionnaires, can complement each other and provide a more rounded view of organizations than can a single instrument.

In "Peppercorn Dining," JoAnn Carmin, Todd Comen, and Yariels Kerr provide an account of the diversity of information that may need to be collected to shed light on an organization's problems. The consultants show that considerable data can be gathered in only two days. This raises issues, however, about how to organize and analyze the plethora of data and feed them back to the client organization, a university dining facility.

I. Leticia Ramirez and Jean Bartunek, in "Community Health Center," show what it is like to do OD as an internal change agent in a health-care facility. The case describes the problems inherent in this internal role and discusses how an external person can act as a shadow consultant to the internal person to help her or him solve those issues.

"The Mercurial President," by Gordon Walter and Theodore Gerstl, presents a fascinating account of the pitfalls of doing diagnosis and feedback when an open and trusting relationship between the chief executive and the consultants is lacking. The case underscores the fact that data alone are not sufficient to motivate change in people.

In "The Apartment Complex," Laura L. Goode describes the complexities of trying to change something as simple as the mailboxes in one's apartment building. The consultant shows how OD can be applied to your personal life, particularly in something as loosely organized as an apartment complex.

Commercial Fertilizer (B)

Achilles A. Armenakis
Auburn University
Henry B. Burdg
Auburn University
J. Taylor Pursell
Auburn University

Achilles Armenakis and Henry Burdg were discussing the Commercial Fertilizer information they had collected. The project was scheduled to begin the next week, so they were preparing for their first day of interviews. Because there were so few managers, they had decided to collect the data for the diagnosis by conducting interviews and observing the behavior and interactions of the managers.

The time and cost involved in designing a tailored questionnaire couldn't be justified with just 13 managers. A prefabricated questionnaire wasn't practical either because Achilles and Henry did not know of one designed to gather information on management practices. The interview method would permit them to develop needed credibility and trust with the managers, while they were learning more about the operation of the company and the interaction of the managers. Furthermore, interviews were more personal and would provide a catharsis among the managers by letting them talk through issues that they confront daily.

DESIGNING THE INTERVIEW PLAN

Henry and Achilles agreed to interview the 13 managers, ranging from the CEO to the plant superintendent. In addition, the wife of the CEO, who was a member of the board of directors and part-time employee, would be interviewed. Among the managers were Jimmy's two sons and daughter. Consequently, the entire family, which makes up the board of directors, was interviewed.

Because the managers were going to be the focus of the project, Achilles and Henry agreed they would use the management practices model to guide their questioning and organize the data. That is, one conceptual framework for describing what managers do comprises the functions of planning, organizing, staffing, directing, and controlling. However, they wanted the diagnostic questions to be somewhat disguised so they could gather the information on actual practices in a subtle way. They decided to ask four broad questions and use more specific questions for probing. The four questions were:

1. What activities do you perform in completing your job?
2. What are the company strengths?
3. What are the company problems/constructive criticisms?
4. What are your expectations regarding the consultants' involvement with the company?

The information obtained from the question concerning job activities would help in understanding the overall business, as well as the managerial practices and interaction patterns of managers. The questions regarding strengths and problems not only would reveal additional information on the managerial practices, but also would help in understanding the organizational culture. The question on expectations would be helpful in minimizing the potential for misunderstanding the role of the consultants.

OBSERVATIONS AND INTERVIEW DATA

The interviews were conducted on two days. As planned, the first day was spent with both Achilles and Henry interviewing, in tandem, a single manager. This helped them synchronize the content and manner in which questions were stated so the data collected during the second day of solo interviewing would be comparable. During the three-hour round trip, they discussed the information collected from observing and interviewing managers. In addition, it was helpful to jointly analyze the data.

The notes taken during each interview were content analyzed to produce key terms and phrases descriptive of the information collected. The data collected from each manager were then summarized into fewer meaningful categories that could be used to describe managerial attitudes and behavior. Exhibits 1 and 2 list the key terms and phrases for the two interview questions on strengths and problems. Each key term and phrase is coded to protect the confidentiality of the managers.

Company Strengths

The company strengths, listed in Exhibit 1, were refined into three major categories. The category discussed most readily was labeled *personal relations*. Comments such as "good people," "family orientation," and

---

EXHIBIT 1 Interview Question #2—What Are the Company Strengths?

1. Good people. M1(1), M3(3), M4(3), M6(1), M7(2), M8(1), M2(1)
2. Family orientation. M1(1), M4(4)
3. Christian orientation. M1(1), M4(2), M6(3), M2(1), M9(3)
4. Fringe benefits are good. M1(1)
5. Diverse. M3(4), M4(8)
6. Strategy has been good. M3(5)
7. Small company. M3(2), M4(1), M5(13)
8. Good reputation. M4(5), M9(1)
9. Responsive to customer needs. M4(5), M9(1)
10. Emphasis on product quality. M4(7), M9(1)
11. Autonomy of personnel. M4(9), M5(1)
12. Top management support of lower level decisions. M5(10)
13. Management and production facility located in same location. M4(11)
14. Good geographic location to serve Southeast U.S. M4(12)
15. Area of the business. M6(4)
16. Integrity. M7(1)
17. Restricted entry into industry. M2(5)
18. Twenty-eight years of operating experience. M2(6)
19. Recession-proof industry segment. M2(6)
20. Low market share among many competitors. M1(1)
21. Not being big. M8(1)
22. Ability to work problems out. M8(1)
23. Low employee turnover. M9(2)

Note: Each key term and phrase represents answers to the diagnostic question. The letters and numbers are codes that can be used to identify the respondent and the specific statement by each respondent, taken from the consultants' interview notes. For example, M1(1) is statement #1 made by manager #1. The code numbers were randomly assigned to insure confidentiality. Therefore, this exhibit represents the content of the responses and their frequencies.

"Christian principles" were used frequently to describe the people and culture. Another strength was labeled *business attributes*. This category comprises comments such as "customer responsiveness," "good reputation," and "quality products." The third strength related to the CEO. "Experience" and "management style" were most descriptive of him.

Company Problems

As expected, more time was spent on discussing problems/constructive criticisms than on the other issues. Both Achilles and Henry had experienced this in the diagnostic phase of other studies. They concluded it must be easier to recall aspects of organizational life perceived as unsatisfactory. Three major categories of problems were formed from the responses to the interview questions.

Corporate Structure. The company consisted of three subsidiaries, although the CEO did not treat them as such—at least in an accounting sense. The company's business operations resulted in one consolidated profit-and-loss statement. The performance of each subsidiary received no direct attention. The CEO would periodically remark "our bottom line is weak" without realizing that one of the operations was contributing to the poor performance of the company.

Many managers worked with all subsidiaries. Some of the managers thought their good work in one subsidiary was countered by the poor performance in another. No clear definition existed of who was responsible for different subsidiary operations.

Company Strategy. It was determined that the company strategy was more adaptive than planned. There was no evidence of a written plan for the business including a budget. To date, much managing was conducted by the "seat of the pants." The recent growth produced more activity than the CEO was used to managing. Two examples to illustrate this finding.

First, the company sold approximately 300 different products, but the mix of the products was not systematically determined. When making decisions regarding scheduling of production, pricing of products, and marketing, the full cost was not considered. Rather, the decisions were based on producing as much volume as possible. Consequently, production capacity was being used without systematically determining the benefit to the company. In one case, low-margin products were being scheduled because of the philosophy of keeping the production runs as high as possible. The company's information system did not produce the relevant information to make beneficial decisions. Therefore, company strategy was not being planned.

Second, the company was shipping huge volumes of low-margin products to one customer over 1,000 miles away. When freight costs were added, a negative contribution was realized. Not only was the gross margin for the order too small to justify, but also the effort and sales cost involved in obtaining the order was not justified. Potential customers close to home were not being developed as vigorously as they should.

Management Practices. The remaining data collected from the managers during the interviews were categorized into planning, organizing, staffing, directing, and controlling.

Planning. The consensus of managers was that there was inadequate direction from the top, no formal long range planning process had been

---

EXHIBIT 2   Interview Question #3—What Are the Company Problems/
Constructive Criticisms?

---

1. Inadequate communication/staff meetings. M1(1), M4(7b), M4(9), M7(2), M8(1)
2. Inequitable merit pay raises. M1(2), M4(7c,3), M4(1), M4(5)
3. Salary levels are inconsistent. M1(3)
4. Procedures are not adequately formalized. M1(4), M3(1), M4(7a), M8(5)
5. Marketing manager based in major city (120 miles from company location). M3(2)
6. Understaffed. M3(3,4), M4(15), M4(16), M5(3), M6(1), M6(7), M10(2), M7(3), M8(1)
7. No direction from the top. M3(5), M4(6), M6(8), M7(2), M7(1), M8(1)
8. Trademark problems in the West. M3(7)
9. Lack of formalized management functions. M4(1), M8(1)
10. Lack of company goals. M4(2)
11. Lack of long range planning. M4(3), M4(8), M6(2), M8(1), M9(1)
12. Lack of departmental goals. M4(4), M4(7c2), M9(1)
13. Lack of individual goals. M4(5), M4(7c2)
14. Poor/no job descriptions. M4(7c1)
15. Inadequate performance review. M4(7c3)
16. Inadequate input and data for decision making. M4(10), M4(11), M4(21)
17. Field salesmen operate too independently. M4(12)
18. Computer not being fully operational. M4(14)
19. Some personnel not adequately trained to meet requirements of the job. M4(17), M4(18), M8(1)
20. Resistance to change. M4(19), M1(1)
21. Lack of respect for corporate management by field sales personnel. M4(20)
22. Company car treated as "perk." M4(2)
23. Trucking division is suspect. M4(4), M4(6), M4(8), M7(3)
24. Resentment between some personnel. M6(3), M6(4), M6(5)
25. Limitations of present production equipment. M1(3)
26. Inadequate office space. M10(1)
27. Supervision problems with going to a second shift. M7(2)
28. Cyclical nature of product line. M1(1), M1(2)
29. Loosing control of business. M1(1)
30. Weak "bottom line." M1(1)
31. Lack of personal work discipline. M7(1)
32. Logistics of growth. M7(1)
33. Lack of organization. M2(1)
34. Overemployed and underpaid at plant. M2(1)
35. No delegation of authority. M1(1), M3(1)

Note: Each key term and phrase represents answers to the diagnostic question. The letters and numbers are codes that can be used to identify the respondent and the specific statement by each respondent, taken from the consultants' interview notes. For example, M1(1) is statement #1 made by manager #1. The code numbers were randomly assigned to insure confidentiality. Therefore, this exhibit represents the content of the responses and their frequencies.

---

instituted, no company and departmental goals had been set, and policies and procedures were not properly formalized.

Organizing. No organization chart existed, although the pattern of formal relationships was known. Authority was centralized with inadequate delegation of authority to all managers. Consequently, managers believed they were being held responsible but were not delegated the appropriate authority. Managers often found decisions being made in their areas by the CEO, who did not first communicate his actions. In some instances, this was ineffective and costly to the company. Furthermore, this behavior circumvented the affected manager's ability to deal with subordinates. Titles of managers were not consistent. No job descriptions existed.

Staffing. There was a general feeling that the company was understaffed. There was an inadequate performance review system. Managers thought merit pay was inequitable, and salary levels were not systematically established. Resentment existed among some managers. In general, managers demonstrated a lack of personal work discipline.

Directing. The managers did not think they communicated adequately. That is, they did not believe the horizontal or vertical communication was as effective as it should be. Also, the delegation of authority and holding one accountable for results were not executed properly.

Controlling. Because the prior functions were not being performed adequately it was believed the controlling function was also being performed inadequately. For example, objectives were not being set and the information system was not producing the relevant information to determine whether the company or the managers were performing adequately.

Expectations

Achilles and Henry were concerned about being able to meet the expectations of the managers. They had discussed the importance of understanding what the managers expected from the project. In response to the expectation question, the managers used phrases such as "help us" rather than "tell us."

PLANNING FOR FEEDBACK

The steps in problem solving include creating an awareness, developing motivation, proposing alternatives, and then deciding on and implementing appropriate tactics. The feedback session was the next crucial step. Achilles and Henry would create the awareness and motivate the managers to address the issues. The management practices model was helpful in collecting and organizing the data. In preparing for the feedback session, it seemed the managers would readily identify with the model; after all, these were their data.

Achilles and Henry admitted the information they had accumulated was not as simple as it appeared—neatly organized into the strengths and problems. Numerous interrelationships complicated the apparent simplicity. The purpose of the interviews was merely to collect data. The remainder of the diagnosis should separate the symptoms (those results observed) from the causes (the behaviors responsible for the symptoms). For example, the managers believed the company was understaffed (item 6 in Exhibit 2). However, Henry and Achilles thought this was a symptom that was caused by any number of potential causes. There was considerable duplication of effort (because no job descriptions existed, item 14 in Exhibit 2). Also, the managers were not making proper use of their time since there was lack of a personal work discipline (item 31), lack of individual and departmental goals (items 12 and 13), and inadequate delegation of authority (item 35).

Another symptom was the weak company strategy as evidenced by not systematically determining product mix (focusing on volume instead of cost). This may be attributable to poor planning, such as not setting goals (items 7, 10, 11, 12, and 16). Achilles and Henry did not intend to present the data summarized in Exhibits 1 and 2, although it was necessary to simplify and identify the data with each manager. Confidentiality of the data was important. Therefore, in order to present the data in an easily interpretable form, Henry and Achilles prepared Exhibit 3. This figure maintains confidentiality and simplifies the explanation (the distinction between symptoms and causes) of the findings.

One strategy for the next phase of the project could be designing solutions with little or no input from the managers. Another strategy could be to work with the managers to analyze the problems and strengths and to develop their own solutions with the consultants acting largely as facilitators.

The response of the managers to the question concerning their expectations of the consultants was helpful in proposing a strategy for the remainder of the project. The managers seemed to be saying they wanted to participate in planning and implementing solutions to eliminate the causes of the ineffectiveness. Therefore, Achilles and Henry decided to propose to Jimmy that a series of work sessions be planned and conducted with the managers.

The benefits to this approach are numerous. For example, the managers would be focusing on the specific practices they identified as being inadequate. Moreover, they would be addressing behaviors and attitudes they defined as being inappropriate, such as poor communication (item 1), lack of input into decision making (16), a resistance to change (20), and resentment (24). In short, by working as a group, the managers

EXHIBIT 3

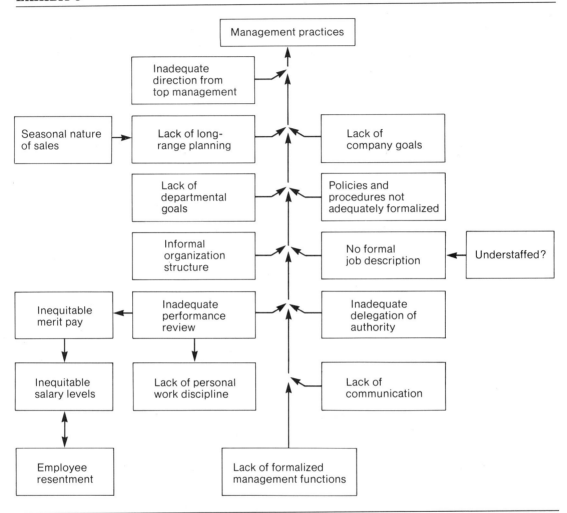

Source: A. Armenakis and H. Burdg, "Planning for Growth," *Long Range Planning* 19 (1986), p. 96.

would also be improving their process skills—communication, problem solving, and decision making.

QUESTIONS FOR DISCUSSION

1. What are the various methods for collecting data during an organizational diagnosis? When is it appropriate for each to be used? Was the interview method the most appropriate in Commercial Fertilizer (B)?

2. Why did Achilles and Henry conduct tandem interviews the first day?

3. What is a diagnostic model? Give examples of diagnostic models. What are the advantages and disadvantages to framing the questions and subsequently the responses around any diagnostic model? Around the management practices diagnostic model?

4. The information provided in Exhibits 1 and 2 has been coded (to protect confidentiality), refined (to minimize irrelevant data), and summarized (to facilitate analysis). Did all managers provide relevant data? Do you agree with the categorization and organization of the data in Exhibit 3? Do you agree with categorizing the company strength data (Exhibit 1) into the categories provided in the section titled "Company Strengths"? Do you agree with categorizing the company problem data (Exhibit 2) into the categories provided in the section titled "Company Problems"? What other symptoms and causes can be identified from the data provided in Exhibit 2?

Engineered Materials

W. Warner Burke
Columbia University

The company, a wholly owned subsidiary of a multibillion corporation, manufactured certain engineered materials, largely for the automobile industry but for other customers as well, such as aerospace companies. The company had been acquired in 1980 by the much larger parent corporation, which could easily be called a conglomerate. The client company's competition was in the United States and in Europe and Asia, so it was developing a global business implementation strategy.

At the time of this case, the CEO was only the second in the company's long history, the founder having died during the late 1970s. The founder had always been the CEO and was a single-minded, tough, autocratic, highly controlling individual. The founder's successor was quite different, more participative in his approach, an accountant who had earned an MBA, rather than a manufacturing person like the founder.

A consultant was engaged at the time by the parent corporation to conduct sessions on leadership and managing change for managers and executives who attended programs at the corporation's management development institute. The client contacted one of the staff members at the institute requesting a consultant with expertise in managing change. The consultant was then contracted by the management development institute staff member to work with the client.

To the consultant's surprise, the client (CEO of the subsidiary) had already scheduled an off-site meeting of his top 40 managers to address the implementation strategy problem. The consultant was being asked to help design the meeting and to make a presentation on "managing change."

SOME PERSPECTIVE

Many consultants would be uncomfortable accepting such an assignment (see, for example, Burke, 1982). Labeling the problem as one of strategy implementation does not tell us very much. Moreover, addressing the problem with an off-site meeting as the action step but with such little clarity and specificity as to overall purpose is like providing a solution to something—but to what?

An option in this case would be to design a meeting for these executives along the lines of Richard Beckhard's "confrontation meeting" (Beckhard, 1967). The confrontation meeting is a highly involving set of activities designed to generate a lot of information in a short time (e.g., one day), and is largely diagnostic in nature. Before a session with the CEO to discuss the meeting, a copy of Beckhard's article was sent to him as a way of stimulating a possible approach that might help clarify the implementation problem.

Part of the consultant's intent in sending the CEO a copy of Beckhard's article was to communicate the message that the kind of off-site meeting he apparently had in mind—a presentation by an outside consultant and discussion—was probably too simple and ill defined. Moreover, the consultant was uncomfortable with how he was entering this potential assignment. In consulting language, the process was out of phase, an intervention was planned without a prior diagnosis. Furthermore, this particular consultant was a strong believer in conducting a thorough diagnosis as an integral if not primary part of any consulting effort. In essence, a good diagnosis practically determines what the subsequent intervention should be.

Wanting to be responsive and cooperative and not wishing to create a problem at the onset for his colleague, the staff member at the management development institute, the consultant agreed to a one-day exploratory meeting.

INITIAL MEETING WITH THE CLIENT

About two weeks before the scheduled off-site meeting of the top management group, the consultant met with the CEO and the director of human resources. After two hours of discussion, it became clear that matters were anything but clear. The purpose of the planned off-site meeting seemed vague. The consultant then asked permission to spend the rest of the day interviewing some of the company vice presidents to ask them about the forthcoming meeting and what its purpose should be (see Exhibit 1 for a chart of the group). At the end of the day, the CEO and the consultant planned to meet again.

Three interviews were conducted. The consultant asked each individual what he knew about the forthcoming off-site meeting. All three stated that (1) they had no idea as to the purpose of the meeting, (2) it had not been discussed at any of the CEO's regular staff meetings, and (3) such a meeting was premature. At the end of the day the CEO and the consultant met again as planned. The consultant summarized for him

EXHIBIT 1 Organization Chart of Top Management

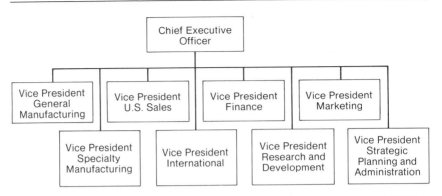

underline individual

what the three persons said. The consultant explained that if these three were representative of his top management group, there was little or no commitment to this planned off-site meeting. It was further suggested that more work was needed to achieve greater clarity about what specific problems such a meeting might address.

As a consequence of the outcome of these interviews and the subsequent discussion with the CEO, the off-site meeting was canceled. The lack of clarity regarding the purpose of the meeting, not to mention the insufficient commitment to such a process, warranted the decision, the CEO and consultant both agreed.

The consultant then suggested the alternative of digging deeper by interviewing individually most of these top executives. The interviews would be open ended, to cast the diagnostic net widely. The CEO agreed, and 26 interviews were conducted.

THE DIAGNOSTIC PHASE

Six major questions were asked in each interview:

1. What are the strengths of the company?
2. What are the primary, current problems the company is facing?
3. What gives you a sense of personal satisfaction in your job?
4. What are some barriers, if any, that prevent you from doing the kind of job you would prefer?
5. What are your feelings about and assessment of the relations between your company and the parent corporation?

6. What are your feelings about and assessment of the company's strategic plan?

The first two questions were organizational, while questions three and four focused on the individual. Another feature of these first four questions was that the first and third accentuated the positive, while the other two probed for negative concerns and issues. Questions five and six were more specific to this particular client organization. Also included in the diagnostic phase was the consultant's reading of the company's strategic plan. See the appendix for an abbreviated version of this plan.

THE FEEDBACK PHASE

Table 1 provides a partial summary of these interviews. This summary was reported back initially to the CEO and then to the vice presidential group—eight executives. Their reaction to the interview summary was twofold: First, they thought the information was accurate (e.g., "That looks like us all right"). Second, they reacted in a ho-hum fashion (e.g., "So what? What does it really tell us?").

Knowing these initial interview results, while fairly comprehensive, were only scratching the surface and highly symptomatic, the consultant had analyzed the interview results somewhat, that is, considered the information beyond just a simple summary. Because some people had positive opinions about the parent corporation while others were negative (no one seemed neutral), the consultant suspected these two groupings of the interviews might reveal something beyond the simple summary. Indeed it did! The consultant hypothesized there were two "camps" within the company. Camp 1 believed that business and the management thereof should be conducted one way, while camp 2 believed something quite different. Although overly simplified and incomplete with respect to a thorough description, Table 2 shows what was presented by the consultant to this top management group.

The hypothesis of two camps is based on thinking similar to what others have referred to as a "center of gravity" or "strategic driving force" for a company in a particular industry (Galbraith, 1983; Tregoe and Zimmerman, 1980). The idea is that an organization has a primary driving force or center of gravity as a result of what its executives believe about the best way of doing business. What's the best way of making money in this industry, at least for our firm? Executives' beliefs about and their answers to this question constitute the

TABLE 1 Summary of 26 Executive Interviews Rank Ordered From Most Frequently Mentioned to Least Frequently Mentioned (to be included, a minimum of two executives had to make the point explicitly)

Strengths

Our management information system
Improvements have been made in product quality and marketplace
Family atmosphere/positive work climate/good people
Interface with parent company has improved us
Brand name recognition; position in the marketplace
Strategic planning/global thinking
We are the best in the business in all respects
Business improving
Lots of potential
Consolidation of factories/upgrade of divisions
We have a lot of talented people
There is better coordination
Efficiency is slowly growing
Good benefits/job ratings/retirement package

Problem areas

Too much paperwork
Business climate bad—no growth industry curerntly, tougher competition
Our management information system (MIS) looks at a lot of numbers
    without much integration/not well supported/seen as a burden
Poor downward communication (it comes either laterally or through the
    grapevine)
Too much planning/too slow making decisions/not a quick company anymore
We're always playing "catch up"; not fast enough
Motivation a problem—no one fired up
Coordination of internal products/product change/getting the right product
    on the shelf
International structure does not meet the needs of the products/no
    cooperation on international products
Need a professional marketing group/more international marketing
Too many performance appraisal systems/people do not like to get feedback
Consolidation has led to layoffs that have, in turn, led to less employee
    motivation
We bitch too much and blame too many of our shortcomings on the parent
    company
People want more information about vision and plans for the future; they do
    not know where the company is going
Feelings of threat about each of our little worlds
Departments need to be better grouped; need to cooperate more
Price has become more important than quality or service
People withhold information
Lateral empire building is a problem

TABLE 1 *(concluded)*

We wait and hope the problems will go away

With business tougher we are admonished to cut, when being aggressive in the marketplace would be better

Confusion about direction—"Are we making products or paper?"

People are having a problem letting go of the good old days

Job satisfaction

Challenging job/high personal involvement with the company and the work

Good rapport with the people/family atmosphere

Good benefits, pay, and rewards

High involvement

High autonomy

Barriers

Decisions take too long/not enough personal freedom/cannot be an entrepreneur

Too much paperwork, meetings, programs

Our history and certain personalities, get in the way

No direct communication with top management

No performance feedback

Parent corporation

Good corporate benefits, retirement package, opportunities for young employees

Merger seen as positive; better resources, organizational security, business

Parent company programs are imposed/they have forced a structure on us

We prefer to stay private

Corporate parent doesn't really give a damn about us—"They are not warm people"

They do not understand our business/reward structure

People, especially middle management, are reluctant to be a part of the parent organization

Business has gone up since the merger; there have been more sales to other corporate family companies as well

There's been an increase in meetings and paperwork

People are good as long as they stay within corporate parent policies and guidelines regardless of the outcome/there is little autonomy/creativity

Our strategic plan

Needs to include and involve more people—a short explanation should go out to all employees

The business changes too quickly to plan 5 years ahead—must not miss the trend, ride the wave <u>now</u>

Necessary/great plan

Strategic plan somewhat unrealistic; we are simply hoping that sales will reamin the <u>same</u>

Strategic plan is a snow job; too many guesses, phony numbers

It is just creating more paperwork

TABLE 2   A Summary of the Hypothesized "Two Camps" within the Company

Camp 1	*Camp 2*
Parent corporation good	Parent corporation bad
Rational approach to business (MBA)—mental	Work directly with customers and respond to them quickly and energetically—emotional
Wear ties to work	Some dirt on one's hands is a good thing—no ties
Future: strategic plan for a changing marketplace	Past: we already know how to succeed in this business
Marketing: must conduct market research and plan/manage accordingly	Manufacturing/sales: must stress productivity/quality and sell, sell
Reward those who plan; then implement	Reward action

company's primary, if not singular, driving force. Of course, the less there is agreement among executives about this belief the less there is a common driving force or *center* of gravity. In this case, there were two belief systems (i.e., two driving forces or centers of gravity). While these two sets of beliefs overlapped, camp 1 was more "downstream" in its beliefs about doing business successfully (i.e., product development according to market need). Camp 2 was more "upstream" (i.e., produce large volumes almost like a commodities business and push sales).

The purposes of this brief presentation were to test the hypothesis and to provoke further discussion, debate, and action. The two-camp interpretation the consultant presented was accurate, the eight executives grudgingly agreed, but they apparently needed to challenge him further. One of them said, "OK, Mr. Consultant, tell us which of us is in which camp!" The consultant took the challenge and classified four of them in camp 1 and four in camp 2. Each executive admitted the classification was correct except the sales manager, who saw himself as "straddling the fence between both camps." At that stage, the consultant and executives had had their fun with this confrontation, and they then unanimously agreed that much work now needed to be done.

problems

camp1   camp2

QUESTIONS FOR DISCUSSION

If you were the consultant in this case, what next steps would you recommend if not urge? Some questions to consider:

1. There were two belief systems or two subcultures, one of which (camp 1) matches the corporate strategy closer than the other. What might be done to help the top group deal with, and with any luck at all, even resolve their two-camp differences?
2. What about the larger picture, their relationships with the parent company? The two subcultures are indeed different.
3. Is there a structure problem? Aspiring to be a global business, is the company organized appropriately?
4. What about the CEO and his role? What action, if any, should he now take?

#1 up rive → produce — sell

#2 down river → respond to customer needs, wants

APPENDIX

Company Mission

Leverage global capabilities via marketing, engineering, and manufacturing to achieve a number one position worldwide as a supplier of engineered materials.

SUMMARY
- Expand marketing and distribution globally.
- Expand product and process development to meet the needs of different market environments.
- Rationalize manufacturing capacity.
- Manage break-even programs to improve overall profitability.
- Double sales by 1992.

SITUATION SUMMARY
- Slow growth for engineered materials in major industrialized nations.
- Global customer expectations are changing.
  Supplier rationalization.
  Transfer of costs to suppliers.
  Computerization (order entry, invoicing, funds transfer, part processing, inventory, etc.).
- Technology and innovation in engineered materials are coming from outside the United States (Japan and West Germany).
- Worldwide competitive mergers and strategic alliances.
- Worldwide overcapacity in the industry.

IMPLICATIONS OF SITUATION SUMMARY
- Future growth must come from penetrating competitor strongholds and enlarging our customer base with small and medium users.
- Worldwide market penetration demands:
  A competitive worldwide standard product line.
  Performance equal to world class competition.
  Cost and quality parity with world class competition.
- We must gain position with worldwide builder/distributors to gain aftermarket sales and supply the necessary products.
- Worldwide prices will be very difficult to increase due to overcapacity and competition for market share—requires us to be a low-cost producer.
- Major customers seeking to reduce number of suppliers may require that we expand our product/service scope in order to retain preferred supplier status.

REFERENCES

Beckhard, R. "The Confrontation Meeting." *Harvard Business Review* 45, no. 2 (January–February 1967), pp. 149–55.

Burke, W. W. *Organization Development: Principles and Practices.* Boston: Little, Brown, 1982.

Galbraith, J. R. "Strategy and Organization Planning." *Human Resources Management* 22, no. 1/2 (March 1983), pp. 63–77.

Tregoe, B. B., and Zimmerman, J. W. *Top Management Strategy.* New York: Simon & Schuster, 1980.

Legal Defense Corporation

Joan G. Dahl
California State University, Northridge
Alan M. Glassman
California State University, Northridge

In 1984, the Metropolitan County Board of Supervisors confronted the following dilemma:

1. With increasing frequency, the Public Defender's Office was unable to provide indigent defense representation due to both inherent conflicts of interest (e.g., one of the multiple defendants in the same case demanded a separate attorney) and caseloads that prohibited the acceptance of additional cases.

2. When the public defender could not provide the necessary representation, the court appointed a private lawyer to represent the indigent defendant(s) and the county incurred the costs. An analysis by the *Metro Times* newspaper indicated these costs were exceptionally high and the existing system lacked the controls necessary to prevent cronyism and fraud.

3. The *Metro Times* article embarrassed the board majority, which prided itself on efficient management and cost-cutting programs, including the privatization or contracting of work traditionally performed by government agencies to private-sector firms.

Initially, the board debated two diametrically opposed approaches to the problem: creating a second Public Defender's Office to represent indigent defendants (supported by board members who advocated strong government) or contracting the work to one or two legal firms through a bidding process (supported by board members who favored maximum privatization). After lengthy debate and extensive media coverage, the political compromise, enacted by board ordinance, was the Legal Defense Corporation (LDC).

The concept for the Legal Defense Corporation was simple:

1. The Legal Defense Corporation would be a private legal firm, incorporated under California law with its own board of directors. Its sole activity would be indigent defense.

2. The county would be the firm's only client and would conduct a nationwide search for an administrator to establish/manage the firm. The county would negotiate a contract with the administrator and pay the agreed upon salary.

3. The administrator could hire five lawyers initially and negotiate their salaries; a pay classification system, somewhat below the Public Defender's Office, was established. All subsequent requests for additional professional staff had to be approved by the board.

4. Most important, as a private firm, the Legal Defense Corporation attorneys would *compete* with other lawyers to gain court-appointed cases. The county would maintain liaison through a staff person in the office of the chief administrative officer for the county.

The challenge in establishing the Legal Defense Corporation was formidable. First, the legal community condemned the concept as an attempt to undermine the legitimate efforts and fees of practicing lawyers who received court-appointed clients; that is, an attempt to focus on costs, not quality of representation. Second, nearly all the county employee associations attacked the proposal as additional evidence of the county's commitment to privatize all services. After all, if legal representation could be contracted, no employee's job was safe. Third, many people in government doubted that judges would accept the Legal Defense Corporation's attorneys. In cases involving indigent representation, the judges had developed long-standing relationships with independent lawyers and several law firms.

In late 1984, the board appointed a well-known criminal defense attorney as the administrator. After recruiting the five other lawyers, the process of "selling" judges on their qualifications (and cost benefits) began. The success of this effort was extraordinary.

By 1988, the Legal Defense Corporation (1) had been fully accepted in 16 of the 34 courts in Metropolitan County and in most instances was the appointment of first choice, (2) had grown from the original group of six lawyers to fifty-five lawyers and a support staff of ten in four main offices and four ancillary locations, (3) had saved the county between $1 and $2 million per year for the last three years, when compared by an independent auditor to the average cost of private representation, and (4) had been praised locally for the quality of its work and nationally as a model experiment in privatization. It was expected that from 1988 to 1990, the Legal Defense Corporation would expand into six or more additional courts.

INTRODUCTION AND ENTRY TO THE LEGAL DEFENSE CORPORATION

In early November 1987, Alan Glassman received a telephone call from Sharon, the liaison person for the County Administrative Office (CAO) to the Legal Defense Corporation (LDC), asking whether he was interested in conducting an in-depth study of the Legal Defense Corporation.

Sharon explained that despite its recognized success, the LDC had recently experienced internal difficulties. These included expressed complaints over working conditions (e.g., poor physical designs/locations), the increasing number of work rules, the existing salary schedule, and the lack of additional benefits. Also, some attorneys perceived John, the administrator, as arbitrary and sometimes capricious in his decision-making behavior. Subsequently, a number of small episodes resulted in John submitting his resignation to the CAO, effective at the termination of his contract in about 10 months. This was not announced to anyone, including organization members and the board of supervisors. In their conversation, John and the CAO agreed to a study to determine the underlying causes, if possible, of the rising internal discontent.

As Alan expressed interest in conducting the study and asked more detailed questions, Sharon elaborated:

1. Both she and the CAO were convinced John did not really want to resign, but needed both external and internal recognition of his accomplishments during the past three years (he was feeling underappreciated).
2. The CAO was personally committed to retaining John and believed that much of the success of the LDC was directly due to the teamwork between John and Sharon when making presentations to judges.
3. This was a critical time for expansion for the LDC, and a change in leadership was perceived as untimely and could possibly weaken the organization.
4. The exact nature of the study and methodology was undetermined.
5. John would interview two or three potential consultants, each known from previous work with county agencies, review our proposals, and make the final decision.
6. Funding for the study would be worked out between John and the CAO.

As Sharon and I were discussing the potential study and some of the operational details of the Legal Defense Corporation, I underwent an approach-avoidance reaction. For the past 15 years, nearly 60 percent of my OD activities had involved public organizations, and my somewhat positive reputation was based on a willingness to tackle "messy" situations, including a current project, in its third year, with one of the county's largest departments; the LDC offered another highly visible and potentially risky challenge. Moreover, privatization/contracting was an area of current research, and the opportunity to gather data on this "hybrid" organization was compelling.

On the other hand, Sharon described the LDC as needing "a form of crisis intervention" and given my personal reluctance to engage in short-term projects, the surrounding politics, and the lack of project clarity, I was hesitant to become involved. Also, although never stated, there was a suspicion that the selected consultant would be part of a concerted effort by the CAO to retain John.

As the conversation progressed, Alan shared with Sharon some ideas for data gathering and feedback. After approximately 75 minutes, Sharon asked Alan to meet with John. Alan agreed. Two days later, John called and a breakfast meeting was set up for the following week.

The Meeting

The meeting between John and Alan began with both noting that this was an initial session with no commitments. Alan shared his conversation with Sharon and explained how he usually gathered data and provided feedback to the client system. John noted that the proposed study was something the CAO wanted and that he personally hoped would help his successor. Both discussed their past experiences.

After the preliminaries, John reiterated the history of the Legal Defense Corporation and assessed the current situation. From his perspective, the increased dissatisfaction could be attributed to approximately 15 percent of the attorneys, who could not adjust to the high performance standards or who could not accept the increased controls needed in a larger organization.

With some prodding, John explained that these attorneys wanted the best of two worlds—the high salaries, plush offices, and freedom of a private law firm and the security of a steady, although often overwhelming, caseload. From his perspective, these unhappy attorneys fell into two categories: (1) attorneys who had failed in managing their previous outside practice (i.e., they couldn't attract enough clients or collect client fees) and (2) those who were poor performers and were disappointed in their compensation level. He summarized by suggesting that they should leave—"let's see if they can make it on their own."

> Throughout the early stages of this discussion, John was rather unemotional and I felt as though I was listening to a well-rehearsed summation. Only when John spoke about the dissatisfied attorneys did I detect that he was quite angry and that he viewed the situation as a personal rebuff.

Equally important was John's perception of his role as administrator. First, he was emphatic in noting that he worked for the county, despite the Legal Defense Corporation's legal status as a private firm. After all, his contract was with the county, he negotiated for resources with the county, and he answered to the County Administrator's Office. Second, his primary administrative concern was quality representation at reasonable cost to the county. Throughout the conversation, John referred to the need for cost containment—the lack of budget to do more. He voluntarily acknowledged that some of the work locations needed upgrading, but to seek too much funding at once would undermine the organization. He also cited his own salary as an example to the organization of the need to be frugal, his salary being nearly three times lower than his last year of private practice. Third, he saw himself as the protector of the LDC's hard-earned reputation and image. John asserted, "I do not want to be viewed as another county organization where workers do what is minimally necessary to retain their jobs," and "My job is to enforce the rules to make sure the county gets a fair day's work and even more from the employees of this organization."

Alan and John exchanged several stories about abuses by government employees. Throughout the conversation, Alan interjected some opinions and elicited additional information on what John perceived as the major issues within the organization. Surprisingly, John asked Alan only a few questions. At the conclusion of the meeting, it was agreed that Alan would submit a proposal for a data-gathering and feedback project that could be completed within three months.

I found John likable. He was an independent, self-made individual with a strong work ethic. During our meeting (and in subsequent conversations), I learned he had put himself through law school at night, he had established his practice in one of the poorest areas of Metro County and had always focused on indigent representation. He had resisted offers to join larger, established law firms, preferring solo practice or a partnership with one other attorney. In 1983, he was honored as the top "capital crime" defense attorney in the state. Commenting on his success, he often stated, "I'm not any brighter than the attorneys I encounter, but I am always better prepared. No one spends more time preparing a case than I do."

I also enjoyed his antiestablishment orientation. For example, he was the first attorney in the state to challenge the State Bar's ban on publishing both success rates and fee structures. Also, as previously noted, he accepted the position of administrator for the Legal Defense Corporation despite the opposition of the legal community to the concept. Regardless of setting (e.g., meetings, office, court), John wore combat boots.

As I reflected on the meeting, I had little doubt that I would be awarded the contract. Although John had made me work for my information, we did establish a reasonable initial level of trust and we did seem to share many common values about helping people and working hard. Moreover, he was very receptive to my suggestion that we focus the study on quality-of-work-life issues and professional needs. As an aside, I thought John was particularly pleased that I did not immediately cast him as the villain.

At the same time, I was still troubled by several questions: the CAO, as expressed by Sharon, seemed intent on retaining John as the administrator, while John was insistent on leaving when his contract expired. Was John sincere about leaving? Could I depend on John for support during the project? Who was my client?

Establishing the Ground Rules

During the next week, Alan asked Joan Dahl to help him put together a proposal that included developing a questionnaire, interviewing *all* members (i.e., professional and staff) of the organization, analyzing the data, submitting a written analysis, and conducting two feedback sessions—one with John and Sharon and one with all organization members. Three weeks later, the contract was signed. At Alan's urging, the Legal Defense Corporation was identified as the contracting client (and payee) and John as the focal executive.

In two follow-up conversations among Alan, John, and Sharon, it was decided (1) John not announce his resignation until after all the data were collected (this pleased the CAO, who continued to withhold this information from the board of supervisors), (2) John would not initiate any "significant" organizational changes during the project period, (3) the data would be shared with John before the final report was prepared, and (4) the organizational members would receive the same data as John at their feedback session. It was also agreed that Alan would have access to all secondary data maintained by the Legal Defense Corporation (e.g., compensation levels, audit reports) and he could gather additional data for his research interests.

> While I still did not know if John was a willing participant, I had decided that to place him in any other role courted disaster.

Logistically, Alan would conduct a meeting at each major office to explain the purpose of the study and to distribute the questionnaires. Completed questionnaires would be mailed directly to Alan at the University. Interviews would be conducted by Alan, Joan, and two other colleagues.

A CLOSER LOOK

The four main locations were close to the courts they served. Until this point, Alan had seen only the downtown location, which was attractive, containing one- or two-person offices. The other sites were much less attractive, ranging from cubicle spaces to "bullpen" areas to incredibly cramped space and shared desks. The site with the latter, located in one of the poorest, highest crime areas in the county, was often referred to as *Siberia*. Except for the downtown site, all lacked privacy and adequate space for files (e.g., cartons of records

EXHIBIT 1   Summary Analysis Respondent Questionnaires
(47 respondents)

General Satisfaction with:
Intrinsic rewards
Co-workers
Career at LDC

Some Satisfaction with:
Working conditions
Benefits
Supervision

Neither Satisfied or Dissatisfied with:
Pay
Performance feedback

Strengths:
Commitment to profession
Commitment to the organization

Problem Areas:
Increasing role ambiguity (with respect to goals, expectations, and performance standards)
Lack of participation (with respect to goal setting and decision making)
Restrictive work rules, policies, and procedures
One-way communication
Concentrated control

EXHIBIT 2   Content Analysis Respondent Interviews (46 respondents)
(Decision rule: Minimum of 8 respondents referred to item)

Item	Number	%	Representative Statement
Job Positives			
Satisfying work	42	91.3	I like helping a variety of clients and interfacing with judges. Time goes fast, I'm busy.
Enjoyable people	23	50.0	I like the camaraderie of a small office that lacks competition.
Independence	19	41.3	I like being handed a stack of cases and told to "do it"—I'm having a great time.
Lack of business worries	8	17.4	It's nice to practice law and not think about finding clients, managing an office, and collecting money.

EXHIBIT 2   *(continued)*

Item	Number	%	Representative Statement
Job Problems			
Overworked and overly stressed	15	32.6	Sometimes I'm so busy I can't think.
Oppressive climate	9	19.6	Upward communication is not wanted. They don't want to hear your problems and are arbitrary about everything.
Job Improvement Suggestions			
Additional staff support	14	54.3	Free law clerks or legal specialists to help manage the work load.
Better work site	12	26.1	The workplace is a sty; I'd like a private office.
Job/Career Aspirations			
Remain at LDC	38	82.6	If the salary stays comparable to other public service organizations, I'll stay at LDC.
Organization Direction			
Expand/ Save money	32	69.6	I assume as long as we're cost effective, we'll continue to expand.
Organization Exceeded Expectations			
Personnel	21	45.7	The high quality of the attorneys has led to acceptance by the bar and other attorneys.
Work quality	11	23.9	We provide much better representation than the public defender does.
Organization Failed to Meet Expectations			
Evaluation/ Rewards	17	37.0	The approach to evaluation is negative; the money won't meet my long-term needs.
Organization Needed Changes			
Supervision	18	39.1	Have less "personality" in supervision and more reasonable rules.
Evaluation/ Rewards	17	37.0	Institute a fair salary structure with standards known to all.
Hiring/Training	12	26.1	Hire only attorneys with 5 years of criminal trial experience; offer internal seminars. (Note: also many comments on the need for support staff hiring and training.)

EXHIBIT 2 *(concluded)*

Item	Number	%	Representative Statement
Leadership:			
Administrator/Supervisor Relationship			
Fear/Lack of authority	21	45.7	[Administrator] doesn't delegate authority; they're mere message carriers. The supervisors often act out of fear instead of reason.
Positive to excellent	9	19.6	[Administrator] encourages supervisors' input on topics but makes the ultimate decision—it's a good relationship. The supervisors play by the rules; it gets them what they want.
Leadership: Overall Assessment			All respondents commented on the administrator. Three conclusions appeared interwoven in their assessment:

1. The administrator was instrumental in gaining acceptance by the judges and in establishing the high standards for LDC attorneys. It was generally agreed that without the administrator's extraordinary skills and guidance, LDC would have failed.
2. As LDC has grown, the administrator has become more autocratic, seemingly more concerned with keeping costs down than with the professional needs of the professional staff. Many of the attorneys considered many of the rules petty, bureaucratic nonsense. On the other hand, a large minority supported the concept of clear-cut rules.
3. Everyone agreed that leadership meant only one thing—the administrator.

---

were stacked in hallways or small storage areas). On the other hand, the cohesiveness of the attorneys appeared much greater at the non-downtown sites.

At the group meetings, most comments and questions focused on the confidentiality of the information, Alan's relationship with John, and the overall usefulness of the data gathering. While nearly all agreed that the 16-page questionnaire asked the right questions, few expected any changes. Comments ranged from, "I know John wants to improve the internal operations of the organization, but I'm not sure he has the managerial knowledge" to, "This is just a charade by John to make it look as though he really cares."

During the next two months, we interviewed 52 attorneys and 10 staff (5 attorneys had been with LDC less than four months, not enough time to provide adequate data, so they were dropped from the study). The forty-seven returned questionnaires were processed and the data analyzed. Summary findings from the questionnaire and interview data, shown in Exhibits 1 and 2, indicated a moderately healthy organization, undergoing some of the normal problems associated with growth and change.

As I reviewed the data, I began to picture a fractionated organization with little chance of reconciliation and with John as the scapegoat. It appeared that regardless of issue (e.g., selection of office supervisor, method of accountability, caseload distribution), cliques existed within each office. Moreover, offices tended to be unaware of events in other offices. In short, these were independent-minded people, and I wasn't sure I could do anything to help them.

On the other hand, John's preoccupation with small administrative details and his inability to delegate to his office supervisors certainly seemed to exacerbate the situation. My conversations with John, however, indicated he was not going to change either.

I was also convinced John would leave.

Informal Pressures

As the interviews progressed, John became increasingly eager to announce his resignation. In a conversation with Alan, he noted that unless 90 percent to 95 percent of the people supported him, and that was unlikely, he was leaving. It was clear that all issues were to be viewed personally. Alan also received numerous telephone calls from attorneys offering additional information and insights. In nearly every instance, however, other agendas operated.

During this time, Joan conducted all the interviews at the Siberia site, resulting in some vast perceptual differences between Joan and Alan. Joan's only direct contact with the organization at this time was with the attorneys in Siberia. These attorneys argued convincingly that Siberia was used (1) to punish those attorneys who most vehemently disagreed with organizational mandates and (2) the location received far fewer resources than other locations.

The Siberia office looked like a combination slum/battleground. The fixtures were the latest in modern office vogue, circa 1940. Files littered the floor in front of overstuffed file cabinets. Placing a chair near an attorney's desk for a client often involved a major rearranging of furniture. The neighborhood was the scene of drug deals, muggings, and an occasional rape. My interviews with the nine Siberia attorneys and two staff were conducted in an overheated, underventilated room often used by juries.

The "Siberia 9" were at first noticeably reluctant to talk with me. Some were openly negative. I saw that my first task was to deal with this negativity so the interviews could proceed. There was a pervasive feeling that Siberia never got its share of resources, from clerical help to paper clips. Several expressed the belief that their work site always "got the leftovers"; even in this instance they didn't get a "real" consultant, just Alan's secretary. The first part of most of the interviews was spent building rapport and reassuring the attorneys they had indeed been given a "real" consultant.

When a level of trust was established, the Siberia 9 began to candidly discuss their feelings about the organization and about John's leadership style in particular. Even though these were defense attorneys, their "prosecution" of John was most convincing. The image of John's style that I was given was quite heavy-handed and unsympathetic. The more data I collected, the more they corroborated the idea that the organization's problems stemmed basically from John's personal style. From this it seemed evident that any intervention needed to focus on him.

Knowing only this unidimensional image of John and having never met him, Alan's need to help John was a bit baffling. My image of John had been formed by the Siberia 9. Alan's attitude toward John was formed by decidedly more temperate inputs. Even with these differing perceptions, Alan concurred that John's style seemed to be a focal point of the organizational data we were collecting.

PREPARATION FOR FEEDBACK SESSIONS

Soon after the data gathering was completed, John (and the CAO) announced John's resignation. When we scheduled the feedback session with John, we learned Sharon would also attend. John also asked us to consider whether a total group feedback session was still needed—wouldn't access to the final report be sufficient? If a group feedback session was conducted, should he and Sharon attend?

Our primary task over the next several weeks was to analyze the data and to determine an appropriate feedback structure that would avoid the unproductive placing of guilt/blame as was currently happening in the organization. At the same time, we both thought we needed to find a framework that would help us and the organizational members put events at the Legal Defense Corporation into perspective to help all parties understand what had occurred in the organization over the last four years.

QUESTIONS FOR DISCUSSION

1. How would you explain the current situation?
2. How would you design the feedback session with John and Sharon?
3. Should a second feedback session be conducted for attorneys and staff? Why or why not? Explain.
4. If a feedback session was to be held for attorneys and staff, should John and/or Sharon attend? Why or why not? Explain. How would you design such a session?

IVT
Subgrouping
Growth
Endsment
Man Style

EVT
Acceptance of LDC
Placement of offices
Career opportunities

2) - Non-judgementally
   - cyclical sandwich - positive, negative, positive
   - Interpretation focus
   - methodology ?

3) - overheads v handouts
   - should be conducted - point of contact
      - they took time, they want to know

Informatics Inc. and Framus Computers

Marcia V. Wilkof
Rutgers University

In early 1985, I received a call from a colleague, Greg Durt, who told me he was doing training at a company I will call Informatics Inc. He explained that top management of Informatics was concerned about the company's relationship with Framus Computers:

> Informatics is a company that purchases computer hardware, adds its own software, and resells the complete system (a hardware and software package designed for a specific use) to its own customers. Framus Computers is a computer vendor from whom Informatics purchases its hardware. Informatics is having a terrible time with Framus. They just can't seem to work together, and Informatics doesn't know what to do about it. I told the chairman of the board, Joe Nettles, that he should talk to you because of your extensive experience with high-technology companies. Because you understand the kinds of internal and external relationships they need to maintain for successful performance, I thought you might be able to help them out. Joe asked me to have you call him if you're interested.

I called Joe, and after a brief discussion of the problems, he asked me to meet with him, Harry Torren, president, and Bernie Clark, vice president of New Product Development, about the problems with Framus. At the meeting, Joe said Informatics wanted to learn how to deal more effectively with Framus.

Joe Nettles

> Our biggest issues with Framus are reliability, performance, and parts. Framus doesn't provide the kind of service that lets us keep the machines running at an acceptable level of performance. I don't think they're used to putting equipment in an environment that requires their machines to operate at a high availability rate (i.e., with negligible downtime). And when their machines are down, the average time it takes to bring a system back up is unacceptable. We can't tolerate the number, frequency, and length of system outages. And it's their fault, not ours. We've tried repeatedly to handle these problems with various people at various levels at Framus, but to no

avail. What I don't get is that we're one of their largest customers in this industry and they don't seem to care about our problems. Davis (the president of Framus) doesn't seem to understand the dimensions of the problem.

Bernie Clark

Framus's attitude is that the problem is ours, not theirs. They tell us that no one else experiences problems with this hardware.

Harry Torren

And our relationship with critical players at the local, regional, and corporate levels is terrible. We have no faith that this situation will get better, and we're so dependent on their machines that we can't change to another vendor. But we can't continue to live with these problems. It looks to us like the situation is deteriorating, and we don't know what to do or how to influence Framus.

The three wanted me to work with them to improve the relationship between the two companies. Before agreeing to take on the project, I contacted appropriate personnel at Framus to determine their interest and willingness to participate. Framus personnel were pleased that Informatics wanted to address the problems and indicated they would cooperate fully.

I conveyed this message to Informatics's top management and told them I was willing to consult as long as both parties agreed that, while Informatics was funding the activities, I viewed my client to be the "relationship between the companies," not Informatics. When both companies agreed, I proposed a comprehensive action research project. However, Informatics agreed only to the first, diagnostic phase with a review at its completion to determine what further steps, if any, should be taken.

INITIAL DATA GATHERING

The first step was to talk with the people from the two companies who frequently interact. Informatics provided a list of these key people. I interviewed all, focusing on the areas Joe, Harry, and Bernie had identified in our meeting as problematic:

1. Informatics was concerned about the number, frequency, and length of system outages. A system outage is when a computer system fails (i.e., stops running) or, as people who work with computers talk about it, the system "goes down." Informatics believed too many systems were going down, that any one system went down too often, and that when a system went down it was down for too long. While Informatics was generally satisfied with the length of time that any one system was up and running between system outages (i.e., mean time to failure was generally good on Framus machines), it was not satisfied with

I proposed a comprehensive action research project because my approach to planned organizational change is based on a collaborative effort between the client and the consultant to improve organizational performance. It centers on working with the client system to identify strengths that enhance performance and weaknesses that impede performance. Together we then develop focused action projects to improve specific areas of performance, implement and evaluate these changes, and generalize successful interventions. Unlike many consultants, I do not believe analyzing a situation and writing a report detailing recommendations is the end product. Too many consultants disappear after submitting a final report, leaving the client to implement the recommendations.

It is also true that many clients are not really committed to changing behavior, but simply want their own beliefs about a particular situation reinforced and/or don't want to see other points of view. Getting a commitment up front for a comprehensive project that includes diagnosis, alternative solutions, and implementation is one way to test the client's seriousness about actually taking steps to change a situation. Implementing agreed to changes is often the most difficult and fragile aspect of improving performance. Working closely with clients in all phases of a change effort and tailoring work to their specific needs is an integral part of every engagement.

In this case, in the area of organizational performance Informatics was interested in improving its relationship with Framus. The project, then, would focus on identifying and understanding both the positive and negative aspects of the working relationship between Informatics and Framus.

My suspicion was that whatever the problems were, both parties would need some assistance in changing patterns of behavior that had probably become second nature. Therefore, I wanted a commitment up front to act on any findings and recommendations for improving the relationship. However, top management at Informatics was not willing to make the commitment. Joe explained that Informatics "does not use outside consultants" and wanted to approach this situation very cautiously. Given their lack of experience with consultants and their uneasiness with the whole situation, I thought it would be best to begin and build commitment to the process along the way. It was my belief that if I could gain their trust, they would be more receptive to an implementation phase down the road.

the length of time it took to repair a system that was down (i.e., mean time to repair was bad).

2. Informatics used both old and new types of Framus computers, all of which were supposed to run the software Framus provided. Informatics fine-tuned this software for its own applications and found that the software did not perform well on all types of Framus machines. Informatics was concerned about rumors that this software "would not now or ever operate efficiently on" some of the machines.

3. Informatics lacked trust in Framus personnel and information. For example, it appeared to Informatics that local Framus personnel were afraid to involve higher management when appropriate; Informatics was concerned that Framus was going to stop development of its newer product line even though Framus had told Informatics that was not the case.

4. Informatics was dissatisfied with its relations with Framus corporate personnel and considered them to be insensitive to Informatics' problems.

Informatics Interviews

I met first with two vice presidents from Informatics, Bob James, vice president for Applications Systems, and Bill Cramer, vice president for Customer Service.

Bob James

> In my opinion, field service is the biggest problem. Framus treats our software problems as a stepchild, just because we've modified the software. If Framus can't easily diagnose a hardware problem, they immediately blame the software. I don't think they really look to see if the hardware might be the culprit.

When I asked Bob to talk more about this issue, he said,

> Well, actually we're pretty satisfied with the frequency of hardware failures. They don't fail that often, but when they do, it's the length of time it takes to repair the computer that's unacceptable. When there's a problem, the customer calls us and we call Framus regardless of whether it's a hardware or software problem. We have a specific procedure to follow for handling problems. It seems like the field service person Framus sends out when we first call them is a trainee. When we call a second time, we get someone with 1½ years' experience. When we call a third time, we finally get someone qualified to deal with the problem. Once we get the right people involved, it's not a big deal.

Bill, vice president for Customer Service, interjected that it is easy to get Framus to come out when there's a problem, but Framus personnel aren't competent.

Bill Cramer

> There's no one to fix the problem unless you go to the regional level. Framus doesn't seem to have a procedure for escalating the problem to a higher level after a certain period of time has passed without the problem being solved. We're the ones who have to escalate the issue. As for the software, we decided to modify their software for our purposes, but we let them know what changes and improvements we've made so they can integrate that information. Then we have trouble with them when there's a software problem.

Bob said they're all frustrated because, "we don't know where the pressure points are at Framus. We can't find anyone to talk to who can deliver results."

Listening to this description, I tried to identify in my own mind what "the problem" was. I found myself confused. What I heard was that the problem is with the software Framus provided, but if Informatics modified the software, how could it expect Framus to correct it? Then Bob seemed to suggest the problem is incorrect diagnosis, that Framus does not really diagnose the problem carefully and is too quick to blame the software, when Bob thinks that much of the time it is a hardware problem. But then they seemed to be saying the length of time it takes to get a system working again is the problem.

Both feel it's hard to find qualified field service personnel. They also said Framus has no procedure for escalating a problem to higher levels to get resolution after a certain period of time has passed. When questioned about the types of problems encountered, they said that actually the severity of the problem is limited to one kind of hardware in one geographic region. An underlying theme was they do not know how to influence Framus, who to talk to get appropriate action.

I decided it was time to talk with Framus personnel.

Framus Interviews

I met with Tom Reynolds, the district sales manager in the area where Informatics is headquartered.

Tom Reynolds

Informatics is afraid that we will become a competitor by selling complete hardware and software systems directly to customers in their industry. Even though we tell Informatics we're not going to become a competitor, they don't believe us. Two years ago things blew up. There were three big issues with field service: parts, training, and responsiveness. As of one year ago, responsiveness was the only big issue. The noise level is down from Informatics. Responsiveness doesn't seem to be a big problem; it's improved tremendously. Our uptime stats improved more than either of us expected.

When I talked with him about who can get things done at Framus, he replied:

The district manager runs the business. That's the pressure point. The district manager has leverage with the field service district manager. The district manager can go anywhere in the company and get things done.

With respect to service problems, Tom pointed out:

> Informatics has cut back some of its service contracts. We didn't agree with them about doing that, but they did it anyway. Maybe our field service managers haven't been over there enough in the past six or nine months, but Informatics reverts too quickly to an adversarial relationship. We like to work tactically and strategically with a customer. Informatics just calls us when there's a problem, and usually when it's already out of control. They don't want to work strategically with us. They just want us to put out fires.

Tom suggested I talk with others involved with Informatics. I met with Tim Daniels, senior sales representative; Dave Harmon, senior field service account manager; and Ray Harris, sales executive.

Dave Harmon

> We coordinate our interactions with Informatics through an account manager who has a team of sales, field service, software, and operations personnel.

Ray Harris

> Originally, we had one account specialist for Informatics who served as a fire fighter. Two years ago, we added a senior manager to focus on the relationship, current products, and future product needs. Four months ago, we added an account manager who manages operations vis-à-vis Informatics. One to two years ago, Informatics was a local account and now it is a major account. Up to one or two years ago, we had one or two main contacts with Informatics through Bob James's group (vice president for application systems). Now we deal with about 50 Informatics people on a weekly basis.

Dave Harmon

> We used to have centralized call handling for field service problems, but the operators were unsophisticated and they had problems. We now have decentralized that function, assigning about 14 Informatics customers to each operator to create a sense of customer identification.
>
> When there's a problem, we have an automatic escalation procedure that works 85 percent of the time. We're working to get it up to 97 percent.

Ray Harris

> Informatics pushes our machines to the extreme. They don't have redundant hardware and the systems they buy are medium, not high, availability ones. In addition, their users are unsophisticated and environmental conditions contribute to the problems. Why they don't make their customers clean up their environments is beyond me. We've talked to them about it and they don't do anything. They think we're making excuses.

Dave Harmon

> We've pushed Informatics for months to work with us to draw up a plan to analyze performance, but they see us as a vendor and don't want to hear about our problems. They just see us as adversaries. We've made changes in management so that outages are handled better, but they don't seem to care. Actually, the lower levels at Informatics are cooperating, but they would be told not to if their upper management knew. Upper levels are aggressive.

They always operate in an attack mode. When we talk to them about working as a team, they think we're being arrogant.

Tim Daniels

Informatics's technical capabilities are very good. They know the hardware and they have a good handle on the software. But they optimize the parts and the short term. They don't take a systems, long-term view. Nobody there ever looks at the whole. Informatics is crisis management; everything is priority number 1 to them. If there's no flame, they don't care.

Dave Harmon

Informatics only cares about outcome measures of performance, not process measures.

After talking with the first half dozen people, I was confused and overwhelmed. Nothing made any sense. Stories weren't the same. Perceptions as to the nature of the relationship between the two companies were contradictory. Many people said that if the two companies were not so financially and functionally tied to each other, they would have ended the relationship years earlier. Personnel from both companies disliked interacting with each other in general and dreaded interacting with each other when problems arose. Given that top management at Informatics saw no way for the two companies to extricate themselves from the relationship, they were committed to finding a way to work out the problems. Lower level employees from both companies, for some reason I did not understand, were committed to working out their problems.

ADDITIONAL DATA GATHERING

I suspended my confusion and simply followed every lead I was given by personnel from both Informatics and Framus. I talked to everyone who was mentioned as a key player in significant interactions between the two companies. In all, 18 people were interviewed, often several times, based on this network "mapping" of the problem areas. I suggested setting up meetings with personnel from both companies. I would design and facilitate the meetings so we could together discuss a particular issue. Informatics management would not agree to have their employees sit down with people from Framus.

Several times I set up meetings with groups of people from one firm to flesh out all issues related to a specific problem area. This allowed me to better understand, for example, how software, hardware, environment, communication, and structural issues caused or exacerbated a system outage problem, at least from one company's perspective.

After my initial discussions with Informatics and Framus personnel, I decided to talk with people about specific critical incidents to develop a more detailed understanding of the situation.

System Availability

Both companies were concerned about system availability. Simply put, a system is available if it is doing the job the client wants done, and it is unavailable if it is not. One measure of availability is the percentage of time the customer wants the system to be available that it actually is available.

Some companies and industries need "very high availability" systems (e.g., the airline industry for air traffic control, the phone industry for routing calls). For example, Bell Telephone System central office switches are intended to be high availability, and their goal is to have something like two hours of downtime per 40 years. Air traffic control systems are also meant to be high availability ones. If and when there is a problem in the system, the client is alerted so repairs can be done. At the same time, mechanisms to compensate for the problems kick in so either the system does not go down or is down for a very short time.

Techniques to assure high availability include redundancy in computers, disc data, and/or software; use of special components in building systems; extensive testing to uncover and correct problems before they occur.

According to Ray Harris, Framus sales executive:

> Informatics thinks it has high availability systems, but we keep telling them the systems are only medium availability ones. They push the machines to the extreme with no redundant hardware, with no high availability characteristics, and with unsophisticated users.

I needed to discover what were each companies' definitions of high, medium, and low availability and what did they see as the boundaries between the points. Both companies had thought about this issue only in the broadest of terms and even then did not agree. Joe Nettles, Informatics chairman, wanted the company's systems to have 99 percent availability. But personnel from both Informatics and Framus targeted 98 percent as the availability goal to be achieved through service activities, not characteristics of the product. Not only was there disagreement between the two companies, but also Informatics's top management and lower-level management did not agree.

I knew that level of availability is always a subjective issue. In this case it led to serious disagreements and differences in expectations between the two companies.

Environmental Problems

I asked about the environmental problems, and the comments of Bob James, Informatics vice president for application systems, were representative of those expressed by both Informatics and Framus personnel.

> I can't get Harry (Informatics president) to put pressure on our own field personnel to clean up our customers' environments. Seventy-five percent of the Framus systems work fine and 25 percent are a problem. Twenty-five percent of the problems may be due as much to lax environmental conditions at our client site as hardware or software problems. Our own managers as well as Framus managers feel that we could do more to insist on more appropriate environmental conditions at our customer sites.

System Outages

I also focused on the issue of how each company responds during a system outage. The following, based on many interviews, summarizes the situation. When a system outage occurs, Informatics goes to the customer site to diagnose the problem. If, after a certain period, the problem cannot be solved or Informatics decides it is a hardware and not a software problem, then Informatics calls in Framus's field service personnel. At this point, the system could have been down for four or more hours and both Informatics and the customer are frustrated and angry (remember, they think these are high availability systems).

Framus comes in and follows its standard diagnostic procedures for dealing with outages, a process that requires several hours. The time it takes for Framus to run diagnostics and follow its outage process seems redundant and unreasonable to Informatics, which believes (1) Framus's actions duplicate Informatics's previous actions and thus are unnecessary, (2) Framus is trying to deny that the problem is a hardware one and puts the issue back on Informatics, or (3) Framus has incompetent field service people who are incapable of diagnosing the problem.

To further complicate the issue, some Informatics personnel believe Informatics could and should improve its own procedures for handling outages. For example, according to Jonathan Speckler, Informatics manager of customer support:

> Informatics does not always let Framus know about recurring problems. Sometimes we go through several levels of diagnostics before calling Framus. By the time Framus becomes involved, our clients and our own personnel are totally frustrated. We blame Framus for the problem, but in a way it's our own fault.

Michael Evans, senior application specialist at Informatics, gave another example:

Sometimes when Informatics and Framus are working well with each other during a system outage, our higher-level managers become dissatisfied with the situation because they think it is not being handled properly or because they receive a call from a higher-level manager at the customer site. Then our management jumps into the situation and makes demands from higher-level Framus managers without first checking with Informatics and Framus personnel who have been involved with the problem. This behavior creates a great deal of tension in the situation and does not help solve the problem.

It was clear to me by this point that the two companies so distrusted each other that they attribute the worst of motives to any action taken. And then any explanation given by the other company is seen as an attempt to cover up its own inadequacies. In other words, both have their own beliefs and no amount of data changes their perception.

It was also clear that the two companies view their relationship from two fundamentally different perspectives. Informatics sees it as a basically poor relationship that sometimes becomes absolutely intolerable. Framus sees it as a basically good relationship that sometimes experiences problems but is much improved now. The one attitude that was strongly shared by both groups of people was their deep interest in and commitment to doing whatever was necessary to improve the relationship.

Documentation

According to Michael Evans, senior application specialist at Informatics:

We have no data about the accuracy of our major diagnostic procedures. We run the diagnostics, make a determination about whether it is a hardware or software problem, and proceed from there. The problem is we never go back to check whether what we identify as the problem turns out to be the real problem. For all we know, what we initially diagnose as a hardware problem could turn out to be a software problem or vice versa. We just don't keep the records to check this.

Dave Harmon, Framus senior field service account manager, told me the following:

Both Informatics and Framus used to keep records about system performance, but the companies started arguing about whose records were accurate, so we stopped collecting certain data. In addition, no trend analysis is done by either company that would indicate if there are specific geographic or technical areas that have been problem free or problematic over time.

> Interviewees talked at great length about the problem areas, often describing specific critical incidents in great detail, including names of key individuals from both companies who had been involved. When talking with personnel from Informatics and Framus, their perceptions of the same critical incident were sometimes so different, I was not always sure they were talking about the same relationship or incidents. Most troubling was that they were in fact talking about the same specific situation. Additionally, some people saw the situation as improving, others saw it as staying the same, and yet others saw it as rapidly deteriorating.

Yet both companies quote statistics about system performance and these statistics are contradictory.

I reviewed records of system availability to ascertain how serious the field service and outage problems are. The records I reviewed were not compiled in a way that made it easy to identify problem areas (e.g., easily indicating system outage due to hardware, software, or environmental conditions).

> Based on this record review, it was obvious to me that people's perceptions are based on historic incidents they were involved in or heard about, not data collected and analyzed over time. This lack of useful record keeping or data analysis aggravates the perception of the problem, if not the problem itself.

ASSESSMENT OF GENERAL MANAGEMENT ISSUES

During my data-gathering activities related to technical issues of system availability, field service, and software, I paid particular attention to any general organizational issues that could also account for the problems between Informatics and Framus. Six issues emerged as critical to the relationship. Each is briefly described below.

General Management Style

Informatics and Framus have very different organizational structures and corporate cultures. Informatics is more formal, bureaucratic, and hierarchical than Framus. A fairly rigid chain of command exists; position and hierarchy are the major determinants of power. Control over tasks and activities tends to be centralized with major decisions made by high-level management.

Many rules, regulations, and standard operating procedures exist, giving people very little autonomy or discretion. Situations are handled in a proscribed fashion following the chain of command. Success and performance are based solely on outcome measures. Job responsibilities and areas of authority are detailed and formal. While there is a fairly collaborative spirit among lower levels in the organization, an adversarial norm, resulting in little trust and cooperation, pervades the top management level.

Framus is a more informal, decentralized, nonbureaucratic organization. Technical expertise and interpersonal skills, not hierarchical position, are the major determinants of power. It is a participatively run organization that places a high value on collaboration in the process of working with people to identify and solve problems. Personnel tend to share responsibility for activities, ignoring positions and chain of command when necessary.

Success and performance are based on both process and outcome measures. Personnel often feel they have a great deal of responsibility with little or no authority to make things happen, except through influence and cooperation. Things happen when people can convince others of the activity's benefits.

The Field Service Organization

Informatics is the primary interface with its clients; it holds the maintenance and field service contracts with Framus. When maintenance or service is needed, the client contacts Informatics, which then handles the issue itself or decides to bring in Framus.

The field service relationship between the two firms is complex. Depending on the type of situation, the firms have pooled, sequential, and reciprocal interdependencies between them. Pooled interdependence occurs with general maintenance issues, where Informatics plays the dominant role in maintaining the software and Framus handles scheduled hardware maintenance.

When a system outage occurs, the relationship resembles sequential interdependence. The client contacts Informatics, which has specific procedures to follow to diagnose and correct the problem. After completion of these problems, Framis is called in. If the problem is not just with hardware, then the interdependence takes on a reciprocal form; both companies, working with the client, attempt to diagnose and correct it.

Framus personnel suggested that part of the field service problem Informatics experiences is due to Framus's field service being organizationally and geographically decentralized while Informatics's customer services are handled centrally. The situation has improved somewhat since Informatics divided customer service at low levels of the organization, giving customer service representatives responsibility for specific customer sites. This change puts Informatics representatives closer to their customers as well as the local Framus field service office. While Informatics, not its customer, has the field service contract with Framus, personnel from both organizations think it would be advantageous for the customers to develop relationships with their local Framus field service office.

Organizational Interface

Both companies believe there is no single voice from Informatics to Framus or from Framus to Informatics. While each has established procedures for handling outage situations, each company does not necessarily agree with the other's procedures or courses of action. However, representatives from the two companies do not work through disagreements to set up systems acceptable to both.

Because these issues are never resolved, there is constant friction in the relationship. People have become so dissatisfied with the procedures and the level of help received from those formally responsible in the other organization that they have found other people to go to for assistance. As soon as there is a problem, because of the lack of trust between the companies and the established procedures, people "end run" each other, ignoring the established channels and activating their informal channels. Because those formally responsible for an area or a situation are no longer informed of problems, they believe the situation is improving. People in the other organization, however, are dealing with situations through their informal networks and perceive the technical situation to be the same or worse, even if they do get better informal managerial assistance.

One of the consequences of this situation is that neither company knows who to listen to in the other company. The problems and issues become so clouded and confused it is difficult to get a handle on what the major problem areas are, which things are getting worse, which areas are staying the same, and which areas are improving. The lack of agreed on or appropriate documentation and trend analysis makes any position virtually impossible to support or refute, which once again allows people to fall back on their opinions, gut-level feelings, and historic reactions. This vicious cycle further erodes the relationship and reduces the level of trust.

Informatics personnel suggested that while there are a number of people involved in various Framus-related issues, there should be one person who represents Informatics to Framus.

Approach to Measuring Performance

Informatics and Framus have different attitudes about measuring performance. Informatics is more concerned with outcome measures of performance than process ones. It just wants a problem fixed; it does not want to know how it is being fixed or what procedures Framus is developing to improve the effectiveness and efficiency with which problems will be handled in the future. Framus, on the other hand, evaluates performance based on both outcome and process measures. Framus prefers to work with its customers as a team to identify and solve problems together at both a tactical and strategic level.

Both Informatics and Framus personnel perceive Informatics as adversarial in its relationship with Framus. Informatics views Framus as a vendor that should solve its own problems and not bother Informatics with the details of how these problems are solved. When Framus tries to explain to Informatics that new procedures are being worked out to handle a problem, Informatics thinks Framus is making excuses or using delaying tactics to cover up an inability to correct a problem. From Framus's perspective, Informatics just wants the problem corrected and is uninterested in how it gets handled. Framus personnel believe their efforts go unrewarded and unappreciated.

Lack of Trust

Because the relationship between the two companies has historically been problematic, a serious lack of trust has developed between them. Personnel from both recount many stories of when personnel from the other company did not follow an agreed upon procedure, did not do what they said they would, did not perform adequately, did not behave cooperatively, or did not correct serious problems in a timely fashion.

Informatics ends up feeling as if there is nothing to do to get action from Framus, that Framus has written them off, that Framus is unresponsive to pressure, or that Informatics has no sense of where the pressure points are in Framus. On the other hand, Framus believes that no matter what Framus does, it is never enough, that Informatics will never be satisfied with Framus's efforts or performance.

Corporate Relations

Informatics and Framus never established good relationships at a district, regional, or corporate level. The highest-level Framus managers in Informatics's home area have not developed a relationship with Informatics top or middle management. This situation reinforces the lack of trust because, at the local level, the two companies do not have a good sense of each other. In addition, Informatics top management has never developed a good relationship with Framus corporate management.

The two companies do not regularly work strategically or tactically with each other at a top or middle management level. Without a good relationship with appropriate corporate personnel, when Informatics top managers are dissatisfied with Framus's performance, they have no top manager to consult with at Framus.

My goal initially was to understand what each individual said in the context of the other information I had received, often sharing with the interviewee other perceptions of the problem I had heard, although always maintaining the anonymity of my sources. Attributing specific comments to specific people would not only have violated my assurances of source confidentiality, but it also would have inflamed an already badly inflamed situation. As I became more familiar with the content of the problems, I kept searching for a framework that would organize my thoughts and guide my actions.

QUESTIONS FOR DISCUSSION

1. Why did these two companies have such a wide variety of problems with each other? Is there a unifying framework that could be used to develop an understanding of what was occurring? What is this framework?
2. What kind of role would you develop as a change agent to work with these two companies that had such major incompatibilities?
3. What would be the first step in improving the working relationship between these two companies? Why not simply attack the technical problems and work through each to arrive at solutions that would increase performance?
4. What technical recommendations would you make for improving performance?

First National Bank

D. D. Warrick

University of Colorado

Following a keynote address at an annual State Bankers Association Convention, I was approached by the executive vice president of a small bank of 25 employees and $55 million in assets. The title of the talk was "Developing A High Performance Organization in Turbulent and Opportunistic Times." The major themes were: (1) our changing environment and the implications for organizations and (2) a step-by-step process for developing a high performance organization using a model I developed called the Organization Excellence Model (see Exhibit 1). The model helps managers understand the primary targets for change in a change program. Another model I find useful in helping managers develop a systems understanding of change is Ralph Kilmann's Five Track Model (Kilmann, 1989).

The executive vice president, who was one of three equal partners who had purchased the bank approximately two years before our meeting, quickly grasped the application to his bank and wanted to explore the possibility of retaining me. I would describe him as a highly motivated, intense mover and shaker with a low key style. He was in his upper 30s and was the youngest of the owners. Before becoming a partner in the bank, he had a thriving certified public accountant (CPA) practice in another city.

After about a hour of discussing the bank and what the executive vice president would like to accomplish, four central issues emerged: (1) the three owners were not an effective team and had strained relations (one partner carried the title of chairman of the board and the other, whom he suspected to be an alcoholic, was the bank president); (2) he wanted to improve employee morale, motivation, and productivity; (3) he wanted the bank to be a "fun" and "enjoyable" place to work and not "so oppressive"; and (4) he wanted to develop a process for managing a bank so he and his partners could begin to acquire other banks.

He believed any program that could accomplish the first objective would be worthwhile and accomplishing the other objectives would be a

EXHIBIT 1 Organization Excellence Model

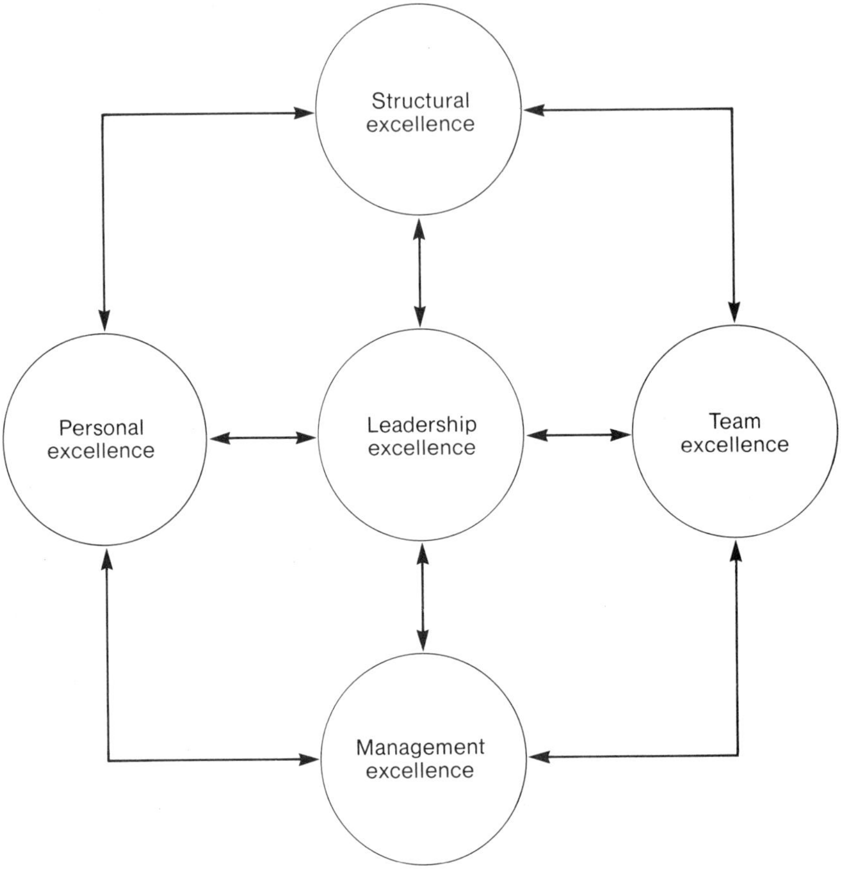

bonus. It was clear the executive vice president had very strong feelings about the issues. He asked if we could meet again in three weeks at a conference he would be attending in Denver.

PROPOSAL AND PROGRAM DESIGN

I met with the executive vice president in Denver and outlined a possible OD program for his bank. He liked the ideas, made a few additional suggestions, and agreed informally to a program. In fact, he wanted to get started in two weeks! The quick action was a welcome change from the months of negotiations and approvals I am accustomed to in working with larger organizations. He asked for a formal proposal that he could take to his partners.

Before parting, I explained the commitment that would be needed by the partners and the need for at least one of them to champion the program. He made clear his commitment and his willingness to champion the program. However, he wasn't sure how committed his partners would be, although he was certain he could persuade them to do the program.

This information presented an interesting challenge and became even more interesting when he informed me that the president had just entered a one-month alcoholic treatment program and would miss the first two weeks of the program. We discussed the need for the involvement and commitment of the three partners and the possibility of delaying the program. However, he expressed an urgency to get started and thought we could update the president when he returned. I decided to go with the agreed upon date, assuming the executive vice president was essentially the informal leader of the bank and was the most likely person to make or break the program.

In writing the formal proposal, I called the executive vice president several times to check ideas and assure that the proposal fitted what he wanted to accomplish. I was concerned that I had no contact with the other two owners, but the executive vice president assured me he was keeping them informed. The proposal was sent within a week of the Denver visit and was immediately accepted. In the proposal, I included a sample memo explaining the program. The memo was to be signed by the partners and sent to all employees before my arrival.

COMMITMENT BUILDING

When I arrived at the bank, I met with the executive vice president and chairman of the board to develop a clear understanding of the program and reinforce the importance of commitment from top management. The chairman of the board was difficult to read as he was intermittently friendly and supportive and somewhat skeptical and caustic.

The meeting lasted about two hours and was followed by a meeting with all bank employees to explain and build commitment to the program. I made a short presentation on the urgency for organization excellence in changing times and introduced a model I developed that creates a climate for positive change and minimizes resistance or disruptive behavior.

The model discusses "problem solvers" (problem-solving style facilitates problem solving), "resisters" (problem-solving style creates obstacles to problem solving), and "hardcore resisters" (problem-solving style blocks problem solving and becomes the problem) (Warrick, 1984). Employees are asked to rate themselves regarding the percentage of their behavior that fits in each category. The model seems to produce a high level of interest, stimulates many questions, and quickly sensitizes people to behaviors that facilitate or block problem solving and change. While most employees appeared to be very interested in the training and program, some appeared apprehensive.

ORGANIZATION SURVEY

After my presentation, I administered an "Organization Assessment" questionnaire to all employees that asks employees to evaluate the organization, the department they work in, and their immediate supervisor. In addition, employees were asked to evaluate the three owners using a "Personal Awareness" questionnaire. An important issue surfaced during administration of the questionnaire. Several employees were not sure which department they were in or who their supervisor was. The executive vice president answered their questions so they could complete the questionnaires.

TOP MANAGEMENT TEAM BUILDING

The remainder of the first morning was spent doing a short team-building session with the chairman and executive vice president. The purpose was to address questions regarding the program and the role of top management in the program, provide training in managing change, and surface key issues top management was concerned about. The focal issue became the relationship of the partners and their roles and aspirations. The executive vice president was very straight about his concerns. The chairman would express concerns and then back off, making his position unclear. It became apparent we were dealing with sensitive, high-stake issues. My role would be a delicate one of keeping the discussion constructive and sensing how willing they were to address the real issues.

ORGANIZATION INTERVIEWS

For the remainder of the day and all of the following day, I interviewed all of the employees that were available (60 percent of the employees). Ideally, I prefer to analyze the results of the survey before starting interviews. In this case, I quickly reviewed the questionnaires to identify obvious issues to probe. In general, I use a few minutes of interviews to build commitment to the program and alleviate concerns. Then I try to ask questions that parallel the questionnaire so I can have a cross-check of objective and subjective data. The interviewing guidelines I try to follow are described in Exhibit 2, and some of my favorite general questions are shown in Exhibit 3. While a few employees were reluctant to be open, most were eager to express their perceptions of the organization.

GENERAL FINDINGS

First National Bank serves a rural community and the surrounding area. The bank is an interesting contrast of state-of-the-art banking technology and rural, down-to-earth employees with limited exposure to the fast-paced, rapidly changing environment of larger cities. Although the bank had been very profitable, primarily because of the technical expertise of the executive vice president, it faced many new challenges because of the depressed farm economy, prospect of numerous bad loans, and need to foreclose on several farms and businesses, many of which belonged to friends and relatives of employees. The approximate organization chart is shown in Exhibit 4. A formal organization chart did not exist at the beginning of the intervention, and many of the employees were unclear about who they reported to or how the organization fit together.

Although the three owners had owned the bank for more than two years, their duties had never been defined or agreed upon, resulting in numerous misunderstandings and tensions among the owners and confusion among the employees about the roles of the leaders.

The chairman of the board had an MBA and had spent most of his banking career with the bank before becoming an owner. He was a leading citizen, well liked by employees, and seemed to like his status as chairman. His title was misleading because his actual job was to manage the Loan Department. He was becoming cynical and discouraged because of his role in dealing with bad loans, many of which involved long-time friends and acquaintances. He also felt pressured by the executive vice president to work faster and more efficiently and "bite the bullet" on loans that needed to be collected or written off. I found that I was not the only one who had difficulty reading him. At times, he had a tendency to be sarcastic, leaving employees confused about the true meaning of his statements. After spending an evening with him and his family at their home, I found him to be very interesting and intelligent.

The president did not have a college degree but had been in banking more than 25 years and came from a family active in banking. Most of his banking career had also been spent at the bank. His role in the bank was unclear, although most of his efforts were in the Loan Department. He was perceived by employees and his partners to be very knowledgeable in banking but was underutilized because of his drinking. Employ-

---

EXHIBIT 2   Interviewing Guidelines

---

1. Provide a comfortable and private place where there will be no interruptions. There should be few barriers, such as a desk between you and the interviewee.

2. Introduce yourself and ask for the name, department, and job of the interviewee. You may also need to know the name of this person's boss. Briefly describe the purpose of the interview. Point out that you are looking for trends and will not report any information that would identify the source without permission from the interviewee. Ask for permission to take notes. Interviewing provides a good opportunity for you to personally build credibility and to promote the program you are involved in.

3. Try to be as natural, warm, and friendly as possible and do not overreact to what is said. Overreactions will stimulate or hamper continuance on a subject. An alert body posture and good eye contact are important.

4. You should be aware that the questions you ask and comments you make are likely to be reported to others after each interview.

5. If a survey is also being used, it is best to administer the survey first so the results can be used in developing questions for the interview. It is also helpful to use questions that will serve as a cross-check with the survey and reveal the subjective data behind the numbers.

6. Take notes in your own readable form of shorthand. Skip quickly over unimportant items. Your objective is to: (1) *identify major issues,* (2) *solicit facts about these issues,* and (3) *ask for possible solutions.* Learn to write without having to constantly look at your paper and also learn to save note taking for later when it might reinforce a "hot" comment.

7. Encourage the interviewees to talk about strengths as well as weaknesses. An overemphasis on weakness causes discouragement and guilt.

8. Objectivity is extremely important! *You must record what is being said*—not what you were primed by others to believe ahead of time or what you want to hear. Check your perceptions thoroughly if you have any doubts about what is being said.

9. You can end an interview at any time by asking, "Is there anything else that you think I should know?" Don't prolong an interview when a person has little to say. When you finish, thank the interviewee for his or her time.

10. Summarize the interview at the conclusion of the day according to the following format: (1) major strengths, (2) major issues along with their supporting facts and possible solutions, and (3) miscellaneous information.

---

ees liked him well enough, but they were confused about his role. The unspoken but apparent tension between the president and the other two partners was growing. They were concerned about his lack of productivity and agitated about several potentially bad loans he had persuaded

---

EXHIBIT 3   General Interview Questions

---

1. In your opinion, what are the major strengths of your organization?
2. What are the major weaknesses or opportunities for improvement?
3. What do you personally like best about working here?
4. What words would you use to describe your organization? Call off the first words that come to mind.
5. What words would you use to describe the culture or norms in your organization?
6. If you were to rate morale in your organization on a 10-point scale, with 10 high and 1 low, what number would you choose?
7. What factors tend to contribute to high morale and what factors tend to contribute to low morale in your organization?
8. On a 10-point scale, with 10 high and 1 low, how valued do you feel as an employee in this company? Why?
9. What does your company do to make employees feel valued? Devalued?
10. If you were to rate how free you feel to be open on a 10-point scale, with 10 representing very open and 1 very guarded, what number would you choose?
11. What obstacles, if any, keep you from utilizing your full potential?
12. Does your work environment encourage innovation, improvement, and new ideas?
13. How does a person get ahead in your organization?
14. Does the organization do a good job of valuing, recognizing, and rewarding the employees with the best performance and the best attitudes?
15. What are some of the major motivators and demotivators in your organization? What would motivate you more?
16. Can you think of some things that would improve motivation and morale?
17. Do you have a clear understanding of what is expected of you and how you are doing?
18. How good are the working conditions and benefits in your company?
19. How would you describe the management style of the leader of your organization?
20. How effective is the top management team?
21. What does top management do to provide vision, direction, and inspiration?
22. How good is teamwork within and between departments?
23. How client centered is your organization?
24. What are some of the concerns that you hear other employees talk about?
25. Does your organization do a good job of providing training and professional development opportunities?

EXHIBIT 3 (*concluded*)

26. How are major changes typically made in your organization? Can you provide an example?

27. If you had unlimited power and resources, what improvements would you make to increase performance or morale?

---

them to grant to relatives. When he returned from the treatment program, I spent as much time as I could getting to know him and trying to update him on the change program. He seemed enthused about the treatment and talked openly about his experience.

The executive vice president functioned as the president of the bank, although his title and compensation didn't reflect the level of his responsibilities. He kept very up to date on the latest practices and technologies in banking and had developed a technical, computer-based system for managing the bank and keeping it financially successful.

While his technical and conceptual skills were exceptional, his people skills were sometimes lacking. Many of the employees were intimidated by his task-oriented and somewhat autocratic style. He was eager to close out any bad loans, acquire other banks, and commit his bank to excellence. His frustration with a lack of movement and challenge, lack of teamwork with the other owners, and small-town environment, where he never felt fully accepted, was growing. He had desired a situation that offered more collegiality for himself and his family. The owners and their families rarely socialized outside of bank activities.

The bank was filled with intrigue. The former owner, who managed with a strong autocratic style, still had an office in the bank, was retained as a consultant, and wielded a subtle, but apparent influence on the owners and employees. An affair between two employees had caused a stir and recently resulted in one of the parties being asked to leave. Several employees had risen to their level of incompetence but were retained as employees because they or members of their family were deeply indebted to the bank and they needed a secure job to pay off the debts. Gossip was difficult to control because the bank was intimately involved in the lives of most of the people in town. One item of gossip centered on the "For Sale" sign in the yard of the chairman of the board. In reply to my inquiry about it, he told me he did it as a joke!

While morale was low, most employees took an "I don't care" or "we do as we are told" attitude because the bank was the best and most secure job in town and had a generous profit-sharing plan. Tensions existed over who got promoted, the status of various titles, and a variety of small issues that became big issues, possibly as a reaction to the unhealthy aspects of the organization. The supervisors were untrained,

EXHIBIT 4 First National Bank Approximate Organization Chart before OD Intervention

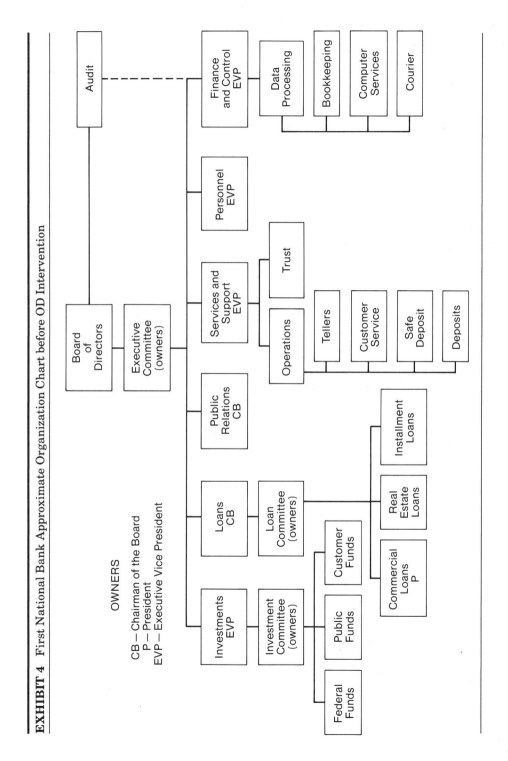

unclear about their responsibilities, and in some cases were not sure who they were supposed to supervise. In response to a question about how she liked supervising, the supervisor with the largest number of people replied, "I don't like being a supervisor and don't really think of myself as a supervisor." The executive vice president did all of the year-end performance reviews, although there was was no formal performance review system.

One other significant factor was that the design of the bank placed the loan-related employees on one side of the bank and the transaction and service people on the other without easy access between the two groups. This created what became known as the north and south groups and resulted in communication problems and some conflicts between the two groups.

RESULTS OF THE ORGANIZATION DIAGNOSIS

The results of the organization diagnosis were provided two weeks after the survey so the information would be fresh and interest in the results high. I try to make reports as user friendly and useful as possible by summarizing strengths and opportunities for improvement followed by survey results and summaries of open-ended questions. This keeps reports brief and easy to use in survey-feedback/problem-solving meetings.

There are two major difficulties with this approach. Writing the strengths and opportunities summaries is very time consuming and requires a number of judgment calls based on my interpretation of the survey and interview results. To compensate for my judgment errors and increase ownership in the data, I go over the results and then have the recipients use the results and any other data they believe is relevant to develop their own prioritized list of strengths and opportunities. This approach also diffuses efforts to discredit the data. The other difficulty is editing open-ended comments to capture what is being said but eliminate inflammatory or confusing remarks and singling out of individuals in destructive ways.

In reporting the results, I developed a profile for: (1) the organization, (2) each department, (3) each supervisor, and (4) each owner. Occasionally, I also break out the data to include teams. It has been my experience that the more you personalize the data, the greater the interest, impact, and likelihood of change. Simply reporting organizationwide data limits the changes that can be made at various levels. An issue I have wrestled with for many years is how to show dispersion. Scores can be very misleading if there is not some measure of dispersion unless the sample size is large. I show a spread of how many people chose 1, 2, 3, 4, 5, 6, or 7 on each item because of the understandability versus using a statistical approach.

A summary of the organization strengths and opportunities for improvement is shown is Exhibit 5. The overall organization, department, and supervisor results are shown in Exhibit 6 and the owner personal awareness results in Exhibit 7. The owners each received the total results. Departments received the results for the organization and their own department. Supervisors received their own supervisor profile. The personal awareness profile was used to accelerate needed changes by the owners because it was important they become pacesetters in the change process. I met with each owner and supervisor to debrief their results and coach them in making personal and departmental changes. It was apparent from the diagnosis that significant changes were needed for the bank to more fully realize its potential.

EMPLOYEE FEEDBACK

A meeting of all employees was held from 5 to 9:30 P.M. on the same day the managers and supervisors received feedback. The meeting was used for several purposes. An hour was used for training. The focus was "How to Succeed Personally and Organizationally in Changing Times." The next activity was feeding back the organization results and meeting in mixed teams (each team had a cross section of employees in terms of levels and jobs) to evaluate the results of the survey, prioritize strengths and opportunities, and share the results. Then the key issues were identified, and employees chose which issues they would like to work on so recommendations for improvement could be made. A follow-up team was chosen consisting of a representative from each of the action teams and the executive vice president to consider all of the recommendations and choose a few high-priority items to begin working on. Feedback on their recommendations was to be given to all employees one month later. The final activity included following a similar process to focus on department issues. In most cases, it was the first time department members had ever met together to communicate and discuss ways to improve.

This meeting resulted in a significant change in momentum. The employees had never experienced this type of involvement and problem solving, and their enthusiasm and excitement became evident. Only four or five remained guarded and skeptical and showed resistance to change. Many problems were solved, new ideas for improvement introduced, and the process of improving communications from top to bottom began.

The obvious problem with this approach is that it can be too much too fast. I felt like I was running a three-ring circus, moving from one group to the next, helping groups with the process, intervening when groups got stuck, and trying to manage the whole process at lightning speed.

While the time available was inadequate by textbook standards, it was all I had. It was great fun!

QUESTIONS FOR DISCUSSION

There are many ways to approach an OD intervention and, particularly in this case, the entry and diagnosis phases. The choices are a function of what is needed, what the client is willing and has the resources to do, and the strengths and philosophies of the consultant. Assume you were the consultant in this case and address the following:

1. Discuss the strengths and weaknesses of the entry phase. What would you have done different?
2. Follow the same process in evaluating the diagnosis phase.
3. What are some principles you believe OD practitioners should follow in the entry and diagnosis phases?
4. After evaluating the information offered in this case, rank in order what you consider to be the five most important issues.
5. Based on the results of the diagnosis, design a one- or two-page OD program proposal to be submitted to the executive vice president assuming you had 12 consulting days and a maximum of seven months to complete your involvement in the program (these are the realities I was faced with in designing a program).

REFERENCES

Kilmann, Ralph H. *Managing beyond the Quick Fix*. San Francisco: Jossey-Bass Publishers, 1989.

Warrick, D. D. *Managing Organization Change and Development*. Chicago: SRA Associates, Inc., 1984.

EXHIBIT 5 First National Bank: Major Strengths and Opportunities for Improvement

Major Strengths

The bank is very open to progressive ideas and uses many methods used by much larger banks.

Excellent management of the bank's resources and assets.

Excellent employee/asset ratio.

Owners are experienced and capable bankers.

Minimal technical mistakes.

Considerable employee talent and potential throughout the bank.

Employees take pride in working at the bank. It is a prestigious place to work in the county.

Good working conditions (pay, benefits, profit sharing, stock, facilities, etc.).

Owners' genuine desire to have a first class bank that is progressive and a pacesetter.

Resources available for accomplishing work (equipment, staff support, funding, etc.).

Willingness to respond to needed changes.

The department ratings revealed that each department has a strong commitment to excellence. They are ready and willing to make needed improvements.

Flexible policies that account for personal needs.

Major Opportunities for Improvement

Communications. Employees would like to be kept better informed. They learn of important information and decisions regarding the bank from outside the bank.

The organization structure needs to be re-evaluated and redesigned for better organization results.

Lack of understanding of the bank's mission and philosophy.

The need for top management to work as a united team and take a leadership role in providing vision, direction, and inspiration throughout the organization.

Employees would like to have clearer job responsibilities and more feedback on where they stand. Some employees are not sure who they report to.

Morale rated low.

Employees seldom felt recognized for their good efforts but were criticized for mistakes.

Managers need to be trained in state-of-the-art management skills. Some individuals in management positions did not fully understand the role of a manager and what is expected of them.

EXHIBIT 5 *(concluded)*

It would be helpful to evaluate bank procedures, policies, reporting requirements, etc., to minimize red tape and bureaucracy for both employees and customers.

The bank needs to become more employee centered. Items such as concern for employees, value and respect shown employees, and efforts made to involve employees in sharing ideas received average ratings.

Efforts should be made to develop more teamwork within and between departments and to train employees in problem-solving and conflict-resolution skills.

The organization culture (the feel of the organization) needs to be revitalized so the bank will bring out the best in employees.

The department ratings revealed a number of problems between employees and that some employees need to develop better attitudes and make greater efforts to be part of the solution rather than part of the problem.

An effective performance review system is needed with reviews given by immediate supervisors.

Ways need to be explored to improve teamwork between departments and between the two sides of the bank.

Telephone coverage is not consistent.

Interpersonal communications is somewhat closed. People are reluctant to share ideas.

More involvement and innovation could be used to improve customer service.

EXHIBIT 6 Summary of OD Program: Summary of Diagnosis Results

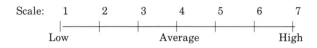

Organization Results   *Department Results*

Organization Philosophy	
1. Commitment to excellence	5.0
2. Concern for employees	4.2
3. Concern for clients	4.6
4. Clarity of mission and philosophy	3.6
Leadership	
5. Leadership provided by top management	4.2
6. Efforts of top management to inspire excellence	3.8
Management	
7. Management skills of managers and supervisors	4.7
Organization Structure	
8. Clarity of organization goals	3.4
9. Organized to achieve results	4.0
10. Minimal red tape and bureaucracy	4.8
Working Conditions	
11. Pay, fringe benefits, facilities, etc.	5.4
12. Resources available for accomplishing work	5.7
Human Resource Management	
13. Value and respect shown employees	4.1
14. Efforts made to train and develop employees	4.8
Capital Resource Management	
15. Management of the organization's resources	6.1
16. Response to needed change	5.8
Management of Organization Processes	
17. Organizationwide communications	2.4
18. Cooperation between individuals and groups	3.8
19. Efforts made to involve employees	3.6
20. Constructive resolution of problems	3.6

Department Philosophy	
1. Commitment to excellence	5.7
2. Concern for employees	4.9
3. Concern for clients	5.3
Leadership	
4. Supervisor inspires excellence	4.6
Management	
5. Management skills of my supervisor	4.8
Department Structure	
6. Organized to achieve results	4.8
7. Clarity of goals	4.8
8. Clarity of job responsibilities	4.3
Working Conditions	
9. Pay, fringe benefits, facilities, etc.	5.3
10. Resources available for accomplishing work	5.6
Human Resource Management	
11. Value and respect shown employees	4.9
12. Efforts made to train and develop employees	4.8
13. Recognition and rewards for high performance	4.5
14. Equality and fairness shown employees	4.0
Capital Resource Management	
15. Management of the department's resources	5.2
16. Response to needed change	5.1
Management of Department Processes	
17. Department communication	4.1
18. Constructive resolution of problems	4.1
19. Relations between department members	4.8
20. Relations with other departments	4.4
21. Effectiveness of department meetings	4.0

EXHIBIT 6 *(continued)*

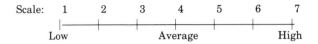

Scale: 1   2   3   4   5   6   7
          Low   Average   High

Organization Results		*Department Results*	
Organization Culture		**Work Culture**	
21. Work environment stimulates excellence	4.1	22. Positive attitude of department members	4.6
22. Healthy behaviors valued and rewarded	4.1	23. Work environment stimulates excellence	4.4
23. Encouragement of innovative thinking	4.8	24. Friendly and supportive work environment	5.0
Organization Results		**Work Culture**	
24. Productivity	4.9	25. Encouragement of innovative thinking	5.1
25. Morale	3.4	26. Trust level between department members	5.0
		27. Freedom to communicate openly	4.3
		28. Commitment to success of department	4.9
		Department Results	
		29. Productivity	5.3
		30. Employee satisfaction	4.1
Overall average for all items	**4.3**	**Overall average for all items**	**4.8**

EXHIBIT 6 (*concluded*)

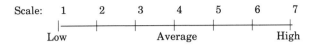

Scale: 1   2   3   4   5   6   7
Low   Average   High

Management/Supervisor Results

Leadership

1. Ability to inspire and motivate employees — 4.6
2. Ability to provide clear direction and purpose — 4.1
3. Sense of priorities (knowing what is important) — 4.9

Management

4. Creates an environment that stimulates excellence — 4.9
5. Planning skills — 5.1
6. Organizing skills — 5.3
7. Decision-making skills — 5.5
8. Follow-up skills — 4.3
9. Delegation skills — 4.7
10. Elimination of unproductive activities — 4.9
11. Communication skills — 4.5
12. Ease in talking openly with — 5.1
13. Listening skills — 5.0
14. Problem-solving and conflict-management skills — 4.8
15. Honesty and straightforwardness — 4.8
16. Employee motivation skills — 4.3
17. Skills in letting you know where you stand — 4.3
18. Value place on employee involvement — 4.6
19. Recognition of employees for good work — 4.1
20. Ability to get results — 4.9

Overall average for all items — **4.7**

EXHIBIT 7 Owner Personal Awareness Profiles

Scale:	1.0–2.0 Poor	2.1–2.9 Low	3.0–5.0 Average	5.1–5.9 Good	6.0–7.0 Excellent
			Board Chairman	*President*	*Executive Vice President*

	Board Chairman	President	Executive Vice President
Attitude			
1. Positive	5.4	4.9	5.4
2. Genuinely interested in others	5.1	4.7	4.8
3. Unselfish	4.9	4.7	4.5
4. Forgiving	5.2	5.0	4.4
Personal Style			
5. Results oriented	5.4	4.9	5.4
6. Organized	6.0	5.1	6.1
7. Sensitive to the needs and feelings of others	4.4	4.6	4.2
8. Diplomatic	4.4	4.7	4.4
9. Makes you feel at ease	4.6	4.7	3.9
10. Straightforward	5.1	4.9	5.2
11. Expresses true feelings	5.0	4.6	4.9
12. Open minded	4.7	5.1	4.7
13. Dependable	5.4	4.5	5.2
14. Even tempered	5.1	4.8	4.4
People Skills			
15. Easy to talk openly with	5.6	4.5	3.9
16. Excellent listener	5.4	4.7	5.2
17. Gives feedback constructively	5.1	4.8	5.0
18. Receives feedback constructively	4.8	4.9	4.7
19. Willing to level and confront	5.2	4.3	5.1
20. Makes others feel valued	4.3	4.4	4.1
Group Skills			
21. Excellent team player	5.1	4.8	4.7
22. Encourages and supports other team members	5.2	4.7	4.9
23. Strong contributor to the success of the team	5.5	5.0	5.4
Problem-Solving Skills			
24. Effective problem solver	5.1	4.8	5.1
25. Reasonable	4.6	5.1	4.7
26. Seeks best solution	5.2	5.1	4.9
27. Stays objective during problem solving	4.8	5.0	4.8

EXHIBIT 7 *(concluded)*

Scale:	1.0–2.0 Poor	2.1–2.9 Low	3.0–5.0 Average	5.1–5.9 Good	6.0–7.0 Excellent
			Board Chairman	*President*	*Executive Vice President*
28. Encourages open discussion			5.8	5.4	5.7
29. Considerate of the views of others			5.1	5.2	4.8
30. Offers innovative ideas			5.2	4.9	5.7
Stress Management					
31. Rarely appears stressed			5.4	4.0	4.7
32. Patient with others			4.7	4.8	4.4
33. Rarely overreacts			4.6	5.0	4.4
34. Manages stress effectively			4.8	3.8	4.4
Leadership and Management Skills					
35. Takes the initiative to make things happen			5.5	4.5	5.8
36. Inspires, encourages, and motivates others			4.8	4.4	4.6
37. Strong skills in managing people			4.8	4.1	4.5
38. Strong skills in managing resources			5.5	5.4	5.7
Performance					
39. Productivity			5.6	5.2	5.4
40. Quality of work			6.0	5.8	6.3
Overall average for all items			**5.1**	**4.9**	**4.9**

Peppercorn Dining

JoAnn Carmin
Cornell University

Todd Comen
Cornell University

Yariels Kerr
Cornell University

The partners of Square One Consulting were having lunch at Peppercorn Dining on the campus of All-American University. Although Square One was headquartered nearby, most of the consultants' business was conducted in other cities. The partners were enjoying having the opportunity to attend a seminar on a campus in their hometown. By chance, Drew Randall, the manager of Peppercorn, noticed the trio and recognized Erica, who had worked her way through college as a student manager at the dining unit. Drew pulled up a chair and started to catch up on the two years that had transpired since she had graduated. The other consultants, Roger and Lynn, listened as they began to reminisce about the "good old days" at Peppercorn.

Erica recalled the time a swim test coincided with her first shift at the dining hall. She called to let the unit know she would be detained, and she finally arrived about an hour late. When Erica entered the unit, she was greeted by a supervisor who took her downstairs to change into the uniform of blue pants, blue-and-white-checkered shirt, a hair net, and a name tag, an outfit similar to what was being worn by the current employees. Erica was then taken to the dish room and informed she was receiving a verbal warning for being late. As the group laughed, the consultants chided Erica further by commenting that her sense of timing hadn't changed. Drew, however, suggested that times had changed.

DEVELOPING A CONTRACT

The consultants were eager to learn about Peppercorn, and Erica, eager to learn about the changes Drew had alluded to, asked about current operations at the unit. Drew, sipping on his coffee, commented, "Staffing is a nightmare. We can't find qualified people anywhere; recruiting and retention has become a constant challenge." Drew went on to explain that the labor market in the county had become tight due to the prosperous Reagan years. Garden County had become a boomtown and, as a result, the university was having difficulty gaining employees. Roger wondered aloud about the general steps Peppercorn had taken to offset the current labor shortage.

Drew, sensing the consultant's interest, openly discussed his perceptions of the dining unit. He stated:

> I would like to make Peppercorn a more pleasant place for everyone to work. I get great productivity out of these guys and they really care. It's just that there needs to be something more. Maybe morale is a little low. There's not much creativity involved in most of the tasks, but the cooks feel great when they sell out of stuff. However, when we sell out, it's probably because the forecast was incorrect rather than as a response to a good product. I take a humanistic management approach, maybe they just need some kind of support. On the other hand, I may give them too much autonomy since I let them manage themselves to a large degree.
>
> I believe that scheduling is management's right. I base my scheduling on operational need. Ultimately, the manager is responsible for the success or failure of the operation, therefore, I should have the right to put the people where I deem best. You know, niche management. Although, I did inherit a lot of the schedule.

As Erica tentatively nodded her head in response to Drew's comments, Roger and Lynn caught each other's gaze and shrugged inquisitively. By the consultants' behavior, it was apparent they were wondering about the meaning behind Drew's words. However, because he was obviously in the mood to talk, the consultants did not interrupt.

Warming up to his listeners, Drew continued, "Some employees have been at Peppercorn, working in the same position, for 20 plus years. Bob, the day cook, has been working here for 28 years. Can you believe that Doug, the night cook, has been here for 10 years and is waiting for Bob to retire so that he can transfer to the day shift? Doug may have to wait a long time since Bob won't be retiring for at least 15 years. It's hard for me to believe that Doug looks forward to that time and that he refuses to transfer to another dining unit."

"That's amazing," said Roger. "You seem to have loyal employees. It must be easy to manage people who know their job so well."

Drew responded:

> It's not that simple. The union contract forms a second set of rules and operating parameters. The contract deals with turnover, sick leave, pay, promotion, and all of the other usual stuff. It seems that there is no reward for non-sickness, but there is a reward for sickness. Now people get one and a half times the pay for sick days if they are on overtime. If they are on overtime, absenteeism is more of a contractual issue than a workplace issue.

Frankly, I believe that staffing affects attitudes and attitudes affect quality; both of which affect productivity. Increased productivity means making better use of time. Perhaps I should structure the tasks in a better way, but managing and working behind the lines makes it difficult for me to see the trees through the forest. There's no time for anyone to stand back and see what's happening.

Drew paused and, as if speaking more to himself than to the consultants, said, "Since I've been so busy, maybe I've lost track of some of my priorities." Turning to the consultants, Drew inquired about their experience with situations of this type and what advice they might offer.

The partners explained they are usually contacted by organizations when management believes an external opinion could provide a fresh outlook on operations. They went on to state they normally begin their work by performing an operations audit, the results of which are presented to management. Additionally, when the situation warrants, strategic interventions are designed to facilitate the achievement of management objectives. The partners further indicated they believe it is essential to become familiar with an organization before appropriate suggestions can be made.

Without hesitation, Drew said to the consultants, "The situation here at Peppercorn has been concerning me for quite some time. I know that you must be very busy, but perhaps you could find the time to work with me. Erica already knows a lot about the operation, and it wouldn't take long for her to become reacquainted."

Because the consultants were planning to be in the area for several days to attend the seminar and to complete some paperwork, Erica suggested they observe operations at Peppercorn. The group, discussing Erica's suggestion, agreed that the first stage should be a preliminary evaluation of the unit, followed by a feedback session with management. Then, based on the outcome, management could conduct an in-depth operations audit. Drew concurred that evaluation and feedback could be useful first steps in achieving his goals. He restated that his goals for Peppercorn were to increase productivity and to improve morale among the workers.

The consultants concluded their discussion by telling Drew they would drop off a written contract by the following afternoon. The contract would include their fee structure as well as a schedule of the dates and times they would like to be on the premises.

REVIEWING BACKGROUND INFORMATION

Two days later, the team gathered around the table in Roger's office to discuss the Peppercorn consultation. Roger and Lynn initiated the discussion by reintroducing the subject of Erica's objectivity. It became obvious that all three of the partners were concerned about how Erica's past experiences would bias her view of the operation. The partners also discussed the fact that Erica's views would influence Roger and Lynn's perceptions of the dining unit. Although Erica believed she could recognize and work with her bias, she suggested she focus on gathering current managerial data. Because their time was limited, Lynn recommended that Erica also conduct a few on-site interviews with people who would be more candid with an old friend than with strangers.

As he was reaching for a notepad, Roger asked Erica about the general operating procedures and the key personnel at Peppercorn. Erica began outlining the operation:

> Peppercorn's hours are 11 A.M. to 7:30 P.M., Monday through Friday. When I first started, we served about 1,500 to 1,600 lunches and 900 to 1,000 dinners daily. By the time I graduated, the counts were down by about 30 percent at lunch and approximately 50 percent at dinner.
>
> When I was a student worker at Peppercorn, there were full-time employees, all of whom were union members. There were also student workers, and we had our own student management staff. When I first started working, there were more student workers than when I graduated. Some of the gaps were filled by full-time temporary workers.

Lynn pointed out that it would be important to determine if these changes were affecting the operation. Erica agreed and indicated that by the time she had graduated, minor conflicts were arising between student and temporary workers at Peppercorn. Erica continued her briefing by providing an overview of the key personnel during her tenure with All-American Dining, the parent organization of Peppercorn.

Erica stated:

> Drew is obviously the manager of Peppercorn. He was also the manager of the Salt Mill over at the "B"-School. He was responsible to Stan O'Malley, one of the assistant directors of All-American Dining. Stan supervised Drew and Beth Clarkson, the manager of food service in the student union.
>
> John Cerrano was the receiving clerk. He always worked closely with Drew. There never seemed to be any problems with his work; he always knew where everything was because he received the goods and then put them in storage. John, or "Bo-bo" as we called him, was the shop steward. He had a close relationship with most of the employees and a bunch of us used to go out drinking with him regularly.
>
> Matt Copperfield was definitely a key player. Matt was the professional supervisor who handled inventory, purchasing, scheduling, and other administrative tasks. It always seemed as if he was at the heart of the operation. I can't remember her name, but there was a secretary who was also in a pivotal position. She had access to a lot of information and she was the source and respondent of all official Peppercorn communication.

The student supervisors were the only other key players that I can think of at this point, and they had extensive responsibilities which included daily management, scheduling, and hiring of the student workers.

The partners' conversation shifted to the amount of time available for the investigation. Lynn asked her partners how much time they thought was necessary for conducting the initial investigation. "Well, Lynn," replied Roger, "based on the information we have so far, it's possible that the longtime employees may not be as open as we might like. They may be protective of their turf." Lynn agreed but added that they shouldn't jump to any conclusions. She noted that often it was the old-time employees who were most interested in talking about their work.

The consultants agreed that three days should be an ample amount of time to gather the necessary data and to develop a presentation for the management of Peppercorn Dining. The consultants concluded the meeting by agreeing that Lynn would concentrate on the production areas of the unit while Roger would survey front-of-house operations.

DAY ONE: INTERVIEWS AND OBSERVATIONS

Lynn was the first to arrive at Peppercorn the following morning. As she approached the facility, she noticed that three female employees were smoking cigarettes on the loading dock, joking around with a purveyor. Lynn introduced herself and lingered with the workers for a few minutes.

Back of House

Entering the kitchen from the loading dock, Lynn noticed it was clean and most of the equipment looked relatively new. The kitchen had fairly good fluorescent lighting, and natural lighting was provided by windows in the pot washing and food preparation areas.

As Lynn placed her coat and briefcase on a rack in the storage area, she observed that the dry goods were neatly arranged, although the supplies were not plentiful. From the storeroom doorway, she could see that the workers were busy, but not rushed. The members of the kitchen staff chatted as they worked and they appeared to know what tasks to perform without needing direction.

The kitchen was divided into five areas (as shown in Exhibit 1). After introducing herself to the workers and taking a brief tour of the kitchen, Lynn positioned herself near the walk-in cooler where she could easily see most of the kitchen operations. She noticed that the walk-in cooler and freezer were clean and were stocked with a moderate amount of supplies. She also observed that the workers' uniforms were clean. However, some of the workers were wearing aprons and some were not. As if reading her thoughts, a student worker passing through the room commented to no one in particular, "We're out of aprons again. Oh well, it's no big deal." Lynn wondered what else might not be a "big deal" to the workers.

The doors to the dining facility were opened at 10:55 A.M. at which time the pantry workers took a break.

Bob, the day chef, was grilling sandwiches in the tilt brazier while Robert, the day cook, was breading pork. Robert moved between food preparation, the fryer, and the steamer. During lunch service, the kitchen staff appeared to be relaxed. Although there was not much talking, they did joke with each other from time to time.

Shortly after 11:00 A.M., a man wearing a chef's uniform entered the kitchen and greeted the other workers. He then took a clipboard and a stack of computer printouts to a table near where Lynn was standing. Lynn felt a bit awkward until he introduced himself as Doug, the dinner chef.

Lynn explained she was observing the facility in order to become familiar with the operation. Doug showed interest in Lynn's curiosity and stated:

> I want the kitchen to run as smoothly as possible. I believe that it takes organization, morale, communication, and a system to have an efficient operation. Communication is important. I ask the servers how things are working out so that I know if I should change anything. I try to maintain a routine system so there won't be many questions during service. I train all of my workers and I enjoy having the opportunity to teach. I've been in food service for 25 years and at Peppercorn for 10 years. I started working in the food service industry when I was about 11.
>
> I think that Peppercorn has the best food on campus. Some of my own recipes have been accepted by management and are now a part of the menu computer bank. I've also developed ideas that have been adopted here and at other campus dining facilities. For example, I started the trend of keeping plastic tasting spoons by the steam kettles. I'm also the person who started using a yellow marker to highlight important items on the computer printouts.

As Lynn and Doug were talking, a man came over and listened to their conversation. Doug's speech became hesitant in this man's presence. After only a few minutes, the man left. Lynn wondered who the man was and why he had such an effect on Doug. From the way he was dressed, there was no way to determine if he worked at Peppercorn, was from the union, or was part of the All-American management staff.

Coincidentally, Doug explained to Lynn that the man was Larry, the professional supervisor. He went on to say Larry plans the menus

EXHIBIT 1 Floor Plan of Peppercorn Dining

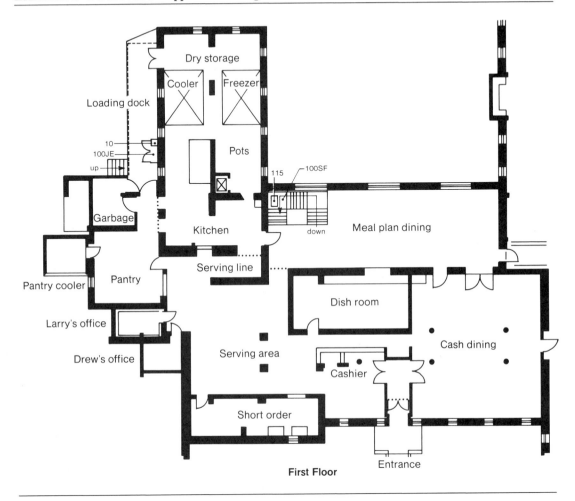

First Floor

and tries to balance the use of ovens and kettles so the equipment is not overloaded. According to Doug, Larry prints out the menus from a computer located in the office. Doug added that the computer system does not always work the way it should. The system is supposed to print menus, compile order lists, and check the inventory. Doug commented, "Sometimes it works well, and sometimes not. Sometimes the menus have to be changed at the last minute because of short stock. We haven't had any salt all semester. This is mostly a result of computer errors."

Doug went on to talk about some of his co-workers. Bob, the lunch chef, has been at Peppercorn for 28 years. Chris, the assistant dinner chef,

EXHIBIT 1 (*concluded*)

Basement

has been with the unit for about three years. Chris, who moved to the kitchen from the short-order station, was trained by Doug. They enjoy sharing ideas and they always try to prepare the food a day in advance.

While Lynn was talking with Doug, she could see the cafeteria line by way of a pass-through window. She noticed that a steady flow of diners was entering the facility. Realizing that Doug enjoyed talking about the unit and being curious about Doug's responses, Lynn felt comfortable continuing the conversation. Observing a student supervisor restocking the hot food line, Lynn asked Doug how he felt about working with students.

He replied, "Some student workers are reliable, while others are less committed." Lynn asked Doug about the role of the student supervisor and in response Doug called the student over. The student seemed unhurried and went on to explain that student supervisors do not have any power over the regular workers; only over temps and other students. Students have their own management structure that includes a student coordinator, managers, and pay clerk. The student personnel coordinator handles complaints. Temps and regular workers take complaints to the regular personnel worker. More temps have been needed recently since there are less student workers at Peppercorn than in previous years.

As Lynn, Doug, and the student were talking, Larry entered the kitchen again. When the student noticed him, he quickly went back to work restocking the food line.

The activity in the kitchen seemed to be getting busier, and Lynn decided she should move to another position so Doug could continue his work. Before she left, Doug commented about the union. He stated, "Skilled workers are on the same union contract as unskilled workers. I think that this arrangement holds back the skilled workers and helps the unskilled to get ahead. It doesn't work well, and we don't even have a shop steward. The only way that I can move up in the organization is to become part of management."

Lynn bid Doug farewell and went into the service area to get some lunch. As she went through the cafeteria line, she noticed Roger observing the cafeteria service. Lynn invited him to join her for lunch, but Roger declined, saying he had just begun his observation and he wanted to spend some time watching service during the busiest hours.

Service Areas

Roger immediately noticed the line servers interacted a great deal with the customers. He also noted there was no portion control. The students would ask the line servers for "a little more spaghetti, just meatballs, no

---

EXHIBIT 2 Line Servers Setup

Starch	Vegetable	Backup	Entree	Entree
Soup	Vegetable	Entree	Entree	Entree

Server 2	Server 1

---

corn, more sauce, or a small cup of soup." Each customer wanted the standard portions or combinations of food items altered to meet their personal needs, and they were accommodated.

The first line server plates the entrees and the second worker serves the side dishes (see Exhibit 2). The workers must communicate in order to properly fill each order. The overall atmosphere in the serving area was relaxed. Roger timed the service and discovered it took two to four minutes for a customer to enter the line and be served during a busy period.

As the flow of customers slowed, Roger initiated a conversation with a line worker who introduced herself as Carrie. She told Roger she had been at Peppercorn for 10 years and was a door checker for 9½ of those years. She explained the door checker made sure that only diners on the university meal plan were allowed in the noncash dining area. She went on to say she had become bored with her position. She was also dissatisfied with her former hours, which were from 11 A.M. to 7:30 P.M. Carrie attained her new position with Drew's help. He facilitated a trade between her and a line server. Now that the swap is final, Carrie believes the other woman, who is now the door checker, may not think the trade was equitable.

During his conversation with Carrie, Roger saw the chef come out of the kitchen and pick up an empty pan. The chef lingered for a minute. He appeared to be watching the line service. Roger returned his attention to Carrie and continued the conversation by asking her about line staffing. Carrie explained, "Usually there are three main workers on the line, two full-timers at one station and one student or temp at the other. We choose our own positions on the line and we usually stick to the same spots. When it gets busy, additional student workers fill in. Today one full-timer is sick, so a temp from another area filled the position. Sometimes they can't find substitutes, so we just have to work that much harder."

Roger stepped aside as a student worker carrying a tray of soup cups began to restock the service line. Roger apologized for any inconvenience and explained he was a member of a group learning about the operations at Peppercorn. Roger asked the student if he could take a moment to tell him about the relationship between student and nonstudent workers.

The student explained that Peppercorn is supposed to be staffed primarily by students. The students are grouped into three segments: student managers, student supervisors, and student workers. However, he said, "Since the supply of students has been diminishing over the years, more temps have had to fill the positions. There's a lot of tension between students and temps as well as between students and full-timers. This isn't surprising since the students supervise the operation. They call us 'students' as opposed to 'supervisors' and we seem to be stereotyped."

He clarified his statement, saying, "There's a discrepancy with age, economic status, and experience in many cases. Only the full-timers and the professional managers are not under the supervision of students. Students have a difficult time supervising older people, and older people have a difficult time taking orders from young people who they probably consider similar to their own children."

The student went back to work, leaving Roger to his thoughts. He was reminded of the conversation that he had with his partners about the conflicts between student and nonstudent workers. It was becoming clear to Roger that this was an important issue.

Just as Roger was beginning to consider the problems that can arise from role conflict and role ambiguity, he was startled by the sound of shattering glass. Roger turned in time to notice a student stepping away from a broken glass, acting as if nothing had happened. Several dishwashers, on their way to the drink station, also saw the broken glass as they walked by. Roger was curious to see how long it would take for someone to clean up the mess. Two minutes later, a dishwasher returned and swept up the glass. During this time, a student supervisor was informed of the problem. Roger noted she never returned to make sure the situation was corrected.

Roger followed the dishwasher toward the dish room. As he rounded the corner of the serving area, Roger heard the sound of blaring rock music. Roger had to weave his way through a narrow passage that was blocked with customers at the cashier's station.

As he entered the dish room through an open doorway, Roger was greeted by a mixture of machinery noise, loud music, and a hot, humid atmosphere. The machinery was arranged in a pattern that allowed many people to perform different tasks simultaneously. The five workers gave Roger a cursory glance and continued with their tasks.

Roger, feeling a bit out of place and self-conscious, stood to one side of the work area and watched the activity. There was a lot of joking, talking, and interacting as the workers sorted and cleaned dishes, silverware, glasses, and trays. Full dish trays were stacked at the rinse station. Each rack was rinsed and then sent through the dishwashing machine. When the dishes completed their cycle, a worker sorted the dishes. Roger noted the worker put several freshly washed dishes into racks with dirty dishes. He also noticed the silverware was run through the dishwasher twice.

Roger wanted to know why the silverware had to go through the wash cycle two times, so he asked the dish sorter who was positioned at the end of the line. The sorter said, "We're concerned that plates and especially the silver are clean. We wouldn't want people catching something from someone else."

The sorter asked Roger what he was doing in the dish room. Roger explained and then asked the worker how long he had been at Peppercorn. The worker said he had been at Peppercorn for a year. Further discussion revealed the worker is on a split shift. He works from noon to 4 P.M. and then from 6 P.M. until 10 P.M. He said he likes having a midday break in order to get things done in his personal life. He explained that he knew three of the other workers before he started the job. Because he was the newest employee in the dish room, he was stationed at the hottest position. He pointed out that the two full timers he worked with had held their positions for four and two years, respectively. The other three workers, including him, were temps.

The worker finished sorting and left the dish room to get his coworkers a cold drink. Roger went over to the area where workers were scraping and sorting dirty plates. The dishes and filled racks were piling up. Roger noted the dish machine was not able to keep up with the demand. He also saw that the paper items were shredded with the food scraps and that Styrofoam was sorted separately.

The oldest woman in the dish room yelled out from time to time, "Come on, keep it movin'." Roger spent a few more minutes observing. As he recalled Erica's story about her first day at Peppercorn, Roger wondered why there were no students working in the dish room. As he was leaving, a student supervisor came in to get trays for the service area.

Roger proceeded to the cashier station where he found the dish sorter chatting with the cashier. After a minute, the sorter returned to the dish room. Roger struck up a conversation with the cashier. After briefing her about his project, the cashier proceeded to tell Roger about some of her observations and experiences at Peppercorn.

She explained that the cashier's job is a full-time, nonunion position she has held for two years. She replaced the person who is currently the secretary. She enjoys having the opportunity to meet people and getting to know the regulars, but she has found that some of the students are rude.

The cashier stated, "I usually get along well with management. Everyone has their good and bad days. I was a manager in my previous job, so I understand what Drew has to deal with. I also understand the problems that the student supervisors have." Roger wondered what the cashier meant by this statement. What does Drew have to deal with and what problems do the student supervisors really have to deal with? Thus far, he had noted that the operation appeared effective, although some communication problems were evident.

The cashier, seeing Drew passing by, stopped him and asked him for more change and small bills. Roger asked if it was standard procedure for her to ask managers for more money, or if she was able to get it herself. She replied she is authorized to get cash, but it is difficult for her to leave her station.

While the cashier was waiting for Drew to return, Roger asked her about work conditions. The cashier replied:

> I get cold in the winter because I'm so close to the entrance and the wind blows in. It's ironic because the rest of the workers complain about it being too hot at their stations. Peppercorn is built over heating ducts, so it's very hot everywhere except at my station. People's biggest complaint is the heat. There isn't adequate ventilation or air flow. Another common complaint is that there's not enough room in the dining, kitchen, and service areas. This is because Peppercorn used to be a riding stable.
>
> In the winter I get sick easily, but I only miss about five days per year. I've learned to live with not feeling well on the job. I have a sore back every night because I set on a bar stool all day.

Before Roger could inquire if she had ever talked to management about her work conditions, she stated, "I'm the only cashier. I have to call on the secretary when it's really busy, but I know she has a lot of work to do. I also restock silverware. This entails shutting down the register, running to the dish room, and then restocking before the register line gets too long. Our job descriptions say that if someone sees something that needs doing, they are supposed to do it. Therefore, during slow periods I help clean tables, do the menu board, and look around for other things to do."

Roger asked the cashier about her plans for the future, and she explained she would like to have a secretarial job so she could get away from food service for a while. The cashier went on to say there are temps and students that make more money than she does as a full-timer and this disparity makes her resentful. The wages seem to be based on job position or union membership. Only four positions are nonunion. These positions include the cashier, secretary, supervisor, and manager. The rest of the workers at Peppercorn are temporary, union members, or students. The cashier added there are only five single people on the staff.

When Roger asked the cashier about the relationship between student and full-time workers, she replied there is a lot of pressure in the dish room. She believes the pressure builds up because the student supervisors never send student workers in to help. The supervisors' excuse is that they are short of help elsewhere. Drew returned with the cash, and Roger went to see if he could find his partners.

Administrative Information

Roger found Lynn and Erica sitting in the dining area. Erica was telling Lynn she had arranged for them to have dinner with some students that evening. Roger sat down with his partners and asked Erica if she could clarify some details about the organizational structure.

Erica responded, "There are three tiers of management at Peppercorn (Exhibit 3). There is the professional management staff, which consists of Drew and Larry. They oversee the full-time workers. There are also

EXHIBIT 3 Peppercorn Dining Organizational Chart

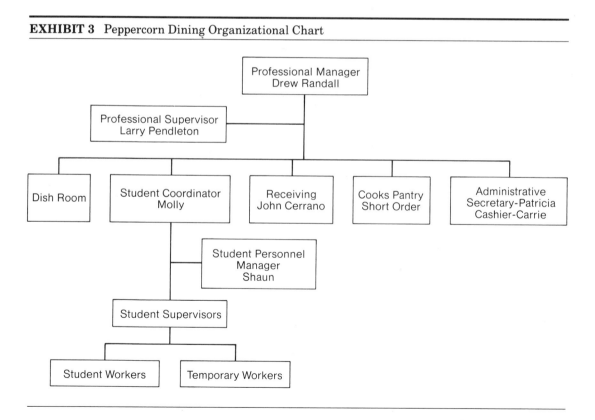

student managers and student supervisors. The student managers oversee student supervisors as well as the student workers. The student supervisors are responsible for daily operations. The student workers and the temporary employees report to them. It seems, however, that the temporary workers also report to, and are trained by, the professional managers."

Roger and Lynn interjected that they had noticed difficulties between the students and the other workers at Peppercorn. Lynn asked Erica if she would clarify the distinction between the different levels of employees. Erica clarified the organizational structure stating:

> There are full-time union employees, full-time nonunion temporary employees, and student labor. Full-time employees hold the positions of cooks, short order chefs, pantry workers, and cashiers. In past years, students filled all the other supplementary positions, including dishwashers, servers, cooks, helpers, short order helpers, pantry helpers, beverage servers, and serving area floaters. For the past four to five years, fewer students have wanted jobs at Peppercorn. This phenomena has resulted in the addition of the third type of employee, the full-time temporary worker.

Erica went on to tell her partners that she had gathered enough information to update them on the key players at All-American Dining. She explained that Larry Pendleton is the new professional supervisor, replacing Matt Copperfield at Peppercorn. In the central office, Nancy Lawrence is still the director of All-American Dining (Exhibit 4). She has been spending a great deal of time traveling to different universities in order to analyze their food service operations. Stan O'Malley is still an assistant director of All-American Dining. Although there is a central office, each unit is independently operated.

Roger asked Erica is she had the opportunity to speak with any employees and if she had been able to uncover any information about management-employee relations. Erica told her partners she had spoken with John Cerrano and some of the pantry workers.

Erica went on to say she and John spoke about changes that had occurred at Peppercorn since she had left. John told Erica the lack of student help has hurt operations at the unit. For example, a special dining event that Peppercorn sponsored last night was difficult for the workers. There were virtually no students on the staff. As a result, the full-time workers and temps had to pick up the slack.

John also commented that Larry doesn't listen to his advice about ordering food. John spends a lot of his time getting food items that should have come in from the suppliers from the other units on campus. According to John, Larry doesn't have the respect of the staff. He doesn't take anyone's advice and acts like a know-it-all. The situation is made worse because Larry doesn't do his job very well.

EXHIBIT 4 Department of Dining Services

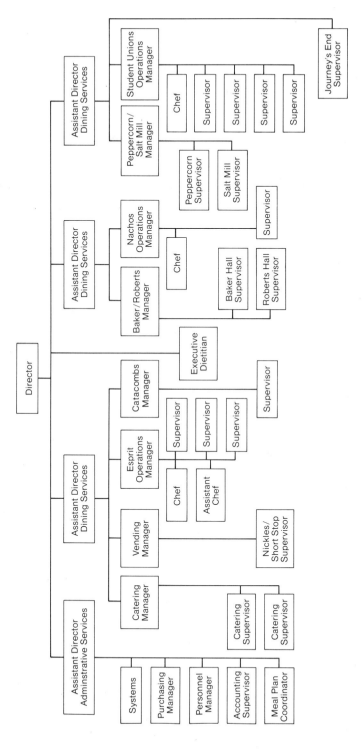

Erica went on to discuss the pantry workers stating:

The workers seemed to indicate a general belief that the management of All-American Dining, as well as the management at Peppercorn, doesn't really care about them. They mentioned how All-American's previous personnel director used to visit the different dining units at least once a month and talk with the full-time employees. During that time, the workers felt that someone cared about them. They said that the new personnel director doesn't come around at all and probably doesn't even know who the full-time employees are.

The workers also told me that there is minimal union representation for food service employees. According to the workers, food service members are a minority faction of the union and aren't considered important unless a strike is in progress. Apparently, the union's primary concern is with maintenance workers, groundskeepers, janitors, and bus drivers. There's no shop steward and union officials don't come to Peppercorn unless there is an official grievance.

Lynn added that Doug had also commented on the union. She stated, "Based on what we have heard so far, no one is thrilled with the union. Workers and management alike seem to find the union a burden."

Roger asked Erica about how each unit on the campus was staffed. Erica explained that the units were independently staffed and at the beginning of each semester, the different units held recruitment campaigns.

Erica became quite excited as she stated, "OK, enough of the routine stuff. One thing that I found out today is that the university is building a new 400-seat dining facility. Also, a privately funded food service operation that will include a variety of dining concepts is opening nearby. Of course, these things will impact Peppercorn, but the scoop is that Drew will be the manager of the new facility!"

Erica, acting quite pleased, sat back, smiled, and waited for her partners to respond. Lynn paused only for a moment and then, turning to Erica, said, "This isn't making much sense, but, before I ask the obvious, why don't you tell us the rest of the facts?"

Erica, a little disappointed at the response her comment evoked, went on to explain that Drew would be leaving Peppercorn in about five months and that Eric Weston, the current vending manager, would take charge of the unit as soon as Drew left.

As Lynn and Erica began to engage in an intense discussion about the future of Peppercorn dining, Roger, in true form, looked at his watch and stated, "Well, not only do we have a contract, we also have a dinner engagement in 20 minutes. Let's get some fresh air before we meet with the students!" The partners began laughing and, recognizing the sanity of Roger's comment, decided a break was in order.

Dinner with Student Managers

After freshening up, the trio returned to Peppercorn to meet the students for dinner. Molly, the student coordinator, and Shaun, the student personnel manager, were waiting for the consultants at Peppercorn's main entrance. The five of them went through the cafeteria line and then entered the dining room, where they found a quiet table to have their dinner.

Shaun seemed to know why the consultants had asked them to dinner and began to tell them about his tenure at Peppercorn. Shaun explained that when he had started at Peppercorn four years ago, there were two to three times the number of student workers. He went on to say more students made the work fun and the operation ran more efficiently. Shaun explained it is hard for the students who have been at Peppercorn for a long time because they know how it used to be.

Molly agreed with Shaun, saying students would work at Peppercorn because it had a reputation for being social. "To attract student workers," Molly said, "Peppercorn must become special, more conducive to meeting students' needs. In the early days, students were proud to be Peppies and looked forward to seeing their co-workers." She proceeded to say they have to treat students well because they can't risk alienating anyone. They can't afford to fire students or give them too many warnings.

Erica asked the students to comment on working with the temporary workers. Shaun said, "The temp-student relationship is not great. Temps are under the student supervisors' authority, but it doesn't really work that way. Temps are less efficient than students, but they are needed to fill the vacant positions. They are probably not as efficient because they have less loyalty to Peppercorn than the students."

Molly interjected, "This year, no students and temps work in the same areas except for emergencies. Temps are trained by the professional management but are supervised by students. Last year, it was unclear who was in charge of the temps. This year it is better. Most things are written in manuals.

"The regular and temporary workers don't talk much to the students," continued Molly. "Temps and full-timers think students are stupid; they have an attitude toward students. It's hard for the students to get cooperation and respect from the temps."

Lynn asked the students about their relationships with Drew. Shaun and Molly explained that while most students don't interact with Drew frequently, they, as supervisors, meet with him regularly. Most of the students think Drew is rude and cold and unapproachable, but they have found he can be very patient. Additionally, many students don't believe Drew is knowledgeable about food service operations. Molly and Shaun have discovered that he is, in fact, an astute person. They attributed his reputation to a lack of accessibility, noting that Drew is generally more accessible to the full-time and temporary workers than to the students.

Lynn further inquired about the students' reactions to the forthcoming management changes. Molly replied, "Since most of the students don't work closely with Drew, we really can't foresee the change having much of an effect on them. Most students don't have any preconceived ideas about the new management."

Shaun disagreed with Molly stating, "It's going to be hard for a new manager to come in mid-year. The transition will cause problems since the new manager won't have the experience. I think that the new manager should change things quickly. New student workers are recruited by us in the spring and meet their supervisors when they begin working in the fall. They immediately have some respect for their supervisor. I think that the new manager will be in a bind."

Molly said she believed the change would have a greater effect on the full-time and temporary workers than on the students. She has heard some workers mention they are concerned because Peppercorn's future is unclear. Many of the full-time workers are loyal to Drew; they have become comfortable with his management style.

Roger, addressing Molly, asked about communication at Peppercorn. Molly responded:

> Communication has been a major problem. The students thought that if they left me notes, things would get done. I would take the notes to management, but important things were not noted as being important. Mostly, the problems were repair and maintenance issues. People brooded that things didn't get done quickly. They didn't realize that most things have to go through a lot of channels, which takes time. There is so much paperwork involved. Now the students make special notations when issues are urgent so that I can establish priorities.
>
> An area that is related to communication is ordering. There are a lot of problems with Larry. Last year, we had a problem with the person who filled a similar job but the job description has changed. Last year, the kitchen workers were getting burnt out. Larry revised the menus and for a while the kitchen seemed better. Larry just doesn't do his job well and we constantly run out of things.

Roger asked about the student pay structure at Peppercorn. Molly told him the pay rate has been changed twice. The effect is that workers are kept on the same pay grade because the raises push people back to level one. The only workers who benefit from the changes are the student managers.

Shaun noted that one of the most frustrating situations at Peppercorn was the lack of student interest, something that could not be controlled. Even when the wages were raised, no one applied for jobs. Shaun added that the student supervisors are upset about paying for their meal plan tickets because many of them worked their way through school.

It was getting late and the students had to attend classes the next morning. The consultants thanked the students for being so candid with them. After the students left, the consultants discussed their impressions of Peppercorn.

Roger commented that their earlier concerns about the willingness of employees to speak with them were unfounded. Lynn agreed, noting that although most of the workers seemed to be quite open, Doug was an exception. He was eager to talk, but the discussion seemed contrived. He seemed to be conveying information that he thought she should know and was careful to portray himself and the operation in a favorable light. Lynn said she thought he was concerned about possible repercussions from his responses.

Lynn went on to recount the interactions she had observed earlier in the day between Larry, Doug, and the student supervisor. She then commented, "Larry is an interesting player. All of the workers mention him. He seems to have a lot of power over the other workers, yet he seems to govern by fear. The workers become timid in his presence, nonetheless, they don't appear to have much respect for him."

Picking up on Lynn's train of thought, Roger noted that in his conversations and observations throughout the day, he had begun to wonder about the social system at the unit. He commented, "Although the organization was highly stratified, operations still seem to run smoothly. While workers may be timid around Larry and even fear Drew, the fact that operations are smooth and that the workers appear to be loyal indicates that personality conflicts and role ambiguity are symptoms of a larger problem."

"That's true," said Erica. "The unit always had a reputation for being a social environment. In the past, we were able to overlook personality and role conflicts because there was a strong culture at the unit."

Noticing that the cleaning crew was beginning to break down the dining room, the partners decided to call it a night.

DAY TWO: INTERVIEWS AND OBSERVATIONS

Erica arrived at the dining hall at 10:30 A.M. As she climbed the stairs beside the loading dock, she noticed a worker was in the car wash, hosing down the trash cans. As she entered the kitchen, Erica spotted Drew helping out in the pantry. They greeted each other cordially and chatted for a few minutes. Drew, taking off his lab coat, said he was due at a meeting on the other side of the campus.

Erica left the kitchen and went into the office to gather more information on the structure and operations of Peppercorn. When she entered through the open office door, she found Larry working at the computer, placing orders with the central purchasing system. Larry explained to Erica that the computer system had not been working properly. It is supposed to generate order lists and inventories based on the menus that he inputs. He indicated, however, there must be some problem with the system because the orders are not coming in, and when they do, they frequently are late. After providing Erica with some literature such as employee handbooks, Larry suggested she talk to Patricia, the secretary at the main office.

Erica followed Larry's suggestion and on her way out of the unit she met Roger. She explained she was planning to visit the main office and said she would meet her partners in the late afternoon to discuss her findings.

Roger wandered around the unit for over an hour, observing the lunch service. During the first hour, the cafeteria was packed with customers. Roger noticed the student supervisors were busy refilling the salad and beverage stations. Shaun helped by restocking glasses and trays. The cafeteria line became long and at one point, Drew, having returned from his meeting, helped serve food. Roger noted that by the end of the lunch period, the cafeteria was short on silverware.

As the lunch service slowed, Roger decided to take a look at the student office. As he entered the downstairs dining room, he immediately noticed it was very hot, that a large percentage of the tables were dirty, and that many of the light bulbs in the dining room needed replacement. Roger located the student office and what appeared to be a small gathering or meeting area.

From the open office doorway, Roger could see a bank of time cards on the wall. Roger also noted the office contained a suggestion box. As he peered in the door, he was greeted by the sound of a woman's voice. Roger entered and introduced himself. In response, the woman identified herself as Sarah Lange. Roger asked Sarah if she would be willing to discuss her work experiences at Peppercorn.

Sarah began by saying she had worked at Peppercorn for three years and had been a student supervisor two years. Sarah stated, "Working at Peppercorn is not as much fun as it used to be. Although the job was never easy, it has become increasingly difficult. As supervisors, we don't really manage any more, and the upper-level student managers like Shaun don't work and don't care. He won't even help out when we are short staffed."

Sarah described an incident when Naomi, another student supervisor, was working a snack shift that was understaffed. Shaun, aware of the problem, stayed downstairs at his desk. When Naomi went downstairs to ask him for help, he acted ambivalent. Shaun finally helped in the dining room for about 20 minutes.

"In contrast to Shaun," Sarah commented, "Molly is willing to pitch in when we are short staffed, but this has caused her to become burnt out. Molly has a hard time dealing with problems that arise among the student supervisors. A few days ago, she called a meeting and told us there was a new policy restricting the snacks that we were allowed to eat. She also told us that we were scheduled to work on special dining programs, which are always at dinnertime. The whole time that Molly spoke with us, she was really curt and acted like she was annoyed. We don't even have a student rep to complain to anymore. At least Molly is leaving at the end of the school year."

Sarah said that although she is not very happy working at Peppercorn, she does not want to quit. She has loyalty to both her fellow workers and to the unit. Sarah said she would definitely quit if some of her friends, who are also supervisors at Peppercorn, stopped working at the unit.

Roger thanked Sarah for talking with him and wished her luck in the future. As he walked up the stairs to the service area, Roger made a mental note to talk to his partners about information flow and to further discuss coalitions within the unit.

While Roger had been observing service, Lynn, who arrived at 12:30, had entered the unit from the loading dock. Hoping the workers would be less self-conscious if she was undetected, Lynn quietly observed operations for almost an hour. During that time, Lynn noticed the steam kettles were draining, and much like the previous day, the kitchen workers appeared unhurried but attentive to their tasks. The manner in which they worked seemed highly professional and reflective of the long years the employees had worked together.

When Doug finally noticed Lynn, he greeted her warmly and began to chat with her. As Doug and Lynn were talking, a man who Doug said was a short-order cook walked through the kitchen. He stopped and stared at Lynn for a moment and then asked, "Are you with the health department or the union?" Lynn introduced herself and explained the nature of her project. The man stared at her again briefly and then walked away.

Doug excused himself and Lynn, left to her thoughts, wondered if the man had accurately stated the paranoia she had perceived in Doug the previous day. Doug returned a few minutes later with a cup of soup and offered it to Lynn, saying he thought she should have the opportunity to taste Peppercorn's good food. As Lynn was finishing the soup, she saw two students walk through the kitchen carrying tacos. They proceeded to the loading dock and began to eat their meal. Lynn, wanting some fresh air, went out to the dock and began to converse with the students.

The students told Lynn they had worked at Peppercorn for three years. One of the students said, "Peppercorn used to be a better place to work. We used to have more students working here. The unit always used to be cheerful, and they used to buy beer and have parties on Friday nights."

Lynn asked what had caused the situation to change and the second student replied, "Drew is much tighter about things. The management is only concerned about customers and not about workers. When I first started working here, we had to mop the floor, but there were a lot of students so it was more fun. Then they didn't make us mop any more. Now we have to mop again, but there is not as much camaraderie among the workers."

The worker continued, "What makes the situation worse is that we can't even mop properly because we are always short of supplies. We haven't had any bleach for a week."

Doug came out to the loading dock and said he was going on break. He wanted the students to come inside so he could give them instructions before he left. Doug told the students that because there was not much work to be done, they could work at a slow pace or even sweep the floor so they could work their full shift.

Lynn followed Doug and the students back into the kitchen. Bob and Robert were finishing the lunch cleanup, and Chris was looking at the dinner menu while eating a snack. When Chris saw Lynn standing alone, he approached her and immediately began to tell her about his work experiences and views of Peppercorn.

Chris told Lynn he likes working at Peppercorn. In the same breath, he said he had recently seen ads for positions at a hotel and plans on applying for jobs. Chris said, "I think the food service industry is hard. We're always working when other people are off, and it's hard to get good financial compensation."

Chris went on to explain that the management at Peppercorn does not give the kitchen staff feedback. He believes this is because management does not eat at Peppercorn often. He also said the management is very cost oriented and won't bring in the best quality products.

Chris went on to state:

Dining used to pay for us to attend professional culinary classes. Now they don't want to spend the money, so they present lectures by campus chefs. It doesn't accomplish much since we are usually taught things that we already know how to make or things that are not within the budget constraints. It doesn't make sense that they are willing to shell out bucks for things like unit specials and management classes and not spend any money on us.

It's hard to get new recipes on the menu. I've tried, but I'm usually met with resistance. I guess that in large quantities they can't afford mistakes. Once, they let us try to test market a new recipe by putting out small chaffing dishes in the meal plan dining room and then asking students for comments on the product. It worked out fairly well and we've used the recipe several times.

As Lynn was wondering about Drew's comment on being a participatory manager, Erica entered the kitchen and came over to tell her she was able to gather some information from the main office. Lynn thanked Chris for speaking with her, and she and Erica went into the service area to find Roger. Roger was chatting with some customers near the salad bar. When he saw his partners approaching, he concluded his conversation.

The consultants each purchased a beverage and on their way to the dining room, Roger told his partners that customers generally had a favorable impression of Peppercorn. They like the food but thought the service was too slow. The only other comment the customers made was that the dining areas were too warm. Erica added that when she had worked at Peppercorn there were rarely any complaints about the food, but they constantly received negative feedback about the heat.

After the consultants were seated, Roger asked Erica what she was able to discover about the structure of the All-American Dining organization. Erica showed her partners copies of the organizational chart, mission statement (Exhibit 5), and goals and objectives (Exhibit 6). Erica went on to describe a few of the things she had discovered that day. For example, menu and staffing changes had to be approved by the central office. She also found out that managers are frequently transferred between units.

Erica then asked her partners what their thoughts were on the structure of All-American Dining and what effect it had at the unit level. Roger suggested that from the information that Erica had gathered, the organization seemed highly centralized. However, workers at the unit level are interested in making their own decisions. He added that the structure of the organization could be contributing to the problems that Drew perceived with productivity and morale.

Lynn, looking over the mission and goal statements that Erica had collected, commented, "All-American professes to be decentralized. Also, Drew believes he is a participatory manager. It seems as if this organiza-

---

EXHIBIT 5 Mission

The mission of All-American Dining is to meet the nutritional, social, aesthetic, and economic needs of the university community with varied and innovative dining services. By meeting these needs we:

- Exert a strong and positive influence on community life.
- Provide educational opportunities for students, staff, and faculty.
- Create a living environment that will help maintain All-American's position as an outstanding center of learning.

The challenge is to accomplish all this within the framework of the enterprise concept.

EXHIBIT 6   Goals and Objectives

The goals of All-American Dining are closely interwoven with those of the Division of Campus Living and the University. These goals and related objectives are outlined below.

I. **Customer Satisfaction.** The primary goal is to provide the All-American community with a nutritious, economical, and quality dining program. The objectives are to:

- Provide high-quality cuisine at an affordable price.
- Conduct surveys to determine customer satisfaction and provide guidelines for change.
- Maintain a variety of quality dining services, including: cafeterias, professional catering, vending, and retail food outlets.
- Offer special dining experiences such as gourmet cuisines, unit specials, and community dining events.
- Create flexible and cost-effective meal plans and options that give customers a wide choice of dining times and locations.
- Maintain the highest standards of health and safety.

II. **Excellent Facilities.** The department's goal is to maintain dining facilities in superior condition.

   The objective is to continually assess and maintain the functional and aesthetic design of facilities in the comprehensive context of the following:

- An ever-changing and varied customer market.
- The need to assure that production and service areas are clean, safe, efficient, and comfortable.
- Budgetary constraints.
- Department and university master facilities planning processes.
- Energy conservation goals.

III. **Professional Management.** Recruit and maintain a professional management staff that can meet the challenges of a dynamic food service enterprise. The objectives are to:

- Encourage a participatory, decentralized management style.
- Recruit exceptional talent and support internal promotions.
- Provide a stimulating work environment through interunit transfers, challenging staff assignments, and intradepartmental competition of programs and services.
- Maintain a compensation program that attracts and motivates an innovative, skilled staff.
- Maintain open and positive lines of communication among management, staff, and customers.
- Provide and encourage education and training opportunities that promote professional and personal growth.

EXHIBIT 6 (*concluded*)

- Conduct regular performance evaluations that are based on predetermined goals and objectives.
- Maintain policy and procedural manuals that will ensure consistent and efficient administration.

IV. **Sound Financial Management.** Develop and maintain effective financial accounting and reporting systems that facilitate effective planning, decision making, and accountability. The objectives are to:

- Be financially self-sufficient.
- Encourage financial responsibility by providing timely, accurate statements, emphasizing the management budget process and requiring managers to be financially accountable.
- Maintain an effective system of internal controls.
- Control labor costs through efficient use of employee time and control the costs of goods with purchasing, menuing, forecasting, and precosting policies and procedures.
- Protect the department against fluctuation in meat costs through hedging in the commodities market.
- Evaluate and budget effectively for future facilities and equipment replacement needs.
- Conduct thorough cost-benefit analyses of potential programs and products.
- Cut costs with a comprehensive energy conservation program.
- Use resources in a reasonable manner.
- Evaluate short-term possibilities with long-range perspective.

V. **Contribution to the University Mission.** Dining's program must contribute to the educational, economic, and community service goals of the University. The objectives are to:

- Support the educational goals of the University through staff teaching and lecturing.
- Provide educational opportunities for the students.
- Use the diverse dining facilities as laboratories for student research and job training.
- Contribute professional time in support of the community.
- Encourage staff participation in University committees and projects.

VI. **Industry Leadership.** Maintain Dining's position as a leader through continual educational and professional contributions to the food service industry. The objectives are to:

- Develop active and creative food service leaders.
- Participate in professional organizations and committees.
- Communicate our ideas and problem-solving techniques to others in the industry.

tion doesn't play by its own rules. I haven't seen any indication of participation, let alone adequate communication between management and line employees."

The consultants continued to talk for a while about the tension they had noticed at the unit. Since Drew was leaving, they wondered if their presence at the unit would have any affect and if the feedback session would really serve its purpose. The consultants decided they would spend several hours the following morning reviewing the information they had gathered. In order to facilitate their meeting, they quickly constructed a partial list of the individuals they had encountered during their observations. This list included characteristics the consultants believed might be important to their analysis (Exhibit 7).

As the consultants sat at the table, several of the employees came over to speak with them. The workers seemed relaxed and joked with the consultants. Doug commented he was working on putting his résumé together, and Chris told the partners about some new recipes he was developing. The pantry workers and dish room workers made small talk until the consultants said they had to depart. Roger, Lynn, and Erica thanked the workers for being so cooperative and said they hoped to see them sometime soon.

EXHIBIT 7   All American Dining and Peppercorn Dining Personnel Chart (partial)

Name	Job Title	Education	Seniority	Age	Full-time	Part-time Student	Management
Peppercorn							
Drew	Manager	A.S.-Restaurant	8 yrs.	37			X
Bob	Day chef		28 yrs.	48	X		
Robert	Day cook	Navy cook	11 yrs.	44	X		
Doug	Night chef	Navy cook	10 yrs.	36	X		
Chris	Night cook		3 yrs.	31	X		
Carrie	Server		10 yrs.	28	X		
Larry	Supervisor	A.S.-Mgmt.	1 mo.	32			X
John	Receiving		11 yrs.	35	X		
Bonnie	Cashier		2 yrs.	28	X		
Molly	Coordinator	Senior-A&S	4 yrs.	21		X	
Shaun	H.R. manager	Senior-E.E.	4 yrs.	21		X	
Sarah	Supervisor	Senior-Gov't.	4 yrs.	21		X	
All-American Dining							
Nancy	Director	A.S.-Restaurant	12 yrs.	41			X
Stan	Asst. director	B.S.-Hotel	9 yrs.	32			X
Larry	Supervisor	A.S.-Mgmt.	6 yrs.	32			X
Eric	Vending manager	B.A.-English	8 yrs.	34			X

QUESTIONS FOR DISCUSSION

The following morning, Lynn, Erica, and Roger gathered at the office conference table to review their notes. After all the partners summarized their findings, the consultants realized they had amassed a sizable body of data. In order to facilitate the meeting, the partners listed the following questions that needed to be answered before they could address the management of Peppercorn Dining:

1. What framework is appropriate for organizing the data?
2. What ideas, models, and concepts should be used to analyze the data?
3. How should the feedback session be designed?
4. Where do we go from here?

Case 11

Community Health Center*

I. Leticia Ramirez
Brigham and Women's Hospital
Jean M. Bartunek
Boston College

EL CENTRO DE SALUD

In early January 1986, Ernesto Smith, the administrative director of a community health-care center called El Centro de Salud (CS), approached me with the challenge of working on what the executive committee (EC) of the center termed a management development project. The EC, which is made up of the five senior managers of the health center, had been discussing the center's internal problems. Ernesto summarized some of the problems. He said the EC members felt overworked because all decision making was constrained at the top levels, and they were unable to focus attention on some long-standing problems that needed attention. Department heads who reported to the EC members were complaining of their frustration in having no input in the decision-making process. Additionally, their work roles and reporting relationships were unclear and frequently changing.

At the same time the EC was beginning work on the management development project, it was completing a restructuring of the managerial and supervisory roles by making most of the department heads second-level managers. The EC thought this restructuring would address some of the problems the center was encountering.

---

*This case is told from the perspective of Leticia Ramierz, who was acting as an internal consultant. She began the intervention while she was a graduate student in Jean Bartunek's Seminar in Organization Development and continued it the following year. During the course of the intervention, Jean acted as a "shadow consultant" with whom Letty talked when she was encountering dilemmas, a number of which occurred during the action planning phase of the intervention. In our presentation of the case, we are placing the reader in the role of shadow consultant. We describe the intervention up to the action planning phase and then ask for your suggestions about what should be done in response to the dilemmas.

General Description

El Centro de Salud is a community health center located in the heart of a low-income, multi-ethnic community in the northeastern United States. Since its inception, CS has offered a comprehensive high-quality health-care service targeted to its population, which includes a large percentage of high-risk mothers and children. The center is an outpatient department of County Hospital, a prominent teaching hospital, and is known within the hospital structure as being able to adjust to the unique demands of the clientele it serves. It annually provides approximately 30,000 service visits to 6,000 users.

Administrative Structure. Similar to the structure of its parent hospital and to the structure of many health-care facilities, CS has a formal triple hierarchy whereby the three functions of medicine, nursing, and administration have equal power in decision making. As is true in many health care organizations, this triple hierarchy creates problems, because people in the three functions tend to operate out of different perspectives. Members of the administration tend to focus on the management of health-care operations, with a primary concern being the efficiency of these operations as a support to patient care. The administration is also most concerned about linking the health center with the external community. The medical staff places its highest values on patient care, service, and medical research. The nursing function carries out the most extensive individual patient care, as well as the primary management of the health center's medical technology. They share with physicians a value on patient care and service, balanced with an appreciation of the administration's needs for coordination.

The executive committee of CS was made up of the administrative director, the assistant administrative director, the medical director, the nursing director, and the director of human services. According to the restructuring being done, the department heads (of pediatrics, nutrition, speech/hearing, etc.) would report to the EC members. An organization chart that reflects the restructing is shown in Exhibit 1.

Historical Background

El Centro de Salud was developed and planned between 1965 and 1966. In 1967, it received its first maternal, infant, children, and youth grants and began operations. Today, CS is one of the oldest comprehensive health centers in the state. Over the years, CS has continuously updated its programmatic emphasis and has acquired new staff expertise as the demands of the patient population indicated a shift in priorities or meth-

EXHIBIT 1 Organizational Chart el Centro de Salud, County Hospital

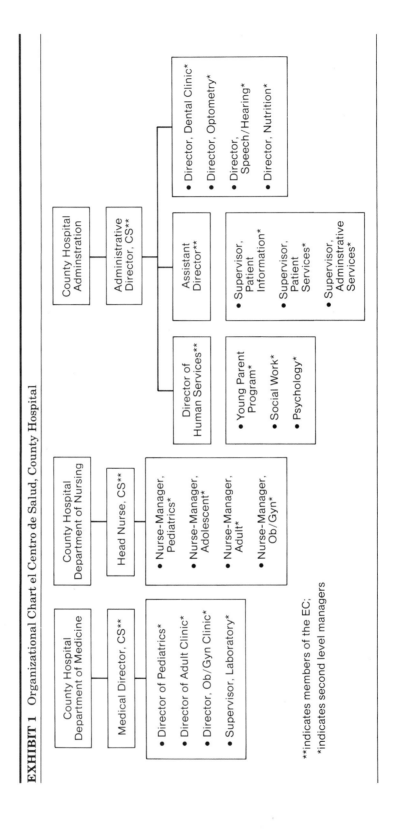

**indicates members of the EC;
*indicates second level managers

ods. However, a family-centered approach to health care remains a constant feature of its program.

Evolution of the Health Center from 1979 to the Current Period.   Between late 1979 and early 1982, CS underwent a major survival crisis characterized by severe program cutbacks, a hiring freeze, layoffs, and severe cost control measures. An administrative director was fired in early 1980 and a new one (Ernesto Smith) hired. At the hospital level, the associate director left his position, and a successor, the current associate director, entered the picture. The new associate director was committed to developing the health center and demonstrated this by her presence at the center, her direct communication with staff at meetings, and her immediate response to staff concerns for resources.

The EC is the sole decision-making body of CS. It evolved in 1982 to replace the previous decision-making body, the program committee, which had been made up of the 16 department heads and which the medical director and administrative director had determined to be too large and unfocused to make effective decisions. Although the disbanding of the program committee had increased decision-making efficiency, it had also caused the department heads to lose all direct input into the decision-making process.

Internally, the health center was changing rapidly in an attempt to remain competitive in the current environment. The executive committee represented one such change. A second was that committees and task forces became the primary form of addressing specific problems on a short-term basis. A third was the hiring of new staff to occupy vacancies that had occurred because of turnover in medicine and nursing.

The Consultant.   I had been employed at the health center since 1980. I had clinical and administrative responsibilities as director of the hearing and speech department and had also acted as internal consultant to the administrative director concerning marketing and strategic planning activities. Before coming to the center, I had been employed by the parent hospital as a diagnostician and speech and language pathologist for one year. At the time the intervention began, I was finishing an MBA program.

THE EL CENTRO DE SALUD OD PROJECT

Entry/Scouting

My first contact with the administrative director about this project occurred in early January 1986. Ernesto presented me with a written proposal that described the EC's objectives for the management development project it wanted me to help carry out as (1) clarifying the roles of the departmental heads and second level managers; (2) developing job performance standards for each of these individuals; (3) identifying projects and ongoing activities the EC could delegate to second-level managers to reduce the workload of the EC and bring about higher levels of performance; and (4) reviewing the organizational structures with a view to giving second-level managers more involvement in the health center's decision making.

Ernesto called the project *management development* because the EC was selecting the second-level managers as a group of leaders and meant to clarify their roles and responsibilities during the organizational restructuring. The committee members wanted to know these managers' skills so they could design training and development activities as necessary.

After reviewing the EC's proposal, I became concerned that the EC had already identified the project's problems and objectives. The group had already determined the second-level managers (whom they had not yet formally identified) needed management developing training and that the focus of any interventions should be directed to that yet unidentified group. Moreover, they had already decided how to implement the management development training.

In contrast to this approach, I spent several long meetings working with Ernesto explaining action research and proposing a project based on this type of methodology, which used a collaborative and analytical approach. I stressed the importance of enlisting the input of the second-level managers (once they were identified) on how they were perceiving the problems to which the EC was responding, especially since the managers would be the group most affected by changes in roles or job descriptions. I explained how data gathering and feedback were necessary in order to achieve a more collaborative effort. I also stressed how much involvement the EC would have to assume in the design, development, and implementation of the project.

On January 21, I presented the same information to the EC. The presentation evoked several responses. Most striking to me was what appeared to be a lack of communication or coordination among the EC group members on the project's objectives. The EC members as a group had not yet discussed how they wanted to proceed with the management development project, and this new information on "action research methodology" was overwhelming to some of them, especially the medical director and human services director. It turned out that Ernesto had written up the information informally discussed by the EC members and discussed it with me before discussing it again with the EC.

Another issue that surfaced during this meeting was a concern for the potential "hidden" effects of the restructuring of managerial roles on the EC. Not only had the EC not identified the middle-level managers, they didn't know how their own roles would fit in with the proposed restructuring. The medical director and human services director wondered how the second level managerial roles would affect their own authority at the departmental level. They raised questions such as: "Will this mean that we will have a whole subgroup of new managers making independent decisions?" On the one hand, the EC members were relieved that restructuring would achieve some task delegation. On the other hand, they were concerned that their authority and power would be diffused. I told the group that before any attempts could be focused on the middle-level management group, the EC would have to reach some consensus about expectations of the managers.

A third issue that surfaced was the candidness of the EC wanting a leadership development training program for the managers rather than becoming involved in an analysis of the organization. They felt they already knew what the problems were and the need was for a leadership development training program at the managerial level. Consequently, I felt a need to describe the difference between management development and organization development. I reassured the group that management development might be one important outcome of an action plan, but if the EC wanted to design an action plan to address a broader array of problems, the approach would have to be broader than leadership development. I also stressed that action research as a methodology would not result in a prescriptive mode of operation. Rather, the process would be the result of a truly collaborative effort between the EC and the management group. The EC members agreed that they liked this approach but were uncertain about the time demands it would involve, not just for the managers but also for them.

A fourth concern expressed by the EC was the potential image problem that might develop because of my dual role as an internal consultant and clinician within the health center. They perceived me more as a clinician and clinic manager than as an organization development consultant. The director of human services, a psychologist, questioned my credibility as an internal change agent because I was not a trained industrial psychologist. The EC members knew of my formal graduate management education. I added that my involvement on this project was being carefully monitored and supervised by an organizational studies professor from my graduate program, Jean Bartunek. This formal affiliation with Jean, a credentialed organizational psychologist, was helpful in allaying the executive committee's concerns that an "amateur" was spearheading the project with little supervision.

After the above concerns were cited, discussion continued about possible advantages of my role on this project. Several pluses were raised.

Having been an employee for approximately six years, I had a great deal of internal information on the history and structure of the organization. The EC also believed the managers, when interviewed, would trust a fellow manager and would be candid and honest in their sharing of information. It was also the consensus of the group that I would have the advantage of knowing what some of the perceived difficulties may be ahead of time, which would prevent me from losing valuable time getting things accomplished.

The meeting ended with an agreement to continue discussing the feasibility of the action research approach and me in the role of facilitator. The EC asked me to prepare a sample interview format I would use to get input from the managers. Despite their concerns about proceeding with the project or with me as the change agent, the group invited me to attend several EC meetings between late January and February, to allow me to gain insight on how the EC functioned as a group and to determine what additional concerns or issues may be relevant to the project.

Contracting

On February 26, the EC and I met in a meeting room at the parent hospital for a full-day retreat. The meeting focused on completing the restructuring of the managerial and supervisory roles, identifying the middle-level managers, and discussing in more detail EC objectives for the project and a tentative plan.

The EC completed the organizational chart shown in Exhibit 1 and the identification of the second-level managers. They also delineated specific job descriptions and responsibilities for each newly identify managerial position. Regarding the action research project, the EC stated the overriding goal was to begin moving toward more collaborative and inclusive management for the center. They developed the following more specific objectives:

1. To give the middle managers increased authority, responsibility, and clear accountability.
2. To increase the managers' involvement in decision making.
3. To communicate where decision-making authority lies for various categories of decisions.
4. To improve the morale of managers and create an atmosphere in which they are encouraged to assume greater authority.
5. To assess the managerial skills and potential for managers and provide training in managerial roles.
6. To reduce the workload of the EC by delegating successfully.

In describing the tentative plan for carrying out the project, I reviewed the action research cycle from problem identification to evaluation. I stressed the need to review the history and structure of CS, and I presented a format I would use to interview each manager on a one-to-one basis. The interview would inquire into such topics as: clear/unclear communication of expectations; perceptions as to whether or not one is able to meet those expectations and suggestions for improvement; specific concerns they would like to communicate to the EC; and personal aspirations for the project.

I asked the EC members to pose any additional questions they would like addressed in the interview. The EC wanted feedback on how it was perceived as following through or not on some of the managers' concerns raised through current communication channels. The EC also wished to know what the managers thought they needed to do their jobs optimally.

The data gathered from the interviews were to be analyzed and interpreted in the form of themes of concern. The information would be digested in a form that would not identify individuals. The focus of the feedback was to be on systemic problems and opportunities, not on specific individuals. The systemic issues could then be addressed in follow-up action planning sessions.

The EC's initial expectation for a quick remedy to the problems was not possible using this approach. We established a four-month time line for the data gathering, problem identification, and feedback sessions. The action planning, implementation, and evaluation phrases would take longer and depend on the action plan designed by the two groups.

The EC agreed to the process and the approach and scheduled a session in late March to introduce the project to the second-level managers. The administrative director chaired that session and introduced the interview process as a means of surfacing managers' concerns and identifying problems they thought might exist in the current system. I then explained how the interview was designed and how it would fit into the large cycle of the project. I reviewed the interview questions and took suggestions on modifications. The managers all agreed to participate.

Data Gathering

Data gathering involved reviewing previous consultant reports, examining organizational charts, reviewing the history of the organization from its inception to its current state, attending middle-management and EC meetings, and interviewing middle managers formally. I also interviewed EC members, but not in the structured and one-to-one approach I had used with the managers. After reviewing all of the above information, with the exception of the middle-manager interviews, it seemed to me that although the concerns and objectives raised by the EC were very real issues that needed to be addressed, they were symptoms of a deeper problem.

The health center had been evolving so rapidly over the last five years, and even more so over the last two years, that the organization was having a difficult time coping with this development. Externally, there were rapid changes in medical reimbursement regulations at the national and state levels, increased competition in the industry, and a changing local consumer market. Internally the parent hospital was analyzing operations within the hospital, and management of the hospital was encouraging this type of activity at the departmental levels as well. All of these factors could easily be contributing to the problems the EC was facing. I described them to the EC members, who said they found this perspective helpful.

During April, I conducted one- to two-hour interviews with the managers. After analyzing the data, I arranged the statements made into themes. I prepared a 28-page master document and a short summary document, which is shown in Exhibit 2.

Feedback and Problem Identification

EC Feedback Meetings.   In April, I met with the EC to present the feedback documents. The EC agreed to review the information and to have comments ready for discussion at the next EC meeting May 7. At that meeting, I asked the EC to respond to two questions: What was your reaction to the interview results? Why do you think people responded the way they did?

The EC members responded in various ways to the first question:

- "People need role clarification."
- "It's a paradox—they want something (for example, role clarification), and then they don't want it."
- "We say, 'you are in charge,' but then we don't let them take charge."
- "The positive comments are gratifying."
- "I felt that it was an honest wish for improvement."
- "I feel a responsibility to do something with the data."

To the second question, the EC members responded:

- "We've failed to set priorities as an organization."

EXHIBIT 2 Summary Results of Interviews with the Second-Level
Managers

STRENGTHS

Theme: *Diverse, friendly, and supportive staff.* People who work at CS are
from diverse backgrounds; they are friendly, cooperative, and committed
individuals.
- "The cooperativeness and friendliness of the staff."
- "The level of commitment and cooperation of people is good."

Theme: *General attitude of freedom.* There is a general attitude of freedom to
be creative and innovative at CS.
- "Having the freedom to think about ways in which to make CS better is
nice."

Theme: *Improvements in facility.* Internal and external physical
improvements in the facility have had a most positive impact on the center.
- "CS has changed physically. Internally departments are beginning to
look more attractive."
- "It's nice to have meetings on the first floor. People are interacting more."

Theme: *Diversity of clientele.*
- "The diversity of the clientele has offered me a unique type of opportunity
and work experience."

Theme: *Improved quality of staff.* The quality of the staff is changing and this
is having a positive impact on the center.
- "A better grade of staff is probably making the difference in getting
things organized."
- "There's a good group of professionals who are well trained, dedicated,
and committed people."

WEAKNESSES

Theme: *Authority and decision making.* There is a need for more
collaborative decision making between top- and middle-level management
and a need for clarity of where authority lies in specific areas.
- "I should have more input into decisions made in my area."
- "This is not well defined in terms of who does what and in what area."
- "It's all constrained at the top level."

Theme: *Job expectations/role classification.* There is a need for clarification of
roles and job expectations.
- "Role clarification is needed, 'What is expected of me?' "
- "Expectations are not clearly communicated and it makes it difficult to
meet expectations as a result."

Theme: *Communication/interactions.* There is a need for more open channels
of communication at various levels.
- "I need feedback from my boss relative to the outlook on my
performance."

EXHIBIT 2 *(continued)*

- "I need to meet regularly with my boss."
- "We need improved communication about decisions which are made."

Theme: *Time management.* The general feeling is that there is so much to do and no time to do it in.
- "Meetings should be on work time. Lunchtime meetings should occur rarely. Now they occur because there is no other time during the day to meet."
- "Better time management in the clinic as a whole is needed."

Theme: *Committees and task forces: selection process/communication.* There is a lack of clarity about the committee formation and member selection process as well as a general lack of knowledge about the status and scope of committees.
- "Individuals aren't able to choose what committees are of interest to them or which ones they want to work on."
- "We need to know what committees exist and what they're doing."

Theme: *Training.* There are training needs at all levels.
- "I need to continue training in my area of expertise, supervision, and in general management."
- "Support staff should be adequately trained and experienced in specific areas."

Theme: *Lack of resources.* The general feeling is that goals and ideas are not implementable because of the lack of adequate levels of qualified staff and other resources to support these activities.
- "I don't have the freedom to do what I feel I need to do because I don't have the support staff."
- "We need adequate staff in terms of numbers of staff available and the types of training which they need to do the job."

WISHES

Theme: *Resources.* To select and to train staff appropriately for CS's staffing level needs and to distribute staff more equally.
- "More equal staffing patterns across the building."
- "Enough staff in all departments where they are needed to run the programs the way they need to be run."
- "More qualified support staff with specific skills."

Theme: *Facility.* To have an improved space and facility to provide appropriate services.
- "We need the space to run our programs the way they need to be run."
- "Expand and/or construct a new facility."

Theme: *Reinforcement/support.* To recognize, appreciate, support, and reinforce employee's talents and worth.
- "A real commitment from top management to recognize each employees' talents and worth."

EXHIBIT 2   *(concluded)*

- "To feel as if we're doing a good job and to get personal satisfaction from that."

Theme: *Clinic focus.* To have a more balanced view of all departments and to target adult clients.
- "That there was a de-emphasis on pediatrics and a more balanced view of all departments."
- "That the serving of adult clients was as much a priority as the serving of pediatric clients."

Theme: *A sense of unity.* To encourage openness and collaborativeness at all levels.
- "I want all employees to be able to give their input, and they should have an opportunity to respond to these types of questions as well."

- "We need to communicate to managers that it's OK to say 'no' within those priorities."
- "What do we want? Do we want managers to meet projected volume levels of patient activity or do we want involvement in decision making?"

Group Middle-Level Manager and EC Meeting. A joint EC–second-level manager meeting was held May 15 to offer managers and EC members an opportunity to review the interview results together and to initiate the follow-up and action planning components. The managers' reactions to the interview results varied from comments confirming that the project was a good beginning to identifying some problems and saying the road ahead was a long one.

The discussion at the meeting raised two new issues as underlying causes of the statements made in the interviews. The first was the "dual clinical/managerial role and the impact of this on the managers." There were mixed reactions to this dual role. Some participants said they were concerned their managerial role outweighed their clinical role. They said, for example, "Having to choose between a clinical and a managerial focus is not a good trade-off." Others emphasized a need for a managerial emphasis to complement the clinical emphasis. Their comments included: "Perhaps those who have years of experience as clinicians need to focus more on managerial skill development." Finally, other participants expressed mixed feelings and cited other complicating factors as affecting the ability to balance the dual role: "How do we bridge that gap between being a manager and a clinician?" "How do I meet my responsibilities at the center and still get in my management training?"

The group felt the need to determine where its emphasis should be and how clinical and managerial responsibilities could be balanced.

The second new issue that surfaced was a lack of a "big picture" message from the EC to the second-level managers. The managers thought programs were often developed without regard to the population the center was supposed to be serving. Additionally, new programs and activities were appearing all the time, and there was little communication or collaboration between departments in implementing them. Added to that frustration was the "trading or sharing" of resources to support the new programs at the expense of already existing ones. What were the mission and purpose of the health center? How do the dual roles fit into that framework? The managers said they needed clarity about the center's focus and direction, so they could have more focus and direction at the departmental level.

Ernesto, who acted as spokesperson for the EC, acknowledged the managers' concerns. He reassured the group that the EC would respond to their need for clarity around the mission statement, and he announced that the next round of joint EC-manager meetings would begin in June.

Action Planning

The EC decided to prepare the action plan initially and have the management group respond to it in June. I advised that a more participative method would be to involve select representatives from the management group to meet with the EC. The EC members rejected this recommendation on the premise that it was their responsibility to address the middle-level managers' concerns. Additionally, Ernesto thought time could be more effectively utilized if the managers had a written draft to respond to. The scheduled meeting with the second-level managers would provide an opportune and sufficient time for the managers to provide input for the action plan.

The EC used portions of its weekly meetings to clarify the mission statement and carry out initial action planning. During these meetings, I attempted to ensure that the middle-level manager group's concerns were being addressed.

Several events occurred that affected the action planning. For example, several of the EC members had hectic clinic schedules and came to some meetings unprepared. As a result, the planning meetings took longer than anticipated. In addition, several members were concerned about the time demands the project continued to take on their schedules. They were becoming increasingly frustrated that the project was such a long process.

Dilemmas Occurring during the EC Action Planning Meetings

During the action planning, the EC members and I encountered several difficult dilemmas. I will present a number of them. On the basis of what had occurred up to this point during the intervention, how should I (and/or the EC) respond to each of these dilemmas?

QUESTIONS FOR DISCUSSION

1. During the EC planning meetings, frequent interruptions due to emergencies in the pediatric or adult departments often called the medical director or the nursing director away. The administrative director often complained that meetings were canceled at the last minute, or that several participants could not attend due to some emergency.

What's a likely reason for these emergencies? What should be done to deal with them?

2. During one of the action planning meetings, a support staff supervisor confided in me that there were rumors among the staff that I was attempting to undermine the authority of the assistant administrative director, and attempting to establish a position for myself on the executive committee. She added that this seemed quite evident to the support staff because of my increased attendance at EC meetings during the project. She said she had tried to dispel the rumors by informing staff members of the project activities and direction. However, she thought she was not successful in allaying their suspicions. This was one of the situations in which I called on Jean for advice.

I informed her of the scenario, and she suggested several possible reasons for the staff responses. For example, she suggested that, as the project unfolded, certain individuals were losing status while others were gaining status. Those losing status might feel threatened by the actions being discussed. Jean reminded me to try to stay objective and not to misinterpret how people were making sense of the change as a personal attack on me. This "objective" stance became even more important for me to assume as we approached the final stages of the action planning.

What should I do in response to this dilemma?

3. At one point, when the EC was discussing the scheduling of future follow-up meetings, the medical director stated she believed she was having to compromise more than most of the other EC members by giving up her research time for the meeting time requirements on the project. She said she resented this; her time was at a premium and other group members were deliberately suggesting she give up her research time to accommodate their schedules.

The nursing and human service directors interjected that they both gave up much of their committee and task force time as well, and there was an equal giving up of other commitments by all members of the group. When Ernesto became frustrated with the conversation, he supported the comment that all were giving up their time. A heated conversation between the medical, nursing, and administrative directors emerged. The medical director accused the group of being unfair and not considering her priorities. She felt pressures from her superior at the hospital to perform on "research-related issues," and she had no time to do all the work required of her. The other EC members responded that they also had superiors with expectations and added responsibilities. The group was deadlocked.

This situation was one I was not prepared to deal with. The EC had previously decided I should not become directly involved in these types of conflicts, since as a clinician I was a subordinate of theirs. However, as a consultant, I felt the responsibility to intervene. I felt caught in the middle and unprepared on how to handle this situation.

What should I do? What should the EC members do?

4. Another dilemma developed regarding the restructuring of the roles. The restructuring process was threatening to a specific group of clinical specialists (nutrition, optometry, dental, speech and hearing) because the administrative director, with the consent of the EC, was creating a new position of specialty clinic manager. This new manager would coordinate and oversee the activities of the four specialty services and would also serve as marketing manager for the health center and act as the key liaison with the external community. Earlier in the project, because he thought I was doing well, Ernesto had offered me the position, but I had turned it down because I felt it important to remain in a neutral, consultant role.

This position was especially threatening to two of the managers in the specialty clinic area. Both managers had been at the center for over 10 years. Both had had many years of being autonomous and reporting directly to the administrative director. Both openly resented the notion of being supervised by anyone else and resented the extra bureaucratic layer between them and senior management.

The optometry manager was the most vocally opposed to the new position. He told several people "management was taking more precedence over medical/clinical issues" and the health center was losing its true mission, which was to serve clients. He claimed the management development project was a front for creating a top-heavy bureaucracy, at the expense of "quality of care service delivery to patients."

This manager refused to accept the change in reporting relationship. Ernesto asked him to reconsider whether he could accept the change.

Instead, he decided to transfer to the parent hospital and left in extremely ill will. He thought that I, as consultant, was responsible for the creation of the position and, thus, also responsible for his resignation. He related this misinformation to the staff in an attempt to discredit me. In addition, he started spreading negative and false rumors about my personal relationships, especially with the administrative director. Once again, I called on Jean for advice on how to respond.

What should Jean, as a shadow consultant, do in this situation? How should I handle the situation?

The Mercurial President*

Gordon Walter
University of British Columbia
Theodore Gerstl
Consultant

BACKGROUND

The Organization

Environmental Testing Services (ETS) was one of four organizations in its field in a multistate region. Its purpose was to provide high-quality, timely, accurate data to both private and governmental organizations in the area of chemical testing of materials associated with environmental issues. It employed approximately 500 people, consisting of approximately 15 percent professional staff (Ph.D. chemists and biologists) and approximately 70 percent technical staff (bench technicians) who did most of the actual testing.

ETS was organized differently than most organizations of its type in that all the professional staff reported to the vice president of professional services, while the operations managers reported to the vice president of laboratory operations (see Exhibit 1 for an organization chart). This created some role confusion regarding responsibility for the ultimate product of the organization. The professionals thought they had legal responsibility (but no authority). The operational managers had functional responsibility but found themselves often dealing with resistance from the professionals. Functional departments of finance, research and development, MIS, and human resources provided staff expertise, but clearly the emphasis was on operations. Since ETS was in an expansion mode, greater emphasis (and greater resource allocation in terms of funds, people, time, and so forth) was being placed on the development of staff departments.

---

*The case is told from the perspective of the senior author who was the primary consultant throughout the project.

EXHIBIT 1   Organization Chart for ETS

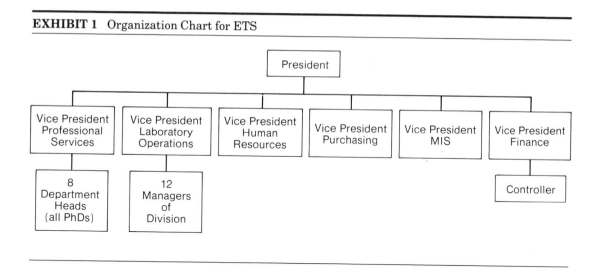

ETS started as a small, single site managed by a group of scientists in partnership and was primarily housed in one large building. However, it had several satellite operations throughout the region for clients' convenience and to maximize levels of service. One of the founding scientists bought out his partners early in the history of ETS and developed it into what it is today. This man was still president at the time of the intervention, 25 years later. Growth was both internal and through the acquisition of other small research and development laboratories. For its first 20 years, ETS carefully cultivated a reputation for quality and timely analysis. Quality and professionalism remained one of the most important features of ETS's core identity, both in the minds of its clients and its employees.

Over time, the president took on equity partners but retained personal control. In the year previous to the intervention, a major out-of-region firm bought 50 percent interest in ETS. The other 50 percent remained in the hands of the president.

How We Became Involved

The organization received an outside grant to pursue a systematic program of leadership development. A search committee made up of the vice president of human resources, vice president of laboratory operations, and her administrative assistant was charged with the task of finding a suitable consultant to help develop a program. About the same time, the parent company president had introduced the concept of corporate culture to ETS in an internal newsletter item, and corporate culture became an item for discussion in the executive committee.

The search committee began a search for possible consultants to perform a needs assessment for a leadership and management development program. We enjoyed an excellent reputation for management and organization development and were referred to ETS by another client. Several consultants were interviewed by the committee.

In the interview, my questioning of committee members raised awareness of significant problems in the organization, especially with regard to its climate. I suggested that this project provided an opportunity to explore the perception of the climate as well as address the leadership and management development question. This was done because of the likelihood that leadership issues would be imbedded in climate issues and a successful leadership development program might be dependent on broader change. (In addition, my interest was more in the area of organizational development than in needs assessment.) The committee reacted positively to the suggestions and expanded the concept of the project.

I discussed the importance of the president in the internal dynamics of the organization and the need to have his involvement and commitment at every stage in the project. It was also clear that the success of the project was highly dependent on consultant/president rapport and that assessing this was a major consideration in the minds of committee members. They invited a written proposal to formalize what had been shared verbally. The committee reemphasized the importance of president rapport in the subsequent contracting letter. (See Exhibit 2 for key elements of both letters.)

What Was on My Mind. I was mindful of a previous intervention where a management development program, aimed at middle and upper management, was inserted into an inhospitable organization. That organization's top management attitudes and the culture were incompatible with the values position of the behavioral sciences (which was the predominant theory base of the management development program). The basic incompatability later turned out to be a problem for the organization. Therefore, I was not attracted to the task of conducting a simple needs assessment that ignored the culture.

I also saw an opportunity to encourage the client to look at more fundamental issues than the ones on which the discussion commenced. Early in the discussion with the committee, I sensed that there were concerns about the president's management and interpersonal style and his direct impact on the culture. I decided to test how open the committee would be with me by putting this issue on the table.

EXHIBIT 2   Contracting with the Client

Item A.   *A key paragraph from the lead consultant's letter to the committee is as follows*:

> It is my understanding that ETS desires to embark on a program that will enhance organizational effectiveness through increasing the knowledge, skills, and general competence of its managers and supervisors. In addition, several members of the top management group have discussed the issue of corpoerate culture, indicating that there might be a need to assess and perhaps change the organizational values and behaviors that shape the existing culture. In order to plan an effort that is specific to ETS's needs, I have suggested to the committee that an organizational diagnosis be undertaken in order to (*a*) determine the type of leadership and management skills most needed at this time, and (*b*) determine what people in the organizational feel about the organization culture (both to discover things that are enhancing the effectiveness and blocking the effectiveness of the organization). As a result of obtaining this data, the management group will have a great deal of information about the state of the organization's health and needs and will be in a good position to make decisions about how and when to proceed with a management development and/or organization development effort.

Item B.   *The committee's contracting letter to me said the following*:

> The approach you propose, incorporating an organizational diagnosis with a training needs assessment, appears to be an appropriate one for our organization's present climate. . . .
>
> We were impressed with the importance you placed on your achieving a working rapport with our president. We want to confirm that should either of you conclude from the initial interview that the relationship is unworkable, the remainder of our agreement with you would be canceled.

Item C.   *The selection committee's letter included explicit guidance on how the relationship should be approached*:

> You are aware of our concern that this study be received positively in the organization. We believe that your communication style and approach will be a major factor in creating a positive experience and producing cohesive results. For these reasons, we would expect that in the first phase of our project all interviews with the president and division directors, feedback sessions, and initial consultations on design of the program would be conducted by you personally.

I explored certain risks (that the president might be a key stumbling block) and received confirmation from the committee members. Simultaneously, there was a dramatic increase in energy and interest in exploring an expansion of the original project. Had the committee not dealt openly and honestly with me on that issue, it would have been a clear sign to me that either (1) there was low readiness for the system to deal with real issues; (2) my style was too "confrontative" for this organization; or (3) I was off base in my perceptions. The committee's positive response was an encouraging signal to me.

Options for the consultant to consider: A choice here was how explicitly to emphasize the values position of the behavioral science interventionist. Is the consultant simply a facilitator, a process consultant, or a virtual tabula rasa incarnate who gathers, stores, and displays data? On the other hand, does he or she stand for something? Does she or he wear a clear *advocacy* hat, along with a process consultant hat? To be merely a process consultant might place the OD consultant in a position of helping authoritarian/exploitative types to practice their craft with more cunning.

The value position of OD is that participation is basically constructive and that more direct communication yields improved organizational effectiveness. At the pragmatic level, the consultant must simultaneously be aware that too much emphasis on the values of OD could prematurely terminate the opportunity but too little might result in either false expectations or a constrained set of intervention options.

Initial Contracting/Entry Issues. The key issues were the relationship between the president and the consultant and an awareness that the interpersonal style of the consultant needed to match with the needs of the organization (see Item C of Exhibit 2).

Another consideration was that the organization had never experienced an intervention of this scale. It was very important to the committee that the project be well received in the organization. I now knew that the organization culture (as a result of the president's interpersonal and managerial style) was a major concern.

Following the formal meeting with the committee, the members informally disclosed that the organization climate was extremely stressful, to the point of "coming apart at the seams." By this, they meant many people were being pushed to the limit in terms of organizational demands (mostly stemming from the president), and the organization was in danger of losing some very good people.

Once I was trusted, they confided a number of concerns that revolved almost exclusively around the president's style. It rapidly was becoming clear that expanding the project to include an analysis of the culture would ultimately be more helpful to the organization by focusing attention on the issues that really matter. (It may have even been a hidden agenda of the two vice presidents on the committtee.) Therefore, there were now two distinct possible directions for the project to take: (1) strictly a simple needs analysis that would result in formulation of a management development program for the organization or (2) a full organizational diagnostic and development effort that combined the needs analysis with a study of the organization's culture.

THE INITIAL MEETING WITH THE PRESIDENT

The purpose of the first meeting with the president was to assess the rapport between us and to begin the process of trust building and relationship building. The president's stated (but not actual) needs for the intervention turned out to include improving cohesiveness of the top team in addition to addressing the points already noted. I experienced the president as open and eager for improvement of his organization. There appeared to be an initial rapport between us. However, the president's troublesome interpersonal behavior was apparent.

Emanating from this meeting, and based on the stated needs of the president for this intervention, I drafted a letter documenting agreed-upon parameters of the project for the president's signature. With a few specific changes introduced by the vice president of human resources, this letter was signed by the president and distributed to all members of the organization who were to be involved in the study.

> I was concerned about writing the letter for the president rather than the president drafting it for himself (especially regarding the president's commitment to the project).

Why I Decided to Accept the Organization as a Client

The positive meeting with the president plus the energy for change expressed by the vice president of human resources and vice president of operations led me to be optimistic about the opportunities for having an impact on the organization. Also, the two key vice presidents had reiterated their opinion that the organization culture was sick and in dire need of change. OD had the potential to solve some of the dysfunctions that were beginning to be identified and thus improve the quality of life of organizational members.

Procedural Contracting/Entry Considerations

A fundamental entry issue was expanding the ownership of the project to include the other vice presidents and the president. This commitment building would help resolve the question of who was the client for the OD aspect of the project. I met with the vice presidents to introduce myself and define more clearly the scope of the project and the specific way the project would proceed. Also, this was an opportunity for the other vice presidents to make suggestions and to shape the project. This not only made for potentially better decisions regarding the project, but also helped to engender their commitment and support.

Two important things occurred in this meeting. First, concerns were raised about the president's commitment to the project (e.g., "Is he on board?"). Also, these concerns were emphasized by a strong emotional undercurrent. Second, the vice president of professional services was conspicuously detached from the discussion, preferring instead to remain silent while taking copious notes.

What Was on My Mind. I was impressed by how much energy there was in the room (especially about the president). There was a real sense of emotional drama in anticipation of both the intervention and possible reactions of the president. The committee members seemed worried about exposing themselves to risk and pain, but not to an alarming degree. The champions of the intervention (vice president of human resources and vice president of operations) were both young and assertive women—without professional degrees. At the same time, the vice president of professional services (a Ph.D. in chemistry in his late 50s) was silent and withdrawn. He was not overly against the intervention but also was not assumed to be a supporter. The vice president of finance was expressing strong concern about the commitment of the president.

My assumption was that this range of reaction represented the themes I would encounter in the total organization. My desire was to move the negative members over to a neutral stance with regard to the intervention and to move the ambivalent ones to positive support.

I did not confront these dynamics at this time because it was too soon in the intervention for me to predict individual reactions to such directness. My sense was that this kind of candor was not the norm of the organization and would not be successful at this time. Also, I did not want to risk alienating anyone so early in the process. I sensed especially that the vice president of professional services would be an important player in change efforts as the intervention progressed.

Client Decision

The committee made its decision to go for the double project. We met again and finalized details about who would be interviewed, what format would be used in the interviews, and the basic approach to communicating the initiative to the organization's participants.

DATA GATHERING

It was six weeks from the initial meeting with the committee to the beginning of the data-gathering phase. A fellow consultant, Theodore Gerstl, and I interviewed about 100 people from all levels and domains of the organization. All interviews were for two hours. Top-level people were interviewed individually and others in groups. An effort was made to put people in groups in which they felt they could talk openly. We took detailed notes of participant responses to the following questions:

1. When we design our leadership development program, what are the areas that would be most helpful to you in learning how to manage more effectively?
2. What do you see getting in the way of this being the most effective organization? What are some of the things that may be blocking you from being more effective or more satisfied in your workplace?
3. What factors contribute to your being effective? What is it about the environment at ETS that you really like?

To allow maximum freedom of discussion, interviews were informal and open ended. To maximize the credibility and the usefulness of the anticipated feedback, we took copious notes in the interviews (writing down as close to verbatim statements as possible). The anonymity of participants' comments was preserved, and this commitment to participants was underscored during the interviews. Specific examples were also gathered to increase the usefulness of the feedback.

The interviews went very well. Word went through the organization that we were easy to talk with, credible, and serious about helping. A good feeling was growing toward us and the project in general. The group interviews went fast and were characterized by high degrees of openness and broadly balanced participation. There seemed to be an atmosphere of mild optimism, mixed with excitement, that something would happen. Large numbers of participants expressed appreciation that they felt listened to and paid attention to.

DATA ANALYSIS

Interpretation of Existing Data

I reviewed the interview data with my partner to surface themes and identify useful quotations and examples to support and/or elaborate on those themes that recurred and were significant. Ultimately, approximately 25 positive and 25 negative issues were identified. A summary of diagnostic observations contained in the written report to the president comprises the Appendix. The initial problems identified by both the president and the top team were confirmed by the interviews.

The interviews produced three surprises:

1. The breadth and intensity of the reactions to the president personally were extraordinary! Almost all issues cited in the interviews could be directly traced to the behavior of the president.

2. Concerns about the behavior of the vice president of professional services bordered on the perception that there was something seriously wrong, either psychologically or physiologically, with him. His dysfunctional behavior was thought to be so out of the ordinary that many people either described him in terms of competency issues or health issues. In either case, his behavior was beyond "normal" behavioral issues one encounters in this type of study.

3. There was concern, particularly at lower levels, that the institution was pressing so hard on volume that quality was being compromised. This concern went beyond pride in workmanship. It had ethical and even legal overtones.

What Was on Our Minds. Now we have a real intervention dilemma! On the one hand, the president-owner-founder is described as brilliant and charismatic by some and, no question, has built a very successful and profitable operation. On the other hand, the president is described as a major problem! He was also perceived as a person who did not listen, who jumped to conclusions, and went around his managers. He criticized people in public so forcefully that they regularly reported feelings of total humiliation.

The data suggested he dismissed and discounted information he didn't want to receive, and he was known to react defensively, punitively, vindictively. People were so afraid of him that they often avoided meaningful interaction. While not completely oblivious to such consequences of his behavior, he minimized the effect it was having on the organization. The president has authorized substantial investigation into the organization but did so under the assumption that the problem was outside himself. Given the data and knowing how he might respond (if the data were accurate), we knew we had to deal with these issues, but how? And when?

Personal doubts were rising fast about the opportunities for success in the intervention as I became increasingly aware of how difficult it was to get time with the president. This inaccessibility reduced informal time to build trust, reduced the amount of feedback that could be processed constructively, and compromised my opportunity to influence the president.

It also may have signaled the president's radically different priorities from those of the intervention. He may not have been serious about the problems identified in the intervention. It may be that he was not as committed as he first appeared or that he was reducing his commitment due to his reading of informal feedback from other channels.

At the same time, however, the consistency of positive reaction to the intervention throughout the organization indicated no need to think the president was getting the word that the intervention was off the mark. Still another possibility may have been a growing resistance on his part, based on information or intuition that we were "on the mark," because he was beginning to feel threatened.

Choices and options regarding timing: Three options capture the range of possible practical actions at this point.

1. We could confront the president with what we have learned. However, such actions could be easily discounted or dismissed as superficial.
2. We could begin a patient process of influencing the president by giving him some warning, "test the waters" about his reactions, and make subsequent moves in light of incremental knowledge of his ability to constructively assimilate feedback.
3. We could keep mum about our insights and concentrate on tightly documenting the information so a formal presentation would have maximum impact.

Organization Readiness

In retrospect, it is clear that the organization's readiness was less than we had anticipated. There was high readiness in terms of motivation for change. However, the organization's readiness to change required the president's readiness to change. He was most emphatically not ready or even interested in changing himself.

Preparation of the Feedback

The next step in the process was to prepare both a written report for the president and vice presidents (the executive committee) and a flip-chart presentation that consisted of supporting material (quotes from the interviews) and an elaboration of all of the major issues. This took five days to produce and consisted of a 15-page, single-spaced typewritten report (covering both the leadership development component and the corporate culture component) and three flip charts of quotes from the interviews to illustrate the issues more graphically.

When this was completed, I was scheduled to meet with each vice president and the president individually to (1) present each person with a "preview of coming attractions," in terms of the data and (2) give each person feedback about themselves privately, both strengths and areas that others perceived might be getting in the way of that person's effectiveness. (The rationale for meeting with each principal player before the feedback session is to reduce the surprise and defensiveness at the session.) These meetings were all scheduled on the same day, with the group meeting scheduled one week later.

There was a slight skirmish between the president and me regarding the meeting time for the group session. At the time, it did not seem too important, but in retrospect, it might have been a very important event. After the meeting with the president in which he was exposed to the issues coming out of the interviews and discussion regarding a change of role for himself and the vice president of professional services (a meeting felt to be very positive and successful), the president's secretary called to ask if the feedback session with the vice presidents could be held sooner than originally planned. I informed him that I had promised the vice president of human resources that the meeting would not be held until she returned from vacation, so a change in date was not possible.

I sensed that he did not want to hold the meeting during its scheduled time (during work hours), so I suggested we meet on a Saturday morning or evening after the vice president returned. He acceded to my request but was clearly disturbed. He suggested, during this conversation, that one of the vice president's subordinates could attend the meeting in her place. I informed him that would be inappropriate, given the sensitive nature of the data. (His not understanding that point signaled that something was very wrong. He was clearly irritated with me now.)

THE LAST INTERVIEW: THE MYSTERIOUS DR. BUTLER

It is important to mention an event that did not seem important at the time, but was to play an exceedingly critical part in this drama. Having interviewed almost 100 people, including all management and professional staff and a sampling of technical and support staff at lower levels in the organization, my co-consultant and I knew the issues well. The last person I interviewed was Dr. Butler, one of the professional staff.

Dr. Butler had a great deal of informal power in the organization, based on his close friendship and long-time association with the president. He was also president of a professional association of biochemists, a group ETS was keenly interested in because its members provided good connections for present and future business.

The interview with Dr. Butler was intentionally very different from the others. Because of the special rapport Dr. Butler had with the president, and because Dr. Butler knew the president well, I planned to utilize Dr. Butler as a resource person in providing advice to me as to how to approach the president.

Dr. Butler conveyed an understanding of the problems the president caused in the organization and agreed with me that he probably was not capable of changing his managerial or interpersonal style. I explored with Dr. Butler the idea of suggesting to the president a change in role, encouraging the president to take a more active external role and a less active internal role. Dr. Butler was in sympathy with that approach and offered his support and assistance, if there was anything he could do.

In the course of our discussion, Dr. Butler coached me on "do's and don'ts" with the president ("He loves peanuts and beer; talk to him in that kind of setting."). The meeting with Dr. Butler was helpful and positive, and I was left with the impression that the project had a real supporter and an important one. This turned out to be a major error in judgment, an error that would change the course of the project and ultimately sabotage it.

FEEDBACK TIME

As the data were accumulated, collated, and placed on flip charts in anticipation of a feedback session with the top team, the imperative grew to make further contact with the president as soon as possible. In this meeting, I would give the president a sense of the data. This had the potential of being a very difficult meeting, because the president would be surprised with both the content of the issues and the intensity with which the issues were felt, particularly the concerns surrounding both the president and the vice president of professional services.

I suggested an offsite meeting of approximately two hours (but open ended if needed), to begin the task of sharing the potentially threatening and stressful information learned in the interviews. The president negotiated the time of the meeting (via his secretary), pressing for only one hour in his office. As a compromise, an 11 A.M. meeting that could continue into the lunch hour was set up.

What Was on My Mind.   What's going on here? Doesn't he know how serious this situation is? I have data that can be exceedingly important to the success of his organization. Why am I having trouble getting time with him? Why is he treating me like this? Is this only indicative of how he treats others, or is there something else going on here with respect to me on this project? I need *at least* two hours, probably four! We should be off site for this, not in his office where we can (and will) be interrupted! Do I accede to his demand for a shorter time in his office, or do I require the conditions I know are needed for this type of meeting?

Options: What would you do?

1. Accede to client demands and hope cooperation will yield reciprocal cooperation.
2. Press for direct scheduling with the president and explain the rationale for offsite meetings with expectations of a rational reaction.
3. Procedurally confront the client (e.g., say, "This is the way I do the task—if you are unwilling to cooperate, I cannot continue").
4. Other options?

What I Did

I chose option number one, hoping the data would *entice* the president enough to increase his perception of the importance of the intervention. Most of what the diagnosis revealed were problems that would respond well to developmental efforts, such as team building and training. The fact that two top people were fundamentally flawed, however, was not solvable in this way. The president was talented as an entrepreneur but a disaster in running this size and degree of formalized organization. The vice president of professional services was either incompetent or in some fundamental way incapacitated. I believed I had to be very direct about issues and suggest it was in the best interest of the organization for the president to become more externally focused.

The organization needed a chief operating officer to replace both the president and the vice president of professional services. We were at a crunch. My sense was that anything less than these steps would not yield what was right for the organization. That is, no developmental interventions would help these people. Either we had to do something fundamental or to continue would be a waste of my time and a sham.

The feedback session was a classic good news/bad news experience. My objective was to give the president feedback in a supportive, but direct, manner. I gave the president an idea of the things people felt positively about, both regarding the organization and himself. While I did not shy away from the critical perceptions of him, I thought the chances of his being able to change a lifelong pattern of managerial and interpersonal behavior were slim to nonexistent. The approach I took with him was to encourage him to think about using his many entrepreneurial strengths externally. I wanted to plant the seed of him thinking about an organizational structure change that would replace him with a professional manager (chief operating officer) and encourage the president to become more active in acquisitions, community relations, and other activities more suited to his skills.

At the same time, I broached the subject of the vice president of professional services. I advised the president that the preceptions of the vice president's competency (both managerial and personal) came up so frequently and with such unanimity that it could not be discounted and must be addressed. The president responded appropriately to both these areas and was willing to explore both changing his role (not his behavior!), making organizational changes, and minimizing the influence and negative impact of the vice president of professional services.

The most contentious and risky issues (from my standpoint) were dealt with openly and appropriately by the president, and none of the defensiveness ascribed to the president by others was evident during this meeting. Everything seemed on track! I was very encouraged and suggested another meeting to continue exploring the data with the president. Encouraged by the thoughtfulness of the session, I pressed for a half-day meeting offsite to dig into the next layer of the data.

Rising Resistance

It is difficult to identify exactly when resistance began to grow. The day after the feedback with the president, his secretary called, trying to move up the scheduled half-day session with the vice presidents. Unfortunately, this would preclude the vice president of human resources from attending, because she was on vacation. (An accident?) Here I could not give in to the pressure of the president. To the president's irritation, the scheduled meeting time was maintained.

What Was on My Mind. I was now immersed in the standard dynamics I had heard described in the interviews and this firsthand knowledge reinforced my sense of the way the intervention had to go. I was becoming increasingly frustrated with the president, increasingly perceiving him as not putting in the time necessary for the success of the intervention and demonstrating a kind of excessive slowness in recognizing the gravity of the issues. His time schedule was increasingly dominating the events and also threatening the success of the project. At the same time, his touchiness and incessant need to dominate were such that I was struggling to maintain the integrity of the intervention without irritating and alienating him.

During the morning, I received a call from his secretary saying, "The president is postponing his meeting with you today until he sees a written report from you." I explained to her that while I could provide him with the written report, I would rather not, because it contains only part of the data, and the report is really meant as a summary of findings only after we had discussed the issues in detail. The secretary reiterated his orders: "He insists on something written, even if it's preliminary, before he meets with you."

What I Was Thinking. I was incredulous! What should I do? I was being blackmailed. The condition of meeting with me was predicated on his getting a written report first. It was against everything that was right, but what could I do? I communicated reluctance to present the written report before face-to-face working sessions because (1) it was only partial and (2) required a discussion of the points raised.

QUESTIONS FOR DISCUSSION

What would you do?

1. Withhold the report until he would meet with me.
2. Give him the report, hoping, once again, that the contents would entice him into rational action.
3. Withdraw from the project (remember, approximately 15 days of time were already into this, and a lot of people took a lot of risks exposing themselves to the consultants in the hope that something good would come of this; in other words, a lot was riding on this).

APPENDIX

Diagnostic Observations Communicated in a Written Report to the President

The report contained 25 strengths and 25 problems for the organization. One section dealt directly with the president's role and behavior. It also contained a section on the leadership development program (the original project). The style of the report was direct yet supportive. For example, it did not shy away from directly noting shortcomings of both the president and the vice president of professional services. However, the general tenor of the report was understanding and optimistic about developing a process to help the organization in these areas.

Organizational strengths

The following were mentioned as items contributing to the effectiveness of ETS and/or to people's sense of satisfaction:

Exciting environments—opportunities for growth, change, challenge—"certainly not boring!"

Lots of freedom and autonomy—people are challenged and encouraged to be creative.

Job content—complexity of tasks. People like what their jobs entail.

The people—people are seen generally as professional; conscientious; competent; supportive.

Opportunities for professional growth and recognition (outside ETS).

Encouragement to seek education.

The size of the company.

Equipment—you get the tools you need to do the job.

Benefits and employee programs; profit sharing, vacations, etc.

Fairness in promotion policy.

Attempts to get employees involved in decision making and companywide programs.

Job postings.

Nonunion.

Safety programs.

Hours; nine-day fortnight; not working weekends.

President himself—charismatic, exciting person to work for.

Service orientation/image in the community is positive.

Less pressure than some other settings.

Lots of money devoted to research.

Good relations among peers.

Excellent support staff, with positive attitudes toward problem solving.

High quality control and efficiency and continued emphasis on quality and service.

Turnaround time has improved.

Good cooperation at lower staff levels.

Problems brought up are sorted out quickly.

Informal atmosphere.

Openness to change; nonbureacratic and nonrigid (compared to hospital setting).

No smoking policy.

Job security.

Competitive salaries.

A feeling that management cares (e.g., this project).

Independence and trust to do one's job (don't punch a clock).

Long-service people.

Good secretarial support.

Technical staff support—"extremely positive attitude; produce good work; loyal; 'they deliver!' "

Involvement and consultation on decisions (for some people).

Good relations with manager (for most people).

Entrepreneurial management style allows variety and freedom to grow.

People encouraged to be creative, innovative, progressive with new ideas and programs.

Individuality is accommodated.

Employees are seen as important—feedback and problem identification is encouraged.

Blocks to organizational effectiveness

The following were mentioned as items blocking the effectiveness of ETS and/or getting in the way of people feeling a sense of satisfaction:

The president's management and interpersonal style.

Lack of cohesive team functioning at the director level.

Climate of blame, territoriality, and mistrust.

Crisis management, fire fighting, lack of rational planning and decision making.

Secrecy, confidentiality—lack of openness and trust.

Unclear or unobtainable goals and objective—lack of clear direction.

Unrealistic workload expectations.

Mission of quality of service threatened.

Lack of sense of accomplishment, achievement, job satisfaction.

Lack of performance feedback; avoidance or aggressive modes used (rather than constructive feedback).

Lack of recognition and positive reinforcement.

Lab operations/professional staff relations strained.

Interdepartmental issues.

Intercompany relations (between sister subsidiaries).

Perceived inequities in staffing, workload, remuneration.

Intradepartmental issues (problems within each department).

Physical plant issues (feelings about working conditions, such as old or unkempt facilities).

The Apartment Complex

Laura L. Goode
Boston College

The apartment building in which I live and in which this intervention was conducted is located in a suburban, middle-class, residential neighborhood. There are approximately 50 units in the building, evenly spaced on five floors of a standard rectangular structure. Each floor is accessible by a central elevator and by stairways at each end of a long, straight hallway. The building has three separate entrances. However, the front door is utilized most because of its easy access to the residents' mailboxes and unit door buzzers. This front-door lobby is one of only two common areas in the building, the other being a small basement laundry room.

Several young medical professionals and/or students are renters and make up approximately half of the total residents. The remaining half are primarily elderly persons, most of whom have owned their units for several years. Turnover among residents is low, as most are generally satisfied with their living accommodations and expenses are relatively low.

Despite the apparent homogeneity within the two groups of residents (one due to common occupations, the other to similar age), there was little interaction between them. At the time the intervention began, there were no organized committees, such as a condominium owners' association. Similarly, with few exceptions, people tended not to socialize with others in the building. The primary types of interaction among residents occurred through chance meetings in the building's common areas. This precluded the possibility of the residents working together to address common problems. Most building residents (especially the medical professionals) had external interests that consumed their time and energy. They generally viewed the apartment as little more than a setting that housed their personal living space. With no organized group or apartmentwide goals for residents to identify, there was little (or no) motivation to strive for improvements in the complex as a whole.

The superintendent function was and is handled by a couple who live on the premises and are employed full time by a management company located in another city. At the time the intervention began, the superintendents had been in their positions for three years. Generally, they were expected to ensure proper upkeep of the building and surrounding property, make necessary repairs, and respond to the specific problems and needs of the residents. In theory, they were available by phone on a 24-hour basis.

Ineffective communication existed between the superintendents and residents. Although everyone who lived on the premises was given the superintendents' phone number, residents often found it very difficult to get in touch with them. When no one answered, there was no way to leave a message. Similarly, the superintendents did not share their knowledge of pertinent issues, except for posting occasional notices on common entrance doors.

In this type of physical setting and social environment, problems requiring interdependent problem solving have little chance of being addressed, let alone solved. People tend to be unaware of the extent of the problem and not to know whether others share their concern and frustration. In the apartment complex, for example, there had been a lack of distinct lines and numbers designating the residents' parking places for several years. As a result of the faded markings, residents were often unable to fit their cars into the appropriate space and occasionally were forced to park on the street illegally. Other unsolved, ongoing problems were outdated fire alarms and extinguishers and insufficient snow removal on surrounding sidewalks.

The physical and social characteristics of an environment such as this apartment building are also likely to foster a norm of problem acceptance, rather than problem solving. For example, if one's mailbox did not lock, most people simply accepted the malfunction and lived with it. One resident even had his paychecks automatically deposited in his bank account to avoid the risk of having them delivered to his unlocked box. He initiated this change before making any attempt to have his box repaired because he assumed his problem would remain unaddressed by the superintendents and guessed that other residents with similarly inoperable boxes did not care enough to pursue a solution.

THE PROBLEM

As I noted, mailboxes in the apartment complex were located in the front entrance to the building between the two doors providing access to the inside lobby. The first door was always unlocked, while the second required a resident's key. Thus, the mail area was accessible to anyone. Each unit was assigned an individual box, a small lockable compartment capable of holding standard-size letters only. Magazines, newspapers, and packages were placed on the floor beneath the mailbox area. Occasionally, the mail carrier or package delivery services attempted to notify residents of their arrival by ringing their buzzers. But this did not occur regularly and when deliverers made the effort, residents were unlikely to be home to answer. Thus, packages were frequently left in the front entrance, outside the locked entrance door.

There were separate but related problems with the mail area. First, packages left in the front entrance were being stolen. No one knew whether the thieves were internal or external, but most believed they were external. Several residents had experienced the problem and were concerned and upset about it. However, according to the superintendents and many of the longtime residents, there had been no major effort, collective or individual, to address the issue or propose a solution.

In addition, many locks (including mine) were broken, so the mailboxes did not close properly. As a result, letters often fell out, were subsequently scattered over the floor, and occasionally lost. Some residents expressed frustration over the situation and others seemed not to care. Again, no serious attempts at correcting the problem had been made, although a few people had asked the superintendents to fix their boxes. Despite these requests, the mailboxes had not been repaired.

Another issue surfaced during a casual conversation between the building's mail carrier and me while I was retrieving mail from my broken mailbox. The carrier expressed concern about the broken locks because he was not supposed to leave mail in open boxes. He implied that in the near future he would no longer deliver mail to open, dysfunctional boxes.

It seemed to me that action research might be a very useful way of dealing with these issues. As I planned the intervention, I began by outlining my overall objectives. Specifically, I sought to work with the building residents to solve the mail/security problem while simultaneously educating the participants about action research principles. I hoped to instill in them an appreciation for the benefits of collaborative problem solving and to provide them with an opportunity to utilize some of the methodologies.

The next phase of my planning process involved assessing the abilities of the relevant parties. Although I had not spoken with the superintendents or many of the residents about their knowledge of action research (or any other organizational change models), I assumed their previous experience was limited. Thus, in addition to ongoing education, I anticipated I would need to act directively, at least in the initial stages of the intervention.

Lastly, I reflected on my role as an internal consultant. As a resident of the building, I had a personal stake in the problem and had my own initial opinions about it. However, I also had a responsibility to the project participants to collect data objectively and minimize the impact of my opinions. I hoped that because I was a fellow resident and had spoken casually with some of my neighbors in the past, I would be able to encourage people to more openly reveal their personal experiences and emotions. It would be very important for me to carefully balance the need to establish my credibility as the project leader with my concern regarding solving the mail/security problem.

THE INTERVENTION

My first step in conducting this action research project was to elicit the involvement of at least two additional residents who would work with me on the project, from initial diagnosis through implementation and evaluation of a solution. While collecting my mail, I became engaged in an informal conversation with two retired women who commented on my broken box. These women seemed eager to have the problem solved and, once someone else set a problem-solving process in motion, were willing to commit time and effort toward achieving the goal.

The two women had both lived on the premises for over 15 years, one as an owner and one as a renter. I thought they would be able to provide valuable information in several areas, including any past actions taken toward dealing with the mailbox and security issues. They were also personally acquainted with the superintendents and many of the residents. Both had been victims of the faulty mail system, having lost packages and/or mail. As is understandable, their initial tendency was simply to blame the superintendents for the problem.

I began to establish a relationship with these women and to introduce action research to them, especially a focus on "what," rather than "who" is the problem. Both women had open minds and no preconceived ideas about the approach. I felt that an introduction to action research and ongoing education throughout the project was necessary to foster an environment for problem solving that would enable collaboration and a search for the multiple potential causes of the problem.

Soon after I made my first contact with these women, a notice was taped to the common area door. The note was written by a resident of the apartment complex and read as follows:

> On October 10th a package was delivered here at approximately 11 A.M. and it was addressed to me. However, I never received the package and learned of its delivery only after calling the sender to inquire about it. I am aware that such disappearances have happened before, but if anyone has any information that could help me locate my package I would be very appreciative! M. Kaplan.

I immediately contacted M. Kaplan (Michael) to inquire further. I learned he was a medical professional who had lived in the building five years, and this was the second time he had been victimized. Although he had previously complained to the delivery services, he had never pursued a solution that involved other residents and was not aware of any such efforts ever being made. He had posted the note simply because several other residents had done so in similar situations, and in desperation he decided to try the idea. He was obviously frustrated and upset. After learning about the project, he welcomed the opportunity to join the core group.

Phases of the Intervention

Based on my initial observations of the mail/security problem and the characteristics of the setting, as well as discussions with the core group, I formulated a plan for gathering data to assist in the diagnosis. This involved (1) distributing an informational letter to everyone living in the building, (2) conducting preliminary meetings with the core group and superintendents, (3) conducting an informational session with anyone interested in participating in the process, and (4) interviewing all interested individuals. I would analyze the interview data and feed back the results to interested residents, who together would conduct action planning.

The Informational Letter.   I prepared an informational letter to distribute to all residents, superintendents, and the postal carrier, inviting them to an informal session to be held one week later. I aimed the letter at telling the residents of my intentions to work with anyone interested in diagnosing, analyzing, and solving the mail problem. I chose this strategy for several reasons. First, I thought it was important for everyone to be aware of the project from the beginning. Equally important, they needed to learn about it from me, not through casual conversations. I did not want to rely on informal communication networks to inform people about the project, fearing several important individuals might fail to hear about it and those that did might misunderstand the intentions of the intervention. I also hoped this memo would generate support and commitment to the project.

Preliminary Meetings.   The next phase involved preliminary meetings with the core group and the two superintendents. These meetings, held in my apartment, were used to prepare for the informational session, educate the groups about action research, and obtain their support for the project. I believed it was important to include all of these individuals in a wide variety of the intervention activities, including initial planning efforts.

The core group and I met first. All three individuals were eager to talk about the mail/security problem specifically, rather than focus on the broader context. Thus, they first discussed their initial impressions of the situation. They related their personal experiences, describing the frustration they felt, the inconveniences created by the problem, and the seriousness of the situation. This discussion helped the group clarify the issues and become committed to working together in solving this problem. We then prepared an agenda for the informational session. I tried to avoid being the dominant force and leader. For example, although I wanted to open the group meeting, I recommended that one (or more) of the task force members also speak at the upcoming meeting. The two women were reluctant, but Michael was eager to address the group.

In meeting with the superintendents, I was concerned there might be many barriers to be broken down. The fact that I was a new resident, was much younger than they were, and was proposing a new approach to problem solving could have worked against me initially. However, the meeting was productive. I opened the discussion by asking them to describe their jobs and to offer their opinions about the mail/security system. I needed to assure them that their job security would not be threatened by the intervention and that the goal of the project was to deal with the problem, not criticize them. I emphasized the importance of the superintendents' contributions to problem definition during the upcoming meeting as well as their continued involvement throughout the entire project. The woman offered to address the group to outline her general ideas about the problem and constraints on the system, while her husband preferred to remain silent. I coached the woman on ways of taking a collaborative, rather than defensive, approach.

Informational Session. Eight apartment residents, in addition to the core group, two superintendents, and I attended the informational session. This was very encouraging because it confirmed my initial impressions about the severity and seriousness of the problem. Some residents were there simply because they were curious about the project. But most told me they attended because they were concerned about the problem and wanted it to be solved.

This meeting was held in the large apartment of one of the women who was part of the core group. Several of the attendees commented they had never been in an apartment in the building other than their own. The new attendees were primarily retirees, although two medical students were also present.

I opened the meeting with a brief introduction of myself and action research, as well as a general description of the mailbox problem. I proposed to interview each interested person and then feed back the information to the group for its use in joint problem solving about the problem. When questioned as to why private interview sessions were necessary, I cited advantages such as the ability for each person to openly voice their views in a confidential and less-threatening setting, and the fact that each participant would be able to learn more about me and the project during the interview session. After some discussion, everyone agreed that interviews would provide the best setting in which to accomplish the project objectives.

Michael then presented an overview of the problem and opened the meeting for discussion. The attendees were eager to describe their individual cases. One woman told of staying in her apartment during the day to assure she was home when packages were delivered. Another building resident expressed his frustration when an important letter was lost because of his broken box. He recounted the difficult process of obtaining a duplicate copy of the document.

It was obvious the group had never collectively addressed the problem before. As one person told his or her story, many heads nodded in agreement. They generally seemed both surprised and relieved to learn others shared their problems and frustrations. Each story had the same ending—a failure to solve the problem and/or retrieve the lost letters and packages. As it became increasingly apparent that individual efforts were not effective, the group seemed to grow more eager to pursue a collective approach.

The superintendent spoke next, and her manner and approach were surprisingly effective. Rather than respond defensively to the various cases and complaints raised by the residents, she focused on the mail/security system itself. She described the relevant mechanical details and outlined her perception of the inherent problems with the system, as well as the resource and budget constraints under which she operated. For example, she acknowledged that the mailboxes were very small, yet were probably not replaceable. She also expressed her own frustration, admitting that previous attempts to solve the problems had failed. Most importantly, she conveyed a strong desire to work with the group in generating and implementing a solution. She began to refer to the problem as "ours" and agreed that "we" should work on it. This was a very important step in our group development. I had feared that the meeting might become a finger-pointing, blame-placing session with two distinct subgroups. Instead, we seemed to develop into a cohesive group with a common purpose.

The meeting concluded with a confirmation of agreement regarding the next steps to be taken. Six of the eight meeting attendees, in addition to the core group members and superintendents, arranged individual interviews with me. The data feedback session was scheduled for three weeks later. I left the meeting feeling encouraged and hopeful about the potential for success.

As I reflected on the meeting later, I began to wonder if I had been too quick to assume that there was a lack of conflict between the superintendents and the residents. Although neither group openly stated negative opinions about the other, this could have been the result of the dynamics of the group meeting. Both groups were present and perhaps felt intimidated about openly expressing their views. Each speaker was perhaps being careful about what he or she said in an attempt to avoid a direct confrontation. On the other hand, it was possible that extreme differences did not exist and tension between the groups was truly minimal. I anticipated that in subsequent gatherings it would be vitally important for me to remain open to the possibility that significant differences did exist.

Individual Interviews. Although I initially intended for each interview to last approximately 30 minutes, I underestimated the time required at the beginning of each session to create a comfortable, trusting environment in which to engage in an open dialogue. Thus, each meeting lasted close to one hour and began with a casual, unstructured exchange on topics such as our families, mutual sports interests, and the schools we attended. When the residents appeared to be at ease with me, I gave a brief review of my background, the project itself, and action research principles. After confirming their understanding of this general information, I proceeded by inquiring about the resident's background. By starting with the resident's personal history (rather than on broader organizational data) I obtained a perspective on each person as an individual. People also seemed to enjoy talking about themselves, and a relaxed atmosphere was created as both of us shared personal information.

The next line of inquiry involved the resident's interpersonal relationships, both with other residents and with the superintendents. My initial diagnosis had led to the conclusion that these areas were potentially problematic and required thorough analysis. I asked questions relating to the individual's social interactions within the building. I probed into past relationships, existing ones, and evaluations of both. "Do you have friends in the building? Have you met any while living here, and if so, how?"

I asked how the residents perceived the roles of the superintendents. The discussion included issues such as personal role expectations, the fit between various individuals and their roles, whether additional skills and resources might be required, and any other changes that might be necessary. "Have you ever spoken with the superintendents, either to discuss a problem or engage in a casual conversation? Were these interactions satisfying?"

Closely related to these issues were process-oriented dimensions of the apartment complex. This area probed into what (not who) each person perceived to be influencing the problem with the mailboxes, both positively and negatively. We discussed communication pattems among the residents as well as the problem-solving and decision-making systems (or lack thereof). This flowed into implementation issues such as follow-up procedures with the superintendents, the extent to which changes were actually instituted, and the subsequent impacts on living conditions. "Were you aware of the mail/security issue? If so, have you been victimized and/or learned of it from other residents? What were your greatest frustrations and overall impressions regarding the solution of this problem and others you have encountered?"

From this focus on the existing status, I moved to inquiring about the interviewee's ideal future state regarding the mail and security situation. Where the previous discussions sought to obtain a broad general picture, this next portion of the analysis focused on those issues the residents deemed important and would be committed to trying to change. After various ideas were proposed, we attempted to predict their impacts on both the individual and the group. Specific, technical suggestions about the mail/security system as well as group process changes were analyzed. "Would you be willing to pick up your packages at the post office? How much would you be willing to pay to have the mailboxes replaced? If periodic group meetings of residents and superintendents were held, would you attend? What topics would you want to discuss and in what format?"

The discussion of the problems and possible solutions created a positive, action-oriented atmosphere with which to end the session. The interviewees said they began to believe the potential existed to successfully solve the mail/security problem.

Findings from the Interviews. In analyzing the data obtained, I looked for common themes in the responses. I sought to identify those aspects of living in the building that many residents felt passionately about (both positive and negative). In addition, I attempted to specify and clarify the various components of the mail/security problem that arose during our conversations. I analyzed specific, individual responses and made generalizations regarding broad, structural issues affecting the residents as a group. I then categorized the ideas presented in the interviews into three areas: organizational strengths, existing mail/security problems, and existing group level structures and processes. Table 1 shows the most frequent comments made by the residents under each category.

I reviewed the interview results with the core group, and we planned the feedback/action planning meeting together. We were concerned about maintaining a focus on "what" versus "who" is the problem during the upcoming session. This was important because many participants blamed the superintendents for many aspects of the problem, citing their lack of concern, follow-up, and responsiveness to both the mail/security situation and other issues.

We also attempted to predict possible responses to the new information. Reactions such as self-protection, defensiveness, and frustration

---

TABLE 1   Most Frequent Comments during the Interviews

A. Organization Strengths:
1. The residents in the building are considerate of one another.
2. The building is safe and residents feel secure.
3. The superintendents live on the premises and, therefore, should be able to respond quickly to problems.
4. The neighborhood is safe, quiet, and convenient.

B. Existing Mail/Security Problems:
1. Letters and packages are being lost and/or stolen.
2. The mailboxes are too small and many are broken.
3. There are not enough people responsible for building maintenance, and there is an insufficient amount of money available to make needed repairs.
4. We lack information regarding postal system requirements and laws regarding mail delivery.
5. Our problems are often not solved.
6. It is very difficult to contact the superintendents to report problems or obtain needed information.
7. The superintendents do not respond to our complaints.

C. Existing Group-Level Structures and Problems:
1. There is a lack of communication between the residents and the superintendents.
2. There is no grievance procedure available to handle our outstanding problems and issues.
3. The roles and responsibilities of both the superintendents and the residents are unclear.
4. There is no formal collaboration between the residents and superintendents.
5. We lack a follow-up procedure to ensure that problems are solved.
6. We lack a collective decision-making structure.

---

could be anticipated. However, the group (including the superintendents) had made significant progress toward becoming a unified, cohesive group at the previous meeting. With these thoughts in mind, we prepared an agenda that allowed for a brief presentation of the interview results, in-depth discussions of the key issues, and development of an action plan.

As I thought about the upcoming session, I grew increasingly anxious about it. People's expectations were high and I did not want to disappoint them. This meeting would be our primary collective effort. The interview data definitely pointed out solvable, manageable problems. My task would be to help the group members see this and encourage creative problem solving.

The Feedback/Action Planning Meeting. The feedback/planning meeting was held in the same core group member's apartment, with all of the original participants but one in attendance. I began the session with a brief review of the informational session. I highlighted the importance of collaboration, openness, and honesty. Next, I presented the consolidated results from the interviews (Table 1). When this brief presentation was completed, I opened the meeting for discussion with a few general guidelines.

I asked the residents first to request clarification on any of the problems outlined. They were encouraged to express their perspectives and impressions regarding the statement meanings. For example, one of the topics listed was "Our problems are often not solved." To one woman this meant her complaints to the superintendents were not adequately addressed and no changes were being made. Another woman interpreted the same statement to imply that individual residents fail to speak out about the problems or attempt to generate solutions.

After discussing these two perspectives, the group agreed that both interpretations were applicable. This was an important dialogue as we gained insight into various perceptions of the situation and avoided placing blame on any one person or group. Instead, we remained focused on solving the problems collectively and sharing responsibility for implementation. After agreeing as to the meaning of each statement, I asked the group members to reflect on which problem area seemed most serious, and which they would like to concentrate on addressing. After posing these requests, I waited for a roundtable discussion to begin.

The conversation was very slow in starting. People sat silent, staring at the interview results, and appeared to be thinking about them. Most appeared frustrated and overwhelmed by the list of problems. The core group and I observed deep sighs and looks of confusion throughout the group.

Finally, the silence was broken. One of the residents, a retired widow, pointed out the high degree of interrelationship among most of the problems listed. She elaborated by proposing several examples demonstrating that solving one problem would likely cause others to disappear or at least improve. For instance, she hypothesized that if the group established a committee using acceptable procedures for collaborative decision making, and if that group could work to define specific roles, responsibility for repairing or replacing the mailboxes could be assigned. This, in turn, would likely solve the primary problem of lost and stolen mail. This woman's optimism and ability to consolidate the list proved to be a major turning point. People began to sit up in their chairs, nod their heads in agreement, and engage in an active discussion.

Next, the group analyzed each issue and the interrelationships among them. With little disagreement, we developed a new and consolidated list of problems:

1. Lost/stolen mail and packages due to both the broken boxes and the inability to contact the residents for delivery.
2. Lack of collaboration among the residents themselves, as well as between the residents and superintendents.
3. Unclear roles and responsibilities of the superintendents and residents.

In order to confirm agreement on the three problems identified for specific action planning, I proposed a vote. The group unanimously chose to pursue these three areas.

On reaching this decision, the group turned to me for guidance on how to begin actually solving the problems. People expressed a sense of accomplishment in the progress thus far, but they also realized that important work was still ahead. I recommended that each person reflect on which of the three problems they personally felt most concerned about, most committed to solving, and most able to influence.

After another long (and difficult) pause, one of the medical professionals pointed out that we needed additional information before we could begin proposing potential solutions. For example, in order to solve the first problem, two areas needed to be researched—purchase and/or repair alternatives regarding the mailboxes themselves and the postal service laws and requirements. Further information was also required about the third problem. Specifically, in an effort to more precisely define the superintendents' roles, their formal contracts would need to be analyzed. In contrast, our ability to solve the second problem was not dependent on any outside information. The group agreed with this assessment.

QUESTIONS FOR DISCUSSION

1. Based on these requirements, the overall project objectives, and the apparent energy of the group to deal with the problem but uncertainty about how to act, what should I recommend that the group do next? Outline the recommendations you would make and how they might be implemented.
2. Why have you selected these strategies as opposed to other available alternatives?
3. What results (positive and negative) would you predict regarding resolution of the specific short-term problems and for the broader, long-range future of the building residents?
4. Was the action research model the most appropriate approach to solving this problem? If not, recommend alternative strategies or identify the phases of the intervention that could have been designed more effectively.

5. How might the project have differed if I had not been a resident in the building?

REFERENCES

Alderfer, C. P. "Consulting to Underbounded Systems." In *Advances in Experiential Social Processes,* Vol. 2, ed. C. P. Alderfer and C. L. Cooper. Chichester, Eng.: Wiley Ltd., 1980, pp. 267–95.

Brown, L. D. "Planned Change in Underorganized Systems." In *Systems Theory for Organization Development*, ed. T. G. Cummings. Chichester, Eng.: Wiley Ltd., 1980, pp. 181–203.

## Part III

Intervening

The cases in this part describe a variety of OD interventions—change programs aimed at solving specific problems and improving organizational effectiveness. They address a diversity of organizational features including interpersonal and group processes, technology and work design, reward systems, and strategy and structure. The interventions also involve an assortment of change targets, such as small work teams, unions and management, the total organization, and interorganizational collectives. Although each case has been identified with a particular type of intervention, the change programs often include a mixture of other kinds of changes as they evolve and undergo modification.

In "Lincoln Hospital: Third-Party Intervention," R. Wayne Boss, Leslee S. Boss, and Mark W. Dundon describe how a consultant can help two conflicting persons resolve their interpersonal problems. The conflict occurs in a health care facility and involves the head of the operating room and an orthopedic surgeon, two key players who need to work effectively together to provide quality medical care.

Philip Mirvis shows how effective teams can be created in the companion cases: "Ben & Jerry's (A) and (B): Team Development Intervention." The (A) case shows how a Vermont ice cream producer founded by new-age entrepreneurs gains the management structure necessary to compete in a rapidly growing marketplace. The intervention is aimed at creating a cohesive top management team to run the previously underorganized company.

In the (B) case, the intervention extends to the firm's board of directors where the consultant helps to resolve conflicts both within the board and between it and the top management team. Finally, the change process moves downward in the company to include other managers and employees in implementing the firm's mission statement.

"Penrock Industries, Inc.: Team Development Intervention," by Eric H. Neilsen and Harlow Cohen, describes an offsite, team building effort with the executive team of a large, family-owned manufacturing conglomerate. The case provides a detailed account of the interpersonal issues that often need to be confronted and resolved in building a more effective team.

In "The Entertainment Industry Council on AIDS: Interorganizational Problem-Solving Intervention," Thomas E. Backer describes how he volunteered to develop an industrywide task force to combat the AIDS epidemic in the entertainment trade. The case shows the difficulty of organizing volunteers from a diversity of organizations to tackle a complex health problem. It underscores the strategic choices, politics, and sheer effort involved in applying OD to such large-scale problems.

David J. Nygren and Maurice L. Monette, in "The Catholic Diocese of Louisbourg: Strategic Planning Intervention," report how OD consultants helped a large religious organization develop a process for deciding how best to serve the needs of its members. The case identifies the different stakeholders having a vested interest in the diocese and shows the methods used to gain their participation in and commitment to the planning process.

"The CAMIDS Group (A) and (B): Sociotechnological Intervention," by Barry Batemen, describes a long-term OD effort to help a word-processing group deal with continual reorganization and technological change. The (A) case shows how an internal consultant helped group members address problems under their control. It demonstrates, however, the need to look beyond the boundaries of the group to assess how external forces affect it. In case (B), further reorganization and new workstation technology provide an opportunity to apply sociotechnical principles to the redesign of the group.

In "The Alum Company: Union-Management Cooperation Intervention," Thomas G. Cummings describes his role as a third-party consultant to unionists and managers involved in designing a new chemical processing facility. He shows the problems involved in trying to bridge the traditional adversarial relationship between unions and management and the special role OD can play in facilitating cooperation between them.

Gerald E. Ledford, Jr., in "LIFECO: Reward System Intervention," shows the problems that can occur when trying to administer a skill-based pay system. Acting as an external consultant, Ledford helps members of a customer service department in an insurance company confront the need to modify their reward practices.

"Los Angeles County Sheriff's Department: Transorganizational Intervention," by Alan M. Glassman and Thomas G. Cummings, describes a change process aimed at assessing and improving the relationship between the law enforcement agency and the cities for which it provides services. The case underscores the need to conceptualize such relationships as forming a transorganizational system and the complexities of intervening into such underorganized collectives.

In "Allan Labs: Strategic Change Interventions," Susan A. Mohrman explains the process of helping a large, nonprofit research organization radically transform itself to compete more effectively in a changing environment. The case shows the problems encountered in large-scale change efforts and the need for trust and cooperation among different stakeholders if change is to occur.

Lincoln Hospital: Third-Party Intervention

R. Wayne Boss
University of Colorado
Leslee S. Boss
Organization Research and Development Associates
Mark W. Dundon
Sisters of Providence Hospital

Soon after the election of a new chief of surgery, the president of Lincoln Hospital faced a crisis. Lincoln, a 400-bed for-profit hospital in the southwestern United States, was experiencing severe problems in its operating room (OR). Forty percent of the OR nurses had quit during the previous eight months. Their replacements were significantly less experienced, especially in the specialty areas. Furthermore, not all could be replaced; when the crisis came to a head, the OR was short seven surgical nurses.

Also, needed equipment often was not available. On several occasions, orthopedic surgeons had already begun surgery before they realized the necessary prosthesis (for example, an artificial hip, finger joint, or knee joint) was not ready, or was the wrong size, or had not even been ordered. Surgery then had to be delayed while equipment was borrowed from a neighboring hospital. Other serious problems also plagued the OR. For example, scheduling problems made life extremely difficult for everyone involved. Anesthesiologists often were unavailable when they were needed, and habitually tardy surgeons delayed everyone scheduled after them. The nursing shortage exacerbated these difficulties by requiring impossibly tight scheduling; even when the doctors were ready to begin, the scheduled nurses might still be occupied in one of the other operating rooms.

The surgeons were at odds among themselves. Over 30 of them were widely regarded as prima donnas who considered their own time more valuable than anyone else's and would even create emergencies in order to get "prime time" OR slots—for which, as often as not, they were late. Worst of all, however, the doctors and nurses were virtually at war. Specifically, Don, the new chief of surgery, was at war with Mary, the veteran OR director; indeed, he had campaigned on a promise to get her fired.

Lincoln's president was faced with a difficult choice. On the one hand, he needed to satisfy the physicians, who during the tenure of his predecessor had become accustomed to getting their way in personnel matters by threatening to take their patients elsewhere. The market was, as the physicians knew, increasingly competitive, and the hospital was also faced with escalating costs, changes in government regulations, and strict Joint Commission on Accreditation of Hospitals standards. Could the president afford to alienate the surgeons by opposing their newly chosen representative—who had a large practice of his own?

On the other hand, could he afford to sacrifice Mary? She had been OR director for 13 years, and he was generally satisfied with her. As he later explained,

> Mary is a tough lady, and she can be hard to get along with at times. She also doesn't smile all that much. But she does a lot of things right. She consistently stays within her budget. . . .

Furthermore, whereas Don had long been an outspoken critic of the hospital and was generally distrusted by its administrators, Mary was loyal, a strict constructionist who adhered firmly to hospital policies and procedures:

> She is supportive of me, of the hospital, and of our interests. She doesn't let the doctors get away with much. She has been an almost faultless employee for years, in the sense that she comes to work, gets the job done, never complains, and doesn't make any waves. I really don't understand the reason for the recent problems. I trust her and want to keep her. It would be extremely difficult to replace her.

The last point was a key one; a sister hospital had spent almost three years unsuccessfully trying to recruit an OR director.

After talking with both nurses and doctors, the president decided not to fire Mary. Instead, he told both Mary and Don that they must resolve their differences. They were to begin meeting right away and keep on meeting, however long it took, until they got the OR straightened out.

The results were predictable. Neither party wanted to meet with the other. Mary thought the whole exercise was pointless, and Don saw it as a power struggle that he could not afford to lose. The president, who wanted an observer present, chose Terry, the new executive vice president and chief operating officer. Mary didn't know Terry very well so she asked that her boss, the vice president of patient services, sit in. Don, who "didn't trust either Mary or her boss as far as he could throw them," countered with a request for a second of his own, the vice president for medical services. When the meeting finally occurred, it quickly degenerated into a free-for-all, as Don and Mary exchanged accusations, hotly defended themselves, and interpreted any interventions by the three "observers" as "taking sides."

DIAGNOSIS

At this point, Lincoln's president called me. We negotiated a psychological contract, where the president shared the above historical information, described the problem as he saw it, and identified his expectations of me and for the project. I, in turn, articulated my expectations of the president. We then agreed to take no steps until I had interviewed both Don and Mary.

Later that afternoon, Don expressed his anger and frustration with the hospital administration and, most of all, with Mary:

> I don't want to have anything to do with this lady. She is a lousy manager. Her people can't stand to work with her. We don't have the equipment or the supplies that we need. The turnover in the OR is outrageous. The best nurses have quit, and their replacements don't know enough to come in out of the rain. . . . All we want is to provide quality patient care, and she refuses to let us do that. She doesn't follow through on things.

He particularly resented Mary's lack of deference.

> Mary's behavior is so disgraceful it is almost laughable. She shows no respect whatsoever for the physicians. . . . She thinks she can tell us what to do and order us around; and I am not going to put up with it any longer. When I agreed to take this job as chief of surgery, I promised my colleagues that I would clean up the mess that has plagued the OR for years. I have a mandate from them to do whatever is necessary to accomplish that. The docs are sick and tired of being abused, and I am going to deal with this lady head on. If we got rid of her, 95 percent of our problems would go away. She has just gone too far this time.

In his cooler moments, Don admitted that Mary was only partly to blame for the OR's problems, but he still insisted she must be fired, if only to prove to the doctors that the hospital administration was concerned about those problems, and that something was being done.

> *Observation:* I am always a bit suspicious about the objectivity of someone who has reached the conclusion that someone must be fired. There is almost always something else that is going on that requires more investigation.

Mary was both angry and bewildered. She saw herself as fair and consistent in dealing with doctors and nurses:

Things had gone relatively well until six months ago. At that time, some of the orthopods started scheduling surgeries and then canceling them at the last minute, which, in turn, fouled up the schedule for the rest of the doctors. When I called them on it, Don went on a rampage. He is the leader of the pack, and now he has blood in his eyes. I have tried to talk with him about it, but he won't listen.

And just as Don's assessment echoed, in an exaggerated form, the doctors' perception of Mary as an exceptionally strong-willed woman, Mary's assessment of Don echoed his reputation among the orthopedic nurses and hospital administrators, who feared and distrusted his quick temper and sharp tongue:

Not only that, but I find his filthy mouth very offensive. I am not going to cooperate with him when he behaves like that. Nobody else talks to me that way and gets away with it. Nobody, I won't put up with it. As long as he behaves that way, it is a waste of time to meet with him. I am sure that I am doing things that bother him, and I want the OR to run as smoothly as possible. But there is no way we can deal with these problems unless we can sit down and talk about them without being abusive.

Clearly, both Mary and Don had strong needs to control other people's behavior, while remaining free of control themselves. It is significant that each used the word *abuse* to describe the other's behavior. They did respect each other's technical abilities, but morally, Mary saw Don as "an egotistical jerk," and he saw her as a "rigid, petty tyrant." Neither trusted the other, thus, each was inclined to misconstrue even unintentionally negative comments—an especially disastrous state of affairs in the gossipy environment at Lincoln, where surgeons, nurses, and administrators were quick to relay, and amplify, the signals of hostility.

It was obvious from these initial interviews that Don and Mary were largely contributing to the OR problems; but it was also obvious that many others had a stake in the outcome of their battle. I therefore went on to interview the surgical head nurses, the vice presidents for patient services and medical services, the executive vice president, the president, and 25 physicians.

The vice presidents and the surgical head nurses agreed with the president: Mary might not be the hospital's most personable manager, but she was a good one. Her conservative, tenacious, no-nonsense style had earned the trust of administrators and the respect of OR nurses, as well as some physicians. As one nurse asserted: "Good OR managers are hard to find and certainly Lincoln is far better off with Mary than without her."

The doctors, in general, supported Don, though some of them had reservations. At one extreme, an anesthesiologist began with a classic disclaimer:

Now, I want you to know that I don't have any problems with Mary, personally. In fact, I really like her. We have been friends for years, and we get along just great.

Nevertheless, he was convinced the OR problems were "100 percent Mary's fault. I have no doubt about that." Furthermore, although he claimed to be, as an anesthesiologist, "a completely neutral third party in this whole business," he clearly shared Don's assumption that Mary's job as an OR manager was to keep the surgeons happy:

> Her people hate her. She is a lousy manager. She just can't work with the MDs. Surgeons are a rare breed, and there is no changing them. You have got to get someone in there who can work with them and give them what they want.

His conclusion echoed Don's: "She ought to be fired, if for no other reason than to prove that something is being done to address the problems in the OR."

Observation: I am always leery of someone who says, "It is all her fault." When someone is blamed for 100 percent of the problem, it usually evidences either denial or a coverup. There may be a completely innocent party in an emotionally charged conflict, but I have never met one. Emotionally charged conflicts are always power struggles, and it takes two parties to play that game.

A less enthusiastic partisan, a surgeon who was a 10-year veteran of the Lincoln OR, was very conscious of the way expectations such as those expressed by Don and the anesthesiologist were apt to be viewed by others in the medical community:

> Quite frankly, I am embarrassed to admit that I am a surgeon in this town; by doing so, I am automatically branded as an egotistical dimwit. With only a few exceptions, those guys are a group of conceited, narcissistic technicians who are so caught up with themselves that they have no clue about what is going on around them. Some of them are bullies, and they push the rest of us around because we don't have the patient census they do.

His assessment of blame was correspondingly more moderate than the anesthesiologist's: "A lot of people would like you to think that this problem is one sided, and that Mary is totally responsible for this mess. But that isn't true." And while he supported Don, whom he described as reasonable and willing to listen to logic, his principal wish was to avoid personal involvement: "I am glad he is fighting this battle. I won't. The thought of getting caught between him and Mary scares me to death."

This last wish was vividly elaborated by another surgeon, who also highlighted the general perception of Mary as a strong personality:

> I don't mess with Mary at all. I'm not stupid. It's true that I don't like some of the things that she does. Sometimes she is just plain ornery. But I also am not willing to take her on. In fact, at this point, I will do whatever she wants, whenever she wants it. If the other docs are smart, they won't mess with her either. They can talk big in their meetings, but if they have any sense, they won't mess with that lady. She controls too many of the resources I need to do my job. So far she has been very helpful, and she has gone out of her way to do me some favors. I don't want to mess that up. I think it is great that Don is willing to take her on, and I wish him success. That way, if she wins, it will be him that gets beat up, not me.

The high turnover among OR nurses was a particularly sore point among the surgeons in general, whose frustration was explained by Don:

> I don't think the administration has a clue as to how urgent this matter really is. It takes at least five years for a surgical nurse to gain the necessary skills to be useful. In the last two months, we have lost some of the best nurses I have ever worked with in my life. As a result, I had to start the training process all over again. It has seemed like I've been working with a group of student nurses! This turnover has cut my productivity by more than 50 percent.

Most of the doctors blamed the high turnover on the nursing managers' inability to retain qualified personnel, whereas the managers blamed it on the doctors' verbal abuse. And in fact, a significant number of doctors were widely regarded by some of their peers as well as by the nurses as impatient, intolerant perfectionists who demanded far more of others than they did of themselves.

From the extended interviews, it was obvious that while Mary had greater credibility with the hospital administration and Don had more backing from the doctors, each had a certain amount of power over the other's constituency: Mary controlled the surgeons' working conditions, while Don controlled a significant portion of the hospital's patient flow. The OR problems could not be resolved without genuine cooperation from both of them—especially from Don, who was outside the formal hierarchy of the hospital and could not be coerced by the president.

I met again privately with each of them to determine whether they were honestly committed to improving their working relationship. Both were skeptical about the possibility of real change but said they were willing to do everything they could to help, as long as their own basic values were not violated. Each defined the kind of help he or she was willing to accept from me and the circumstances under which that help was to be given.

INTERVENTION

Only at this point did actual third-party facilitation intervention begin. I used a design that included perception sharing, problem identification, contracting, and follow-up meetings. At their first formal meeting together with me and the three vice presidents who acted as observers, Mary and Don began by writing answers to three questions:

1. What does he or she do well?
2. What do I think I do that bugs him or her?
3. What does he or she do that bugs me?

The very process of writing things down was helpful. It gave them time to get used to this explicitly confrontational situation before either of them had a chance to "pop off" at the other, and it forced an element of rationality into an emotionally charged situation. Also, the questions required specific answers concerning behaviors, not subjective generalizations about personalities. Listing specific behaviors made each of them realize that at least some of the things they disliked about the other could be changed.

They then explained these responses orally, in the order shown in Exhibit 1. Because of their mutual hostility, I thought it safer to require that at first they address their remarks only to the third party, not to each other. Each, however, was required to hear the other's presentation so each would understand the other's perceptions. And because both were guaranteed an uninterrupted speech, each was more likely to listen to the other. Taking up the positive perceptions first helped. As Don later explained:

> I was stunned to hear her say those positive things, particularly the part about me taking care of her family. For a long time, I had seen her as my enemy, and I expected only the worst. I was amazed that she had so much respect for me. As a result, many of my negative feelings for her began to leave. It is really tough to stay angry at someone who says so many nice things about you. I also found that I was much more willing to listen to what I do that bugs her. Somehow, criticism is always easier to take when it is accompanied by something positive.

It also helped that before making any accusations against each other, they were required to examine their own behavior. As Mary acknowledged, neither had ever taken the time to figure out specifically how he or she might be causing problems for the other:

> It had never really occurred to me that I may be doing something that caused Don to react that way. Vaguely, I suspected that I may be doing something that he didn't like, but I was hard pressed to identify what it was. I really had to stand back and say to myself, "What is it that I am doing that is making this working relationship go sour?" I had spent so much time concentrating on what he was doing that bugged me that I hadn't looked at myself.

EXHIBIT 1 Participant Responses to Three Questions in the Third-Party
Facilitation Model

---

1. **What does Mary admire about Don and think he does well?**
   - He is very concerned about patient care.
   - I admire him for his skills as a surgeon. I would have no problem sending a member of my family to him.
   - He is interested and wants to work out issues that we have with each other.
   - He can be very gentle and considerate at times.
   - He is well respected for his skills by his peers and by the OR nursing staff.

2. **What does Don admire about Mary and think that she does well?**
   - She is honest in her work.
   - She has met my needs in orthopedics in getting us the instruments and equipment we need.
   - She has a lot of external pressures on her and she has handled them well.
   - She deals well with the various groups that are pulling at her: patients, staff, administration, physicians.
   - She manages the overall picture very well in the OR.

3. **What does Don think he does that bugs Mary?**
   - I am impatient. (Mary agrees)
   - I am demanding of personnel in surgery, but everyone can't always get what they want, when they want it. (Mary disagrees)
   - She is uncertain as to how much I am willing to support her this coming year. (Mary agrees)
   - I am not the best listener. (Mary agrees)

4. **What does Mary think she does that bugs Don?**
   - I don't listen to him. (Don agrees)
   - I appear defensive at times. (Don agrees)
   - I respond to some directives in a very detailed manner. (Don agrees)

5. **What does Mary do that bugs Don?**
   - She is difficult to communicate with. I can talk to her, but I am not sure that she is listening.
   - She doesn't assume the responsibility for some specific problems, such as not being able to do an operation without a full set of prosthesis available.
   - She doesn't effectively manage the personnel that she supervises in OR. Specifically, there is a great deal of disruption going on. And there are also morale problems, particularly as they relate to their trust of her and her trust of them in the OR.

6. **What does Don do that bugs Mary?**
   - He generalizes and is not very specific with examples, even when questioned.

EXHIBIT 1 *(concluded)*

- The staff labels him as a whiner, in terms of "nothing is ever right," his complaining, etc. This also relates to laying out problems and then walking away.
- He sometimes says one thing but means another—and gives mixed messages. An explanation of this is my asking him how things are going, he says fine, but then I find out that he has problems later in the day.
- I do not feel a full measure of support from him, and that bugs me.
- He doesn't always listen to my concerns.

The oral discussion of this question made it obvious that neither was intentionally causing problems for the other, making both parties less hypersensitive to imaginary insults. Also, because both were much harder on themselves than they were on each other, the milder criticisms they did subsequently direct at each other were not nearly as offensive as they would otherwise have been.

The next step was to identify specific problems for Mary and Don to address. They wrote their responses to question three on a sheet of newsprint, assigning vectors to represent the relative seriousness of the problem. Some of the most serious problems could be resolved immediately; others were going to take longer, but at least Don and Mary now knew what their priorities had to be.

Finally, it became possible for them to agree on specific behavioral changes that might help. Don and Mary each defined what they wanted from the other and negotiated what they themselves were willing to undertake; I moderated the meeting and wrote down the decisions. (At the end of the meeting, Don, Mary, and the three observers each received a copy of these commitments.) Because Mary and Don were interdependent, either could easily have sabotaged the other's efforts. Therefore, in defining each action item, I reminded them to specify responsibilities for both parties:

- What will Don (Mary) do to resolve this problem?
- What will Mary (Don) do to help the other succeed?

This technique made both parties jointly responsible for resolving each problem and thus changed the whole dynamic of the relationship—from mutual isolation to collaboration, from denial of responsibility to acceptance of responsibility, and from a focus on problems to a focus on solutions.

During the next year, I had four more meetings with Don, Mary, and the three vice presidents. Before each meeting, I interviewed each participant privately. At the beginning of each meeting, the participants gave general reports on what was going on, between Mary and Don and in the OR in general. In particular, I asked the two to list positive events and specific behaviors on each other's part that they appreciated. They then reviewed the commitments they had made during the previous meeting. In almost every case, both Mary and Don had kept these commitments, thus building a basis of trust for further commitments during the latter part of the meeting. Where they had not kept the commitments, plans were made to ensure follow-through before the next meeting.

QUESTIONS FOR DISCUSSION

1. How would you evaluate the effectiveness of this intervention?
2. What objective measures would you examine?
3. What subjective measures would you examine?

Ben & Jerry's (A):
Team Development Intervention

Philip H. Mirvis
Boston University

"Two real guys," Ben Cohen and Jerry Greenfield, head Ben & Jerry's Homemade Inc., an independent ice cream producer that has gained market share and public approbation against industry competitors Häagen-Dazs (made by Pillsbury), Frusen Glädjé (made by Kraft), and Steve's. The story of the founders has a romantic, antiestablishment quality to it that reads like a new-age entrepreneur's dream.

The "boys," childhood friends, each dropped out of college in the late '60s, worked at odd jobs for a time, and together opened a small ice cream scoop shop in Burlington, Vermont, in 1978 with scant know-how (they learned ice-cream making through a $5 correspondence course) and less capital (they started with $12,000—a third of it borrowed). But they had something else going for them: a combination of old fashioned values and newfangled ideas.

Neither Ben nor Jerry had any intention of becoming businessmen. From the start, however, both were committed to making the best ice cream possible and to having fun while doing it. More than this, these "self-styled Vermont hippies," as the press calls them, were committed to the simple notion that business draws from the community and is obliged to give something back to it. In the early days, this meant giving away ice cream to loyal customers and worthy charities. As the company grew to sales of near $50 million, B&J's embraced what it calls a *social mission* to improve the quality of life—not only of employees, but also locally, nationally, and internationally—and to do so in an innovative and upbeat way.

The economics of B&J's show fast-track growth over the past several years characteristic of very successful startup companies (see Exhibit 1 from the 1988 annual report). Sales doubled annually from 1984 to 1986

EXHIBIT 1   Annual Report 1988: A Report to Shareholders, Customers, Community Members, Suppliers, and Employees

---

Five Year Financial Highlights (in thousands except per share data)

Summary of Operations:

	Year Ended December 31				
	1988	1987	1986	1985	1984
Net sales	$47,561	$31,838	$19,954	$ 9,858	$ 4,115
Cost of sales	33,935	22,673	14,144	7,321	2,949
Gross profit	13,627	9,165	5,810	2,537	1,166
Selling, delivery and administrative expenses ..	10,655	6,774	4,101	1,812	822
Operating income	2,972	2,391	1,709	725	344
Other income (expense)—net	(274)	305	208	(31)	(13)
Income before income taxes .	2,698	2,696	1,917	694	331
Income taxes	1,079	1,251	901	143	118
Net income	1,618	1,445	1,016	551	213
Net income per common share (1)	$ .63	$ .56	$ .40	$ .28	$ .12
Average common shares outstanding (1)	2,579	2,572	2,565	1,991	1,724

Balance Sheet Data:

	Year Ended December 31				
	1988	1987	1986	1985	1984
Working capital	$ 5,614	$ 3,902	$ 3,678	$ 4,955	$ 676
Total assets	26,307	20,160	12,805	11,076	3,894
Long-term debt	9,670	8,330	2,442	2,582	2,102
Stockholders' equity (2)	11,245	9,231	7,758	6,683	1,068

(1) The per share amounts and average shares outstanding have been adjusted for the effects of all stock splits, including stock splits in the form of stock dividends.
(2) No cash dividends have been declared or paid by the company on its capital stock since the company's organization and none are presently contemplated.

---

and increased nearly 50 percent from 1987 to 1988. The company is today the super-premium market leader in Boston and New York City and distributes its products in grocery stores and mom-and-pop convenience outlets in Florida, the West Coast, and parts of the Midwest. Some 80 franchises operate scoop shops in these markets, and the company's "pints" manufacturing facility and headquarters in Burlington have become Vermont's second-largest tourist attraction with over 600,000 visitors annually.

In addition to expanding this facility, B&J's recently built a novelty plant in Springfield, Vermont, to manufacture ice-cream brownie bars and stick pops and leased space to house its marketing, franchising, promotion, and art departments. Today, over 350 people work at B&J's. Production runs around the clock, staffed by a few dairy experts and many more offbeat people who gravitated to the company because of competitive wages, its funky image, and its social mission. Among the production staff is a team of handicapped employees who have distinct and important responsibilities.

The product side of B&J's blends what *Time* magazine calls "incredibly delicious" ice cream. The story goes that Ben has deficient taste buds, so products have to be particularly pungent to stir his palate. This means "double-fudge" and "big-chunk" add-ins to the ice cream. Funky flavors, like "Cherry Garcia," an assortment of T-shirts, Vermont "cow" paraphernalia, and wacky promotions all make word-of-mouth marketing the key to B&J's commercial success. And, yes, the founders insist on having fun. At annual meetings, Jerry, trained in carnival tricks, uses a sledgehammer to break a cement block over the stomach of the mystical "Habeeni Ben Coheeni."

It is, however, the social mission of B&J's that most distinguishes it from corporate America. The good works of the company are many and range from regular donations to community and social action groups to a commitment to buy only Vermont-based cream from area dairy cooperatives. B&J's embraces socially responsible marketing and has proposed to "adopt a stop" in the New York subway system (which the company would clean and maintain in lieu of advertising) and begun an innovative joint venture with the Knowledge Society in the Soviet Union.

Recently, the company introduced "Peace Pops" as part of the "1% for Peace Campaign." This effort is aimed at encouraging other businesses to join a movement urging the government to devote 1 percent of the defense budget explicitly to peaceful purposes. A new product featuring Brazilian nuts obtained at above-fair-market price from native Brazilians is further evidence of the founders' social commitments.

INNOVATING INSIDE OF B&J'S

Ben and Jerry have been at the edge of innovation since the company went public. Rather than seeking venture capital to expand the business, they drew up a stock prospectus on their own and sold shares to Vermonters door to door. One in every 100 Vermont families bought in to the tune of $750,000. When Häagen-Dazs tried to pressure shopkeepers to keep "Vermont's finest" off their shelves, Ben and Jerry started a grass-roots campaign against Pillsbury replete with bumper stickers (What's the Doughboy afraid of?) and a one-person picket line (Jerry) at the Pillsbury headquarters.

Ben and Jerry have tried to introduce this same funky and socially responsible orientation inside the company. The company's mission and many of its policies and practices (see Exhibit 2) reflect the upbeat and caring values of the founders. A policy of "linked prosperity" ensures that 7.5 percent of pretax profits go to good works and 5 percent is returned to employees via profit sharing. The salary ratio between the top paid and least paid in B&J's is set at 5 to 1. This means, if managers want to earn more, they have to increase the base wage throughout the company.

Employees come in all shapes and sizes. Most are young (under 30) and many have responsibilities well beyond their experience. It is a matter of pride to all that B&Jer's can speak, act, and dress "like themselves." Still, the work is demanding and the pace frenetic. The production room is often awash in cream, and the freezer crew works in chilling conditions. There is nothing akin to market research in the company, demand is fluid and unpredictable, and when I first arrived on the scene, the franchising and sales managers weren't communicating with each other and neither paid attention to the marketing director.

In 1987, it became evident to Ben and Jerry, as well as to managers and employees, that the company's external image—of funk, fun, and love—was out of sync with the atmosphere inside the company. The company was always short on ice cream and long on hours, pressure, and problems. The author was commissioned to work with the founders and board of directors and with the management and work force of the company to undertake organizational development and bring people, functions, aspirations, and directions together.

ENTRY

Henry Morgan, former dean of the School of Management at Boston University and board member at B&J's, contacted me about this project. Henry comes from a long line of New England activists deeply committed to the improvement of the human condition. His family lineage traces to Hawaii where ancestors were missionaries, and Henry has had a career as an entrepreneur, management innovator, and social investor. In addition to his membership on B&J's board, he is active on other boards and is a leader in the Council of Economic Priorities' efforts to promote corporate social responsibility.

Entry through Henry, however, posed some risks. For example, like Henry, I was an outsider coming into B&J's where the emphasis, to this point, had been on "homegrown" innovation. Ben, Jerry, and Jeff Furman, an attorney and longtime B&J's counsel, had crafted the company's innovative employment and investment policies. It was unclear to

---

EXHIBIT 2   Ben & Jerry's Mission and Operating Principles

Ben & Jerry's, a Vermont-based ice-cream producer, is dedicated to the creation and demonstration of a new corporate concept of linked prosperity. The company has three central missions and several key operating principles.

Three Missions

Product Mission: To make, distribute, and sell the finest quality all natural ice cream and related products in a wide variety of innovative flavors made from Vermont dairy products.

Economic Mission: To operate the company on a sound financial basis of profitable growth, increasing value for our shareholders and creating career opportunities and financial rewards for our employees.

Social Mission: To recognize the central role that business plays in the structure of society by seeking innovative ways to improve the quality of life for a broad community—local, national, and international.

Operating Principles

Linked Prosperity: "As the company prospers, the community and our people prosper." 7.5% of pretax profits go to the Ben & Jerry's Foundation for distribution to community groups and charities. 5% of profits are put into a profit-sharing plan. 5 to 1 salary ratio between top management and entry-level production workers. To raise top pay, raise the bottom up.

Community Development: "Business has the responsibility to give back to the community." Donations of ice cream by request to all Vermont nonprofit organizations. Leveraged assistance where B&J will help nonprofits stage fund-raisers selling Vermont's finest ice cream.

Ownership Perspective: "Everybody is an owner." Employee stock ownership, stock grants, and stock purchase plan. All-company "town meetings" monthly.

Integrity: "Two real guys." All natural products. Commitment to Vermont Dairy Cooperatives. "What you see is what you get." People can speak, act, and dress as they wish.

Work Hard/Have Fun: "Bend over backwards." Pledge to meet orders, satisfy customers, make things right for people. "If it's not fun, why do it?" Company celebrations. Jerry's Joy Committee to spread joy in the workplace.

Human Activism/Social Change: "A model for other businesses." 1% for Peace Campaign. Socially responsible marketing. Joint ventures in Israel and Moscow to spread goodwill.

---

me what these three really wanted from an OD program. Was I being brought in to get management "aligned" behind the founders' guiding precepts as a phone conversation with Ben intimated? Or were the precepts themselves open to question and modification via management and employee input? If so, did it require an outsider to stimulate this reexamination? Or was I being set up?

To complicate matters, there was a division in the board of directors. Ben, Jerry, and Jeff were rather more "far out" in their aspirations for the company, particularly in comparison to the more conservative general manager, Fred "Chico" Lager. The former anticipated an outpouring of good vibes once "people power" was unleashed. Chico had more everyday concerns: feuding between management, unclear lines of authority and responsibility, a lack of operational control. More specifically, as an example, a freezer door was broken and neither the freezer, nor maintenance, nor production managers claimed ownership of the problem or took responsibility to see that it was fixed. That, to him, was symptomatic of an undeveloped organization.

Finally, there was the matter of defining OD. Neither Ben nor Jerry nor the board had any inkling about what OD is and what OD people do. I had to educate them about the field and make some kind of action proposal. This would mean getting to know people, getting a handle on their hopes and their problems, and learning something about the ice-cream business and conditions in the marketplace. Where to start? I went to a board meeting to check out members' hopes for organization development and what they wanted from me.

FIRST BOARD MEETING

Ben

> I want our people to love their work and have positive feelings about the company. Love, soul, kindness, consideration, generosity, fairness, heart.

Jerry

> I want a feeling of togetherness and family feeling . . . I'd like staff to feel it was their company.

Jeff

> I'd like to see spirit and energy to make a difference in the world . . . plant seeds of new and different possibilities of looking at our culture and world. Not corporate America.

Chico

> Something special and unique that is making new ground, that will be studied and appreciated years to come.

Henry

> More open communication, listening at the top. More buy-in to shared values. Showing respect for the individual.

Merritt

> Awakened enthusiasm, accomplishment, high morale.

At this first meeting, I asked board members to state their vision of the ideal organization and hopes for the OD effort. Ben and Jerry talked of peace, love, family feeling, and good vibes. Jeff was on a different wavelength: He articulated a political vision where B&J would be an exemplar of a radical new kind of organization. Chico spoke about innovativeness and excellence, without the radical chic or global emphasis. Henry's hopes were addressed to better human relations and human resource management. Merritt, another businessman cum board member, expressed similar sentiments.

I had the board members write their visions on sheets of paper, and then together we burned them to symbolize how energy and togetherness could transform things. Some chanting added to the ritual. It must have seemed a bit hokey to the board, but I have my own preferences and style of doing things and wanted to illustrate my own offbeat inclinations. In any case, Ben had offered me a wizard's hat to signify his vision of my role. The fire trick fit the costuming.

That night, however, I had some misgivings. It was clear that, when pressed, neither Ben, nor Jerry, nor any board member save Chico would provide the day-to-day leadership needed to move development through the organization. On the contrary, the founders wanted to hand off the responsibility to Chico and his to-be-formed management team. My job was to help bring that team into being and to ensure that the team took leadership of B&J's business and social missions. It was also to help bring the work force together in as-yet-undefined ways.

Should I start my work at the top? I had an inkling that the board was not aligned behind any one definition of Ben & Jerry's. However, the board was not, at this time, asking for assistance with its work nor could the members openly talk about problems within the group. The problems, in board members' eyes, rested within the organization. That made Chico and his team the natural focus of intervention. Chico, at this time, had 20 managers reporting to him, with responsibilities ranging from running the manufacturing plant to handling orders for T-shirts and other B&J paraphernalia.

Still, I worried whether OD would directly reach the work force. If I worked from the top down, it might take months (years) to have a direct bearing on people's work lives. The production workers were full of ideas, I was told, and eager to become more involved. Maybe some form of quality-of-work-life program was in order wherein employees could take active responsibility for problem solving in their own areas of responsibility. My question: Were managers and supervisors ready for this?

The next step was to do some fact-finding in the company. I arranged with Chico to conduct interviews with all of his 20 managers, tour the plant, talk with production workers and sales personnel, and generally sniff around. That would lead to a diagnosis of the organization and an action proposal.

DIAGNOSIS

Three months of interviews with key managers and staff at B&J's showed the following areas of strength and concern in the company:

Strengths:
- High commitment to the company and its mission.
- Norms of honesty and straightforwardness.
- Smart and articulate management.
- High interest in growth and learning.
- Founders and general manager as role models.

The interviews affirmed the positive public side of B&J's: Managers and employees were wholly dedicated to the company. Many of the managers had left successful jobs in other companies to come to B&J's because of its funky atmosphere, freewheeling style, and socially responsible orientation. Some had taken salary cuts to come aboard. The managers were smart and each had his or her own view of how the company should develop. These views, taken together, pointed to a more participatory style of management with people charged with higher levels of responsibility. This would require more training, of managers and supervisors, in both technical and managerial areas. They would also need to get organized—with more clarity about who was doing what and why.

The interest was there. Everybody I spoke with was eager to learn more and get better at their jobs. The commitment was also there. Many professed deep feelings of connection to Ben and Jerry and were inspired by the chance to take "their company" and run it. They also looked to Chico to teach them the ins and outs and looked forward to working closely with him as part of the "management team."

Concerns:
- People and systems not keeping pace with growth.
- Lack of clear structure, roles, and teamwork.
- Lack of common mission, direction, priorities.
- People are stretched to the limit.
- Founders and general manager are both company's greatest strength *and* greatest weakness.

The roster of concerns shows that Ben & Jerry's was underorganized for handling the challenges posed by rapid growth in the marketplace and work force. Interviewees talked about the absence of clear goals and agreed-to priorities, problems of communication and coordination, tasks half-finished and new initiatives begun, then dropped. No one had the time to get on top of things or ensure follow-through.

Furthermore, the interviewees depicted the founders and general manager as both the company's greatest strength and its greatest weakness. To this point, Ben and Chico had access to the most relevant information and called most of the shots. But conflicts between the two were legend. Ben would push for better quality, faster flavor development, funkier ads and promotions, while Chico would urge pragmatism, shuffle priorities, mediate tensions, and hawk expenses.

These two titans seemed to be omniscient: They handled hot problems and made all the right moves. But nobody knew how they worked things out or got things done. It was plain enough, however, that the to-be-formed management would have to set more of the direction, solve more of the problems, and develop systems for control and follow-through if participatory management and decentralization were to be accomplished. Furthermore, they would have to get closer to one another personally and develop more trust and confidence in one another, if family feeling and pride of ownership were to prevail.

Thus I pitched the OD effort at helping the board of directors to clarify the company's mission and to cede operating responsibilities to management. In turn, the board was to empower managers to run the company in a strong, unified, and responsible fashion. There were pragmatic issues to address: the managers did not see themselves as a team nor had they worked together to formulate goals and establish roles and responsibilities.

There were also matters of principle on the agenda: many managers had no prior experience leading a company so dedicated to social responsibility. Several, frankly, did not fully buy into socially oriented company policies, including the active association of the company with the 1% for Peace Campaign and the salary ratio of 5 to 1 between the highest and lowest paid members of the corporation. A few were chafing at the mandate of the founders to have "fun" at work while still achieving record rates of production at superior quality standards.

TEAMBUILDING VIA A RETREAT

The 20 managers and Chico went to an offsite retreat where all were blindfolded and roped together in their three work-related clusters and then charged with locating three inner tubes symbolically lashed together maybe 75 yards away. The members of each cluster shouted out instructions or demanded them, took stabs at leading and then pulled back in frustration, while the other groups stumbled along vainly searching for the "goal." One group finally located the tubes, then cheered for their own success and chided the other groups. This experience provided a window into current dynamics in the company and led us to examine teamwork, competition, and cooperation during the rest of the retreat.

Thereafter, the managers climbed ropes, worked on problem-solving initiatives, and trekked in the out of doors, all in the service of finding new ways to work with one another. One evening they talked about their personal lives and values through the medium of "mind maps." Everyone recorded on a silhouette the persons and events that had most shaped their character, how they wanted to be thought of in the company and by their peers, and what mark they wanted their life to leave behind. Several spoke of their scarring experiences in Vietnam, their poignant efforts to cope with family trials, the impact their mothers, fathers, and now their spouses and children had on them. Many cried. There were hugs and cheers.

The next evening, the clusters had the opportunity to put on skits about their part of the organization. The manufacturing cluster drew from a popular game show to show their peers the "jeopardy" involved in making high-volume, high-quality foodstuffs. The marketing and sales group selected a member to wear the beard of one of the founders and joined him in songs and dance about the foibles of competing with less socially responsible companies and the seeming folly of having fun at work.

The search for the inner tubes was repeated at the end of the retreat. The groups quickly joined forces with the others to analyze the problem, work out a plan, figure out roles and responsibilities, and establish procedures to stay in touch with one another. They reached the goal in one third of the time. The retreat concluded with each attendee selecting a "totem" to represent his or her experiences and developing a personal action plan to be implemented in the months ahead.

Why Teambuilding?

My reasons for recommending teambuilding to launch the OD effort at B&J's were threefold. First, it was crucial for managers to begin to think of themselves as managers and as members of a management team. Many of the managers at B&J's were truly supervisors, who worked alongside employees and focused only on the work going on in their own area of responsibility. To cope with growth, it was essential for them to begin to plan, set priorities, and coordinate efforts with one another. This meant they had to operate like real managers and become a management team.

Second, the managers would be assuming new responsibilities heretofore in the hands of the founders and general manager. I thought it important for them to see how much they had in common and how much affinity they had with the founders' vision of the enterprise. Teambuilding provides a good medium for self-disclosure and helps people to open up about who they are and what they believe in. The mind maps and skits were designed such that people could see how they were all in this together. Needless to say, lashing them together to search for an inner tube was a more literal translation of the message.

Finally, managers had to collectively commit to taking on new responsibilities and learn new methods for working together. The several exercises at the retreat were aimed at educating them in group management and problem-solving skills. The ropes course, in turn, emphasized the importance of personal courage and peer support in tackling the unknown. The managers left the retreat closer and charged up about running the show.

However, the rationale for beginning OD with teambuilding was rather traditional and conservative in character. Many OD proponents eschew the top-down approach to development and work simultaneously at many levels in a company. Work teams and worker-management committees are starting points for OD in many organizations. The aim is to get as many people as possible, as soon as possible, involved in organizational improvement. The risk with going company-wide with OD from the start is managerial resistance. Frankly, in this case, I didn't think managers were ready to respond to group problem-solving initiatives by their subordinates and teams. They were not conversant with techniques like brainstorming, force field analysis, and contingency planning—requisites for team leaders. Nor were they ready, in my judgment, to cede responsibility as they were just assuming more of it. Instead, my proposal was to go slow, get management organized and built into a team, and then push OD downward.

FOLLOW-UP: GOALS AND RESPONSIBILITIES

This began months of teambuilding with the newly created management group (see Exhibit 3). Each working cluster was charged with developing a mission statement for its area of responsibility. The cluster groups met several times to translate these into operating goals. The manufacturing group, for example, focused on improving production capacity and quality. Managers from the freezer, production, distribution, and maintenance departments then analyzed work flow, identified their respective responsibilities, and made commitments to one another to maximize capacity and ensure quality standards. The marketing group, in turn, formed a steering committee to bring franchising and sales together and developed a system to control competing pressures on the art department.

In turn, managers also met with their work groups to gather input and incorporate suggestions. In that way, at least, employees were kept abreast of developments and had a chance to be involved. A safety committee was created, staffed by managers and workers, to address a broad range of concerns throughout the plant and headquarters facility.

Several meetings were held to coordinate cluster goal setting. At one session, managers drew pictures illustrating the degree of alignment between functions and the overall vision of the company. One artist depicted the founders as the sun, the functions as orbiting planets, and the market as a streaking comet. Others used stick figures to show the company coming together, people cheering, and craziness all around.

What resulted from these sessions was a series of cluster goal statements, an action agenda for the next year focused on tasks and goals, and closer interpersonal and work relationships. Did teambuilding make a difference? Managers rated themselves as much more of a team and the functions say they are far more aligned:

Understanding of the Goals and Direction of Your Department?

At the start of the process:	3.5 out of 10.0
At this point in the process:	7.5 out of 10.0

Relationship with Other Members of the Management Team?

At the start of the process:	5.1 out of 10.0
At this point in the process:	7.5 out of 10.0

CROSS-TALK

Despite the progress in organizing management, the founders worried whether the funk and fun was being lost in all of this business. There was a heated debate between managers and the founders over growth. The founders hoped to limit growth in order to keep the company small and people connected. Managers pointed out that existing marketing and franchise commitments would require growth and that B&J's simply could not stiff its customers. Back and forth the talk went. It seemed as though the managers had become something of a threat to the founders, who were having trouble letting go of promised authority.

Ben and Jerry then took the initiative to "lift up" the cluster goals into a unifying statement of the company's economic, product, and social mission. To air differences, the newly formed management team and founders then met to examine their differences. Before the meeting, Ben had said publicly that management "wasn't weird enough" and expressed worry that the company's social mission was being sacrificed to growth. The managers first chafed at his inference that they weren't interested in the social mission. Then they took his concerns to heart. Each member of the management team came to the meeting wearing a mask bearing the likeness of either Ben or Jerry and buttons saying "We are weird."

Together, managers and board members talked over issues of trust and relative powers with the founders, fleshed out how management and the board would work together, and made a pact that the company

EXHIBIT 3   Management Teambuilding Model for Clusters and
Departments

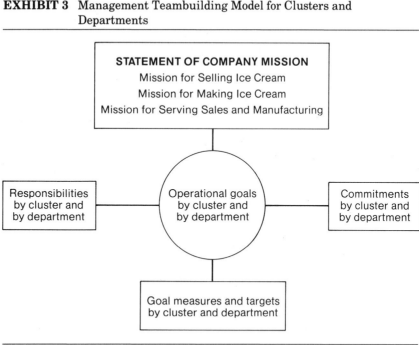

would remain committed to high quality production, good works, and
fun.

Following the session, several actions were initiated to bring ne-
glected aspects of the mission statement to life. A "Joy Committee" was
established to ensure that spirit was kept alive in the company. It hosted
lunches, sponsored social events, and launched several happenings
throughout the company. Employees were encouraged to take a more
active part in the Ben & Jerry's Foundation and contribute directly to
charitable giving. Finally, a budget committee was created to formulate
B&J's first one-year plan.

QUESTIONS FOR DISCUSSION

1. Many OD interventions are undertaken to loosen up an organization. In the typical case, too much centralization, bureaucracy, and functional turfism have created work and relationship problems. Here, by
comparison, organization and teambuilding were undertaken to tighten
up the company.

In doing a diagnosis, what factors are important to consider in determining whether a company is over- or under-organized? What are the implications for planning an intervention?

2. The consultant in this case chose to work OD top down through a program of organization and teambuilding. This is a very traditional model of practice. Other OD models, involving more immediate and direct employee participation, could have been undertaken at Ben & Jerry's. Many employee involvement programs, involving labor-management cooperation and quality circles, are being implemented in many organizations today.

In planning an intervention, what cues recommend a more top-down versus bottom-up introduction of OD? Was the consultant's rationale for going top down justified in this case? What are the strengths and weaknesses of this approach?

3. This case ends with the founders and newly formed management team in seeming agreement over the direction of the company. Do you think this agreement will last? There are bound to be future conflicts between the social mission and the business mission of B&J's. Can OD be applied to these kind of ideological conflicts? What kind of OD?

Ben & Jerry's (B):
Team Development Intervention

Philip H. Mirvis
Boston University

One year of teambuilding with management at Ben & Jerry's resulted in the creation of a solid organizational infrastructure for running the business and a management team working together to manage rapid growth. The confrontation meeting between the managers and board (concluding the A case) smoothed over differences between the founders and managers and enabled Fred "Chico" Lager and his team to run the show. Still, there were lingering feelings of mistrust between the two groups, and weirdness alone didn't define the differences between them.

As Ben Cohen and Jerry Greenfield left everyday operational responsibilities behind, both became more absorbed in the social mission of the company. They attended various workshops led by social activists and found themselves in a growing network of socially conscious organizations, including the Body Shop in Great Britain and Patagonia in the United States. The founders received great kudos for the social achievements of their company and became emboldened by a new vision of what Ben & Jerry's could accomplish. Ben began to talk about B&J's as a force for social change and took an active interest in the "1% for Peace Campaign" (see the A case). He proposed that B&J's launch a "Peace Pop"—ice cream on a stick—whose profits would be partly donated to the new movement.

B&J's board was divided on the venture. Some members were worried that consumers would equate Ben & Jerry's with the newly formed Peace organization. Thus, pains were taken to make sure B&J's and 1% for Peace were legally and physically separate entities. In addition, several managers balked at the idea. A few thought it was too risky for the company to develop and market "cause" products. Others questioned the anti-American sentiment of some early 1% for Peace literature and expressed doubts about the viability of the campaign.

This was an idealogical as well as a practical conflict. It also, to my eyes, had organizational roots. It surfaced, for example, a division within the board over the direction of the company. Ben, Jerry, and Jeff Furman were primarily pushing the company's social action emphasis. Chico, plus the two outside directors, seemed more focused on the business and human sides of the company. This signaled a need to work with the board to sort things out.

Furthermore, the Peace Pops project brought Ben and Chico into conflict—not only over ideology but also over their respective powers and roles. Chico, as head of the management team, and Ben, chairman of the board, had been at loggerheads in the past. Heretofore, however, each had counterbalanced the other and conflicts between them had been amicably resolved. Now the two were in a win/lose struggle over the future direction of the company and what it would stand for.

My questions: Was the tension encountered between the board and management or just between Ben and Chico? Could I continue to do OD with managers and employees without active mediation between Chico and Ben and between factions on the board?

Board meetings became contentious over the next months, with Ben issuing, in the eyes of managers, a report card on how they were doing on the social mission and never giving them anything more than passing marks. Chico was alternately feisty and withdrawn at meetings. He began to identify with his team and fight Ben over every issue.

TAKING OD UPWARD: BOARD OF DIRECTORS

To get to the root of the problem, I began to work with the board of directors to address its purpose and role in the company. The rationale was that the board couldn't expect management to be aligned behind the company's mission if the board itself was divided. Nor could management take responsibility for achieving B&J's product, economic, and social mission (see the A case) if the board second-guessed their leadership and commitment to the social agenda. A short survey was administered to board members to ascertain their own degree of alignment on goals and roles.

The diagnostic survey revealed several areas of commonality and effectiveness in the eyes of board members:

- Board has necessary mix of skills and perspectives.
- Board examines all aspects of problems/looks for creative options.
- Board is able to air disagreements and listen to different opinions.

This attested to the problem-solving capability on the board. Its members are smart, interested in a wide range of issues, and able to look at all sides of an issue or problem. The board may not have a disciplined approach, but it hunkers down when a situation requires a decision or a problem needs resolution.

At the same time, there were sharp differences in the board over its role in company matters, and members clearly defined some process problem in the group. The board's areas of ineffectiveness are:

- Board divided on whether it has too much or too little influence over management.
- Board puts off conflict until it escalates and seldom comes to firm agreement over value differences.

This shows ambiguity over the board's role in the company. One faction of members thought the board should act as an oversight committee—ensuring that management accomplished its key goals and aggressively pursued the social mission. Another faction believed the board should delegate more responsibility to management and concentrate on longer-range issues.

On the process side, all agreed that board members were strong willed but able to listen to diverging viewpoints. On the downside, there was a tendency for individual members to push their own agendas, sometimes at the expense of agreement and the good of the organization. Furthermore, board members all reported that the relationship between management and the board was not satisfactory.

I observed that disagreement within the board was sending a mixed message to managers. On the one hand, managers were supposed to assume responsibility. On the other, they were second-guessed and held closely in check by the board. We talked over the conflicts and agreed that management and the board had to get together to resolve this.

By this time, Chico's management structure had been fleshed out into two tiers. At the top was an operating committee composed of Chico and the heads of marketing, manufacturing, human resources, and corporate planning (see Exhibit 1). Below them were middle managers representing each of the functions. It was this operating committee that met with the board in an intergroup conflict resolution session.

SURFACING CONFLICTS BETWEEN MANAGEMENT AND B&J'S BOARD

The conflict-airing session was designed such that management and the board first met separately to define their views of the situation. The managers perceived that they were being treated like second-graders when called to task by the board. The board members believed that management was not accountable for key problems concerning quality im-

EXHIBIT 1   Ben & Jerry's Management/Organization Structure

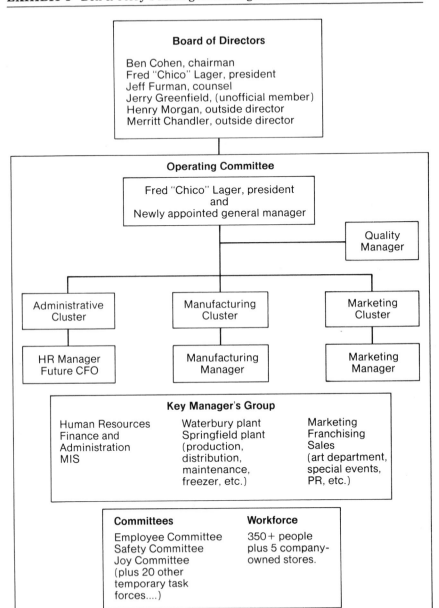

Board of Directors

Ben Cohen, chairman
Fred "Chico" Lager, president
Jeff Furman, counsel
Jerry Greenfield, (unofficial member)
Henry Morgan, outside director
Merritt Chandler, outside director

Operating Committee

Fred "Chico" Lager, president
and
Newly appointed general manager

Quality Manager

Administrative Cluster

Manufacturing Cluster

Marketing Cluster

HR Manager Future CFO

Manufacturing Manager

Marketing Manager

Key Manager's Group

Human Resources
Finance and
Administration
MIS

Waterbury plant
Springfield plant
(production,
distribution,
maintenance,
freezer, etc.)

Marketing
Franchising
Sales
(art department,
special events,
PR, etc.)

Committees

Employee Committee
Safety Committee
Joy Committee
(plus 20 other
temporary task
forces....)

Workforce

350+ people
plus 5 company-
owned stores.

provement and the introduction of a low-fat product. Both sides agreed there was a lack of mutual trust and support between groups.

The real heat centered on the social mission of the company. Ben complained that management wasn't backing the social mission and had been singularly unresponsive to his proposal to produce Peace Pops. Managers shot back that the company's social mission was a "moving target." One month it meant support for Vermont dairies and the arts. The next month was peace and social change. A board member likened Ben and Jeff to seagulls who dropped new ideas into the organization. To the gulls, it was only natural. To managers, it just looked like more "shit" coming from on high.

These respective viewpoints were aired in a fishbowl meeting. First, while observed by board members, managers met in the fishbowl to talk about their frustrations. Then the board met, while observed by managers. I kept a roster of issues indicating where views were held in common and where there were divisions. This yielded a list of issues and the frustrated feelings they engendered.

To air these latter issues, four-person groups of managers and board members then took "walks in the woods" to discuss the findings and clarify disagreements. The groups were structured so managers and board members having conflicts were put together with more neutral parties and those with particular facilitation skills. The walks were scheduled to last 30 minutes. Instead, they took two hours.

The session concluded with a roundtable meeting that identified issues for immediate resolution and for further work. Two proposals emerged from the meeting. First, the board and operating committee refined ground rules for working with one another. This further clarified the respective authority and responsibilities of each group. It was agreed, for example, that management would preconsult with the board on capital and human resource decisions but would have final say on most matters. In turn, the board would review the performance of management when projects were undertaken involving board approval and intervene when specific management commitments were not being achieved.

Second, principles were established to minimize second-guessing, "gotcha" games, and other process problems in board-management meetings. It was understood that old habits would be hard to break. Thus, these paper principles would have to be practiced and my role would be to act as a process facilitator/enforcer as needed.

Dealing with conflicts over the social mission proved more difficult. The second proposal advanced was to create a committee, representing the board and managers, to clarify the firm's social mission, set priorities, and adjudicate conflicts. The "Jive Five," as it would be known, was charged with fleshing out B&J's social mission and with bringing it to life in the company.

Ben and Chico's Relationship

Working with Chico and Ben was harder still. To begin, it needs to be recognized how difficult it is for anyone to run the founders' business. A general manager so positioned is always subject to second-guessing and has the dual responsibility of protecting the owners from too many employee gripes and protecting the work force from the owners' quirks. In B&J's history, Chico served that function ably and the operative norm was to "let Ben be Ben."

In dealing with these two, furthermore, it is tempting to typecast Ben as the liberal and Chico the conservative in an ideological system of checks and balances. Certainly they served these roles in the company. However, to label Chico a *conservative* is relative. His office includes signed portraits of role models such as Mr. T, J. R. Ewing, and other cultural icons. Moreover, Chico kept close ties to a work force that included many gays and lesbians, lots of hippies and a few bikers, a plant manager dubbed "Darth Vader," and a human resource manager who read the *Whole Earth Catalog* like the Bible—hardly the mark of a reactionary.

However, Chico was the businessman in the company, having proved himself through ownership of an offbeat tavern early in his career, and carefully expanded B&J's through prudent hands-on management. Fred Awards, given to employees who proposed money-saving ideas, say something about his businesslike orientation.

It was his deeply felt commitment to the business that so troubled Chico when Ben proposed redefining Ben & Jerry's as a vehicle for social change. Frankly, Chico was worried about its implications for the company. He had watched People Express Airlines' decline in the marketplace because of imprudent moves and inattentive management. He saw B&J's future as equally fragile. Ben was tinkering with the magic formula, in Chico's eyes, and he worried that grandiose ideas would stretch resources, cause confusion among customers, and perhaps bring the company down.

One-on-one discussions with Ben and Chico led to a full airing of their conflict with fellow board members and managers. Each was given support for his perspective, but the board tried to help the two see how positions were being exaggerated and differences magnified. Common ground was found, at least on the Peace Pops controversy, and Ben and Chico's respective levels of authority were redefined. It was decided that Chico would have full operating responsibility for the company, and he was accordingly elevated to the presidency. This would give him leadership over the operating portion of the board's agenda and allow him to determine which, if any, of his managers would participate in board meetings. At the same time, Chico acknowledged that his doubts about Peace Pops were sabotaging the project. He agreed to give it full backing and sent appropriate signals to managers and employees.

Ben and Chico did not, however, kiss and make up. After long bouts of soul searching, Chico decided he would leave B&J's within two years to rethink his career and rebuild his personal life. I had recommended he put off such career decisions until he and Ben worked on their relationship and he could think clearly about his next moves. Chico listened to my counsel and he and Ben began to meet privately to work on their relationship problems.

OD DOWNWARD: PUSHING THE MISSION

With conflicts on the board and between Ben and Chico sufficiently worked through, the company's mission statement was unveiled at an all-employee meeting. Ben introduced the social mission to the tune of "What's Wrong with Love?" Jerry described future product developments, promising to begin his own "low-fat" campaign. And Chico detailed the company's economic mission to the sounds of "Money, Money." The day was completed when Mr. Clean made a guest appearance to celebrate the start of the "cleanliness campaign."

Concurrently, work was undertaken to prepare managers and employees to carry out the mission. Two consultants were brought in to conduct human relations and basic management training for wholesale and retail managers. Skill training then moved into teambuilding for these managers and their supervisors. A series of visits were sponsored where managers could learn more from other progressive companies. Bruce Dillingham, a plant manager who developed a high-performance/high-commitment workplace at Digital Equipment, came in to talk about new work designs. B&J's manufacturing managers visited Edie's Ice Cream to see a sociotechnical work design in operation and Springfield Remanufacturing Company to see how a gain-sharing system might work. A film about the Body Shop was shown to employees to illustrate how one company put its social mission into operation. Significantly, the company also began to issue social responsibility awards to go along with those offered for cost savings.

Finally, there was a redesign of all-staff meetings. Group facilitators were trained to lead small-group discussions at all-staff meetings and report on problems and suggestions. The company began to issue a newsletter, updating people about births, weddings, and divorces, developments in the business, and the company's social agenda. "Letters to Raoul"—a section containing questions, gripes, and ideas—read like something out of Zap comics.

Interviews of the work force two years after OD was begun at B&J's show the progress has filtered down to them. Most production people say new systems and process improvements have made work easier and less chaotic. A "fruit-feeder" task force has made major improvements in work technology. The marketing side is aligned behind Peace Pops and more generally behind a social mission focused on social change. Employees from Burlington scooped ice cream at the Soviet-American sail in New York just recently and 1% for Peace T-shirts are prominent throughout the plant and offices.

There's talk of redesigning production areas along sociotechnical lines, of reorganizing marketing to focus on specific products, and of conducting teach-ins to raise social consciousness among the work force. All of this is in next year's OD plan. Meanwhile, Paul Hawken, of PBS's "Growing a Business" series, visited B&J's to put the company's efforts into a larger perspective. He put it aptly: "Big business is not where it's at today. You guys are heroes (to Ben and Jerry). You folks are really making a difference! (to the work force). We look to you. We learn from you."

QUESTIONS FOR DISCUSSION

1. Most OD specialists say the climate has to be ripe to undertake OD in an organization. In this case, what could/should the consultant have done to test the board's readiness to support management teambuilding in advance of the cited conflicts?

Given the board's division over its role and conflict over the social mission of the company, was teambuilding with management a setup for later problems? If so, was it realistic for the consultant to intervene with the board early on? Why and why not?

2. Some theorists differentiate between structural and interpersonal problems in organizations. To what extent, in your view, were the problems between Ben and Chico related to their roles versus their values? How do you view the consultant's interventions with them? What else could have been done?

3. For this next year, the consultant has proposed to continue teambuilding through the company, to assist in the formation of a manager's steering committee and employee steering committee to bring more systematic input into company decisions, and perhaps conduct an employee survey. Managers think it sensible—in formulation and sequence. Ben thinks it conservative—isn't it just an extension of what was done last year? What do you think?

4. Finally, looking over the A and B cases, how would you rate the overall intervention program? How about the depth of interventions and their sequencing? What would you have done differently?

Penrock Industries, Inc.: Team Development Intervention

Eric H. Neilsen
Case Western Reserve University
Harlow Cohen
Case Western Reserve University

Penrock Industries was a small ($75 million annual sales), privately owned manufacturing conglomerate headquartered in a major city in the eastern United States. The founder, Thurmond Penrock, had started in the metal stamping business, making parts for manufacturers of everything from metal trays for the lower end of the housewares market to encasements for microwave ovens.

Thurmond had no formal education beyond high school. However, he had developed an excellent business sense over the years it had taken him to transform the stamping plant from a startup operation to a highly profitable business doing $15 million in sales in 1970. According to his son Calvin, Thurmond could walk into any small business on a sales call and, within a couple of hours of conversation, determine the company's technical and manufacturing strengths, its major markets and growth potential, how well people were getting along with each other, and whether the ownership was making a decent profit.

In 1970, after an especially successful year, Thurmond agreed to buy out the owner of small ($8 million annual sales) toy manufacturer. The latter had gotten into trouble by investing heavily in the development of a new line of electronic products that sold poorly during the Christmas rush. Thurmond had made some of the metal parts for the new line, but he had been convinced from the beginning that the venture would fail. From his viewpoint, success could only come from a mass marketing effort that would take the toy company out of its traditional word-of-mouth hobby shop market and into competition with much larger and well-entrenched toy manufacturers that advertised nationally. His client and old friend, by contrast, was convinced the traditional marketing channels would suffice because of the new product's sheer attractiveness.

A NEW INTEREST: ACQUISITIONS

Soon after taking over the toy firm, Thurmond reoriented all of its products back to the hobby shop market. He and two of his closest assistants from the stamping firm (the company controller and the chief engineer) also went over every aspect of the toy operation in minute detail and made a number of other changes in policies, standards, and decision-making procedures. With these changes, the firm soon returned to profitability.

Throughout this reorganization, lasting approximately six months, the original owner had remained on the payroll with the intention of retiring as soon as the new management was familiar with the firm's operations. However, it was not long before Thurmond persuaded him to stay on permanently as general manager and chief operating officer in return for a percentage of the unit's yearly profits. The only caveat was that Penrock and his team could intervene if the firm got into trouble again.

This success experience led Thurmond to pursue further acquisitions on a continuous basis. During the next 14 years leading up to the time of the intervention, the company acquired six other small manufacturers. All of the latter were within 300 miles of the original stamping plant and were located among what had only recently been the last of the farming communities outside the urban sprawl of major cities. Such locales were now becoming attractive manufacturing sites due to somewhat lower labor costs and access to major highways.

Two of the acquisitions proved barely salvageable and were resold as soon as they could attract a break-even price. One of the remaining four, a manufacturer of garden tools and implements, became highly successful. Two others, an oven maker for the restaurant industry and a manufacturer of auto antitheft equipment, were barely breaking even, although in Thurmond's eyes there was enough promise to warrant keeping them for the foreseeable future. The newest acquisition, a stamping business that made metal boxes for the personal computer market, had just been acquired and was being reorganized.

THE ORGANIZATION

At the time of the intervention, the company's headquarters staff was divided nominally into two groups (see Exhibit 1). Thurmond and the two colleagues who had helped him with the first acquisition formed the development team. They spent much of their time on the road, sometimes working very hard at making new deals. At other times, they simply maintained good relationships with the numerous minority position partners whose equity had been necessary for subsequent acquisitions.

EXHIBIT 1   Partial Organization Chart of Penrock Industries, Inc.

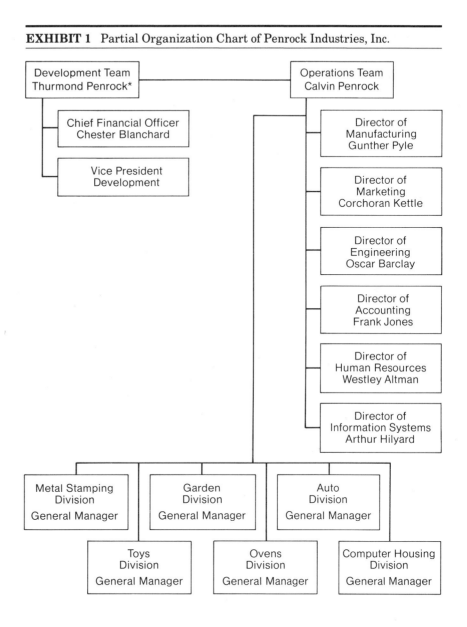

*Names included for persons mentioned in the case.

The second group was called the corporate operations team and was headed by Thurmond's son Calvin. This group now did most of the follow-up analysis of each new acquisition. More importantly, its ongoing task was to make the current acquisitions as successful as possible.

The team was comprised of the corporate directors of manufacturing (Gunther Pile), marketing (Corchoran "Corky" Kettle), engineering (Oscar Barclay), accounting (Frank Jones), human resources (Westley Altman), and information systems (Arthur Hilyard). While all of these people officially reported directly to Calvin, they were also variously involved with the firm's development activities and, alongside their operations duties, were often engaged in projects assigned by Thurmond Penrock. The rest of the corporate staff, about a dozen in number, were assistants to all of these individuals.

Each of the businesses was functionally organized, headed by a general manager, and had its own directors of manufacturing, marketing, engineering, accounting, human resources, and, in three cases, an information systems manager. Each functional head within a business had a staff ranging from as few as three people for some human resource functions to as many as 250 in the larger manufacturing units.

Integration within the operations side of the corporate group was accomplished nominally through the hierarchy and a set of weekly meetings, starting with the Monday morning operations meeting, attended by Calvin and his direct reports, and cascading into meetings with other subgroups as necessary. However, by far the most important vehicle for integration was one-to-one interaction between any member of the corporate group and either Calvin or his father. No chain of command, preplanned work flow, or decision-making protocol stood in the way of the owners' personal choices or involvement.

It was not unusual in a given week for Calvin and/or Thurmond to have separate one-to-one meetings with six members of the corporate staff who would present their cases and promote their interests regardless of the dictates of formal structure and procedure. The meetings were not trivial; at times, they led to shifts on important decisions or exceptions to normal procedure.

The official company stance was that the corporate team existed (1) to serve the corporation as a whole by maintaining certain companywide operating policies and (2) to serve the businesses in particular through consultation as requested by the latter. Its members had access to all data with respect to their particular functional areas in each of the businesses, but they were not to intervene directly or usurp the authority of a general manager unless ordered to do so by Calvin or his father. In reality, this policy was followed extensively only for the three most successful units. Businesses that were new and/or even slightly in trouble were fair game for attempted improvements by the corporate staff.

THE PEOPLE

Thurmond Penrock had maintained the practice of inviting the original owner of each acquisition or this person's chief operating officer to stay on as general manager, in return for a percentage of the unit's profits. While most of the original owners had agreed initially to this arrangement, only the toy company president and the previous owner of the newest business were currently on the payroll. New general managers as well as the corporate staff had been hired largely through the network of contacts Thurmond Penrock had accumulated in his continuous search for new businesses. For example, it was not unusual for him to cut off efforts for a particular acquisition while hiring away one of the managers from the potential acquiree.

More recently, Calvin had hired the directors of information systems and marketing through contacts at the school where he had recently received his MBA. All of these people were on salary, with the general managers also receiving a percentage of their unit's profits.

With the exception of Thurmond Penrock, all of the managers in the corporate group had undergraduate degrees, and with the exception of the toy company general manager, so did all the general managers of the businesses. Further data on the backgrounds of the corporate operations team can be found in Exhibit 2.

In contrast to the corporate directors and the general managers, only about half of those who reported directly to the general manager within each of the businesses were college educated, and still fewer people at the next level down had attained this level of education. There were no unions in any of the Penrock businesses, and most of the hourly work force had grown up in or near the communities where the units were located.

BUSINESS STATUS

At the time of the intervention, the operations side of the company was doing well financially. The two oldest units as well as the garden implements manufacturer were quite profitable, and all except for the newest business were at least breaking even.

However, several problems were becoming increasingly troublesome to Calvin and his father. First, turnover among general managers had been 30 to 50 percent for three years in a row and had not been limited to the less successful businesses. By contrast, turnover in the corporate group had been very low for over a decade and nonexistent for the past three years.

Second, the recent acquisition of the sixth business had made the company, and the family in particular, strapped for cash. The economy,

---

EXHIBIT 2   Personnel Profile

Thurmond Penrock—*age:* 61; *education:* high school; *background:* began his career as a production laborer in a large stamping plant, worked his way up to the rank of production superintendent by age 33, started his own stamping firm with the help of a disgruntled customer two years later.

Calvin Penrock—*age: 37; education:* B.A. history, MBA marketing; *background:* worked in marketing at another firm upon graduating from college; joined the family business seven years ago when the marketing manager at one of the units died; assumed the role of vice president of operations three years later when the prior encumbent was fired by Thurmond Penrock; earned MBA by attending school at night.

Chester Blanchard—*age:* 63; *education:* B.S. accounting; *background:* spent his early career in a small accounting firm, became acquainted with Thurmond Penrock soon after the latter started his own firm, went to work for Penrock as the company controller a year later.

Gunther Pyle—*age:* 44; *education:* B.S. economics; *background:* worked in a large assembly plant while attending college at night, met Thurmond Penrock when he was a guest speaker for the school's small business club; hired by Thurmond as an assistant production superintendent for the company's third acquisition, soon became superintendent and then corporate director of manufacturing when this acquisition was sold; has been in that role for almost 10 years.

Corchoran Kettle—*age:* 42; *education:* B.S. history, MBA marketing; *background:* four years in the Navy following college, began civilian career in sales at another family company, moved into marketing there as that company grew, met Calvin while attending night school for his MBA; has been with Penrock as director of marketing for four years.

Oscar Barclay—*age:* 41; *education:* B.S. engineering, ROTC; *background:* four years in the Army Engineering Corps after graduating from college, began civilian career as part owner and the only engineer in his family's garden tools business, became director of engineering for Penrock Industries when it was acquired by the latter eight years ago.

Frank Jones—*age:* 36; *education:* B.S. accounting; *background:* was hired upon graduating from college to replace Chester Barclay as controller for the original stamping firm when Chester became involved with acquisition activities; remained in this position, with duties expanding as Chester's assistant in acquisitions, until two years ago when the director of accounting role was created for corporate operations.

Westley Altman—*age:* 37; *education:* B.A., M.A., Ph.D. philosophy; *background:* was a university instructor until completing his PhD at age 28; had been taking courses in business administration as a contingency and joined the personnel department of a large company when he

---

EXHIBIT 2   (*concluded*)

could not find an acceptable position in academia; met Thurmond Penrock through a friend of the family; hired as director of personnel three years ago.

Arthur Hilyard—*age:* 36; *education:* B.A. business, MBA information systems; *background:* had worked for several firms, primarily in accounting, got interested in information systems when a firm he was working for automated its accounting system, returned to school evenings to earn his MBA, met Calvin there; Calvin created the position of director of information systems for him four years ago in a drive to automate the accounting functions at all the units and build in automation and decision support systems where feasible in engineering and manufacturing.

---

moreover, was making it difficult to initiate cash calls from the other partners. This was increasing the tension between the corporate group and the other businesses because the latter were constantly proposing plans for renovation and expansion that required significant capital investments.

Third, Calvin Penrock was beginning to feel stretched in his role. The number of details he was required to attend to on a day-to-day basis was now nearing his limits, given the way the firm was organized. With more acquisitions anticipated as soon as the current economic crunch was over, he began to search for advice on how to manage the human side of the company's growth more effectively.

DATA COLLECTION AND FEEDBACK

The authors were brought in as consultants to Penrock Industries, Inc., in response to the concerns noted above.[1] In several hours of conversation with Calvin (Thurmond Penrock preferred to take a backseat to the project), the three reviewed the history of the organization, the nature of the industry, and the issues with which Calvin was now concerned. They agreed that the most important next step was to find out how other people in the organization were experiencing the current operations. In particular, data were needed on whether the current structure and operating policies were experienced as satisfactory and in what areas, if any, energy existed for change.

---

[1] For a summary of the first author's approach to organization development, see Eric H. Neilsen, *Becoming an OD Practitioner* (Englewood Cliffs, N.J.: Prentice-Hall, 1984).

While it was clear from the beginning that some changes would be useful with respect to Calvin's office in particular, the consultants and their primary client wanted to see whether this change could be couched in a larger program that would benefit as many members of the organization as possible and, at a minimum, not make matters worse from other people's viewpoints.

To accomplish this task, an interview/feedback process was undertaken with all members of the corporate staff, including secretaries, staff to the functional directors, assistants to Thurmond Penrock, and the other managers in the development side of the organization. The general managers of the six businesses were also included in order to put the data collected from the corporate group in a still broader context. The process involved one- to two-hour interviews with approximately 35 people. The following questions were covered:

1. Please tell me about your job.
2. What has your career been like so far?
3. Whom do you work with most closely on a day-to-day basis? What do they expect of you? What do you expect of them? How well are these expectations being met?
4. How do the structure and policies of the larger organization help and hinder you from doing your job effectively?
5. What trends do you see in the way the organization has been evolving over the past several years?
6. Suppose you had three magic wishes about how to change the organization in any way you wanted. What would they be?
7. What do you personally want to do more of or start doing, continue to do at about the same rate, or do less of or stop doing?

Exhibit 3 summarizes the more pertinent findings and observations from the consultants' preliminary report to Calvin and his father. This report was given to them at the end of the interview process with the intention of using it as a springboard for a discussion of how to conduct the feedback sessions.

After talking with Calvin, these and other data were fed back by the consultants to all the participants. The presentation was made with flip charts (no written documents were circulated) at an all-day meeting held in the ballroom of a hotel located near the company headquarters.

The presentation was followed by meetings of subgroups, arranged by rank or job group (general managers, corporate operations team, top management, middle management staff, etc.). The task of each group was to discuss what was revealed in the presentation (all the flip charts remained taped to the walls for easy access) and to prepare a short presentation on what was of most concern to its members, what warranted elaboration or correction, and what they thought should be done next.

EXHIBIT 3 Representative Comments and Quotations from the
Consultants' Report

Career
People's ideas about career progress seem to be tied to the idea of further
business expansion:

- I would like to see more acquisitions so some of us could become group
  managers.
- I'd like to see more acquisitions so I can do more work with them.
- I don't know what the next step in my career is, but I want to progress, and
  I don't see us growing as rapidly as I would like.

Relationships
There are many two-person relationships, based largely on work
interdependence and/or shared longevity throughout the organization.
Specifically, many people seem to have an ally or close confidant for sharing
ideas, expertise, and commiseration. By contrast, far fewer people have
several close colleagues who form a stable work group.

Numerous "teams" exist on paper within the corporate group. Their
members acknowledge their composition and typically describe the other
members as candid, open, and forthright with each other. However, they also
note they are not really a team as yet in the sense of a unified, cohesive,
well-coordinated group. This condition is attributed, depending on the
speaker, to the leaders' management style, the short life of the group thus far,
travel demands that inhibit interaction, and lack of explicit attention to team
development. Regarding this topic:

- None of us knows what the rest of us do. We should be a group, not a
  collection of individuals.
- All of us have cordial relationships, but we don't work together effectively
  as a team.
- We share a common target but need much better coordination with each
  other.
- We are just in the formative stages. We're babies not yet in kindergarten in
  terms of working as a team.

The Organization
Positive comments were forthcoming about the organization's structure and
policy regarding the amount of personal autonomy it provided, the apparent
appropriateness of the design given the general economic health of the
organization, the informality of the work environment, shared commitment to
success as a visible underlying theme to all policies, and a basic appreciation
for Calvin's leadership and in particular his participative style relative to his
immediate predecessor. On the negative side were complaints about
procrastination and a "wait-and-see" attitude by the leadership:

- There are times when we allow a GM to ruin an eight-year employee. Then
  what happens is that there's a vacancy for a long time and someone has to
  do two jobs—that's how they get burned-out.

EXHIBIT 3 (*continued*)

- When a supervisor is bad they wait till it gets *too* bad so you lose two or three good employees.
- We predicted this would happen a year ago when we hired this person, but it's taken until now for us to act.

A particular critique of top management is its failure to articulate a clear corporate mission or a stable planning process:

- We spend too much time fighting fires and not enough planning for the future.
- When you get a bunch of young, enthusiastic managers, each with his own area to develop, and no clear direction from the top, people end up doing things that others haven't agreed on. This leads to confusion, overlap, and frustration.
- Upper management wrote MBOs for themselves last year, but to my knowledge they weren't shared widely or followed up on. I haven't seen my boss's, so I'm not sure I'm coordinating my own goals with his.

Lack of clarity regarding the corporate group's relationship to the businesses is another big issue. People both point to this directly and demonstrate this by voicing different views about what the relationship should be:

- Corporation to businesses . . . we send memos and they send memos back and we send them again . . . so we keep butting heads with GMs.
- We showed them our plan, and they said they would adopt it. When we came back a while later, they hadn't. So we ended up playing "gotcha."
- The hardest thing for corporate to do is to walk into a business and say, "I'm here to help you." They give you a fake issue or say they' re doing fine. You may know something is wrong but you have to walk away.
- Our job is to act as a support system to the businesses . . . to provide the services and expertise they don't have, as needed.
- The more liberal people around here like to feel democratic, but that's bullshit. We should tell them we are not a support staff.
- We're the policy arm here for the businesses. We have to decide whether we're here to service or control.
- Right now there is no direction because we confuse them with our messages versus our actions.

Another theme regarding the management group as a whole, with the exception of those at the top, is the desire for a more consistent set of rules, styles, and policies:

- I've lived under tight and loose control styles and feel I do well under both. I simply need to know the rules of the game.
- There's nothing documented in my area or other areas. When you are continually bringing in new people, they apply their past experience and we get a patchwork quilt. Knowledge and procedure aren't formulated in the Penrock way.

EXHIBIT 3 *(concluded)*

- If you're good, you get all the candy. The problem is there are no baseline criteria. Say to us, "These are the rules." The only clear rule is that they (the Penrocks) have the right to tell you when to shut up. They own the place.

Communication was also a problem:

- The corporate executive team has its meetings, but we aren't always informed of what has been discussed that is relevant to us, or what has been decided that will affect us. This often affects how we do our jobs.
- I often learn about a change in corporate policy from people in the businesses, when I am supposed to be representing the corporate group!

The presentations were followed by an open discussion and some final comments from both Penrocks.

Three major thrusts were agreed to that day and elaborated on a week later in a memo by Calvin to the corporate staff and the general managers: First, the family and the closest associates would go to work immediately on developing a corporate mission statement, accompanied by both short- and long-term objectives. At the all-day session, Thurmond Penrock had gone into considerable and much-appreciated detail to explain why such a plan had yet to be created. The essence of his story was that the firm had recently been facing so many opportunities and contingencies that he had wanted more time before making up his mind. However, given the now apparent impact of his delay on the rest of the company, he was now willing to go ahead with the development of a plan.

Second, the corporate executive committee would engage in a team-building session several weeks hence and with the help of the consultants (1) delineate the particular tactics and operating strategies necessary to meet the mission and objectives that by then would have been formulated, (2) clarify their respective role relationships with each other and the rest of the organization, and (3) work with the consultants to develop their skills as a team.

Third, a separate meeting would be held later in the year with the general managers in order to clarify their relationships and responsibilities to the corporate group once the latter had gotten its act together.

THE TEAMBUILDING INTERVENTION

Soon after the aforementioned memo had been circulated, further contingencies in the environment prevented Thurmond Penrock from going to work on a corporate plan. This was disheartening both to the corporate staff team and to the general managers, and there was talk of putting the entire project on hold until the plan was completed.

Nonetheless, Calvin and several others on the corporate staff were eager to move ahead. They did not want to lose the momentum already created by the interview/feedback project and thought progress in some areas was better than nothing. The consultants found their arguments reasonable and, with Thurmond's blessing, agreed to go ahead with an offsite meeting. The revised plan was to work on "becoming a more unified team" at this session, using the task of clarifying team roles and team members' expectations of each other as the primary focus. Implementing the corporate plan would be handled later in the year at another offsite meeting.

The first step in preparing for the teambuilding session was for the consultants to reinterview each of the corporate operations team members, as well as Chester Blanchard, the CFO, who would also attend the meeting. In this round of interviewing, the focus was on (1) the elements of each person's job as he or she experienced them, (2) the dilemmas and challenges each person typically encountered in attempting to perform each element, and (3) each person's experience of the way the corporate operations team worked—its strengths, weaknesses, bad and good habits, productivity and satisfaction.

These interviews took two to three hours per person and were seen as useful problem-solving activities in and of themselves. Many of the issues surfaced had little directly to do with other team members, so no plans were made to present all of the interview data at the workshop. Nonetheless, discussion of non-team-related issues with the consultants often brought up new action strategies for the interviewee and seemed to strengthen relations between the team members and the consultants.

Those issues identified as suitable for discussion at the upcoming session were summarized by the consultants in a brief memo to the interviewee a week or so after their meeting, with corrections and clarifications being made thereafter. The resulting document became the personal agenda for the interviewee, which he or she could use as desired.

Besides these role analyses, each preparatory interview also involved a discussion of how the interviewee viewed the team at work. The consultants took notes on particular alliances and rivalries that were consistently identified across interviews, on the personal styles and habits attributed to each member, and on what norms of behavior appeared to be in effect. These data revealed that almost all of the members of the corporate executive team were dissatisfied with the way the team operated. The Monday morning meetings, when they were held (and they were canceled often), were seen as a waste of time. Each member was characterized consistently by colleagues as having a very definite style, almost a script, from which he rarely deviated and which determined the way he would approach each agenda item.

For example, Calvin was seen as inclusive and participative at the beginning of every meeting and would start it with a clear agenda and great enthusiasm, but he was also seen as quickly losing interest when an action plan was not immediately forthcoming. When this happened, he would let the conversation wander without attempting to redirect it, or he might even leave the room for a few minutes. Unfortunately, Calvin's losing interest seemed to happen with great frequency. Whenever an issue came up that another member of the group either disagreed with or did not want discussed at that time, Calvin would use his own characteristic response to block effective discussion.

As another example, Westley would get into a battle over the semantics of how the item was being presented. Frank would feign sleepiness and seemingly ignore entire periods of conversation, only to reenter with facts or opinions that would cloud the issue as soon as a decision appeared imminent. Oscar, who always sided with wherever Calvin seemed headed, would pick fights and rant and rave about others' lack of loyalty to the company. Corky would state all his concerns in terms of questions and then look hurt and upset if others' answers were not in line with his own. And Arthur and Gunther would spend their time throwing barbs at each other, either directly or indirectly, and would then aim their hostility at anyone (Calvin excepted) who broached an issue having to do with their functions. Typically, once these patterns developed, Calvin would let the conversation run its course for a while and then move on to the next item with no clear resolution on the decision made.

According to the team members, the real work requiring cooperation got done in private one-on-one conversations during the rest of the week between each team member and Calvin or, less frequently, his father. The choice of whom to approach depended on who was present and which leader seemed more amenable to the team member's desires. Disagreements between father and son were infrequent, and it was obvious to all that they consulted each other at length on most important decisions, thereby obviating any real advantage regarding whom to approach first.

This, however, did not prevent the team members from trying to block each other's objectives by means of these behind-the-scenes conversations. The result was that Calvin in particular (both because of his role and because his father was more often on the road seeking new deals) was bombarded with several sides of every story and, in the absence of productive group interaction, was often left to make most of the decisions for himself.

Both the data gathered during the interview/feedback project as well as the follow-up interviews with each team member made it clear to the consultants that the corporate operations team was highly dependent on the family leaders for direction and support. As one member had put it, "They own the company, and if they say jump, you jump!" While there were important lateral relationships within the committee, they were invariably superseded by each person's relationship with either Calvin or Thurmond Penrock.

Personal styles and norms of conduct that inhibited collaboration were clearly understood and articulated by team members during the interviews, and yet attempts at changing them had occurred infrequently and to date unsuccessfully. Calvin reported experiencing being "heavily depended upon" and was beginning to burn out as a result. On the other hand, transforming the forthcoming mission statement into a workable document for guiding day-to-day operations, developing better relationships with the unit managers, and creating a viable solution to Calvin's work overload would require a greater level of collaboration with the group.

The Offsite Meeting

The last half hour of each of the preparatory interviews focused on the logic of the workshop itself, and possible activities were described. The protocol listed in Exhibit 4 was then developed in light of the managers' responses to various options discussed.

An annotated version of this protocol, with all activities spelled out in detail, was shared with Calvin a couple of weeks before the workshop was to occur. Calvin thought the contents looked reasonable but profferred that he was relying on the consultants to do what was best for the team. Two of the other team members called one of the consultants during the week before the workshop to discuss again what was planned. The consultants' basic posture was to be as expansive as the client wanted in describing the protocol, but always to note that the plan might be changed in collaboration with the whole group at the workshop. This was a tentative plan, not something carved in stone.

The workshop started smoothly. Everyone arrived at the site (a country resort) on time and enjoyed leisurely cocktails and dinner. After dinner, the participants adjourned to a very comfortable meeting room, furnished in two sections with two circular tables and wooden club chairs at one end of the room and several couches and easy chairs arranged in a circle at the other. There was even a piano at which one of the members subsequently entertained his colleagues during various breaks throughout the weekend.

One of the consultants began the formal proceedings by reviewing the agenda and asking for further comments and requests for clarification. The general tenor of the response was, "Let's do it!" and the toy block

---

EXHIBIT 4   Teambuilding Workshop Protocol

Friday Late Afternoon
Introduction—cocktails and dinner, followed by an overview of the workshop.

Toy block construction exercise—a group activity that generates data on how members clarify objectives, define and allocate roles, execute plans, and cope with important contingencies. To be used here as a springboard for articulating basic concepts regarding group dynamics.

Saturday Morning
Consensus decision exercise—another group activity designed to provide data on how the group works and to use these data to generate new work norms.

Saturday Afternoon
Role analysis discussion—objective is mutual understanding, clarification, help, and, ultimately, agreement on ways to behave with each other that will make each person more productive and enthusiastic.

Saturday Evening
Role analysis for vice president of operations—the vice president of operations' role is central to the team's effectiveness, so discussion of this person's role warrants a somewhat more elaborate procedure.

Sunday Morning
Interpersonal feedback opportunity—an interpersonal feedback session oriented toward exchanging constructive advice about each other's professional development.

Sunday Afternoon
Planning reentry—at least 45 minutes needs to be spent discussing how the results of the weekend's activities will be reported to the rest of the organization. At a minimum, members need to agree to the levels of confidentiality with regard to what has been said, the level of detail to be gone into in discussing even informally what happened, and the requests for new behavior to be made to the rest of the staff at this point.

---

construction exercise was started immediately. The group was divided randomly into two teams for this exercise. The atmosphere in the room was raucous. People were falling all over each other and kidding about whether they should have eaten so much at dinner. The two teams successfully completed the model within a couple of minutes of each other.

After a short break, each group was asked to meet separately again for about 15 minutes in order to list what they had done well and poorly in building the model. The two lists were then shared with the entire group. The focus of these readouts, as is typical, was almost entirely devoted to content issues with little attention to group process. For example, the items listed referred to issues such as whether appropriate maps had been drawn for each layer of the model, whether code names for the various pieces had been chosen correctly, and whether the north-south axis of the model had been appropriately designated with each instruction.

This is what the consultants had anticipated, and they now took the opportunity to distinguish between process and content and to dwell on examples of group process through the notes they had taken throughout the exercise. They reinforced the latter through a brief handout, which members were encouraged to review along with their role analysis descriptions, before retiring that evening.

Overall, the first evening seemed to go as planned. The participants had gotten a chance to interact with each other in a nonwork setting and to become oriented to the consultants as facilitators. The consultants had been given the opportunity to check out the current quality of relations among the group's members and the general mood of the group so they could assess whether the agenda was appropriate. All signals indicated the participants were on an even keel with each other and in the mood to proceed according to the protocol.

Saturday morning's activities also went very much as expected. The consensus decision exercise was done in a single group comprised of everyone but the consultants. This involved coming to a series of agreements about the elements of a problem, using the principle of consensus as the desired decision-making strategy. Despite clear instructions to try a different way of working together, it was uncanny to the consultants how quickly the behavior of each member reflected what had been said about his typical meeting habits during the preparatory interviews. The group's score was significantly better than the average of the individual scores but significantly worse than two of the members' individual scores, those of Corky and Arthur. The latter two individuals were the newest members of the group, and the dynamics of the exercise suggested they had yet to gain much influence with the other members.

This was the first time the consultants had been able to watch the group at work other than at two sessions designed to discuss the OD project, which had been highly focused on themselves. For various reasons, several attempts at arranging opportunities to observe the group at its Monday morning meetings had all fallen through.

The participants, on completing the exercise, were asked to list what they had done well and poorly, emphasizing group process and in particular the extent to which they had tried to reach a consensus.

Once again, member behavior mirrored almost exactly the habits pointed to in the preparatory interviews. Westley argued with several people over whether the group had made any decisions. Corky, despite several invitations for him to state his own opinion, kept asking the consultants whether they thought the group had done a good job in drawing people out. Oscar attacked Corky for not being more assertive in the exercise (several people had booed upon learning that Corky had had the highest individual score). Arthur and Gunther, both of whom had scored very poorly on the individual questionnaire, worked hard at convincing the group that the situation was too artificial to have been taken seriously. During this discussion, Calvin took the opportunity to answer some phone messages.

The consultants were beginning to worry. Clearly the group would have to change for the activities planned for the afternoon to be successful. After summarizing what they had heard the group members say, the consultants went back over a step-by-step explanation of what a consensus-oriented decision might look like in the context of the exercise just completed, pointing to alternative ways of behaving that each member could have engaged in at different points in the discussion. The participants listened attentively and seemed highly interested and intrigued with the concrete alternatives suggested.

But then, by way of rounding out the discussion and hooking it into the real world, the consultants asked the team to discuss the ways in which their behavior during the exercise did and did not mirror their normal meeting behavior. Once again, the group acted out the very behaviors they had reported as typical of themselves. And this time, moreover, they could come to *no* agreement with each other that the session was representative. Not a single person had changed his style to fit some of the suggestions just offered.

The consultants next intervened by listing on a flip chart the behavioral strategies reported in the interviews, this time without any names attached, and they invited the group to consider various incidents that occurred during the preceding two hours in terms of these behaviors. Perhaps by removing or separating the behavior from the individual (the person from the problem), people would be able to see their activities more objectively and be able to make more informed choices about them. That tactic worked. The group now could agree on excellent examples of each type of behavior.

Trying to bring matters full circle, one of the consultants suggested these behaviors represented the group's shared technology for getting in each other's way, even though particular behaviors were associated with particular members. The latter comment was met with considerable skepticism. People did not like the idea of taking responsibility for their colleagues' bad habits. Nonetheless, it was generally agreed that the group as a whole bore some responsibility by repeatedly allowing each tactic to happen.

The rest was easy. Members' acknowledgment of how they had cooperated in creating the problem seemed to make it apparent that they also had the power to solve it. The consultants asked them to come up with a new, more desirable set of behavioral norms. By the end of the morning, the group had not only developed a new list, but its members had also

---

EXHIBIT 5   New Norms for the Corporate Operations Team

- Every member must be "fully present"—no snoozing, wandering in and out, running to the telephone.
- When you think a decision has been made, say *out loud* what you think it is and the logic behind it.
- No arguing for argument's sake—no getting lost over semantics, no getting loud when you aren't winning.
- Spread airtime around the group. People can be silent if they want to, but a raised hand needs to be responded to in sequence.
- No sandbagging—coming in late with information that should have been reported earlier.
- Make declarative statements instead of asking questions that test whether the other person is thinking as you are.

---

begun to change their individual behaviors to be in tune with these norms (see Exhibit 5).

New Openness, New Rules

The atmosphere at lunch, served in the same meeting room, was noticeably quiet. Several members excused themselves in order to read their role analyses. There was a noticeable absence of the endless stream of jokes that had dominated all the other breaks. The afternoon session began with the consultants reviewing the proposed procedure and then inviting anyone to volunteer to start.

Westley Altman, corporate director of human resources, agreed to lead off. The dilemma he opened with concerned his responsibilities to the units about the staffing process. Westley had spent most of the past year instituting an open job posting program in all the businesses, something new to all but one of them. Whenever a vacancy occurred, the job would be posted on the company bulletin board for two weeks, and people internal to that business could apply for it at this time. External recruiting was also permitted, and a manager was not obliged to pick an internal candidate if an external candidate's credentials were clearly better. However, interviews would not start for either group until after the two weeks ended.

This procedure had been discussed at length at each unit and agreed to as a companywide policy. And yet, it was frequently being violated. The tactics for getting around it were probably as old as the procedure itself; for example, writing a job description so tightly that the only person who could qualify was the one the manager had picked before the entire procedure had started, or appointing one's preferred candidate into the slot on a temporary basis and then using performance already achieved as an excuse for rejecting all other candidates.

Westley reported he was receiving complaints that only the jobs no one wanted were being filled according to the spirit of the program, while all the desirable jobs were being allocated unfairly. When he followed up on a complaint and pushed the issue to a confrontation, the net result was a worsened relationship with that particular business unit or with the particular managers involved. As he saw it, he faced a major dilemma, which he wanted the group's help on: (1) let enforcement of the new policy slide and end up with a program having no credibility or (2) enforce the policy and end up with poor working relationships.

Discussion of this dilemma was lively because almost all of the team members had experienced such policy violations. The dialogue quickly changed into a series of attacks on the units for their supposed lack of attention to corporate policy in general, untrustworthiness, and so on. The consultants reminded the group that these were difficult matters to resolve without the unit managers present. They asked Westley whether there was any aspect of this situation that dealt with people in the room. After a long silence, he said, "Let's face it, we're all doing this to each other."

He followed this statement with the review of a recent incident: Gunther (manufacturing) had spent two weeks at one of the businesses, advising on the startup of a new assembly line. During this time, he had been instrumental in the firing of three people and the restructuring of several work groups. All three replacements had come from outside the unit. One of them was known to be Gunther's neighbor. A second had been introduced to the company by Calvin and had been working in a less attractive job at a nearby unit. And the third was a good acquaintance of Oscar Barclay (engineering).

Westley had come prepared and, at this juncture, handed out the résumés of these three people along with the resumes of two in-house candidates from the business unit. It was clear that one of the latter was superior to the person who got the job he had applied for, and the other in-house candidate's credentials were little different from the person who had gotten his desired slot.

"I think this is a symptom," Westley went on, "of what you fellows think of the human resource function in this organization."

He then shared several more incidents that highlighted the fact that human resource policies were frequently given lip service and then ignored. Gunther and Westley soon were engaged in an argument over the definition of one of the policies being violated. Spontaneously, with no cues from the consultants, the rest of the group pointed to the flip chart with the new norms on it and said, "You're both doing it!"

Silence followed. Finally, one of the consultants asked the group whether, despite particular details, Westley was essentially correct. Several people agreed, and Frank (accounting) actually apologized to Westley for his role in one of the incidents just discussed. The consultants then suggested that people talk for a while about how they had gotten into this situation. Not much headway was made in coming up with an explanation, but some factors were identified, for example, the need for people one could really trust in the units, the need for quick action, the fact that things had always been done this way.

The consultants' next gambit was to ask whether the group would be willing to make some new agreements to remedy this situation. It was important to make them concrete enough to be testable and realistic enough that there was a reasonable chance the parties involved would follow them.

Westley asked Gunther to keep him up to date on what his intentions were about "facilitating" the hiring or firing of anyone when he was doing a project in a unit. Gunther suggested it might be possible if Westley would refrain from reciting the rule book before listening to all of Gunther's story and would work with him to achieve his objectives in a legitimate way. The two agreed to this and to check with each other in six weeks to see whether each thought the agreement was being lived up to. Several other agreements were reached with Westley, and the group took a break. An hour and a half had passed.

Not every team member's issues generated as much discussion or tension as Westley's. A pattern seemed to develop in which one person with especially difficult issues was followed by someone with a much lighter agenda, who was in turn followed by someone with a more serious one. An informal procedural norm also seemed to develop whereby the description of an issue was kept to just that—description—until everyone was satisfied that he could imagine in vivid detail the event or condition being discussed, and how it connected to the dilemma or predicament its author was trying to express. Only then did the group turn to an open discussion of the causes of the situation described. The latter discussion was brought to a close by attempts at making specific one-on-one contracts that would be checked out in six weeks.

By 6:00 P.M., only four people had had a turn. It was agreed that the group would continue with this task through the evening. It was 1:30 A.M. when the last person, save Calvin, had said he was ready to give up the floor.

There was little socializing after the role analysis discussion ended. The consultants decided not to hand out the additional readings and the personal feedback questionnaires that had been planned. Discussing Calvin's role and dealing with reentry would be enough for tomorrow. People were exhausted but seemed pleased with how much they had covered. As one person put it, "It's hard to believe we had so much to talk about."

A Turn in Events

The group started at 9:30 Sunday morning instead of the intended 8:30. Calvin began by saying how pleased he was at what had happened thus far. He was sure this was what the team should be doing, and now that it was his turn, he also had some important things to share. He said he had been thinking a lot over the past few weeks about the kind of contribution he wanted to make to the company, and he was closing in on the decision that the vice president of operations role was not the right one for him.

He was becoming more and more involved in business development activities with his father and was anticipating the day when Penrock Sr. would retire and he, Calvin, would be in charge of the whole organization. In line with this, he was thinking about stepping back from the operations side over the next several weeks and looking for a replacement for the vice president of operations role. This interim period, he thought, might be a good time for the team to practice working as a team. He would attend the Monday meetings but essentially abide by the consensus decision-making process.

The group's immediate response was largely silence. Two of the team had apparently already heard about Calvin's impending decision and voiced their support for his new direction. Others stated their appreciation for his leadership to date, noting how much he had contributed to the development of the corporate group.

The serious possibility that Calvin would actually change roles was new to the consultants, although he had hinted he was thinking along these lines in a conversation with them a few weeks before. While they said the idea of this particular team working always by consensus was rather startling to them, given the prerogatives and traditions of the family, they also expressed their interest and enthusiasm for seeing how it would work.

They also suggested, however, that group members spend some time talking about what they would expect from a new vice president of operations and what this person could expect of them. There were some tasks this person could do more effectively than any other member by nature of his or her position of total oversight, as well as the more direct reporting relationship with the organization's top leadership. This suggestion was rejected by several people and then by the group as a whole. Several thought the team, with all of its new agreements and resolutions as well as its introduction to consensus decision making, could benefit from some time working with each other before deciding what would be ideal for the vice president's role. Calvin went along with this, and the consultants acquiesced.

The group spent the rest of the morning going over each of the one-on-one agreements and personal resolutions made the day before. These had been listed on flip charts that draped the walls of the room. Regarding the agreements, the task at hand was to read each item and ask (1) whether the parties involved were still willing to try it out and (2) what implications this might have for other people in the organization.

The task went smoothly, with only a few changes being renegotiated, and the discussion turned naturally toward what the group as a whole would say about the workshop to the rest of the organization. It was agreed that Calvin would have each person's resolutions and the total list of agreements typed and circulated to the team. Members were free to say what they wanted about the workshop to other people, since all agreed that they would do so anyway and that most of the incidents that had been discussed had been known through the grapevine almost since their occurrence.

More importantly, Calvin agreed to talk to his father about what had gone on during the workshop. While Calvin had not shared his dilemmas in light of his decision to withdraw from the role, he had been a very active participant throughout the proceedings and had become party to a dozen agreements. Several of these dealt specifically with the commitment to develop an explicit corporate philosophy, a strategic business plan, operational objectives, and discipline-based objectives.

Making headway with regard to the first two of these objectives would require his father's approval and active support. Chester's presence and quiet support throughout the meeting had been taken as a sign of Thurmond Penrock's support in principle for the project as a whole. It remained to be seen how far this support would extend.

After lunch, the consultants reviewed what the group had accomplished and went over the parts of the agenda that had been discarded. The group agreed to have another workshop in 90 days to explore the original Sunday agenda as well as to check on progress. By that time, a new vice president of operations presumably would have been picked, and the agreements people had just cemented would have been fully tested and refined.

The workshop ended with each person having a chance to reflect out loud on his learnings. By and large, the team members voiced great enthusiasm and even greater exhaustion. More than a little anxiety, however, was also expressed in the way people looked at Calvin, their oblique references to his possible shift in roles, and their expressions of need for his continued support.

QUESTIONS FOR DISCUSSION

1. One of the focal objectives of this workshop was for the corporate operations group to become a more unified team. What did the consultants do to accomplish this task? How well did they succeed? How

was their strategy consistent and/or inconsistent with your knowledge of how groups develop?

2. Develop an alternative workshop agenda for facilitating the corporate team's development. Clarify the objectives of each activity you suggest and your theoretical rationale for the sequence in which you place them.

3. Was doing a workshop with the corporate operations team the most appropriate intervention at this time in the project? List some alternatives and possible reasons for them.

4. How might the consultants have behaved more effectively in (*a*) preparing for the workshop and (*b*) conducting it?

5. What impact, if any, do you think this workshop had on Penrock Industries, Inc.? What should the consultants do next in this consulting relationship?

The Entertainment Industry Council on AIDS: Interorganizational Problem-Solving Intervention

Thomas E. Backer
Human Interaction Research Institute

PROLOGUE

You can almost hear the breathlessly eager writer telling the story idea to a weary producer in some movie studio office building: "A terrible crisis befalls this entire industry, see, and a lot of people start dying of this strange disease. At first, everything's kept secret, with lots of rumors and whispers, and doctors faking death certificates, and nobody wanting to believe it is happening. Then a leader of this industry gets sick and comes back home to die as the only passenger on a chartered jet. Now nobody can pretend it isn't happening. So there's a panic, and people do some really irrational things. But then the industry's top executives and union leaders get together, and they put aside their differences to help deal with this crisis. They have this big conference, and. . . ."

But before the writer can finish, the producer cuts him off with a polite rejection, and the writer moves on to his next story idea, secretly relieved he won't have to bring such an improbable tale to life in a script.

But this improbable story really happened, and it happened in the very land of improbable stories: Hollywood. This story is about how an entire industry—the entertainment industry—mobilized to deal with the AIDS health crisis.

The story actually starts with the first people who contracted the virus that causes AIDS because they included members of the entertainment industry in New York and Los Angeles. But the world's attention was riveted first by the image of a 747 jumbo jet landing at Los Angeles International Airport in July 1985, bearing the dying movie star Rock Hudson.

Like so many other images involving movie stars, this sad event changed the world's perceptions, moving us irrevocably into the "age of AIDS." And for the Hollywood entertainment industry, major changes also were afoot. In the months that followed, there was an intense controversy about actors playing scenes for TV shows or films that involved open-mouth kissing, about makeup artists applying makeup to actors who might be infected, about discrimination in hiring actors who might be gay.

Then a seminar was held in December 1985 by the Alliance of Motion Picture and Television Producers (the collective bargaining agent for management in the industry). Presentations from health experts about the nature and risks of AIDS provided facts on which to base company and union policies. The Screen Actors Guild and the Makeup Artists and Hairstylists Local 706 (two of the most concerned unions) both issued statements after the seminar that helped calm the panic.

Through these actions, the Hollywood entertainment industry by 1986 already was a pioneer in developing an appropriate, humane response to the AIDS health crisis, at a time when few companies outside of San Francisco were even paying attention to this growing national problem. Celebrities such as Elizabeth Taylor also were helping to raise funds for AIDS research and treatment, and others were contributing their services to education campaigns through the mass media.

But there was still much to be done. At the beginning of 1987, only a handful of workplaces in Hollywood had AIDS policies or programs, and incidents based on fear, prejudice, and misunderstanding were common. In a geographically concentrated industry with a work force that includes many independent contractors (actors, technicians, and so on) who move from company to company working on films or TV shows, a coordinated, industrywide AIDS program would make great sense, but it wasn't happening. Some executives were apprehensive about getting involved—"somebody might think I've got it, or that I'm gay." Others were just too busy with the pressures of their jobs. For more than a year after the AMPTP seminar and its immediate outcomes, not much happened.

When change did occur, it was through an interorganizational problem-solving intervention I helped coordinate as a volunteer OD consultant. Because it started partly by a happy accident and flowered rapidly, much of the story I'm about to share was analyzed only after the fact. Most of the challenges this OD intervention has faced have been only moderate in intensity, but they have been continuous. As with many Hollywood stories in three acts, good fortune occurred along the way—some of it related to basic principles of OD applied in this unusual set of circumstances.

Like all good stories, at its heart are a couple of simple themes. One is the theme of *information utilization*—to develop organizational capacity to respond to a very complicated challenge, comprehensive information is needed (including data on how other organizations have responded to similar challenges). Also needed are strategies for getting this information utilized effectively (e.g., by presenting it from a credible source). The other is the theme of *participation*—to make a system intervention like this work, many players need to be involved, most of them through informal networking, and they must accept that what develops belongs to them, not to some outsider. Participation in this case has been helped immeasurably by an entertainment industry tradition of helping co-workers who need health care or financial aid—referred to by the catch-phrase "we take care of our own."

ACT I: SETTING THE STAGE AND GETTING THE PLAYERS TOGETHER

In April 1987, a conference was held at the Directors Guild of America theater in Hollywood, bringing together more than 100 concerned television, radio, and film professionals to discuss ways in which the entertainment industry could help America respond to AIDS. The conference was underwritten by NIDA, and coordinated by EIC, as part of a three-year project to mobilize the mass media in educating the public about drug abuse and the risk of AIDS. (See Table 1, "Cast of Characters," for definitions of EIC, NIDA, and other players in this story.)

At this conference, I gave a presentation about what American workplaces—Wells Fargo Bank and Levi Strauss in San Francisco were then the leading examples—were doing to help their work forces deal with AIDS. At the end of my talk, I asked for a business card from anyone interested in starting a volunteer task force to look at what the entertainment industry could do on this subject for its work force. A half dozen cards were later thrust into my hand.

This OD intervention began informally. I had not planned in advance to ask for people's business cards; the idea just seemed right when I said it. No one had retained me as a consultant; no one asked me to undertake this job. It interested me because of my long-standing work in the entertainment industry, because of my consulting work for NIDA and EIC, because of my institute's AIDS in the workplace activities—and because it needed to be done.

As an experienced OD consultant, I knew this intervention would be tricky business, especially given the emotional complexities surrounding the AIDS health crisis. There would be resistance from some, hesitance from others, and a battle to get commitments of time from busy executives who may already be involved in volunteer work.

Perhaps more than many industries, entertainment rests on informal networking and behind-the-scenes negotiations (multimillion-dollar films typically start production under informal "deal memos,"

TABLE 1   Cast of Characters

The Industry—The fabled film and television industry in Hollywood has some 230,000 workers. It is a geographically concentrated industry, with much of its work taking place within a few square miles of greater Los Angeles, especially in such cities as Hollywood, Burbank, and Culver City. It is an industry with wild excesses of profit and loss and many changes brought about by recent mergers and acquisitions (example: Time Inc. and Warner Communications), technology (example: home video), and other factors. It is a stressful industry, with high rates of substance abuse and other lifestyle-related disorders; and it is a tight-knit, "cottage" industry, dependent on teamwork and cooperative decision making. Its "we take care of our own" philosophy is exemplified in such unusual institutions as the Motion Picture and Television Country Home, a hospital and retirement facility for members of the industry.

The Management—Key executives of the major film and TV companies have notoriously short job tenures; those who head these companies' human resources and benefits departments are not in the same fast track and are the key representatives of management involved in this story.

The Unions—Representatives of unions for creative and technical workers in a heavily unionized industry often are involved in issues related to the welfare of their union memberships, and AIDS has been no exception.

The Consultant—For 20 years, I have been an educator and management consultant in the entertainment industry. Much of my work has been pro bono, offering seminars and training programs for unions and for educational organizations like the American Film Institute. I've also been a consultant to a wide range of entertainment companies and unions. After all these years, I'm something of a "known commodity" in this industry, with some day-to-day familiarity with the workings of Hollywood: I read *Daily Variety,* go to the awards shows, have made a dozen educational films, and have a file cabinet full of unproduced projects and ideas like everybody else in the industry! This breadth of experience gives me a unique kind of "outside insider" status.

As I'm also a psychologist and a professor at UCLA Medical School, I have credentials as a health professional. I'm often called on by Hollywood organizations to consult on health-related issues, from drug abuse to stress management.

And my larger work is relevant: for that same 20 years, I have conducted research on organizational change, concentrating on health and human resources issues, an area in which I have also worked as an OD consultant with organizations of all types. For the last several years, this work has included consulting with organizations on AIDS policies and programs. That background in change management, and especially in understanding the intense psychological dynamics surrounding change that involves values-laden issues and uneasy collaborations, was instrumental to the intervention described here.

TABLE 1 *(concluded)*

The Information Resource—The Human Interaction Research Institute is a nonprofit social science research center. Since January 1987, it has been conducting research and gathering information on AIDS in the workplace. It now has one of the world's largest collections of data, training programs, and policy materials on this subject, and it is conducting an ongoing research study for the National Institute on Drug Abuse concerning AIDS and drug abuse education in the entertainment industry.

Other Players—The Entertainment Industries Council (EIC) is a nonprofit organization whose principal mission involves using the power of the entertainment industry to fight drug abuse and related social problems. The Entertainment Industry Referral and Assistance Center (EIRAC) is a nonprofit employee assistance program providing substance abuse counseling and other services to the entire industry. The center was started in 1983 by many of the same management and union representatives who figure in this story.

The National Institute on Drug Abuse (NIDA) is the federal agency having leadership responsibility for developing community responses to drug abuse as a risk factor for AIDS. NIDA provided some early support for the development of EIRAC, believing that supporting the industry in an effort to better handle its own internal problems of substance abuse would increase its capacity to assist in public education—a philosophy that carried over to NIDA's support of the activities detailed in this case.

not full contracts). I had the contacts, but using them would take time, energy, ingenuity, and help from others. And like all the others who have collaborated on this industrywide campaign, I would be working as an unpaid volunteer, though much of what I would be doing would relate to other activities in my work. To be truthful, however, these considerations stand out only in retrospect; in April 1987, I just believed this needed to be done and I could play a part in making it happen, so I moved ahead.

My first step was to arrange a luncheon meeting with Jan Valentine, vice president for human resources at the Burbank Studios and a long-time friend and colleague. Valentine is widely recognized in the entertainment industry as "one who's always there" where social or health issues are concerned. Her studio had the first AIDS policy, one of the first drug abuse policies, and has been a pioneer in many other efforts to provide health services to workers (see Rawlinson, 1989, for a profile of Valentine). We had already worked together on EIRAC's development and other projects.

At our lunch, she agreed to join the volunteer committee, and we outlined how we might respond to several challenges we saw ahead:

1. The task force needed to be developed and led *for* and *by* people who are full-time in the entertainment industry (even though I'm accepted in the industry as consultant/educator, I'm still seen—appropriately—as a part-timer); if it was seen as "my group" rather than "an industry group," it wouldn't work. We identified other human resources and labor union executives who could be invited to the first meeting and planned to ask this group to nominate still others so we could have a wide range of both management and labor representatives, from the major movie studios, the television networks, the large production companies, and the most important creative, craft, and technical unions.

2. These are all busy people, and few had any prior background with AIDS. Thus, it was up to me and my institute to develop the informational resources we needed, supplemented by pioneering efforts within the industry, such as the AIDS policy Jan Valentine already had developed for her company. Unless I was willing to make this commitment to "do the group's homework," it was unlikely to be successful. Moreover, we agreed that my presence on the task force as a health-care professional was a critical element to its credibility, and that my serving as chair would both bolster this credibility and allow all others to come on board without the possible pressure of making the more major time commitment of being chairperson.

3. As a small, all-volunteer group, the task force would depend for its existence and success on the dedicated efforts of its members. Thus, we decided not to solicit for membership top industry executives who might lend their names but then rarely show up at meetings. We needed people who could do some work, and we knew just where to turn: to the same human resources and union executives who had helped with the foundation of EIRAC (there is now at least a 20 percent membership overlap between the two groups).

4. This small group also needed a bit of financial and service support to get it started—this was provided through some modest funding from NIDA and EIC, from services contributed by several major entertainment companies, and from my own institute. Getting this support together also took energy and much informal networking, sometimes involving both Jan Valentine and myself "drawing in due bills" from people in the industry we'd done favors for in the past.

5. We needed some visibility, but not too much until we had something concrete to offer. From the beginning, we wanted to have the task force keep a relatively low profile, until we had held a number of meetings and decided how we could best have impact.

6. We needed to be courageous in our planning and commitment making, but also realistic. If we undertook too much, we would end up accomplishing nothing, a common failing for volunteer groups taking on worthy causes.

7. We also needed to be sure none of our actions would reflect negatively on the organizations the task force membership represented. Thus, we started with a standing policy that any public action or press release would be reviewed in advance by the entire task force membership before release. We learned later that this policy was instrumental in persuading several Hollywood organizations to send a representative to our group.

About a dozen people came to our first meeting. We talked about how to best expand our membership, and we defined the following limited mission:

- To provide leadership and effective communication among organizations in the entertainment industry in developing humane, cost-effective policies and programs concerning AIDS—for workers with AIDS or ARC, for their co-workers, and for education and prevention in the industry as a whole.
- To provide information and access to technical assistance for those organizations needing it in developing or enhancing an AIDS policy or program.

From the beginning, we also made some deliberate decisions about what we would not do, and we discussed these openly. We would not be a fundraising organization on behalf of AIDS services (there are other organizations doing that); we would not be an advocacy organization; and we would not be concerned with the depiction of AIDS in the entertainment or news media (there also was another group, started about the same time, that did have the latter as its main mission, and I have served on that body, called the Entertainment Industry Coalition on AIDS, from its inception).

We agreed we would meet about once every other month, and at each of the next several meetings (summer and fall 1987), we would define a program of activities for 1988. The group selected me chairperson, and I made several promises about what I would do in that role. First, I promised to keep a flow of information going to the members through memos and telephone calls; many volunteer groups fail because they have no apparent life between face-to-face meetings. Second, I responded to one member's concern that "we not do anything that would embarrass my company" by promising to limit our contact with the media to informational releases, rather than taking positions on issues (as discussed below, a crisis nonetheless developed in this area). Third, I promised at least a one-year commitment to the group, to allay concerns that it might wind up leaderless in just a few months.

ACT II: PUTTING THE SHOW ON THE ROAD

The newly formed task force agreed that its first purpose was to gather information from employers and unions concerned with AIDS both inside and outside the industry. Resources from the Human Interaction

Research Institute's AIDS in the Workplace Initiative were summarized and presented to the task force, providing a portrait of American work organizations' response to the AIDS health crisis. This helped us see what was needed for Hollywood and identified specific resources and information we could adapt to the entertainment industry. Having written several of the business periodical articles among these resources added to my credibility as the consultant/change management specialist.

We interacted with a number of key groups in the industry. For instance, in January 1988, I made a presentation to the business agents of the 45 unions representing craft and technical workers in the industry, facilitated by a good word from a key union official already on the task force (I also had done much non-AIDS volunteer work with entertainment unions). We strove to hold task force meetings in locations that symbolized broad industry support. For example, an early 1988 meeting was held in the board room of Lew Wasserman, chairman of MCA-Universal. We noticed this meeting was especially well attended.

And just like a company getting ready to start production of a motion picture, we placed notices in the trade papers, like *Variety,* announcing our existence and hoped-for future. Several additional members of the task force came to us after seeing these notices.

We confronted some crises early on, though the interpersonal functioning of the group was generally smooth and healthy. This was partly because many in the group had worked together before and partly because we took steps early on to minimize the potential for disruptive conflict.

A key member of our group was required to withdraw from participation in the task force by this individual's employer, one of Hollywood's largest companies. This was a significant loss so early in our existence. I knew privately that the decision had been sparked by some personal concerns of a top executive with this company about the AIDS issue. However, in consultation with the departing member of the group, we agreed it would be far better for the task force's morale to downplay this unfortunate episode, and the low-key strategy worked. No other member has had participation questioned by a superior, and most are there at the specific directive of their organization's leadership.

Several members of the task force advocated strongly for involvement in fund-raising for AIDS services, even though that was not our stated purpose, and expressed displeasure when the group voted them down. By allowing them to express their views and then voting on the matter, we were able to keep these members on board with us, even though they were disappointed with the outcome.

On other occasions, I had private discussions with members to suggest likely outcomes of their presenting a given issue, so they could modify their statement to avoid loss of face. Or I would volunteer to bring up an issue myself so it wouldn't be identified with one particular member or his or her organization. This strategy helped to reduce conflict between the various organizations represented on the task force (e.g., between labor and management).

We had a series of conflicts about whether there are, in fact, a significant number of intravenous drug abusers working in entertainment companies. Despite clear evidence to the contrary, some members of our task force were reluctant to believe "this could happen in my company," and thus resisted the task force investing energy in promoting information or education efforts for this risk population. Some behind-the-scenes dialogues, in which we could discreetly reveal to the doubters some facts about each of their companies, helped to dispel this conflict. This again reinforces the importance of the change agent's ability to have private, off-the-record conversations to deal with sensitive issues.

In one case, an organization whose representative seemed initially to have many doubts about how we were addressing AIDS policies and programs was much more supportive after I provided some pro bono consultation on the organization's own activities in this area. Volunteers in this kind of interorganizational effort need to feel there is some kind of reward for them as individuals to remain involved, whether that is recognition, direct assistance, or some other benefit.

By the end of 1987, we were ready to make our first major public commitment—a conference in April 1988 to bring together labor representatives and managers from the industry. Rather than mounting our own conference, we decided to become part of a larger event (co-sponsored by the Human Interaction Research Institute) aimed at the overall Los Angeles business community. The task force committed to doing this at a time when many businesses in Los Angeles were still somewhat skittish about being identified with a disease associated mostly with gay men and IV drug abusers.

We selected key players for the conference event carefully: our keynote speaker was J. Nicholas Counter III, president of the Alliance of Motion Picture and Television Producers, the bargaining agent for management in Hollywood. The chairperson of the event was Jan Valentine, already described as a person with much credibility in the industry. Each of the session speakers were industry executives with practical experience in developing AIDS policies and programs, from both the union and management sides.

We decided to make an award to an outstanding employer. The award was given to George Spiro Dibie, president of the Photographers Guild Local 659, for his determined leadership in the way his union treated John Johnson, a computer programmer with the union who has AIDS. When Johnson came to Dibie with his situation—half-expecting to be fired—Dibie responded by insisting his union board (unanimously!) permit Johnson's workload to be reduced, his work schedule to be altered, but for him to be kept on at full pay. In receiving his award, Dibie said simply, "The human thing is always the right thing to do."

We succeeded. Our conference was well attended; we got significant attention in the Hollywood trade press; and the task force was bonded together by the positive experience of the conference. *Variety* printed verbatim the next day much of the text of Nicholas Counter's keynote speech, a speech that focused on what AIDS was costing the industry financially and that formally accepted (on behalf of the many companies his organization represents) the 10 principles for AIDS in the workplace advanced by the New York/New Jersey Citizens Commission on AIDS.

A second major task in 1988 was to conduct a research study intended to learn more about the incidence and impact of AIDS in the entertainment industry. The study was conducted on a pro bono basis by the Human Interaction Research Institute and coordinated by a graduate student research assistant, Robert Wegbreit of Claremont Graduate School. A mail survey and personal interviews with key executives revealed that major employers in the entertainment industry have experienced an average of 17 cases of AIDS, compared with only 7 cases per company in a recent national survey. One large entertainment employer initially reported 150 cases, though the number was reduced when only those cases confirmable by medical documents were included. The respondents to this study indicated that much had already been done by major employers, but there was still widespread fear, ignorance, and "response paralysis"—again, findings consistent with studies of other American industries.

The task force weathered another crisis related to this study. Several members thought the report "painted a negative picture," suggesting the entertainment industry had more cases of AIDS than other industries (which statistically is true, as reported by several studies in addition to ours).

These members were especially concerned about their companies' names being attached to a report that could generate controversy. As a result, we decided to withhold the study results until we could also announce how the task force was going to respond. One of the major observations of our interviewees in the 1988 study was that smaller employers for the most part could not afford the responses that large corporations were already engaging in (such as retaining consultants to develop policies and programs). Small employers needed simple, inexpensive methods tailored to their special needs. We decided that our response should focus on meeting the AIDS-related needs of smaller employers.

The task force received a grant from the Permanent Charities Committee of the Entertainment Industry to produce an "Information Kit," released in April 1989, which contains a wealth of resources for the smaller employer to use and is distributed free. At the same time, we launched a technical assistance consultation program, offering volunteer speakers from the task force membership to assist any company or union in the industry wishing to develop an AIDS program or policy. Both activities were based at EIRAC, which also had received a small grant from EIC to help in providing information on AIDS and drug abuse to the entertainment industry. EIRAC's activities include maintaining a resource library for use by the industry, seminars, and industrywide informational mailings.

Yet another crisis occurred in mid-1988, when a Los Angeles television reporter investigated alleged discrimination against AIDS patients by the Motion Picture Health and Welfare Fund, the industry's main self-insured insurance provider for technical and craft workers covered by union contracts.

As chairman of the task force, I was asked to appear on TV, which I wisely declined, but I was not so wise in agreeing to be interviewed by a reporter from *Variety* who took my tentative interpretations of this situation and turned them into a front-page story assuring readers that our task force was launching an "immediate investigation" of a body that included several members of our task force on its board! This was not true, but the statement appearing in print caused some concern and embarrassment. I immediately wrote an explanatory memo to the entire task force. The tempest eventually turned out to be only teapot size, but it reinforced the importance of keeping a low profile on task force activities, given the level of emotionality associated with AIDS.

ACT III: BEYOND THE TASK FORCE

As of this writing in mid-1989, we are launched well into the next phase of the task force's activities. We have just conducted a second major conference, held at the Los Angeles Theatre Center and attended by more than 110 persons. This conference addressed the issues of AIDS and drug abuse, educational programs for minorities, benefits and cost concerns, and legal issues.

The conference also involved for the first time the live theater in Los Angeles (a theater trade association, Theatre LA, was a co-sponsor of the event, and a series of followup activities for theater organizations now have been planned). The Focus Project, conducted by the Human Interaction Research Institute and funded by the National Institute on Drug Abuse, served as co-host of this event. Now the Focus Project, in collaboration with the task force, is examining how entertainment employers and unions can work together in providing targeted education for workers on AIDS and drug abuse, including programs aimed at women and minorities.

Once again, the task force is in a position of leadership. Just as our

"Information Kit" is one of the first publications aimed specifically at smaller employers in a particular industry, so our new activities concerning drug abuse, women, and minorities turn out to be ground breakers. In fact, a recent national review of AIDS education activities revealed that almost nothing has been done yet by American employers to provide education targeted specifically to blacks and Latinos, even though these are the two minority groups most affected by AIDS.

We are now looking for ways to maintain the vigor of our program. A task force committee is developing a series of one-minute film clips on AIDS, which will be shown in advance of private screenings of feature films by various industry organizations (where most members of the audience are workers in the entertainment field). Recently, we have approached the recording industry, adding a new member who has been a pioneer in drug abuse education in that arena. Through his participation, we are hoping to expand our membership and activities with recording companies and music publishing companies.

And the leadership of the task force is evolving: since the fall of 1988, I have been co-chairperson of the group, with Glenda Megna, human resources administrator for the Burbank Studios. This reinforces the task force's image as an industry-directed entity and is the first step toward a future transition. Already Glenda Megna has taken over significant responsibilities for the task force's activities, and the next step will be to appoint another co-chairperson from within the industry, when it is time for me to step down from this post.

At our most recent meeting, the task force voted to become a part of the Entertainment Industry Referral and Assistance Center, which already administers most of our programs. The task force, as a volunteer committee, has no legal status and cannot receive funds. By becoming a subpart of EIRAC, we can begin to institutionalize our efforts as part of a major organization that already helps the industry "take care of its own" in many ways.

QUESTIONS FOR DISCUSSION

1. In addition to absorbing the Entertainment Industry Workplace AIDS Task Force into the Entertainment Industry Referral and Assistance Center (a permanent organization with full-time staff and offices), how can the industrywide AIDS campaign be institutionalized?
2. How could the task force's work in Los Angeles be transferred to New York, where there is also a large entertainment industry?
3. How can the task force's strategy for developing an industrywide - response to the AIDS health crisis be transferred to other industries, especially those that are geographically concentrated?

REFERENCES

To learn more about what's in this case:

Shilts, R. *And the Band Played On.* New York: Morrow, 1987.

Institute of Medicine. *Confronting AIDS: 1988 Update.* Washington, D.C.: IOM, 1988.

Backer, T. E. "Managing AIDS at Work." *Healthy Companies,* April 1988, pp. 22–27.

Wegbreit, R., and Backer, T. E. *Study of AIDS in Entertainment Industry Workplaces.* Los Angeles: Human Interaction Research Institute, 1988.

Tusher, W. "AMPTP's Counter Keynotes Industry AIDS Conference." *Daily Variety,* April 28, 1988, pp. 3, 19.

Rawlinson, H. "Filling the Role in Hollywood." *Personnel Administrator,* May 1989, pp. 48–51.

Robb, D. "Industry AIDS Benefits up 83%." *Daily Variety,* June 7, 1989, pp. 1, 18.

Arnot, M. "Hooray for Hollywood." *Executive Briefing,* Fall 1989, pp. 1, 4.

The Catholic Diocese of Louisbourg: Strategic Planning Intervention *

David J. Nygren
Boston University
Maurice L. Monette
Boston University

The Diocese of Louisbourg was created in 1944 to serve the Roman Catholic population of a 24-county region of the upper Midwest. In four decades, it has grown to include 63 parishes with a total membership of 80,000 people, approximately 8.5 percent of the region's entire population. Twenty-one parochial and diocesan schools operate in the diocese. In addition, the diocese sponsors counseling and service agencies and has links with four hospitals and a college owned by a religious congregation operating in the diocese.

Bishop Campbell, then the chief executive of the diocese, had initiated a planning process for the diocese in 1983, in part, as an effort to resolve long-standing tension between the parish priests and the department heads in the chancery, many of whom were members of the diocesan clergy. The chancery is the central administrative office of the diocese.

The chancery was perceived by the parish priests as being out of touch with their needs and the needs of their people. The priests on the chancery staff thought of the parish priests as stuck in their ways and unwilling to promote changes mandated by the Vatican Council as early as 1963. The parish priests preferred a less centralized model of governance, one that would allow them to exercise authority and direction over their respective programs. They believed the chancery staff should be working for them—they were certainly spending their money. The priests working in the chancery believed the best way for the diocese to

---

*This case study reports the authors' postevaluation of a strategic planning intervention by another set of consultants.

be organized was with a central hierarchy and a central office managing all programs and services. The contrast between a philosophy of control and service was often used by parish priests to describe the chancery. They obviously preferred to have the chancery function as a service.

Bishop Campbell had observed the repeated resistance by the parish priests to nearly every attempt by the department heads to initiate programs and changes in services. His plan was to organize a presbyterial council that would serve as the working body to generate programs in collaboration with the priests whose parish needs the programs were designed to serve. He believed the greater the involvement of the presbyterate through its council, the more likely the voted programs would be implemented. At the very least, he knew he had to do something to minimize the polarization that had existed now for nearly a decade.

Bishop Campbell was also faced with significant personnel and financial issues that he thought could be resolved with a planning process. Among his concerns was the fact that the institutions of the diocese, specifically the churches, were not serving the populations most in need. What were once thriving parishes were now thinly attended, and areas of significant growth were underserved. In addition, many priests had built up their parishes to a degree that satisfied a limited number of parishioners. These same priests were very reluctant either to move to another location or to expand the nature of their services to a changing population.

Because each parish had assumed a fair degree of autonomy over the years, financial reporting was limited at best. Many of them were barely viable from the perspectives of either finances or mission. Although it was expected that the parishes would support the chancery staff salaries and programs through their annual contributions to the bishop from parish funds, a few pastors simply refused to contribute, thereby registering disregard for their membership in a larger corporate enterprise as well as their unwillingness to be controlled by "chancery bureaucrats." Bishop Campbell saw that without some flexibility in the personnel pool and stewardship of financial resources the real needs of the diocese would never be served.

Bishop Campbell hoped to utilize a planning process that would generate a larger vision of the church, its corporate spirit, and the opportunities that existed for all members. Even though he had no clear process in mind, he hoped to establish a sense of the future that would enable the priests to buy into a larger vision.

That vision would include expanding the responsibility given to the lay members of the church, perhaps restructuring the offices and services of the diocese to reflect a collegial model of governance, eliminating the polarities that were now prevalent between the chancery officials and the parish priests, and serving populations not previously served. He believed that an attractive alternative to the present realities would tap their willingness to cooperate. Bishop Campbell died unexpectedly in a car accident only nine months after his installation, and well before his vision could be realized.

THE NEW BISHOP

At the beginning of its fifth decade, a new bishop was appointed to lead the diocese. Bishop William L. Futrell, a native of the region, took office in June 1984. He is a tall man with a broad smile. Upon meeting him, the most pervasive impression is of a man enthused by the work he does while still holding onto a youthful idealism and a little naiveté. Despite his initial reluctance to assume the role as bishop of the Diocese of Louisbourg, he bears the position in an increasingly poised manner. He served as vicar-general under two bishops, both of whom were strong leaders.

Although the church's leadership selection process is very secretive, Futrell's appointment was, to his way of thinking, "a result of my knowledge of the diocese from having worked closely with two bishops and the general sense that I would continue the direction set by Bishop Campbell." Futrell admits at the same time, "I neither sought nor wanted the position as bishop, but, since I have been chosen, I will do my best not only to carry on what my predecessor had envisioned but also to expand the vision to include what I perceive to be the future."

In speaking to the priests at a regional meeting, Bishop Futrell indicated the background of the planning process. "We got into planning under Bishop Campbell. The need for that came about because of the tension between department heads (who were viewed as consumers) and parish priests (who were viewed as the producers of the hard earned cash needed by departments). That tension was very real. Bishop Campbell's game plan was to mediate that situation by getting us to look at our operation, all aspects of it."

Bishop Futrell thought that even if he could manage the complex problems of the diocese without external support, the intricacies of the planning process and his history in the diocese required greater expertise than he was willing to claim for himself. Expectations were running very high because of the remarkable vision set by Bishop Campbell.

Bishop Futrell turned to a private foundation for support in pursuing the planning process begun by Bishop Campbell. The foundation, in turn, recommended Tom Fairhurst, director of the Newport Consulting Group, a scholar known for his expertise in strategic planning and non-profit governance structures. Fairhurst ultimately became the primary consultant to the bishop. His extensive background included a doctorate in planning from a prestigious Northeast university. He was assisted by Michael Chambers, a priest, whose background included extensive work with church groups and a doctorate in administration from a notable East Coast university. His role in the consultation process was to provide Fairhurst and various committees with feedback about the process. He also independently directed parts of the process.

The consultants were invited into the pilot process to determine the major issues facing the diocese and to recommend some form of intervention. Fairhurst did a preliminary assessment of the diocese and then proposed subsequent planning steps. Once the foundation agreed to fund the planning project, designed and written largely by Fairhurst, Fairhurst was hired as the chief consultant. Michael Chambers was then hired to assist him in the project.

The bishop admitted that the question posed by the consultants, "What is your vision for the diocese?" really stumped him. He realized he had neither a clear vision nor any idea of how he might move the planning process forward. His initial perception was that "there are no sacred cows. All I really want to do is listen to the priests and to be collaborative."

Bishop Futrell's desire to function effectively as the leader was further manifest by his choice to attend a four-week executive management program at which Fairhurst was a contributing faculty member in the area of strategic planning. The program solidified his conviction about the need for planning, and it also strengthened his confidence in Fairhurst. He had also concluded that the comprehensive planning perspective of Bishop Campbell was not focused sufficiently for him to proceed with confidence. He began to talk of strategic planning as distinct from comprehensive planning.

The shift in language gave rise to cynicism among many, especially the priests, who accused Futrell of reinventing the wheel. Nonetheless, he returned to Louisbourg a learned disciple of strategic planning. In a very significant way, Futrell became a recognized internal change agent, albeit one a little suspect because of his fervor after the management program.

Bishop Futrell identified strategic planning as "a process of making choices based on a unique mission within the context of specified financial and human resources to maximize the impact of our presence." His hope for the planning process was that change could occur both structurally and pastorally at the diocesan level, at the deanery level, and at the parish level. He knew at the outset that winning the support of the clergy would be difficult. Because he had come from within their ranks, he needed to prove himself as a leader.

He was also aware that the priests would likely make attempts to sabotage the efforts of outside consultants whom they perceived as "elitist and uninformed of the real state of affairs in the region." But Bishop Futrell made his intentions clear to the deaneries when he stated, "We must throw out the antiquated, bring on the needed, and insist on accountability."

Based on the recommendations of Fairhurst's initial assessment of the diocese, Bishop Futrell began a three-part study of how best to go about planning in the diocese. First, the bishop consulted with his advisors and the presbyterial council. Second, equipped with an overall understanding of alternate approaches to planning and with a growing sense of the needs he intended to address, the bishop and an aide visited the leaders of three other dioceses with reputations for effective planning in order to learn about their successes and failures.

Third, the bishop appointed and convened a 13-member planning design committee, which later became the steering committee, composed of seven lay members from the diocese, a woman religious, two priests selected from the presbyterial council, the vicar-general, the chancellor, and himself. This committee was charged with the task of preparing the proposal, which ultimately received funding, to the foundation outlining the purposes of, and approach to, planning for the diocese.

Despite the bishop's strong determination to promote change within the system, overall he lacked adequate and competent support staff for the project. He did name his vicar-general, Fr. David Austin, to direct the planning process. Fr. Austin, a bright, articulate, and gentle man, was known as a troubleshooter. Many of his assignments had been to parishes in the diocese that were riddled with conflict or disarray. In addition, his work as vice-chancellor and then as vicar-general prepared him for increasingly complex responsibilities in the diocese.

As director of the planning process, the goals Fr. Austin established were: (1) assess the needs of the diocese composed of 10,000 square miles, 1 million people, 8 to 9 percent of whom are Catholic, 115 priests with a median age of 42, and a chasm between their liberal and conservative ideologies and (2) examine the mission and identity of parishes as they will exist in five years, and determine which parishes should be expanded or consolidated, how finances should be managed, how evangelization might occur, and how education can be conducted. Fairhurst remarked that Austin's goals were not necessarily entirely reinforcing of the direction set by the bishop.

Chambers emphasized that throughout the planning process, Fr. Austin was solicitous about doing all he could. Yet, his loyalty to the bishop and his constant offers to help covered the fact that he did not want the job. In Chambers's words:

> He seemed chronically tired—he sometimes dozed off at meetings and always looked ashen. He became agitated whenever he heard rumors of clergy discontent with the process or whenever a key diocesan decision-making body like the clergy council or the finance committee questioned in the least some aspect of the planning process. He did not leave us with the impression that Austin could take charge of a process as complex and potentially explosive as strategic planning.

According to Chambers, two factors strongly influenced the relationship of Fairhurst to both the bishop and Fr. Austin: Fairhurst's consulting style and his image of the bishop and Austin. According to Chambers, "Fairhurst's style could be characterized as spontaneous. Often, no one but himself knew the steering committee agendas." Chambers was confused about this at first. "I felt guilty that I was not doing more to prepare for the meetings. I expressed to Fairhurst my eagerness to help, but still, I was rarely given agendas. I came to understand that Fairhurst does not prepare agendas far in advance. He works alone and thinks on his feet, expecting little from others."

Second, the consultants were both of the opinion that the bishop and Austin were not in touch with the total flow of the planning process (i.e., the gestalt, the big picture). In fact, the consultants spent almost eight months explaining the process and defining terms for the bishop, Austin, and the steering committee. Chambers remarked, "Few of these people ever understood the whole planning process in such a way that they were able to guide it."

Consequently, the primary consultant filled the internal leadership vacuum, rode with the bishop's trust, and took charge of the process in consultation with the bishop. The consultant often took tasks onto himself that in other settings he would have left to others within the organization, such as the environmental scan and the chairing of the steering committee meetings. Because the bishop had been so impressed with Fairhurst during the management program, he easily deferred to his expertise and status. In some ways, he realized he was getting more from the contract than he had bargained for and this seemed acceptable.

THE PLANNING PROCESS

The proposal, written largely by Fairhurst and discussed by the planning design committee, highlighted specific choices about the church's role in education and social services, the allocation of resources, leadership training, new structures for governing and advisory bodies, and a renewed sense of ownership and direction among the parishes of the diocese and their members with regard to specific priorities for action in the diocese through the early 1990s.

The purposes of the planning project were:

1. To reflect on the security, identity, and support the church and church membership give to the people of the diocese today.
2. To create a new sense of expectation about membership in the church—specifically about what it means to be a Catholic today.
3. To teach the people of the diocese to assess and meet each other's needs and the community's needs as part of their Christian discipleship.
4. To teach the people of the diocese to be "convicted" to the values of the Gospel and to live them in the Catholic and sacramental tradition.

In addition to the purposes outlined in the proposal, the committee also generated a list of some 220 ideas suggesting areas for investigation. Out of this list, the committee selected several priority issues including:

1. The need to create a vision and an integrated sense of direction to guide choices for the future of the diocese.
2. The need to foster a sense of history and tradition within the church without getting stuck in that history.
3. The need to formulate an effective response to the different levels of faith development and to the educational and leadership needs in the diocese and its parishes.
4. The need to implement a planning and decision-making process in the diocese that counters the sense that each parish and agency operates as an independent business unit and generates a sense that it is part of a local church composed of many unique but interdependent units.
5. A desire to learn to be more businesslike as an aid, not an obstacle, to the spiritual mission of the church.

In September 1985, the foundation approved the funding of the project, and the planning design committee was designated as the steering committee. With Bishop Futrell, this committee would oversee the project. The diocesan chancery and agency staff were organized to provide support services.

Bishop Futrell inaugurated the major planning effort at the 1985 Chrism Mass held during Holy Week and attended by priests and people from every area of the diocese. In that address, he described both his perception of his leadership role and his vision of the church, which he labeled *Model B*.

> In Model B, the Church is the People of God. Jesus calls each member of the Church to take an active role in his mission. It is primarily in the parish community that all this happens. That is where God's People are challenged to say to themselves, "What would Jesus do? What does Jesus want us to be and to do in our community?" The bishop's role in this model as I envision it is to teach the word of God, to preside over Christian worship, to choose and direct helpers in the ministry, and to discern the special gifts that the Spirit gives his people.
>
> A diocesan pastoral center and the bishop's staff, in Model B, would exist primarily to strengthen parish life, to help and support pastors (and parish pastoral teams) to call forth, validate, and train people in ministry. Model B is not the one presently existing in the local Diocese of Louisbourg. Our current model, as I see it, I will call it Model A, reflects an ecclesiology which emphasizes the hierarchical and institutional character of the church. In this model, there is great stress on the role of the bishop. The bishop is regarded as an administrator, a builder, a fund-raiser, as one who gives permission, makes assignments, sends out directives, settles all arguments, brings the calm of peace to situations. In Model A, the Chancery is the center of the diocese.

There frequently is a feeling by many pastors, and to some extent among other people in the diocese, that the diocesan offices are big bureaucracies cranking out all kinds of programs and laying them on the back of already overworked parish staffs. Pastors, generally, have one goal in Model A: cut off the funds so such bureaucracies will go away and leave them alone. My vision is to somehow take us from Model A into Model B. I admit that as I strive to develop an ecclesiology described in Model B that my feet are planted in our present model, Model A. One does not walk out of "set" concrete easily. It is my prayer that down the road you will find yourself sharing my excitement and that the end result will not be "mine" but "ours."

The bishop's cooperative intentions met their first test in a meeting with the consultants and presbyterial council. The chief consultant proposed a strategic planning format that would be steered by a committee of representative priests and laity. According to the bishop, "Ultimately, the presbyterial council accepted the proposal presented so convincingly by Fairhurst, but this decision was, in hindsight, one of our biggest mistakes; people were selected because they were representative rather than because they were leaders."

Similarly, combined clergy and laity task forces were established to study major concerns. Although each member of the steering committee also served as a member of a task force, the chairpersons of the task forces were selected from the other members. "The lack of role clarity for the chairs and little coordination between the steering committee and the task forces created major difficulties in the process," according to the bishop. "It seemed one consultant worked with the steering committee and the other worked with the task forces." According to the consultants, the plan involved each consultant facilitating a discrete part of the process. Accordingly, it made sense to them to divide their labor between the steering committee and the task forces.

"There was no lack of communication between the task forces and the steering committee, but there was a lack of leadership," according to Chambers. He was constantly in touch, over the telephone and through the mail, with the chairpersons. He attended all of the meetings of one task force and most of the meetings of another that asked him to attend because of leadership problems. A third task force was having leadership conflict and required several phone consultations for each meeting.

From Chambers's perspective, the problems sensed by the task forces stemmed not from the lack of contact but from the very selection process for membership on the committee and the task forces. Neither was chosen on the basis of tested competency. Chambers said, "The steering committee was representational in nature and the task force leaders were selected with the help of local pastors whose assessments of their nominees were uncritically accepted by Austin."

According to Chambers, two of the task force chairpersons were incapable of effective leadership. Their groups were torn by dissent and misunderstanding. "In at least two cases," said Chambers, "the steering committee members on the task forces further exacerbated the problems by getting emotionally involved and taking sides with one or another faction." Bishop Futrell wondered if "perhaps the consultants weren't talking with each other on some of these matters."

Fr. Austin observed that although he was the coordinator of the planning process, only the consultants seemed to know where the process was headed. "I never felt the consultants trusted me . . . and they may have been right." By the end of the process, Austin concluded the consultants did not trust him to coordinate the process but they could choose not to confront the issue.

Austin believed the steering committee was "appointed in-house from the chancery." The steering committee nominated members to the task forces on the basis of, in his opinion, an individual's expertise in the area of concern. In his perception, the mandate to the task forces was unclear, and the result was that the steering committee and the task forces developed overlapping interests and agendas.

Even though steering committee members had been assigned to the task forces, he commented, "There were never any reports from the task forces to the steering committee. Reporting from both the task forces and the consultants was generally behind schedule, and this put me in the position of covering up for them." According to Chambers, the task forces submitted extensive reports to the steering committee that were never evaluated in a critical manner. Consequently, their input had little effect on the outcomes of the process.

DATA GATHERING

The theoretical design of the planning process set forth by the consultants is depicted in Exhibit 1. Since Bishop Futrell had studied the model in the management program, he understood each of the components.

Once accepting the model, the steering committee established four major strategies to gather data for the planning process. These included:

1. A portrait of the diocese.
2. A profile of the diocese.
3. A diocesan assembly.
4. A convocation of the bishop and all the priests.

From September 1985 through May 1986, the committee's primary energies were focused on developing a strategic history of the Diocese of Louisbourg. Two kinds of information were incorporated into this strategic history: (1) a portrait, fashioned from interviews and some written documents, of the life and service of the diocese and its people and (2) a profile consisting of specific statistical data about the current status and trends of the diocese's resources, its parishes, and instrumentalities.

EXHIBIT 1 Strategic Planning (A schematic outline)

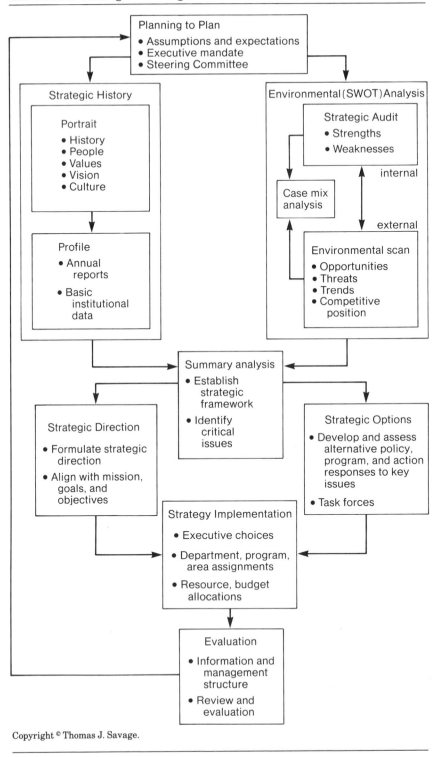

The portrait was not meant to be a complete or comprehensive documentation of the diocese. It involved rather a qualitative method to generate a narrative impression of the diocese—its people, their values, the geography of the area, and the strengths and weaknesses of the diocese. The portrait attempted to reveal not only a historical and cultural perspective, but also the feelings associated with membership in the organization. The portrait was ultimately published in tabloid form and distributed to every Catholic household and institution in the diocese.

The profile was intended for use as background information and to provide a context for the work of the task forces. It called attention to key events, decisions, and actions of the past that have shaped the diocese. The profile also included a detailed financial analysis performed by a financial consultant hired by the Newport Group. Finally, the profile pointed to specific changes and challenges that should be taken into account in planning for the future.

To construct the portrait, members of the steering committee proposed to conduct over 100 interviews of people in the diocese recommended by pastors and members of the committee. The interview sample was not chosen randomly. The selection process was, however, designed to ensure that a variety of voices and multiple perspectives would be incorporated into the portrait. The narrative was developed from both tapes and typed summaries of the interviews by Fairhurst and reviewed in several drafts by members of the steering committee.

Although Fr. Austin takes pride in the outcome of the portrait process, he worries that too much of the agenda and ultimately the plan itself came out of the portrait.

> We only interviewed about half the number we intended to see, and of those I interviewed 50 percent of them. I know I colored perceptions. We did the best we could in the four-month period, and, surprisingly, I think the portrait is fairly reliable except that members of religious orders and rural parishes are underrepresented.

According to Fairhurst, Austin only interviewed about 25 percent of those required to complete the portrait. Fairhurst did substantially more interviews than Austin. Fairhurst also took responsibility for condensing the data into the final form. In his opinion, Austin did not unduly influence the interpretation.

To construct the profile of the diocese, specific statistical data were compiled by Fairhurst with the assistance of the financial consultant. Interviews of all of the diocesan personnel resulted in two reports: "Financial Analysis of the Diocese of Louisbourg" and "Viable Structures for the Diocese of Louisbourg: A Report to the Bishop." Key financial indicators and financial goals were identified (see Appendix A).

From the results of the portrait interviews, the steering committee surfaced the diocesan issues that seemed most pertinent for analysis. By May 1986, the issues were clearly outlined and task forces chosen. In

June, an overnight training session was held for the chairpersons and co-chairpersons of the five task forces.

The task forces were established to consider the following major themes:

1. Renewal of Catholic identity.
2. Parishes, priests, and people.
3. Viable structures of accountability.
4. Christian service in the modern world.
5. A strategy for finances.

From September 1986 through February 1987, the Steering Committee monitored the task forces and planned the diocesan assembly. The assembly, part three of the planning process, was held in February 1987. It was attended by over 400 people, including most of the diocesan clergy, the task forces, and randomly chosen people from the diocese.

Resistance to both the plan and the process was strong among the priests. They refused to break into small groups with the laity to discuss the plan. Nonetheless, the assembly offered reactions to the diocesan portrait, the profile, and the proposals of the five task forces. After the assembly, the task forces reconsidered their proposals in light of the assembly recommendations and submitted these to the steering committee. In June 1987, the final recommendations were submitted to the priests of the diocese at a four-day clergy convocation.

The clergy convocation was the first time the priests of the diocese met independently to review the results of the planning process. There was a high degree of frustration and a low degree of investment in the process at that point. According to Bishop Futrell, "The priests did not own either the mission statement written by Tom Fairhurst or the outcomes of the task forces." The priests had generally viewed their role in the structure of the church as pivotal to ideas and progress since they are responsible for implementing any innovations in their respective parishes.

The only planning issue in the convocation to instill any enthusiasm was the concept of the renewal of Catholic identity. Underneath the enthusiasm around this question, the bishop suspected that "At the heart of the issue is the role of the priest in this constantly evolving church. Perhaps their dissatisfaction was really an effort to acknowledge their own pain at the losses of power and prestige they had encountered in recent years."

Fr. Austin viewed the convocation somewhat differently. For him, it was a turning point in the planning process. Among other things, the priests seemed to value the fraternity expressed in being together. He saw some value in their being able to express their feelings to the bishop and to one another. In the course of the convocation, they began to see certain programs as necessary to the diocese, and they softened their aggressive edge. In his view, the most important outcome was that "the bishop went into the convocation as chancellor and came out as bishop."

PRINCIPLES OF ORGANIZATION

In addition to the qualitative information presented in the portrait and the quantitative results presented in the profile, an environmental analysis was undertaken to consider how both internal and external factors to the diocese would likely influence the future. The environmental assessment highlighted what reasonable assumptions might guide the decision making and implementation process over a five- to seven-year period. Operative strengths and weaknesses were then delineated to bound the strategic choices available to the diocese (see Appendix B).

The steering committee built its strategic direction for the Diocese of Louisbourg from the various data sources, particularly the task force reports. Subsequently, strategies and goals for achieving each objective were established. Exhibit 2 summarizes the plan.

In order to support the strategic direction set forth in the plan, the steering committee established three principles to ensure that the structure of the diocese would support the strategic objectives.

Principle 1.   Deaneries: The proposed structure of the diocese was intended to reflect the bishop's desire to decentralize the governance of the church by encouraging the local church as the people of God gathered around the bishop in local communities, primarily parishes (Exhibit 3). The local clusters of churches would be organized by deaneries. Each area was asked to evaluate the configuration of parishes that met the criteria of viability and to propose realignment where necessary. At least one deanery would be composed of special ministries and would be represented in the deanery structure of the diocese.

Principle 2.   Pastoral services: Within the office of the bishop, all pastoral services and programs would be organized under pastoral offices accountable to the bishop (Exhibit 4). The cabinet would be composed of the vicar-general, the chancellor, and the heads of the five pastoral offices. The pastoral offices would have both service and regulatory functions.

Principle 3.   Bishop's advisory groups: The bishop would receive advice from four groups: consultors, the finance committee, the presbyterial council, and the strategic planning committee.

At the end of June, the steering committee held its final meeting, most of which was spent discussing a proposed organizational chart for the diocese. Later that summer, the principal consultant handed the bishop a document titled, "A Strategic Discovery Process for the Diocese of Louisbourg: Providing Recommendations for Diocesan Activities into

EXHIBIT 2 Strategic Directions (Diocese of Louisbourg)

Objective I
RENEWAL
Call the people of the Local Church to a renewed Catholic identity through outgoing personal conversion.

Strategies

1.1 Implement the RCIA in every parish.
1.2 Implement the Renew Program in the diocese by Fall 1990.
1.3 Communicate a broad awareness of Mission, Values, and Objectives.

Tactics and Goals

1.1.1 Provide opportunities for ongoing education of clergy and laity in RCIA.
1.2.4 Form parish Rewew teams for implementation on the parochial level.
1.3.1 Utilize *The Sunday Visitor* as the primary tool to communicate the Mission, Values, and Objectives of the Local Church.

Objective II
OUTREACH
Reach out to our inactive and unchurched brothers and sisters and those in need

Strategies

2.1 Devise processes for evangelizing the inactive, unchurched, and those searching for full communion in the Catholic Church.
2.2 Educate the baptized to their responsibilities in the ministry of peace and justice.
2.3 Encourage the people of God to live out their baptismal call through the active practice of the corporal and spiritual works of mercy.

Tactics and Goals

2.1.1 Facilitate the establishment of an Evangelization Team in every parish for the purpose of identifying and serving inactive Catholics and the unchurched.
2.2.2 Raise social consciousness and a sense of Christian responsibility through and annual observance in every parish, appropriate to the liturgy of the day.
2.2.3 Investigate the possibility of selecting a Sister Diocese from a Third World country.
2.3.3 Encourage the establishment of parish social ministry committees and work with existing committees to identify and respond to parish social needs.

Objective III
VIABLE PARISHES
Build up and sustain parishes

Strategies

3.1 Develop an understanding of the term *viable parish.*
3.2 Peovide meaningful liturgy (Mass, Sacraments, Para-liturgies) in every Catholic Faith Community.
3.3 Provide formation and education for all members, young and old.
3.4 Enhance proper pastoral ministry and management.

Tactics and Goals

3.1.4 Conduct self-study in each parish.
3.2.1 Establish Pastoral Office for Worship and Adult Formation and delineate areas of responsibility, including RCIA, liturgy, Renew, evangelization and adult education.
3.3.1 Establish Pastoral Office fot Youth Formation and delineate responsibilities.
3.4.1 Develop models and guidelines for parish finance councils and parish pastoral councils.

Objective IV
STEWARDSHIP
Exercise responsible stewardship of human and financial resources

Strategies

4.1 Enhance effective organization of diocesan structures.
4.2 Provide for development of diocesan personnel.
4.3 Improve stewardship of financial resources.
4.4 Develop additional sources of funding for diocesan programs based on priorities identified through planning.

Tactics and Goals

4.1.1 Define primary roles and responsibilities of all diocesan offices.
4.2.1 Formulate and implement an effective procedure for due process.
4.2.2 Formulate and implement a pilot performance appraisal system for lay personnel.
4.3.1 Establish a Christian value- driven diocesan investment policy commensurate with good stewardship.
4.4.1 Appoint a Director of Development to formulate and implement a comprehensive development plan for the diocese.

EXHIBIT 3   Structure of the Local Church

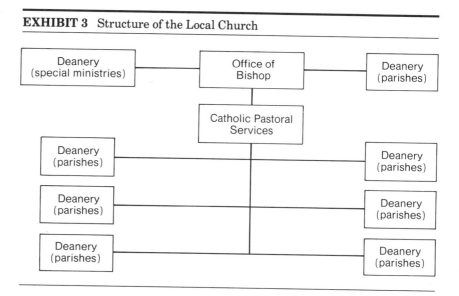

the Early 1990s." This document contained the recommendations emerging from the planning process as expressed by the main consultant. Both the foundation grant to support the planning process and the consultant contract expired simultaneously without any definitive implementation plans.

Bishop Futrell was generally satisfied with many of the outcomes of the process. In particular, he believed he had assimilated the role as leader of the diocese as a result of the planning process. He remarked, "Now the task is to drive the plan down to the ranks." His initial statement that "I have no sacred cows" was reconsidered shortly after the conclusion of the planning process when, after disbanding the personnel placement board, he assumed sole responsibility for the placement of priests.

Apart from the planning process, Bishop Futrell had envisioned an innovative funding campaign to eliminate parish taxes and assessments. The "Fruitful Harvest Campaign" was established as a biannual drive that guaranteed the local churches would benefit from any excess of revenue produced after the specific goal for a parish had been met. The formula for the fund drive was based on parish income as a percentage of total parish income in the diocese and parish membership as a percentage of total diocesan membership. A parish would receive a 10 percent rebate if it met its goal, and the diocese would do a 50–50 split if it exceeded its goal.

The bishop initiated this innovation immediately, rather than wait for the implementation phase of planning to suggest a time line. He believed the campaign represented the view of the church that he had been

EXHIBIT 4 Organization of Pastoral Offices

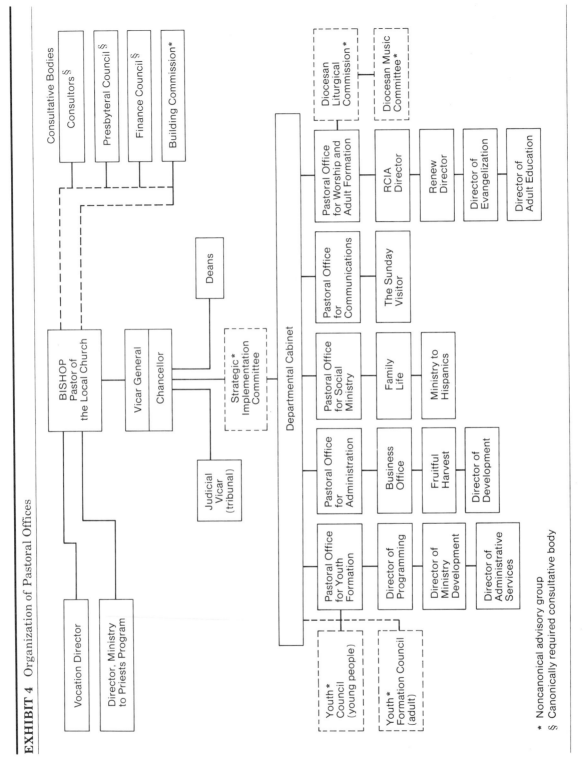

* Noncanonical advisory group
§ Canonically required consultative body

attempting to instill since he first contrasted his Model B style of leadership with the Model A style. With the campaign in progress, the major
issue facing him was how to construct an implementation plan that
would motivate his middle managers, the priests of the diocese.

QUESTIONS FOR DISCUSSION

1. In what ways did the consultants help or hinder the organizational
   development project? Did their leadership to the various constituencies in the process, especially the bishop, further the ends set out by
   the bishop?
2. How effective was the strategic planning framework as an organization development intervention? What other interventions could have
   assisted the organization in its desire for development?
3. What other techniques might have been employed to resolve the interpersonal tension between the chancery staff and the parish
   priests?
4. What should be the role of middle managers, in this case the priests,
   in any strategic planning and implementation processes?
5. What type of implementation plan might effectively promote the conclusions of the planning process? What factors will most influence
   the middle managers' willingness to cooperate? How can they make
   a significant contribution to the implementation process?
6. Design an implementation process that includes the strategy you
   would use with the group, a chronology of events, the key players,
   activities, and measures by which you will measure the success or
   failure of the process.

APPENDIX A

Key Indicators and Financial Goals:
For Actual and Projected Years as Specified

	Actual			Annual Compound Growth %
	1985	1986	1987	1982–87
Key indicators for diocese				
Total population	1,065,000	1,065,000	1,019,946	(.9)
Catholic population	90,253	89,730	88,795	.5
Catholic % of population	8.47%	8.42%	8.71%	.8
Total baptisms	2,101	2,066	1,986	4.1
Number of parishes	64	63	61	—
Number of missions	2	3	3	—
Total diocesan priests	92	87	90	1.4
Total religious	145	145	159	.1
Total lay teachers	267	283	254	5.5
Support and revenue (000s)				
Fruitful Harvest Campaign	1,339	2,600	1,764	—
Gifts & bequests	55	62	113	(3.6)
Dividend & interest income	699	826	666	.5
Managed property	79	73	217	—
Insurance assessment	135	111	137	3.1
Publications	155	182	192	11.8
Fees & misc.	20	29	91	—
Support & revenue total	2,482	3,883	3,180	9.3
Deductions (000s)				
Program services				
Parish revenue sharing	132	946	140	—
Social services	495	349	598	—
Pastoral	70	76	95	—
National catholic org.	148	130	143	12.8
Publications	131	192	215	26.6
Education	114	164	149	9.9
Support services				
General & administrative	370	348	362	16.8
Managed properties	104	62	56	—
Development	175	98	126	—
Depreciation	74	100	137	21.4
Interest expense	11	9	5	(18.6)
Deductions total	1,824	2,474	2,026	2.6
Change in fund balances (000s)	675	1,407	1,154	—

	Projected				Annual Compound Growth %
1988	1989	1990	1991	1992	1987–92
1,010,000	1,000,000	990,000	980,000	975,930	(.9)
89,000	89,500	90,000	90,500	91,000	.5
8.8%	8.9%	9.0%	9.2%	9.3%	1.3
2,050	2,225	2,300	2,400	2,428	4.1
61	61	62	62	63	—
3	3	3	3	3	—
89	88	87	86	85	(1.1)
150	145	140	135	130	(3.9)
260	270	275	280	290	2.7
1,700	1,300	2,000	1,400	2,000	2.5
80	90	120	130	150	5.8
670	680	690	700	710	1.3
75	75	80	80	80	—
180	190	200	150	150	3.3
325	350	360	360	370	14.0
90	95	100	105	110	3.9
3,120	2,780	3,550	2,925	3,570	2.3
600	150	600	150	650	—
675	725	775	790	810	6.3
180	225	260	275	310	17.7
160	170	180	190	200	6.9
322	350	370	390	410	13.8
185	195	205	215	225	8.6
320	350	360	375	380	1.0
65	70	70	70	70	4.6
150	100	130	150	170	6.2
165	250	275	300	330	19.2
6	8	8	10	10	14.9
2,828	2,593	3,233	2,915	3,560	11.9
292	187	317	10	10	—

APPENDIX B

Environmental Assessment

Demographics. The demographic indicators for the 24-county region suggested that by 1990 the population will be approximately 1.1 million with the only significant increases in population to one region known for its fertile land. Overall, the elderly population will remain over the national average (approximately 12 percent of the total in 1982), while the number of children under the age of 18 will remain close to the national average (approximately 27 percent in 1982 and declining since then). The percentage of people who are Catholic in the region will remain under 10 percent through 1990. The income level, political affiliation, and cultural identities of the 24 counties will continue to make the diocese an amalgam of heterogeneous communities. The geographic dimensions of the diocese will remain the same.

The rural and farm economies of the respective counties are likely to continue to struggle against manufacturing decline in the region, farming foreclosures, and foreign competition. At the same time, the preference for local services and the prospects for economic development partnerships with several Japanese companies give reason to hope to many of the smaller communities.

Although the number of citizens of the counties represented who completed high school exceeded the national average by 9 percent in 1980, those who completed four or more years of college is well below the national average. It is anticipated that family values and structures will be reinforced at the same time that the number of people living outside traditional family structures and single-parent families will increase. Similarly, the region anticipates divorce rates that exceed the national average.

Within the church itself, lay participation will only increase, and women will assume increasingly significant positions of leadership at both the parish and diocesan levels. Priests will be required to collaborate in nearly every way in the leadership and management of the parish. Until lay roles are more clearly negotiated and specified, the church will expect confusion and some conflict within pastoral settings.

Organizational concerns, such as diocesan structures, personnel, and resource distribution, will dominate over the more strategic concerns such as the development of an apostolic spirituality for the laity and continued renewal of the sacramental life of the church.

Parish life will continue to focus on the traditional family unit even though fewer Catholics in the region will be living in such settings. The percentage of people "unchurched" in the diocese will remain above the national average.

Organizational strengths. The diocese has an energetic and well-informed bishop who willingly leads with strong initiatives and an invitation to others to continue the renewal begun with Vatican II. A strong core of priests and laity committed to service in the geographically dispersed region presents significant opportunities for local leadership and innovation. The relatively malleable chancery organization could be altered to serve the specifically identified needs of the population. The chancery staff is reasonably balanced between long-term employees who know the traditions and the history of the diocese and those who are newer appointees who bring a fresh perspective. The diocese presents a relatively stable financial picture.

Organizational weaknesses. The identity of the diocese springs more from the discrete parish units than from any corporate or "regional" understanding. The governance structure of the diocese and the success of any parish unit has been typically tied to the bishop or the local priest respectively. This personalist style has led to leadership transition difficulties and to program uncertainty. Without management policies to assist in planning, budgeting, and personnel evaluation, little consistency can be found in the operating units of the diocese. Since most parishes view themselves as independent units, most parish financial records remain unaudited, and some communities fail to see the validity of the overhead administrative costs of the chancery.

Task force conclusions. The steering committee had appointed task forces to study the five areas of concern using the various sources of data, including the portrait, the profile, environmental analysis, and financial data. The steering committee received its recommendations and from them established the strategic priorities for the diocese. The steering committee report was eventually distilled into four areas for strategic development. Exhibit 2 indicates the organization of their recommendations according to strategic objectives, strategies, and goals.

The CAMIDS Group (A):
Sociotechnological Intervention *

Barry Bateman
Block-Petrella-Weisbord

Jerry's impossible. Ever since he took over, he's been on this centralization kick. We've worked hard to make CAMIDS into something more than just a word-processing department. We have capabilities that we never had before or that any publications group here has. We have our own clients who come to us directly. Now they want us to give up what we've accomplished and receive all of our work from technical writers and editors. Most of those turkeys don't even know how to spell. Their idea of a good time is to keep us busy trying to read their scribbling. And this whole idea of reorganization—we've been reorganized twice already. They treat us like we're replaceable parts or just another piece of equipment. Sometimes I don't think it's worth it. I've been thinking about giving it up.

It was a snowy winter's day in 1981, typical for the upper Midwest. I was having lunch with one of my internal clients. Susan was a supervisor of CAMIDS, a group of computer operators at SIG Corporation's Computer Systems Division. The CSD produces computers for the government and is schedule driven; consequently CAMIDS, as a support organization, was always under pressure for quick turnaround times.

The more we talked, the more apparent it was that Susan was trying to keep her people motivated while her own spirits were sagging. Jerry was Susan's new boss, who now reported to Jim, the head of the newly constituted Documentation Services organization, to which Susan and her group now belonged. Both Jim and Jerry were promoted as a result

*The author wishes to gratefully acknowledge the encouragement and help of Dr. Charles Manz, Bower Research Fellow, Harvard University, without which this case would probably not have been written.

of the reorganization and were in total support of the move toward greater centralization of the division's publishing services. Susan, on the other hand, was concerned about many things, not the least of which were the effects of the recent reorganization on her people and of a brewing conflict with Phil, a manager of 30 technical writers and editors in a separate Publication Services group, which was now to "give them work to do."

CAMIDS had originally been part of Engineering Services, intended to provide document production services to design engineers and programmers. The group was now being absorbed into the larger Documentation Services organization; eventually all word-processing services in the division were to be consolidated under one organization. Exhibit 1 shows an organizational chart of the newly constituted Documentation Services organization in early 1981.

I worked in the division as an internal consultant. I was originally assigned to work with Susan's small group of 15, helping them form a problem-solving group known as an action team, similar in intent to a quality circle. My formal entry was as an action team coach.

As an internal consultant, I viewed the action team process as a way to help management learn to let go of decisions and problems that could be better handled by work groups. At the same time, work groups would learn group problem-solving and decision-making skills and begin to ex-

EXHIBIT 1   The Newly Constituted Documentation Services Organization in 1981

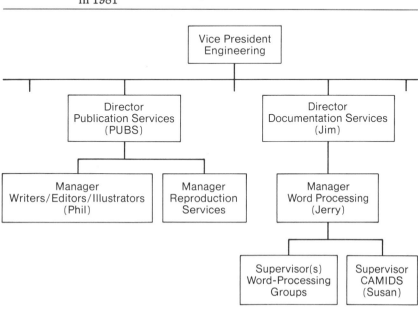

ert some control over their lives at work. Since becoming an action team was a voluntary activity, the teams also seemed to be excellent vehicles for identifying and gaining quick entry into work groups that were ready for change.

Susan had been trained as an action team leader, and we had been working for about six months identifying, defining, and addressing problems the group had. The group was made up of 13 women and 2 men. They were well regarded by the engineers, and their reputation for responsiveness and superior service had attracted more and more work, both within and beyond the engineering department.

The charts they produced were becoming a standard in presentations by many of the division's most influential managers. Program Management and Marketing, two key and powerful functions within the division, were CAMIDS customers. As a result, CAMIDS was getting a lot of visibility and took special pride in the work even though the work was repetitious and boring.

Before the reorganization, the group had formed an identity of its own. Susan, who had been an operator before becoming the group's supervisor, was committed to preserving as much of that identity as possible. Also high on her list was maintaining the relative autonomy the group enjoyed.

The new reorganization, among other things, threatened the group's sense of itself, and the members were struggling to hold on to what they had. For now, they were still together as CAMIDS, a small group in the larger Documentation Services organization. Eventually, if things continued in the same direction, they would become part of a group of 50 word-processing employees, all of whom would receive their work from technical writers and editors. This was seen as more efficient than receiving work directly from the larger CSD organization and its many departments.

"Susan, how can I help?" (a standard, somewhat worn out, but still useful question to be asked by a consultant at this point in a discussion).

I don't know. I don't know if anybody can help. It's more complex than Jerry's obsession with centralization. We have some personality conflicts going on too. I just can't seem to communciate with Phil, and the Publication Services group in general is a problem for us. I think he sees us as being in a battle for territories and all of a sudden we're a threat. Combining us with Word Processing is also a problem. We do a lot of word processing ourselves, but most of the word-processing groups have been decentralized, so there really hasn't been a problem. Now, with the reorg, we'll have clear overlaps. Also, I think centralization is the wrong way to go. We started out centralized, then we decentralized for a few years, and now we're centralizing again. It just doesn't make sense.

Up to that point, I had been working with Susan and her group to identify their problems. It seemed they were getting more clear about them and were growing in their ability to work as a group. Yet what she had just revealed about how she and her group felt about the reorganization had the potential of blocking their progress. As we talked, it seemed to me something needed to be done that would help her and her group deal with the conflicts they were having.

Schooled in the traditional organizational development belief that communication was at the heart of all problems, I offered to facilitate a meeting with Phil and then, if necessary, Jerry and Jim or all of them together. The presence of a third party usually has several effects. One is that it makes everyone extremely uncomfortable, sometimes to the point that they will do almost anything not to have to repeat the exercise and so are more motivated to work their issues. Second, the consultant may, on a rare occasion, actually make a contribution that will make a difference—help clarify, offer options, help people listen to each other, provide a safer, more open environment, and so on.

Unfortunately, it is not always easy to arrange. A consultant can't usually just call a meeting so others can work through their problems. In this case, I had a contract to help only one party, Susan and her group. I lacked a direct relationship with Jim, Jerry, and Phil. The definition of my role as a coach to CAMIDS limited how I could behave in my relationship to Jim, Jerry, and Phil. While it was expected that I would help CAMIDS with its problems, there was no expectation or desire on Jim's part for me to begin working with other departments of the Documentation Services organization. Until I was called in to help what was essentially a new client group (i.e., Susan, Jerry, and Phil), by either them as a group or by their boss, the engineering vice president, my hands were tied.

One option was to bring in an external consultant. I had been an external consultant before joining the company and so was aware of the advantages an external consultant would have, particularly in getting Jim and Jerry on Susan's side long enough to deal with some of their problems.

As an internal consultant, I had the advantage of living day-to-day in the organization and thus had a better feel for what would work or not work. Also, I had more information on how decisions were made and who made them. On the other hand, I was also part of the system—I had probably lost my ability to see things clearly after the first two months. Also, conventional wisdom among many managers in organizations would say that relying on an internal consultant to help deal with departmental rivalry and conflict is risky business—"you never know for sure whose interests they are representing: yours, the organization's, or their own. While an external may not understand how we do things around here, at least you know whose side they're on (and who pays their bill)."

While bringing in an external consultant may have helped, organizational norms prevented me from seriously considering this option. Internal consultants were expected to do the consulting. If you needed to bring in someone, it meant you weren't doing your job. Also, I was personally stumped about how to get someone in when only one party was willing to work on the issues. I felt ethically bound not to go directly to Jim unless it was OK with Susan, which at that point it wasn't.

The other option was for Susan to talk to Jim and Phil *directly* about the issues she was concerned about, suggesting some changes needed to occur. After we talked it over, Susan agreed to try it. I also let her know I would be available to help her develop a plan for the meetings. A few days later we met again and talked about her options. The plan that emerged from our discussion was simple: she would meet with each of them individually, talk about the problems she saw, and then, if she felt it was appropriate, suggest I be brought in to help. If necessary, I would come in and help save them from themselves and each other and everyone would live happily ever after.

Susan met with Jerry and Phil independently, as planned. They both gave the idea of change about three minutes' consideration, and each decided the notion was absurd. As far as they were concerned, these were normal problems in all reorganizations and time would take care of them. Jerry told Susan not to worry about it. Her focus should be in getting her people to do their work and make sure they didn't get into areas that "weren't their concern." Besides, there was a plan to move them to a new work area, so "there will be less likelihood of people fighting with each other."

Susan returned to her office bruised but not beaten. Eventually, 15 (mostly female) CAMIDS operators and 35 word-processing operators (all female, all with less than five years' and most with less than two years' seniority) were relocated to the basement of a three-story building housing approximately 5,000 other division employees.

The Publication Services people, editors, technical writers, and illustrators (50 employees, all male with an average 15 years' seniority), stayed on the top floor of the building, "so they could be close to engineering and other professionals." Other word-processing groups were still spread out in other buildings the company owned because of a lack of space in the large building and because executives in the smaller locations thought they needed in-house support.

No one had given much thought to work flow except that all work should be given to word processors by the editors, illustrators, or technical writers. CAMIDS operators and the word-processing operators, the lowest-paid employees of the Documentation Services division, were simply told to find a way to work it out. Susan and her group were left feeling helpless, down, and a little more angry. The problems mentioned before were still not solved. CAMIDS continued to take work directly from its outside customers, Program Management and Marketing. Work from editors and technical writers was changed by word processors, usually for the better, but this continued to upset the professionals. The enhanced computer technology went essentially unused, besides, "in a year or two we'll be replacing it with something else."

A NEW FOCUS

With one failed attempt to make order out of chaos under our belts, Susan and I talked about what to do next. As an internal consultant, I had little positional power at that time, except that I could cross organizational lines. I didn't know Jim, Jerry, or Phil well enough to influence them and could see no clear way to approach the subject without violating Susan's need for confidentiality. She clearly preferred that I "not fight her battles for her," and I had no wish to do so. I also had 15 other action teams to think about and was about to become involved in a "cultural change" effort directed by our CEO. My time was becoming someone else's. Susan felt rebuffed and put down by her meetings with Jerry and Phil but still wanted to do something.

We finally returned to the list of 150 problems the group had generated in action team meetings, and we noted that most of them, beyond the relationship issues already discussed, seemed to originate outside of Documentation Services.

Action teams were only given the charter and the tools to deal with problems they had direct control over. The problem-solving process was a seven-step method with specific tools that were to be used by the teams. To say the process was rigid was an understatement. Also, it was clear there was a lack of fit between the problem-solving tools and CAMIDS's situation. Since the director of the action team program thought it was important for all teams to be using the same set of tools, artificial barriers prevented me from introducing CAMIDS to other tools and methods. Such a departure would be "outside the action team process." Once again, I experienced a double bind around my role as coach.

This bind wasn't resolved until I experienced what one of my colleagues referred to as "a blinding flash of the obvious." Since my role in general within the division was not limited to being an action team coach, I had some flexibility I had not considered: I could switch hats! With a wave of the magic wand and Susan's agreement, I became her department's *consultant,* instead of the *action team coach.* It now became possible to do something more appropriate for the situation. This bit of recontracting may seem a small thing, and a bit absurd when one thinks about it, but it was a critical turning point in how I saw myself in relationship to the CAMIDS group, as well as how it came to see me. As internal consultants, how we see ourselves at any given time is probably one of the most critical aspects of our effectiveness. Everything we do and how we do it will follow. It also taught me an important lesson: contracting is not an event, it is a continuous process. It is also a difficult one.

I still believed Susan and I had been on the right track before—even though our strategy didn't work. The need for CAMIDS to deal with the outside world was evident from its list of problems, and Phil and Jerry were clearly part of their outside world. Yet it was also true the situation wasn't confined to Phil and Jerry.

As we began to talk about the problems as a whole, their true complexity emerged, and the next step became obvious: the group had to get a much better handle on what was happening outside its boundaries. Workable strategies would begin to emerge only after a much more thorough analysis of the external environment was conducted. A new approach was needed. We began to put together what we knew about CAMIDS's environment. Interviews of key customers and stakeholders by group members provided the information in Table 1 on the demands placed on CAMIDS, including the unknowns the group dealt with on a day-to-day basis.

TABLE 1 Demands on CAMIDS

Key Stakeholder	*Demands*	*Unknowns*
Publications	Immediate (unrealistic) turnaround time	We never have previous notice of schedule
	Nonstandard formats	Why we can't have standard formats
	More passes on a job than we normally bid	
	Expect us to meet schedules they set up without checking with us first	

TABLE 1 (*continued*)

Key Stakeholder	Demands	Unknowns
Technical Writers	Different projects establish different formats, which we have to accommodate	Don't usually know when work is coming in
	Usually documents have to be handled on "RUSH" schedules, although not unrealistic	We don't know what jobs they are bidding on to have input on format, schedules, etc.
	Expect us to handle document control (maintain data base)	We don't know relationships of documents to each other
		Real schedule not the same as that first requested
Design Automation	Expect us to handle document formatting	
	Expect us to maintain their files	
VHSIC	Expect us to work with elements they have keyed in for final format	
	Expect us to maintain their files	
	Sometimes expect rush turnaround	
UYK 43/44 (Program Management & Marketing)	Immediate turnaround	Usually have no previous notice of work coming in
	We always handle their garbage (difficult) work	
	Expect us to keep track of their bits and pieces	
AMERICAS (Program Management & Marketing)	Expect us to handle formatting	We don't know how documents affect each other
	Expect us to maintain their files	We don't know who is bringing in documentation
	Expect documents on time, but reasonable	No previous notice of incoming work

TABLE 1 *(concluded)*

Key Stakeholder	Demands	Unknowns
Systems Software Department	We handle format even if technical writers specify otherwise	Real schedule required
	We maintain their files	Whether they talk to each other about common data
	Reasonable turnaround time	
	We are responsible for document history (charge packages)	
	We must control common data between books	
IR & D	We must handle difficult formats	We don't know what overall schedule is or how it is affected by late author input
	Demand high quality	
	Demand overall schedule be met	
	Demand we rekey things that could be "updated only"	
	Demand CPT transfers	
Proposals (Marketing)	Ridiculous turnaround	Real schedule is never known
	Expect us to know standard format for proposals, but they change it every time	Real format requirements never known
	Demand that we take abuse (verbal, back stabbing)	Advance knowledge of scheduled work
	Demand overtime	We don't know what they are saying about us

QUESTIONS FOR DISCUSSION

1. Discuss the appropriateness of centralization/decentralization when acquiring new technologies. What is the expected impact on people?
2. How can the CAMIDS group utilize the stakeholder data to plan for the future?

Case 21

The CAMIDS Group (B): Sociotechnological Intervention *

Barry Bateman

Block-Petrella-Weisbord

The main outcome of CAMIDS's planning and problem-solving work in 1981 was to give it a more complete understanding of the situation. It inspired more hope, positive activity, and a sizable action plan. Eventually, the group was able to exert some control over the environment. Jerry, Susan's boss, had been keeping track of the effort and was intrigued by what he saw. Susan and I began to talk with him about other things that could be done, especially the need for a more systematic and system-focused change process that would involve others in his organization.

Unfortunately, it was too little, too late. Events in motion at this time threatened to block any further progress by the group. Some of these events were mentioned in Case A and were expected, such as the consolidation of CAMIDS and Word Processing. As a result, CAMIDS ceased to exist as a separate work group. As Susan had predicted, the consolidation made little sense and caused more problems than it solved. Unfortunately, this is an old story. Consider the following:

> We trained hard . . . but it seemed that every time we were beginning to form up into teams, we would be reorganized. I was to learn later in life we tend to meet any new situation by reorganizing, and a wonderful method it can be for creating the illusion of progress while producing confusion, inefficiency and demoralization.
>
> Petronius Arbiter, 66 A.D.

In relationship to the history of the CAMIDS group, no truer words were ever spoken. The consolidation caused many operational problems, and

*The author wishes to gratefully acknowledge the encouragement and help of Dr. Charles Manz, Bower Research Fellow, Harvard University, without which this case would probably not have been written.

the newly constituted Word Processing Department slipped back into crisis management and fire fighting. Not to be daunted, management forged ahead. In late 1982, more reshuffling occurred. Another reorganization force-fit the already confused, consolidated Word Processing group into a new larger and more centralized Documentation Services organization, as indicated in Exhibit 1.

This reorganization exacerbated operational issues even more for several reasons. The new Documentation Services combined ex-CAMIDS personnel with their old adversaries, Publication Services (PUBS). Higher-paid editors, illustrators, and technical writers, exclusively male, still disdained of working with "the girls in the basement." These dynamics heightened previously unresolved conflicts; the status and gender issues were difficult for the group to acknowledge, much less deal with.

A general breakdown in trust and communication followed, inhibiting the organization's ability to set project priorities. Coordination of work between groups, which each played a different role in the production of a complete document, was lacking. Jerry later moved to a new position outside the Documentation Services group. The work that Susan and I had done persuading him to see the benefits of a systematic change process went out the window.

As an internal consultant, I was not operating at a high enough level to help make a difference. Management support and sanction, required

---

EXHIBIT 1   Centralized Documentation Services Organization in 1982

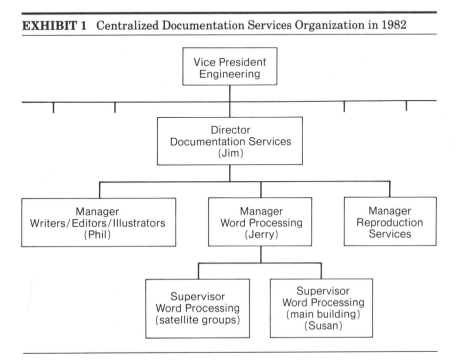

to make significant and meaningful change a reality, were no longer possible in the near term. As for the new Documentation Services group, some stability was needed. Yet, it was clear the organization needed help. The question was what to do.

Unfortunately, there are times when an organization must simply fail before it learns to do things differently. For consultants, there will always come a time when no matter what they do, nothing seems to work. For me, CAMIDS in 1982–83 was such a time. I finally decided to back off. Although I was convinced there wasn't much I could do to help until they were more ready, I had a hard time getting over the feeling I was abandoning a client in need. The CAMIDS action team was also reorganized to include others, and another coach was assigned to work with them as I went on to other things.

I kept in touch with Susan for the next two years. Mostly I listened. Susan's job and her responsibilities were expanded. She now had a much larger group to supervise, so our meetings were less and less frequent. When we did meet, our conversations always came back to the idea of systematic and large-scale change as being the only viable option. We seemed to have the answer, but we both agreed the timing was wrong.

By 1984, Susan and I had risen in our respective organizations. She was now manager of Word Processing and most of my clients were vice presidents. I was reporting to the CEO on the overall cultural change process in the division and, with lots of help from my staff and some future-oriented line managers, had successfully implemented a quality-of-work-life effort. The climate was improving for the introduction of new ways to structure work, and my group's efforts in the factory were showcased as managers made presentations on their successes and learnings in a conference on work innovations attended by over 80 percent of the division's managers.

Predictably, the situation in the two-year-old Documentation Services organization had changed for the worse. The slow but sure deterioration of productivity, service quality, and morale brought on by the reorganizations and poor working relationships was evident as customers began to complain about errors, lack of coordination, and missed schedules. To complicate things even more, another wave of technological change was on the horizon. This time there seemed to be no escape, no easy way out. This time Susan wasn't alone in her concern.

The change was actually a complex mixture of three different types of change coming from three different directions:

1. *External to the company:* The company's primary customer, the U.S. government, gave notice that within five years the company was to convert to an electronic data base. All records and documents that had previously been submitted only in paper were to be converted to magnetic tape that could be read by the government's mainframe computer systems. This directive affected Documentation Services directly. It would have to find a way to comply.

2. *Internal to SIG, external to Documentation Services:* In order to take advantage of new local area network (LAN) technology, Documentation Services would, as a part of a five-year SIG automation plan, be hooked up to all departments electronically. This would allow documents to be sent over the network directly from Documentation Services' customers. The Information Systems Division (ISD) was the force behind the automation plan, and it had top-level support for its charter. Automation had become roughly equivalent in meaning to "good for you."

3. *Internal to Documentation Services:* An investigation into advances in workstation technology indicated that new pagination and illustration computer hardware and software were available that would, in theory, allow one person to produce a finished document, complete with text, graphics, and page layout. Before, such a feat took in the work of several different departments. In addition, the completed document could be viewed on a computer screen, just as it would look when printed out. This technology was affectionately referred to as a *whizziwig* (what-you-see-is-what-you-get).

These changes would have profound impacts, both positive and negative, for the Documentation Services organization. True, the department could avoid some pain of change by deciding not to go ahead with procurement of the new pagination and illustration workstations, but the potential advantages to such systems were so great that turning away from the technology was unthinkable. The other two changes were givens—decisions from on high that were beyond the department's control. In the end, there was really no choice but to forge ahead.

In thinking about how to cope with what seemed to be the inevitable, Jim, who was still the director of the Documentation Services organization, had several dilemmas. Changes would be required, and, in particular, new skills would be required. He knew some employees would simply not be able to adapt. At first blush, these challenges seemed to be nothing new—he had been there before. Some of the issues were more or less problematical—difficult, but solvable. People could be retrained and repositioned and, if necessary, transferred or let go.

What Jim could not get his arms around, however, was one issue that had plagued him from the time he had first heard about the new pagination system. This question became the straw that finally broke the camel's back, in terms of my eventual reentry into the work system: *who to give the new pagination and illustration workstations to?* Like the other new systems that preceded it, the new workstations would be too expensive for every employee or even departmental unit to have one. Yet, even if it were affordable, no one person had all the necessary skills to fully utilize the power of the new workstations. Underutilization of the technology would be guaranteed. And then there was the problem of the organization itself.

As previously shown, Documentation Services was traditionally organized. Functional managers and supervisors directed the activities of departments of specialists. Six departments reported directly to Jim, including the people formerly in Publication Services (editors, technical writers, and illustrators) and Word Processing, which housed some remnants of CAMIDS, but was mostly word-processing operators.

The flow of documents was essentially as follows:

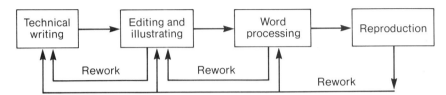

Jim's first inclination was to give the workstations to the illustrators and editors, who were the highest-paid specialists. Yet the workstations would also eventually be the primary text-entry tool. Typing, or text-entry, as it had become referred to, was a skill that would be critical in the use of the workstations. Typing skills were in short supply in Publication Services (technical writers, editors, and illustrators), yet were in great abundance in Word Processing. Word-processing operators were also younger, potentially more adaptive, and already accustomed to working with the company's mainframe computer system. Yet, as far as editors and illustrators were concerned, the word-processing operators knew "next to nothing" about technical writing, editing, or illustration. They were also the least paid.

Given the status differences and communication problems that already existed between these groups, every option seemed to be a lose/lose proposition. The amount of rework the organization was producing was thought to be partly related to the ongoing conflict, and Jim had little interest in making things worse. Yet it was clear that the new pagination workstations would become the focal point of document production, and the operators, whoever they were, would gain status and higher wages.

This dilemma became Documentation Services' Achilles' heel and brought the issues that had been plaguing the organization for years to the surface. It wasn't until later, when I had gained reentry into the organization, that a way of framing Jim's dilemma was coined to his satisfaction: "Jim, if you automate this mess, all you'll end up with is an automated mess!"

The way out of Documentation Services' dilemma was finally created by a convergence of different political interests that revolved around how to get a handle on the seeming inability of the division to implement new technology effectively. Since early 1983, my role in the division had gradually shifted from being an all-purpose consultant and facilitator to a change agent. This role shift was a direct consequence of my work with the CEO on the cultural change process, which had recently been redefined as an *organization change process*. The CEO was clear with me about my role: he saw me as a change agent—someone who would push him, his staff, and the division to change the way that work was managed. My charter was extensive and my access to top management was high.

My staff and I had been looking for a demonstration site undergoing substantial technological change. Documentation Services seemed exactly right for what we had in mind: a simultaneous redesign of a work system and its technology—a "whole system" approach to deal with "whole system" issues. With project support wired into top management, and Documentation Services in agreement, we could help them fix their mess before they automated it. Also, I still had an unfinished feeling about Documentation Services and hadn't forgotten Susan.

My staff and I, through our network of contacts in ISD and Engineering, began to talk about the possibility of a project in Documentation Services. The feedback we received was that Jim was interested because he had finally admitted he had a big problem on his hands. ISD, the organization responsible for the five-year automation plan, was interested because Documentation Services was key to its plan. Susan was interested because she was trying, once again, to survive the change. Yet there was still some hesitation. While Jim could see that change was inevitable, he was basically a cautious man. After all, things had always worked out before. Why was this any different?

After waiting a month or two with no indication that Jim would, on his own, decide to go ahead, Susan and I sat down once again and discussed strategy. She was willing to push one more time and I was willing to pull out the stops to help get things moving. On the same day that Susan went to see Jim, I went to his boss three levels up. When I finally sat down with Jim, it was at his request. In Beckhard's language, I had used the commitment strategy called *power*.

Getting Documentation Services' agreement wasn't hard this time. True, it helped, especially later, to have the project "hard-wired." Yet Jim had realized he was truly up against a wall and appreciated the words of encouragement and support he received from his boss. Also, the approach we outlined made sense to him. In some ways it was the ultimate leap of faith on his part, and in others, it was the only viable way out of Jim's lose/lose dilemma.

The core aspects of the strategy, taking a whole system view and turning much of the work of finding a solution over to his employees, was appealing. After thinking about it, Jim agreed fully with the principle, once proposed, that those who were to be affected most by the change had the right to participate in its design. He was also willing to admit that together they had more information on what the impact would be and therefore what the most appropriate response would look like. With special attention paid to building commitment to the change, the organization could potentially come together in a way it never had before.

With the help of an outside consultant, ISD, and an internal OD specialist, a plan was conceived that would empower Documentation Services employees at the lowest level to design and implement their own futures. A design team, made up of word processors, editors, illustrators, technical writers, and one supervisor, would work for the next six months on a new design for the organization. They would report to a resource and support team, comprised of Jim and his managers.

Both teams would receive process consultation from internal and external OD consultants and help on understanding technological issues and options from ISD. A technology group was also organized to begin the search process for appropriate hardware and software. A solid working relationship between these four groups produced, over the next nine months, a learning environment conducive to simultaneous design of the organization and its technology.

The design team was given a full charter, within wide parameters, to change what needed to be changed. Employment was the only guarantee given to people in the organization. It was generally understood that everyone's job would change. Everyone in the organization was invited to volunteer for the design team. Of the 10 design team members selected from 60 volunteers, 3 were from the original CAMIDS group of 1982. Their familiarity with open systems planning and group problem solving seemed to help them stand out as strong candidates for this work.

A visioning and stakeholder analysis process, much like the one used in 1982 by CAMIDS, was conducted by the steering committee, which turned the results over to the design team as a guide for their design. I believe it is safe to say the managers, with the exception of Susan, were surprised by what they heard when they talked to Documentation Services' customers. They were rudely awakened to the impact their infighting and lack of coordination had on customer service.

A sociotechnical analysis and design methodology, with its focus on controlling key variances and optimizing the interaction of technical and social subsystems, was used to produce the new organizational concept. Among other things, it was discovered that documents were "thrown back and forth over the wall" between Word Processing, technical writers, editors, and illustrators an average of 6 times and as many as 15 in some extreme, but not infrequent, cases. More than 125 variances, or points of error, were identified. The amount of work generated by the severely fragmented organization was a frightening discovery.

The social analysis revealed poorly designed jobs, a low perceived quality of work life, a general lack of career paths, the negative impact of status differentials, issues of gender, and the inadequacy of the current compensation system. All in all, few rocks were left unturned. A flowchart of the steps in the project is provided on the next page.

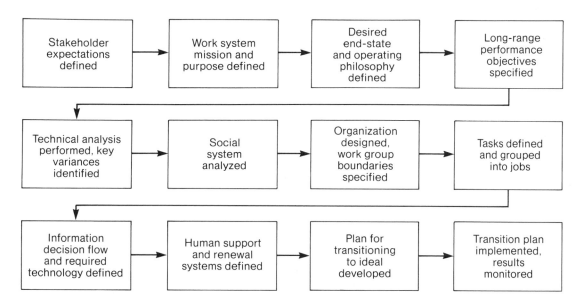

In the end, the design team proposed an organizational concept that was as elegant in its simplicity as it was revolutionary in its design. Within two years, a totally different type of organization existed. In 1988, Susan informed me Documentation Services had finally stabilized.

QUESTION FOR DISCUSSION

What issues need to be resolved during implementation? Predict the outcome.

The Alum Company: Union-Management Cooperation Intervention

Thomas G. Cummings
University of Southern California

The Alum Company is a large, multinational firm operating in the chemicals industry. The company is over 80 years old and is ranked in the Fortune 50. It has multiple chemical-processing plants scattered primarily throughout the United States. Alum has a long history of enlightened management practices, including a deep interest in sociotechnical work design and employee involvement.

At the time of this case in the late 1980s, the company was introducing an innovative technology into one of its larger plants in the Midwest. The technology was originally developed in Europe by a key competitor and drastically improved the yield of certain chemical-processing operations. Under a licensing agreement, Alum was the first American firm to acquire the technology, thus gaining a competitive advantage if implementation went smoothly at the Midwest facility. Corporate executives believed a sociotechnical approach to designing how employees interfaced with the new technology would help to assure its successful operation.

CONTACTING THE CONSULTANT

My involvement in the new technology project was initiated by human resources personnel from corporate headquarters. They were responsible for providing organization development and industrial relations help to the Midwest plant, and they contacted me as a potential sociotechnical systems resource. Over the course of several phone conversations, I learned the Midwest facility was moderately profitable and heavily unionized. Employees were represented by a large, international union with a strong reputation for promoting safety, health, and quality of work life for its members. Union and management relations at the Midwest plant were characterized as cautious and not overly friendly with a history of intermittent conflicts over wage rates, job classifications, and other grievances.

Alum intended to implement the new technology at a site located adjacent to the Midwest plant. Because the new site would fall within the jurisdiction of the existing local union, corporate management thought the union would have to be involved in any change efforts that might modify work designs, job classifications, and other working conditions.

Under the existing labor agreement, the new site could be treated differently from the existing plant if both sides agreed. However, extreme caution would have to be taken to assure that changes at the new site did not spill over to the existing plant and undermine its current labor agreement. The labor agreement was part of a statewide bargaining process that included similar chemical firms and, consequently, could not be altered unilaterally at the local site level.

My role, if I was chosen as the external consultant, would be to act as a neutral third party helping plant management and local unionists to design collaboratively the work of the new site. This would include facilitating joint problem solving, offering sociotechnical expertise and training, and recording the activities for official notes of what was transpiring.

An initial meeting between representatives of the union and plant management was scheduled next. The purpose of the meeting was to explore the possibility of working together on the design of the new site. Secondarily, the meeting would give both sides a firsthand look at me and would help the participants decide if they wanted me as their third party. I had already passed a preliminary assessment in which both management and unionists had checked my references and reputation. A major plus on my side was that I had previously worked with members of the same international union at another chemical company. They described me as fair and honest with a good sense of humor and a willingness to get my hands dirty on the shop floor.

I anticipated the meeting with a good deal of excitement and apprehension. Working as a third-party consultant to unions and managers requires considerable interpersonal skills, diplomacy, and patience. Based on previous experience, I knew that both sides would be watching me closely to assess whether I could relate to them and their situation and especially whether I could be impartial and fair to each party. I would have to be extremely careful about not appearing too much like a business school professor who was preferential to managerial viewpoints. On the other hand, I would have to guard against overcompensating on the side of the union.

Because I was unfamiliar with the new technology, the dynamics of the Midwest plant, and the participants, I obtained and read as much material as I could get about the situation. I also prepared to do a good deal of active listening during the meeting.

> I envisioned my role at the meeting as facilitating a process that would allow both parties to make informed choices about proceeding together on the design of the new site. This would include gaining a shared understanding of the new technology and the design tasks, sharing expectations about working collaboratively, and arriving at a decision to proceed or not. I would help to assure that everyone got a fair hearing and that the discussion stayed on track. I would also share my experiences with this kind of collaborative effort if appropriate.

THE INITIAL MEETING

This two-day meeting took place off site at a resort hotel. Participants included two members from the international union, the local union president, the site manager where the new technology would be implemented, the labor relations specialist at the Midwest plant, and me. The night before the meeting, we met informally for dinner to get acquainted and to talk about the new technology.

The participants asked several questions about my experience in these kind of efforts, and the international union members explicitly asked where I stood on unions. I answered that I had once been a member of the United Auto Workers, and that although unions had their positive and negative sides, I believed they played an integral role in the nation's industrial relations system. Moreover, I said I had recently co-written a textbook on labor relations with a balanced view of unions and management and that I would send them a copy if they were interested. They asked for a copy and seemed satisfied with my answers.

Next, the topic turned to the new technology. The unionists showed considerable interest in it, particularly in what it might mean for hiring new employees, designing jobs, and determining levels of pay. They frequently questioned the site manager about his preconceptions on these issues, and he typically answered: "That's for all of us to decide if you want to be involved." The unionists showed some skepticism about management's true intentions for the joint effort, often relating, in a humorous manner, stories where plant managers had not followed through on their word in the past. The labor relations specialist typically joined in on these tales with his own version of what occurred.

I was impressed that both sides showed a good sense of humor, a willingness to speak up, and an ability to give and to take. I also thought the unionists were no fools. They were not about to rush into a collaborative effort with management without considerable testing, clarification, and internal debate. I went to bed that night feeling good about the participants but apprehensive about whether they could truly collaborate, given the conflictual nature of their past relationship.

The next morning we generated an agenda for the meeting that included:

The issues and givens of the new site.

Specific design tasks needed to start it up.

Sociotechnical systems concepts and approach.

Decision to proceed and next steps if any.

The site manager listed all of the issues and givens related to the new technology. This included a description of the technology, its location, construction budgets and schedules, and the company's belief in adhering to the existing labor agreement. The union participants strongly endorsed that belief, but otherwise they said very little during this presentation. A potentially troublesome constraint on the joint design effort was identified: the severe time schedule before startup of the new technology, which would occur in about a year. It was questioned whether this would give us sufficient time to design jointly the new site, particularly since selection and training of employees would have to occur in about eight months.

We next identified design tasks that management and the union would have to perform before startup. These are listed below in temporal order and show the magnitude of work ahead in the next several months:

Develop a values statement to guide the design efforts.

Organization/work design including shift schedules.

Wage rates and classifications.

Job duties and responsibilities.

Selection and hiring.

Training programs.

Evaluation and control systems.

Information systems.

Relationships with rest of Midwest plant.

Before starting the next item on the agenda, sociotechnical concepts, the local union president forcefully stated: "We cannot talk about cooperation outside of our past relationship with management." He then proceeded to recount a list of "bitches" the local union had with plant management. These included such complaints as contracting out work, failing to recognize the union as the real voice of employees, having poor feedback and communication, and imposing too much management authority on workers. He recounted specific examples of these abuses, often punctuating his narrative with statements like: "How can you cooperate with people who are trying to screw you?" The site manager and labor relations specialist listened patiently to these gripes and said little about whether they agreed or disagreed with them.

In the interest of fair play, I asked them to recount any problems they had with unionists at the plant. They responded more cerebrally than emotionally, mentioning such issues as absenteeism, thefts, shoddy workmanship, too many two-party grievances, and people's unwillingness to grow on the job. The union participants listened attentively but neither agreed nor disagreed that these were real problems at the plant.

Rather than try to get the meeting back on track, I thought it was better to let both sides air their complaints about each other. There was considerable emotion underlying these gripes, and letting participants voice them would provide some cathartic relief and help to clear the slate so we could continue to explore the possibility of collaborating on this project. It would also allow each party to acknowledge the other's legitimate right to participate in the governance of the plant. Fortunately, the "bitch session" had its intended effect, and both sides thought the air had been cleared enough to proceed with the meeting agenda.

Next, the meeting involved conceptual input from me about the sociotechnical approach to organization design. Using a flip chart, we reviewed the concepts of open system and of joint optimization of both social and technical aspects of work. We also outlined different forms of work design with particular attention to self-regulating work teams, which the participants had special interest in. They asked several questions about how such "leaderless" groups functioned, and both sides seemed interested in the possibility that less hierarchical management might be needed in the new site. This part of the meeting ended with a brief overview of the change process needed to design and develop sociotechnical work designs. This included the use of a union-management design team that would perform the design tasks on behalf of the total site.

The final item on the agenda involved a decision about whether to proceed with the joint design effort. From the union's side, a positive choice would mean the local union president would recommend the joint effort to his bargaining committee, which in turn would have to approve the project on the union's behalf. On management's side, the site manager had the authority to commit the company to the collaborative effort, and he stated sincerely that he favored the project and hoped the union would also agree.

The unionists had some reservations about management's sincerity and whether the two sides could really bridge their traditional adversarial relationship. Despite these questions, however, one of the international union members argued strongly that the union should be open to management's offer to bridge the union and management gap and should give the project a chance. "If things don't go well," he said, "the union can always bail out." The union president then agreed to recommend the joint effort to the local bargaining committee and to let it make the final decision about whether to proceed.

The meeting ended with a frank discussion of my role and acceptance as a third party to the joint effort if it continued. The union participants, who continued informally to question my opinions about unions throughout the meeting, stated that they liked my input, impartiality, and especially my sense of humor. They questioned, however, how I could maintain my neutrality because management was paying for my services.

The management participants also had positive assessments of me but similarly questioned the issue of my neutrality. I responded to the feedback by saying I would like to work on the project but only if both parties saw my input as useful. Moreover, in order to remain neutral, I would work under a contract where either side could dismiss me at will. Thus, although I would be paid by management, the union would have the right to fire me for whatever reason at any time.

The participants thought this solution to the neutrality issue would be workable, and they agreed to use my services if the project continued. The decision to proceed now rested with the local union bargaining committee, which would address this issue in the coming week.

THE SANCTIONING MEETING

The bargaining committee addressed the possibility of a joint design effort for the new site at its next monthly meeting at the union hall. The local president reviewed the two-day meeting and recommended the committee go forward by meeting with site management to officially sanction the project.

Although I was not present at this meeting, I heard later from the union president that there was a spirited debate about whether management could be trusted and whether management was using the joint effort to co-opt the union to its way of thinking. Because the bargaining committee had serious reservations about management's sincerity and intentions, it decided to postpone an official decision about cooperation until it met with site management at the sanctioning meeting. Then, if the committee's questions and reservations were addressed satisfactorily, it would agree to proceed officially with the joint effort.

The two-day sanctioning meeting took place off site about two weeks later. All participants from the initial meeting were present in addition to the union bargaining committee and line managers from the new site.

The local president and site manager jointly gave background about how both sides had come to the possibility of working together on the design of the new site. They reaffirmed the basic premise that either side could end the joint effort if it did not like what was happening.

They then introduced me, and I talked about my experience with union-management projects and my potential role in this effort. I stated I would help them create a process for designing the new site. This would include: developing a union-management design team; helping it decide how to tackle the different design tasks; providing conceptual inputs for the design tasks; facilitating team meetings; and recording the official minutes of the meetings. I further stated I would not under any circumstances do the designing for them. In effect, my role would be to facilitate them doing their own designing activities. After all, they had far better knowledge of the situation than me, and they needed to own the design and be committed to it if they were going to implement it successfully. I also discussed the issue of my neutrality and that my contract would allow either side to dismiss me at will.

Finally, the representatives from the international union talked about their role in the union and warned participants that the goals of union and management are fundamentally different. They did hold hope, however, for this collaborative effort only if it proceeded cautiously, respected the existing bargaining agreement, and was limited to the new site and not the total Midwest plant. One international member emphasized this last point by saying: "We can't let what's happening at the new site get over the fence to the plant. This could set a dangerous precedent that could undermine the current labor agreement."

The rest of the sanctioning meeting followed the same agenda as the initial meeting. The site manager described the new technology and the constraints and givens related to the project. Then, I reviewed the design tasks the union and management would have to perform jointly to start the new site. This was followed by a ritual gripe session where separate subgroups of unionists and of managers listed complaints about each other and then shared them in a total group setting.

The gripes were essentially the same as those identified at the initial meeting, and the behavioral dynamics entailed a good deal of finger pointing, particularly by unionists. For example, one union member claimed management was trying to break the union by contracting out work to nonunion shops. He said this practice was growing rapidly and often forced unionists to work side by side with nonunion subcontractors. A manager countered by saying subcontracting was necessary for economic survival because of the high wage and benefits package of union workers.

My role in this exercise was to see that each side actively listened to and acknowledged the complaints of the other side. I encouraged participants to be as empathetic as possible and to focus on understanding rather than rationalizing the gripes. I was not always successful at this effort.

At this point, the union participants said they had heard enough about the joint effort to decide about proceeding. They retreated for a caucus in a separate room and asked me to attend. What followed was a lively discussion of the pros and cons of working with management and of the steps the joint effort might take.

On the plus side, the joint effort would get the union greater access to managerial information and thinking, would likely result in more interesting and rewarding jobs, and would probably improve the existing union-management relationship. Negatively, union members might accuse the bargaining committee of being in bed with management; managers might try to dominate the design team and co-opt the union into supporting their preconceived ideas; the project might fail and the blame be laid on the union.

The pros and cons were judged to be about equal, with no clear direction about what choice to make. The discussion turned time and again to one underlying issue: What was management's real commitment to the joint effort? When no clear answer was forthcoming, the union president asked: "Why not get the new site manager in here and ask him face to face?" Members readily agreed and asked him to come to the caucus and give his views about management's commitment.

The site manager reiterated the importance of the new technology to the Alum Company and management's strong belief that a joint union-management effort would help to implement it successfully. He further stated that although site managers did not have much experience with joint efforts, they were willing to learn together with the union how to collaboratively design the new site. Of course, there would be mistakes and problems with the project, but management and the union would be in the same boat trying to work things out together.

Believing in the sincerity and integrity of the site manager's views, the unionists decided to proceed cautiously with the project, knowing that at any time they could withdraw if necessary. They informed management of their decision, and both parties drafted a joint statement of their intention to work together on the new site design. This would be disseminated throughout the Midwest plant and was intended to communicate the innovative yet tentative nature of the project.

Next, I gave a short lecture on sociotechnical concepts and design guides and reviewed the design tasks we would have to accomplish. We also discussed the composition of the design team responsible for carrying out these tasks, and participants strongly believed everyone at the present meeting should be a member with the exception of the representatives of the international union. The meeting ended by scheduling a series of meetings to perform the design tasks. The next meeting would take place in about two weeks and would address the development of a joint values statement to guide the design effort.

> I felt strongly at this point that both sides were extremely cautious about working together. It was very difficult for participants to consider collaboratively designing the new site outside of the context of their past relationship, which had often been conflictual. My major attention was getting participants beyond this negative frame by showing them it was in their vested interests to work together on the new site. For the union, this could result in a better quality of work life for members working at the new site. For management, this could produce a successful implementation of the new technology at the Midwest plant. Hopefully, the joint design activities would demonstrate to both sides that it was possible to collaborate without violating the existing collective bargaining agreement.

CREATING THE VALUES STATEMENT

The initial draft of the values statement was developed at a two-day meeting held off site. At the start of the meeting, we identified norms that participants believed should guide their behaviors as they performed this task as well as subsequent design activities. Members felt strongly that they should "participate actively in the design tasks; listen to each other's inputs; speak up frankly when they had something to say; and start meetings on time." Members also agreed to set aside time periodically to check progress on these norms and to call attention to norm breaking when they saw it occur. I agreed to do process consultation during the meetings in order to help the members operate more effectively as a design team.

We started the task of developing a values statement for the new site by discussing the reasons for such a statement and what it might include. The statement would provide broad guidelines for designing the new site and for subsequently operating it. It would serve to inform site managers and employees about how to act, how to relate to each other, and how to interface with outsiders such as customers, suppliers, and the rest of the Midwest plant. The statement would include the kinds of performance and human outcomes desired for the new site as well as the kinds of organizational conditions needed to achieve those outcomes.

Participants voiced some confusion during the abstract discussion of value statements and asked me for concrete examples of what such documents looked like. I provided several examples of values statements from other companies, including some that had been created by union-management committees and some that were only management determined. This led to an interesting discussion of the wording and tenor of the statements, particularly those that seemed to favor management. For example, the union's reaction to one statement in a similar chemical company was: "No union people could have been involved in creating this" and, "It's self-serving for management."

In order to get a better feel for what participants really valued for the new site, we broke into subgroups composed of union and management members and generated multiple endings to the following three statements:

A new site employee should _____.

A new site manager should _____

The new site should _____.

The subgroups then came back together and shared their responses. Examples included:

- "A new site employee should come to work on time, work safely, work effectively with others, be willing to accept responsibility."
- "A new site manager should lead by example, treat people fairly, be willing to delegate decision making, understand the new technology."
- "The new site should provide meaningful work, minimize status differences, provide stable employment, be profitable."

There was considerable discussion about what the different statements actually meant and whether participants really believed in them. Over time, members gained a clearer understanding and deeper commitment to the values embodied in the statements. At the end of the first day of the meeting, a subgroup of the design team met to consolidate the different statements into a preliminary values statement for the new site.

Starting the next morning, the design team reviewed the values statement word by word and made necessary modifications. The completed statement appears in Exhibit 1. The discussion included a number of salient issues, such as concern for employees' family life, which is troublesome in round-the-clock operations, and the integrity of the bargaining agreement, which is addressed in the last paragraph of the statement. The union participants were particularly interested in how employees at the Midwest plant might respond to the statement and in management's commitment to employee control and involvement in the operation of the new site.

Although these issues could not be resolved at this time in the joint effort, members felt more comfortable having raised and discussed them. The next task would be to design the work structure of the new site using the values statement as a guide. This would take place in about three weeks at another two-day meeting.

EXHIBIT 1 Joint Union-Management Values Statement for the New Site

---

PURPOSE

We, The Alum Company, Midwest plant, and Local Union 104, are going to design the organization to operate the new site in such a way as to meet human needs for safety, health, meaningful work, fair and equitable pay and treatment, preservation of our environment, and to enhance the employee's family life. In order to accomplish these purposes, we understand that the new area will be operated in an efficient and profitable manner.

HOW WE PROPOSE TO ACCOMPLISH THIS

Work environment

We expect to staff the new site with employees who want to work together in an open and trusting climate. We further believe that this type of environment will enable people to work together with maximum effectiveness. Our efforts will be directed toward supporting employees in operating more effectively to meet mutually agreed-upon goals and objectives. We expect that individual differences will occur. We will try to resolve them within the group.

Work design

The work design will be such as to provide the greatest opportunity to work effectively together, helping each other to succeed. Work design will enable employees to operate with as much freedom and discretion as possible.

Management

We expect management to provide the leadership that will enhance the success of our goals and objectives. Management will also provide the necessary goods, services, and information.

Information

Employees working in the new site can expect to be fully informed on matters affecting plant operations so they can participate effectively in decisions. They can expect to hear about problems before solutions are offered and to play a part in the decision. Areas will be provided for necessary exchanges of information.

Facilities

Wherever possible, the new site facilities will be designed with people in mind.

Training

Training will be provided to new site employees in various ways, such as formal training, on-the-job training, and by other training methods. Training will be designed to include self-development on a day-by-day basis. We recognize that people learn at different rates and plan to take that into consideration as we do our training. It is understood that individual and group work knowledge and experiences will be shared with employees.

Relationship to complex

The new site will be operated to produce quality products and with consideration for the balance of the Midwest plant.

EXHIBIT 1   *(Concluded)*

Union-management relationships
The company and the union recognize that the integrity of the collective bargaining agreement must be maintained. The company and the union expect to work together on common problems.

The process of creating a values statement is as important as the content included in such documents. Participants need to have good group interaction, open communication, and active listening if they are to understand each other's values and arrive at a sufficient consensus to permit joint action. This is particularly true in union-management projects where participants are likely to have divergent and often conflicting interests and values.

Consequently, I spent considerable time at this meeting helping the group work through process issues, such as members interrupting each other, differential levels of participation, and disagreements over the meaning of certain words. I also helped members identify and work through certain value conflicts, such as the union's desire for employment security and management's wish to be highly profitable. Although addressing and resolving these issues took time, members increasingly behaved consistent with their norms.

Before finalizing the values statement, I played the devil's advocate, confronting participants about what it would be like to behave consistent with the values and whether they really thought such behavior was possible at the new site. This resulted in a values statement that was both realistic and strongly supported by all participants.

REACTIONS AT THE PLANT

At the beginning of the work-design meeting, participants addressed two issues having to do with the relation of the joint effort to the rest of the Midwest plant: how employees and managers from the plant were reacting to the values statement which had been disseminated widely, and how communication from the design team to the rest of the plant could be improved. The union stated that its members generally liked the statement but had serious reservations about whether management could live up to it: "They've been taking names and kicking ass for 20 years; they are not about to change overnight."

Employees also had many preconceived notions about how the new site would be operated. The operations people were generally excited about the possibility of working in an enriched environment with greater employee involvement. "It's about time we had some say over things. We know more about what's going on than most supervisors." The craft maintenance people, on the other hand, felt threatened by the possibility that operations people might take on more of the maintenance function: "We're being sold down the river." "Operators had better stay away from craft work; we're the only ones classified to do it." We noted this as a serious issue that would have to be addressed in our design activities.

The management members of the design team stated corporate executives as well as other managers at the Midwest plant were impressed with the values statement and endorsed it: "This is the way we should have been managing the plant for years." The union responded skeptically: "A lot of old-line supervisors sure don't behave that way." The new site manager replied he would try to select managers who could behave according to the values. He concluded, however: "But if they don't fit in, we'll have to find other opportunities for them."

The union also reported that employees requested more specific communication about the new technology and the design team's activities: "What's really going on?" "We're being left in the dark." So far, communication had been limited mainly to posting the minutes of the design team's meetings on plant bulletin boards and to informal contacts with members of the design team. Employees needed more interactive communication, where they could ask questions and probe answers.

To remedy this problem, the new site manager agreed to hold monthly question-and-answer sessions at the union hall. The first meeting would begin with a slide show showing the new technology and the physical layout of the new site. Then, the latest activities of the design team would be discussed and questions and answers would follow. The meeting would end by asking employees for any input they would like to give the design team.

DESIGNING WORK

After addressing these plant issues, the design team turned to designing work at the new site. Following a sociotechnical approach, members first laid out the work flow of the new technology, which involved a sequential series of continuous chemical processes. They then identified production variances that could arise from the technology and the nature of the raw material and examined how they were interconnected.

Variances include significant deviations from production standards that can hamper performance and outcomes. Because the different phases of the work flow were highly interdependent and closely linked in time, variances occurring earlier in the production process would have drastic effects on later stages of production unless they were rapidly controlled. Consequently, a technical criterion for designing work was to control production variances as quickly and as close to their source as possible. From the values statement, a social criterion included designing work to allow employees as much freedom and discretion as possible.

Given these technical and social criteria, participants next explored work designs that would jointly satisfy both standards. I encouraged members to be as innovative as possible and to use previous conceptual inputs from me about sociotechnical work design to guide their efforts.

After several alternative proposals and considerable discussion and debate, members arrived at a work design that appeared to satisfy both criteria. The total production process would be assigned to a self-regulating group for each shift. Members of the group would be multiskilled and would be responsible for performing all of the interrelated tasks necessary to process chemicals for their respective shift. Over time, as the group developed and gained skills and experience, it would have discretion over task assignments, work methods, and relationships with others, such as support groups, suppliers, and customers. This work design would promote the coordination and discretion needed to control technical variances; it would also be consistent with the values statement pertaining to enriched work design.

> My major role in work design was to provide conceptual inputs about how to analyze the technology and how to link variance control with values about work design. I also encouraged participants to move beyond their past experience with traditional work designs and to think of innovative alternatives that might be more appropriate to the new technology and to the quality of work life of employees. Members had trouble breaking out of the traditional frame, and I was uncertain how to help them. Perhaps creativity exercises might have helped.

THE STALEMATE

Although both union and management members agreed the group design was highly appropriate to the new site, a major disagreement emerged concerning who should lead the groups. The new site manager proposed that the group leaders should be shift supervisors who are members of site management. He argued: "We need to have management control and accountability over the production process." Having supervisors lead the groups would also give them the clout necessary to handle the increased demands and complexity of the new leadership role. Leaders could not act traditionally but would have to help groups develop skills and autonomy and relate to their environment.

The union members strongly opposed this proposal. They countered with the recommendation: "Group leaders should be called *master pro-*

cess controllers and should be located within the bargaining unit." This would give union members more discretion over site operations, provide greater promotion opportunities, and allow greater flexibility because group leaders could also do bargaining unit work if necessary.

Management reiterated that it did not feel comfortable having this key job located outside of management: "We need to have accountability for the shift teams located within management." It would be willing to reduce the number and role of shift supervisors as the groups developed, but, essentially, this would remain a management job.

At this point, tension within the design team was extreme, and cooperation between the two sides declined rapidly. The unionists accused management of having preconceived ideas about work design that give management maximum control over employees. They concluded: "This shows that management does not trust us and is not really willing to collaborate on the design of the new site. The need to have team leaders as part of management has nothing to do with sociotechnical design but is an attempt to gain strike insurance so management can run the plant in case of a walkout." For the union, the real issue underlying management's proposal was finally out on the table.

Both sides were at a stalemate. I pointed out that this is essentially a matter of trust: "Management does not trust union members to hold key leadership jobs at the new site, and the union sees this as a sign that management is not really collaborating on the design of the new site. Each side has been defending its view with little listening to or empathy for the other side's perspective." The participants agreed with this interpretation and decided to give the issue further thought and to meet again in one week to resolve it. The meeting adjourned without the customary smiles, handshakes, and goodwill displayed at the close of previous meetings.

I was surprised and dismayed by this quick turn of events, particularly in light of the strong cooperation on the values statement. Once we got down to concrete design choices, fundamental differences over control and trust between the parties surfaced. The group leadership issue was a symptom of a far deeper conflict over power and control in the workplace.

Each side saw the new site from the perspective of the traditional adversarial relationship where one party wins at the expense of the other. Management wanted to keep the production process under its control and saw the union proposal as undermining its right to manage. The union also wanted to control production and saw management's proposal as reducing the union's power and especially its ability to carry out a successful strike if necessary. Unless this adversarial frame could be broken, I had serious doubts about whether the joint project could continue.

QUESTIONS FOR DISCUSSION

1. What are the advantages and disadvantages of labor-management cooperative efforts when designing organizations?
2. What are the major values of using a sociotechnical approach in this case?
3. As the consultant in this case, what actions would you take next to resolve the stalemate?

LIFECO: Reward System Intervention

Gerald E. Ledford, Jr.

University of Southern California

The life insurance industry witnessed tremendous changes during the 1980s. The vast majority of its customers once were satisfied with basic whole life policies that were simple to service and lucrative to sell. During the last 10 years, most new customers turned their backs on whole life and instead chose from among a plethora of life insurance products that, in general, were less profitable, more difficult to explain and sell to customers, and more complicated to service.

Increasing regulation by state insurance commissions, poor investment of premium income by many companies, and changing federal tax rules all added uncertainty and pressure on industry earnings. The life insurance industry in general had experienced poor profit margins for years, and this led to increasingly fierce competition.

In this environment, the most profitable companies were not the industry giants, but a new breed of smaller, innovative, and nimble companies. One of the new breed was LIFECO (a pseudonym). LIFECO had a reputation as a very well managed smaller company. In general, its executives were younger, better educated, and more aggressive than the industry norm.

LIFECO'S CUSTOMER SERVICE STRATEGY

LIFECO used a different strategy for selling its products than did most insurance companies, and this proved to be a key source of competitive advantage. The company did not sell its products through full-time or independent insurance agents who lived in the communities where LIFECO policies were sold. The full-time field agents employed by some companies were difficult to recruit, train, and supervise, and their commissions were very expensive. Independent insurance agents, who sold the products of multiple companies, not only were paid expensive commissions but also their loyalty to any particular company was always in doubt. For these reasons, LIFECO elected to market its products solely through direct advertising and to serve customer needs from toll-free telephone centers.

The majority of employees at LIFECO worked for the customer service division (CSD), which consisted mainly of three toll-free telephone centers. Kelsey Taylor, the vice president of customer service, believed the way in which her group was managed could be a critical source of competitive advantage for the company. She thought most financial services companies designed their customer service organizations in ways that were fundamentally flawed.

In the typical life insurance company, as in banks and other financial services organizations, back-office operations were structured like the factories of an earlier era. Division of labor was extreme; job titles and functional departments proliferated to such a degree that no individual and no department did much of a job of servicing customers.

Separate departments handled the paperwork associated with sales of new policies, answered inquiries about old policies, processed routine premium payments, pursued delinquent premium payments, terminated policies, processed claims against policies, and so on. Over time, the number of functional departments tended to proliferate as new departments were created to handle new or special service problems.

Kelsey Taylor strongly believed this way of organizing made outstanding customer service impossible. Employees felt responsible for their own department's narrow task, not the total job of serving the customer. Because employees lacked the technical knowledge to manage or coordinate their own work, extensive supervision was required. The span of control was about even in a typical operation, which greatly inflated operating expenses.

No employee knew very much about all the different tasks needed to serve the customer. As a result, all too often customer inquiries were shuttled from one department to another as employees attempted in vain to find someone with the knowledge relevant to the customer's problem. Also, there were many missed opportunities for selling company products, because only the sales department was allowed to recommend products to customers. Taylor believed these problems were the predictable result of poor organization design.

REDESIGN OF THE CUSTOMER SERVICE DIVISION

Taylor found an excellent opportunity to try a different design when three regional customer service centers were consolidated into one new center. The new center would eliminate the extra costs associated with operating three different facilities, including the costs of maintaining three separate management staffs. Also, building a new facility permitted the installation of an improved telephone system and a state-of-the-art computer information system.

The old centers would be shut down in phases as parts of the new center came on-line and replaced them. Employees and managers of the old centers were allowed to transfer to the new center. However, two of the three old centers were in distant states, so new hires would constitute most of the staff of the new center.

The operations manager of the new customer service center was Harry Simkins. Simkins was a 35-year industry veteran who had risen through the ranks at LIFECO. He was extremely knowledgeable about unit operations. Simkins also was known as a people person, and he was very well liked by his peers and subordinates.

Kelsey Taylor used the design of the new facility as an opportunity to redesign the human organization. The redesign effort was led by a design team that included six employees and three managers, representing different levels and functional departments. The design team was headed by Harry Simkins, and it reported regularly to Kelsey Taylor. She attended some key meetings of the group, but generally she gave it considerable latitude to develop proposals for change. As a member of the senior executive group for LIFECO, Taylor took design team recommendations to top corporate management when this was needed.

The design team's plan was innovative. The new organization would be built around self-managing teams, each serving a defined geographic territory. Within its territory, the team was responsible for most of the tasks needed to service the customer, from sales to policy service. This built identification with and knowledge of customer needs. One important goal of the design was to train employees so any team member could handle almost any phone call from any customer. The teams would be responsible for managing their own performance. There were to be no first-line supervisors for the teams; rather, area managers would be responsible for assisting several teams.

THE SKILL-BASED PAY SYSTEM

One of the innovations of the new organization design was a skill-based pay (SBP) system. The SBP system gave employees incentives to learn new skills. The design team believed such incentives were critical to ensuring employees had the technical knowledge they needed to serve the customer and to manage their own performance in the teams.

The tasks the teams were required to perform were defined and organized into 12 skill blocks. Each skill block was a set of related skills. The skill blocks were roughly equivalent in difficulty, so each block typically required about four months for an employee to learn through training and use on the job. Employees were entitled to ask for certification in a new skill block four months after their hiring date, and afterward, four months after their last certification. Any employee passing a certification test was eligible to receive training in a new set of skills.

There was no guarantee that every employee who wanted to advance could be certified every four months; problems with providing training, work-load problems, or other factors might slow the training and certification process. Under ideal conditions, however, an employee could acquire the skills associated with all 12 blocks in three years.

Each time an employee passed the certification examination for a new skill block, he or she received an increase in base pay. The pay increases were considerable; employees moving from the entry rate through all 12 blocks would more than double their base pay. Needless to say, skill-based pay represented a powerful incentive, and it was effective in building employee commitment to training and job rotation.

PROBLEMS WITH SKILL-BASED PAY: YEAR 1

Although skill-based pay was popular with employees as a concept, the system did not work well at first because of startup problems at the new customer service center. The training department was overloaded and behind schedule from the beginning in putting together the training packages needed for employees to prepare for certification examinations.

The new computer information system, which was critical for responding on-line to customer inquiries, was plagued by software problems for nine months. Ultimately, the program had to be revised extensively. This meant all employees who were trained initially on operations that involved the computer system (such as handling customer calls) had to be partially retrained before their skills were usable. Those for whom training or the technology was not ready could not advance as rapidly as they hoped.

By the end of the first year after the new center opened, employees who were present from startup (some 80 percent) were about 10 months behind schedule in advancing through the SBP system. Employees had been told at the time of hiring that there were no guarantees of advancement every four months—four months was the fastest it was possible to advance. However, employees tended to forget this message and even to deny that it had been given to them, despite proof to the contrary. There was near consensus among employees that it was unfair to keep employees from advancing because of the failures of other people (such as the training department and the software programmers).

One year after startup, the original hires had expected to be certified in three skill blocks and consequently to have received three sizable pay increases. Instead, almost none were certified in more than one block. The design team became the vortex of the storm over skill-based pay. The design team developed a compromise that would preserve the overall concept of SBP, yet respond to employee complaints.

The compromise called for all those hired after the first year to be advanced through the skill-based pay system as it was originally designed. This was reasonable, because the problems with training programs and software had been solved, and it was possible for new hires to advance at the planned rate of one block every four months. The work teams also would emphasize to new hires that they might not be able to progress if problems arose.

The compromise also called for those hired during the first year of operation to be "grandfathered" for a year. That is, they would receive one extra pay increase to compensate for the loss of two training and certification periods during the startup year. During the coming year, it was the responsibility of all "grandfathered" employees to make up the extra skills for which they were being paid.

Kelsey Taylor and the rest of the executive group at LIFECO accepted this compromise reluctantly. The executives viewed the original skill-based pay plan almost like a contract. They were willing to keep their end of the bargain, which would pay LIFECO's back-office employees handsomely by industry standards. In return, they wanted proof that employees had the skills for which they were being paid. They ratified the compromise only because of the fervor with which it had been advocated by the design team.

PROBLEMS WITH SKILL-BASED PAY: YEAR 2

The compromise worked as planned for the new hires. However, there continued to be a problem with the original hires. The main reason for this was LIFECO's accelerating success. Heavy overtime was needed to handle all the new customers, leaving less time than was desirable for training. Veteran employees were able to keep up a normal pace of advancement, but only 10 percent made up the skill block for which they were receiving extra pay by the seventh month of the second year.

In the eighth month of Year 2, the design team began to consider how to handle this problem at the insistence of the executive group. Kelsey Taylor personally relayed her own and the executive group's concerns to Harry Simkins. The executive group would not approve paying employees for skills they did not have in violation of the design team's original plan and the later compromise.

The executives were unsympathetic to claims that forces beyond employees' control were the cause of lost income. They never promised employees they would receive pay increases on a regular timetable, come hell or high water. They saw the design team's task as finding ways to accelerate the training and certification process so employee skills could catch up to pay levels. If this was not done, several key executives would favor scrapping the novel SBP system, on the grounds that it was more expensive and troublesome than it was worth.

The design team struggled unsuccessfully for several weeks to meet this challenge. To help the group, Kelsey Taylor asked me to be a process facilitator at an all-day workshop the following month. She and the rest of the executive group had been preoccupied with other matters, not the least of which was the threat of a hostile takeover by a larger company. She had not been able to meet with the design team for some time, and she would not attend the workshop. She briefed me, however, and also suggested I call Harry Simkins in preparation for the meeting. I did so.

MY ROLE AT LIFECO

I had worked at LIFECO over a period of four years. Most of my work had been with the senior executive team. Two years before, when the design team began considering skill-based pay, I had conducted a day-long workshop on the topic to help launch the design process. Thus, I knew the key players at LIFECO and the customer service center personally, if not well.

Taylor asked me to work with the design team as a process facilitator, not as a technical consultant on skill-based pay. She believed the team was having problems working together as a group because it seemed unable to come up with effective, creative solutions to apparently straightforward problems. Thus, although my expertise on skill-based pay was a plus, this expertise was not the reason for my invitation to the workshop.

THE DESIGN TEAM WORKSHOP

The design team workshop did not go well. The team had a different agenda than the one specified by LIFECO executives. The team spent most of its time on one theme: there was no way for the veteran employees to make up the skill block they owed, given the overtime workload. As a result, many design team members wanted to go back to the executive group with a proposal to grandfather the veteran employees for another year, as long as these employees were making reasonable progress under the skill-based pay plan. In essence, they wanted to maintain the status quo.

Members of the design team emphasized how hard they were working, the good performance record of the teams, employee dedication to learning all the tasks in the teams, and the progress in the certification process. One member said:

> The least the company can do to reward the people who built this organization up from nothing is to cut us some slack on this grandfathering. It wasn't our fault that the computer didn't work, or that training didn't have its act together, or that we've had an ungodly amount of overtime this year.

A number of heads nodded in assent.

The team knew the executive group disliked the grandfathering scheme. However, team members wanted to believe (wrongly, I thought) the executives would consider extending the compromise. No one from the group strongly expressed the position that the design team should find ways of accelerating training and certification.

Simkins did not take much of a leadership role at the meeting, and he did not even relay Kelsey Taylor's thoughts to the group. His main response to the group was to agree with it. Nearly all of the informal leadership in the group was provided by the members who were from work teams, not from management. The informal leaders seemed defensive and self-righteous.

Most of my process interventions, which became increasingly active and confrontational, went nowhere. For example, I pointed out, "You can't say that it is impossible to accelerate the training and certification process. You haven't tested your assumption by engaging in serious problem solving on how to speed up training and certification." The group's response to this comment was silence.

At a break in the meeting, I expressed my concerns to Simkins. In response, he restated the view of the nonexempt employees on the design team, and he said it would be "heartbreaking" to deny them continued pay increases when they were working so hard and performing well. He also was more concerned about keeping the peace in the center than anything else.

He said a disaster could befall the center if the self-managing teams became disenchanted with the company. Employees might refuse to work overtime, make deliberate and costly mistakes, join a union, or do any number of other things. There was more danger of this than in a traditional organization because employees were essentially unsupervised. No one was making any threats now, but it could happen, he said. After the break, Simkins's behavior did not change, and neither did the group's.

I was becoming worried. It looked like the design team and LIFECO executives were two camps with hardened positions. The design team believed the compromise was fair and did not want to change it—ever. Team members believed they were making good-faith progress at learning new skill blocks. Also, they viewed the executives as ungrateful for not appreciating all the veterans had done to make LIFECO a success.

The executives saw the design team's compromise as reneging on the original deal. This made them suspicious of the integrity of the design team; some began to wonder if they had a "union without a union down there." They viewed the design team as ungrateful for not appreciating the extra costs involved in the skill-based pay plan and for not realizing that veteran employees had something during the first year that other people didn't—a job.

My best guess was that if design team members went to the executive group asking for (or demanding) an extension of the compromise for another year, without having seriously considered how to meet the terms of the original compromise, they would be flatly rejected. Much worse, I feared that such an encounter would be so hostile it would jeopardize much that had been built during the last two years. The entire SBP plan might be abandoned by the executives. Also, the credibility and future success of the design team were threatened. The group had been a tremendous asset to the company, but it might never be trusted in the same way by the executives on matters other than SBP. Indeed, a number of members might become so disenchanted they would quit the group.

MY OPTIONS

The workshop was half over, and little progress had been made. What should I do? My options, as I saw them, included the following:

1. Do More of the Same—or Nothing. My contract was to facilitate the workshop, not to act as a content expert on skill-based pay or to ensure the group achieved any particular outcome. Perhaps I should simply fulfill the terms of my contract, whether or not the group welcomed my interventions. Doing nothing (or nothing different) is always an option for consultants and facilitators, and it should always be considered. I thought carefully about whose interests any action would serve. I also thought about whether any action would serve the needs of the group as opposed to serving my needs to feel effective.

This option had both pluses and minuses. On the positive side, I would avoid violating the role for which I was hired. I would not, for example, detract from the group's sense of responsibility for its own behavior and decisions. Moreover, I did not want to impose my agenda on the group. On the negative side, I thought it likely that unless something changed, the group was headed for a potentially disastrous collision with the executives.

2. Confront the Design Team with the Executive Perspective.

This option would require stepping out of the process facilitator role and acting as a consultant with expert information. My diagnosis was that the failure of Simkins and other management members of the design team to convey the executive perspectives was a critical problem. Team members sized up the situation in a smug, self-righteous way, without understanding what the executives thought and how deeply they believed it. They were courting disaster without realizing it.

This option had advantages, but it was risky. The advantage of this option is that it might permit the group to react in an informed way to the executives. Also, in my view, the group would not take seriously the possibility of meeting the terms of the original compromise unless it was forced to do so by external pressure. In the end, the group still might decide it was impossible to meet the terms of the compromise, but the group had work to do before it could make this decision in an informed way.

There were several dangers in this option. One was that it could threaten my ability to work with the group, because I would be seen as a "management tool" rather than as an objective third party. Indeed, it would seem peculiar for me to convey the executives' views when neither the executives nor the managers on the design team had done so in the past. Another possibility was that the group might react so angrily to my confrontation that the meeting would end. Finally, the group might lose its sense of responsibility for its own decisions and react with passive resignation.

I also felt ethical qualms about this option. Would I be imposing myself where I did not belong, in the middle of a dispute over pay between workers and managers? Would I be doing employees any favor by decreasing the ardor with which they fought for more pay? Or would I be helping preserve a system that made them among the best-paid back-office employees in their industry?

3. Call Kelsey Taylor.

I believed the design team never would have gotten stuck if Kelsey Taylor had attended group meetings. She would not have been shy about representing the executive perspective, and the group respected her. Perhaps I could arrange for her to come to a future meeting. I thought this might be a good thing to do, but it was relevant to my actions for the rest of the workshop only if I chose the first option. She was unavailable to the group that day.

4. Mediate between the Design Team and the Executive Team.

Obviously, both the design team and the executive team misunderstood the other's position. Perhaps the issue was one of intergroup conflict, not the failure of the design team to solve a problem effectively. Rather than risk appearing to take the executives' side, perhaps what was needed was someone to help each side understand the other better. I could suggest suspending the meeting until intergroup issues were resolved and could suggest processes for resolving the intergroup conflict.

On the positive side, intergroup conflict was obvious and real. Both sides might be receptive to this idea. It would leave responsibility for the issues and decisions to LIFECO personnel, rather than with me. On the negative side, this option would postpone resolution of the conflict for some time, certainly until an intergroup meeting could be held. Moreover, there was no guarantee the intergroup conflict would be resolved. It might be that each group would understand the other better, but that both sides would simply understand better why they thought the other was unreasonable.

QUESTION FOR DISCUSSION

What course or courses of action should I choose?

Los Angeles County Sheriff's Department: Transorganizational Intervention

Alan M. Glassman
California State University, Northridge
Thomas G. Cummings
University of Southern California

In October 1988, we were asked by the commander of the Contract Law Enforcement Bureau of the Los Angeles County Sheriff's Department (LASD) to conduct a two-day conference for the management of the LASD's Field Operations' regions and the city managers and administrators of the incorporated cities for which the LASD provided contract services.

The conference, the second annual, would focus like the first had on examining and improving the relationship between the LASD and its contract cities, according to the commander. He added that although the first conference, which had been facilitated by another consultant, had been considered a good starting point, there had been no follow-up or tangible results, thus we could expect some skepticism. Also, only 12 of the 37 city managers and administrators had attended the first conference. This year's conference was scheduled for late January 1989.

We agreed to facilitate the conference because the LASD was a long-standing client of the senior author's and we had both worked previously with some of the city managers/administrators. Based on our previous consulting experiences, we quickly agreed on interviewing some of the participants and reviewing materials from the initial conference.

Personally, we were hesitant to undertake this effort. First, although the conference was already scheduled, there was no clear idea on what was to be accomplished. Second, the risks seemed quite high; the parties had little experience working as a large group and we had only a short time to do our preliminary work and design the conference. Third, from the description of last year's efforts by the previous consultant, we thought that he would have a much better sense of the participants' needs than us. Although we raised each of these issues with the commander, his attitude was, "We want you, and we know you'll do a good job."

THE LOS ANGELES COUNTY SHERIFF'S DEPARTMENT

The Los Angeles County Sheriff's Department provides law enforcement services to approximately 2 million persons living in an area of about 3,200 square miles. The department consists of nearly 9,100 police classification and civilian employees and has an annual budget that exceeds $800 million. As shown in Exhibit 1, the department is headed by an elected sheriff and 11 executive officers (i.e., undersheriff, assistant sheriffs, and chiefs) and is divided into five divisions and three field operations regions.

The department's decentralized investigative and patrol services operate on a 24-hour basis from 20 stations located throughout the county. Station detectives investigate local crimes, supported by a centralized detective division that specializes in certain specific crimes including arson, homicide, narcotics, and vice. Additional centralized support is provided by Special Enforcement Bureau (SWAT), Aero Bureau, Emergency Operations Bureau, Crime Laboratory, and Records Bureau.

Contract Law Enforcement

Contract law enforcement refers to an intergovernmental agreement between an incorporated city and the Los Angeles County Sheriff's Department through which the department provides the needed patrol, investigative, and ancillary services (i.e., traffic enforcement, community education programs) requested by city officials. Cities can contract independently or as partners in regional programs with other contract cities.

The monetary savings to a participant city can be substantial primarily because of the sharing of resources, facilities, and overhead expenses. In theory, each city pays only its proportionate "user costs." In 1989, 38 of the 86 cities in Los Angeles County contracted with the LASD at an annual cost of approximately $91 million. In addition, tax revenue provides all cities with specialized services such as transportation of prisoners, use of the crime laboratory, and policing of special events.

EXHIBIT 1 Los Angeles County Sheriff's Department Organization Structure

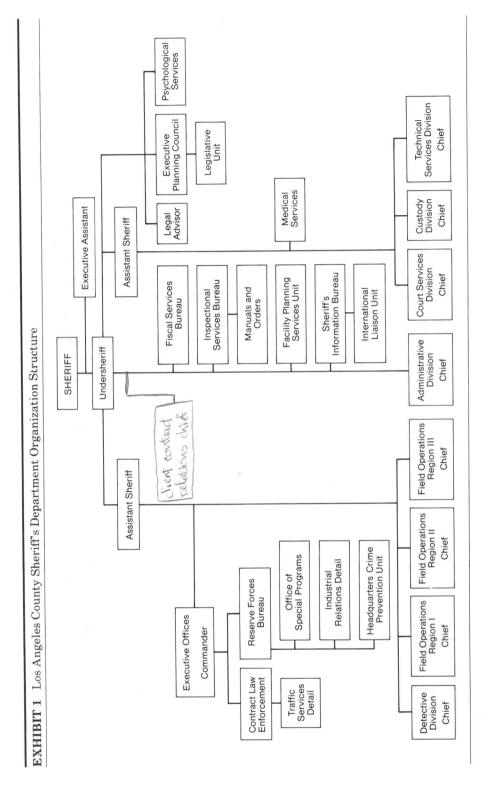

Each patrol station is usually commanded by a captain who fulfills the role of chief of police for the contract city/cities served by the station and who maintains a close working relationship with city officials. The contract law enforcement commander works directly with the three field operations regions' chiefs and regional operations commanders to provide functional supervision over the station captains. The contract law enforcement commander is the LASD's liaison with the contract cities and is involved in all aspects of program development and contract administration.

PREPARING FOR THE CONFERENCE

As a starting point, we reviewed last year's conference report written by the previous consultant. This included both the preconference data-gathering findings and the conference outcomes. From our perspective, the report, not the data, was disappointing.

First, the preconference data simply listed verbatim the actual responses of the respondents to four questions:

What is the role of the city manager/administrator in law enforcement?

What is the role of the sheriff's station captain in the administration of the city?

What are your views concerning Los Angeles County contract law enforcement as contrasted to city police departments?

What problems would you like to see discussed at this conference?

As expected, respondents' perceptions differed significantly, suggesting many potential conflicts and the need for a systematic framework for using the data. Yet, no analysis of the data (134 statements) existed, and it was difficult to determine how it was used at the first conference. Exhibit 2 offers examples of respondent statements.

Second, and more important, based on these perceptual differences, the previous consultant identified the major problem as communications and designed the initial conference as an information-sharing session. The exchange of ideas seemed to duplicate the preconference data, and there was no attempt to push the parties to further action. This offered a clue why no postconference activities had occurred during the past year. At the same time, we were delighted to have the data, which provided an excellent foundation for our forthcoming interviews.

EXHIBIT 2   Representative Responses to First Consultant's Preconference
Survey

Q: *What is the role of the city manager/administrator in law enforcement?*

- The city manager must be actively involved and responsible for the delivery of proper law enforcement services in the community.
- The city manager plays a variety of roles related to law enforcement, including providing the financial resources for law enforcement and acting as a communicator between the city council and the sheriff's department.
- Help keep the cost of law enforcement down while maintaining a safe level of service. To be supportive of a reasonable request to increase the level of service.

Q: *What is the role of the sheriff's station captain in the administration of the city?*

- The station captain serves as the department head of the law enforcement function in the city. He is accountable to the city manager and is responsive to the city's law enforcement needs and problems.
- To serve as a department head, just like any other department head. He/she should be an intregal part of the city management team.
- I see the role of the station captain as being a communications facilitator, idea innovator, and project implementer.
- To work closely with the city manager in the area of public safety; to maintain an absolute line of communication; to be supportive of the city manager; and, most important, to stay out of city politics.

Q: *What are your views concerning Los Angeles County/contract law enforcement as contrasted to city police departments?*

- Higher quality of services. Better trained personnel. Less politics associated with the contract model. Better backup services.
- In contrast to a chief, the station captain is not the final decision maker on matters concerning policy, funds, and personnel.
- City officials need to occasionally be advised that contract cities can't dictate changes in policy.

Q: *What problems would you like to see discussed at the conference?*

- How cities can influence change in the Los Angeles County Sheriff's Department.
- A general discussion of how the station captain can be more responsive to the city administration.
- Elected officials' roles, conflicts of city policies and sheriff's policies, incorrect perceptions of each other's priorities.
- Relationships between the city manager and station captain—how to keep them positive.
- The rising costs of law enforcement, the future of city government, the recruitment of qualified personnel.

The Real Issue—Client-Centered Service

After interviewing a small number of LASD operational officers, the commander of the Contract Law Enforcement Bureau, and several city managers/administrators, it became apparent a fundamental shift was occurring in the relationship between the LASD and the contract cities:

1. The contract cities were seeking increased awareness of local priorities and increased responsiveness to local law enforcement needs by the LASD. This was particularly important to those cities with the greatest cultural diversity.

2. The contract cities were seeking increased involvement in local community activities by LASD station personnel. This was perceived as a means for developing greater commitment to the local community.

3. The contract cities were seeking increased input/consultation in both resource allocation and operational decisions. This was considered critical to those city managers being criticized by city councils and citizen groups for their lack of knowledge concerning LASD activities.

As summarized by one of the LASD field operations chiefs:

> Our contract program is seemingly based on a "this is what we do and this is how we do it" premise, when more properly it should be based on meeting local needs as perceived by the people who engage our services. Our attitude, like most of law enforcement, is that we know best, what is best, for the citizen.

As we learned more, we began to define the relationship between the parties as a transorganizational system; that is, a group of organizations (i.e., contract cities, LASD) that have joined for a common purpose (i.e., law enforcement) and are experiencing conflict in defining service delivery and role responsibilities. We then perceived the conference as a "convention" of key participants in the transorganizational system. It would provide a face-to-face forum within which participants could jointly decide how best to structure their roles, responsibilities, and interrelationships.

Redefining the Conference

In early December, we met with the commander of the Contract Law Enforcement Bureau and proposed the conference be reframed from focusing on the relationship between the LASD and its customers (i.e., contract cities) to analyzing how the LASD and the contract cities jointly function as a single system.

We also noted that our specific focus would be on identifying common problems and concerns of the members of the system and that significant postconference work would probably be required to resolve them. Unless the LASD was willing to be an active participant in pursuing these issues, it was best not to adopt this framework—it would do more damage than good. Lastly, we requested that the sheriff and/or undersheriff attend the conference as one of the major "players" in the system.

The commander was very supportive of our approach, noting, "It's time for a candid discussion of the total relationship," and "I believe the department is prepared for greater equality in the relationship—I don't believe you'll encounter much defensiveness or resistance."

During the next week, the commander obtained the support of the three chiefs, the undersheriff (who would attend), and the sheriff (who could not attend because of previous commitments on the dates of the conference). We then drafted a letter to the 37 city managers/administrators indicating a different conference than last year's—a conference that could "substantially change the relationship between the LASD and its contract cities." We received acceptances from 31 city managers/administrators. The LASD would be represented by all station captains, regional commanders and chiefs, the undersheriff, and members of the Contract Law Enforcement Bureau totaling 34 members.

THE CONFERENCE

As we began to plan the conference, we recognized that the relationship between the parties was typical of most transorganizational systems—underorganized. There was considerable ambiguity about the law enforcement needs of the different cities and about how the LASD should relate and provide contract services to them. Consequently, if the conference was to have a significant impact (our goal), we would have to play an activist role in providing direction and in mediating conflicts (Cummings, 1984). We decided on a dual format for the conference:

- To include brief lecturettes as an educational tool to help the participants frame their relationship and identify systemwide issues. Specific topics included, "Societal Change and Organizational Life Cycles," "Transorganizational Systems," and "Organization Design and Product Delivery." Underlying each was the concept of client-centered service.
- To organize the bulk of the conference around small-group data generation and large-group feedback sessions to explore interpersonal relationships and differences in organizational and personal values, the latter being critical in understanding responses to potential changes.

We also chose to follow an action-research model throughout the conference. Each segment could be modified to reflect outcomes from the previous segment. This provided the flexibility necessary to "stay with the data" and to jointly determine future steps.

Outcomes

The discussions precipitated by our lecturettes resulted in the following consensus:

• The LASD is a very mature (i.e., very bureaucratic) organization (1) exhibiting extensive control systems, rules, and procedures, (2) seeking new growth oportunities (i.e., contracting with additional cities, offering new services), and (3) valuing its reputation for quality. Key questions included: Can the LASD, a mature, elaborate bureaucracy, avoid a declining relationship with contract cities seeking a new type (although ill-defined) of relationship? Can managers who "grew up" in a stable, dominating bureaucracy overcome their normal resistance to change and explore new internal and external relationships?

• The LASD was appropriately structured to deliver a generic service/ product (i.e., contract law enforcement) at a minimum cost. The obvious tradeoff for cost-effectiveness was the inability to respond quickly and adequately to specialized customer (i.e., a contract city) needs.

On the other hand, many of the issues raised by the contract cities suggested a desire for a more specialized, perhaps individually oriented, contract law enforcement service. Since it was recognized that the costs of this approach would be prohibitive, it was suggested the LASD could be more client-centered if it loosened its present structure slightly and provided some add-on to the generic services and products available.

• The participants accepted that they were part of a transorganizational system, they were pursuing their own vested interests, and conflicts existed between city managers/administrators and members of the LASD. They concluded they needed to develop new conflict resolution mechanisms within the system that allowed for early identification and amelioration of normal conflicts.

While nearly everyone agreed there was nothing new in these conclusions, they also recognized it was the first time they had thought of themselves as a single team. As noted by one city administrator, "Seeing an issue from the point of view of the LASD and some of the other city administrators and being responsible for resolving the issue to the satisfaction of nearly everyone provides a very different perspective."

Many of the specific issues generated by the subgroups were explored during these discussions. Exhibit 3 summarizes the output of the initial mixed groups in identifying issues within the system. During these group sessions, the undersheriff acted as an observer; he then participated in the larger discussion. Although initially viewed as inhibiting some LASD openness, he soon became an active, candid participant and helped establish some open exchanges.

EXHIBIT 3 Systemwide Issues Identified by Mixed Groups

Group 1
1. Stability of assignment of sheriff's personnel (i.e., frequent movement is viewed as a positive step in career development) and its impact on deputies' loyalty to city versus loyalty to department.
2. Inability to tailor equipment to special demands of city (note: discussion ranged from city seals on patrol cars to weapons).

Group 2
1. Timely responses to city needs/requests for information.
2. Deputies need to better understand their relationship to the city manager/administrator and city council; develop training programs, set standards of accountability.

Group 3
1. Identification of deputies with city.
2. Communication disparities within and across LASD commands.
3. Degree to which cities should influence LASD priorities/philosophy.
4. Need to resolve inherent conflicts between local city concerns and sheriff's countywide concerns.

Group 4
1. Minimizing cost of law enforcement (i.e., current emphasis on   civilianization of LASD positions) versus public demand for sworn personnel.
2. Improvement of formal communications between LASD and contract cities (e.g., quarterly meetings between LASD executives and city managers/administrators to discuss policy issues).

Group 5
1. Relationship of the deputy to the community.
2. Avoidance of "us" versus "them" mentality.
3. Need for greater LASD decentralization—structure too cumbersome for effective interaction.

Group 6
1. Greater emphasis on personnel development to meet city needs, including recruitment and retention of qualified people within city and management development programs.
2. Better information/understanding of financial aspects of the relationship (e.g., risk management, cost studies).

Throughout the two days, we were very directive in our role. We forced the participants to (1) identify root causes for identified issues, (2) provide specific examples of behaviors they liked and disliked, (3) relate their discussions to our lecturettes, (4) challenge each others' assumptions, and (5) confront conflicts. Additionally, we summarized data for them and continually explored issues beyond the point where they felt comfortable. In short, while the participants were keenly aware they were dealing with substantive matters (we received much private, positive feedback throughout the conference), they were equally aware of their high dependence on us.

Near the end of the conference, the group began to struggle with the question of how to proceed after the conference concluded. Proposals ranged from assigning the Contract Law Enforcement Bureau the responsibility for using the conference data to further improve the relationship beween the LASD and the contract cities, to establishing several mixed groups to make recommendations on specific issues, to reflecting on the conference and meeting again in four months to take the next steps. This search for direction was not unexpected, given their lack of experience as a team, the substantial amount of data generated, and the far-ranging discussions that occurred. After approximately one hour, a city manager turned to us and pointedly stated:

> It's obvious that we will not reach a satisfactory conclusion on this question. My fear is that next year we will be asked to attend another retreat; they are fun, and we will again wonder why nothing of substance occurred during the year.
>
> I'll grant you that this conference generated some excellent discussions and solid ideas for further improving relationships, but how do we capitalize on our desire to do something? You are the experts; how do we sustain our focus on a transorganizational system and not revert back to single city or LASD parochialism? What do you recommend?

Others quickly affirmed their commitment to working as a group on the identified issues, but they noted many constraints such as lack of time, distance, coordination problems, and frequent LASD transfers. As the discussion ended, it was our turn, one more time!

QUESTIONS FOR DISCUSSION

1. Discuss the appropriateness of initially defining the relationship as a transorganizational system (include factors that support this framework and factors that suggest that it was a mistake). Can you defend another framework?

2. Develop a recommendation to the group for utilizing the conference data during the year. What role should the OD consultants play?

REFERENCE

Cummings, Thomas G. "Transorganization Development." In *Research in Organization Behavior,* vol. 6, ed. Barry Staw and Larry Cummings. Greenwich, Conn.: JAI Press, 1984.

Allan Labs: Strategic Change Intervention

Susan A. Mohrman
University of Southern California

Consulting for an organization undergoing strategic redirection requires infinite patience, a strong constitution, tolerance of ambiguity, fascination with organization, love of puzzles, and optimism about people. This case, which focuses on the early stages of such a change effort at Allan Labs, illustrates why.

Allan Labs is an interesting organization. It is a nonprofit organization consisting of 15 laboratories, with 250 to 1,000 employees each, performing highly sophisticated research in the areas of health, nutrition, and the environment. I was immediately drawn to its diversity—to the large number of highly specialized scientists and technologists who populated the 15 laboratories. Employees in each specialty speak a different technical language and see the world through a different set of lenses. They have to find ways to work together to solve complex problems about which any one set of lenses gives only partial clarity.

The work of Allan Labs is fascinating to me. Within these labs are people at the cutting edge of knowledge, working to solve real-life problems like cancer, AIDS, the disposal of toxic waste, and the preservation of the ozone layer. Finding a solution to these problems requires systematic, patient, careful, steady, and intense investigation. On the surface, the pace at times seems at odds with the urgency and severity of the consequences of the problems for humanity. These people work at the levels of the atom, the genetic code, and chemical processes—far removed from the pollution and human suffering experienced by most of us, yet at the very heart of the efforts to address these problems.

Each laboratory has its own facilities and is composed of multiple research teams. Each research team is different. Its size, diversity, schedule, budget, and goals are all determined by the nature of its research agenda and the contracts that govern it. Various special roles exist to link the specialties—people who can bridge several disciplines or people who are good at sitting down with diverse contributors and helping them understand and work with one another. Norms protect professional autonomy and standards. People are bound together by their quest—not by loyalty to an organization.

I was attracted by the organizational challenges this posed. In my first consulting project with this organization, I had worked closely with a lab that was looking for ways to neutralize certain toxics. In that project, I was struck by the dichotomy between the way people described the work they did and the way they described the organization.

Work was intrinsically interesting and inherently exciting. They spoke of the "aggravations" of dealing with people from different disciplines—chemists, software engineers, microbiologists, and so forth—and of trying to relate to the "strange understandings" they had of the world. Nevertheless, they understood they needed each other, even if they often avoided dealing with each other. They loved their work and would willingly spend hours telling you about their piece of the intricate puzzle that had to be solved in order to make progress. I was a willing listener. I found the content interesting and was attracted by the depth of knowledge and dedication of the scientists.

On the other hand, the organization was described as a pain in the neck: "It" worked to thwart rather than facilitate work. "They" had no idea of what it took to run a lab. There was no strategic leadership—resources were spread too thin and in too many directions. People were feeling choked and unappreciated. Innovation was precluded by the bureaucrats in the "tower" (administrative offices) who made it difficult even to hire the people needed to do the job. In fact, they said, good people were being driven away despite the interesting work.

ORGANIZATIONAL STRUCTURE

This dichotomy reflected a structural division in the organization. Allan Labs has two presidents: one for science and the other for administration (see Exhibit 1). Originally established by a large grant from an inventor/philanthropist, the organization's charter stipulated that research scientists were to choose their own leadership using a collegial system similar to that found in universities.

For several decades, the organization had operated as a loosely coupled group of relatively independent labs, each responsible for raising its own contract research funds, each receiving a share of the general endowment income to invest in new endeavors, and each having a small administrative support group. In the late 1960s, as the environment be-

EXHIBIT 1   Allan Labs Organization Chart

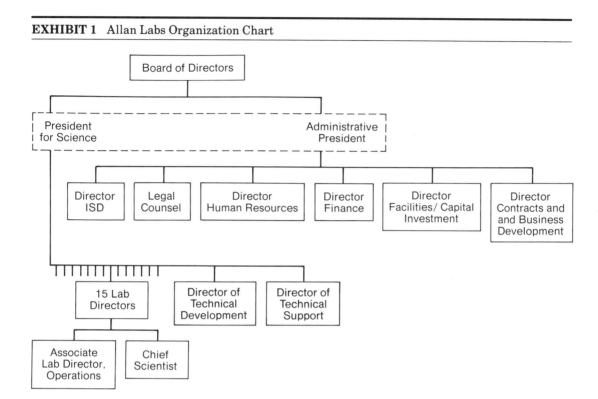

came more complex, research funds became harder to get, and the cost of research skyrocketed, administrative services were centralized, and an administrative structure grew up parallel to the technical governance structure. Legal, human resources, finance, information systems, facilities/capital investment, purchasing and contracts/business development became central support groups that grew in size and activity level during the 1970s but not in acceptance.

By the late 1970s the board of directors recognized that the increased competition for shrinking research dollars and the complexity of the environment required both a more aggressive marketing posture and the attainment of considerable internal economies. The organization could no longer afford to have the labs competing with one another for funds. The recession brought with it a severe curtailment of operating funds as funding agencies slowed payment. For the first time, Allan Labs laid people off.

During this period, an administrative president was appointed to work with the president for science with a mandate to establish closer ties with the funding community and to bring operations expenses under control. The administrative support groups encountered muffled opposition as they slowly introduced standard practices and systems and centralized decision making in such areas as facilities, purchasing, and salaries and other human resources practices. The processes by which they imposed limits, guidelines, and audits of practices, and wrested final control over purchasing of equipment and development of computer systems, left scars that would be painful and sensitive through the decade of the '80s.

The strategy of centralization and standardization worked successfully to get Allan Labs through very difficult times. The labs regained financial strength and secured a number of highly prestigious large contracts. Research productivity remained high.

Nevertheless, by the late 1980s, there were new clouds on the horizon. Research funding was again becoming more competitive, granting agencies were becoming more concerned with how funds were spent, and less slack could be built into budgets and schedules. The cost of doing research was soaring largely because of the expensive equipment and computer systems required. Most importantly, the key resource of the labs, its technical people, were becoming scarce. Competing organizations were raiding Allan Labs and open requisitions were at an all-time high. Demographic projections indicated this problem would get worse in the coming decade.

The arrival of a new administrative president triggered a fresh look at the organization and its strategy. After a year on the job, he knew the organization was not well positioned to address the challenges that would face it in the next decade. Together, the two presidents decided to systematically examine the organization's strategy.

ENTRY

Based on the relationship I had developed during an earlier project and my familiarity with the organization, I was recommended by the manager of organizational development, Jim Meyer, to work with him and the two presidents in this process. Jim's OD unit had been established to help work through the interunit conflict that had erupted during the centralization of staff functions.

Jim now had two people who reported directly to him. Their work consisted largely of teambuilding, coaching, and process consultation within and between the labs and central departments to which they were assigned. They primarily helped with the ongoing process issues of developing effective project teams when new research contracts were obtained. Jim's specialty was organization design, and he had helped the organization establish its administrative structure and helped various labs with the ongoing redesign needs that stemmed from the fluidity of contracts. Jim was trusted and respected in the organization and had an excellent sense of the politics and pitfalls of Allan Labs. I felt fortunate to be working with such a competent and enjoyable internal consultant.

My initial contract was to serve in two capacities. First, I would consult to Jim, who had never consulted to a large-scale strategic change process. Second, he and I would constitute a team of consultants with the two presidents as clients. This turned out to be a very large project, involving a long and involved change process with a large number of interventions.

Throughout the process, Jim and I have acted as a team consulting to the overall change effort first with the two presidents and then also with a top-level steering committee. In addition, I have consulted to Jim and to his staff to help them prepare to deal with the multiple thrusts and inherent complexity of systemic change. My collaboration with Jim and his consultants was very comfortable. They were well schooled in the fundamental tools of their discipline and very quick learners about the nature of large-scale change. It seemed to me we developed a mutual respect for each other and a trust that enabled us to work independently or in collaboration as the situation demanded.

A number of changes have developed—efforts such as management and supervisory training and climate survey-feedback that have extended into the labs and across the corporation. Most of these have been consulted to by the internal organizational development specialists, often with me as a shadow consultant. My contract has emerged month to month. I am comfortable with this. I see my role primarily as positioning internal people to carry on. Whenever possible, that means internal consultants, change agents, and change sponsors should play the prominent roles.

In my view, large-scale organizational change must not be dependent on external consultants. The consultant must be almost invisible to the process if organizational members are going to take ownership and enact change in their daily work lives. Consequently, I see my role as an external consultant as doing a lot of behind-the-scenes planning and coaching. Such a posture enables increased trust and collaboration between me and internal consultants and change agents.

This case focuses on the initial interventions that set the stage and started the change dynamic in Allan Labs. It then keys in on a particular leadership group and the challenges it posed to the change strategy.

LAYING THE FOUNDATION FOR CHANGE

Although both presidents expressed a desire for a strategic planning and change implementation process, Jim and I suspected their images of this process were different. We held separate interviews with the two clients to ensure that we understood what they hoped to accomplish through this process and to ascertain their initial impressions of the scope and magnitude of the task.

There were differences in their expectations. The technical president anticipated a several-hour process in which they identified key needs in the organization and initiated a few task forces to make the changes. The administrative president anticipated a process that systematically examined environmental forces and organizational strengths and weaknesses and involved organizational members in the process. At an initial agenda-setting meeting, they recognized quickly the need to spend time together to develop a shared set of expectations.

The Initial Dialogue

For three months, Jim and I facilitated weekly meetings between the two presidents, at which they shared perspectives about the organization and its strategic direction, learned where they had common and differing viewpoints, and reviewed a great deal of information about the organization and its environment. We helped structure this process of mutual exploration and data collection, but the energy to pursue various paths of inquiry came primarily from the two presidents. They were both highly articulate and very well informed about their business and the challenges it faced. They were equally knowledgeable and cared intensely about the environmental issues targeted by the work at Allan Labs. I found myself caring very deeply about these issues as well.

On the other hand, the two men knew very little about each other. At first, they were both quite cautious about exposing their inner selves. Through these intense discussions, they came to fully appreciate both the differences in their views and how their two viewpoints complemented one another and formed a systemic view of Allan Labs and its environment.

Although they were impatient to "get on with it," they realized the integration of these perspectives was the essence of the strategic and organizational task that lay ahead. We provided them with a list of questions to stimulate their process, but the discussions were wide ranging and open ended. We extracted shared views and points of disagreement that required further discussion and identified areas where data would be essential. We also steered them to consider issues they seemed to be overlooking.

Based on an environmental scan (conducted with the help of various staff specialists who collected a large amount of relevant data for them), they believed it would be possible to limit the scope of the process. They were happy with the current research focuses of the organization. They thought Allan Labs had targeted not only the most pressing issues, but also those most likely to receive ongoing funding throughout the next decade. They believed that the organization should continue to seek the same mix of funding as it had historically received, although they thought this funding would become increasingly more difficult to obtain and would require a closer relationship to funding agencies and the larger scientific community that influenced such decisions.

They concluded Allan Labs did not need a change in *what* it did; rather, it needed a change in *how* it worked—an organizational strategy that enabled it to achieve increasingly stringent performance standards. For example, they believed Allan Labs needed to find ways to achieve synergy between research programs and labs that had previously functioned almost as independent entities. Through their weekly sessions, they generated a tentative agreement about the key strategic needs of the organization; only then were they comfortable beginning to test and supplement their assumptions and ideas with input from others in the organization.

It was a somewhat risky consulting strategy to have them proceed so far without their staffs becoming involved other than as sources of requested information. Would they now be truly open to considering input from below? Jim and I allowed the process to unfold as it did because we were sure that unless these two quite different men could achieve a sense of comfort with one another and of shared organizational leadership, it would be difficult to get the two sides of the house to move together.

Gradually they came to trust that they had common values and intent and to agree about the need to link many stakeholders into the strategic direction that emerged. The danger was lessened that the strategic direction-setting process would create a leadership schism. One factor that contributed to our comfort with letting this first stage be encapsulated at the top was the remarkable openess of both of the presidents to information. They sought it, digested it, and incorporated it into their already rich understandings. Now, however, it was time to pulse the organization.

Diagnostic Interviews

The next intervention, planned collaboratively with the two presidents, was an "interview-feedback" process. In-depth interviews were conducted with 200 organizational members, including top managers, chief scientists and other key stakeholders, opinion leaders, and people with multiple (sometimes competing) perspectives from all parts of the organization. I was one of five interviewers. The others were Jim and another internal OD consultant and two high-potential managers who were also opinion leaders in the organization. Each of us pulled out the major themes from our interviews and then shared and compared them in a process designed to ensure that the data we gave the presidents were relatively raw—that is, as much as possible unbiased by the views of any of us.

The interviews (see Table 1) elicited respondents' views of the challenges the organization would have to face in the coming decade, the strategic directions and needs they saw, and organizational capability to meet these challenges. The interviewees were eager to talk—most were sharp, highly concerned individuals who had well-defined views of the organization and preferences for the future.

Once again I was struck and intrigued by the varying perspectives and "slices of reality" held by organizational members: biologists who saw the entire future of the labs as depending on attracting biogeneticists with a particular expertise; a financial officer who saw the labs as primarily "a complex business that just happened to generate knowledge"; a contracts administrator who viewed the organization as in a network of relationships with funding agencies and with the applied labs that were consumers of the knowledge generated by Allan Labs; lawyers who saw the key strategic aspect of the business as the handling of various mechanisms for patenting and licensing knowledge that ensured a stream of investment cash for the future, and so forth. For any large-scale change to work, the new direction would have to intersect with a large number of realities. A key task of the consultants, as I saw it, was to plan interventions that enabled various groups to come together to iron out new and common understandings of reality.

TABLE 1 Partial Interview Schedule: Organizational Strategic Diagnosis

1. How would you describe the current strategy of Allan Labs?
2. What is going on in Allan Labs' environment that the organization must respond to or anticipate? What kind of response is called for?
   In its funding agencies?
   Among its competitors for funds?
   Among the users of its research?
   In the work force?
   (and so forth)
3. What are the key vulnerabilities of Allan Labs?
4. Describe the organizational strengths and weaknesses of Allan Labs.

Note: In addition to these open-ended questions, a number of questions probed the specific issues the two presidents had identified as key.

Establishing the Preliminary Direction

In several intense working sessions, the two presidents and Jim and I reviewed the relatively raw data and the integrated lists of themes that emerged from the interviews and tried to make sense of areas in which there were conflicting themes. The initial strategic concerns and directions formulated by the two presidents were largely confirmed through the interviews. Most individuals in the labs felt proud of the quality of the research generated and of the contribution to solving social problems. They were content with the research focuses.

The challenges posed by the organizational environment that had been identified by the two presidents were echoed in many interviews: the need to establish closer ties with other entities, to become more cost-effective, and to be attentive to a dwindling technical work force. However, the diagnostic interviews indicated the organization was much less well prepared for the challenges it was facing than the leaders had believed. There was more distrust between labs and the "tower" than the presidents had perceived; morale was lower than they had hoped; there was little faith in the managerial capability at the middle levels of the organization to lead the organization through change; and people's frames of reference were more segmented than they had hoped.

Discussing the patterns and meanings of the raw interview data enabled the two presidents to develop a much more finely tuned sense of where they needed to lead the organization and what aspects would have to change.

During this process, both Jim and I helped clarify what we heard interviewees say and helped organize the data so they weren't overwhelming to the two presidents but also were not presented in such a way that conclusions were foregone and determined by our own biases. This fine line is made especially difficult because the client is looking to the consultant for organizational expertise and for help in understanding the data. I see my role as providing heuristic frameworks to help the clients process the information, helping them accept the information with a minimum of defensiveness, working with them to develop possible alternative directions, and providing examples of creative ways in which other organizations have addressed similar issues.

The need to proceed carefully and cautiously was clear. Large-scale change interventions, if successful, create momentum for change by disrupting the current equilibrium of the organization. This was an organization that was highly successful at producing splendid research. This high-quality research was the link between the organization and its invaluable technical staff. Organizational change efforts that interfered with the research were likely to alienate this group. Furthermore, Allan Labs is an organization that works on the basis of many logics. Those multiple logics had to be employed in the process of interpreting the data and determining action implications; yet, any particular constituency was only likely to identify with one of the logics. Laying the foundation for change would require a process to broaden perspectives.

Based on their own previous work and the interview data from within the organization, the two presidents identified three key strategic emphases: (1) the attraction and retention of technical employees; (2) the cost/value of the research knowledge produced; and (3) the effective linkages to key environmental entities such as funding agencies, competing and complementary research and development labs, the greater scientific community and companies, agencies, and applied research labs that are the consumers of their knowledge.

They formulated the following preliminary change directions for the organization:

1. To become an employer of choice in the area of health and environmental research.
2. To create synergies between the various research labs through sharing of knowledge, equipment, people, and other resources.
3. To increase teamwork in the organization; not only between various labs and various specialties, but also between the administrative and technical sides of the house.
4. To reverse the trend toward large, powerful administrative staff groups and the proliferation of paperwork and controls.
5. To strengthen the linkages of the various labs with key organizations in their environment so the work of Allan Labs remains state-of-the-art, highly visible and respected, and is effectively applied.

As can be seen, these strategic directions were primarily in the area of organizational capability rather than in the form of a changed mission or domain of activity.

Creating a Sense of Need and Vision of the Future

Jim and I advised the two presidents that the first challenge of the transition process would be to establish an understanding of the need for change throughout the organization and to get further input and buy-in to a vision of what the organization needed to become. It was decided to start with the top 100 key managers and scientists, representing both the technical and administrative sides of the organization. A three-day offsite meeting was planned to review the data indicating need for change, share the preliminary change directions, and start an input process that would eventually lead to a shared vision.

It was decided to create this mixed group in order to begin to counteract the strong divisions between various groups that were identified by many interviewees and to contribute to the expressed overarching organizational need for people to work together. One of the key themes from the interviews was the extreme segmentation of the organization, the tendency of various groups to jealously guard their autonomy and/or power, and the massive coordination voids this created. The decision to conduct the feedback in this large mixed group created some tension, of course, with the dual pyramidal structure. Such a process did not cascade through the normal organizational lines, nor did it occur within the relative safety of the more homogeneous scientific and administrative subgroups.

At this meeting, we started by having each of 10 subgroups spend 45 minutes anticipating some of the themes they thought would be present in the data. We did this to get them actively involved in thinking critically about their organization, and we hoped it would reduce their defensiveness. Then the two presidents shared the summarized themes from the interviews and their own thinking about strategic direction. They skillfully demonstrated the commonality they had discovered and the shared leadership they were prepared to exert.

The participants discussed the data in their small groups, nominated additional strategic thrusts, and requested clarification or discussion on the objectives presented. This process enabled people to raise their concerns and to hear a dialogue that began to clarify what was meant in each of the areas and why it was included. Most of the additional areas identified at the meeting could be fit under one of the existing directions. A key outcome of this component of the offsite meeting was that participants witnessed the high level of agreement that existed between the two leaders.

The second offsite activity involved breaking into 10 heterogeneous groups, two of which examined each of the strategic directions and discussed what it would take for the organization to accomplish it. The lists of areas that needed to be addressed for the five directions were in general complementary and to some extent overlapping. People left the session with a notion of how these strategic directions fit together, how they challenged the status quo, and the thinking of the two leaders in identifying these thrusts. They did *not* necessarily leave convinced of the desirability of the changes that would be required. Nor were they in all cases comfortable with the directions. For example, several of the administrative managers were uncomfortable with the fourth objective that dealt with strength and size of the staff groups.

Each manager present at the meeting was asked to take the strategic directions as they had been slightly modified and expanded, share them with their organizational units, and discuss their desirability and feasibility. From a change perspective, the organization was in the midst of the front-end processes of developing a sense of need for change and starting to create a vision of where the organization had to move (Tichy and Devanna, 1986). Given the large number of diverse stakeholders, we had designed the process to include strong leadership from the presidents, who created a framework for the change process, but strong participation and input from a wide diversity of stakeholders to refine the directions, build in responsiveness to stakeholder needs and interests, and develop ownership and common purpose.

This meeting had been conducted largely by the two presidents, with process assistance from Jim and his staff. My role was as an observer of the final day only, in keeping with our intention to position internal people as the highly visible change agents. I was there when the groups reported back about what they saw as necessary to achieve the strategic directions, and I was able to sense the effect on the group.

I focused on the multiple strong perspectives voiced by various participants. This large, heterogeneous group was able to react to and discuss data, strategic needs, and organizational directions in a thoughtful and congenial way; yet, I knew that, in practice, strong vested interests would work against each of these objectives.

The change process would have to enable the legitimate interests and concerns of a large number of groups to be expressed and acknowledged, at the same time forging progress on the basis of shared directions that enabled gradual progress toward a vision. Such a change process would require systemic thinking from people unaccustomed to thinking that way. Furthermore, this change effort, like other large-scale organizational change efforts, would involve the purposeful upsetting of a delicate equilibrium that governed current organizational performance. In such a highly successful organization involving so large a number of specialties, this caused me anxiety. Embarking on this effort required a great deal of confidence in the organizational diagnosis and in the judgments of the two presidents about the future environmental demands the organization would experience.

A month later, the two presidents received input and reactions from the staffs of each of the managers who attended the meeting. It largely took the form of additional thoughts about what needed to be done to achieve the strategic direction or concerns about unanticipated consequences of moving in these directions. For example, creating synergies between labs would require joint seminars and conferences designed to share information. Reversing the trend toward large, centralized staff groups would require accountability systems for lab managers. Being the employer of choice would require sabbaticals for technical employees.

This input, from lower in the organization, tended to be more insular and more concrete than the information gathered at the offsite meeting. In general, staffs appeared to be cautiously optimistic about the benefits to be derived from these new directions but overwhelmingly negative about the ability of the organization to pull it off. They were concerned about past attempts to manage change and about the willingness and skills of middle managers to truly support the change process.

Here was yet another of the difficulties of this change effort: the difficulty the organization had implementing change was a symptom of the organizational segmentation that the strategic change process was designed to overcome. Thus, the change process itself would have to be designed in such a way that it established organizational capability to act in an integrated way. On the other hand, the power and influence within the organization was currently vested in highly segmented units that would have to alter their own behavior patterns in order for the envisioned organization to become a reality.

This aspect of fundamental organizational change is what I find most interesting and challenging—the fact that successful organizational transition demands the very capabilities it is trying to achieve. An organization is never truly ready for such change; rather, the change process has to develop readiness by putting organizational members in situations where to be successful they have to adopt the new behaviors that are the goal of the change process.

This is most easily done in new units and structures as, for example, in a cross-unit steering committee designed explicitly to integrate multiple stakeholder viewpoints or in a one-time offsite gathering of 100 diverse individuals. It is less easily accomplished in existing organizational units, teams, and leadership groups whose members have adopted well-developed norms and values that have supported the organizational status quo. These units too will have to transform themselves. They hold the keys to organizational change: ability to reward and recognize behavior, power over careers, and power over resource allocation.

Consequently, we decided to begin the change process in three ways (see Exhibit 2): (1) develop a special leadership group (steering committee) to plan and manage the transition for the organization as a whole (Beckhard and Harris, 1987); (2) develop the two top staffs of the organization (technical and administrative) to advocate and support change in the behavior of the organizational units for which they are responsible; and (3) encourage and facilitate initiatives from within and across the various labs and departments that could serve as pilots and exemplars. Our ultimate plan was to combine the two top staffs into a strategic advisory group and develop them as a team for that purpose. However, because of the deep-seated mistrust between and within the two groups and a governance structure that had explicitly been established to allow technical autonomy, we decided it was best to first develop the teamwork and change leadership capabilities of each staff.

EXHIBIT 2 Role of Steering Committee in the Change Process

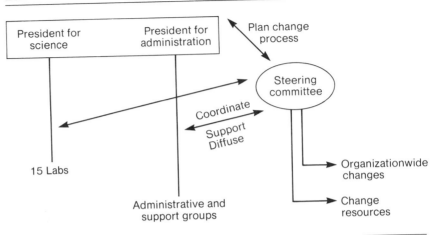

BEGINNING THE TRANSITION

The Steering Committee

The steering committee was composed of six individuals chosen because they were well respected leaders representing key perspectives necessary to the change effort. Administrative leadership was represented by two individuals from the staff of the administrative president: the director of human resources and the director of contracts and business development. The technical side was represented by one member of the central staff of the technical president, the director of technical support. In addition there was a laboratory director, a laboratory associate director, and a chief scientist, each of whom were from different labs and represented different technical backgrounds.

The mandate for the steering committee came directly from the two presidents: to work closely with them in planning and coordinating the change process; to initiate specific change efforts; to identify resources that would be needed to make the transition; and to encourage, coordinate, and diffuse learnings from changes occurring in various parts of the organization. They were empowered to establish necessary task teams and to call on various organizational groups and units for support.

These six people started about as slowly as any steering committee I have ever dealt with. It quickly became evident that mistrust permeated the group. Each individual came with a personal agenda based on his or her role in the organization. This group was a microcosm of the many divisions that existed between various parts of the organization.

Most of the members had been with Allan Labs a long time, and several had a history of unpleasant dealings with one another. The lab director had been adamantly opposed to the centralization of staffing functions and had lost no opportunity in the past several years to complain about human resources's services. The director of technical support had previously controlled contracts and business development and had established his own shadow organization, which continually challenged the work of the contracts and business development function.

The divisions between members from the labs and those based in "the tower" were particularly deep and painful. They were based on the steady erosion of laboratory autonomy during the past decade and the resentment that had caused both within the labs and also within the central staff groups who had been the targets of resistance and criticism that only got worse as power became more centralized. Both groups saw the other as unwilling to consider the overall good of the organization and in some cases as being deceitful in advocating their own needs. In addition, four of the six members were technically oriented and had almost no experience thinking organizationally. Consequently, they had to learn a whole new way of looking at Allan Labs in order to steer the change process.

Although it took what seemed like an inordinate amount of time for the steering committee to begin to trust one another sufficiently to start to constructively work on the task, it did happen. For the first three months of biweekly half-day meetings (an offsite meeting would be "impossible" given their busy schedules), they fled the task, preferring instead to endlessly share and discuss their views of the world and to periodically engage in skirmishes with one another that further sidetracked the process. Non sequiturs were the dominant mode of interaction.

I was becoming discouraged. None of the tried-and-tested techniques I had used so often with other similar groups engaged this one in anything other than a momentary glimpse into each other's worlds. Visioning, expectation setting, experiential learning, videotaping and playing back their own vividly counterproductive behavior—all seemed successful only as temporary diversions from their main purposes of establishing the legitimacy of their own viewpoints. Even when they agreed on an issue, they continued to try to convince one another. During the frequent visits from the two presidents, the group would seem to make progress at further delineating their mission and the key issues they had to deal with. However, this solidarity tended to be short lived, based on the realization that their bosses were expecting them to deliver plans and recommendations.

Finally, the group became tired of its own ineffectiveness and determined that as a team it would bring the process under control and move ahead. They had worn each other down. They started verbalizing frustration with the process and anxiety about their lack of accomplishments. My major contribution was to recognize when they had reached that point, for it was only then that they were willing to examine their own performance and set improvement targets.

I helped them articulate what they didn't like about how they were functioning and what they would have to do to be effective. They established norms to help them move ahead. They planned a three-day offsite meeting to tackle their task, including some badly needed educational input about organizations as systems, teams as performing units, and organizational change processes. From then on they began to share, integrate, and take a systemic view of the organization. They began to formulate a transition plan. I was relieved. On the other hand, I had come to understand in a very vivid manner the extent of the divisions of perspectives within the organization.

Teambuilding with the Administrative Management Team

During this period, I began working with the administrative president to develop the change leadership capacity of his staff. He understood that his staff would have to model the teamwork, interunit cooperation, and emphasis on good people management implied in the strategic directions. He had a good grasp of the shortcomings of the staff he had inherited—a staff that had been with the organization for between 10 and 30 years and had lived through a rags-to-riches transition in their own influence in the organization.

They looked back with pride on the years in which, in their view, the centralization of support staff and of organizational decision-making power had created order and organizational health out of chaos and organizational entropy. They had been well rewarded for the roles they had played in that process and had come to believe in and enjoy their new status. They believed that, in most issues, they knew better than the labs and could therefore make unilateral decisions. The failure of the labs to immediately accept the wisdom of their decisions and the importance of their changes cemented their notion that the labs were not interested in the welfare of the organization and consequently could not be trusted to make important decisions.

The administrative staff had never been managed as a group. The previous administrative president had rarely held staff meetings and believed the organization was best run by clearly delineating the areas of authority of each staff member and designing the organization so they stayed out of each other's ways. Each functional group was housed on a different floor of the tower, so they rarely had to deal with one another. Careers were largely confined within one functional area, and individuals had a great deal of in-depth knowledge of how to accomplish the responsibilities of their function in this particular organization and in

the environment of basic research labs. On the other hand, they had almost no knowledge of the broader picture and especially of life in the
labs.

The administrative president, who had had very little experience
managing a team process, was easily persuaded to begin with a teambuilding process that examined how the staff was currently functioning
and how staff members would have to function to provide leadership in
the strategic change process. He knew that he had to learn to behave
differently in order to instill trust and cooperation, but he did not have a
sense of how he was perceived.

Although passionately dedicated to the labs and their broader social
purpose, he was viewed by his subordinates as cold, impersonal, inexperi-
enced, and punishing. Because he was so intellectually engaging and eager to learn, he grasped concepts quickly. His attempts to change his behavior, however, were stiff and uncomfortable. I hoped that through an
intense offsite experience with his staff, a greater degree of interpersonal
comfort would emerge and more trust and common understanding would
result. In addition, new roles and ways of relating could be defined.

The staff members reluctantly agreed to a teambuilding process, pro-
testing mightily that they had never functioned as a team and, judging
from their success, there was no need to do so. They protested that strategic leadership was not their responsibility, and they would be "good
soldiers" if the president just told them exactly what he wanted from
them. They also let him know that "his" strategy was establishing unrealistic expectations within the organization that were causing them
trouble in getting their job done. Specifically, the objective to reverse
the trend toward large, powerful central staff groups was leading people
in the labs to openly resist influence from their staffs.

The team development process began with a series of interviews that
Jim and I conducted with each staff member, their direct reports, and a
sample of their "customers" in the labs. The interviews were designed
to get an idea of how the functioning of the administrative staff group
was perceived, its strengths and weaknesses, how this group helped or
hindered task accomplishment, and what would be needed from this
group if the new strategic direction were to become a reality. The plan
was to begin a two-day offsite teambuilding session with the feedback of
the results. Because the change processes were beginning to unfold
quickly in several parts of the organization, Jim and I decided I would
conduct the session without him. This also seemed desirable given that
his boss, the human resources director, was part of the team.

The data were among the most negative I have ever seen. The initial
interviews were of the staff members. They described their own group
quite negatively and generated a clear list of the ways in which they im-
peded each other's task accomplishment and of the needs they had from
one another. It was clear this group of individuals did not work as a coor-

dinated team, a fact they all acknowledged in advance of the interviews. Beyond that, the team members in many cases were at war with one another, paying each other back for historical slights or perceived inadequacies. The notion of being required to work together was strongly resisted by several members, who justified their stance based on their belief that teamwork "wastes time." Their behavior, however, suggested fear concerning their own capability to operate effectively in a teamwork environment.

The data from subordinates and from key customers were just as negative. Table 2 illustrates some of the data from a short survey filled out by each interviewee. The failure to work together at this level in the organization was causing problems throughout the organization. People saw their bosses working at cross-purposes, creating an extremely negative environment and providing no leadership in resolving systemic problems in the organization. They perceived a defensiveness and protection of turf that precluded good relations with employees in the labs and with employees in other administrative departments. They saw the administrative staff as a group of individuals concerned about their own personal power and distrustful of all others in the organization. Furthermore, several interviewees said they had been instructed by their bosses to give only positive information in the interviews so the president would not feel the need to continue this teambuilding process. Others said their bosses intended to sabotage the whole process by going through the motions of attending and through superficial participation.

Shortly before the interviews were completed, I was approached by two staff members who informed me they and two others believed the new strategic direction was dangerous to the organization, and they were prepared to do anything necessary to prevent it from being implemented. They thought the president was not fully aware of the needs of

TABLE 2 Sample Results from Survey about Top Administrative Team

Does the team ...	*Strength*	*Neutral*	*Weakness*
Provide consistent direction	7	17	21
Solve problems cooperatively	3	19	23
Share information openly	6	13	26
Have clear roles and responsibilities	14	22	9
Model cooperation between various parts of the organization	9	20	16
Push decisions and accountability down	8	13	24
Treat people as important assets	7	11	27

Note: (N = 45)

the organization and that he was acting out of ignorance. They also reiterated a theme that had emerged in the interviews, that a number of staff members distrusted him as a person and thought he had personally harmed their careers and their health by putting unreasonable performance demands on them. They believed none of the conditions existed for successful teambuilding and urged me to persuade the president to cancel the event.

Shortly thereafter, I was approached by two staff members who had initially been supportive of the plan for the teambuilding. They spoke of the amount of resistance building in the staff and expressed their fear that the two days would be wasted and might actually do more harm than good for the strategic change process. They even mentioned that two staff members had threatened to quit or retire if this teambuilding process got "out of hand."

Once again I was being confronted by the extreme divisions within this organization. Now, however, it was not the richness of the multiple viewpoints that impressed me; rather, it was the pathology of a system where so many distrusted and feared so many others and where self-protection drove out any semblance of cooperative behavior. I found myself not wanting to spend two days with this group. I began to have doubts about the wisdom of tampering with a system that showed so little apparent capacity or inclination to change.

The excellent science done at Allan Labs was apparently happening despite the organization; perhaps that is inherent in the nature of scientific work. Although this was the intriguing issue that kept me emotionally tied to this project, I was beginning to be concerned about the amount of upheaval this change process might cause.

As I sat down with the president to discuss the interview data and to plan the teambuilding session, I pondered whether to recommend that it be postponed until more groundwork could be laid or even canceled.

QUESTIONS FOR DISCUSSION

1. The consultant was obviously feeling some hesitancy about the advisability of proceeding with the teambuilding for the administrative staff. In a micro sense, the hesitancy came from concern that the conditions for a successful session were not present. At the macro level, the whole issue of upsetting the equilibrium of a "successful" organization was troubling. Did the organization have the resources necessary to deal with the upheaval and create a new way of being? In your view, what are the risks and benefits of proceeding with this intervention at the administrative staff level? Should the teambuilding occur? If so, how would you design the teambuilding process? If not, what are the appropriate next steps?

2. What is the appropriate role between an external change agent and internal change agents? Was it appropriate for the external consultant to take a less visible role in key events? What are the risks and advantages of such an approach?
3. In what ways is consulting within a large-scale strategic change process different from other consulting?

REFERENCES

Beckhard, R., and R. T. Harris. *Organizational Transitions: Managing Complex Change*, 2nd ed. Reading, Mass.: Addison-Wesley, 1987.

Tichy, N. M., and M. A. Devanna. *The Transformational Leader*. New York: John Wiley & Sons, 1986.

## Part IV

Practitioner Roles and Ethical Dilemmas

The cases in this part describe the diverse roles played by OD practitioners and the ethical dilemmas they encounter in helping client organizations improve themselves. There is no universal role appropriate to all settings, and change agents must modify and adjust their behavior to fit the situation. In playing different roles, practitioners often encounter complex ethical issues that can hurt client members. Addressing these issues professionally is often the cornerstone of competent OD practice.

In "The Hostile Director," R. Wayne Boss describes the reluctance to participate and anger shown to him by one of the participants in what should have been a fairly routine teambuilding intervention. The case raises ethical issues about confronting such problems in group settings.

Susan G. Cohen, in "Utilco Corporation Consumer Advisory Panel," shows the complexity of the consulting role in working to empower a consumer advisory panel of a regulated utility company. She encounters a variety of political issues and is faced with an ethical dilemma when a panel member and a corporate executive appear to make a secret deal that could jeopardize the integrity of the panel.

"McLaughlin School," by Jean M. Bartunek, describes changes occurring over a school year in the administration of a private school. The consultant acted mainly as an observer of the change process and is asked at the end of the year to present data feedback to the administrators. This raises interesting issues about the consultant's role in designing and conducting the feedback.

In "Universal Technologies," Gerald E. Ledford, Jr., describes his role as a shadow consultant offering advice and counsel to an internal change agent. The context of the case is a union-management quality-of-work-life project, and Ledford is faced with the problem of whether to actively intervene when the project's survival is threatened.

The companion cases "SDF Company (A) and (B)," by Rex C. Mitchell, describe a long-term change effort for improving the productivity and quality of work life in a consumer electronics products firm. In the (A) case, Mitchell recounts his role as an external consultant in helping the firm to create an employee learning program and to improve its production planning and management processes. Although the project appears successful, the consultant is worried that the firm is too dependent on his initiative and lacks the internal resources and commitment to maintain the changes.

Case (B) occurs about one and a half years after the end of Case (A) and describes a teambuilding intervention with the human resources department. Members of the department and key external stakeholders have serious misgivings about the performance of the human resources director, and Mitchell is faced with the problem of how to help him turn things around.

The Hostile Director

R. Wayne Boss

University of Colorado

PSL

Bedford, a county social services department located in the eastern part of the United States, had been involved in an organization development (OD) project for one year. The previous OD interventions included an organizational diagnosis and development of an action plan, followed by changes in the organization structure. Specific interventions included third-party facilitation between physicians and nurses and among nurse managers, role clarification sessions, confrontation meetings between interdependent departments, and a teambuilding meeting with the CEO and the administrative council. John, a newly hired assistant administrator, attended that teambuilding meeting during his first month on the job.

Within three months after the top-level teambuilding meeting, John participated in a similar meeting with six managers: the director and assistant director for adult services, the director and assistant director for youth services, the director of family therapy, and the director of emergency services. Unlike the other two directors, the family therapy and emergency services directors had no assistant directors reporting to them.

Before the teambuilding meeting, John and Wayne, the consultant, negotiated a psychological contract regarding their expectations of each other, what they hoped to accomplish during the session, and how they would work together to build this new group into an effective team. John clearly understood his responsibility for the meeting's success. When John asked Wayne who should participate in the meeting, Wayne suggested he include those with whom he intended to work most closely and whose cooperation was essential to ensure an effective organization. Therefore, he decided to include all six managers.

Before the three-day teambuilding meeting, which was scheduled to begin Monday, Wayne conducted diagnostic interviews with all participants. Normally, such preliminary interviews occur the day before the session but, because of scheduling problems, the interviews had to be conducted Monday morning. Wayne met separately with each of the seven participants and asked them the same four questions:

1. What do you see as the major problems facing this group of managers?
2. Do you have any issues or problems with John?
3. Do you have any issues or problems with any of the other five people who will be attending this meeting?
4. Ideally, what would you like to accomplish during this three-day meeting?

The answers to these questions helped identify the group's problems and, therefore, determined the design of the three-day meeting.

The first five interviews were uneventful. However, the interview with Bill, the emergency services director, took a different twist. He had agreed to meet with the other three directors in a three-day teambuilding meeting. However, he had not agreed to have the two assistant directors participate. The interview went as follows:

Wayne

The reason I am meeting with each of you is to find out what you see as the problems facing this group and what you would like to accomplish during the next three days. Briefly, let me outline what will happen the next few hours. I will be asking you the same four questions that I have asked everyone else and that I reviewed with you earlier. I will be taking notes, primarily because I am not smart enough to remember what everybody said. However, no one will see them but me. After the interview, I will read back to you what I have written down to make sure it is exactly what you meant. I will then meet with all seven of you, share a summary of the problems facing the group, and help you develop an agenda for this meeting.

The first question is, "What do you see as the problems facing this group?"

Bill

Is it true that the assistants will attend this meeting?

Wayne

Yes.

Bill

Is it true that you advised John to have them come?

Wayne

John asked me whom he should include, and I suggested that he invite the people whom he intends to include on his administrative team.

Bill

That is the most irresponsible and incredibly stupid thing I can imagine. Had I known before last Friday afternoon that they were coming, I would have insisted that they stay home. In fact, I should never have shown up this morning. I feel that strongly about it. Anybody who knows anything about this business at all knows that we can't talk about problems among the directors with the assistant directors there. The rule is: "Never talk over problems with your peers in front of your subordinates. Never!" It just can't be done.

Wayne

I disagree. But please tell me more. I would like to hear what you have to say.

Bill

What do you mean?

Wayne

Why do you believe it can't be done?

Bill

I don't have to answer that. You're supposed to be the consultant. You're the expert. Frankly, I am very disappointed and surprised that you're so uninformed about organization theory and the basics of how a team should be built. This is not the way to do consulting. I'm surprised that you weren't more thorough in your diagnosis. I have some real questions as to whether you know what you're doing.

Wayne

What are your questions?

Bill

Read my lips. I don't think you are competent. Do you understand me?

Wayne

I am very interested in what you have to say, but not this way. Please tell me what you would like to know.

Bill

What skills do you have?

Wayne

What skills do you think are important in order for me to be of help?

Bill

I don't know. What can you do? Can you do anything at all?

Wayne

Yes.

Bill

Like what? I don't think there is one thing in this world you can do well. Name me one thing you can do.

Wayne

Well, I breathe pretty well.

Bill

Don't play games with me. I want you to be creative.

Wayne

What does "be creative" mean?

Bill

I don't have to answer that. Anybody who's as good as you're supposed to be should know what I'm talking about. What can you do that will be the least bit creative?

Wayne

I've never really been accused of being especially creative. I am not even sure I know what that means.

Bill

You really think you are hot stuff, don't you! Well, you're not. What can you do for us? The truth is that you can't give us anything. Our hiring you is a waste of money—no question about it.

Wayne

What are the problems facing this group?

Bill

What do you mean by the word *problems*? We don't have any problems, except for the fact that we have to put up with you for three days. What is the purpose of this meeting, anyway?

Wayne

We have two major goals for these sessions: problem solving and skill building. We have been called in because problems exist in the organization, and . . .

Bill

I want to know what kind of work you do, because . . .

Wayne

Bill, you interrupted me. Now, we have been called in because problems exist in the organization, and either the people inside the organization lack the skills to resolve those problems, or they have not been empowered to use the skills they currently have. Everything we do in this meeting will be designed to help achieve those goals. However, before that can happen, we need to talk . . .

Bill

I want to know what it is . . .

Wayne

Bill, you interrupted me. Now before we can achieve these goals, we need to talk with everyone to find out what their problems are and what they would like to accomplish. I always do a diagnosis before I prescribe treatment. As I understand it, there are two things that are major sources of frustration for you. First, you don't like it when you are not consulted in advance about decisions that directly affect you. Is that right?

Bill

You're darn right.

Wayne

Second, you don't think the assistants should be attending this meeting because they will have a detrimental impact on any good that can be accomplished. Is that correct?

Bill

Yes.

Wayne

You also have some concerns about my competence. Is that right?

Bill

That's for sure.

Wayne

Do you see any other problems facing this group?

Bill

It's the wrong group for teambuilding. It can't happen.

Wayne

Any other problems?

Bill

No.

Wayne

Do you have any issues or problems with John?

Bill

None, except that he listens to you. I really can't believe he could be that stupid.

Wayne

Do you have any issues or problems with any of the other members of this group?

Bill

None. It is just the wrong group to be meeting. Do you understand what I am telling you?

Wayne

I really think so. You don't like it when you aren't consulted in advance about decisions that directly affect you, and you don't think the assistants should attend this session. Is that right?

Bill

Yes.

Wayne

What would you like to get out of the next three days?

Bill

It's not my job to decide that. You're the consultant. You're the expert. That's why we're paying you big bucks—to decide those things for us. I don't intend to do your work for you.

Wayne

>Is there anything that you'd like to accomplish during the next three days, in the ideal sense?

Bill

>Is it true that trust is very important to healthy groups?

Wayne

>Yes.

Bill

>Is it true that in order for a consultant to be successful, the participants need to trust him?

Wayne

>It helps.

Bill

>Well, I want you to know that I don't trust you as far as I could throw you.

Wayne

>I picked that up.

Bill

>How are you going to build trust in this group? Tell me what you're going to do, specifically, to help us trust each other.

Wayne

>I am not sure that I can answer that at this point.

Bill

>Why?

Wayne

>Because I haven't yet talked with all of the players.

Bill

>What are you going to do today?

Wayne

>I don't know for sure.

Bill

>What are you going to do tomorrow morning?

Wayne

>I don't know, at this point.

Bill

>What is going on here? You mean to tell me that we're going to spend three days with you, and you don't even know what you will be doing?

Wayne

>Not at this point. I always do a diagnosis before I prescribe treatment. I still need to talk with John. After we finish this interview, I'll meet with John and ask him the same four questions. I will then share with him a summary

of the problems facing this group. I'll also share your concerns, as well as my concerns about what you have told me. By that time we'll have a better idea of how we'll spend the next three days.

I will then meet with all seven of you, share a summary of the problems facing the group, and help you develop an agenda for this meeting. By that time we will all know the direction we will be going during the next three days.

Bill

Well, don't expect anything out of me, because I won't cooperate. I don't intend to do anything. In fact, I'm not going to say a single word.

Wayne

I can respect that. I don't think you should have to do anything you don't want to do. Nobody is going to be forced to do anything they don't want to do. That's the antithesis of what we are trying to accomplish.

Bill

Well, that's a good thing, because you won't hear a single word out of me.

Wayne

Is there anything you would like to see this group accomplish during the next three days?

Bill

I don't want to even be here.

Wayne

I sensed that that might be the case.

Bill

Very funny! You have no idea of the amount of pressure I feel. I have two major projects and a manuscript due for publication in the next three weeks. I also have a major grant due in Washington by Friday. I refuse to waste three days with you in this teambuilding session that will fail—AND IT WILL FAIL. I refuse to waste my time on these mindless activities.

Wayne

Why don't you just excuse yourself and go back to the office?

Bill

I've thought about it. I'd like to. But I told John that I'd be here, and I *always* keep my word.

Wayne

Tell me what you plan to do during the next three days.

Bill

I won't do anything to sabotage you. I won't hurt you, although I could do a number of things to make your life very miserable; and, quite frankly, I would enjoy that. But I won't. I am not that kind of person. But I want you to know that I won't do anything to help you. You're on your own. By the time this whole thing is over, everyone involved will know that you don't know what you are talking about.

Wayne

Anything else I need to know that we haven't talked about?

Bill

No. I'm not telling you anything else. You're not getting any more information out of me.

Wayne

One of my own personal values is to provide maximum opportunities for people to make choices, and it seems to me, at this point, that you have some choices to make. You can either stay here and participate with the others, or you can leave.

Bill

I'll stay, but I told you I'm not going to say a single word.

Wayne

Another choice you'll have to make is how you're going to behave during the session. It may be possible that John will send the assistants home. But I doubt if that will happen. So if they don't go home, then you will have another choice to make: you can sit in the corner and pout because you didn't get your own way, or you can make the best of it and tough it out, in spite of the fact that things aren't set up in the ideal way, from your point of view. Whatever you decide to do is perfectly OK with me. It will be interesting to see what you choose to do.

Before we finish, I would like to read back to you the notes I have taken, to make sure that what I have written down is what you meant. (Wayne then reviewed his notes.) Is that information correct?

Bill

Well, congratulations. You finally got something right.

Wayne

Does that mean that what I have written down is what you meant?

Bill

Yes.

Wayne

Thank you for taking the time to visit with me.

Wayne then interviewed John and asked him the same four questions he had asked everyone else. At the conclusion of that interview, he summarized the problems facing the group. That part of the interview went as follows:

Wayne

Bill's attitude is the biggest single problem facing the group right now.

John

Tell me about it.

Wayne

He's upset because he didn't know the assistants were going to be here, and he didn't find out about it until late last Friday. He's so concerned about it that he said he won't say a word as long as they are here. He believes it's against the rules of organization theory to talk about problems with peers in the presence of subordinates.

John

It sounds like he has some issues with me.

Wayne

I agree.

John

That's funny. He seemed perfectly natural to me this morning and hasn't said a word about his concerns.

Wayne

Sounds like a bit of passive aggressive behavior, doesn't it? One thing is clear: he certainly isn't willing to address his issues with you at this point.

John

Why?

Wayne

He's probably afraid of what you might do to him. He seems to be pretty nervous and insecure.

John

If he sits quietly for three days, it will be the first time in his life!

Wayne

He also said he has some major issues with me. He appeared to be quite angry, and he really got after me when I met with him.

John

What should we do?

Wayne

The first thing for you to decide is who is in charge of this meeting.

John

There's no question in my mind about that. This is my team, and I am in charge.

Wayne

Then it seems to me we have some choices. We can ignore his threats and hope he is bluffing. Or we can address the problems head on and talk about the discomfort people feel in being here.

John

What do you suggest?

Give them
a choice

Wayne

If we address the problems directly, you'll know where Bill stands within 30 minutes. If you avoid the problem, you may not know where he stands three days from now.

John

I guess that settles it.

John and Wayne then joined the rest of the group, and Wayne shared a summary of the responses to the four diagnostic questions. The issue with Bill was addressed in the following way:

Wayne

There seems to be a misunderstanding about the purpose of this meeting and why this particular group of people was chosen to attend this session. John, perhaps you could take a few minutes and explain what you want to get out of this meeting.

John

I made the decision on who should come. I asked Wayne whom I should invite, and he told me to bring the people I've identified as *my* leadership team. That's why you're here. You are the key players I've chosen to help me build this organization. I expect you to work together and not to play the games that have been played in this organization for years. I don't have time for it, and I'm not going to put up with it. We have too much to do.

If we're going to work together effectively, you're going to have to shoot straight with me, and you're going to have to shoot straight with each other. That means that if you have issues with each other, I expect you to address them directly. I promise you that I will do the same. If you have any problems with what I do, I want you to address them as well. If you aren't willing to live up to those expectations, I need to know that right now, because I don't want to waste my time and your time building a team that isn't going to work.

Everyone remained silent for a long three minutes. Wayne then said, "Any comments about what John has just said?" Five members of the group individually expressed their reactions and pledged their support to helping John be successful. Bill remained silent and looked at the floor. Wayne then asked, "Bill, do you have any comments?" Bill said nothing for almost 60 seconds. The conversation then went as follows:

Bill

I just don't like to be surprised.

Wayne

Can you say more about that?

Bill

I expected that this meeting would include John, me, and the other three directors. I didn't know that the assistants would be here until late Friday afternoon, and then I had to learn it from someone other than John.

Wayne

And the fact that John didn't tell you was problematic?

Bill

Yes. It bothered me a lot.

Wayne

Because you had a different set of expectations concerning what you would talk about with just the directors?

Bill

That's right.

Wayne

John, any comments about that?

John

I didn't make up my mind about this until late Thursday morning. I tried to reach you on Thursday afternoon, but you were out of your office. I was gone on Friday, so I asked my secretary to call you and let you know what was happening.

Bill

(Looking relieved and smiling.) Well, that makes sense. I guess I misunderstood what was going on. It's not that I strongly disagree with them being here. I just hate to be surprised. In fact, as I think about it, having them here seems like a pretty good idea. I can also support what it is that you're trying to do. It is perfectly consistent with how I like to manage my area.

Wayne

Any other comments? (The group was silent.) If not, then perhaps we could take a break for a few minutes.

Bill was the last to leave the room. As he walked past Wayne, he stopped, looked at him, and said with a frown on his face, "I don't appreciate what you just did to me." He then left.

QUESTIONS FOR DISCUSSION

1. What is the problem? *expectations, power struggle, resistant*
2. Whose problem is it?
3. What is the consultant's responsibility?
4. How do you deal with hostile, aggressive people?
5. When do you keep information confidential?
6. Who has the power/responsibility to resolve the problem?

Utilco Corporate Consumer Advisory Panel*

Susan G. Cohen
University of Southern California

During the June meeting of Utilco Corporation Consumer Advisory Panel, the following dialogue ensued:

Tim (small-business representative)

The [consumer advisory panel's] regulatory subcommittee caucused during the breakfast period and discussed the draft decision by the Public Service Commission. . . . The panel's conclusion, I think, is that we are of the same opinion still. We thought the company's proposal was fundamentally wrong; we continue to think so. We think the Public Service Commission decision is, at best, worse than the original proposal by the company. . . . I have agreed to draft a statement on behalf of the subcommittee . . . and if we [the panel] can agree upon that statement, we can represent our views directly to the service commission in whatever procedural mode is available to us.

Sarah (second-level consumer services manager)

Will the expressions you make to the service commission be as individuals or as Utilco's consumer advisory panel?

Tim

That will depend on whether we can get panel agreement on the statement. First, if the subcommittee can agree on the statement. Second, it will depend on whether the panel at large agrees.

John (vice president, external relations)

I think this goes back to a discussion we had before. . . . We talked about what is the role of the panel and . . . I believe we concluded the discussion

---

*The names of the organization, managers, and panelists have been changed, as have certain other details, to protect the anonymity of the participants. Utilco Corporation is a pseudonym. I would like to thank several managers and panelists for their comments on previous drafts of this case.

with general agreement that the panel was advisory to the company and that as individuals each person was free to go back to their own constituency and act individually.

Ralph (professional consumer advocate)

I think it is a very important issue and I have never been of the understanding that the panel is only advisory to the company. I thought we had evolved past that. . . .

John

I would have to disagree with that. . . .

Freda (consumer advocate)

We have two issues on the table. One issue is the rate case and the other issue is what the role of the panel vis-à-vis the company and any public stand is, whether it is the media, service commission, politicians, whatever. . . .

Susan (facilitator)

I think Freda's point is right that there are two issues: a substantive recommendation on the rate case that needs to proceed and the issue of what is the role of the panel and what does it mean to be advisory, which has come up many times during my tenure. . . . Let's separate the two issues and deal with the recommendation on the rate case first.

Carolyn (consumer advocate)

I am confused and frustrated and this is my last panel meeting because of this. We, as a subcommittee, have worked many hours on this issue. . . . We were united as never before on this panel. . . . It touched the fabric of almost every one of us. And I think we did a lousy job collectively, as a subcommittee, telling the panel of our fervor, our hard work, our research, and the issues in detail. As a result, the panel chose, as was appropriate, not to go forward either with a public statement or movement on this issue. And effectively it died at the December meeting. . . . Now we are seeing the prospect that it is not a dead issue. . . . But I think it is too bad that for the first time in the four years or more that I have worked on the panel, we have handcuffed ourselves by not making a written statement, which is probably not going to be any different than the written statement we came up with back in December. . . . And I am sorry because I regret leaving the friendships and hard work that I have done on this panel. . . .

Thomas (minority consumer representative)

My comment goes directly to Carolyn and also to John. Carolyn, first, I'd like to prevail upon you to reconsider your resignation. . . . John, the company would be well advised by me to rethink its position of how this panel goes public on issues that affect their constituencies. . . . We are already being challenged by some outside groups as being a rubber stamp of the company, and that aggravates me more than anything I know of to be identified in that manner. And I think that if the company has some real problems with accepting a public statement that a consumer panel makes about an issue that affects its constituencies, then I think this panel serves no real purpose to the company. . . .

Susan

> Let me try something else. I think I can help here. What we are reviewing is something that happened in December, which was that the subcommittee had a recommendation, and the discussion got stopped without the panel ever coming to some agreement or disagreement about the recommendation. Instead, a motion was made to accept the work of the subcommittee, so there was never a sense of closure for the subcommittee, and the whole panel never took a stand. All right, this is where we are right now in this groove, because we don't know really where the full panel stood on that subcommittee recommendation. But what has happened is that the big bugaboo has always been does the panel take an outside stand, and I think the panel is really divided on this issue. So, as a way of proceeding, first, we don't know where the whole panel is on the subcommittee recommendation; and second, once you have that information, there is still the issue of whether the Consumer Advisory Panel takes an outside stand.

As the meeting continued, panelists did not respond to the facilitator's request to consider and respond to the subcommittee's recommendation on the rate case. A few panelists voiced opposition to the panel taking a public stand, but they were drowned out by the stridency of the others. A vote was taken on a motion to send a letter to the service commission, and it won by a 2-to-1 majority, even though the letter would arrive after the deadline for public input.

BACKGROUND

Consumer Advisory Panel

This was the last panel meeting of my first year as a facilitator for Utilco Corporation Consumer Advisory Panel. Utilco established the Consumer Advisory Panel 10 years earlier, when the consumer movement had just begun to hit its stride. The company recognized a need to communicate more directly with customers and to establish an ongoing dialogue with consumer leaders. A university sociologist was asked to help the company assemble a consumer panel, and he became its first outside facilitator. I am the panel's fourth facilitator.

The Consumer Advisory Panel is composed of 15 consumer representatives from all areas of the state, representing a wide range of constituencies including: senior citizens, minorities, handicapped, low income, small business, students, consumer activists, and state government organizations. Members serve staggered three-year terms, although no limit exists on the number of terms members may serve. Approximately one third of the members have been on the panel since its inception.

The panel meets once a month from September through June. Its agenda is set by panel members and company representatives and includes issues such as rates, regulatory matters, customer service, outreach programs for special groups, and billing formats. Members select the subcommittees on which they wish to serve, and subcommittees meet monthly as needed.

The Company

Utilco Corporation is a regulated utility company. Its rates and tariffs are set by the state Public Service Commission. It provides service to approximately a million customers and has over 10,000 employees. Its revenue and sales are over $1 billion. Its nonregulated subsidiaries account for only a small percentage of revenues and sales. The company views the existence of a consumer panel as an efficient mechanism for being responsive to consumers in its predominantly regulated business environment.

The company has four managers from its corporate relations group who work most directly with the panel. These managers are direct reports of one another, representing four levels of Utilco's hierarchy. In addition, other company representatives regularly attend panel meetings, including a government relations manager, a customer service manager, and an operations manager. The corporate relations manager meets once a month with the facilitator to plan the upcoming panel meeting.

The Facilitator

At the time I accepted the position as facilitator, I was completing my dissertation on group empowerment. Before my doctoral training, I had worked as a social worker, community organizer, and administrator of nonprofit organizations. During my doctoral training, I did research and consulted with corporations aspiring to achieve high performance by creating conditions for employee self-management. Symbolically, I viewed this consulting position as an opportunity to integrate my past with my present career. More practically, I was leaving a full-time job so I could finish my dissertation, and I needed the money.

My personal goal was to increase the influence of the panel on company policies that affected consumers. I wanted members' voices to be heard, their recommendations to be considered and responded to by the company. I wanted the panel to be an effective group, disciplined in its decision-making processes. My vision differed somewhat from the previous facilitator who conceptualized panel meetings as an opportunity for communication and dialogue among individuals with different perspectives. Freedom of expression was important to me not as an end, but as a means of getting things done.

Facilitator Selection Process

The previous facilitator, a friend of mine, had recommended me and one other person for this position. A facilitator selection committee, comprised of three panelists and three company representatives, reviewed several résumés and decided to interview seven individuals. The interviews occurred in a small room in the Sheraton, the hotel where the panel usually met. Interviews were semistructured and 40 minutes were allotted for them. The highest-level manager from the company asked the first question, followed by a panelist, followed by the next manager in the pecking order. The formality of the interview contributed to my nervousness. Later, I was told I shredded my coffee napkin into small pieces during the interview.

The most interesting question was asked by Tim, an attorney and the panelist representing small-business concerns. He asked how I could maintain my independence as a facilitator when Utilco would be paying me. I responded that in order to be effective and help the panel influence the company's policy-setting process, I had to maintain credibility and trust with both the panel and Utilco. This necessitated maintaining my independence as a third party. Although my response was honest, I knew I would be walking a fine line managing a difficult tension. The question of "who is the client" continued to plague me during my tenure as facilitator.

The previous facilitator told me I was one of the top candidates, although there was some concern on the part of the company about my nervousness during the interview. If I were selected, I knew I needed to discuss this problem directly with the company, and indicate my openness to continued feedback. I was offered the facilitator job. I checked with the previous facilitator in order not to violate her trust, and she encouraged me to discuss my nervousness with the appropriate company manager. During my first preparatory meeting with this manager, I raised this concern. Although I was uncomfortable beginning a project with a discussion of a potential weakness, our discussion established a foundation for a collaborative relationship.

Diagnosis and Feedback

In my contracting with Utilco Corporation, we agreed I would initially interview all panel members, company representatives to the panel, and company officers. Feedback would be presented verbally at my first panel meeting, and a written summary would be provided to company officers.

Interviews with panelists provided an opportunity to meet them in their job settings or homes and learn about their reasons for participation, as well as their perceptions of panel strengths and weaknesses. Interviews with company officers helped me learn about the business and their perceptions of the panel's role, strengths, and weaknesses. In addition, officer interviews enabled me to begin establishing credibility with the leadership of the company. Individual interviews with company representatives provided an opportunity to hear their perceptions off the record, not just what they would say when meeting as a group with me. Through these interviews, I was able to identify similarities and differences between the panelists' and company's perceptions of panel effectiveness.

I interviewed 23 individuals and spent approximately 10 days collecting and analyzing interview data. The understanding I had with the company was that it would pay me for the time I spent on this process. No estimate was made in advance, however, of the length of time the process would take.

In the midst of conducting these interviews, I informed the highest-level manager with whom I had negotiated my contract about the time spent on data collection and analysis. He told me not to be concerned about it. As instructed, I submitted my bill to his subordinate, two levels down, who handles the day-to-day work of the panel. Later, I learned from her manager, positioned in the middle, that they "freaked out" about the bill. They were over their budget, and their boss had never told them he told me not to be concerned. I was angry, but prepared to negotiate innovative payment arrangements with them. In a planning meeting with these three managers, I reviewed the work that had been completed, and they seemed reassured. They agreed to pay me on receipt of invoice, and their concerns about the budget faded over time.

The interview process was exciting and enjoyable. From panelists, I learned about problems of consumer credit, difficulties faced by disabled people in dealing with utilities, the subtle discrimination against the small-business owner, the not-so-subtle discrimination against the state's minorities, the hardships of seniors, and the level of poverty that remained hidden in this relatively affluent area of the country. From company executives, I learned about the impact of regulation on their industry, the company's strategic plan, and their view of the role of the panel given broader business goals.

The early time spent in the company was instructive. One of the senior officers said to me during his interview: "You're working with the panel. Why would you want to do a thing like that?" A few managers with no panel affiliation, whom I casually met in company hallways, giggled when I said I was working with the panel. I shared these vignettes with company representatives to the panel, and they responded that gaining credibility within the company had been an uphill battle for the panel.

On the other hand, senior officers told me the company valued the panel, it served as a useful and efficient way of staying in touch with the state's consumers, and it kept the company honest, particularly when panelists said things the company did not want to hear. The company respected the expertise of panel members and viewed the panel as creating change in Utilco. The company had some concerns that the panel might not be representative of consumers in the state and that no method existed for membership rotation.

By and large, panelists shared the same impressions of the panel's strengths and weaknesses. Panelists viewed the group as influencing the company, and they valued its independence. They thought the group had become more cohesive and effective over time. Some panelists talked about the lack of membership rotation. Yet, most panelists viewed the panel as benefiting their constituencies and as being more than window dressing.

The company and panel had similar perceptions of the company's role. The company was viewed as reluctant to share information in a timely way. It was viewed as responsive to requests from the panel but not proactive in asking the panel for assistance. Utilco was perceived as unclear regarding boundaries defining consumer issues.

One notable difference between the company's and panelists' perceptions concerned the panel's role. The company viewed the panel's role as advisory and asserted that advisory means the panel provides input, but the company effects change. Panelists stated that the meaning of an advisory role was unclear and ambiguous.

Everyone interviewed advised the facilitator to run an orderly meeting and control discussions. I was instructed to be objective and neutral in my third-party role and to feel free to help the group improve its process. I was cautioned not to try to do too much in my first year but to concentrate on building credibility and rapport.

The first meeting went very well. A feeling of anticipation and excitement pervaded the meeting. Potential new members attended the first half of the meeting, and voting took place to select three new panelists from a pool of eight. Company representatives and panelists validated my data feedback and agreed to some preliminary action steps. Utilco's chief executive officer attended the meeting and expressed his continued respect for the panel process. Utilco indicated its intent to file a rate case with the Public Service Commission in the middle of October, and the panel voted to have its regulatory subcommittee review it. We were on our way.

Meetings Leading to Current Situation

The October through December meetings focused on this rate case. Panelists had been telephoned for their individual reactions in September. Although some were supportive, panelists expressed concern about the impact of this increase on those below the poverty line, small businesses, and nonprofit organizations. Many panelists were upset the company provided them with such little warning. The subcommittee understood the company's reasoning but had reservations about Utilco's plans.

At the October meeting, subcommittee members expressed their reservations about Utilco's intent to file this rate case. A few panelists went on record indicating their opposition on behalf of their constituencies. Much heated discussion ensued, culminating in a unanimous vote (with three abstentions) to oppose Utilco's filing. The panel asked the subcommittee to continue its work on defining potential exemptions to this case. The panel asked the company representatives to inform company decision makers of its vote. In response, company representatives asked the subcommittee to draft a resolution to be shared with company decision makers. Utilco indicated its intent to file the case but stated it was open to the panel's concerns.

Company representatives left the meeting surprised and angry. They were surprised because more opposition had been expressed at the panel meeting than at subcommittee meetings or in one-to-one discussions with panelists. Some company representatives blamed others who had worked directly with the regulatory subcommittee for not doing a better job of controlling it.

Although no one directly criticized the facilitator, I was sure that some believed I should have done a better job of influencing the outcome. John, the vice president of external relations, told me he viewed voting as inappropriate and discussion of issues should suffice. Utilco was afraid the panel's vote would be shared outside the company with constituencies opposing this rate case.

Before the November meeting, several subcommittee and company meetings took place. The subcommittee developed recommendations concerning potential exemptions. The company did not support most of these exemptions, and consequently, positions remained far apart. Company representatives found themselves in the uncomfortable position of trying repeatedly to justify the company's position to the subcommittee. This frustrated subcommittee members.

I met with company officers, company representatives, and the regulatory subcommittee. As a response to the company's interpretation that its managers had not done a good job in presenting information, I sent a memorandum suggesting that panelists were representing the interests of their constituencies. In company meetings, much time was spent reviewing worst-case scenarios and potential company responses. For example, if the panel decided to testify at the hearings or release press statements critical of the company's position, what would the company do?

At the beginning of the November meeting, I attempted to set the stage for what I knew would be a potentially contentious discussion. Before the discussion of the rate case, we reviewed and discussed the purpose and role of the panel. I introduced the concept of "groupthink" and said groups are most effective when they weigh costs and benefits of alternatives before making a decision.

The discussion of the rate case followed, with the subcommittee presenting its resolution opposing the company's filing, and the company presenting its rationale for its decision. The company modified its plans slightly and accepted the subcommittee's recommendation for one exemption. However, apart from this exemption, the company's stand remained the same. Much discussion followed, somewhat repetitive of the October and subcommittee discussions. At the end of the meeting, the vice president said the company would still consider panelist input. Some panelists were distrustful of John's comments because they viewed the company's position as fixed. The company had bought some time. During this time, John tried to influence other company executives to reconsider the panel's concerns, but Utilco's position remained firm.

The December discussion repeated ground that had been covered previously. Neither the company's nor the subcommittee's position had changed. Utilco indicated it had reached its final position and would not consider the remainder of the exemptions the subcommittee had proposed.

Some confusion existed about whether the panel should formally take a stand on the subcommittee's recommendation or whether the vice president should communicate his sense of the panel's position to the company. John argued strongly against formalizing a position, saying he could do a better job of representing the panel in the company if the panel did not vote. By a majority vote of eight to seven, panelists indicated their preference to deal with the subcommittee recommendation informally. Ironically, the panel voted in order to decide not to vote, because voting was the only mechanism available for panel decision making, given strong disagreements among members. To give the subcommittee a sense of closure, a panelist moved to accept the subcommittee's work with commendations for its outstanding and persistent effort. That motion was accepted by a vote of 14 to 1.

At the end of the December meeting, the company was relieved and the facilitator was upset. I disagreed strongly with the vice president about his stand on panel voting. I thought the panel needed a way to resolve controversial issues. While facilitating the meeting, I believed I could not disagree publicly with John's stand on voting. In a private conversation with him, I expressed my opinion, and we agreed to disagree. The rate case discussion was over. Dissention, however, did not disappear; it just went underground.

The meetings between January and May were more routine. The structure for the remainder of the panel year needed to be developed. Issues were brainstormed, and panelists selected priorities. Secondary issues were delegated to subcommittees. New panel members selected subcommittees to join. The foundation for the remainder of the panel year was laid.

The panel then addressed its priorities. The panel heard presentations on Utilco's strategic plans, repair and maintenance activities, corporate donations, and utility service as a public entitlement. An ad hoc task force, composed of a few panelists and company representatives, reviewed concerns about the degree to which the company shared information with the panel and the timeliness of company responses. Although this concern was not fully resolved, the company agreed to bring issues to the panel sooner and let the panel know how issues were resolved.

Utilco had downsized through a voluntary retirement program. As a result of retirements, extensive employee redeployment was necessary. Two Utilco panel representatives were redeployed and replaced by other middle managers. One of these managers was new to Utilco, having worked previously as a public relations manager for another utility. The other manager, his new boss, had been at Utilco for his entire career, but he had never worked with the panel before. Panel continuity remained at the officer and administrative levels, but the critical liaisons to the panel were new. These new managers began their tenure in January, with the previous managers helping them make the transition. After four months of developing trust between myself and the previous Utilco representatives, I had to begin again.

In some ways, the calendar year marked a new beginning for the panel. The panel determined its working structure, brainstormed issues, and selected priorities and work methods. New company representatives were introduced. However, the lack of closure about the rate case and the ambiguity concerning the panel's role continued into the new year.

The June Meeting and Its Aftermath

As the transcript at the beginning of this case suggests, the June meeting brought the unresolved issues to a head. The Public Service Commission had issued a draft ruling on the rate case, which the subcommittee thought was worse than the original company proposal. The subcommittee proposed to draft a letter to the commission on behalf of the panel. Emotion in the room was heightened by a panelist announcing her resignation because of frustration concerning this issue.

Although Utilco's vice president argued strongly against the panel taking a public stand, panelists voted to send this letter to the service commission, and a motion to reconsider the vote failed. The panel voted also to consider at the September meeting whether its role included taking outside stands. John, the vice president, was shaken by the vote and encouraged panelists to call him directly, so he could more accurately reflect their opinions to the company.

Tim, the attorney representing small businesses, who had agreed to draft a letter, called me two days after the meeting. After speaking with another panelist, Tim was no longer sure he wanted to send this letter. He realized the letter would arrive at the Public Service Commission after the deadline for public input, and it would not have its intended impact. In addition, one of Tim's clients was about to declare bankruptcy and needed some urgent legal help. Tim said he did not have the time to write this letter because he had to respond immediately to his client's needs.

Tim told me he had called John earlier that morning. Tim said he told John the panel needed to be taken more seriously by the company. Tim believed the company would be more likely to take the panel seriously if its caliber were improved. Tim told me he and John made an implicit agreement in which Tim agreed not to send the letter and John agreed to help to improve the caliber of the panel by soliciting new panelists with statewide and national reputations for the open positions.

I was upset. On the one hand, I disagreed with the panel's decision to send a letter to the commission. Panelists had not reviewed or even discussed the content of the letter they proposed to send. The panel had not reached closure on the subcommittee's initial recommendation. Given the hearing deadlines, it was not possible to review and send a letter that would be considered by the Public Service Commission. Instead, the panel's decision was the product of anger and frustration with Utilco Corporation. The panel was not going to let itself be pushed around by the company this time.

On the other hand, the panel did vote to send a letter to the commission. Ironically, Tim was the panelist who suggested this strategy and had volunteered to draft the letter. As facilitator, I had some responsibility for making sure panel decisions were implemented.

Furthermore, ethical issues were involved. If it were true that Tim and John had a private agreement, I was not sure I wanted to remain as facilitator. Because Tim called me to seek my opinion on what he should do, I potentially was compromised. I could not ignore the situation.

The broader issue of the role of the panel remained. The panel and company had committed to begin a process of reaching agreement about the panel's role at its September meeting. However, the panel had existed for 10 years, and no operating guidelines had been defined. Its role had stayed ambiguous.

As facilitator, I had some decisions to make. Should I resign? How should I handle Tim's change of heart? What about the unresolved issue of the panel taking outside stands?

CURRENT ASSESSMENT

I had to come to grips with the immediate situation before I could consider the broader question of the panel's role. Tim's reversal, supported by an implicit agreement with an officer of Utilco, put the panel in jeopardy. However, Utilco's reaction to a letter from the panel to the Public Service Commission opposing its rate case might ultimately put the panel in jeopardy. Utilco would close managerial ranks and be less willing to share information about substantive issues. I was between a rock and a hard place, needing to decide between process and outcome. If an appropriate process were followed, the outcome most likely would undermine future panel effectiveness. If the letter were not sent to the commission, a more appropriate outcome, then the process of panel decision making and ultimately panel effectiveness would be compromised. A year's worth of my work as facilitator seemed to disappear as a result of the June meeting and its aftermath.

I had a good relationship with Tim and a more distant, but solid, relationship with John. Tim liked being in the heat of battle and enjoyed political intrigue. John was a perfectionist, highly competent, but sometimes indirect. Occasionally, John avoided conflict by being ambiguous about his position. Perhaps I misinterpreted what Tim had said and no quid pro quo existed. I wondered if Tim and John had really made a deal.

If I were to resolve the immediate crisis, I needed to deal with the underlying question of the panel's role. Utilco asserted the panel was advisory to it, and advisory meant the panel could not take public stands, although individuals were free to act on their own or on behalf of their constituencies. The panel asserted that the meaning of an advisory role was unclear, and members disagreed as to whether or not the panel should take stands in the public arena. Thus, the problem had been defined as a question of the appropriate panel role. But wasn't the real issue about power?

The Consumer Advisory Panel is dependent on Utilco Corporation for information, education, staff support, access to decision makers, to be listened to, to be taken seriously, and for its recommendations to be implemented. The Consumer Advisory Panel's very existence is dependent on Utilco Corporation. The inverse does not hold. Utilco will continue to exist, provide services for its customers, and make a profit for its stockholders, with or without a consumer panel. Emerson (1962) defined power and dependency as the inverse of one another, that people hold power to the degree that others are dependent on them to achieve the goals they desire. The consumer panel cannot successfully influence the policy-setting process on behalf of its constituencies without Utilco's support.

Furthermore, the Consumer Advisory Panel is composed of a diffuse group of individuals representing multiple constituencies. It is unbounded and underorganized, lacking a formal leadership structure. Indeed, the role of a facilitator substitutes for a formal consumer leader. In contrast, Utilco is a billion-dollar corporation, with a clearly defined managerial hierarchy. Decision making tends to be centralized and hierarchical. John, the only company officer to regularly attend panel meetings, is clearly in charge, and panelists and company representatives look to him to speak for Utilco Corporation. The structural differences between the company and panel contribute to the relative powerlessness of the panel.

The debate over the role of the panel occurred only when a controversial issue was on the floor. The panel threatened to take an external stand and become a player in the regulatory process when it felt stymied in its attempts to influence the company. The panel's threats, its extension of its mandate, were aimed at equalizing the power imbalance. The Consumer Advisory Panel wanted a meaningful voice. It wanted to get Utilco's attention. Over time, members learned the company paid attention to threats of negative press releases or letters to the Public Service Commission.

Therefore, the establishment of clear ground rules that forbade the taking of external public stands might destroy the major source of panel influence on the company. As facilitator, I had to be careful I did not unintentionally reduce the panel's power base by pushing for clear guidelines.

The company may have viewed the existing ambiguity as serving its interests as well. Concerns about confidentiality and external use of information served as an excuse for some departments not to share timely information with the panel. The potential threat of the panel taking an outside stand gave the consumer relations department leverage over other departments with which it disagreed. The panel could be and was used as ammunition in internal Utilco battles.

The lack of clear and agreed-upon guidelines resulted in relatively low trust between the company and panel. The company did not trust the panel to keep confidentiality, and it feared the panel might publicly embarrass it. Utilco's paranoia, at least partially, was based on historical fact. Similarly, the panel did not trust the company to provide substantive information in a timely way and to truly listen and respond to its recommendations. Again, the panel had good reasons for its mistrust. The consequence was relatively low panel effectiveness as a decision-making body.

As facilitator, I was committed to improving panel effectiveness. However, I was not certain this commitment was shared by either the panel or the company. I experienced confusion about my role and responsibilities. Although I strongly believed I needed to maintain my independence as a third party, I was not always sure how to translate this into behaviors. Because of the events following the June meeting, I knew I had to do something. But what should I do?

QUESTIONS FOR DISCUSSION

Initial Confusion/Conflict Concerning Panel Structure and Process

1. What are the appropriate role and responsibilities of a consultant when working with a consumer advisory panel for a corporation? What are the expectations of the company? What are the expectations of panelists? Should the facilitator concern herself only with running panel meetings? Is it possible to simultaneously chair panel meetings and provide process interventions? How much initiative should the facilitator take for creating change? Should the facilitator be concerned only with panel process and not with content? Should the facilitator work with the company to improve its procedures or relationships if she thinks they have some bearing on panel effectiveness? Should the facilitator make sure the company follows through on its commitments to the panel? Should the facilitator make sure the panel follows through on its decisions?

2. Who is the client? Utilco Corporation? The panel? Both? If both, how can the facilitator consult effectively given the conflicts between the panel and company? What about the monetary arrangements? Perhaps the facilitator is kidding herself and the company is really the client because it pays for her service. Perhaps the client is neither the company nor the panel, but the idea of improving panel effectiveness? Can an idea be the client?

3. What should be the consultant's primary working relationship in the company? Should it be with the officer who has the most power and ultimate responsibility for the panel but is not involved in its day-to-day activities? Should it be with the fourth-level manager, who signed her contract? Should it be with the third-level manager who has the responsibility for working with the panel on critical issues? Should it be with the second-level manager who handles panel administration and has the longest tenure with the panel, apart from the officer?

Resolving the Consultant's Personal Agenda

    1. How should a consultant respond to the ethical dilemmas that may arise from this work? What are a consultant's ethical and professional obligations? Should the facilitator view the reputed agreement between Tim and John as an ethical problem? Under what conditions should the facilitator resign?

    2. Does the facilitator's personal involvement undermine her effectiveness? The facilitator describes herself as being committed to improving panel effectiveness. Has she taken responsibility for a goal that should be "owned" by the client?

    3. What are the facilitator's blind spots? How have they influenced her analysis of the situation? How have they influenced her assessments of members' behaviors?

Determining What to Do Now

    1. What should be the facilitator's response to the reputed agreement between Tim and John? Should she maintain Tim's privacy and implicitly agree to his arrangement with John? Should she arrange for a face-to-face meeting with Tim and John to openly discuss the situation? Should she talk to John privately to obtain his perspective after informing Tim of her intentions to do so?

    2. How should the facilitator respond if a private arrangement had been made? Should she resign for ethical reasons? Should she keep their secret and help Tim and John determine the best way of dealing with the panel? Should she attempt to persuade them that their agreement was not in the panel's best interest, and get them to reverse their stand? Should she tell them she had to support the panel's decision as facilitator, and she would make sure a letter was drafted and sent to the commission (either by doing it herself or getting another subcommittee member to do it)?

    3. What should the facilitator do to inform the panel that Tim was no longer willing to draft the letter to the Public Service Commission? Should she do nothing and hope the situation blows over by the September meeting? Should she attempt to convince Tim of the importance of his communicating his change of position directly to panelists? Should she agree to inform panelists for Tim? Should she let the company inform panelists on Tim's behalf?

    4. What should the facilitator do to deal with the ambiguity concerning the panel's role and the underlying issue of its powerlessness? Did the existing ambiguity serve the interests of the panel and company? What about resistance to change? Did the June meeting create a readiness for change that had not been there before? Does it make sense to encourage the company and panel to establish operating guidelines?

5. What approach should be taken to define the panel's role and operating guidelines? Should the role and guidelines be collaboratively defined or should the company take responsibility for clarifying its expectations? What interventions should she use? How should she structure the September meeting?

REFERENCE

Emerson, R. M. "Power-Dependence Relations." *American Sociological Review* 27 (1962), pp. 31–41.

McLaughlin School*

Jean M. Bartunek
Boston College

COORDINATING THE CURRICULUM AT THE McLAUGHLIN SCHOOL

In 1986, I asked a friend who was familiar with several private schools in Ohio to find a school there that was planning an organizational change and that would allow me to observe the change process and interview major participants over the course of the 1987–88 school year. In return, I would volunteer to feed back my observations on the change to the people involved.

My friend contacted the principal of the McLaughlin School, who was interested in my proposal. McLaughlin was introducing a new academic director position, which would replace a previously established curriculum coordinator role and was aimed at increasing coordination of curriculum among different administrative units. The principal and I arranged that, assuming it would be acceptable to other administrators, I would visit the school on a regular basis during the 1987–88 school year. We also eventually agreed that at the end of the school year, I would feed back my observations to the administration. Thus, the year's interviewing and observation would be diagnostic from the perspective of the school. I would start by coming in May to talk with the other administrators and gain their approval for my study.

Background Information about the School

The McLaughlin School enrolls approximately 550 girls and young women and is organized into three main administrative units, a lower school (K–4), middle school (5–8) and upper school (9–12). A chart listing

*I am grateful for the openness and honesty of the administration and faculty at the McLaughlin School, the assistance of Robin Reid, and the helpful comments of Cary Cherniss, Judy Gordon, and Sandra Waddock on earlier drafts of this case.

EXHIBIT 1   Administrators at McLaughlin

Role	Name	Tenure at the School (as of September 1987)
Principal	Mary Anne Walters	6 years
Upper school head	Carol Rooney	16 years
Middle school head	Claudia Lindhorst	3 years
Lower school head	Judy Gallagher	18 years
Academic director	Karen Kerns	12 years
Business manager	Penny Dalton	11 years
Former curriculum coordinator	Janice Luebbe	3 years

---

the administrators and their tenure at McLaughlin is shown in Exhibit 1. The principal was Mary Anne Walters. The upper school head was Carol Rooney, who was perceived by herself and others to have considerable competence at counseling relationships with the students but to be less competent in developing curriculum. Karen Kerns, who would become the academic director, had been middle school head since 1981. Mary Anne and Karen were good friends, and Mary Anne was widely viewed as Karen's mentor. The lower school head, Judy Gallagher, had been at McLaughlin longer than any of the other administrators. The curriculum coordinator, Janice Luebbe, had just accepted a position for the next year as principal at another school.

In addition to the administrators, there were seven department chairpersons— science, social science, English, foreign languages, physical education, fine arts, and mathematics. On the average, the department chairpersons had been at McLaughlin for 12 years, with the range from 8 years to 18. The physical education and fine arts departments extended from K–12. All the other departments operated primarily in the upper school.

I have been interested for several years in a type of organizational change in which some members of an organization (*not* formal change agents) try to change the organization in a way that, consciously or not, involves a change in the shared understandings, or culture, out of which their organization operates. Based on the information I'd been given about the planned change at McLaughlin, the change in roles would imply change in these shared understandings, especially with respect to the understanding of coordination. On the basis of prior research I had conducted, I had developed a process model I thought this type of change followed. Work at the school would give me a chance to observe a relatively small and contained organization undergoing this type of change, so I could explore the applicability of my model.

The process model I had developed (described in detail in Bartunek, 1988; Bartunek & Moch, 1987; Moch & Bartunek, forthcoming) suggested that organizations typically have certain shared understandings that guide the way members act. These shared understandings are sometimes reflected in the metaphors people use to describe their organizations. They are expressed in recurring patterns of behavior, which in turn strengthen the shared understandings. Change begins with a dramatic challenge to a shared understanding and the development by some members of an alternative. There are conflicts and power struggles between the proponents of the original and new understandings, the outcome of which is some new understanding. If the new understanding is satisfactory to powerful organizational members, the process ceases; if not, still newer understandings and conflicts regarding them occur. The process of change in shared understandings is often difficult, involving strong feelings such as shock, anger, defensiveness, a sense of loss, and ambiguity. Although the difficulties and conflicts are due in large part to the change process itself, they are likely to be attributed to, or blamed on, individual people.

Understanding of this type of change requires understanding of the past conditions and understandings that give birth to the attempted change. Consequently, before describing what happened during the 1987–88 school year, I will present a summary of McLaughlin's recent history. I learned about this history from personnel at the school and from several people who had been curriculum coordinators during the 15 years before 1987.

McLAUGHLIN'S RECENT HISTORY

As had occurred in several private schools in the late 1960s, McLaughlin had taken a number of steps to broaden its student population. For example, in 1969, it had substantially increased the number of minority scholarship students enrolled. Steps such as this had increased the social awareness of the staff and student body, but they had also led many students to withdraw and had weakened McLaughlin's academic reputation in the city in which it was located. Consequently, the person who became principal in 1970 focused her attention on enhancing the school's enrollment, endowment, and external reputation, and she and Carol Rooney allowed the department chairpersons considerable autonomy in building the academic strength of the departments. Carol had given the department chairs responsibility for a wide variety of functions, including departmental curriculum and hiring. The different departments did become academically stronger but also very independent of the administration.

Mary Anne Walters was hired as principal in 1981. From the time she arrived, she was aware of a high degree of autonomy within the different departments and schools. At the time she was hired, no one had an overview of what happened to each student. In fact, the various academic departments used different grading systems. In addition, students often spent all night working on their assignments because the different departments did not coordinate assignments and test schedules. Mary Anne (and some of the other administrators) believed the lack of coordination hurt the overall educational effort by placing too many disparate demands on students.

Before 1987, Mary Anne had already taken several steps to try to increase coordination. In 1982, she had insisted, against the upper school faculty members' considerable opposition, that they serve as academic advisors, so they would have a sense of the "whole" student rather than only activities related to their own discipline. She had significantly upgraded the student affairs staff in order to achieve a more holistic approach to education. She had also redesigned the curriculum coordinator role two times. Three people served in some variety of that role between 1981 and 1987.

The Curriculum Coordinator Role

The role descriptions of the curriculum coordinators had stressed work in the upper school, although they had been expected to do some work in the middle and lower schools as well. Mary Anne believed their efforts had had some positive effects. However, neither Mary Anne nor the past curriculum coordinators thought they had achieved adequate coordination. The curriculum coordinators believed they had been able to accomplish far less than they had hoped because of resistance they encountered from the departments and from the upper and lower school heads.

The Curriculum Coordinators and the Department Chairpersons. The curriculum coordinators said they had frequently experienced a kind of passive resistance by the department chairpersons to their curriculum coordination efforts. For example, one former curriculum coordinator said the response to her coordination attempts seemed like shadow boxing. She described her experience of trying to get teachers to coordinate homework assignments across departments as "slow, Chinese water torture."

The Curriculum Coordinators and the Upper and Lower School Heads. The curriculum coordinators had felt blocked by Carol. From their perceptions, Carol was threatened by their attempts to coordinate curriculum. She would make it difficult for them to achieve their purpose, frequently by becoming angry and withdrawn or by telling them they were overstepping their reach. The normal pattern of the curriculum coordinators when she did this was to back down. For example, one of the former curriculum coordinators said she had tried to "relate to her as an equal," but Carol was "defensive and obstructive," so she eventually decided to back down and primarily report to her. After that, her relationship was smoother. However, this curriculum coordinator then left unable to accomplish the objectives of her job.

The curriculum coordinators had also felt blocked by Judy Gallagher, the lower school head. One of the curriculum coordinators said, "Judy ran a tight little school into which outsiders did not get." They described Judy's actions as making them sufficiently unwelcome that they did not attempt to intervene in the lower school.

The Design of the Academic Director Position

In the spring of 1987, Mary Anne decided to make another attempt to improve coordination of the curriculum. She decided to change the curriculum coordinator role into an academic director position. Mary Anne discussed the new job with the administration during the spring and obtained apparent approval for it.

In contrast to the curriculum coordinator, the academic director would have responsibility for curriculum from grades K–12. Moreover, to strengthen the position, the academic director would not only coordinate the curriculum, but also coordinate preparation for an accrediting evaluation to take place in the spring of 1988. The academic director would also coordinate textbook ordering (an activity previously carried out in the individual schools), which would ensure continuity and lack of duplication of texts across grade levels. The chairpersons of the fine arts and physical education departments, whose activities extended across school lines, would report to the academic director. Finally, the academic director would be the school's liaison with the academic subcommittee of the board of trustees.

Unlike curriculum positions in some other schools, the academic director would not be an assistant principal but would coordinate with the heads of the schools. One responsibility on the job description read, for example, "the academic director supervises the overall design of the curriculum and the delivery of instruction in conjunction with the heads of the schools and the department chairs." Mary Anne wanted the academic director and the heads of the schools to share authority.

When Mary Anne decided to create the academic director position, she also decided to appoint Karen Kerns to the position. Karen would be replaced as middle school head by Claudia Lindhorst, who was a teacher in the middle school. Mary Anne believed the job description for the academic director position fit Karen's expertise very well. Moreover, this job would be a natural progression in the development of Karen's administrative skills.

My Introduction and Entry to the School

On my first visit to the school, after an introductory discussion with Mary Anne, I met with the administration as a group. I proposed that I distribute a questionnaire (not discussed in this case) to the faculty at the beginning of the school year, feed back the results to the administration and faculty later in the fall, and visit the school approximately every three weeks during the school year. At the end of the school year, I would review with the administration the results of my year's observations and reflections regarding the implementation of the academic director role. I also said I would act as a consultant during the school year in a narrowly specified way. In my written proposal, I included:

> I would be happy, if/when McLaughlin requests it, to act as a consultant with regard to the academic director role. I would not expect to make definitive pronouncements on how to solve problems with the role. I would, however, give feedback based on the results of the interviews . . . to administrators and faculty dealing with the role. The feedback would give you some idea, from my perspective, of how the role is being understood and addressed, as well as some of its impacts.

The administrators agreed to the study. Then I met with each administrator individually. I used the opportunity to get to know them and their perspectives, to have them get to know me, and to answer their questions. When I talked with them, I listened in particular for metaphors they used to describe the school. Four of the administrators used the following phrases to describe relationships between the different academic units:

- "Each school is a fiefdom."
- "The biggest problem is the departments who think they're queens of the world."
- "Each department is its own kingdom."
- "Each department is a fortress unto their own."

These metaphors seemed consistent with the school's reputation as a place in which a high value was placed on autonomy.

I talked with Janice Luebbe, the outgoing curriculum coordinator, who was not optimistic about the likely success of the new academic director job. She thought her own job had had "little identifiable domain beyond what a good secretary or registrar could do." She believed that even with the redesign of the job, Karen would end up primarily as an executive secretary for the heads of the schools. Karen, however, was optimistic. She said she knew Janice had had a tough time, but she had a different style than Janice; she was better at selling ideas to people and quite capable of fighting for ideas she considered important. So although she was nervous, she thought she would do all right.

IMPLEMENTATION OF THE POSITION

During the summer of 1987, Mary Anne asked all of the administrators to draw up job descriptions for their own jobs. She thought this would enable them to be clear about whether their job responsibilities overlapped with those of the academic director, as well as about the specific duties of the new job. The administrators discussed the job descriptions at their planning meeting in August. It was here that the first difficulties with the new job surfaced.

Judy Gallagher, the head of the lower school, said there was overlap between the academic director's job duties and her own, and that the academic director should not coordinate curriculum in the lower school. Karen and the other administrators were upset at Judy's reaction; they thought the academic director's job duties had already been agreed on by everyone in the administration. Consequently, the year started with what Carol called a "huge conflict in terms of what Karen should be doing."

The Beginning of the 1987–88 School Year

The curriculum coordinator's office had been physically located in the upper school. Because the academic director position would be oriented not only to the upper school but also the middle and lower schools, there was a need for the academic director to have a new office. Construction of the new office (and other parts of the school) began during the summer. However, the office was not complete in September. Consequently, when the school year began, Karen had to use a desk situated between two school secretaries in an open office immediately adjacent to Mary Anne's.

In September, at the opening orientation session for the faculty, Mary Anne described the academic director position by saying:

> Karen's role is a curricular growth role. She will be working on curriculum programs K to 12 and will be working on professional growth with the individual department chairs. Work with her so she can get to know the total curriculum as much as possible. If you're doing an overview, tell her. She's not the one who solves problems related to faculty, students, and parents. So if someone is failing math, go to the head of the school. And she doesn't write the faculty evaluation. This isn't an easy role description to work with.

One of the faculty told Karen later that day that Mary Anne had said "more what the job doesn't entail than what it does." As a consequence, Karen told me she was concerned the faculty wouldn't know what her job duties really were.

Early in September, Karen introduced to the faculty the process they would use to prepare the self-study for the accrediting evaluation to occur that spring. Several of the faculty and administration said she did "a superb job" of introducing the evaluation. She wasn't sure, however, exactly what else she should do and said she was "trying to find her identity in the job."

Mary Anne's Ulcer

In late September, Mary Anne developed a gastric ulcer and was gone from the school for three weeks. The board of trustees appointed Penny Dalton, McLaughlin's business manager, as acting principal in her absence. While Mary Anne was away, Karen moved from the secretaries' office into Mary Anne's.

About this time, Karen learned the math department had made a decision in which she felt she should have been involved, and she told me she was feeling shut out by the departments and by Judy Gallagher. She believed Mary Anne had to return and reinforce her authority as academic director if she were to have any authority. Penny Dalton told me, "Karen is more gloomy than she should be. She's finding a passive resistance in that she doesn't get included in things. People are not interested in having her tread on their turf."

> I visited the school soon after Mary Anne got sick. I observed an event that, while only tangentially related to the academic director position, affected my expectations for the year. The night before I came, the father of a middle school student had called Claudia Lindhorst, the new middle school head, complaining that one of the teachers was treating his daughter unfairly. Claudia had good reason not to believe the father, but because she was new in her job, she wasn't sure how to respond. She asked Karen for help. While I was with Karen (in Mary Anne's office), she called the student's father and virtually demanded that he come to the school the next week to meet with her and discuss his complaint. Karen proposed several dates on which he might come, all of which he rejected. It sounded to me as if he were somewhat intimidated by her response. When she got off the phone, she said to me and Penny, who was also in the room, "No one is going to do that to one of my teachers."
>
> This event made me think that, as she had told me in May, Karen really was capable of fighting for her ideas. I started to think that although the curriculum coordinators had backed down when their efforts were challenged, Karen was not likely to do this.

Mary Anne's Return

Mary Anne returned to McLaughlin in mid-October, so Karen moved back to the desk between the secretaries. This was difficult for her. She told me, "I need to have my own space . . . being between two secretaries makes you feel like a third secretary."

Soon after this, Karen said she wasn't sure, and she didn't think the other administrators were sure, where she fit in the school. This lack of clarity was frustrating. When I talked with her that day about Karen's role, Carol commented that after the previous curriculum coordinator, "Academic is back in my jurisdiction. Karen doesn't deal with academic content or students' academic problems." When I asked if she had done any coordinating with Karen, she said no, "We haven't had a time to sit down together."

In late October, Karen and Mary Anne talked with each other in depth for the first time since Mary Anne had gone into the hospital. Mary Anne told me later that Karen had been wondering "if she has the right to go in a classroom. I said, 'You are going into the classrooms.' Judy just asked me why Karen is visiting science classes. I said, 'Because I asked her.' " As a result of the assistance from Mary Anne, Karen had finally started visiting classes, especially in the lower school. She believed the visiting she was doing was essentially "secretarial stuff, . . . but with a purpose. I've got a wider vision."

The effects of Karen's visits to the lower school were positive, at least as far as Judy was concerned. She told me, "Something has clicked in Karen's mind regarding her job and how she sees it. . . . She wants to be there as a resource. In that view of herself, she's been very helpful to me. She's bending over backwards not to overstep."

Early in November, Karen organized committee meetings preparing for the evaluation. Karen was excited about how well they went and thought she was finally doing her job well.

The Development of Tensions in the Administration

Later in November, a shift began to take place. It began with some tension in Karen's and Mary Anne's relationship. Karen was getting frightened that the preparation for the accrediting visit wouldn't all come together. She thought Mary Anne was also nervous about the accreditation and said that was adding to her own anxiety.

At an administration meeting, Carol brought in a proposal from the science department for money for new equipment. As Karen recounted the story,

> I thought the proposal should go through me . . . Carol asked Mary Anne if the equipment goes in the regular budget. They just kept talking. I tried to get in the conversation. Mary Anne gave it back to Carol. . . . Mary Anne said later she'd made the right decision about who should be in on the discussion. I said Mary Anne should have had Carol and me decide.

Karen added, "I felt like Janice Luebbe—I had been end-runned."

Karen's office was ready at the beginning of December. She moved in and said that as a result, "I feel human again." Early that month, the coordinators working on the self-study for the accrediting evaluation met with Karen and Mary Anne to discuss the committees' work. They said the committees had uncovered some core issues among the upper school faculty of "alienation, isolation, and lack of trust." The committee coordinators agreed that these issues needed to be addressed at the next faculty day, which would be early in January.

In mid-December, a school librarian, who reported to Karen, suddenly announced she was quitting. Karen was upset enough about what had happened that she called me to talk about it. She felt guilty about the librarian's decision, that she had done something wrong. She talked about feeling "paralyzed" about her work, no longer able to get anything done. The problems of alienation and mistrust she had discovered seemed gigantic, and she felt responsible for determining some way to deal with them. She said Carol wasn't very helpful in dealing with these problems. "She just hangs her head and says she's at fault."

Karen told me her relationship with Mary Anne was still strained. For example, during January, she would have to be gone for four days, making an accrediting visit at another school, and Mary Anne had scheduled a meeting Karen would ordinarily attend at the same time. That upset her.

I had mixed feelings about this phone call. I was glad Karen had wanted to talk with me about the librarian's quitting and other difficulties she was experiencing—it suggested that she trusted me, and it gave me helpful information about what was going on at the school. On the other hand, I wasn't sure how to respond to the call. I felt like I was being asked to play more of a counselor role than researcher role.

In May, I had agreed to give feedback, if it was requested, on ways problems were being "understood and addressed." So I responded to Karen on the basis of what I knew about the curriculum coordinators' experiences as well as my awareness that the type of change being attempted was usually difficult and that, in most situations, the difficulties were blamed on individuals instrumental in the change. I told Karen it was possible some of the problems she was experiencing were due to difficulties inherent in implementing the academic director position, not just her personal issues. She had been at the school long enough to know the problems the curriculum coordinators had experienced, and it seemed likely the factors that had caused the problems for the other people were still present.

Over the next few months, as I continued to talk with Karen and Mary Anne, I felt fairly frequently that I was being asked to play a counseling role. I continued to have mixed feelings about this—both gratitude that they trusted me and uncertainty about how I should respond.

Karen's and Mary Anne's Relationship

In early January, the faculty members met in several small groups during a faculty day to continue their self-study. Two of the upper school groups had what Karen called "a deep discussion of isolation and mistrust among the upper school faculty and between the faculty and administration." Karen told me the next day that she felt good she had facilitated difficult issues coming out in the meeting, but she was still having a hard time relating to Mary Anne. She especially felt she wasn't receiving enough affirmation from her.

Mary Anne was aware of Karen's feelings, but she saw the situation differently. She told me:

> I may have the wrong personality in the job. There's not a question in my mind that we need the job. But the present person is getting very unhappy, even though a lot of the job is getting done. . . . To make the situation worse, I'm a problem in her life. . . . There's an overdependence . . . she really wants affirmation. . . . She has department chair coordination under control. It took time, but that doesn't surprise me. She planned a super thing (for the faculty day). She's succeeded in all these things. As she succeeds she gets more and more miserable.

As Karen's and Mary Anne's relationship worsened, Penny Dalton found herself becoming an arbitrator between them. She told me she had been spending a lot of time with Karen recently. She said, "Karen feels, as I'm sure you know, that Mary Anne isn't totally supportive. . . . Karen should feel more comfortable in what she's trying to do. She feels and expects that people will be thrilled to have her walk in the door and help." Penny echoed Mary Anne's sentiments that Karen was doing much of her job well: "The evaluation process is going very well. . . . The organization has been superb."

By the end of this visit to the school, I was also feeling a little like a third party between Karen and Mary Anne. I felt that I was being drawn into their relationship problem, that both of them were talking almost as much about each other as about the academic director position.

One consequence of the visit and the phone call from Karen that preceded it was that I realized I needed to be very clear for myself about who my "client" was in this increasingly difficult situation. I decided it had to be the school as a whole, not any of the individual people. If I would be called on for assistance, I would try to help school personnel understand underlying issues (especially organizational issues) in the change process, but not take individual sides. This seemed to be the most ethical position.

Developing Problems in the Implementation of the Academic Director Position

Early in February, Carol told me she believed the academic director job was going well. Karen had established a meeting of the department chairpersons as a curriculum committee. This committee had met for the first time, and she had a sense that Karen "feels 100 percent better than in October, because the evaluation committees were moving."

Mary Anne told me she thought Karen was struggling in a very complex process of change and was trying to take too much control over it. However, she added, "I'm still convinced this is going to work."

Karen was feeling overwhelmed with work. She was about to start having individual meetings with the department chairpersons and to develop staffing plans for the next year, in addition to working on the self-study. She thought the first curriculum committee meeting had gone well, but she wished Mary Anne had given her some positive feedback on it. Instead, she said Mary Anne had told her, "That was not a curricular meeting, but a department chair meeting." Despite this, Karen said she was determined to be pleasant to Mary Anne, regardless of what happened.

The issues of isolation and mistrust had come up again at an upper school faculty meeting. Karen thought that for the first time there was real give and take on this issue and people were listening to each other. That was exciting to her.

During mid-February, Carol told Mary Anne that Karen was "stepping on my toes." She was insisting that the upper school faculty sign a calendar aimed at coordinating test schedules, which to Carol had nothing to do with Karen's job description. Mary Anne told me she thought Karen was trying to deal with too many areas only tangentially related to curriculum (like the test calendar) and consequently wasn't getting her own work done. At the same time, Karen told me she thought that Mary Anne and Carol were making decisions behind her back. For example, they had approached Larry Maddock, the chairperson of the physical education department, to fill a vacancy for the next year in the student affairs staff. Karen believed she should have been part of that decision because Larry reported to her.

The Self-Study Report

The self-study report for the accrediting team was due to be submitted in early March. The school heads were all expected to make sure certain sections discussing their schools were written. As far as Karen could tell, however, Carol wasn't working on her section of the upper school report, and she was anxious about what would happen if it didn't get done. So one Sunday in late February, Karen and three members of the school's student affairs staff who were friends of hers spent the day at the school and essentially wrote a draft of the upper school report, which Karen later gave to Carol for further revision. They didn't tell Mary Anne that Karen was doing this or that the student affairs staff was involved. While they were working, Karen told the student affairs staff she thought that she wasn't getting affirmation from Mary Anne. They agreed that she wasn't getting the support she needed. One of them told me about this session the next morning.

Mary Anne didn't know what had happened. When I asked her how Karen's job was going, she responded, "I think she's done very well. My sense is that it's growing slowly better all the time. . . . Right at the present moment she's very busy getting everyone pulled together on the evaluation, and that's taking a lot of time."

That day Karen arrived at school wearing a neck brace. When I talked with her that afternoon, she attributed the difficulties with her neck to arthritis exacerbated by cold weather. She told me she was still not getting along with Mary Anne. I suggested that her determination to be pleasant to Mary Anne regardless of how she was feeling might be a cause of her neck problems. She agreed but insisted she would still try to be pleasant. She was worried abut the upcoming evaluation and believed that if it didn't go well "there's going to be a scapegoat, and I'm the most likely prospect." She said Janice Luebbe had "left very disheartened," and she was afraid that would happen to her. Shortly after this visit, Karen started talking with several people—including other administrators and some faculty members—about how Mary Anne wasn't supporting her.

> This was a difficult visit for me. I was very surprised that Karen had managed to pull off working on the upper school report with the student affairs staff without Mary Anne knowing about it, and I wondered what would happen when Mary Anne found out, as I assumed she would. I wondered if the difficulties between them would spread to include other people who would be drawn into taking sides between them.

Completion of the Evaluation Report

In early March, Karen gave the upper school faculty a draft of the upper school evaluation report, presenting it anonymously. The draft included a description of problems of alienation and mistrust, because these had been part of the faculty's discussion in their communities. The next day the faculty met to discuss the report. Some of them said alienation and mistrust weren't really issues. Those who had helped write the report were afraid to say they had been involved, so they kept quiet. When I visited the school shortly afterward, Larry Maddock told me Karen was upset when the upper school faculty "changed its mind" about affirmation and trust not being present. A member of the student affairs staff told me Mary Anne had found out how the report was written and was very upset about it.

When I talked with Carol that day, she said, "Karen is in a very bad space right now. . . . There is a real alienation between Mary Anne and Karen." She added,

> I'm doing some liaison between the two. Karen's had it. She can't do anything right. I talk to Mary Anne and she tells me one thing and I go to Karen and she says something else, and we don't have two people talking to each other . . . but here's an upper school report Karen didn't let me in on. . . . It's hard to rewrite some things in the report you didn't know to begin with.

Penny Dalton was concerned about whether Karen would succeed in her job. She said, "We misjudged her working style . . . she's so overextended, there's a lot not getting done . . . then she does some things too thoroughly."

Mary Anne felt caught in a dilemma about how to deal with Karen, largely because Karen had started telling so many people about the problems she and Mary Anne were having. Mary Anne said, "If I should ask her today how her job is coming, that's interpreted as pressure. If I don't ask her, it's interpreted that I don't care. . . . For the last 10 days, I know now, she's been talking with everybody about the fact that I'm not supporting her. She's putting me in a very, very difficult position." Mary Anne thought Karen's distress was "so out of proportion right now she's (talking with others) without even knowing it."

That afternoon I asked Karen how the evaluation report was coming along. She said it was almost done. She then said Carol had had a conversation with Mary Anne and, as a consequence, Mary Anne was "being nice." Karen didn't believe this shift, however, and thought she was being placated. Karen also said she was exhausted from all the work she was doing, and it wasn't getting done as quickly as it should, so people were upset with her. The self-study report was completed and sent to the accrediting team in the middle of March, three weeks after it was due.

Another Job Offer

Karen told me about a significant event that had occurred recently. A friend of hers from another private school, someone who had previously taught at McLaughlin, had called her and described a job opening similar to her current one—except with what appeared to be a much clearer job description—in the school where he presently taught. He wondered if Karen was interested in considering this job. She said, "I'm thinking about it. . . . I feel awful for thinking about it, but the fact that there is a possible job makes me feel better. . . . There's a 99 percent probability I won't act on it, but knowing their is an escape route is reassuring."

Karen's friend had called her again and suggested she put in an informal call to the principal of the other school. She had made the phone call, but she told me the conversation, and the fact the other school was interested in her, had given her the freedom to stay in her present job.

The Evaluation Visit

The evaluation occurred in early April and didn't go well, beginning from the first night. That night the accrediting team met with McLaughlin's administration to discuss how the evaluation visit would proceed. The accrediting team suggested plans for a faculty meeting that differed from McLaughlin's typical procedure. Most of the administration favored the plan, but Karen, with some support from Judy, objected. The accrediting group reluctantly went along with Karen's proposed alternate plan for the faculty meeting, a plan that required her to develop a "guiding question" for faculty discussion by Monday night.

Monday morning, when the accrediting team was introduced to the school as a whole, chairs were set up for the accrediting team, Mary Anne, and the school heads. Karen complained about this, saying that because she had been in charge of preparing the evaluation, she should be sitting in the front of the room with the others. That day Karen worked on developing a guiding question but couldn't do it. Mary Anne said she would help her, so on Monday night Karen and Mary Anne met to discuss the question. They ended up having a three-hour meeting that Karen described as a fight and that left Mary Anne with a "raging headache." During that session, Mary Anne asked Karen why she was so upset. Karen told her, "Everyone had a place to go with the evaluation team but me. . . . I felt like a fifth wheel."

Karen was so tired at the next morning's team-administration meeting that she started crying when someone asked her a question. One result of these events was that the accrediting team kept asking Mary Anne about Karen's role. They reaccredited the school. However, in their exit report at the end of the evaluation, they strongly recommended that Karen's role be clarified by the following September.

Just after the evaluation ended, Karen told me, "I'm feeling borderline stupid. I've made a jerk of myself." Mary Anne told me she was disappointed that the accrediting team had focused almost entirely on the academic director job and had missed the rest of the school. She said, "The accrediting team . . . asked all week long . . . , not about the school, but Karen. 'Did she want my job? Why aren't you taking a stronger stand?' " Shortly after the evaluation, Mary Anne started revising Karen's job description, and told Karen that Karen's job description and her own overlapped, and where they overlapped, Karen's would have to change.

Karen told me, "I've changed the way I look at myself 2,000 percent this year. . . . I see things in a whole other perspective. It's a very tumultuous and confusing time." As Karen reflected on her behavior during the evaluation, she said, "I got a sense Mary Anne was disappointed by the evaluation, and I feel really bad. . . . I felt guilty because I might have gotten them off track."

When I visited the school later in April, I asked Mary Anne what she would most like Karen to understand about her actions. Mary Anne responded, "I'd like her to come to grips with the fact that this is a service job for which she can have a lot of influence. . . . She's accountable to the school heads for things in their schools . . . and I'd like her to understand the job in relation to the principal and then, having come to grips with that understanding, decide whether she'd like to do the job."

Mary Anne asked me to work with her on reviewing Karen's job description. The original job description had a "mission" statement in it, and she said she intended to remove this statement. She asked if I would return later in the day to talk more about the job description, which I agreed to do.

After this conversation, I spoke with Karen. She said, "The last couple of weeks since the evaluation I've been so depressed. . . . It's like there's almost a cold war (between Mary Anne and me). We only speak when we absolutely have to." Karen said her current feeling was "sort of like being paralyzed, because you're afraid to move without knowing in advance she'll say it's OK." However, if she didn't figure out how to act appropriately, she'd be "rendered incompetent," just as the curriculum coordinators had been.

Later in the afternoon, I talked with Mary Anne about Karen's role description. After discussing various possibilities, Mary Anne decided to retain most of the specific duties of the role, but to cancel the duty of liaison to the education subcommittee of the board of trustees. I suggested that, to check overlap and so Karen's job wouldn't be considered in isolation, Mary Anne have everyone on the administration write out short descriptions of their job responsibilities. She thought that was a good idea, and the next week she asked the administrators to write brief descriptions of their jobs for her.

> I felt very awkward working with Mary Anne on Karen's job description. This was the first occasion on which I was being asked to give advice relating to the conduct of the school, rather than acting as a sounding board or helping people think out the issues they were grappling with. I dealt with my awkwardness by encouraging Mary Anne to look at Karen's job description in relation to those of the rest of the administration, as well as to maintain the original reporting relationships. Afterward, I felt somewhat guilty about giving any direct advice.
>
> I was also aware of feeling very sad about what had happened in the implementation of the academic director position, that Karen's experience in the position seemed similar to that of the curriculum coordinators. It was very painful not only for the school personnel to live through but also for me to listen to.

End of the School Year

Toward the end of April, Carol and Karen had a confrontation. At a curriculum committee meeting, Karen made a recommendation about study halls that she recognized "strayed into Carol's area of responsibility." After the meeting, Carol came over to her "with flame in her eyes and said, 'This is the problem: you're in my area.' " Karen told her she was sorry, but she immediately walked away and hadn't spoken to her in several days.

Karen forgot at first to give her short job description to Mary Anne. When Mary Anne reminded her, she immediately typed it, but added a copy of the job description of the other school that had contacted her, saying only that a friend had showed it to her. Mary Anne said this alternative job description "would overlap with the school heads." Karen told me on my trip to the school in May that Mary Anne thought she (Karen) was "on a power trip and wants the final word." But her own impression was that the heads of schools were making decisions she should be involved in and forgetting her job was there. She said, "If I hear Mary Anne say one more time, 'that's the heads' job,' I think I'll scream. . . . The thing that worries me is that with all the nonsense going on, I feel less and less productive. After the incident with Carol, there were three or four days when I couldn't do anything."

On that same trip, Judy told me Karen was having a hard time, that she and Mary Anne were "having a type of war." Judy said, "Sometimes Mary Anne thinks Karen's trying to take over. At times, I see where she might give that impression." One of the times she had given this impression was when Mary Anne had been away sick in the fall, and Karen "took over her office and sat down in her chair."

Carol was upset that Karen had, to her mind, spent so much time focusing on the upper school, when the academic director position was supposed to focus on all three schools. She wondered what effect that had on others' perceptions of her job; if people knew what she was doing at the school. She wondered what the faculty were thinking about who was in control—"How many hands are on that rudder?"

In mid-June, shortly after graduation, I was to present a feedback report to the administration on my observations of the year. Mary Anne and I decided that would be a good time for the administration to consider any final revisions in Karen's role. So as part of the plan for the day, I was to decide how to engage the administration in considering these revisions.

At an upper school faculty meeting shortly after graduation, two of the faculty made a formal proposal that the seniors carry out a senior-year project. They had previously gotten approval from Carol to raise this issue, but they hadn't mentioned it to Karen, who was very upset that Carol had let it go through without her. She wondered, "What is it they want me to do, if not be involved in curriculum?"

PREPARATION FOR THE FEEDBACK SESSION

The feedback session was scheduled for the following week. I had to decide how to design this session. My primary aim was for the administration to think about what had happened during the year in a "bigger" context than personality or interpersonal issues, one based on the model of the process of change in shared understandings I had developed. Related to this aim and to my earlier concerns, I wanted to be sure I wasn't seen as taking any particular individual's side, but as acting from the perspective of the school as a whole. Finally, I had to incorporate clarification of Karen's role within the context of the feedback.

QUESTIONS FOR DISCUSSION

1. How should I design the feedback session in a way that would achieve these aims? How can I help the administration see what had happened in an "organizational," rather than "personality," context?
2. What should I do to ensure that I am seen not as favoring any particular individual or individuals, but as concerned about the school as a whole? How should I design the discussion of the clarification of Karen's role? What is the outcome of this session likely to be?

REFERENCES

Bartunek, J. M. "The Dynamics of Personal and Organizational Reframing." In *Paradox and Transformation: Toward a Theory of Change in Organization and Management*, ed. R. E. Quinn and K. Cameron. Cambridge, Mass.: Ballinger, 1988, pp. 137–62.

Bartunek, J. M., and M. K. Moch. "First Order, Second Order, and Third Order Change and Organization Development Interventions: A Cognitive Approach." *Journal of Applied Behavioral Science* 23 (1987), pp. 483–500.

Moch, M. K., and Bartunek, J. M. *Creating Alternative Realities at Work*. Cambridge, Mass.: Ballinger, forthcoming.

Universal Technologies

Gerald E. Ledford, Jr.
University of Southern California

Several years ago, I was part of a four-person action research team helping to establish a quality-of-work-life (QWL) program in a large organization. The organization, which we will call Universal Technologies was a manufacturing subsidiary of a Fortune 500 corporation. Most of its facilities were located in one multiplant manufacturing complex employing about 8,000 people. The complex dated back to the founding of the company, and its products remained a core business of the corporation.

THE ORGANIZATION

Universal's organizational structure was extremely complicated. Even after several years of working with the organization, we in the consulting team often became confused about important details of organizational structure and reporting relationships. Each plant in the complex was interdependent with one or more other plants. This meant that changes in one part of the organization had ramifications for other parts. Also, informal communication channels were active, which meant major changes in one part of the system quickly became the subject of discussions and rumors in other parts.

The characteristics of the production technology, such as the degree of automation, the degree to which employees worked in interdependent work groups, and the uncertainty of the production process, varied across plants within the location. For most employees, however, the technology was moderately to highly complex, technical, and difficult to fully understand.

Historically, the organization had been consistently profitable, even though it was never the leader in its industry. Like many U.S. manufacturers, the company suddenly faced a dramatic increase in competitive pressures in the early 1980s, as a sleepy and mature industry suddenly heated up. New foreign and domestic competitors, changing production technology, customer dissatisfaction with the quality of the company's products, and a host of other factors led executives of the organization to seek means of dramatically improving performance.

A wide variety of changes were adopted, including management training, new technology, quality improvement efforts, changes in organizational reporting relationships, trimming layers of management and the number of hourly employees, and the union-management QWL program that is considered here. These changes were loosely coordinated at best, which meant, at times, they worked at cross-purposes. For example, it was difficult for the union to trust management fully in the QWL effort when more than 10 percent of union members were being laid off and when the union leadership sometimes received no advance information about key changes affecting hourly employees.

THE UNION

The QWL program was the product of collaboration between the organization and an international union that had represented Universal Technologies employees for decades. The union had a national reputation for toleration of labor-management cooperation, and the union previously had been involved in QWL efforts with other companies. At Universal, the union leadership offered general support of the QWL program, but it remained wary about management's motives for QWL and its competence to make the needed changes.

The union was a very decentralized organization. Local presidents were elected by the membership and could not be replaced except in extraordinary circumstances by international union officers. This meant most of the union power was at the local level; local presidents determined how far the QWL effort would go from the union side.

The union did not see Universal Technologies as one complex but indivisible organization, but rather as several different organizations located in one place. In keeping with the union's definition of organizational boundaries, the organization was divided into seven union locals, each headed by its own autonomous president. Regional officials appointed by the international union offered some coordination between locals, but it was not always easy to develop consensus on the union side about how to respond to management initiatives that affected the whole multiplant complex.

The work force represented by the union was extremely diverse with regard to age, sex, and ethnic origin. The education level was moderately high; high school graduation was a minimum requirement for employment. Universal had little trouble recruiting capable new employees because of its reputation as a stable, high-paying employer.

THE QWL PROGRAM

The primary goals of the QWL effort were to improve the quality of work life for employees and to improve organizational effectiveness by means of increased employee involvement. These broad goals were widely accepted at Universal, in part because they allowed different people to interpret QWL goals in light of their own needs and interests. Like many union-management QWL programs, a multilevel structure of joint QWL committees was created to realize these goals.

The QWL effort was guided by a joint union-management QWL steering committee. It was comprised of high-level managers for the subsidiary, a number of union local presidents, and the regional business agent for the union. The steering committee formulated overall policy for the QWL program, monitored progress, and acted as a final appeals board for QWL suggestions that were advanced and rejected at lower levels of the organization.

Reporting to the steering committee were joint plant committees, representing the management and local union leadership at each plant within the complex. Working within guidelines from the steering committee, each plant committee set up its own QWL structure and made its own initiatives. Some of the larger plants also set up joint department committees to facilitate the effort.

The final level in the hierarchy of QWL committees was the shop floor committee level. During the several years that the author worked with this company, over 1,000 employees were members of the 100 shop floor committees at one time or another. There were several different types of shop floor committees. Most resembled quality circles in that they included volunteer employees from a common work unit, selected their own problems to solve, received training in group problem-solving skills, continued their existence indefinitely, and so on. Other shop floor committees were more like task teams, with a defined problem to solve within a specific time frame.

All of these QWL groups were parallel structures—that is, they existed side by side the normal management hierarchy. The groups were empowered to make suggestions for change, but they were dependent on the normal hierarchy for implementation. They suffered from many problems common to quality circles and other parallel structures, including inconsistent management support, long lead times for change implementation, frustration by nonmembers with the perceived "special privileges" of group members, and so on. The steering committee adopted the parallel structure approach to provide some form of employee involvement throughout the organization as quickly as possible and to provide management and the union with enough experience to determine whether they wanted to go further with their joint employee involvement efforts.

The parallel structure model was not the one we in the external consulting group preferred. We believed the parallel organization model afforded a limited and tenuous form of employee involvement. However, the strategy for the change process was the client's to formulate. We were willing to help them implement the type of QWL process they preferred, while continuing to point out that broader and deeper changes might also be required.

EARLY QWL INTERVENTIONS

During the past three years, the QWL effort focused on making the shop floor committees as successful as possible. The types of changes suggested by these groups ranged widely. Many of the changes addressed hygiene issues, such as buying comfortable chairs for offices and improving food in the cafeteria. These proposals generated much resentment because they were seen as trivial time wasters by nonmember employees and managers. However, a wide variety of work-related issues were addressed as well. These were concerned with cost savings, quality improvement, the adequacy of equipment and tooling, communication and coordination between parts of the organization, work process documentation, and many other issues.

No attempt was made to precisely quantify the costs and benefits of the QWL program. However, it appeared the savings generated by the shop floor committees more than paid for the entire change effort. This was primarily because of the success of a few key groups that were able to develop cost-savings suggestions that together saved the company millions of dollars. On the other hand, most QWL groups struggled even while a few groups enjoyed impressive successes.

EXTERNAL AND INTERNAL CONSULTANTS

The external consulting team of which I was a part included four experienced action researchers. Over the first three years of the program, the roles of the consultants shifted. Our most senior consultant was involved only briefly. He worked at initial entry with senior management and the steering committee in helping them define program strategy. The second most senior consultant was heavily involved from the beginning. I was next in seniority and experience within the consulting team, and I joined the group along with a more junior person soon after the project began.

The three most active consultants loosely coordinated their endeavors and frequently worked in pairs. In many situations, we divided the overall consulting task and the parts of the client organization. We were often glad to have each other to talk to in working with Universal Technologies. The client was so huge and the changes it needed were so deep that we often felt overwhelmed by the consulting task. One of the ongoing tasks called for by our contract was training and development of the internal QWL consultants.

Twenty internal consultants worked in a QWL department from the human resource function. They provided training to QWL groups at all levels, group facilitation, and some limited consulting services to management. Except for the two QWL department managers, none of the internal consultants had previous experience as higher-level managers. Some had been hourly employees, others had been in staff positions such as management training, and a few had been first-level supervisors.

With few exceptions, their services were greatly appreciated by the QWL teams, especially at the shop floor level. However, most of the internal consultants received much less respect from certain key managers, who viewed the internal consultants as low in status, power, and skills. This assessment, while uncharitable, was not without foundation. It nevertheless was our judgment that some of the internal consultants were talented and capable of becoming competent.

The internal consultants were eager to learn from the external consultants and from their own experiences. Our relationships with the internal consultants were generally cordial and mutually supportive. This did not mean there were no conflicts between internal and external consultants. The internal consultants often felt unappreciated, understaffed, and undertrained, and they sometimes reacted defensively to statements we made to the steering committee that they thought implied shortcomings in their role or performance. The two managers of the QWL department also had very strong views about the most appropriate change strategy, and they were not disposed to have the external consultants advocate another point of view at steering committee meetings or elsewhere.

In particular, the external consulting team believed the parallel organization model was only a stepping-stone to much deeper and more powerful forms of employee involvement. The internal consultants were more interested in perfecting the parallel model, which was familiar to them. Both groups tended to reach opposite conclusions about difficulties in the QWL effort based on the same evidence. We saw low enthusiasm for QWL among nonmembers of QWL groups, slow problem solving, lack of management support, and related problems as basic flaws in the parallel model. The internal consultants saw the same conditions as symptoms of inadequate training or facilitation.

JOB DESIGN OPPORTUNITY

For some time, we had argued to the steering committee, top managers, and union leaders that a new direction was needed if the QWL effort was to continue to develop. In particular, we believed that changes in the design of the work were needed. We saw a basic contradiction in asking for a high level of employee involvement during meetings of special groups for an hour a week, yet leaving the day-to-day work very tightly controlled by supervisors, machine pace, industrial engineering standards, and external rules and procedures.

Very traditional job designs were used throughout Universal Technologies, and our assessment was that these were the wrong job designs for most parts of the operation. We saw all the symptoms of job designs that did not allow adequate worker discretion and self-control, including poor coordination across interdependent departments and functions, poor quality, poor understanding by employees of how their work fit into the bigger picture, high turnover despite high pay, and job dissatisfaction. In our minds, job redesign experiments were needed both to help address organizational problems and to help the QWL effort avoid stagnation.

We believed self-managing work teams would be ideal in many parts of the operation. Such teams had been used successfully many times in other companies using similar production technologies in order to solve similar organizational problems. We also believed the work force would be receptive to such a change. Thus, we continually looked for good potential job redesign opportunities at Universal.

An opportunity arose from an unexpected direction. Sam Keller, the plant manager of one of the large plants in the complex, decided to sponsor a job redesign effort. Previously, he was not noted for his support of the QWL program. He had been appointed to the steering committee by the president of Universal Technologies, but he had attended only one or two meetings in three years. Keller believed the QWL program was a waste of time and money, and he was especially irritated by the focus of many groups on hygiene issues. Keller was known as a maverick; he had come from another company, and he prided himself on being an innovator and a man of action.

Keller came to the same conclusions as the consulting team about the inappropriateness of the job design in the plant. However, he tried to change the job design without bothering to go through the formal QWL process. He set up a job improvement task team that included both hourly and management representatives. This group was originally to report only to Keller. After behind-the-scenes pressure from the union, an internal consultant, and human resource managers, he agreed the group would be responsible to the union-management plant committee.

At its first meeting, Keller, with the blessing of the plant committee, gave the job improvement task team its charter. Within three months, the group was to propose a new work design to the plant committee that would improve product quality, increase employee job satisfaction, and enable the plant to make changeovers to new products more quickly. Keller did not attempt to specify the group's design in advance; the task team was given free rein to propose any kind of change it desired. The group was allowed to meet as often as it thought necessary, even if this meant meeting every day, and to request whatever resources it needed to get the job done.

One of the most able internal consultants, Bob Hays, was assigned to the task team. Hays, a former first-line supervisor, was excited by this assignment. He wanted to get some experience in a job redesign effort, and this was a golden opportunity. The consulting team was glad Hays had been assigned to the group as well.

Keller's initiative came at a bad time for the external consultants. All three of us were overloaded with other commitments in Universal Technologies and other companies. We simply did not have much time available during the three months the task team would do its work. I had the most time available. I offered to be Hays's "shadow consultant"—someone he could continually talk with about what to do. Hays called me several times for advice on how to proceed. However, Hays would sink or swim mostly on his own. This did not disturb plant manager Keller at all. He was not convinced that either the internal or the external consultants were essential to the changes he hoped to see.

I attended three of the group's first 15 meetings. My major direct contribution to the task team came early, when I conducted a one-day workshop for the task team to help members understand different job designs and the appropriate conditions for applying each. This was very well received, and the task team used some of the ideas I presented to help organize its thinking during the remainder of its existence.

The group plunged into its task. The group met for two days a week at first, but soon it was meeting three days a week on developing a change proposal. The group was both exhilarated and exhausted by its work pace. The task team began to doubt it was possible to do its job within three months but decided to press ahead as far as possible anyway.

THE BLOWUP

About six weeks into the group's existence (the midway point in its lifetime), I received a worried phone call from Bob Hays. Everything seemed to have gone wrong during the two weeks since my last meeting with the group.

The elected chairman of the task team was a vocal union member, "Sonny" Martinez. Martinez was a former shop steward. Martinez, however, had no real experience at leading problem-solving groups, and he was insecure in his role. He also was very worried about the potential for the job design change to conflict with collective bargaining contract provisions concerning such matters as job classifications, bidding, seniority, and possibly pay. Even though the plant committee (including union officers) had told the task team to be creative and not to feel constrained by the past, Martinez insisted nothing could be considered that was even potentially in conflict with the contract. He had become far more strident since I last saw the group.

Hays reported that most members of the group, especially on the management side, had become very frustrated by Martinez's behavior in the two weeks since I last met with the group. Privately, some called him "a broken record" or "Sonny one-note." The group was stuck because it was very difficult to develop any meaningful changes in job design that did not have at least some contractual implications, and Martinez tried to block all such discussion.

At the task team meeting earlier that day, Martinez announced the leaders of the union local were very disturbed about what they were hearing (presumably from him) about the deliberations of the task team. He said they were especially concerned about possible violations of the contract that were being considered by the task team. The president of the local and the other union members of the plant committee insisted on attending the task team meeting in three days to discuss these issues. Martinez added that this meeting would "once and for all settle the issue of whether this task team was going to get away with violating the contract."

The task team was incensed at this announcement. A management member bluntly accused Martinez of sabotaging the group through misrepresentations to the union leaders. She told Martinez his inappropriate and premature actions had jeopardized all the work of the group so far and possibly poisoned the well to the extent that the union leaders would never be receptive to reasonable proposals that required negotiating new contract provisions. After an acrimonious discussion, the group could agree only that it would meet the next day to plan the meeting with the union leaders.

Bob Hays felt overwhelmed by this turn of events. He was afraid the conflict level was so high that the group was in danger of being torn apart, and he feared that a golden opportunity for job redesign would be lost. Unspoken was his fear that he would be blamed if the group collapsed.

He asked whether I could attend the planning meeting or the "summit meeting" to help facilitate. He was sure that all those attending would welcome my attendance at either meeting. However, I had previous commitments for the days of both meetings that I could not break. What should I do?

I thought resolving the task team's issues was very important to the future of the entire QWL effort at Universal Technologies. I believed job redesign was badly needed, yet the company might decide job design was too sensitive a topic for union-management groups to consider. I also felt bad for Bob Hays, who was trying hard but might be in a no-win position.

In my mind, there were three key issues. First was the role of internal versus external consultants. It was part of the job of the external consultants to help the internal consultants learn to be successful, not to make the client dependent on us for handling every difficult situation personally. On the other hand, it would be irresponsible to leave Hays in a situation where he was destined to fail, if my direct involvement might turn failure into success. Thus, I had to estimate Hays's chances of being successful without my direct involvement.

The second key issue was the role of the task team. The argument over the role of the task team vis-à-vis the collective bargaining agreement had become very heated, but was not without foundation. What would the plant committee do if the task team came up with recommendations that conflicted with the contract? This had never really been addressed by the plant committee.

The final issue concerned the psychological development of the task team as a group. An obvious possibility was that the group might simply be passing through an angry "storming" stage of development that could be resolved successfully with the help of skillful facilitation.

I talked over options for action with Bob Hays. We consider the following options.

MY OPTIONS

1. *Try to delay the meetings until I can be there to help.*

Our best guess was that the task team and the union officers would be receptive to this possibility. Obviously, this was the most direct way to offer my help. Hays might learn more about handling difficult group issues by watching me in action and would not be blamed solely if resolution proved impossible. Perhaps this was the sort of difficult situation in which an experienced external consultant was needed. On the other hand, I was concerned that I would undermine Hays's role and prevent him from gaining an invaluable confidence-building and learning experience if I came in and did what he was capable of doing without me.

What are the real pluses and minuses of this option? If you prefer this option, what would you say to the task team and union leaders to propose it?

2. *Coach the internal consultant in order to help him work more effectively on his own at the meetings.*

This would avoid making an emergency out of the meeting with the union officers. If this option was successful, it would increase Bob Hays's self-confidence and would help the group feel ownership over the outcome of the meetings. If it was unsuccessful, it might severely damage his effectiveness as an internal consultant.

What are the real pluses and minuses of this option? If you choose this option, what would you say to Bob Hays to help him diagnose the situation and to help him act effectively?

3. *Arrange for another internal consultant to be there to help.*

This option might make sense in combination with option 2. Perhaps another internal consultant could offer some help at the meeting to Bob

Hays and make some on-the-spot interventions more effectively because of greater objectivity. At the very least, this person could give support to Bob Hays. There were one or two internal consultants as skilled as Hays, and who might be able to play this role.

What are the real pluses and minuses of this option? If you choose this option, how would you prepare the internal consultant for this role? What would you need to do to pave the way for him or her to attend the meeting?

4. *Make behind-the-scenes calls on key members of the task team.*

I could use this option in combination with any of the others. I might call members of the task team to size up their positions, to better diagnose the situation, and to help plan future interventions. I could use this information myself if I choose option 1 or to help prepare Bob Hays if I choose option 2. Note that this option raises the same concerns about client dependency on me as option 1. Also, this option raised the question of whether I would be failing to deal openly with group issues, which might undermine the group's effectiveness in the long run.

What are the real pluses and minuses of this option? If I choose this option, what do I say to the people I call? Who do I call?

5. *Make behind-the-scenes calls on key players in the company and union from outside the group.*

Perhaps I might call Sam Keller to let him know what was happening and to try to get him to attend the meeting. Perhaps I needed to call the union leaders to better understand their views, to reassure them that nothing objectionable was happening in the task team, or to give us the information needed to plan better for the summit meeting. However, this option raised ethical questions even more intensely than option 4 concerning failing to deal openly with group process issues.

What are the real pluses and minuses of this option? If I choose this option, who do I call and why? What do I ask them?

In my mind, however, there was little doubt about the course of action that made the most sense.

QUESTION FOR DISCUSSION

Which options or combination of options did I choose?

SDF Company (A)

Rex C. Mitchell
California State University, Northridge

SDF was a medium-sized company designing and manufacturing consumer electronics products in Southern California. It had 900 employees, in one location, and about $100 million in annual sales. SDF faced very tough competitors from the Far East. Most former U.S. competitors were now defunct. SDF's heyday was perhaps 10 years earlier, when it had a preeminent position in the industry. Then, it experienced a slow decline; lower-cost foreign competition eliminated U.S. companies and cut into SDF's business. It had been forced to lay off roughly 50 percent of the work force about 18 months before my first contact.

SDF was one of 10 companies in the parent corporation, which was privately owned (see Exhibit 1). SDF was strictly a design and manufacturing company. All marketing and distribution were handled by a separate company within the parent corporation. The parent corporation had been restructured six months before the first contact with me. At this time, manufacturing and marketing had been divided into separate companies. SDF began with an adverse financial position in terms of transfer prices (largely dictated from the top) that were very unfavorable to it and very favorable to the marketing company. Therefore, SDF was losing money and under much pressure to "make a profit." It had serious employee relations problems and a number of production and quality problems.

The president of SDF, Ken, had been promoted from within six months ago, at the time of the corporate reorganization (see Table 1), and he was pushing hard to improve the performance and financial position of the company. The manufacturing vice president, Neal, was well liked by the production people and had very good access to the informal system, but he was not sophisticated in terms of modern operations management. The human resources vice president, Hal, was a traditional human resources person and a nice man; I learned later he was not respected by the president.

EXHIBIT 1 Organization Chart (relevant parts)

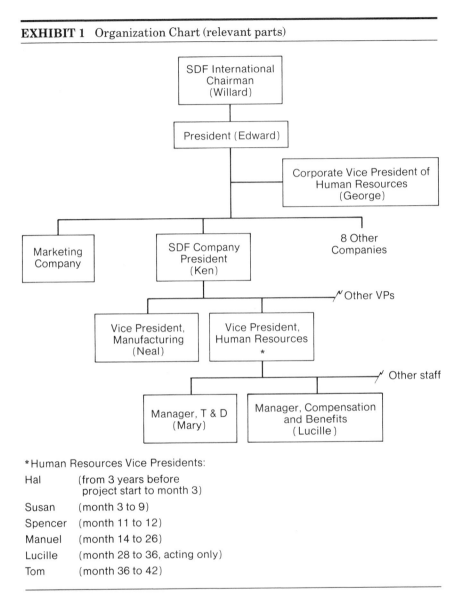

*Human Resources Vice Presidents:

Hal	(from 3 years before project start to month 3)
Susan	(month 3 to 9)
Spencer	(month 11 to 12)
Manuel	(month 14 to 26)
Lucille	(month 28 to 36, acting only)
Tom	(month 36 to 42)

About 700 of the 900 employees at SDF were on production lines or in direct support to them. Most jobs were relatively low in skill requirements and pay. About half of the production work force was women. About 50 percent of the production employees were Indo-Hispanic people of the Americas (Latino, as an imprecise shorthand); another 30 percent had Oriental and other ethnic origins. Many had minimal English communication skills. The percentage of illegal aliens was estimated to be about 15 percent in 1985.

TABLE 1 Background Information on Key Individuals

Willard:

> Chairman and largest owner of the privately held, parent corporation, SDF International; 63 years old; founded the original form of the SDF Company about 25 years ago.

Edward:

> President of SDF International; 49 years old; in present position since its creation one year ago; in top executive positions with SDF for 15 years.

George:

> Corporate vice president of human resources; 45 years old; in present position since its creation six months before Case (B) (three years after the start of Case (A); previously had his own executive search firm and handled the recruiting of Tom as one of his last projects.

Ken:

> President of SDF Company; 45 years old; in present position since its reorganization six months before; with corporation for four years.

Neal:

> Vice president of manufacturing; 57 years old; in present position 10 years; with SDF Company since its founding 25 years ago; moved into staff position 1½ years after start of Case (A), then retired nine months later.

Hal:

> Vice president of human resources at start of Case (A); 52 years old; with SDF in present position for three years.

Tom:

> Vice president of human resources at start of Case (B); 36 years old; with SDF in present position for six months before Case (B).

INITIAL RELATIONSHIP

My first contact with the company was a phone call from Neal, who had heard of me from a mutual acquaintance in another organization. He told me briefly about a pet project of the chairman of the board. After some mutual exploration in this phone conversation, we agreed to have a meeting with Hal, who was accountable for the project, but was out of town. I learned that they were talking with two other consultants.

This meeting seemed to be positive for both sides. I followed it with a brief letter proposal. They expressed interest. This was followed by several steps: I met with Ken; then had another discussion with Neal, Hal, and Ken; a meeting with Edward, president of the parent corporation; and a private meeting with Willard, chairman/CEO/major owner of the corporation. They selected me. We agreed on a plan and a first-year contract for the estimated three-year project.

The impetus for the project came from Willard, a very capable and successful businessman who also had some humanistic, socially oriented values, especially toward hourly workers. He wanted to establish a school for production workers on company premises and company time. In some fashion to be determined, the employees would go to school when they finished their work for the day and learn about whatever they desired, not necessarily something to do with the company's work. He thought this would be such a positive experience for the employees that they would be happier and, almost as an afterthought, that it would be beneficial for the company also. He had sent down the assignment to make his idea a reality soon.

I introduced some of the findings from the research on job satisfaction and productivity (particularly the dearth of evidence that satisfaction results in improved performance) in an attempt to help put this experiment into a business context. However, the focus of the project remained constrained—and I had to decide if I wanted to become involved.

This was an uncomfortable decision at the contracting stage, which basically reduced to: (*a*) agree to do a project in which the (unusual) intervention was already specified, at least at a conceptual level; or (*b*) reject the project because it did not allow for the conventional OD model of rather unconstrained data collection and diagnosis before designing an intervention.

Some positives for doing the project were: the very unusual, interesting, and interested chairman; the fact that I liked the president and two vice presidents; high internal commitment to the project from the top down; a company faced with tough challenges; an unusual project; a relatively low-skill multicultural work force (different from most of my projects); and favorable timing (the very intensive first few months of the project would occur during the summer, when I had considerable time away from the university).

Some negatives for doing the project were: they were starting with a solution, lacking clarity on the problem or objectives; the chairman was insisting on a very tight time frame; there was a lot of skepticism in the organization after seeing many highly publicized projects that never "got off the ground" or disappeared quickly; and they had limited skill in internal staff resources. It was clear that, if I became involved, I would have considerable role ambiguity and at least some role conflict.

My decision to do the project was not a difficult one, given the positives above (plus the fact that I had just finished a major two-year project with one client and was interested in starting another sizable project). The major factors against taking the project (the lack of clarity within the organization on the objectives for the project and constraints on the methods) could be managed, I believed, by redefining the objective(s) of the project to integrate the various objectives and make it appropriate to use a school for production workers as part of the solution. I didn't identify significant role or ethical difficulties in redefining the objective of the project, as long as I was explicit at the outset in doing this and made sure all the stakeholders had a chance to understand and react to the redefined objective.

THE PROJECT

I redefined the objective of the project as: to improve both the quality of work life (QWL) of the employees and the productivity of the organization through developing an employee learning program (ELP) and integrating it with a revitalized, integrated production planning and management process. I defined a project plan that was somewhat backward in sequence (to satisfy constraints): (*a*) develop and implement an employee learning program, (*b*) integrate it with existing production planning and management processes, then (*c*) improve the production planning and management processes. Step *a* and the beginning of *b* were to take about a year; step *b* would be the primary focus during year two and continue during year three; and step *c* would begin during the first year and take at least three years.

I put this objective and a fairly detailed work plan into an expanded proposal, discussed it first with Ken, Neal, and Hal, and then discussed it with Edward and Willard. They all agreed on the objective and work plan, which I started to implement.

The project was started with the challenging objective of having an employee learning program in operation in six weeks. Early work included detailed discussions with many people in production and human resources to introduce to them the concept of the project, get them thinking about it, begin to build understanding and acceptance for it, and obtain their ideas about the project and related matters. These discussions ranged from individual ones to 10 people at a time and with individuals from production employees through the chairman.

Pilot ELP Program

The project began with a pilot program that was operated for three months. The major reasons for starting with a pilot were: (*a*) rapid startup (a requirement dictated by the chairman); (*b*) modest disruption to production processes and results; (*c*) increased probability of success through selecting two work centers with enlightened, supportive management, and by allowing considerable direct, personal contact with participating employees; (*d*) creating an early success and building on this with both employees and management in the remainder of the company; and (*e*) learning from a specific experience before expending major resources.

All of these advantages were realized, and it is clear that starting with the pilot program was important. Two of the 18 production lines were selected because of their good performance, able supervision, and potential to recognize the value of the program and help it begin successfully.

An important factor in the pilot program was the steering committee formed to provide ideas and to be a two-way communication link with people in different work groups and in various levels of the company.

I had defined the need for and role of the steering committee in the original expanded work plan. I identified the functions and levels to be represented on the committee and worked with Hal, Neal, and production supervisors to identify the specific individuals to be invited to participate.

Individuals were selected who were both informal leaders in their production work groups and who were expected to be able and willing to give ideas and candid comments about the plans that were being developed. We wanted individuals who would both contribute to the planning meetings and also be effective in a two-way communication link with the informal system at all levels in the organization. After individuals were identified, I arranged for them to be invited to participate by Neal. The direct supervisor joined in where appropriate.

The resulting 12 members of the steering committee represented various functions and levels from production workers through vice presidents, comprising: one production worker, one lead person, and the supervisor from each of the two work groups involved in the pilot program; three other production workers from three different work groups not involved in the pilot; the human resources staff member working directly with me on the project (Bob); and the vice presidents of human resources (Hal) and manufacturing (Neal).

This committee met at critical points in the pilot program to provide ideas and to critique tentative plans for next steps, to provide feedback from their peers, and to go back to their work places with the latest information and understanding about what was happening and what would happen next. A preliminary description of the program was generated, summarized in a two-page paper (printed in English and Spanish), and distributed to all individuals in the two work groups, each in a meeting called by their supervisor, with the consultants present to assist and to meet the people.

Next, individual interviews, usually about 15 minutes long, were held during working hours with each of the approximately 45 persons in the pilot group. The individuals were given the option of bringing an interpreter and/or friend and about 20 percent did. There were three main purposes for the interviews: (1) to increase the understanding and answer questions of the participants about the program, (2) to find out what learning topics would be of most interest to each participant, and (3) to help develop rapport with the individuals and spark their interest in the program and its potential value to them.

These interviews were very important in the success of the pilot program; questionnaires or group meetings would not have produced the same benefits. At the same time, frequent discussions were held with the two first-line supervisors involved, plus their management—to involve them in the planning and to develop their interest and ownership for the project.

There was a fairly involved process to identify and recruit potential volunteer instructors from the staff at SDF (this was a desire of the chairman at the outset, based on effectiveness rather than cost considerations, and made good sense to me). Only one outside professional instructor was brought in for the pilot program classes.

> I identified a list of about 30 potential volunteer instructors by networking through the informal system and by having announcements made at all of the regular departmental staff meetings. We narrowed the list to about 15, considering those able to teach topics most likely to be used in the pilot program (based on the needs analysis that was part of the individual interviews with all participants) and those with some background in teaching/training.
>
> I interviewed the 15 and identified a pool of instructors from which we would draw during both the pilot and main program. I provided a set of resource materials on teaching and conducted one teacher training session with the five teachers selected for the pilot program. I met individually with each instructor before and after each class meeting for the first several weeks and then met with them individually and as a group frequently during the remainder of the three-month pilot program.

There also were many discussions and design decisions during the last three weeks before implementing the pilot program involving various individuals up through the president. Several rounds of written and oral communications occurred shortly before the kickoff meeting. This meeting began with light refreshments and informal mingling of the 45 participants and about 20 members of management and human resources staff. This was the first time most of the workers had met Ken and Edward.

The pilot program basically consisted of a series of one-hour classes during work time, meeting once every two weeks for three months, plus the accompanying work discussions, recognition, and attention. The participants chose five classes to be offered (English as a second language, exercise and self-defense, introduction to computers, reading blueprints, and selection and operation of hi-fi components) and individuals chose which they would attend.

There were ongoing efforts to obtain feedback from participants and others. Information thus gained was used to provide a basis for decisions and design of the main program.

Main Program

The main program extended the potential for participation to all production workers and their supervisors; however, each production line would have to meet certain performance criteria to be eligible to participate. It was decided to operate the program on a monthly cycle: (a) performance results for one calendar month are analyzed to determine which lines will be eligible for the monthlong classes to begin during the following month; (b) classes of high priority for the eligible lines (as determined in a needs analysis survey) are offered as potential classes, and the people in those lines select the classes that will be given by their signup preferences; and (c) each individual participates in the class he or she chooses (from those the employees collectively select) for one hour each week for four consecutive weeks.

Design, preparations, and communications for the main program were performed during the three-month pilot program, so the main program could begin immediately after the pilot. A new steering committee was organized to help with the main program, in the same ways that were found to be vital with the pilot program steering committee. Some of the members had been on the pilot steering committee.

A new needs analysis was conducted by written (trilingual) questionnaires. Extensive written and oral communications were used with the participants and their direct supervisors, plus many other individuals and groups, including: the president and his staff, all production management, other production workers not participating in the program yet, instructors and their management, the steering committee, all management, support groups, and key individuals in other parts of the parent corporation.

Considerable work was necessary to identify and clarify key performance objectives and measures and to improve systems to make it possible for production supervision to focus on specific results and measure performance against them. Then, performance criteria for participation in the ELP could be established. There had to be many compromises in this part of the project because the production management systems were so primitive. The initial criteria for participation remained relatively unchanged during the first 18 months. The groups eligible for participation were those that met their established performance criteria during the month.

My role during roughly the first 18 months of the project was a very active and direct one, for several reasons. First, this was the company's desire at the contracting stage. It recognized that it had limited internal resources, considered hiring a full-time person to design and manage the program, and then decided to hire a consultant.

Second, the company assigned one human resources staff member, Bob, to handle much of the ongoing administration of the program; however, his time and experience were limited (and he left the company about seven months into the project). The various human resources vice presidents were very interested, supportive, and helpful; however, the impact of their involvement was limited by the turnover in this position.

Third, this project was experimental and quite different from anything that had been done before. Fourth, there were a large number of "messy" realities and complications that had to be managed (see Table 2 and discussion in a later section).

Basically, I initiated every new action; managed almost all of the design and operations; and performed a majority of the design, analysis, coordination, training, coaching, and communication tasks during all but a few of those first 18 months. For example, I designed and organized the training needs analysis, plus had the data scored and analyzed outside the company, then prepared a summary with implications for use in design. With volunteer instructors, I trained (briefly) and oriented them, negotiated support from their bosses (as necessary), managed logistical support, visited their classes, provided coaching, and provided and arranged for "strokes" and recognition for their efforts.

I arranged for the manufacturing vice president to take the lead in determining the performance criteria and system to determine eligibility for participation in the program, and I helped him arrange for extensive participation by his managers and supervisors. Then, I helped him simplify the system and prepare briefings for management and training for supervisors who would administer it. I initiated and participated in almost all sessions to help them improve their production planning and management processes.

I established rapport with most of the key individuals in the informal system at SDF and spent some time at least one or two days each week "out on the lines"—talking with people about the project, the company, and their interests. I wrote all communications, including letters from the president, and wrote or drafted all talks or verbal communications by the management staff.

SOME MESSY REALITIES

There were many nontidy realities about the company and the context for the project, which necessitated special efforts and trade-offs. These messy realities included the list in Table 2. The first five items in the list

---

TABLE 2 Some Untidy Realities in the Project

1. Diversity, vagueness, and idealism in company's "presenting objectives."
2. Contradictions in priorities of various key stakeholders (e.g., social largesse of Willard while holding Ken accountable for major improvements in profitability).
3. Job security fears.
4. Skepticism about company programs not happening or lasting.
5. Company aversion to surveys (even data gathering in general).
6. Demographics (large majority were Latino, sizable other ethnic groups, many with limited English skills and little formal education, large group of temporary and agency employees).
7. Serious limitations in production system and information systems.
8. Frequent changes in products, production lines, and work assignments.
9. Supervisors and managers busy putting out fires.
10. Difficulty in creating coherence, understanding, ownership, support.
11. High turnover (including production supervisors).
12. Turnover in human resources (6 vice presidents in the three years after the start of Case (A)—with accompanying difficulties in maintaining continuity in contracting and internal roles.

---

had been addressed adequately during the early months of the project. The others remained active and troublesome throughout the project.

Let's consider particularly some of the complications introduced by the last reality in this list: high turnover in the human resources department, especially at the vice president level. The six heads of human resources are listed in Exhibit 1, with their periods of service. The vice president at the time I started consulting with the company, Hal, was doing a fairly good job with respect to the project; however, within the first week, I learned that the president, Ken, was unhappy with him for several reasons. Within three months after the project began, he was "eased out" (encouraged to resign, with a modest severance package and outplacement assistance).

He was the person who contacted me initially, was my official company contact for the project, and was very helpful both with the project and in helping me gain access to people and become accepted in the company. Ordinarily, the departure of an individual filling such key roles could have a considerable effect on a consulting project. However, this first change in vice presidents did not cause any disruption for me, for several reasons:

1. Because of the high corporate visibility of the project, the president was an active party to the contracting and had been involved in all stages.

2. As soon as I learned of the severity of Ken's unhappiness with Hal, I made sure I developed a solid connection with Ken (I also made a serious attempt to facilitate the conflict between Ken and Hal, but Ken took a firm stance that things were beyond the point of no return).

3. I was already established in the company because of the intensive level of work in the first few months and early success of the project.

4. Hal, with my encouragement, assigned a human resources staff member (Bob) to work with me on the project; he was capable and was well involved before the change.

5. A replacement for Hal was recruited before he was told of the decision; therefore, there was not a break in staffing. The new vice president (Susan) was excellent, and she also enjoyed the full approval of Ken.

The next six months (before Susan left) were very successful for the project and were the smoothest period for me during all my work with SDF. Susan not only had the usual initial support from the president derived from his selection of her, but also proved to be very effective and a good fit with the company. She earned a high degree of respect from Ken, the other vice presidents, her staff, and people throughout the company. She and Manuel (the fourth vice president in the sequence during my work with SDF) were the only ones who would have been welcome to remain with the company.

About four months after Susan arrived, Bob resigned to take another position. For a variety of reasons, another human resources staff member was not assigned to work with the project, and Susan personally filled that role. When Susan left, conditions were different and there was moderate disruption:

1. Susan left before the company found a replacement. I met with her and Ken and we agreed that I would take complete responsibility for the project during the staffing gap (this was later continued under the next vice president, Spencer) and that I also would provide support and informal guidance for the human resources staff during the gap (I had managed a large human resources department for five years a few years earlier, so this was not moving outside my expertise). It was not practical to assign another staff member to work with me at this time.

2. Susan and I had been working out details of my second-year contract. The timing of her departure complicated this because the president wanted the new vice president to be a party to contracting; I was doing special work outside the original scope of the first-year contract; the company was in the middle of final budget negotiations; and so on.

3. Susan and I had been planning a major effort for the coming year to help improve the company production planning and management processes and to integrate the ELP with them.

4. I had relied on Susan to manage most of the coordination with Ken. This was a result of several factors: (1) I was now spending much less time at SDF (in contrast to the first few months of the project, when I was there at least part of two to three days every week), (2) I wanted to support her in developing her role, and (3) she did it very well. Therefore, her active role left more of a void than occurred during the previous transition. However, I had maintained good rapport with Ken and within the company, so this was not a serious disruption.

5. The third vice president (Spencer) turned out to be a mutual disaster for him and the company. Spencer started with the company about six weeks after Susan left. I did not provide any consulting assistance in the selection process, although I offered to assist (this didn't seem to interest Ken and I didn't push it). Spencer was a nice man in his early 30s with modest human resources experience, who had been "between positions" for several months. I spent two sessions with him, briefing him on things that could be useful about the company, the project, and suggestions for working effectively with Ken and others.

He was eager, but seemed to lack organizational sophistication and other dimensions necessary for success in his position (I would place this position considerably above average in difficulty among human resources vice president positions). About two weeks after he started, Ken said to me, "I think I have made a terrible mistake" (referring to his decision to hire Spencer). He was gone after six weeks.

By this time (about 12 months after the start of the project), I was frustrated, particularly because of the complications for me and the project created by the turnover in vice presidents. The project was progressing well, and there had been considerable improvement in company performance. However, there had been only modest improvements in the production management system (and there were some signs of backsliding).

My original plan and efforts to "work myself out of a job," to develop internal resources and gradually transfer responsibilities for the project to them, had fallen apart since Susan left the company three months ago. I didn't want to continue to run the project or continue to provide informal direction for the human resources staff, but felt I should continue—on professional, ethical, and personal grounds. Also, I was being asked to by Ken. I could not define a reasonable alternative to suggest to them. I did not want to see the project (in which I had invested considerable time and interest) fall apart, with what I anticipated would be resulting losses for me, employees, and the company.

I also was concerned directly about the turnover in human resources vice presidents and wanted to influence a change in this. Ken welcomed my involvement in his next selection, and we agreed on several aspects of my consulting role for the transition period. I continued to run the project and provide informal guidance to the staff during the month gap before the fourth vice president (Manuel) started. I helped Ken clarify key selection criteria and define a process for use in this staffing selection.

Manuel had about 15 years of solid human resources experience, was very competent technically and a reasonable manager, was Latino and fluent in both Spanish and English (an important asset with the employee population at SDF), and had good organizational skills. I briefed him on various things, took him on a plant tour and introduced him to people, and as quickly as possible moved back into the sidelines. This transition between vice presidents was focused primarily on disentangling myself from the emergency human resources roles I had been playing for the over four months since Susan left and supporting Manuel in his entry.

The 12 months Manuel was in the position (before he took a higher level human resources position with another company) were characterized by intense competitive and financial pressures on the company and steady improvements in the human resources department. However, progress in the department and on this project were hampered by staffing and financial constraints. The internal assignment on the project was given to a human resources staff member; however, she was responsible for so many other things that her most conscientious efforts to work on this project still resulted in limited attention to it.

Simultaneously, there were severe limitations on funds to hire me for work on the project because of both the continuing financial squeeze in the company and the fact that it had already spent more than its year's budget for me in obtaining the emergency backstopping help during the two, near-continuous transitions between vice presidents. The net effect was to reduce work on the project to a maintenance level during the rest of that second year.

RESULTS AND LEARNINGS FROM THE FIRST TWO YEARS

The number of work groups and employees eligible for the ELP increased steadily and substantially during the first year of the program, as a result of higher performance. The overall performance of the company improved significantly (e.g., during the first 18 months of the program, financial losses were cut by more than 50 percent, sales volume was up 20 percent, backlog and scrap rates were down, employee turnover was down by 25 percent). Further, the approximately two thirds of the production groups that particularly embraced the ELP/QWL program had markedly better performance improvements than did the other third.

The design of the ELP evolved over its first two years, although only modest changes were necessary after the first nine months. Some of the key design and process elements found to be important for the ELP are summarized below:

1. Having active, visible support from management at all levels.
2. Integrating the program into normal management responsibilities, as an aid in achieving good performance, rather than allowing it to be an optional, "somebody says I have to do it" type of program.
3. Providing a clear, believable process for employees to become eligible to participate in classes. They need to believe there is a reasonable, fair method to decide when they may participate and that the requirements aren't far beyond their reach.
4. Involving employees at all levels in planning, design, and change of the program.
5. Giving the participating employees ample opportunity to identify and choose what they want to learn (and not limiting it to work-related topics).
6. Providing extensive communications to participants and others at all stages.
7. Ensuring that all classes are of high quality, including providing very capable, interested instructors for all classes.
8. Supplying support, recognition, even rewards for volunteer instructors.
9. Ensuring good follow-through on mundane logistics such as making sure instructors are there on time and prepared; rooms are available, open, clean, and at a reasonable temperature in advance; chairs and equipment are in place; supervisors remember to release people in time to get to classes.

During the first two years of the project, there were 19 sets of monthly classes, in addition to the classes during the pilot program. Two to 11 production lines, involving 50 to 400 employees, participated each month, with many groups repeating extensively. Seventeen of the 18 production lines in operation during at least part of the two years participated in the 149 classes, covering 31 topics. Reactions from the participants were very positive, with a widely shared desire to earn future participation.

At the end of year two, I wrote a second annual report. This included discussion of needs for further development of the program under five major issues: (1) obtaining a supply of motivated, capable instructors on a continuing basis, (2) offering a greater range of learning opportunities, (3) improving program administration by SDF staff, (4) improving the production planning and management processes, and (5) integrating the ELP with production performance management processes. There had been reasonable success, but much more work was needed.

DECISION POINT NEAR THE END OF YEAR TWO

I was frustrated about the status of the project near the end of its second year. At first examination, this seemed to be an inappropriate feeling. We had achieved reasonable success in improving the QWL of the employees. The employee learning program was successful and seen as an unusual positive by the employees. The project had resulted in some additional, relevant training for supervisors—and the frequency and quality of work discussions about production and quality had increased considerably. There had been significant improvements in the company performance (although there were a number of other factors contributing to this besides this project).

> Why was I frustrated? In short, the QWL/performance improvement project had not become very well stabilized. Most of the improvements, even in the manufacturing system, were reactive and in response to efforts I initiated. Very few individuals yet had much of a vision of how the company and its manufacturing system could be significantly better, or how programs such as the present QWL effort could be integrated with its production planning and management processes to the advantage of both the company and the employees.
>
> Most of the first-line production supervisors didn't yet envision how they could take a more active role in the production planning and management process. We had not developed the internal staff resources and involvement necessary to ensure continued operation of even the features already in place without substantial involvement of an outside consultant.
>
> Further, because of special budget constraints, the company has been limiting severely its use of outside consultants during the last year and was likely to continue this during the coming year. Not only had I failed to "work myself out of a job" quickly enough, but there was the prospect of seeing a major deterioration in the gains already made.
>
> I could note adverse circumstances beyond my control, especially: turnover in human resources vice presidents (four in two years) and in human resources staff involved with the program (now working with the third in two years), and budget problems that had reduced my consulting support to an ineffective level halfway through the project. However, the reality remained that the last two years of effort on the project would be largely a waste if the project were put in a maintenance mode at this time, and the resources necessary to move the project ahead to a stabilized point seemed not to be available.

QUESTIONS FOR DISCUSSION

1. Critique the consultant's original decision to undertake the project, knowing some of the complexities and constraints. What would you have done? Under what conditions? Why?

2. Do you have any concerns about the consultant's role in redefining the project objectives at the beginning?

3. Discuss some of the pros and cons for the consultant's very active role in determining the direction of and managing the project during most of the first 18 months.

4. What issues and difficulties were likely to be introduced by the consultant accepting the added role of taking full responsibility for running the project and also providing informal direction for the human resources staff during the transition period between vice presidents (the more than four-month period from Susan's departure in month 9 until Manuel arrived in month 14)?

5. What would you as the consultant do at the end point of the case (nearing the end of year two) relative to the existing project and your future involvement at SDF? Discuss your reasons.

Case 31

SDF Company (B)

Rex C. Mitchell
California State University, Northridge

This part of the case occurs 3½ years after the start of the project, as described in Case (A). During the 1½ years since the end of Case (A), I had not been consulting with the company, at my choice. I made this decision because SDF lacked and seemed unable or unwilling to develop the internal resources and consultant funding necessary to complete the original project and bring it to a stabilized stage where it could have a reasonable degree of self-sustaining momentum. SDF also had changed human resources vice presidents two more times.

The employee learning program (ELP) was still in operation, with minimal support from the human resources department to manage the ongoing administration. In my opinion, it needed to have a major overhaul and revitalization or be stopped because its impact on performance and QWL had deteriorated during the 1½-year period of little attention.

On the other hand, the improvements in the production management system we had started two years earlier had been continued and improved somewhat. The company was still having financial pressures, despite considerable improvements in productivity and costs, because of external competitive pressures from foreign companies plus the still-unfavorable transfer prices between SDF Company and the marketing company.

I had been approached by SDF and agreed about one month ago to undertake a new, small project for the human resources department.

A TEAMBUILDING PROJECT

It is past midnight and I am sitting in my study, thinking about a project I am doing for SDF: a teambuilding project for the human resources department staff. I am particularly aware of three upcoming discussions and actions I need to decide how to handle:

1. A meeting in three days with the vice president of human resources (Tom) to plan the next steps in this teambuilding project. I had met with Tom yesterday to provide feedback from interviews with department staff and key stakeholders outside the department. There was considerable critical feedback both with respect to the department and Tom, personally.
2. Lunch with the company president (Ken) in two days, at his request. I expect Ken will want to talk about Tom's performance, Ken's continuing frustration with Tom, and the teambuilding project.
3. A long-distance call I will receive in the morning from the corporate vice president for human resources (George), wanting to talk further about Tom, problems with Tom's department, the teambuilding project, and possibly about a second project initiated by George's boss, the corporate president (Edward).

As I reviewed my notes, I recalled how these two projects had begun. About six weeks ago, I had received a call from the manager of Training and Development (Mary), who reports to Tom; she had been hired by SDF about four months previously, and I did not know her very well. She asked a number of questions about teambuilding, what were some designs, how it could be initiated, and so on. She had a specific work group in mind, but was very cautious to avoid identifying it. It was not hard to guess that it was the human resources department. About two weeks later, I received another call from Mary, who identified the work group as the human resources department, elaborated on some of the problems that led her to believe a teambuilding project was needed, said she had gained the support of Tom to have such a project, and asked me to join in a meeting with her and Tom to discuss this.

We met a few days later; this 1½-hour contracting meeting proceeded smoothly, with no unusual features. We agreed to do a limited-scale teambuilding project focused on plans and priorities for the department over the next one to two years. We agreed I would gather data on perceptions of the department and its effectiveness through individual interviews with the 10 people in the department, plus about 10 key stakeholders outside the department including Ken and George (we identified a tentative list).

I would organize the data in a way to avoid revealing who said what and provide a preview of the data to Tom. Then, he and I would plan the next steps, tentatively centered around a one-day work session with the human resources staff to be scheduled about a month later. Tom agreed to communicate, within the next two days, to his staff, Ken, and the other outside stakeholders about the project and ask for their involvement.

On the third day, I started calling people to set up appointments for interviews. I quickly learned that Tom had briefly communicated to part of his staff, but not to Ken or others about the project. I smoothed the pique Ken expressed at Tom for not telling him about the project directly. The interviews were quite candid, helped considerably by the fact that I knew all of the individuals from previous work at the company. (See Table 1 for examples of data from the interviews.)

There were two noteworthy aspects about the data. First was the high degree of dissatisfaction with the current priorities and effectiveness of the human resources department and also with Tom's performance. During the seven months since Tom joined the company, he had been pushing very hard to change the priorities and primary emphasis of the department from a fairly traditional one to taking the lead role within the company to change the manufacturing system toward use of a variety of sophisticated techniques and systems (e.g., a just-in-time [JIT] operation, with continuous process improvement [CPI] groups). There was a large amount of data critical of these changes, of cutbacks in other human resources efforts to provide these changes, and of the speed and style with which the changes were pushed.

Second, the agendas and interrelationships of key stakeholders were even more complex than in most organizations. For example, Ken was extremely frustrated and dissatisfied with the changes in human resources priorities and department operation that Tom had made during his seven months with the company, stated that the situation was intolerable and must change, and said he had told Tom this repeatedly.

Three of Tom's staff, who had direct relationships with Ken, reported conversations with Ken in which he had expressed his frustration with Tom and the department—and in which they had expressed some of their own frustrations directly to Ken. Several of the department staff were unhappy with the changes in focus Tom was trying to make and also were concerned that the department's credibility and influence in the company were deteriorating badly. They saw this as a result of Tom's changes and lack of congruence with Ken's priorities.

Tom reported he thought his and Ken's priorities were in good agreement, and the major issue was to get some of his staff to move ahead to become proactive in changing the manufacturing system to incorporate some sophisticated techniques and systems, rather than spending most of their time on "employee relations and other traditional personnel crap."

The corporate human resources vice president, George, had a very mixed set of considerations: (*a*) before joining the parent corporation, SDF International, in this just-created position about six months ago, George had operated his own executive recruiting firm and had been paid by SDF for recruiting Tom, so George had a vested interest in having Tom seen as a good selection; (*b*) George and Ken had a long history and friendship, so he had both respect for and interest in Ken's concerns; (*c*) some of the indications of conflicts involving Tom and some staff with

TABLE 1   Examples of Data from Interviews

The data appear in the verbatim words of the individuals as far as possible. They are organized under several major categories that seemed to fit the data and are grouped under three types of sources (external to the human resources department, internal to the department, and Tom). Although only about 20 percent of the data are given, the comments are representative (except that almost none of the comments about specific individuals are shown here).

Overall Impressions of Human Resources Department
and Its Present Effectiveness

External
- There are good people and most are trying hard, but the department's priorities are not my priorities (from Ken).
- They seem overly interested in special programs and automated systems.
- The fundamentals are not getting done.
- They are not accessible or available.
- Fairly good—despite all their problems. It's made it really hard to have so many changes in VPs and direction—it's hard on them and hard on us.
- The level of contact with employees in the shop is up.
- We've had some good experiences with training.
- Still disorganized; can't count on delivery of things promised.
- Doing some good things, e.g., safety program.
- They pass the buck and pass you around—not helpful or accommodating.
- SDF is not a clean, calm business: there are a lot of crises, planning tends to be chaotic and largely short range, things are not stable, there are not established traditions and a bureaucracy. I wonder if Tom can adapt to and be comfortable with this reality.
- They have moved toward a big emphasis on long-term future projects and aren't doing the necessary day-to-day things.
- Establishing and maintaining good working relationships with others is a central part of every HR job, and vital to accomplish anything. A couple of individuals (named) seem to think that this is separate from successful performance of the HR people.

Internal (except Tom)
- We have serious problems and need to address them ASAP.
- I think the department image is near an all-time low. I'm really concerned.
- Tom's and Ken's priorities are quite different.
- People are working really hard—but are not recognized outside.
- The instability at the top of HR has been our biggest problem; we just get adjusted to the direction of one VP when another one comes in with completely different goals and approaches.
- We have an identity crisis: outside people don't know what we are doing, inside we don't know how we fit into the company.
- I think outside opinions of us are getting a little better.
- We're doing a tough job and pretty well meeting demands—but they don't appreciate us.

TABLE 1 *(continued)*

Tom
- Things are better than under my predecessors, but people are looking for scapegoats.

Communications and Work Relationships
between Human Resources Staff and "Customers"

External
- Excellent with some of the staff, terrible with others (named).
- Tom seems not to have any idea how to operate with Ken.
- Support is there if we need it, but we have to go get it—this is a little strange and different.
- It's hard to get support from our HR rep (named), as she has her own agenda and takes an adversarial role automatically on everything. It's real obvious that she is very interested in JIT and special training projects—and not in taking a proactive role in employee relations or in other traditional personnel roles—we need support.
- I have tried to call our rep, but don't get much help—so now I don't call much.
- My personal interfacing with HR is very comfortable and good. People act and respond to my needs and problems. . . . I'm very impressed with my rep (different one).
- If someone says they will do something, I can't rely on it happening (but there is some improvement from last year).

Internal
- The other VPs have good working relationships with Ken. Tom and the department badly need him to develop one. Tom seems not to "read" Ken (examples from several people).
- People outside don't know what we do.
- We need to be much more accessible.

Tom
- I think my priorities and Ken's are in good agreement; we get along fine.

What Customers Would Like from Human Resources

External
- My number 1 priority is excellent communication (up, down, across). Then and only then can we develop shared goals (Ken).
- What I want first from HR are the fundamentals: an excellently run department, common goals, people working together, accessible, providing the company with basic tools (e.g., wage and salary structures, up-to-date policies, consistent policy administration), helping maintain good employee relations, good recruiting, supervisory training, accurate and accessible data (Ken).
- They have too much emphasis on projects and not enough on fundamentals.
- HR to help maintain a level of employee relations—e.g., so that. . . .
- Promote consistency in policies: definition, implementation and application,

TABLE 1   *(continued)*

same in both plants, especially in disciplinary actions, provide supervisor's manual and employee manual.

- Put realistic costs on issues/programs, rather than push them because they are a good idea—identify realistic costs and what we can gain.
- Define to supervisors what they need to be doing on the floor relative to managing people (and staying out of trouble).
- Keep commitments—this is critical in business.
- A basic personnel system (things can't be tracked). They need to design some basic personnel systems before worrying about computerizing them.

What Human Resources Would Like to See

Internal

- For the department to establish better relationships with our customers, and to gain respect (and ability to get things done).
- Active leadership from Tom.
- For Tom to establish a good working relationship with Ken and his staff.
- For us to be out on the floor more and have more visibility there; they don't know who we are or what we do.
- Support from Tom for staff in outside meetings and in disputes with managers.
- Better communications inside HR and with the outside.
- Consistency in policy practices in the two plants.
- Clear definition of jobs and responsibilities in HR.
- We're not getting the basics done.
- We need to make the day-to-day company functions run smoothly; a first step is to prepare and make available: salary structures, policies and documents, supervisors' guidebook, employee handbook.
- Publish information to let managers know who does what in HR.
- We need to work together more—everyone's off doing their own work.

Tom

- We need to focus on doing what we need to do to support the company business. My major priority is to support Ken in the business; we need to get JIT (a just-in-time manufacturing system) going.
- My top priority is getting all the pieces in place for continuous product improvement (CPI): a plan for all 18 work centers, training for line and management, in-group problem-solving sessions with facilitations, cross-functional area meetings. . . . The HR staff need to make the transition to focusing on this, rather than the traditional personnel stuff.
- I hope the HR staff does or can feel we're making progress and supporting the business. Do they understand some of the things we're trying to do?

Shared, Understood Goals and Priorities within Human Resources

External

- What Tom seems to want as the department's priorities are not my priorities (Ken).

TABLE 1 *(continued)*

- I don't think they have common goals.
- They need to define their mission clearly.

Internal
- We clearly don't have common, understood goals.
- I don't think Tom's and Ken's goals are in agreement. We're caught in the middle.
- We need to develop goals that we all understand and ways to get them done.

Tom
- We need to establish common goals, get on the same wavelength.

Clear, Understood Rules and Responsibilities within Human Resources

External
- I don't know who does what—or where to get help.
- I don't know who to call for services.

Internal
- Tom tells us to do what we know needs to be done. Sometimes we need more direction or coordination than that.
- I'm not sure how to sort out some things; Tom just leaves it up to us.

Tom
- We have some issues regarding who has to do what.

Communication, Rapport, and Work Relationships within Human Resources

External
- Staff in HR are feeling afraid and frustrated.
- There is a lack of cohesion in HR; we can see it. They need a clear sense of direction, of how they will operate.
- There is dissension within the department.

Internal
- There are serious tensions within the department.
- People are split into two camps.
- Most people are working hard; a couple are not.
- (Many specific comments, omitted here.)

Tom
- Things are pretty good within the department, but I'm not comfortable with my managing in the department; they haven't received enough management from me; I haven't performed up to my potential.

Improving Manufacturing System and Company Performance
(Including JIT/CPI Projects)

External
- Absolutely, we need to and will eventually evolve to have some of the sophisticated systems that Tom wants to see. But, we need to build toward that— rather than taking a flying leap and crashing.

TABLE 1 (*concluded*)

- Some of the HR people make JIT sound like a religion—you have to accept it all or nothing, and you're a sinner if you don't accept it all right now!
- The pilot for JIT just didn't work out. . . . We weren't sufficiently prepared and/or didn't make enough management commitment. It left a very bad taste on both sides.
- They have too much emphasis on projects and not enough on fundamentals— we need support.
- Production is not sold on JIT, etc. We need to work on a real foundation first— to develop a manufacturing system you can rely on. We're making good progress, are in a healing mode now, to repair a manufacturing system. We don't need another program right now (no matter how good).
- There were problems with the way it was presented.
- It's difficult to see this as a responsibility and pet project of HR.
- To start this, if we are serious, I would. . . .
- We need healthy systems in place before starting into major JIT changes.

Internal
- All Tom seems to care about is JIT.
- He wants us to drop everything else and concentrate on JIT but seems to ignore the needs and requests of managers and Ken—how are we supposed to ignore these?
- Production people don't seem very interested in JIT; why are we pushing it so hard?
- We're not a very sophisticated company and most of our work force is minimum wage and marginal. I don't think we can expect to operate in ways that would fit a top-flight aerospace company.

Tom
- My major priority is supporting Ken in the business; we need to get JIT going.
- I want management agreement on what is JIT/CPI at SDF. We need to do statistical process control on the lines.
- My top priority is getting all the pieces in place for continuous product improvement (CPI).

---

others in SDF Company had come to the attention of George and his boss, Edward, so George could not ignore them without personal risk as well as neglecting his corporate responsibilities.

> Since a number of the stakeholders, including Ken and George, wanted to talk with me about the human resources department situation and their concerns about Tom, not just be interviewed to provide data, I had to make some decisions about how to handle this. I defined a stance from which I would operate in discussing the project outside the human resources department (your instructor may supply information on this after you discuss the point in class).

I also had to make decisions about how to handle data feedback to Tom because there was so much negative data about his redirection of the department and about him personally. I normally provide comprehensive and uncensored data feedback to both the "boss" and to the group in a teambuilding project, with the provision of protecting against revealing who said what.

I usually provide analysis and tentative conclusions but also provide generous amounts of actual verbatim statements that led me to these tentative conclusions—in ways that can be examined and disconfirmed by the people receiving the data. The rare exceptions to this rule have been situations where there seemed to be serious risk of causing emotional injury to individuals through normal data feedback processes. I decided I did not need to use unusual feedback processes in this case, based on inputs from Tom and a staff member who had worked with him for several years and seen him receive and handle difficult feedback data previously.

Accordingly, I finished my data analysis and prepared materials for a detailed data feedback session with Tom. These consisted of a modified version of Table 1 (but using the full data set) and another set of feedback data about Tom and his performance. We met for three hours as I explained the written summary materials, and we discussed the data.

Tom was moderately defensive at first, but he soon listened and ask mostly clarifying questions, with only minimal defensive statements. I watched carefully for signs of overload, but he stayed alert, tracking what we were discussing and giving signs of comprehending the material quite well. Near the end of the session, he commented, "It seems that things are more serious than I thought."

Later, after he had talked some about his assessment of the data, he asked me, "Do they think they would be better off without me?" I told him I believed this was not the case and pointed out a number of sample quotes in the data he had before him that led to my conclusion. I also told him, with Ken's permission, that Ken did not want him to leave, but he did want to see some significant changes.

We discussed briefly that the data seemed to be calling for a significant turnaround in some of the priorities of the department and in its latest mode of relating with its "customers." I told him I believed this could be done very successfully and I had some ideas on how to do this. He jumped (too quickly, I felt) to say, "I'm going to do it; I have never run away from anything before and I'm not going to do it now."

I suggested that he allow himself a few days to reflect, rather than feeling he had a duty to commit to change today. I also gave him two one-page preliminary briefs on, respectively: (1) several excellent opportunities to build human resources credibility at this time and (2) some possible next steps. We agreed to meet again in three days to discuss the data further and to plan actions.

DECISIONS TO BE MADE ON NEXT STEPS

One of my (and your) immediate tasks is to prepare for an uncertain next work session with Tom in three days. The stated purpose is to discuss the data further and plan actions. However, it is uncertain what stance Tom will take and you must be prepared for anything from he resigns to he wants to begin an immediate, full-scale turnaround effort.

A second immediate task is to anticipate what issues Ken is likely to bring up relative to Tom and this project at the lunch meeting in two days (he initiated the meeting) and how you will handle yourself in discussions about these. You know Ken well; you both like each other and have mutual respect. He has been your ultimate (and often direct) client throughout the work you have done for SDF during several years. He has talked candidly with you about his frustrations with Tom and how the present situation "cannot continue." He has direct input from at least three human resources staff members about their issues and concerns. He is aware you had a data feedback session with Tom yesterday. Ken has not seen any of the data.

The third immediate task is to think through how you will handle the telephone call from George tomorrow. He is out of state attending a trade show and his message today said he will call again tomorrow morning and would like to talk about "how the session with Tom went today." He talked candidly in an interview last week about his serious concerns regarding Tom's performance and poor relationship with Ken.

Among the underlying factors that may enter into his stance and your response are: (*a*) his vested interest in avoiding the image that his recruiting of Tom was not a success; (*b*) his long-term friendship and relationship with Ken; (*c*) his corporate loyalties, including primary allegiance to his boss, Edward—there has been some hint that George and Edward are judging Ken on the troubles with the human resources vice president; and (*d*) the fact that Edward approached you with George last week to ask if you would assist SDF Company in another project.

QUESTIONS FOR DISCUSSION

1. Discuss the classic question, who is my client? with respect to this project. What professional and ethical issues must you deal with and what kind of "alignment" with respect to the organization and stakeholders do you establish as you do this project?
2. Describe how you will prepare for the work session with Tom in three days, including your role, strategy, and ways to deal with the uncertainty in Tom's stance. Consider how you will handle the session under at least these three stances by Tom: (1) he has decided to resign,

(2) he has decided to stay but wants to make as few changes as possible—only enough to mitigate the most serious criticisms and allow him to continue on his present course, and he wants to suppress most of the feedback data; (3) he wants to start immediately a full-scale effort to make drastic personal and departmental changes.

3. Describe how you will prepare for and handle the lunch meeting with Ken in two days. What role(s) will you take? Do you anticipate any role or ethical conflicts? Discuss these in depth, with your reasoning and strategies.

4. Discuss in depth how you will prepare for and manage the scheduled telephone conversation with George tomorrow, including the role(s) you will take and any anticipated role or ethical conflicts.

Part V

Integrating Cases

In each of the previous parts of this book, the cases intentionally highlight a specific dimension of organization development—entering and contracting, diagnosing, intervening, and practitioner roles and ethical dilemmas. Yet, as stated in the introduction and seen in the cases, the practice of OD rarely involves only one aspect; rather, it is a complex, often messy process. The cases in this part show that OD is an interrelated cycle of activities, thus providing a more comprehensive picture of the practice of OD.

In "American Research and Development (A-D)," Robert T. Golembiewski describes the process of helping a research laboratory shift its focus from searching for discoveries through such traditional disciplines as chemistry and biology to designing and building new products based on molecular biology and genetics. After diagnosing the situation and intervening, Golembiewski receives confidential information that may undermine both the project and the relationship with one of the internal consultants. Further events make it necessary to reestablish the psychological contract.

"Mega Corporation (A-D)," by Larry E. Greiner and Arvind Bhambri, explains how a new chief executive officer, acting as an internal change agent, and an OD consultant, serving as an external change agent, work together in facilitating strategic change. The case allows for examination of the internal-external relationship and the mutual learnings that can occur. Throughout the case, the authors accentuate the importance of careful planning before intervening.

In "Los Angeles County Probation Department (A-D)," Alan M. Glassman reports how an OD consultant helped a large government organization change its strategic direction and reestablish leadership in its field. The case contains a complex problem—the top executive initiates and fully supports the change effort, while his executive committee resists. Many questions emerge about how best to institutionalize change.

Case 32

American Research and Development (A-D)*

Robert T. Golembiewski
University of Georgia

AMERICAN RESEARCH AND DEVELOPMENT (A)

A three-year set of interventions in a work force of approximately 350 scientists and technicians was stimulated by the appointment of a new director of research at site P, hereafter also called American Research and Development. Site P was the largest research and development (R&D) unit in a multinational firm, and it was engaged (among other projects) in exploiting an important scientific breakthrough at one of the firm's European R&D units. As shown in Exhibit 1, separate sections existed at site P for the research and development functions, each headed by a director. These two individuals reported to the vice president, worldwide research and development. The vice president also had responsibility for several other sites throughout the world. The major internal actors are underscored in Exhibit 1.

Two internal members of the organization, A and B, played major roles in the planned change effort. As implied in Exhibit 1, they had similar jobs at the same location, but at different levels of the organization. Both individuals had composite jobs—operating activities associated with human resources administration, plus an organization development component. They were joined by Bob Golembiewski, an external OD consultant. He had worked with both A and B, individually and in combination, over a number of years, and Bob had also consulted with the vice president, worldwide research and development.

Entry was quite direct and uncomplicated. "Bob, we've got another live one for you," director A said one day over the telephone. "It will

---

*For additional learnings from the case series, see Robert T. Golembiewski and Ronald Fox, "OD in Industry," in *Visions of Tomorrow, Actions of Today*, ed. Paul R. Milo (Plainfield, N.J.: Organization Development Network, 1980), pp. 247–54.

EXHIBIT 1   Major Corporate Actors

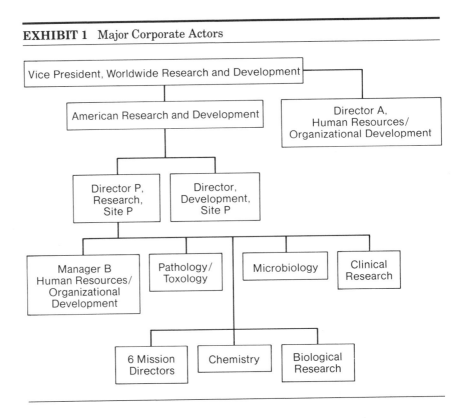

take a lot of time. When can you get started?" Contracting was quick and rudimentary, resting essentially on our long history of common experiences—many of them difficult, most successful, and a few that drew attention beyond the firm.[1] Within 20 minutes, we had an agreement.

Bob had a good map of the firm, gained over a decade of experience at all levels. Over the years, he had co-trained weeklong T-Groups for approximately 350 managers, often with director A; and he was a common consulting presence at headquarters and in the field in times of both

---

[1]Reports about interventions in the host organization appear in the research literature, and they include: Robert T. Golembiewski and Arthur Blumberg, "Sensitivity Training in Cousin Groups," *Training and Development Journal* 23 (1969), pp. 18–23; Robert T. Golembiewski and Stokes B. Carrigan, "Planned Change in Organization Style Based on Laboratory Approach," *Administrative Science Quarterly* 15 (1970), pp. 79–93; Robert T. Golembiewski, Stokes B. Carrigan, Walter R. Mead, Robert F. Munzenrider, and Arthur Blumberg, "Toward Building New Work Relationships," *Journal of Applied Behavioral Science* 8 (1972), pp. 135–48; and Robert T. Golembiewski, Keith Billingsley, and Samuel Yeager, "Measuring Change and Persistence in Human Affairs," *Journal of Applied Behavioral Science* 12 (1976), pp. 133–57.

growth and cutbacks. The late 1970s were very good times for the firm, and Bob was pleased to continue working on what he often publicly referred to as "the corporation in search of its new soul." The parent corporation had been unusually effective because it was responsive to people and their needs. But a blockbuster of a new product was affecting the corporation, especially R&D. Sales had increased several-fold in a few years, inducing its share of stresses. Moreover, R&D was playing "Can you top this?" in the search for a successor product, while major changes in the way science would be done also had to be made.

The Current Situation

The interventions were to occur in the research function at site P. The research and development focus was shifting dramatically—away from the empiric approach of *finding in nature* agents that had efficacy in gross biological systems and toward *designing and making medicinal agents* tailored to specific events/structures in specific organs or tissues at the molecular level. This new approach is rooted in molecular biology and genetics, while the earlier approach is based on conventional disciplines such as biology and chemistry. Specifically, this new science would mean major retraining for many existing personnel, hiring cadres with new and—most difficult of all—sometimes exotic skills, and providing for those individuals who would not be able to find comfortable places within the new research and development functions.

The new director of research at site P believed he would remain in his new position for perhaps five years, assuming reasonable performance. At the first meeting with his trio of consultants—Bob, A, and B—director P noted that he saw his job in long-run terms, but he wanted to take advantage of the anticipated "honeymoon" following his appointment. He added:

> My mandate is not to shake 'em up and then leave. Oppositely, I want to induce a sense of great stability, even though the research function will be undergoing significant, even radical, changes in how we perform our tasks.
>
> I need your help in quickly building a strong team of managers and in developing a number of effective and flexible interdisciplinary teams at the several work levels. Yet, we must avoid further destabilization. In a sense, I am asking you to both hurry up and wait.

The meeting celebrated a challenge. P was the fourth director of research during a seven-year period, and the mix of short-term and long-term considerations certainly reflected the difficult realities of the situation. But the four men had long-standing relationships, especially director P, A, and Bob. Moreover, they liked one another. And the three consultants were unanimous in their opinion that director P was the right person for the job. His selection delighted them, in fact.

We agreed that during the next several weeks manager B would conduct interviews with all research and development executives and managers, of whom there were 50. The purpose was simple—"to determine how to intervene to aid the new director." Before we parted, A and B shared their view that under the previous director, who built strong one-to-one relationships with his immediate subordinates to overcome prior leadership instability, the research section had become balkanized. That is, the missions were the basic units of organization and initially were intended to function as temporary projects. But they had developed into permanent entities with stable staffs and budgets, a strong desire for autonomy and secondary regard for the flexibility of the total research initiative, and isolated scientists and technicians working on different missions.

The Data

The interviews were structured to elicit three themes, but in ways tailored to individual respondents. Willingness to disclose was almost universally high, even for those who had reason to be threatened by director P's appointment. "It's about time that we faced our problems," typified the general reaction. In general form, the interviews touched three topics:

1. What things are going well?
2. What are the major problems?
3. What are your personal priorities for change and renewal?

Some useful details emerged from the interviews, but the exercise contributed more to consciousness-raising about future change than to generating new information. As the diagnostic summary in Exhibit 2 reflects, the interviews basically confirmed several potentially self-canceling imperatives. As intervenors, we had to:

- Get something meaningful started quickly, capitalizing on the new director's "honeymoon" period.
- Encourage an integrative thrust in an environment characterized by balkanized self-interests.
- Proceed in humane ways while being responsive to pressing corporate and subsystem issues.
- Plan for an implementation period of several years.
- Avoid unnecessarily traumatizing an already shaken research function.

EXHIBIT 2   Initial Diagnosis of Major Features of R&D Organization at Site P

1. Individuals at site P generally feel one-down in a parent corporation with several comparable R&D capabilities, one of which had recently generated a breakthrough product.
2. This immediate source of one-downness exacerbates a long-standing set of deficits under which most R&D members believed themselves to be operating. To illustrate:
   - R&D contributions are seen as insufficiently valued by corporate officials.
   - R&D exhibits symptoms of a "maturing organization."
     —Many employees consider themselves "stuck" or "topped-out" in their present jobs.
     —Opportunities for advancement by internal growth are slim, in part because the research section at site P is considered to be at its maximum size, and because research personnel are not considered as broadly employable in other site P functions.
     —Turnover is low because the corporation is seen as a very good and well-paying employer, because the pace of activities is at least comfortable, if not leisurely, and so on.
     —R&D is aging if not yet aged: new positions are scarce and turnover is low.
3. Managerial style over the previous 5 years strongly tended to be nonconfrontal and "smoothing," which—in part reasonably and in part pure rationalization—was considered by the vice president the only strategy capable of bringing on-line a breakthrough product to which R&D at site P contributed significant work but which derived more centrally from work at another corporate facility.
4. Major componets of the R&D thrust are insufficiently integrated, if not in actual conflict; thus, the robust identifications with a mission often create barriers—between missions and between individual scientists on different missions.

- Overcome cultures in both research and development, as well as corporate, that discouraged vigorous and especially adverse personnel actions.
- Build on strengths but acknowledge basic weaknesses.

Additional Limitations

Three major constraints limited our design process for acting on the diagnosis. First, the development function could not be included in the design. While tensions between research and development functions clearly constituted a major source of difficulty, the new director opposed any joint interventions. He was unwilling to "export anxiety," both personal and for others, during his "settling in" period in research.

Second, the corporate as well as the research and development cultures did not encourage aggressive action in personnel matters. For example, approximately 85 percent of all employees were rated in the top appraisal category, but many also were at the top of the salary range for their position. This precluded a sense of progress for those many employees who had bumped against the salary ceiling and were not promotable into management. While a dual promotion system was in the early stages of implementation, it promised no early impact on our efforts.

Third, the new director opted against immediate reorganization of the research missions. Such changes would be a longer-run goal only. "We'll go with what we have for now," the director declared. "Let's give everybody a chance to do their best under my direction. Your job is to design a program that will provide that chance. Then we'll see."

QUESTIONS FOR DISCUSSION

1. As the external consultant, do you agree to move on to designing interventions, or do you decline because the constraints are too confining? Does your decision change if you are the internal consultants (i.e., A or B), or an external like Bob?
2. Assuming you agree to continue, what kind of OD design promises progress, yet respects the client's constraints?

AMERICAN RESEARCH DEVELOPMENT (B)

Unlike his predecessors, who dealt individually with each mission and each of the scientific disciplines, the new director P wanted a more fluid, collaborative system. He also was willing to pay the upfront costs in both time and dollars; hence, his early initiation of a research operations committee (ROC), with the enthusiastic support of his three consultants—A, B, and Bob Golembiewski. The ROC was composed of P's 10 direct reports detailed in Exhibit 1. The basic goal was to move the ROC toward robust decision-making status and oversight of the research missions. There was mixed enthusiasm among the direct reports at the start, but major resistance focused on the membership of manager B, who was not a physical scientist, but a part of director P's plans for building the kind of committee he wanted. The resistance diminished, but never disappeared.

About three months after his selection, the director of research gained substantial agreement among his major direct reports to begin team-building in the ROC. Conventionally, director P sought to develop shared perceptions and norms for his new committee, as well as to begin defining its mission and role. Additionally, the director desired to move definitely (if cautiously) toward interdisciplinary monitoring of the several research missions via the ROC, whose members represented the full panoply of required scientific and managerial skills.

Director P expressed his vision directly. To paraphrase him:

> In order to speed up research and to increase our effectiveness, we have got to focus all skills on developing priorities and on monitoring the progress of each mission. No one person can do that, even if things go at a snail's pace while the director tries to swallow the whole thing. We need a powerful team. Absent that, we'll have a director struggling futilely to keep abreast of complex science and technologies, and autonomous missions. The director will lose, most of the time.

Teambuilding

The change quartet—director P, A, B, and Bob—always realized that building an integrative ROC would be no easy task. All ROC members were carryovers and were accustomed to one-to-one relationships. Moreover, ROC members included forceful personalities, several of whom had openly indicated their strong preference for being left alone to do their scientific work; they wished to avoid administration as much as possible. Finally, with so much of the current focus on the missions, enthusiasm for building a strong ROC was mixed. In fact, several ROC members were committed to the greatest possible autonomy for the missions, and, of course, for themselves.

Despite the challenge, the change quartet saw no other alternative but accepting the status quo, which was seen as a last resort only; hence, the unanimous decision for teambuilding, despite the concerns about success. "We are not here to reinvent the status quo" became our informal motto. "Let's go for it."

The design of the initial two-day teambuilding experience emphasized the sharing of perceptions and expectations, following the regenerative model of interaction that seeks to increase openness, owning, and trust, while reducing risk.[1] As prework, all ROC members were asked to develop individual lists of their perceptions of the new director. Table 1 presents the effort of one ROC member, and it overlaps substantially with most other lists. These perceptions were compared against each other and against a "managerial credo" prepared by the director concerning his philosophy, principles, and style (reproduced in Table 2). The general contrasts and complimentarities between Tables 1 and 2 were worked through in the context of the specific policies and issues

---

[1]Robert T. Golembiewski, *Approaches to Planned Change*, vol. 1 (New York: Marcel Dekker, 1979).

TABLE 1   Sample of Pre- and Postmeeting Reactions of Members of Research Operations Committee to the Director

Premeeting Perceptions of Director	*Postmeeting Reactions to Director*
1. A chemist who has learned enough biology to know how biologists work and to distinguish mediocre from good ones.	1. Refine this knowledge further—applying it can only upgrade research.
2. Quick grasp of complicated problems and implications of proposed solutions.	2. Dont' slow down!
3. Provides solid support for us.	3. Continue.
4. Has more faith than I do in committees.	4. Increase reliance on one-to-one decision making.
5. Pragmatist—has sound grasp for the extent of the possible in improving working conditions.	5. Continue to avoid ideologies and catchphrases that influence passions and evoke unrealistic expectations.
6. Idealist—makes high demands on senior scientists for quality of scientific output.	6. Continue or increase this. It brings out the best in people.
7. Listens some.	7. Listen more!
8. May be reluctant to make changes "better for the company" if an individual may be hurt.	8. May need to seek alternatives to protect individual and company interests.
9. May wish to accomplish too much too soon regarding company development.	9. May not be possible with increased regulation by government.
10. Personal style encourages and allows open, frank discussion.	10. Continue.
11. Everything black or white.	11. Would like a little gray occasionally.
12. Quick decisions.	12. Like this in him and still see it.
13. Gets into small details.	13. Could let go of some of these.
14. Great confidence he is right.	14. Necessary in his role, and I still see it but do not always like it.
15. He will work the interfaces with good intent, full effort, and cooperation even when it looks impossible to succeed.	15. Will have to confront the problems himself if collaborative approach isn't working.
16. Everything must be done regardless of present commitments/work load.	16. More aware and considerate of time problems.

TABLE 1 (*concluded*)

Premeeting Perceptions of Director	Postmeeting Reactions to Director
17. Emphasize personnel issues to achieve top-notch professionalism.	17. Should focus on key issues that deal with progress of research.
18. Concern for image of P—particularly opinions from other areas and levels.	18. Guided but not directed by opinions of others.

TABLE 2 Director's Managerial Credo

Philosophy and Principles

1. Achieve success for individuals and corporation through technical excellence in pursuit of well-chosen objectives.
2. Will not compromise individual conscience or principles in any way while doing this.
3. Plan ahead and perceive overall environment and individual needs so as to avoid being responsible for personal tragedies [deriving from mismatches].
4. Run a people-oriented administration that demands the best one can produce.
5. Build excellence throughout and not suffer fools lightly.
6. Build bridges to all groups that we interface with, inside and outside the company.
7. Get the job done without walking all over people in the doing.

Style
Open, confrontive; very communicative; attempting to be constructive; informal; moderate level of tolerance for ambiguity or for poor skills; truthful; often in a hurry; technically interested and sympathetic of problems; tough, if necessary.

---

confronting the research department. The related discussions took the bulk of two days.

To provide feedback, as well as a bridge to future action, ROC members were asked toward the end of the two-day session to volunteer a list of emerging reactions to the director and his style (see Table 1). The pre- and postmeeting reactions were shared publicly as the terminal activity of the initial teambuilding.

While director P's three consultants were pleased by the progress toward integration that the data suggested, we also noted several possible defensive or delaying themes. For instance, postmeeting reaction number 4 encourages the director to "increase reliance on one-to-one decision making," a style that would reduce the ROC's role in integrating the research missions and in providing an interdisciplinary review of work. Similarly, premeeting perception number 17 sees director P as focusing on "personal issues to achieve top-notch professionalism." The corresponding postmeeting perception advises the director to focus on "key issues that deal with progress of research." These seemed to be code words for "let my people be."

In their postmortem clinic, the change quartet saw some mixed results of the initial teambuilding, but the signs of overall movement were clear to all four. They agreed to move on, sharpening their sense of a second major design feature. At the same time, additional teambuilding activities would be held for the ROC, to reinforce and to extend the initially positive experience.

Barriers to Creativity Design

The second major early design element for the research department sought to create for all employees a sense of real movement and progress. With the explicit buy in of P concerning the general flow and many details, A, B, and Bob designed a "barriers to creativity" design that sought to simultaneously meet four criteria:

1. To gently (but firmly) start a process leading toward basic changes in research's missions and roles and in individual skills/abilities and attitude relevant to doing science.
2. To provide ample time for isolating problems and solutions.
3. To involve broad ranges of participants in diagnosis and prescription.
4. To reduce the reasoning/rationalizing process dominant among research personnel: "We want to do a first-class job, but there are just too many obstacles in our way."

The barriers to creativity design had three general properties: (1) it initially sought to *deemphasize judgmental aspects* directed at individuals, and thus to reduce personal threat; (2) it sought to highlight *things*—policies, procedures, and relationships—that could be changed to improve research creativity; and (3) it sought to *provide time* for individuals to make appropriate attitudinal and behavioral changes relevant to management style as well as to basic ways of doing research. This progression was seen as fair because research personnel had grown accustomed to "other days and ways" that were legitimated by their employer, or at least tolerated.

But the barriers design was nonetheless insistent. Specifically, its basic flow had two major stages. The design initially emphasized isolating/reducing barriers to effective effort, and then the design promised the evolution of stricter managerial standards.

The *degree* of insistence on the latter point was a continuing issue between the research director and the consultants. Generally, the consulting trio urged some aggressiveness after the first stage, during which "everyone was given a fair chance" to change. The director generally came down on the side of more restraint than the consultants on a range of issues—such as concerning when and how much to try to tighten performance appraisal procedures, which now saw nearly 9 of 10 R&D employees rated in the very top category when the all-but-universal view recognized major performance problems.

The dynamics between director P and the three consultants on such occasions took a typical form. All differences were explored in detail, and, when differences remained, the consultants respected P's sense of pacing even when we did not share it. This in part reflected the common reality: the consulting trio was "on tap," and P was "on top." This reality also was softened by two facts: the trio "won" its fair share and maintained a high degree of respect for P's judgment as well as his willingness to test it.

The barriers design unfolded over time, which can be telescoped here by reviewing three emphases: (1) identifying past and present barriers to creativity; (2) determining methods to reduce or eliminate identified barriers; and (3) creating a more demanding future work site and confronting the challenge/threat for research employees.

Existing Barriers to Creativity. The first stage in the barriers design sought to identify and to deal with real and/or perceived obstacles to effective effort in the research function. Creativity always was defined very broadly as anything that was seen as complicating the work of the research section and its people.

A sample of diagnostic interviews with research personnel was completed about one year after the director took office, or some nine months after the initial session of his research operating committee. (The delay was occasioned by an unexpected departure of manager B, human resources and organization development. The incumbent unexpectedly left for a better-paying job in another area of the firm, and it was another six months before replacement B took over, conducted the interviews, and reported the results to the director.) The snippets below from the new B's report give some sense of his findings, which, in many cases, are reported in terms of the very words informants used:

Productivity versus creativity—Management appears to be more interested in quantity than quality. You are allowed to be creative, but you are expected to be productive. Creativity is not evaluated, production is. Quarterly reports state members, not ideas. There is pressure to submit compounds. People do work to get numbers rather than more interesting, challenging work.

Current missions—Creativity is mission oriented (the mission being the basic unit of organization in research). There is a lack of communication between missions. It is difficult to pursue anything in depth. Going past a certain point exceeds the project objectives. If an idea you have is outside the scope of a mission, who do you go to?

Management styles—Higher-level management is extremely conservative. Management changes programs too often. If they have a good program and good people running it, they should let it run. Some supervisors feel threatened by new ideas and change. Too many managers don't spend time on the bench and because of this they get out of touch with what is happening in the labs. Management is not willing to provide enough time for sufficient exploration of feasibility studies. When you present a feasibility study, you still have all your other responsibilities. This is one more thing to fit into your schedule. We don't hear about long-term corporate goals for research. . . . Nonscientific management has a great control over research.

Lack of emphasis on creativity—We have not looked for creative people. Management doesn't have good measures of creativity. We haven't tried hard to determine who is creative and give them rewards. We don't emphasize creativity or provide incentives for people to use creative talents. We place a fair amount of emphasis on networks and getting things done on time. People come to look at their jobs as tasks. We have tended to hire people who can fit into job openings rather than looking for creative talent.

Infusion of new people—We need to hire more young, creative people either on a permanent basis or postdoctoral program. We need a continual flow of younger employees.

The delay in assembling the barriers was not welcome, but the former B's opportunity was very attractive, and the new B had been a longtime collaborator of both A and Bob. The job was a substantial step up for the new B, however, and would involve some gearing-up time. And the new B did not have the benefit of the network of relationships available to the previous B.

In sum, director P, A, and Bob were of a similar mind concerning the new B. They all would have preferred that the incumbent stay. Since it had to be someone else, however, the new B was a fine choice.

Acting on the Barriers to Creativity. The interviews precipitated another major action by the director and a grudging ROC. After the new B's report, all research managers and supervisors—half of them at each of two two-day sessions—met to provide specific counterpoint to the interviews, which were publicly shared in detail. Participants at the sessions also:

- Developed specific themes about discrete families of barriers, with emphasis on those barriers about which substantial consensus existed.
- Prioritized the themes.

- Developed suggested action plans.
- Confronted the director with their products, made recommendations, and gauged his reactions.

The two 2-day sessions were welcomed outside of the ROC in general, but research personnel seemed more hopeful than convinced. The results of three scales on a postmeeting reaction sheet support this conclusion:

1. Overall, how would you rate the effectiveness of the meeting in terms of addressing the barriers to creativity? 6.3

   not effective |—|—|—|—|—|—|—|—|—| very effective
   0   5   9

2. Overall, how would you rate the effectiveness of the meeting in terms of discussing the barriers to creativity with the director? 4.4

   not effective |—|—|—|—|—|—|—|—|—| very effective
   0   5   9

3. Overall, what probability do you assign to useful changes being made as a result of the meeting? 4.7

   low probability of change |—|—|—|—|—|—|—|—|—| high probability of change
   0   5   9

"Wait and see" also described the posture of the director's research operations committee. After extended discussion, for example, only the director attended the two two-day sessions. One or two ROC members expressed interest in attending, but the thrust of the associated decision making took these two bottom lines: (1) either only the director *or* he and all ROC members should attend and (2) if all members went, that might create problems with airtime, especially for supervisors/managers. It was decided only the director would attend. While we three intervenors saw this as a loss of potential ownership for ROC members, we did not consider the loss crucial, especially with the director planning on being in his present job for an extended time.

In part as a response to these several signs of research function tentativeness, a third phase of the barriers design sought to communicate a sense of progress, *as soon as possible*, with a full report on all themes promised for a later date. About four weeks after the action-planning meetings, the ROC issued several policies in response to some of the priority obstacles. Other actions followed and were broadly communicated.

Six months after the two initial managers' sessions on barriers to creativity, a capstone meeting was conducted. An afternoon meeting followed by dinner was held for all supervisory personnel and attended by all ROC members. After cocktails and dinner, the director presided at an additional session, at which:

- All issues were reviewed.
- All actions were reviewed, whether already taken, proposed, or still pending, with definite targets for completion given in the last two cases.
- Reactions and suggestions were solicited.

Director P and all three consultants were pleased with the momentum that was building for taking action on the barriers to creativity.

The question remained open for the consultants, however. Would director P bite the bullet and signal that he expected better performance as the barriers were recognized and eliminated or reduced? A few days before the capstone meeting, P was still temporizing. But the consultants got a public answer to their question in the closing minutes of the capstone session, after action planning had ended.

Moving Toward R&D's Future.   Director P signaled an escalation of the barriers design at the very end of the session just described, perhaps induced by the real enthusiasm about the action planning. This thrust may be characterized in simple terms: Fair warning about a different day and time coming. The director used some such words in closing the formal part of the summary meeting:

> Let me try to put what we're doing in perspective. This meeting is the beginning of the end of Phase 1—a phase oriented toward reducing or removing any perceived obstacles to productivity. I have tried to bend over backwards—at least in my mind—to do the best we can to get rid of any obstacle that anyone perceived as impacting on what they do and how they do it.
>
> We will over time move into Phase 2—a phase oriented toward a growing emphasis on high performance and productivity. Phase 2 will require attitudinal changes among those of you who have grown—for good reason or none at all—cynical or pessimistic about the chances of change or improvement in research.
>
> Phase 2 will require changes in the ways we do research. We need to become better at motivating and rewarding creative and superior performance. The new ways of doing research will challenge all of us, but the main purpose of Phase 2 is to give everyone a fair chance to succeed.

The character of this fair warning was the subject of discussion up to the very last days before the meeting, and the consultants were pleasantly surprised that the director used terms like those quoted above.

One of the consultants a few days earlier had written the three paragraphs quoted above, and they were discussed between the director and the consultants several days before the meeting. But the director never committed as to whether he would use this particular bridge to the future, until he spoke in public session.

Substantial and sustained applause greeted the director's closing words. Three postmeeting reaction items suggest the applause was genuine and general, if hardly unanimous. In sum:

1. Overall, how would you rate the effectiveness of the summary meeting in terms of addressing the barriers to creativity?

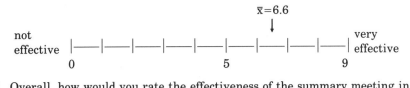

2. Overall, how would you rate the effectiveness of the summary meeting in terms of discussing the barriers to creativity with the director?

3. Overall, what probability do you assign to useful changes being made as a result of the summary meeting?

Coming from tough graders, the average responses suggested general and growing support. The director's sense of timing and pace also seemed pretty good.

The Unexpected Happens

The sense of success felt by the director and two of the intervenors was strained and restrained, however. While the planning for the summary session was in its early stages, the director uncharacteristically closed his door when A and Bob arrived for a regular meeting. "You guys need to know I'm in the running for one of the top R&D jobs in the industry," the director opened the discussion. He added quickly: "And no one else here can know. I don't want to jeopardize 'barriers,' first and foremost.

Realistically, the odds also are low I'll be chosen, and I don't want to appear foolish around here. This is the kind of job I aspire to in 5 or 10 years. Do the best you can to steer people and to avoid false expectations, if it will help people. But I expect your absolute silence, even with B."

When A and Bob recovered from the jolt, they resisted. "That's not how we usually have done business in the past," they insisted, noting their relationship had matured to the point where they all expected they could and would use personal discretion in sharing information with others, except in those rare cases when absolute confidentiality was explicitly signaled.[2]

"Then was then, now is now," chortled the director. "I expect your absolute silence, as well as your help as things develop."

QUESTIONS FOR DISCUSSION

1. Was it reasonable for the consultants to start the barriers to creativity portion of the design so early in the ROC teambuilding and when signs of resistance still existed?
2. Why did the consultants and director P opt against problem solving based directly on the results of the interviews by the new B? Or why not select a small task force from among research personnel to do the job, rather than all research managers and supervisors?
3. Should consultants have agreed to the capstone meeting, as they did, without an explicit understanding about whether director P would signal a subsequent emphasis on increased expectations about performance?
4. What do professional ethics/integrity have to say about confidentiality in general? In cases like the present one?
5. What are the pluses and minuses of various possible responses to director P's demand? Are different responses appropriate from the internal (A) and the external (Bob)?

AMERICAN RESEARCH AND DEVELOPMENT (C)

Director P's demand for confidentiality about his job candidacy inspired much animated discussion and even argument. Internal consultant A and Bob lamented, "We're damned if we do and damned if we don't."

---

[2]For one view of our shared preference about confidentiality, see Robert T. Golembiewski, " 'Promise Not to Tell': A Critical View of Confidentiality in Consultation," *Consultation* 5 (1986): pp. 68–76. See also, "A Statement of Values and Ethics for Professionals in Organization and Human System Development," *Consultation* 5 (1986).

But director P was in the same situation. He could have withheld information about his candidacy for a major executive post, with significant negative consequences for the two consultants and the barriers program. And P saw no alternative to confidentiality if he shared the information with A and Bob.

After cooling down, A and Bob accepted the charge by director P. They rationalized their decision in three ways:

1. Paramountly, extensive positive experience with the director encouraged accepting his charge, uncomfortable though it was for them. In addition, the director's departure was seen by the director and his consultants as highly improbable because the new job was such a quantum promotion.
2. Neither the consultants nor the director wanted to jeopardize the momentum of the barriers design, on which B could better proceed with all reasonable speed if unburdened by knowledge of a low-probability possibility. Relatedly, if by some small chance the director were to leave, at least B's relationships with research personnel would not be compromised.
3. Finally, A and Bob had a long-standing relationship with the director that B lacked, which added a certain credibility to excluding B. Indeed, B had never seen the director until interviewed for his new manager's job, while A's and Bob's relationship with director P extended over a decade.

In any case, A and Bob accepted responsibility for agreeing not to share their new knowledge with B, and it weighed heavily on them. Their responsibility would be most dramatically obvious if the director were to leave. Still, excluding B was the big issue, whatever occurred. "Will he be able to work with us in the future as in the past?" was the central question. "What would he do in our place?" they asked.

Four Major Problems

The director's job opportunity also implied four major problems for the barriers design. First, the momentum of the design was threatened. Thus, the director's enthusiasm for the project might waver during any protracted negotiations. In the worst case, a replacement might have a very different set of goals and values than the present director.

Consequently, the three sworn to confidentiality—director P, A, and Bob—were nervous about preserving all possible credibility for "barriers." The alternatives did not attract: deepened pessimism and perhaps despair among research personnel, deriving from a lost initiative and a violation of the psychological contract that was emerging in R&D. This irony of openness in "barriers" and closedness about the director's job possibility preoccupied discussions between A and Bob, both drawing the men closer and yet raising a challenge that, next time, one of them might be in B's place. "I spend more time with you than my wife," A observed to Bob in one of their frequent discussions about what to do and how.

Second, the director's possible departure seriously compromised the leadership of the barriers program. The director had basically carried the ball, although the research operations committee at his enthusiastic persistence did mandate certain changes and clarifications in policies. However, ROC members did not have enough ownership to satisfy either the director or any of the consultants.

At special risk was a program accepted by the ROC in principle, the comprehensive review program. It sought to meet a major set of issues raised by the barriers design—those related to appraisal and reward for performance. For example, the program proposed that future appraisals were to be made more openly, would be less influenced by idiosyncrasies of individual supervisors, and would give greater attention to the quality of the science. A new and substantial reliance on peer ratings would contribute to realizing all three intentions. Moreover, appraisals would have a strong career-planning thrust and also would provide for early notice when a person's work was becoming unsatisfactory or when a person had "topped out." This philosophic thrust was consistent with the intent to reduce the probability that people "would just die on the vine" and stay there.

The comprehensive review program had moved briskly under the director's leadership and staff work by A and B. Beyond the ROC, the concept was also quickly approved by the next and final level of review—the R&D operating committee, which advised the vice president, worldwide R&D. Virtually all preparatory detail work on the program was recently completed.

Third, for an indefinite period that came to be four months, only A and Bob were privy to the choice making by the director about changing jobs. They prompted numerous discussions about informing B, the closest operationally to the barriers program and the director's staff person for human resources and OD. But the discussions came to the same conclusion. B remained uninformed, at the insistence of the director.

This situation implied strain with B during the interval of confidentiality, as well as later. The issues associated with withholding information from B about the director's job opportunity would be real if P stayed and would assume even greater proportions if the director left.

Fourth, both A and Bob were simultaneously meeting with the vice president, worldwide R&D, concerning an assessment of the total organization of which the research director headed only a part. The vice president did not have an inkling of the director's decision making, again by deliberate choice based on the director's insistence. Manager A and Bob tried to delay the review, but the vice president was insistent, and they feared their open expression of concern about a conflict of interest would blow the cover for director P.

Both A and Bob knew that the vice president might disapprove of not being informed. Consultant A reported directly to the vice president, for one thing.

On the other hand, the vice president understood that on occasion, the ability of ODers to function rested on confidentiality that excluded him, and the vice president respected that aspect of their roles in the past. The enforced silence required a certain wariness with several others, but truthfulness was possible. For example, A and Bob honestly reported in their initial assessments of the vice president's organization that several key personnel losses were possible in the absence of certain aggressive actions by the vice president. "Of course, you are not at liberty to tell me the names of those key personnel," the vice president noted on the report. "Not yet," A and Bob responded, in effect. "But we'll keep in touch with them to try to encourage an exchange. Right now, mum's the word."

The Director Leaves

The director of research was offered the big job and accepted it. His current employer wanted the director to stay on, but the new opportunity was far beyond anything available to the director at site P or at corporate. P announced his departure about two months after the capstone meeting summarizing progress on the barriers effort was held, and his last day at work was about a month later.

QUESTIONS FOR DISCUSSION

1. What should Bob and manager A do now? How should they try to repair their relationship with B?
2. What should be done to cushion the barriers program against the shock of the director's departure?

AMERICAN RESEARCH AND DEVELOPMENT (D)

A multipronged strategy began to evolve with the first broader knowledge of director P's job opportunity, and it shifted to high gear with the announcement of his departure. This strategy—or, more accurately, strands of substantially congruent strategic initiatives—may be summarized briefly under four headings.

1. The Issue between Colleagues.   As noted, director P did not wish to inform B—his own staff resource—of the negotiations about a possible new job. Internal consultant A and external consultant Bob were aware of the matter almost from the start. They agreed to strict confidentiality, despite their reservations about potential problems with colleague B. The latter knew for a time that he was being excluded from some discussions involving his own boss, and he mentioned his concern to A and Bob. They confirmed that his sense of exclusion was correct. "Nobody ever said you didn't have sensitive antennae, but right now we can't say any more." B came to suspect that a broader R&D assessment was the topic of the closed meetings between director P, A, and Bob. No effort was made to persuade B to accept this point of view, but neither was he dissuaded from it.

Priority was given to getting in touch with B as soon as the director's decision was made. Special efforts were made to give B as much notice as possible. B learned of the director's departure and of the withholding by A and Bob at the same time. B was crestfallen, but he agreed to work on the issues between the men.

Immediately after the director made his announcement, testing and repairing the relationship with B emphasized the unusual nature of the case. Some exploration of feelings occurred, especially between A and B. This sharing focused on the organizational conflicts of interest inherent in the roles of the two internal consultants. They not only worked for two other people linked as superior and subordinate, but both A and B had operating as well as consulting responsibilities. Much potential for mutual leverage existed in this situation, but the stickiness of the situation was acknowledged by all.

The focus of these discussions was direct and had five major themes. First, both A and Bob dwelt on this question: "Do you see anything else we could have done, not knowing all of the director's reasons for confidentiality, but nonetheless respecting him and our long-standing relationship with him?" B saw no alternative, while emphasizing that this did not reduce the real discomfort and distancing he felt on learning of his exclusion. "You guys cut me off at the knees," B once told them. At a later stage of the discussion, all three men laughed uproariously at B's view of being an "organizational mushroom": "You know, kept in the dark, covered with fertilizer, and waiting to be canned." The metaphor was not that funny, and tension reduction explained more of the communal silliness than the quality of the humor.

Second, A and Bob stressed to B that his "being out of the loop" had its advantages. B would not have a conflict of interest in moving the barriers program along. Unburdened by knowledge of the director's negotiations, B could not later be second-guessed on any actions if the director did leave. For example, research personnel could not say he led them down the primrose path. The point was granted by B, but he still preferred to have known. Knowing had its costs, but it avoided suspicions that B was less than a full partner.

Third, A and Bob successfully sought a robust role for B after director P announced his resignation. Details appear later, but the general point here is that, as real as the exclusion had been for B, he realized the two colleagues had not made negative judgments about him to the director, and they strongly supported B after the departure of director P.

Fourth, B derived some consolation from the fact that practically everyone else also was kept in the dark. So B definitely was not singled out for special treatment; he was more in a class-action category.

Fifth, some useful public catharsis occurred at a professional meeting where an earlier version of the barriers case was the focus of attention in a public session, and numerous professional colleagues reacted to A, B, and Bob—all seeking to learn about self and others. Generally, A and Bob were berated for respecting the director's demand for confidentiality, and for leaving a colleague in the dark. In fact, in this public session, B defended the actions of his two colleagues as "bad when they did withhold, and tough if they hadn't."

For whatever reason, the issue of B's lack of knowledge never became a broadly serious issue at the work site. Others learned of B's exclusion, but they either accepted the explanation at face value, were satisfied by the evidence of the otherwise-good relationship between the three men, or simply did not consider the matter of general concern in the context of the great loss of P's departure.

2. Conserving Barriers' Momentum.

Two strategic components sought to conserve the momentum of the barriers design in the face of the director's departure. The first component went down easily among the troops to encourage the view that there was far more pull than push in the director's departure, that the director was not simply tossing in the towel. Virtually all observers highlighted the extreme attractiveness of the new job. So substantial was the increase in responsibilities that shoptalk questioned whether the director's previous work experience had left him ready for such a great leap upward. The barriers design also gained a certain enhanced corporate status because of the promotion by a major competitor of the design's champion.

The second strategic component to conserve the momentum—supported first and most vigorously by Bob—was aimed at ego maintenance, if not enhancement, among research personnel. Bob proposed a broadly representative and participative search committee be formed to attract a "super scientist" to replace the director. This suggestion was consistent with the aspirations for excellence in the barriers design, as well as with the evolving prominence of molecular biology and genetic research. The suggestion also acknowledged two darker realities: (1) all research personnel, including some who had their hopes raised by the barriers design, faced the daunting prospect of adapting to yet another director and (2) a few of the more ambitious scientists would soon learn that no one then in research was considered promotable to director. The collegial search for a "super scientist" deliberately sought to moderate both sources of this downside potential.

Other features of the suggested search committee modeled OD values. Thus, the search would be unusually participative, consistent with the barriers design. The search committee would be composed of broadly recognized scientific contributors at several hierarchical levels of the research function, who would be given great leeway by the vice president, worldwide R&D. This procedure was unusual in the firm as well as in R&D.

Bob's suggestion was accepted by the vice president, worldwide R&D, during a telephone conversation. "Son of 'barriers,' " he observed with a chuckle in his voice as he heard the process sketched, "with concern for great openness and the self-esteem of our scientists as major features."

The search committee met initially within the first week after director P's last formal day at work. The vice president deliberately appeared at the kickoff meeting and indicated committee members were on a long leash to take advantage of an opportunity that some might see as a danger. The committee spent two days developing its sense of mission and role, as well as its criteria for choice, which the vice president later accepted with effusive congratulations concerning the seriousness and high purposes reflected in Table 3.

Seriousness and high purposes also got reflected by the search committee in other ways, once their confidence grew that the vice president was not merely waxing eloquent. Determined efforts were made to involve broad ranges of research personnel in suggesting candidates; hundreds of résumés were reviewed for scientific standing by the search committee; a search firm was retained to make selected contacts as well as to provide an initial assessment of managerial and personal features of a few candidates; and the first candidate visited the firm about five months after the initial search committee meeting.

This second strategic initiative got high grades. From the first, all visiting candidates drew raves. And even congenial critics applauded the several virtues of this approach to recruiting the new director, unusual and perhaps unprecedented in this firm. (The eventual first choice accepted the job and remained in office for over five years, when he was later promoted to a worldwide R&D role.)

3. Leadership for Barriers. Although expectations were restrained, two strategic initiatives sought to provide some degree of leadership for the

---

TABLE 3 Search Committee Criteria for Seeking New Director of Research

Scientific Qualities

R* 1. Proven researcher
    a. Problem selection
    b. Execution
    c. Application
R 2. Independent reputation as a scientist
D* 3. Broad scientific interests
R 4. Can appreciate and understand biological science at a molecular level
R 5. Encourages innovative research
R 6. Gets primary job satisfaction from research process (gets kick out of scientific research)

Management Qualities

R 1. Ability to provide an effective environment for research
D 2. Will work effectively through development function interface
D 3. Experience in directing interdisciplinary research
R 4. Is analytical, probing, and constructively confrontive
D 5. Familiarity with drug-discovery process
R 6. Capable decision maker
R 7. Strong advocate of moving from research to upper management

Leadership Qualities and General

R 1. Positive outlook
R 2. Excellent communication skills upward, downward, and laterally
D 3. "Quick study"
R 4. Ability to develop scientists
R 5. Demonstrated leadership qualities (ability to motivate, generate enthusiasm, inspire)
R 6. Willingness to move science into new areas

*R = Required
 D = Highly desirable

---

barriers program while the new director was being chosen. First, of major symbolic importance, the search committee would be headed by the same B who had been cut out of the information loop about director P's job opportunity. Bob was the initiator here, and the vice president, worldwide R&D, quickly saw the several virtues in B's appointment. This argument was most impressive to the vice president who authorized major roles for B:

> If you value B, he needs reinforcement now. He did not know about the director's choice making, and you can well appreciate his surprise and his reactions to being kept uninformed. So you have two alternatives: gut B by benign neglect or provide clear roles for him in the immediate aftermath of the resignation.

Internal consultant B then discussed his choice for an external consultant with the vice president. Both agreed that Bob might be helpful in "getting the search committee off the ground," especially in quickly getting over any initial suspicions of the vice president's serious intent. These two appointments increased the chances that the barriers design might survive under the new director, because both B and Bob were closely associated with the design. The organization grapevine suggested this intent did not escape the notice of research personnel, who might otherwise have grown disillusioned about the life chances of the barriers program.

Moreover, the search committee embodied the barriers ideals and exerted influence concerning the management style of the person selected as the new director of research. For example, the committee's criteria for the new director variously reinforced and reflected the several themes of the barriers design: excellence and joy in research, development of scientists, transcendence of organizational parochialisms and disciplinary walls, with a bias toward inducing regenerative interaction, and knowledge of science at the molecular level.

Second, the hope was that B could sustain barriers activity during the search, via his membership on the ROC. One alternative had B chairing the ROC, an extraordinary possibility because B was not a physical scientist. This notion died, however.

Low expectations were appropriate concerning this second initiative toward barriers leadership. B at first was active in raising barriers issues, but the ROC was generally not predisposed to move until the new director was on board. That this was reasonable did not enhance B's leverage, even if concerns about the ROC's intent were possible. For example, the comprehensive review program was moving toward implementation, and it intended major changes in performance appraisal and compensation. The ROC delayed implementation, thereby reversing one of its own earlier decisions that had also been accepted by the top R&D authority. So backing up, even somewhat ungracefully, characterized the ROC more than moving on, as it waited for a new director.

In other particulars, consultant B moved toward seeking goals consistent with the barriers design, if with mixed results. For example, at B's initiative, the ROC agreed to a pilot teambuilding intervention for one of the missions, the central unit of organization in research. Such an intervention was begun, but it did not go very far until after a replacement for the director was in office.

4. Confidentiality with a Boss. A's boss, the vice president, worldwide R&D, was also among those who were surprised by the director's announcement. The vice president was one of Bob's clients. Soon after the director's announcement, the vice president met with A and Bob. The meeting was serious, yet punctuated with explosions of laughter and the shaking of heads about the coercive nature of some situations.

Stage Base

1. *Re Screening & contact*
2. *contracting*
3. *Diagnosis / analysis*
4. *Select intervention*
5. *Implementation →*
6. *Evaluation*
7. *empowerment*

structure — norm, storm, eventually preform

"Well, I'll be damned," the vice president observed when told of the confidentiality that had excluded him. "You guys seemed confident when you told me I could expect some losses of key people in research, and now I know why!"

The two consultants emphasized this was a tough judgment call and very unusual in that they preferred an understanding with all clients—and especially director P—that they would rely on mutual discretion about how shared materials got used. Without relishing the particular case, the vice president clearly appreciated the general problem. Bob concluded the discussion with the following comment:

> This time, confidentiality threatened our relationship. But at least you know for a fact that we can keep a confidence without peeping or being immobilized by it. And who knows? The next time it may be you who urges confidentiality on us. But we'll all work to keep those times to a minimum.

→ Snagged by Rice

QUESTIONS FOR DISCUSSION

1. How do you evaluate the several strategic decisions to keep the barriers to creativity program alive after the departure of director P? Should the program have been put on hold until a new director was chosen?
2. If you were internal consultant B, how would you react to being excluded from information about director P being in the running for a major executive position with a competitor? Do you have any major unfinished business with director P, A, or Bob? How should you act to reduce that unfinished business, if it exists for you?

Force field analysis

1. *Decide on problem — describe current situation - Why do I want to change*
2. *Carefully and completely describe the desired condition*
3. *Identify driving & restraining forces*
4. *Examine forces which are susceptible to influence*
5. *Add driving, remove restraining*
6. *Implement action plan*
7. *Actions to stabilize*

Charismatic leader

Case 33

*Mega Corporation (A-D)**

Larry E. Greiner
University of Southern California
Arvind Bhambri
University of Southern California

- goal/role ambiguity
- structural constraints
- managerial style/philosophy

Reward System Problems

MEGA CORPORATION (A)

Six months after Tom Rice became CEO of Mega, he invited one of his former MBA professors, Larry Greiner, to visit the company as a consultant. Greiner and Rice had remained close friends and colleagues since Rice's graduation 10 years before. Over the years, Greiner had advised Rice on his career, which had been largely in management consulting, and on several occasions, Rice had asked Greiner to work with him on consulting assignments.

On Greiner's initial visit to Mega, Tom Rice asked him to interview his senior executives for issues "they thought need to be addressed in the development of a long-term strategic plan," as well as "to get a reading on how I am being perceived." They agreed that the interviewing should take about two days, and that Greiner would give both an oral and written report to Rice on completion. The consultant's fees were to be billed on a per diem basis.

The Mega Corporation, with revenues exceeding $500 million, was the fifth-largest marketer of liquefied petroleum (commonly called propane) in the United States. Headquartered in Denver, Mega employed 2,500 people and served over 300,000 domestic, industrial, agricultural, and motor fuel customers nationwide through a network of wholesale and retail outlets. These outlets were fed by a distribution system that utilized pipelines, rail tank cars, a fleet of trucks, and strategically located rail and truck terminals.

---

*This case was prepared by Professors Larry E. Greiner and Arvind Bhambri of the School of Business, University of Southern California, as a basis for class discussion rather than to illustrate either effective or ineffective handling of an administrative situation. Certain names and figures have been disguised to preserve confidentiality.

Performance leads to Satisfaction

Mega was a major subsidiary of Alpha Industries, a $1.5 billion diversified corporation recently taken private through a leveraged buyout (LBO). According to Bob May, chairman and CEO of Alpha, the corporation's previous stock price on the NYSE was undervalued at nearly 50 percent of book value, and he had become worried about a takeover attempt. In commenting on the implications of the LBO for both Alpha and Mega, Bob May made the following observation:

> The LBO flipped Alpha from having $300 million in equity and $100 million in debt to just the reverse. It made us private and more in control, but the cost of the increased debt was $45 million each year in interest. I was unhappy with the performance of Mega and its ability to contribute to paying off the debt, so I brought in Tom Rice to be CEO of Mega.

The decision by Bob May to bring in Tom Rice as CEO of Mega was a difficult one that he hoped would produce a turnaround in earnings at Mega. Bob May had hired Rice as a management consultant immediately after the LBO to assist him in developing cost-reduction programs at three of Alpha's subsidiaries, one of which was Mega. At the same time, and unrelated to Rice's project, Bob May terminated the CEO of Mega and assigned one of his corporate vice presidents to be the interim president until a permanent CEO could be selected. With regard to his selection of Tom Rice, Bob May told the writer:

> I think everybody was shocked by my bringing in a consultant and putting him in a line role, but I think it's something that Tom wanted to do very much, and my feeling was that he had a lot of ability, so why not turn him loose on it.

Tom Rice was an ex-Air Force pilot with a BA in English and an MBA from the University of Southern California. His initial job was in real estate finance for a large bank, but he soon left that job to join a management consulting firm in Chicago. Over the next few years, he moved to two other management consulting firms where he quickly became a partner and senior officer, eventually heading the Chicago office of the second firm. In deciding to take the job at Mega, Rice said:

> Even though I had some qualms about moving to Denver, I took it because I wanted a shot at running a major company. Also, I respected Bob May, and I felt like I had some respect from him coming in the door. I didn't see the Mega job as an end in itself. Once it was up and running, I could move on to something bigger. Bob gave me lots of incentive with an ownership interest.

Arrival of Tom Rice

Tom Rice became CEO of Mega on his 38th birthday. He was introduced to Mega's senior vice presidents by the outgoing and interim CEO at a hastily called meeting. Rice was shocked to learn that the departing CEO had given them no notice of his arrival and appointment as CEO.

We were about to go into the meeting together when I asked the former CEO if he had told them about my appointment and he said, "No." So I suggested that maybe he ought to go in and have a few minutes alone with the people to give them a chance to adjust to the news. He went in and, in essence, said, "I'm going to stay at Alpha headquarters and Tom Rice is going to be the new president.... I'll bring him in" ... and I went in. They were all sitting there looking stunned and demotivated as hell. Nobody had told them why no inside candidates had been considered.

During the meeting, Rice made a few brief comments about how he looked forward to working with the group. "It was very uncomfortable ... they just stared at me." Following the meeting, the former CEO called Tom Rice to tell him he had planned to fire one of Mega's senior executives because he didn't want "to leave Rice with a cancer in the organization." Rice thanked him for the call.

Tom Rice was so angry at the way the ex-CEO had treated Mega's senior executives that he decided not to heed the advice of the former CEO to fire one of them.

I didn't trust the judgment of the ex-CEO. I decided to keep all of the people, give them incentives, go through the annual planning process, and if it didn't work, then clean house.

Tom Rice entered a functional organizational structure (see Exhibit 1) where he found the senior group in a "low state of executive morale." Rice was Mega's third CEO in two years and, according to one senior executive, "teamwork had all but disappeared, with everyone defending their own turf." During his first few days on the job, Tom Rice observed that the senior executives tended to remain in their offices, with no one speaking to him or to each other. "I felt like they all had their eyes on me, waiting for me, and even daring me to do something."

Initial Actions. Tom Rice quickly discovered that Mega was 25 percent behind its annual profit plan, with only five months remaining in the fiscal year. As a result, he decided to meet intensively with his executive committee to plan how the company could meet the annual profit plan. These planning meetings were in contrast to the previous CEO's style, who preferred to deal with people on a one-on-one basis. Rice described the meetings as:

... an excellent forum that enabled me to ask questions and that's why I enjoyed it. Very quickly, I learned a lot about the company. We came up with a laundry list of key issues, and airing them was a major improvement even though we couldn't solve all of them. What came out of all this was a commitment to achieve our profit goal for the year—and to hell with whether it was the right level, we would still try to achieve it.

EXHIBIT 1 Mega's Organization Structure

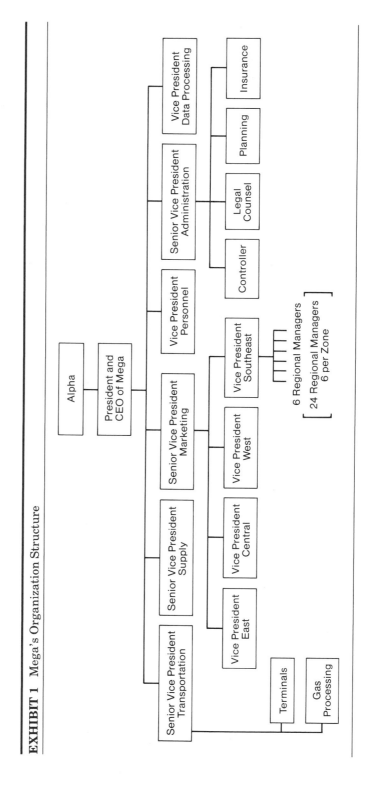

The planning meetings resulted in two major actions by Tom Rice. One step was to negotiate a revised incentive bonus with Bob May for his key executives if they made the annual profit plan. A second decision was to raise prices immediately to increase revenues. The executive committee resisted Rice's pricing decision, but he stuck to it, saying "trust me."

At the end of five months, Mega exceeded its profit plan by 10 percent, with half of its profits coming from the price increase and the remainder from increased unit sales. Rice then called his executive committee together, congratulated them, and told them that they would all receive a substantial bonus. He also gave a gold clock to each member to remind them of "what they could do under time pressure." Rice was not only pleased with their accomplishments, but he believed he could build off their backgrounds and experience (see Table 1):

> From the start, I liked what I saw. They were young, educated, and hadn't been in the company long enough to tell war stories. And then they really pitched in to pull it out.

Following the interviews, the consultant prepared a brief written report (see Appendix) that listed several major issues, including whether Mega should diversify out of propane, the adequacy of its present organization structure, and blockage caused by "turf-protecting" behavior among certain senior managers. Greiner told Rice that while the executives differed over proposed solutions to the strategic issues, they were "uniformly much happier with Rice's leadership." The consultant recommended that a retreat be held where the top group could discuss strategic issues and proposed solutions. Rice agreed because "we seem to be making progress as a team."

TABLE 1 Background of Mega's Senior Executives

Name	Title	Age	Education	Seniority
Tom Rice	President & CEO	38	MBA	New
Pat Cook	Senior vice president of supply	37	BS	5 years
John March	Senior vice president of transportation	43	MBA	7 years
Andy Davis	Senior vice president of marketing	40	MBA	5 years
Bill Hope	Senior vice president of administration	39	MBA	10 years
Sam Smith	Vice president of personnel	44	BA	20 years
Ron Mix	Vice president of data processing	41	BS	3 years
Jerry James	Legal counsel	38	LLB	10 years

Consultant's comments: I felt very comfortable in working with Rice, whom I liked and respected. He had a great deal of experience as a consultant, and his clients usually acted on his recommendations. Yet Mega was a new situation and challenge for both of us—he was the client and I was the consultant. We could dispense with the usual get-acquainted games between consultant and client. I knew we could argue and remain friends because we had done it many times before.

It was exciting for me, too, to be working with a CEO who was smart and "progressive"—many of my prior CEO clients had been the "problem" themselves, and it was an uphill struggle. In working with Rice, I saw the opportunity to move ahead rapidly in making changes that might never be made in many consulting situations. We shared a lot of similar values—a concern for people and process and a rather hardheaded business mentality about achieving results.

At the same time, I was perplexed about where we might go because the company was in a difficult situation with its parent and the marketplace. I was not a strategic planning consultant, nor did I have great knowledge in his kind of business, but I assumed that between Rice and his key people and myself, we could figure it out.

QUESTIONS FOR DISCUSSION

1. What is your assessment of the business issues facing Mega in its marketplace and its relationship with Alpha?
2. Give your evaluation of how Tom Rice proceeded during his first six months. What crucial actions did he take? What were the results and how did these affect Rice's position as CEO and his ability to proceed? Would you have acted in the same way as CEO?
3. Assess the relationship between the consultant and Tom Rice. What are its strengths and weaknesses? If you had been Tom Rice, would you have sought out Larry Greiner or another kind of consultant with different qualifications?
4. Evaluate the way in which the consultant proceeded and comment on his written report to Rice. Is the report what you expected? Do you think a retreat makes sense for proceeding, or would you recommend another course of action? How would you organize the retreat? What should be the roles of Rice and Greiner in the retreat?

APPENDIX

Consultant's Report

Dear Tom:

The purpose of this letter is to expand on what I outlined at dinner. The interviewees were very open and constructive in their comments. As we agreed before my arrival, the purpose of the visit would be to get a feel for the company through confidential interviews and to report the major areas that need further attention from top management. Listed below are the main topical headings and issues that I could decipher.

I. *The Top Group*

How do we structure the group better? Do we need two groups, one composed of Rice and the senior vice presidents to drive strategy, and a larger group to review and set policy? How often should various groups meet, and what should be their character? How can we improve the way we work together informally? How do we improve the level of trust and reduce turf protecting? Can we discipline ourselves more in meetings? How can we divide up various corporate tasks and hold people accountable?

II. *Product Flow or Distribution Process*

Should we develop an in-depth study to determine the real costs of moving propane through the system and the best ways to manage the flow? Can we articulate better how customer problems and inquiries get handled so our response is better? Should we go to a transfer pricing system from supply to marketing? How can the senior vice presidents of marketing, supply, and transportation work more closely together to improve the efficiency of the process?

III. *Corporate Strategy*

What short-term (one to two years) strategies should we set for ourselves? How do we improve inaccuracies in market forecasting? Should we keep the wholesale business? How do we capture greater market share against sleepy competitors? What should be done about the southeastern region? Should we concentrate our focus on certain market segments? What do we do about terminals and gas processing? What long-term (three to five years) strategies should we adopt? What kind of diversification strategy, if any, should we have? Should we develop a supply business for other LPG firms? What R&D should we undertake? What do we do about Alpha and the LBO?

IV. *Organization Structure*

Do we have the right balance in our structure? Is marketing too large as a single organization (80 percent of our employees)? Should we divide marketing into two departments, east and west? Should transportation be folded into supply? Do we have too many levels in marketing? Should data processing and personnel report to the CEO? Should training and safety continue to report to legal? What should be our overall position on centralization versus decentralization?

V. *Corporate Staff*

Do we have too many people in some staff groups, especially accounting and data processing? How do we improve the response of data processing to our information needs? What do we do about the general staff attitude, which seems to be slow and still attuned to the regulation days? Do we have enough high-powered talent below the top level? Do we need a few sharp analysts working directly for Rice and the top group? Do we have enough people in legal to handle lobbying? Are we short on safety people?

VI. *Personal and Team Development*

Tom Rice seems to be well received; he wants us to achieve together. He needs to reflect a positive image to the employees and to the industry. He can be more direct in sharing his beliefs and opinions with us. We are not sure if he really wants to solve problems in a team. We need to do more cross-training and job rotation. How do we learn to solve conflicts better without making them a threat or a personal issue?

Recommendations

The above are the main questions evoked during the interviews. There is a lot of agreement for many of the issues, though a lot of differences in proposed solutions. Everyone expressed a strong desire to work together with you.

My suggestion is that we design a retreat for all of us to meet together to discuss these topics, flesh them out some more, and develop whatever action plans that are needed. If you decide to hold a retreat, we will need to design a format to approach the various issues in the most constructive manner. It may be that some issues deserve more focused discussion, while others can be tabled for another meeting.

You may want to pass a copy of this letter on to the others so they know what I reported to you. It could also serve as a basis for planning a future meeting.

I look forward to seeing you again in the near future. Please give my thanks to the others for their warm reception.

Sincerely,

Larry Greiner

MEGA CORPORATION (B)

The agenda for the first retreat (see Exhibit 2) was planned by Larry Greiner and Tom Rice. They organized it around three broad topics: strategy for the company, organization structure, and the top management team. The retreat was held at a "no-frills" hotel (requested by Rice), lasting from Friday noon to Sunday noon. Rice and his seven senior executives, all of whom were members of Mega's executive committee, attended the retreat along with Larry Greiner and his colleague,

---

EXHIBIT 2   Tentative Agenda for First Mega Retreat

Friday, February 8

12:00–1:00	Lunch
1:00–4:00	*Strategic Issues and Opportunities*

We will try to identify the short-term and long-term strategic issues and opportunities facing Mega. In particular, we want to get a clearer focus and specify the alternatives, along with their pros and cons.

4:00–5:30	*Overall Corporate Organization Structure*

We will analyze the present structure and its strengths and weaknesses. How well does the current structure fit the current strategy? Then, before adjourning, we will begin a discussion on what types of structure best fit with the strategic alternatives identified in the prior session.

6:00–7:30	Dinner
7:30–9:30	*Teambuilding Session*

We will use some self-evaluation techniques to take a closer look at the functioning of the group and talk about plans for building an even more effective team.

Saturday, February 9

8:00–10:00	*Overall Corporate Structure*

We will continue from yesterday by examining the relationship between different structures and the strategies identified yesterday.

10:00–12:00	*Distribution Flow*

We will discuss the present situation and how it can be made more effective, ranging from how to price it, how to measure it, and how to make it more responsive to the customer.

12:00–1:30	Lunch
2:00–5:00	*Corporate Staff Organization*

This discussion will focus on the structure of the staff in Denver and the climate in the office. We will look at how it can be made more effective, ranging from who reports to whom to norms for performance.

5:30–	Dinner

Sunday, February 10

9:00–10:30	*Committee Organization at the Top*

Discussion of what is the best way for the top executives to organize themselves. What kinds of committees do we need, who should be on them, and what should be their charter?

10:30–12:00	*Action Planning*

We will review and summarize the specific plans that we made during the meeting. Who will do what to follow up?

Arvind Bhambri. Rice requested that Greiner serve as moderator while Rice joined the group in its discussions:

> The group is looking to me too much, and I don't have all the answers. They have to become more active and vocal with their points of view.

In opening the retreat, Rice told the group, "I have no hidden agenda. . . . I just want us to dive in and see where it takes us." The consultant began with a short lecture based on Michael Porter's (1980) strategy framework, and then he used the framework in leading a discussion of Mega's competitive situation. Several flip charts were filled when a heated interchange took place between Tom Rice and two members of the group:

Rice:

Why do you guys see so many threats and so few opportunities?

March:

(Vice president of transportation) Because the market for propane is so mature and customers for propane are limited.

Cook:

(Vice president of supply) Besides, even if we could sell more propane, we don't have enough money for investments because all our cash goes to Alpha to pay off the LBO debt.

Rice:

I feel that we can take control of our own destiny, no matter what the external environment says. Don't let's blame others for why we can't take control.

The consultant intervened to suggest that the group divide into two subgroups to "identify" two to four strategic directions for Mega, along with their pros and cons. Two hours later, they reported back, initiating a debate over two particular strategic alternatives: diversification versus an exclusive focus on propane. Mega had already diversified into a limited number of nonpropane businesses before Rice was appointed CEO. Several members of the group questioned this direction. One member said: "There are still a lot of opportunities in propane if we make acquisitions and are more selective in our geographic markets." But another member, Andy, who was in charge of marketing (80 percent of Mega's employees), argued strongly for diversification. Tom Rice remained quiet throughout this discussion, despite having participated actively in one of the subgroups.

The second day of the retreat again involved the use of subgroups to examine different organization structures. The groups met after the consultant gave a short lecture on various structural forms and the conditions under which they might apply. In subsequent reports by the subgroups, one group proposed a decentralized product structure divided between industrial and retail divisions, while the other group advocated staying with the current functional structure.

The general discussion became argumentative and wandering, with one member finally observing, "We can't solve this problem until we decide on our overall business strategy." Everyone seemed to agree, at which point Rice suggested the group return to the strategy discussion. The second consultant then gave a brief lecture on designing a strategy/mission statement. He told the group the statement should "sum up the company's desired identity, be brief and clear, put into writing, and made understandable to all employees." Two subgroups were then sent off to draft suggested strategy statements.

At the end of the second day, each subgroup presented surprisingly similar strategy statements. Both groups agreed that Mega should "concentrate exclusively on the propane industry," "become more marketing oriented," "make acquisitions," and "set high financial goals." Their analyses had determined that Mega, despite being in a mature industry, could still "clean up" because its major competitors were "badly managed" and there were many small "mom-and-pop" operations that might sell out.

The remaining discussion centered on how high the financial goals should be; a central concern was how Mega could generate cash for Alpha and still make long-term investments in acquisitions and additional marketing programs. A way out of this dilemma was found when one member proposed selling nonpropane assets, closing low-profit propane outlets, and cutting operating costs. When another member suggested the company should try to "double profits in five years," Tom Rice said, "I could get very excited by that goal, and I know I can sell it to Alpha."

The retreat ended Sunday with Tom Rice complimenting the group and leading them in a discussion on follow-up steps. It was agreed that each person should draft a separate strategy statement and give it to one member, Bill Hope, for final drafting of a single statement. Rice asked that the final draft be "subjected to some hard market and financial analysis," and "it should be tried out in some group meetings with middle managers for their reactions." Rice then announced the group would meet again in six weeks for a second retreat to "ratify a new strategy statement" and resume discussion on organizational structure.

Second Retreat

The second retreat began with a presentation by Bill Hope of the final draft strategy statement (see Exhibit 3 for agenda). Everyone indicated approval. For the rest of the morning, two subgroups met to evaluate the

---

EXHIBIT 3   Agenda for Second Mega Retreat

Saturday

9:00–12:00
    Fine-Tuning the Strategy Statement
    Key questions:
    1. What is strong about Bill Hope's statement?
    2. What is missing in his statement?
    3. Will it give us direction?
    4. Will it box us in or liberate us?
    5. How can it be communicated effectively?

12:00–1:00
    Lunch

1:00–3:00
    Developing a Management Philosophy Statement
    Key issues:
    1. Values about what level decisions should be made.
    2. Values about involvement of employees in decision making, planning, and goal setting.
    3. Values about performance appraisal.
    4. Values about employee development.
    5. Values about staff orientation.

3:15–5:30
    Reevaluating Basic Organization Structure
    Last time we had two structures proposed to us. Can we examine them to determine how consistent they are with the strategy statement we have prepared? Which is more consistent? How might we make a transition toward one of these structures? What actions are most feasible now; one year from now; two years from now?

5:30–7:00
    Drinks and dinner

7:00–9:00
    Fine-Tuning Present Organization
    Last time we had several suggestions about improvements that could be made within our present organization. What should we do about:
    1. *Supply-transportation interface*—Should they be combined? How can they work together more effectively?
    2. *Marketing organization*—Does it need new functions (e.g., director of domestic sales, director of industrial and national accounts)? Should some functions be divested (e.g., acquisitions, truck fleet, wholesale sales, etc.)? Should regions be consolidated and better balanced?
    3. Do we have some functions in the wrong place? For example, not only some under marketing, but safety and training under legal, training scattered around, wholesale pricing in MIS?

EXHIBIT 3   *(concluded)*

Sunday
8:00–11:30   *Improving the Corporate Staff Organization*
                 Last time we had some alternative models suggested, as
                 well as a philosophy of how staff should relate to the line
                 organization.
                 Key questions:
                 1. Should all staff be consolidated under one senior vice
                    president of administration?
                 2. If not, what is the logic for a second set of staff
                    responsibilities, such as one for administration and one
                    for corporate development?
                 3. What is the position with regard to decentralization?
                    How can that be implemented more effectively?

---

statement against a number of criteria provided by the consultant, such
as: "Do we find the statement exciting and challenging? Is it enduring
but also selective enough to aid in screening major decisions?" When the
two groups returned, they reported that the draft statement met most of
the criteria, but they also wanted it shortened and given a more explicit
focus on propane marketing. A redrafted and abbreviated statement
was then drawn up over lunch by Arvind Bhambri. When Bhambri read
the following redrafted statement to the group in its afternoon session,
spontaneous applause broke out:

> *mission statement*
>
> Mega is a leading marketer and distributor of propane and related services.
> We set aggressive financial goals and achieve growth through market devel-
> opment and acquisitions. Our people establish a competitive advantage in se-
> lected market segments through a unified effort that demands:
> • A strong marketing orientation.
> • High standards of safety.
> • Outstanding service "before our customers need us."

The remainder of the retreat proved far more difficult as the group
turned its discussion to organization structure. The consultant presented two alternatives that had received the most attention in the prior
retreat: (1) a product structure divided between wholesale and retail
markets and (2) the present functional structure. Again, two subgroups
met to review the structures in terms of their pros and cons. This time,
however, each group was asked by the consultant to determine which
structure, or refinement thereof, would best implement the new strategy statement.

On returning from their meetings, both groups indicated a strong preference for the current functional structure, contending the wholesale
market did not show enough profit potential to warrant a separate product group. But here the agreement ended. One member argued for a new

marketing department that would develop new products and sales programs. But this was opposed by Andy, the current head of marketing, who contended, "I can take care of that in my operation." When one member proposed the consolidation of all staff functions under a new senior vice president of administration, the directors of legal, human resources, and data processing all argued that they should continue to report directly to Tom Rice. Time was running out when one member said, "Well, at least we know that we don't want a product structure, but can we ever agree on what we want?"

The retreat ended with Tom Rice expressing his personal commitment to the new strategy statement, adding, "We need to do some more thinking about our organization structure, so let's keep talking about it until our next retreat in one month."

Consultant's comments: During the two retreats, I was impressed by how hard the group worked—they seemed to be driven to find an answer to their differences and uncertainties. I had done many retreats before, but never where the whole future of the company was the main agenda. Several times I felt like it was just an academic exercise and that afterward everything would go back to business as usual. But Tom Rice seemed to step in at the right times to keep the process moving ahead. I don't think he had a preset decision about what the strategy should be, at least he never indicated that to me. I tried to keep some distance from him during the retreats.

A key contribution was made by Arvind Bhambri when he "boiled down" the strategy statement over lunch. He reduced a lot of complexity to a few words that seemed to represent a strong consensus. The organization structure discussion proved to be far more difficult than I anticipated, and I was worried that we wouldn't be able to figure it out. I told Tom Rice that, and he said, "Let's have a planning meeting in advance of the third retreat so that we can help the process."

QUESTIONS FOR DISCUSSION

1. Assess the first retreat. How did the design of the retreat help to facilitate resolution of issues, and where did it inhibit resolution? Why was the group not able to cover all of the agenda? What was the role of the consultant and his impact? What was the role of Tom Rice and his impact? Would you have acted differently in either role? What were the key contributions by other members of the group?

2. Assess the second retreat. In addition to the same questions as above, why is the subject of organization structure proving so difficult to resolve?

3. How would you design the upcoming third retreat? Should the consultant or Tom Rice change their behavior so as to develop a resolution of the organization structure? Should the same group attend the retreat? Would you attempt to address any additional issues beyond organization structure?

REFERENCE

Porter, M. *Competitive Strategy*. New York: The Free Press, 1980.

MEGA CORPORATION (C)

Tom Rice decided to become more directly involved in planning the agenda for the third retreat (see Exhibit 4 for the agenda). He told the consultants:

> We need to move these meetings off the discussion level and into action. I'm ready to move and the group seems ready too. They seem to be waiting for me to make a decision, so I will do it. All our financial and marketing checks on the strategy statement make sense and the middle managers like it but say it isn't us now, so now the question centers on organization structure and who fills what jobs.

During a four-hour planning meeting, Tom Rice and the consultants drew up a new organization structure. Rice wanted to lead off the retreat with a presentation of the proposed structure, including a statement of key charters for each major function. He also wanted to hold an open discussion about who should take what positions, and the consultants agreed to design a format for handling this delicate discussion. Rice further decided to invite only the four senior vice presidents of the major functions to the retreat because, "These guys are most crucial to making this happen, and I have to focus on their anxieties."

The retreat began with Tom Rice presenting the proposed organization structure on a flip chart (see Exhibit 5). The structure contained a new marketing department for developing new programs, renamed the old marketing department as operations, added a corporate development group for acquisitions, combined the supply and transportation departments into a single functional group, and placed human resources, data processing, and legal all under a new senior vice president of corporate services.

In addition, Rice explained to the group that he wanted to reduce the number of zone managers from 4 to 2 and regional managers from 24 to 10 in operations (the old marketing department), so as to "tighten up management and put our best field managers against the market-

---

EXHIBIT 4   Agenda for Third Retreat

Objectives
1. Reach consensus on a shared vision of what Mega should be in the future.
2. Design organization structure, key roles, and personnel assignments.
3. Make commitment to a specific plan of action to implement vision and organization.

Schedule
Friday, June 28, at 1:00 p.m.
   Vision and organization discussion:
   1. Presentation by Tom Rice
   2. Group discussion
      a. Does the vision make good sense to us?
      b. Does the vision fit our first and second retreats' statements of strategy and values?
      c. Does the organization fit the vision?
Adjournment at 5:00 p.m. Casual dinner at 7:00.

Saturday, June 29, at 8:00 a.m.—Continental breakfast
   Personnel discussion:
   1. What are the skill requirements for the key jobs?
   2. Who should fill these jobs? What are the individual preferences?
   3. Who will do what and when?
Adjournment at 5:00 p.m. Dinner at 7:00.

Sunday, June 30, at 8:00 a.m.—Continental breakfast
   Continuation of plan of action discussion:
Adjournment at 12:00. Sunday brunch in the main dining room.

---

place." When Tom Rice had finished his presentation, he invited the four senior vice presidents to "criticize my proposal for how well it implements our new strategy . . . feel free to shoot holes in it."

The discussion started slowly with questions seeking clarification. The most silent member, Andy, the head of marketing, suddenly spoke out with a dissenting opinion: "I'm worried about the new marketing group being separated from my operations group." Rice sharply responded, "Andy, I want us to talk about these functions without putting ourselves in certain jobs." Rice went on to explain that he believed marketing issues would not receive sufficient attention if left in operations, and that he was trying to be consistent with the group's expressed desire to emphasize marketing in its new strategy statement. Other members agreed with Rice's reasoning. When one member suggested that national sales should be placed under the new marketing department, Rice agreed.

Another senior vice president thought 10 division managers were too few, so 4 more were added. After two hours of discussion and modifica-

EXHIBIT 5 Proposed Organization Structure

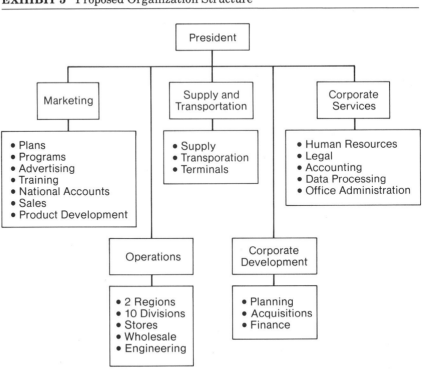

tions, no one seemed to be raising further serious objections to the overall structure, including Andy, who had confined his concerns to the new marketing department. Late in the day, one of the group said, "It looks good to me; let's go ahead with it." The rest of the group vocally concurred, with Andy quietly nodding his head.

The next morning began with an active discussion of key responsibilities for each top position in the new structure. When the group had finished drawing up these responsibilities, Tom Rice said, "Now, I would like to talk about who should fill each job, and I'd like to get your opinions and preferences." The consultant then asked the group to engage in an exercise where each participant "put down on paper which job was their first and second choice, and who besides themselves, from inside or outside the group, would best fit each job."

Much nervous laughter accompanied completion of the written assignment. When the final results were posted on a blackboard, the group was astonished to see exact agreement between their personal job preference and the nominations by others, with one notable exception. The group preferred that Andy take the new marketing job, but he wanted to stay in operations. The marketing job was Andy's second choice.

Much of the subsequent discussion involved members of the group trying to persuade Andy to take the marketing job, but he strongly resisted. Finally, Tom Rice stepped in to say:

> Look, I feel very good about the way we have handled this. We seem to know where our basic talents match up. It's been a long day, so why don't we go off and relax a bit, and then we can return to our discussion after dinner.

Just as Rice was leaving, he quietly told the consultant "to order champagne and dinner for 7; we are going to celebrate." Then he ran out the door after Andy, and they headed off into the woods together. Three hours later, the group returned for dinner where Andy announced he wanted to take the new marketing job. The group applauded, and Tom Rice raised his glass to say:

> I'm ready to go with all of you in new positions, so let's toast our goal of doubling over the next five years and all of us having a lot of fun doing it.

When the consultant later asked Tom Rice what had happened in the woods with Andy, Rice explained:

> I told him I really needed him in the marketing job because he was the best marketing person in the company. He still resisted. So I asked him what it would take to get him in the job, and to my surprise he said he wanted responsibility for recruiting a bunch of young, high potential managers to the company. And I said that was fine with me, at which point he jumped up and shook my hand. I was amazed, because I was ready to let him go.

Consultant's comments: Everything seemed to come together in the third retreat, and it was one of the most exhilarating consulting experiences of my career. The planning meeting before the retreat took a full day. Tom Rice wanted to present an organization plan, but he did not have any strong ideas about it except that it should be different from the present chart.

At first, I thought that step would be too "directive," but Rice seemed adamant in wanting to take the lead. He also felt strongly that he wanted to reduce the size of the group to the key people he thought were most critical for managing the new structure. I went along because we hadn't made much progress on designing a new structure in the previous meetings.

We drew up different organization charts and kept checking alternatives against the strategy statement. We came to a consensus on a recommended structure, and then I agreed to prepare the charts for Rice to use in making his presentation. I also suggested to Rice that he ask the group to criticize the proposed structure and be open to modifications.

During the retreat, the decision to give the participants a say in who should occupy what jobs was made after the first day of the retreat. Rice wanted to hold such a discussion, but he didn't know how to design it. I suggested the paper exercise, while saying I had never done it before. I told Rice it was risky, but he said, "We're on a roll, and I want to see if we can get all of this worked out before we go back to the office."

When Andy held out, I wasn't quite sure if I should intervene—or even what to say. That's when Rice stepped in and asked for the adjournment. Everyone seemed relieved. The dinner party was a real celebration—I think all of us couldn't believe that we had accomplished so much and that now it was actually going to happen. The energy in the room was electric.

QUESTIONS FOR DISCUSSION

1. Assess the change in role by Tom Rice in preparing for and leading off the third retreat. Was he too directive in proposing a single plan, and did he go too far in deciding not to invite three members from the prior retreats? How did these decisions affect the dynamics and the outcomes?
2. Assess the role of the consultant. Did he defer too much to Tom Rice? What contribution did he make, if any, to the third retreat?
3. Assess the substantive changes that were made. How does the new structure differ from the old structure? Was the new structure more consistent with the new strategy than the old structure? Were the personnel changes more in line with getting the most competent people in the right jobs to implement the structure?
4. How should the implementation of the new strategy and structure take place? What specific steps would you, as a consultant, recommend? How rapidly should the plan be put into place? What should be done in handling the three key executives who did not attend the third retreat?

MEGA CORPORATION (D)

The week after the third retreat was a busy one for Mega's senior executives. The CEO, Tom Rice, met separately with each of the three executives not invited to the retreat. One of them, the head of legal, had been nominated at the retreat and approved by Rice to be the new senior vice president of corporate services, which would include data processing, human resources, accounting, and legal. The legal executive was elated to hear about his promotion, but the other two executives were disappointed while still enthusiastic about the overall structural changes. Rice asked the new senior vice president of corporate services to meet immediately with the other two managers to discuss "how they could work together effectively in the new structure."

Mega's CEO also asked the new executive committee, now consisting of five senior vice presidents instead of the earlier four senior vice presidents and three vice presidents, to meet in an all-day session and to come prepared with a "new structure for each of your functions, and bring a list of nominations for persons in each job." This meeting, attended by the consultant, saw the group review, modify, and approve various structural changes within each functional area. During the discussion on personnel appointments, two members argued over wanting to recruit the same manager, and Tom Rice intervened to say: "Why don't you both talk to her and see which position she really wants to take?"

Two weeks later, a large celebration was held in a company warehouse with all field managers and corporate employees in attendance. A large banner, "Double in Five Years," was displayed prominently, and a Dixieland band played. Tom Rice gave a speech about the new strategy and the organization changes. Other senior executives stood up to express enthusiasm for these changes. Employees in the audience seemed excited, and one manager asked Tom Rice, "Will we have the opportunity to buy stock in the company?" Rice responded it would be legally impossible, but "we will try to share the benefits with you."

During the following year, numerous changes occurred in Mega and its performance. The first month saw 39 executives change jobs within the company, including all of the top executive team except Tom Rice. Morale was cited by many employees as having dramatically improved; several people reported numerous examples of senior- and middle-level managers involving their subordinates more in team decision making; and many employees were recognized for their new ideas and suggestions for additional changes. The new head of marketing, Andy Davis, recruited six new young managers, including the captain of the Cal-Berkeley football team. The senior vice president of supply and transportation cornered the futures market on propane and became a supplier to other major propane users at a substantial profit. The asset base of the company changed dramatically as various nonpropane assets were sold and six acquisitions were made.

Midway through the first year, Tom Rice called a fourth retreat for the executive team to "extend the change effort down to the lowest levels of the company." The consultant, Larry Greiner, moderated the meeting, although it was designed by Rice and his team beforehand.

During the meeting, the two remaining zone manager jobs in operations were eliminated and their job occupants transferred or retired, removing one entire level from the hierarchy. Several programs were created and subsequently implemented by different senior executives taking responsibility for each new program. A training program was created for sales managers, and a sales incentive program was introduced. A new profit-sharing plan was also created for all employees.

Finally, all store managers were invited to bring their best salesperson with them to a two-day conference where Tom Rice discussed the new strategic goals, followed by small-group discussions and group reports on how to improve performance at the store level.

A manager two levels removed from the senior group later commented on the effects of these changes on him personally:

> I was just about ready to leave when the lights came on. I got a new boss who finally listened to me. He was giving me more work than I had ever done.

Still another manager at the store level said:

> Before Tom Rice, those guys at the head office rarely ever visited my store, and then it was to find something wrong. Now I feel like they are actually trying to help me. My sales have gone up a lot, and my paycheck is a lot fatter, too.

At the end of one year, the company had significantly exceeded its profit plan, and its return on assets was up 40 percent. A sizable reward distribution was made from the profit-sharing plan. Special recognition was also given to the senior vice president of corporate services who came in $500,000 under budget. After two years, Tom Rice reported to Bob May that Mega would double its profits in less than three years.

Consultant's comments: I played a very small part in this phase of change. Tom Rice and his team seemed to take over. I sat in on the initial meeting to plan personnel changes, where I suggested the celebration event so as to make the changes carry a positive and motivating message. Rice would call me occasionally to tell me what was happening, and usually it was to tell me how pleased he was with the results, although he rarely asked for advice. The fourth retreat was run entirely by Rice, and I sat in with Arvind Bhambri to offer comments and suggestions. Our main contribution was to suggest organizing programs under different senior executives for extending the change effort to the work force.

QUESTIONS FOR DISCUSSION

1. Identify the key decisions and events that took place in implementing the new strategy and organization. How did these affect motivation and productivity among the middle management and the work force? Are there additional steps that you would have recommended or might recommend for the future?
2. How did the CEO's role and the consultant's role differ during this period from the earlier retreats? Who was giving leadership to the changes during this period?
3. Looking back over all four parts, how would you conceptualize the total change process? Did it proceed through certain identifiable phases? The process was largely driven from the top down—were there other alternative approaches? Would the approach used at Mega work in other situations, or did it depend on conditions unique only to Mega? How important were the roles of Tom Rice? the consultant? the top group? in facilitating the change process?

Case 34

Los Angeles County Probation Department (A-D)

Alan M. Glassman
California State University, Northridge

LOS ANGELES COUNTY PROBATION (A)

The Los Angeles County Probation Department is the largest such agency in the western United States. The department employs approximately 3,500 people (see Table 1) and manages an annual budget of about $160 million. The department administers 3 juvenile detention facilities, 15 juvenile camps, and 14 field offices. As shown in Table 2, in fiscal 1987–88, the average number of probationers under direct supervision was approximately 96,000 people.

A Decade of Misery

Between 1974 and 1984, the department experienced three traumatic, externally initiated crises. First, in 1974, a long-standing feud between the Los Angeles County Board of Supervisors and the chief probation officer (CPO) resulted in the dismissal of the CPO for mismanagement. The CPO challenged the board's action in court, a process that lasted eight years, and resulted in the CPO's reinstatement in 1982. During this period, the Board of Supervisors appointed two acting CPOs, one internal (1974–1977) and one external (1977–1982). The previously dismissed CPO returned for two years (1982–1984), then retired.

Interviews in 1984 with department managers indicated the department became fractionalized under the different CPOs (particularly with the appointment of an outsider), both department bureaus and individuals focused only on their own needs, and external relationships with the Board of Supervisors and community groups deteriorated. In short, both internally and externally, the department became highly politicized, resulting in divisiveness and a loss of credibility.

TABLE 1 Staffing, 1987–1988

Executive managers	6
Managers	81
Supervisors	245
Probation officers	2,458
Support staff	693
Total:	3,483

TABLE 2 Average Daily Probation Population

Detention facilities	1,800
Juvenile camps	1,740
Adult field supervision	75,389
Juvenile field supervision	16,963
Total:	95,892

Second, in 1978, California voters passed Proposition 13, an initiative that severely limited the authority of local government to raise property taxes to fund programs. The impact on the department was immediate. As shown in Table 3, between fiscal 1977–78 and fiscal 1983–84, the department lost 1,130 budgeted positions, or 25.65 percent of its work force.

Internally, the loss of positions resulted in layoffs, the demotion of nearly one third of the managerial and supervisory work force, the closing of several offices, the doubling of caseloads, and cutbacks or reorganizations in established programs (e.g., community relations and community day-care centers, family treatment programs, aftercare units, school liaison program).

TABLE 3 Budgeted Position Changes

Fiscal Year	Budgeted Positions	Change	% Change
1977–78	4,406.1	—	—
1978–79	4,098.0	−308.1	−6.99
1979–80	3,972.7	−125.3	−3.06
1980–81	3,665.4	−307.3	−7.74
1981–82	3,391.8	−273.6	−7.46
1982–83	3,204.3	−187.5	−5.53
1983–84	3,276.1	+ 71.8	+ 2.24

During the same period, other departments considered part of the social service system suffered similar reductions, while departments in the criminal justice system (e.g., sheriff, public defender, district attorney, municipal and superior courts) grew by approximately 15.2 percent.

Third, the environment in which probation operated was changing from a focus on rehabilitative programs to a renewed emphasis on sanctions (i.e., punishment) for wrongdoing. This shift in public attitude conflicted with the treatment orientation of many members of the Probation Department. That is, nearly all remaining members (particularly after the layoffs) had joined the department during the 1960s, most with a social service background (i.e., education, work experience) and a desire to engage in casework that would restore probationers to productive activities in the community. As a consequence, as innumerable studies emerged challenging the benefits of clinically oriented programs, members of the department became more and more defensive.

An Aggressive Leader, a Reluctant Executive Committee

In August 1984, I was engaged in a strategic planning project with the Division of Standards and Training for Custody (STC), California State Board of Corrections, when the STC senior staff consultant asked me to meet the new chief probation officer for Los Angeles County Probation. He explained the previous year's events, concluding that although the department was characterized by low morale and a sense of hopelessness, the new CPO wanted to attack the existing malaise.

He also expressed considerable frustration, noting that despite his repeated efforts, the Los Angeles County Probation Department was not in compliance with mandatory state training requirements and immediate action was needed to prevent the loss of much-needed state funds. According to him, the new CPO was willing to engage in a long-term OD project.

This was a very personal discussion. The STC staff consultant was directly responsible for my work with STC and had also helped me gain favorable visibility at the state level. Moreover, we had established a comfortable professional friendship, and he was clearly asking for my help. He wanted to "match" me with the new CPO.

On the other hand, I had just finished a three-year stint with a public-sector organization (which was only mildly successful) and I was anticipating tackling a private-sector client. When I stated I was presently negotiating with two private-sector organizations and did not feel comfortable taking to the CPO, he responded, "Alan, it's important to me—helping LA has possible career implications." Internally, I felt obligated.

As our discussion continued, I learned three additional facts:

- A national debate had begun on the appropriate role of probation in a changing environment; the field was searching for a new identity.
- At one time, the Los Angeles County Probation Department was known nationally for its creativity and boldness in program design and implementation; now it was viewed as a weak "player" with little to offer.
- The new chief probation officer for Los Angeles County Probation was an unexpected choice; the Board of Supervisors was split on his selection, and most expected his tenure to be difficult.

I was now intrigued by the situation and agreed to meet the new CPO, thinking I could offer some reasonable advice on long-term change and perhaps learn something about a field in which I had little knowledge. The meeting (with the STC staff consultant in attendance) took place the next week.

A Different Type of Leader. From my perspective, the new chief probation officer, Barry, was not the typical department head of a government agency. Most notably, he truly had a compelling vision for his organization—in order to survive, the Los Angeles County Probation Department had to become an established member of the criminal justice system. To succeed, all existing programs needed to be reassessed to determine their viability and their contribution as deterrents to criminal activity. Equally important, the department had to establish new cooperative programs with law enforcement agencies, noting, in particular, that the highly regarded Los Angeles County Sheriff's Department rarely supported probation programs.

Also, and most surprising, he understood the underlying constructs for planned change. We were able to discuss both the complexities and the subtleties of action research, overorganized bureaucracies, and systemwide change. Moreover, he accepted the need to begin at the top, and unlike many executives, he did not blame the line and/or line managers for the organization's problems; he did not expect a consultant to go out and fix "them." He accepted responsibility for the situation, was eager to begin a systematic change process, and needed an OD consultant to help him plan the changes and manage the interventions.

Throughout the nearly three-hour conversation, I found Barry to be quite forthcoming when responding to my questions. Together, we explored such diverse topics as (1) the parochial behavior among executive staff members, (2) the lack of motivation by an aging, cynical work force, (3) the absence of managerial development and career development opportunities, (4) the role of probation, and (5) the nature of Los Angeles County politics. When, near the end of the discussion, I mentioned the need to consider survey research, management development, process consultation, inter- and intragroup teambuilding, and strategic planning, he simply replied, "Pretty messy, isn't it? Think you can do it?"

> Most important, however, I considered the conversation to be significant, not because of the range and depth of topics discussed, but because we were "testing" each other's value system (e.g., beliefs about people and organizational responsibilities to multiple stakeholders, personal openness, and willingness to be challenged). I became increasingly aware that given the opportunity, I would like to work with the CPO.

Before adjourning, we each noted that the meeting had exceeded our expectations. However, we also agreed to defer any discussion of a formal contract until I met the members of the executive committee. Barry wanted them to share in the decision process, and I wanted to assess their "willingness to play." It was decided I would attend the committee's regularly scheduled meeting in two weeks.

A Very Typical Executive Group. The executive committee consisted of five deputy directors, each responsible for a bureau (i.e., a major functional area). According to Barry, five interrelated qualities characterized the group:

1. They were appointed by three different CPOs, resulting in "mixed" loyalties and commitment to existing programs and future directions.
2. They were very protective of their own turf, avoiding personal interactions around work issues and smoothing over interbureau difficulties.
3. They were competitors for the authorized position of chief deputy to the CPO (see Exhibit 1), frequently engaging in personal lobbying with the CPO and/or personal put-downs of each other.
4. They were overly concerned with status symbols, often engaging in discussions of office space and furniture, number of employees within their bureaus, and personal accomplishments.
5. They were most comfortable solving operational problems, delaying discussions of policy and strategic issues until absolutely necessary.

All of the members had over 20 years' experience in probation and, with the exception of the deputy director for residential treatment, all had spent their career in Los Angeles County. He was an "outsider" who had served as chief deputy during the term of the external CPO.

After some opening comments by Barry, I sketched out the purposes and traditional types of interventions of organization development. Initially, the members of the executive committee asked some straightfor-

---

EXHIBIT 1 Partial Organization Chart

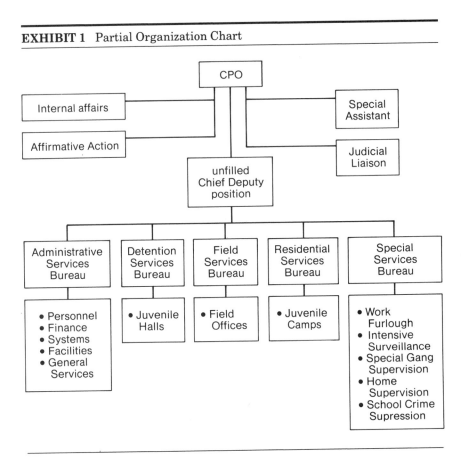

---

ward questions concerning my background and my consulting experiences in both the public and private sectors. Somewhat surprisingly, they eschewed any discussion of underlying values of organization development, the potential benefits and risks of survey research, and the readiness of the organization to undertake a long-term change effort.

Then, a revealing cross-examination began. Very aggressively, several members of the executive committee challenged (1) my personal integrity (e.g., "Isn't organization development just another fad for academics seeking extra income?" "I'm sure we're just another laboratory for some research papers"), (2) my probation knowledge (e.g., "You're virtually ignorant about our field," "We're unique as an organization; I don't see how you can understand our needs," "What can you tell us that we don't already know?"), and (3) my potential role (e.g., "It would seem we could do this ourselves," "Would you report to us?").

I responded candidly to all questions, noting, for instance, that consulting naturally increased my income and that, as an academic, I sometimes published papers (with permission) on my learnings in client organizations. Yet, I did not find this incompatible with my concern for helping people and organizations. Regardless of my responses and my attempts to provide an unbiased perspective on organization development, the group remained hostile and the verbal sparring match continued.

I was not pleased with the situation. I had concluded that the executive committee was a very vulnerable group, seeking simultaneously to protect themselves and to please the CPO. Given the lack of executive level support, could a systemwide OD project really succeed?

In addition, I was concerned about the other managerial levels. Like the deputy directors, nearly all had over 20 years of experience and had been "bruised" during the preceding decade. Would they be any more supportive? Perhaps this was a change effort desired only by the CPO.

I decided to delay making a commitment to the organization and to seek additional information.

Throughout these exchanges, Barry remained mostly silent, occasionally asking a deputy director to clarify a question or whether my response to a question was satisfactory. After approximately 90 minutes, Barry summarized the discussion, stated his personal belief that a long-term change effort was needed, and asked me for suggestions.

After restating (more positively) the concerns expressed by the deputy directors and offering some personal doubts about the readiness of the Probation Department, I recommended that "we" hold a two-day developmental conference for the 80 managerial personnel. I would facilitate the conference, thus allowing the executive committee to assess my style and permitting me to gather additional information. After the conference, we could discuss the appropriateness of conducting survey research. After a brief discussion, all agreed this was a reasonable approach, but funding would be difficult.

After my presentation, the executive committee took a 10-minute break. During this time, I shared my initial impressions of the group with Barry. He indicated he was quite pleased with the outcome and I should begin planning the conference.

A New Beginning?—Maybe

During the next two weeks, I spoke to Barry several times. We reached accord on an offsite location, budget (STC agreed to fund the conference), and dates. Because of vacations and conflicts in schedules, the conference would not occur for nearly 10 weeks. We also agreed upon the following guidelines:

1. My role would be facilitator of the conference; educator on the subjects of planned change, leadership, and planning; and advocate for an organization development project. We jointly decided I would assume a confrontational orientation, continually challenging the group's focus on the past, use of bureaucratic formality in their interactions, and belief in the traditional role of probation.

2. We wanted to emphasize that the conference signaled the start of a new administration, characterized by greater openness and collaboration in identifying and resolving problems. The managers needed to think of themselves as a team, responsible for the future success of the organization. At the same time, it was necessary to hear explicit statements of support from the executive committee members.

3. Since the managers had not met as a group for nearly eight years and because of the parochial nature of the bureaus, we concluded that a negative outcome was possible. Thus, we agreed to a tightly structured framework for the conference. The outline is shown in Exhibit 2.

The Managerial Conference. Barry began the conference by briefly reviewing the recent history of the Probation Department and then emphasizing the need for the department to reestablish its reputation, both locally and nationally. He stated his strong belief in the participants' abilities and his hope that this conference would constitute a new beginning. He intro-

---

EXHIBIT 2 Conference Outline

Day 1
7:00–8:00	Continental breakfast
8:00–10:00	Organizations in transition
10:00–10:15	Break
10:15–12:00	The leadership challenge
12:00–1:30	Lunch
1:30–3:00	A systems approach to planning
3:00–3:30	Break
3:30–5:00	Strategic planning for public agencies
5:00–6:00	Break
6:00–7:30	Dinner
7:30–9:45	Filmed case analysis

Day 2
7:00–8:00	Continental breakfast
8:00–10:00	Filmed case analysis (continued)
10:00–10:15	Break
10:15–12:00	Interbureau problem identification
12:00–12:15	Break
12:15–2:00	Interbureau problem identification and action planning
2:00–3:00	Question and answer—executive committee

duced me, citing my educational background and consulting experience and our joint planning of the subject matter for the conference.

I was pleased with the beginning. As people arrived for the conference, they appeared genuinely glad to be together. There was much hugging and expressions of delight at being off site as a group. Several commented on the nice accommodations.

Barry's comments were well received. Obviously, he had tapped the participants' professional pride and had made them feel special. Moreover, his remarks had linked us, giving me additional credibility. The climate was set.

I began slowly, as educator, discussing the rate of change, the impact on organizations, and, as advocate, the concepts of planned change. The group was attentive, but questions were limited. Just before the break, I linked the presentation to the Probation Department by reading a statement from *Megatrends* by John Naisbitt (1982):

> In the area of the law and justice system in the United States, for several decades we operated under a framework, a paradigm, of rehabilitation. Admittedly, we never did it very well, but until the 1970s, the operating rubric was rehabilitation. That changed. During the 1970s, the operating framework slowly changed from rehabilitation to punishment and that is today's prevailing paradigm.

I added that from my conversations with Barry and my experience working with other members of the criminal justice system, I believed the survival of the Probation Department depended on switching paradigms. The impact of the statement was immediate—people were upset. It was time for coffee.

Nearly all the managers had social service backgrounds and degrees. When they had joined the Probation Department in the 1960s, it was to help, not punish, criminal offenders. They strongly believed in rehabilitation.

I had achieved my purpose. I was now an adversary, albeit a sympathetic one.

During the break, several of the managers engaged me in conversation, questioning my understanding of the role of probation and the applicability of my private-sector examples to public agencies. I encouraged them to raise these issues when we reconvened.

The remainder of the morning was lively. Utilizing questions and comments by the managers, we examined the new demands on managers/leaders, alternative structures for responding to an increasingly changing and perceived hostile environment, and the likelihood of "old-timers" undertaking a major role in a planned change process. Importantly, although we differed significantly on several issues (e.g., can bureaucracy be reformed?), the discussions remained constructive. As we concluded the session, I indicated again that my concern was the Probation Department's long-term survival, but I understood the value the participants placed on rehabilitative programs. In fact, it might be appropriate to let the department die.

The remainder of the day went as planned. Both lunch and dinner were primarily social events. The afternoon sessions on planning (conducted by a colleague) provided an excellent conceptual framework, and the managers showed considerable interest in the subject. Most of the managers, however, indicated the material could never be operationalized in the Probation Department. The evening film was "12 O'clock High," the story of an unhealthy organization (i.e., a bomber group during World War II) and the commanding general's efforts to manage change and restore pride. The parallels were clear.

Throughout the day, the initial positive attitude of the group continued to build. It became increasingly clear that the managers felt treated and enjoyed being together.

Members of the executive committee seemed relaxed, although they offered few comments. In my discussions with Barry, he thought several of the deputy directors were upset with some of my comments; however, he felt comfortable and was looking forward to the next day.

The next day began with an analysis of the film. We systematically linked the film to our previous discussions on planned change and leadership. With increasing frequency, the managers focused on their own organization, providing examples of dysfunctional behavior and personal frustrations. I continued to challenge their thinking, and at times, the atmosphere in the room was very serious. We were testing each other.

After the morning break, the managers were divided by bureau. Each was asked to identify specific problems his or her bureau was experiencing with other bureaus. The discussions were very animated. After a short break, the data was fed back and clarification questions were encouraged. The bureau most often "attacked" was administrative services, seen as an empire hoarding valuable resources—a traditional line-staff situation. The bureau most alienated from the others was detention services, seen as an appendage to the organization.

Having identified many problems, each group was then asked to select one specific problem to resolve with each of the other bureaus during the ensuing months. We concluded the session by establishing interbureau managerial teams to oversee the issue resolution.

The last agenda item was a question-and-answer session with the executive committee. It was important that they be seen as a team. Not unexpectedly, but somewhat disappointingly, it was a very "safe" session. The questions tended toward operational issues, and the executives' answers were tactful. It was evident that no one wanted to risk disturbing the good feelings generated by the conference. Importantly, however, the executives agreed that change was necessary. After a brief time, we concluded the conference.

Aftermath. Several days later, I called Barry to obtain some feedback. He noted (1) the managers' formal evaluation forms (completed for STC) rated the conference very highly, (2) the managers who spoke to him found the conference subject matter interesting, but were disappointed they had not received any "tools" that could be of immediate use, and (3) the deputy directors remained noncommittal. From his perspective, there was a great deal of uncertainty.

QUESTIONS FOR DISCUSSION

1. What are the similarities and differences between public-sector and private-sector organization development?
2. Given the strong support of the CPO and the lack of support from the deputy directors, would you now accept the Los Angeles County Probation Department as a client? Assuming yes, how would you proceed?
3. The management development conference was designed to learn more about the managers. Can you provide an alternative design? Specify your rationale.

REFERENCE

Naisbitt, John. *Megatrends*. New York: Warner Books, 1982, p. 99.

LOS ANGELES COUNTY PROBATION (B)

One month after the conference (December 1984), Barry asked me to meet with him and the senior STC consultant to discuss starting an organization development project in the Los Angeles County Probation Department. He reasserted his commitment to systematic change, stating the managers expected him to follow up on his conference pledge of a new beginning. We scheduled the meeting for early January, noting that our intent was to reach an agreement on the extent of the OD project and concomitant costs.

Establishing the Relationship

The meeting began with some preliminary reflections on the conference. Barry stated the "spirit" generated by the gathering was dissipating and people were beginning to see it as just a "one-shot deal," adding that he felt some urgency in establishing a formal change project. After a brief discussion, Barry and I agreed collecting survey data from the managers and creating a forum for discussing its meaning should be the next step; then, we would use the outcomes of the forum to develop a follow-up set of interventions. We also concurred that the survey should include all managers and should consist of both a questionnaire and personal interviews.

Our only difficulty was funding. Similar to most government agencies, the fiscal year for the Probation Department began July 1, and because no monies existed for this type of project, a supplemental budget authorization would be needed. This would involve the formal approval of the chief administrative officer for the county, development of a request for proposal (RFP), and notification of potential bidders. The process, even if my bid was the most successful, could take several months. This was not acceptable to either of us.

At this point, the STC consultant offered a solution. He indicated that his immediate concern, and his reason for attending the meeting, was the failure of Los Angeles County Probation to comply with the state mandate that all custody personnel (including probation) receive 40 hours of certified, in-service training and development each year to be paid for by the state. Since this was a relatively new law and since Los Angeles County Probation was so large, it was becoming increasingly embarrassing to the STC as it "forced" smaller agencies in the state to comply.

Citing a recently enacted STC provision for funding training need assessments, he suggested Los Angeles County Probation conduct such an assessment and as part of the assessment gather other "related" data. The condition for funding: Los Angeles County Probation would be in total compliance in fiscal 1986. Also, in subsequent years, the STC would continue to fund the mandatory training and development, but the department had to request funding for any other project interventions. After a lengthy discussion of funding arrangements and some tangential issues, we reached a formal agreement.

The Psychological Contract.   After the STC consultant left, Barry and I continued our conversation during lunch and then into the late afternoon.

Once again, our discussion covered a broad range of topics as we established the informal agreements necessary to guide our relationship. Some examples included:

1. Barry would remain at the Probation Department for the duration of the organization development project; my very rough estimate was four to five years.
2. The measures of project success would be (*a*) the Probation Department's return to prominence as perceived by external stakeholders, (*b*) the increased involvement of managers in planning future directions and in operational decision making, and (*c*) an improved working relationship between managers and supervisors.
3. We would meet regularly to assess the project's progress, determine the impact of operational issues, and plan overall strategy. We were to be partners with Barry setting the parameters for change and me designing and implementing the interventions.
4. Our relationship would be a role model for the collaboration we hoped to achieve among the managers and between superiors and subordinates.
5. I would adhere to a "no surprise" rule; that is, any new interventions or shifts in direction would be discussed with Barry before implementation.
6. I would provide process consultation at the executive committee meeting, although my efforts would probably be resisted, and I would have access to all managers and formal committee meetings. I would use my own judgment regarding confidentiality and the sharing of information.

> Throughout the day, I was cognizant of the symbolic aspects. For instance, the meeting took place in Barry's office, ensuring high awareness among the managers, including the executive committee members, who worked in the headquarters building. Similarly, when we decided to extend our discussion, Barry needed to cancel several meetings with departmental members. During breaks, we were often seen laughing and, in our "hallway" conversations with others, we emphasized the newly agreed upon relationship.
>
> I was certain the grapevine would be active. Entry had begun.

The Executive Committee.   Three weeks later, I attended my second executive committee meeting to present the preliminary survey instrument and interview schedule for review and to design the data-collection and feedback process. Barry and I had agreed that the members of the committee had to be actively involved in the startup, regardless of their initial hostility toward me and our belief that they would offer ongoing resistance to the organization development project.

Neither the managerial needs assessment component (derived from the formal job descriptions, a review of probation-related literature, and an analysis of similar private-sector positions) nor the organizational assessment component (taken from a variety of previously used instruments on work-related satisfactions, job involvement and motivation, job context and work role, leadership, and work unit relationships) elicited much discussion. Rather, the executive committee focused on the open-ended interview schedule, asking very appropriate questions (e.g., "How do you intend to ensure objectivity in interpreting responses?" "Do you have some predetermined outcomes in mind?"). We took our time and carefully explored these issues, occasionally concluding that no answer would be satisfactory. The discussion concluded when Barry stated that although there were risks in the process and the data might not be complimentary to everyone, he was committed to working with the current group of executives—they were his team.

Two observations struck me during this dialogue. First, one member of the executive committee was increasingly supportive of the need for the survey and the potential benefits of having hard data and actual comments from employees. Several times, this member buffered me by asserting, "Don't we want to know?" or "I trust his expertise." Second, the executive committee members were fearful that the data would be used to purposefully "hurt" them, that some hidden motives existed. While Barry's comments provided temporary reassurance, I was certain the issue would not go away.

We quickly reached agreement on the logistics:

1. Based on the executive committee discussion, I would make several modifications in the survey instrument and resubmit it to the executive committee for final approval; the interview questions would not be changed.
2. The data would first be shared with Barry, then, approximately two weeks later, with the executive committee, and finally, at a special meeting, with all managers.
3. Once the survey instrument was approved, I would attend the next regularly scheduled managerial meeting in each bureau to distribute and explain the survey instrument, discuss the feedback process and potential use of the data, answer questions, and provide self-addressed envelopes.

4. Initially, data would be organized by bureau; data on specific units within a bureau would be available to individual managers, if requested.
5. Interviews would be scheduled by the staff training office (a unit within the administrative services bureau) and planned for one hour; two of my colleagues would assist in the interviewing.
6. Specific comments assessing members of the executive committee (an open-ended question) would only be fed back to the executive.

The Data

Seventy-seven of the 80 managers (comprising four levels of management) completed the managerial training needs assessment and organization assessment questionnaire. Data were aggregated and cross-tabulated by demographic characteristics, bureau assignment, and units. In general, the demographic factors, shown in Table 4, were not significant.

The managerial training needs assessment contained 75 potential topics classified into six categories: probation competencies, laws/regulations update, community resources, personal skills, administrative/management theory and practice, and behavioral aspects of management. The findings revealed that 17 topics (see Table 5) were perceived as very important or important at the department level by at least 70 percent of the respondents in four bureaus. Interestingly, the deputy directors' responses supported 14 of these topics.

The organization assessment questionnaire indicated most managers had positive feelings about their job and their career, but assessments of organizational processes varied by bureau. Overall, the managers believed the organization was managed autocratically by their bosses, information exchange and support were limited, and they were underutilized. Table 6 provides some selected data from this assessment.

The open-ended interviews were conducted by two of my colleagues who asked managers for a self-appraisal of their job, their bureau, their bureau's external relations, organizational leadership, and needed organizational change. All 80 managers were interviewed, and a report was prepared on each of the bureaus, using verbatim comments. The reports ranged from 11 to 17 pages. Exhibit 3 provides selected comments from one of the bureaus.

Preparing for Feedback. It was now April 1985. I called Barry to schedule the feedback sessions. He stated the data-gathering process had generated much discussion concerning the functioning of the organization, that expectations for change were high, and that he was ready to go forth.

TABLE 4 Selected Demographic Characteristics

Present Bureau

	Administrative Services Bureau	Detention Services Bureau	Executive Staff	Field Services Bureau	Residential Treatment Services Bureau	Special Services Bureau
#	13	18	5	13	17	11
%	16.9	23.4	6.5	16.9	22.1	14.3

Managerial Level

	Deputy Director	Director III	Director II	Director I	Other
#	5	4	25	23	20
%	6.5	5.2	32.5	29.9	26.0

Age

	Less than 35	36–40	41–45	46–50	More than 50
#	1	2	6	20	48
%	1.3	2.6	7.8	26.0	62.3

Sex

	Male	Female
#	64	13
%	83.1	16.9

Education

	Some College	Bachelor	Master	Doctorate	Other
#	5	33	33	2	4
%	6.5	42.9	42.9	2.6	5.2

Full-Time Employment with Probation Department

	0–5	6–10	11–14	15–20	Over 20 Years
#	1	2	7	7	60
%	1.3	2.6	9.1	9.1	77.9

Expected Number of Years Until Retirement

	0–2	3–4	Over 5 Years
#	16	14	47
%	20.8	18.2	61.0

TABLE 5   Self-Perceived Departmentwide Managerial Training Needs

Probation Competencies

No training needs

Community Resources
Constituency building
Media relations

Law/Regulations Update
Juvenile law update
Liabilities update

Personal Skills
Computer use

Administrative/Management Theory and Practice
Budget process
Decision-making methods
Futures planning
Management ethics
MIS
Problem-solving methods
Strategic planning
Productive standards and measurement

Behavioral Aspects of Management
Conflict resolution and negotiating methods
Leadership style and employee motivation
Managing change
Meeting effectiveness

QUESTIONS FOR DISCUSSION

1. How would you assess the highlighted aspects of the psychological contract? What other agreements would you include?
2. How would you interpret the data provided in this case?
3. How would you design the feedback session with Barry? the executive committee? the managers? What factors influenced your decision?
4. In the current situation, what risks exist for Barry? for the consultant?

TABLE 6 Selected Organization Assessment Data

I. Satisfaction with Job Aspects

	Very Unsatisfied	Quite Unsatisfied	Somewhat Satisfied	Quite Satisfied	Very Satisfied
Job					
ASB	1		3	5	4
DSB			2	7	9
EXEC				5	
FSB		1	4	4	4
RTSD			2	10	5
SSB			1	4	6
Totals					
#	1	1	12	35	28
%	1.3	1.3	15.6	45.5	36.4
Cum %	1.3	2.6	18.2	63.7	100.1
Supervisor					
ASB	1	1	4	4	3
DSB		2	5	6	5
EXEC			1	2	2
FSB		1	1	5	6
RTSD		5	6	4	2
SSB			2	6	3
Totals					
#	1	9	19	27	21
%	1.3	11.7	24.7	35.1	27.3
Cum %	1.3	13.0	37.7	72.8	100.1
Subordinates					
ASB	1		5	4	3
DSB			4	10	3
EXEC				2	3
FSB		1	5	6	1
RTSD		1	9	6	1
SSB		1	3	6	1
Totals					
#	1	3	26	34	12
%	1.3	3.9	34.2	44.7	15.8
Cum %	1.3	5.2	39.4	84.1	99.9
Pay					
ASB			4	7	2
DSB	2	3	4	9	
EXEC		1	1	2	1
FSB	2		3	5	3
RTSD		1	2	11	3
SSB	1	1	2	4	3
Totals					
#	5	6	16	38	12
%	6.5	7.8	20.8	49.4	15.6
Cum %	6.5	14.3	35.1	84.5	100.1

TABLE 6 *(continued)*

	Very Unsatisfied	*Quite Unsatisfied*	*Somewhat Satisfied*	*Quite Satisfied*	*Very Satisfied*
Friendliness					
ASB		1	2	10	
DSB	1		6	6	5
EXEC			1	2	2
FSB			4	5	4
RTSD			4	9	4
SSB			3	5	3
Totals					
#	1	1	20	37	18
%	1.3	1.3	26.0	48.1	23.4
Cum %	1.3	2.6	28.6	76.7	100.1
Career progress					
ASB			4	6	3
DSB		7	2	6	3
EXEC			1	3	1
FSB			5	4	4
RTSD		2	2	10	3
SSB	1	3	2	3	2
Totals					
#	1	12	16	32	16
%	1.3	15.6	20.8	41.6	20.8
Cum %	1.3	16.9	37.7	79.2	100.1

II. Goal Involvement

	Strongly Agree	*Agree*	*Neither Agree nor Disagree*	*Disagree*	*Strongly Disagree*
Participate in goal determination and importance					
ASB	2	9	1	1	
DSB	5	5	1	5	2
EXEC	1	1	1	2	
FSB	4	8	1		
RTSD	2	6	3	2	4
SSB	2	6	2		1
Totals					
#	16	35	9	10	7
%	20.8	45.5	11.7	13.0	9.1
Cum %	20.8	66.3	78.0	91.0	100.1

TABLE 6 *(continued)*

	Strongly Agree	Agree	Neither Agree nor Disagree	Disagree	Strongly Disagree
Participate in setting goal deadlines					
ASB	2	9	1	1	
DSB	3	4	2	7	2
EXEC	1	1	1	2	
FSB	3	6	4		
RTSD	1	5	5	2	4
SSB	2	5	3	1	
Totals					
#	12	30	16	13	6
%	15.6	39.0	20.8	16.9	7.8
Cum %	15.6	54.6	75.4	92.3	100.1
Managerial support/ commitment in helping					
ASB	1	3	7	2	
DSB	1	5	3	7	2
EXEC	2		3		
FSB	3	6	3		
RTSD	2	2	7	2	4
SSB	1	3	6	1	
Totals					
#	10	19	29	12	6
%	13.2	25.0	38.2	15.8	7.9
Cum %	13.2	38.2	76.4	92.2	100.1

III. Department Profile

	ASB	DSB	EXEC	FSB	RTSB	SSB	#	%	Cum %
Leadership									
1. Confidence shown in subordinates									
a. None									
b. Little	8	4		4	8	3	27	35.5	35.5
c. Substantial	5	14	5	8	9	8	49	64.5	100.0
d. Complete									
2. Feel free to discuss job with supervisor									
a. Not at all		1				1	1	1.3	1.3
b. Not very	3	4		3	5		15	19.5	20.8
c. Rather free	9	13	5	8	12	11	58	75.3	96.1
d. Fully free	1			2			3	3.9	100.0

TABLE 6 (*continued*)

	ASB	DSB	EXEC	FSB	RTSB	SSB	#	%	Cum %
3. Subordinate ideas sought and used									
a. Seldom	1				1	1	3	3.9	3.9
b. Sometimes	11	7	1	7	9	6	41	53.2	57.1
c. Usually	1	10	4	6	7	4	32	41.6	98.7
d. Always		1					1	1.3	100.0

Motivation

	ASB	DSB	EXEC	FSB	RTSB	SSB	#	%	Cum %
4. Predominant use made of									
a. Fear, threats, punishment, and necessary rewards	1	1		1	2	1	6	7.9	7.9
b. Rewards and severe punishment							0	0.0	7.9
c. Rewards, some punishment, and involvement	10	14	3	10	14	9	60	78.9	86.8
d. Rewards and involvement	1	3	2	2	1	1	10	13.2	100.0
5. Responsibility for achieving goals									
a. Mostly at top	5	1	1	3	6	3	19	24.7	24.7
b. Top and middle	5	5	2	10	6	3	31	40.3	65.0
c. Fairly general	2	9	1		4	5	21	27.3	92.3
d. All levels	1	3	1		1		6	7.8	100.1

Communication

	ASB	DSB	EXEC	FSB	RTSB	SSB	#	%	Cum %
6. Aimed at achieving goals									
a. Very little	2					1	3	3.9	3.9
b. Little	8	5	1	2	7	4	27	35.5	39.4
c. Quite a bit	2	10	3	10	10	5	40	52.6	92.0
d. A great deal	1	3	1			1	6	7.9	99.9
7. Direction of information									
a. Downward	5	1		1	4	2	13	16.8	16.8
b. Mostly downward	6	11	2	10	11	4	44	57.1	73.9
c. Down and up		2	3	2	1	3	11	14.3	88.2
d. Down, up, side	2	4			1	2	9	11.7	99.9
8. View of upward									
a. Suspicion						1	1	1.4	1.4
b. Possible suspicion	1	1			4	1	7	9.5	10.9
c. Caution	8	13	3	9	11	6	50	67.6	78.5
d. Open mind	3	4	2	3	1	3	16	21.6	100.1
9. Accuracy of upward									
a. Often wrong									
b. Censored	3	2	1		3	1	10	13.5	13.5
c. Limited	7	10	3	11	10	6	47	63.5	77.0
d. Very accurate	3	6			4	4	17	23.0	100.0

TABLE 6 (*continued*)

	ASB	DSB	EXEC	FSB	RTSB	SSB	#	%	Cum %
10. Superiors' knowledge of subordinates' problems									
a. Know little	1	2					3	3.9	3.9
b. Some	8	9	1	7	7	4	36	46.8	50.7
c. Quite a bit	3	7	4	4	9	6	33	42.9	93.6
d. Great deal	1			2	1	1	5	6.5	100.1
Decision making									
11. Level formally made									
a. Mostly top	4	3		2	5	3	17	22.1	22.1
b. Policy at top, some delegation	9	9	3	8	10	4	43	55.8	77.9
c. Broad policy at top, more delegation		5	1	3	1	4	14	18.2	96.1
d. Throughout integrated		1	1		1		3	3.9	100.0
12. Origin of technical and professional knowledge used									
a. Top management		3		1	8		12	15.6	15.6
b. Upper and middle management	11	7	2	8	5	6	39	50.6	66.2
c. Certain extent, throughout	2	8	2	4	4	4	24	31.2	97.4
d. Great extent, throughout			1			1	2	2.6	100.0
13. Subordinate involvement in decisions related to their work									
a. Not at all									
b. Occasionally consulted	9	8	2	9	7	7	42	55.3	55.3
c. Generally consulted	2	9	3	4	10	4	32	42.1	97.4
d. Fully involved	1	1					2	2.6	100.0
14. Decision-making contribution to motivation									
a. Nothing, often weakens									
b. Relatively little	5	4		4	5	3	21	27.6	27.6
c. Some	4	10	4	9	11	5	43	56.6	84.2
d. Substantial	3	4	1		1	3	12	15.8	100.0
Goals									
15. Goals established									
a. Formal orders	1	2		3	2		8	10.7	10.7
b. Orders, some comments	4	5		2	8	6	25	33.3	44.0
c. Orders, after discussion	6	6	4	7	6	3	32	42.7	86.7
d. Group action	1	5	1		1	2	10	13.3	100.0
16. Undercover resistance									
a. Strong	1			1	1	1	4	5.3	5.3
b. Moderate	5	4	2	5	10	6	32	42.1	47.4
c. Some, at times	4	12	3	7	5	4	35	46.1	93.5
d. Little/none	2	2			1		5	6.6	100.1

TABLE 6 *(concluded)*

	ASB	DSB	EXEC	FSB	RTSB	SSB	#	%	Cum %
Control									
17. Concentration of review and control functions									
a. At top	1	1		1	2	1	6	7.9	7.9
b. Mostly at top	2	6	3	5	8	3	27	35.5	43.4
c. Moderate delegation	8	7	1	7	5	6	34	44.7	88.1
d. Widely shared	1	4	1		2	1	9	11.8	99.9
18. Informal organization resisting formal									
a. Yes	1	3		3	3	2	12	15.9	15.9
b. Usually	3	1		2	3	2	11	14.5	30.4
c. Sometimes	8	11	5	8	9	7	48	63.2	93.6
d. No, same goals as formal		3			2		5	6.5	100.1

EXHIBIT 3   Selected Responses to Open-Ended Interviews from One Bureau

The Job's Positive Aspects
- I especially like the people I work with; they're competent and highly motivated.
- The responsibility, decision making, planning and organizing are all pluses.
- I like a lot of things about my job: the logistics of getting the work done on time, trying to develop a good team, and trying to turn out a quality product.
- I enjoy doing the work—making a contribution and changing people's lives.

The Job's Negative Aspects
- It's repetitious now; the challenge is long gone.
- The physical plant is dreadfully old, the neighborhood is dangerous, and maintenance is slow.
- I lack control. Too often I'm not in control of the factors I need to get the job done.
- The work load is heavy.

The Bureau's Strengths
- The current bureau leader has concern for people as well as standards.
- We have experienced directors and supervisors.
- We manage a large number of clients.

The Bureau's Weaknesses
- We're a huge group with a large span of control. We seem to be going in different directions.
- Too many people are overconcerned with retirement and used to doing business the old ways—they have a narrow scope in relating to the community.
- There's an age gap. I and other managers have a personal and professional malaise.

EXHIBIT 3 *(concluded)*

Department Leadership

- The current administration is good. It looks like exciting leadership. I'm sorry that the changes are coming so close to the end of my career.
- I don't hear any strong negatives about the group.
- The executive group isn't a group. Barry needs a chief deputy; he can't rely on old relationships much longer.
- There's tremendous backbiting in the executive committee. They are not willing to share and work together.
- They are really trying, but I don't feel that we have a heck of a lot of input into decisions. I don't think the executives are awfully effective, but I don't know why. Lots of people are doing the same thing, in the same way, as the last several years.

LOS ANGELES COUNTY PROBATION (C)

In May 1988, nearly four years after my initial meeting with Barry, we met for our final review of the organization development project. The discussion began by focusing on our generally stated "success criteria." First, we agreed that most external stakeholders now recognized the Los Angeles County Probation Department as a (1) responsible member of the criminal justice system and (2) leader in developing innovative, community-oriented sanctions.

For example, locally, in 1987 and 1988, the chief administrative officer for the county rated the Probation Department among the 3 best of the 45 county agencies and Barry's performance as exceeding expectations. Similarly, in the budget process, many members of the judiciary and the Los Angeles County sheriff now supported additional funding for probation programs.

Statewide, legislators often consulted the Probation Department when contemplating new programs to curb crime and/or revisions of criminal justice statutes. Nationally, the Probation Department gained accolades for developing tough drug and gang suppression programs, while maintaining a focus on helping juveniles. In fact, beginning in 1987, at both professional and academic meetings, Barry became a key spokesperson on the role of probation in a changing society.

Second, internally, we concluded some success had occurred in expanding both managerial role responsibilities and decision-making authority. As the Probation Department had developed new relationships within the criminal justice system, managers increasingly assumed additional responsibilities for representing the department on interagency committees and negotiating program and resource details. Also, we noted the increased use of managerially dominated departmental task forces to examine future issues had resulted in some excellent reports and recommendations for executive committee consideration. Managers now understood, and most accepted, that an important component of their yearly evaluations was their contribution to the Probation Department beyond their specified local responsibilities.

Yet, both Barry and I were aware that, at the unit level, many managers were still hesitant to act without consulting their immediate superior, and many managers were still "playing it safe." While this was not acceptable, we were certain it would change during the forthcoming year. That is, as the expected managerial turnover began to increase at a faster rate, Barry would continue his recent practice of appointing new managers who were more aggressive and expected more autonomy.

Third, we believed the stage was set for greater cooperation between managers and supervisors. For instance, an expressed complaint of many supervisors was the absence of their managers from unit locations because of new committee/task force assignments, resulting in less interaction and slower decision making. We, however, perceived the situation as a learning step needed by both managers and supervisors to understand that their roles were changing, that unit effectiveness depended on a closer working relationship, and that managers had to delegate much more day-to-day operational responsibility to supervisors. In fact, Barry often spoke of unleashing participation throughout the organization, and some managers were beginning to experiment.

Three additional factors offered further optimism: (1) a supervisory development program was now established, providing the cognitive knowledge necessary to understand the impact of the change program on individuals and groups and the need for greater collaboration; (2) supervisors were involved in the development of the strategic plan and as members of problem-solving groups, providing new opportunities for manager-supervisor cooperation; and (3) the first manager-supervisor two-day conference had occurred, signifying the importance of the relationship between the two groups. In summary, we believed both managers and supervisors were at a "ready state."

Throughout the initial assessment, I was aware that we might be engaged in a self-fulfilling "success." Could Barry, given the resources and time devoted to the project, admit it wasn't successful? Could I, given four years of active interventions, admit it wasn't successful?

I was debating raising this issue, when to my surprise, Barry stated, "It's unfortunate that we don't have any quantitative data to show people." I concurred, reflecting on the impracticality of conducting long-term evaluative studies in long-term, real-world situations.

A More In-Depth Assessment

As the discussion progressed, we shifted to a review of the major focuses of the project and the accompanying interventions. The conversation was loosely organized, and we jumped from subject to subject highlighting both successes and disappointments. In reflection, we concentrated on four primary categories: (1) managerial and supervisory development, (2) strategic planning and organization structure, (3) human resource practices, and (4) executive turnover and power redistribution.

Managerial and Supervisory Development. The managerial data on training needs were used to construct a three-year training plan. In establishing the plan, Barry and I had agreed to five underlying assumptions:

1. Training events should emphasize cognitive knowledge, including mandatory topics generic to all managerial functions.
2. Training events should target knowledge and skills directly relevant to the achievement of the Probation Department's goals and objectives; these were linked to the strategic directions set by the County Board of Supervisors concerning fiscal responsibility, program efficiency and effectiveness, and human resource management.
3. Training events should correspond in a planned way with expected changes in managerial practices, technology, and job functions.
4. Training events should develop complimentary expertise within each bureau, thereby allowing managers to utilize each other as support resources.
5. Training events should be developmentally oriented, providing sequential activities to improve performance through training.

For all managers the plan (1) mandated courses on "Leadership Style and Employee Motivation" and "Strategic Planning," (2) mandated a four-course sequence in either "Managing Behavior within Organizations," "Managing Program Productivity," or "Managing External Relationships," and (3) offered electives ranging from computer applications to contract management to office management.

These courses became the most important interventions in the organization development project. The initial, mandated courses provided an opportunity for managers to express both their discontent with the current situation and their belief that significant change was impossible. At the same time, these courses also forced the managers to assess themselves and their personal intransigence. Over the three years, their resistance to new ideas diminished, and the courses became the primary means for developing a consensus about needed changes. Both Barry and I agreed it was this normative-reeducative aspect that pressured peers and, at times, the executives to support additional experimentation and change.

In 1987, two years after implementation of the managerial development program, the executive committee approved a two-year program for supervisors based on the recommendations of a task force comprised of both supervisors and managers. In our critique, Barry and I agreed that the start-up was experiencing some of the same skepticism that initially dominated the managerial program (i.e., most supervisors asserted their relationship with managers had not improved and that day-to-day operations were more difficult because of the increased absence of managers). We were, however, optimistic that by next year we would see a change in attitude.

We also continued to hold an annual management conference as a forum for discussing events of the past year, working on interbureau issues, and preparing participants for potential systemwide interventions (e.g., strategic planning, organization design, career development). Additionally, in April 1988, we held the first managerial/supervisory conference. These events would continue with the executive committee, at its request, assuming planning responsibility.

> At the November 1987 managerial conference, I asked the managers to use a metaphor to describe the Probation Department three years ago and to use the same metaphor to describe the Probation Department now. Responses were written on index cards and collected for discussion.
>
> The data, shown in Exhibit 4, were representative of the responses.

Strategic Planning and Organization Structure. While the managerial and supervisory development programs drove the change process, the introduction of strategic planning committed the Probation Department to radical change. The decision to develop a strategic plan emerged after several discussions within the executive committee that focused on the concerns highlighted in the organization need assessment and the difficulties of managing in an era of limited resources. From these discussions, three sets of questions emerged:

1. *Strategic Focus.* Is the Los Angeles County Probation Department using its resources to best meet the current expectations of our customer—the public? What are the emergent issues within the probation field and how do we best prepare ourselves for these future challenges? Can we provide our employees with a clear sense of direction?

2. *Operational Focus.* Is the Los Angeles County Probation Department properly structured to respond effectively to the demands of its external environment? Can the department generate greater interbureau cooperation? In which areas can productivity be increased by improving internal efficiencies? Can employee involvement in key managerial processes (e.g., problem solving, decision making) be increased?

EXHIBIT 4 Metaphors Describing Probation Department

Three Years Ago	*November 1987*
Cloudy, stormy sea—difficult to navigate	Open waters—horizon in view
Grand Central Station: many destinations	Metro Rail (in Washington, D.C.): fewer destinations, more orderly process of getting there
University without a curriculum	Trade Tech
Band of guerrilla fighters	Drill team with more left feet than marchers
A team of many quarterbacks	Strong quarterback has emerged, team members responding, but still not ready for the big game
Illegitimate stepchild in a fragmented family (i.e., county)	Adoption proceedings under way—family in process of reconciliation
Good head coach and talent, but lacked a winning way/attitude	Like a team with a 5–5 record and improving
A ship out of control	Ship has a rudder, captain, and direction

---

3. *Individual Focus.* Can the Los Angeles County Probation Department construct an internal program that ensures continual employee development? Can we increase commitment and motivation while offering only limited rewards?

The executive committee then appointed 15 members of the department to a departmental mission committee (each deputy director appointed one manager, one supervisor, and one line employee). The committee's charge was to develop a departmental mission statement as a starting point for envisioning a desired future; the mission statement would provide the basis for consolidation around a common purpose, allocation of resources, and determination of appropriate job responsibilities, programs, and controls. At the time, a specific mission statement did not exist.

The initial meeting revealed deeply rooted conflicts as individuals struggled with their personal reasons for entering the probation field, their anger at the loss of occupational status in society, and organizational survival issues. The interplay between committee members was often aggressive, disrespectful, and hostile. After the meeting, which lasted three hours, several members openly questioned their continued participation. I affectionately referred to the meeting as "bloody Wednesday."

Known throughout the department as the mission committee, the group met regularly over a six-month period, slowly developing constructive group norms, assessing stakeholder expectations, conducting a SWOT analysis (i.e., strength, weaknesses, opportunities, threats), always seeking inputs from their individual constituencies (i.e., bureaus, job-level peers), and finally coming to a consensus that the survival of the organization was the only acceptable outcome and that meant moving into the criminal justice system. As indicated in Exhibit 5, the recommended statement was only 33 words, yet as noted in an executive bulletin issued by Barry, "Each word in the statement was literally reviewed, challenged, defended, and reevaluated before the committee members reached consensus."

The statement was approved by the executive committee and received overwhelming support from managerial personnel in an open discussion at a subsequent conference. Equally important, the statement was highly publicized in the community. Everyone noticed that the term *rehabilitation* did not appear and the language used came from the criminal justice field. As an executive of the Los Angeles County Sheriff's Department asked me, "Is probation really going to be different?"

Pleased with the committee's work, the executive committee asked the group to continue its efforts by developing a set of goals and objectives. Utilizing a similar process, the committee completed its work over a three-month period. After extensive discussion and some modification by the executive committee, four major goal areas (i.e., program operation and development, support systems, community awareness programs, and human resource planning and development) and 18 objectives (e.g., design an intensive surveillance program for high-risk offenders) were approved.

In our review, we noted that after the strategic plan intervention (supported by process consultation, teambuilding, and training), the Probation Department was forever different. It was the first strategic plan by a county department and the impact was immediate—external credibility, internal direction.

The plan was implemented in 1987 through the use of a collateral structure. Briefly, eight directors (two for each goal area) were chosen to oversee the development and implementation of specific strategies/action plans. Through a nomination/volunteer process, these directors organized teams for each objective. By late 1987, over 200 employees, at all levels, were participating and enthusiasm was exceptionally high.

Yet, at the time of our 1988 review, we were disappointed—the concept of managing through a strategic plan seemed to be weakening. This was

---

EXHIBIT 5   Mission Statement

To protect the community by recommending sanctions to the courts; enforcing court orders; operating correctional institutions; and incarcerating delinquents.

To design and implement additional programs to reduce crime and to ensure victims' rights.

---

primarily because of (1) the inability to integrate the strategic plan with other department processes (e.g., budget preparation, policy development, human resource decisions), causing increased conflict between the eight directors and the executive committee, (2) the lack of support from nonparticipating managers, resulting in added pressures on their employees who wished to participate (e.g., "It doesn't earn you anything when I do your performance evaluation"), and (3) the failure to view strategic planning as an evolving process, establishing periodic reviews and opportunities to update.

It was clear in our discussion that Barry felt personally responsible for the situation. He understood what had gone wrong and viewed institutionalization of the strategic plan as a top priority in the forthcoming year. After all, it had worked—the direction of the department had shifted, some of the objectives were successfully completed, other objectives had progressed (although with fewer people and less visibility), and it had generated widespread involvement.

I concurred. I believed it was his fault. It was his job.

During this period, we also systematically assessed the design of the department. With the help of an external sociotechnical expert, we utilized a two-day managerial conference and then follow-up data with the executive committee and a task force of 10 directors to develop more logical design alternatives. However, the only major change approved was the elimination of the special services bureau and the creation of two field services bureaus, dividing the special projects between them.

By May 1988, this exercise had been forgotten by most managers. Barry and I, however, had often referred to the design options and their impact at our meetings. At this closing meeting, we both laughingly asserted, "Someday!"

Human Resource Practices. During the first two years of the organization development project, several "common law" human resource practices posed obstacles to the change effort and needed to be challenged. First, the custom that permitted managers to remain within a bureau and/or at a work location for most of their careers increased bureau provincialism and individual resistance to new ideas and decreased organizational flexibility. While the original intent of the practice was to recognize managerial concerns (e.g., driving distance) and interests (e.g., juvenile programs), the current result was a stagnated organization.

Second, the norm of rating nearly all managers very highly in their yearly performance evaluation ensured continued mediocrity by poor managers and increased frustration by high-performing managers because of a lack of recognition or tangible rewards. Also, supervisors and line employees interpreted these high evaluations as an example of management taking care of its own and blaming problems on those further down in the organization. This practice seemed rooted in the "cutback era" as a method of reducing pressure.

Third, many managers did not recognize the legitimacy of either the supervisory union or the line union, perceiving both unions as a constant threat to managerial authority and as uncommitted to the welfare of the department. Consequently, a strained relationship often existed at work locations, resulting in disciplinary actions and grievances. The local situations were exacerbated by the executive committee's perception of the unions as enemies and the Los Angeles County Board of Supervisors' "hard-line" bargaining stance with all unions and public berating of unions for the county's fiscal difficulties.

Beginning in 1985, and at Barry's urging, the executive committee occasionally discussed these practices, finally concluding (1) managers should not have job tenure, but should be placed where they would be most effective, (2) managerial movement was necessary to develop new skills and decrease parochialism, and (3) managerial differentiation was needed if productivity and quality were to have meaning. Also, at my suggestion, they explored methods for improving their relationship with the unions.

In February 1987, I facilitated an offsite meeting of the executive committee to jointly evaluate managers and to discuss the appropriateness of managerial job assignments. A priori, we developed acceptable criteria and work sheets and discussed the process to be followed. The offsite discussions were candid (e.g., several deputy directors acknowledged making promotional or assignment promises to individuals), and at the conclusion, nearly 20 percent of the managers had been rated "unsatisfactory" or "needs improvement." Only 10 percent of the managers were considered outstanding. Particularly important was the assessment of each manager's strengths, weaknesses, and developmental needs and the identification of potential successors to the deputy directors.

On completing the evaluations, the deputy directors focused on their bureaus' challenges/difficulties, reaching consensus on reassigning over 25 percent of the managers "in the best interest of the department." As the session ended, all agreed to provide feedback to each manager and to start documenting poor performance for future disciplinary action.

From my perspective, this was a critical intervention in the organization. For the first time, the deputy directors learned they could work together in a noncrisis situation.

The process also identified tomorrow's leaders. This group soon came to the forefront of the change effort.

In February 1988, a second review occurred. It was equally successful. By May 1988, most of the poor performers had retired, and over 80 percent of the managers had been reassigned at least once. Barry pointed out that the new norm in the organization was "managers will be moved whenever it is organizationally necessary."

Barry also noted that over 20 percent of the managers had been appointed since the start of the project, and during the next two years, because of anticipated retirements, he would appoint another 20 percent. Since these promotions were from the supervisory level, a unique opportunity existed for strengthening local managerial-supervisory relationships. Additionally, we explored methods to build on the supervisory development sessions and further involve the supervisors in the change effort.

A major disappointment was the failure of a task force on career development to show results. We both believed that as management demanded increased productivity and quality, management was obligated to help individual employees better manage their careers in the department. This necessitated an organizationwide program providing career information, skills training, job matching and opportunities, and maybe establishment of a career development institute.

Executive Turnover and Power Redistribution. During the four years, three changes occurred at the executive committee level. First, the "outsider" member requested reassignment, noting both differences in philosophy with Barry and the very negative perceptions of managers in his bureau as reported in the organizational need assessment data. Barry placed him in charge of the department's most important (and highly visible) construction project and appointed a popular manager as his replacement. The performance of the bureau immediately improved, and, over the next two years, the bureau initiated several innovative programs.

The deputy directors reacted very differently to the personal data from the need assessment. For example, my strongest supporter in the group was hurt by his image as a "nice guy," but not capable of representing the needs of the bureau in "battles" with the other deputy directors. Another member who received "mixed" data responded by aggressively asking, "When do we get to tell them what we think of them?"

I fed back the data to each deputy director at an individually scheduled meeting, spending approximately two hours with each discussing the meaning and implications. Although they did not have to share these findings, each did discuss the data with Barry.

From my perspective, it provided both Barry and me with some leverage. For the first time, the deputy directors had to admit they were not perceived as doing as good a job as they claimed. They were vulnerable.

Near the end of the first year of the project, the deputy director most critical of Barry announced his retirement. After consideration, Barry did the unthinkable—he appointed a personal specialist from another county agency as deputy director of the administrative services bureau, reassigning two of the other deputy directors. The new deputy director had an excellent reputation, at one time had worked for the county's chief administrative officer, and was more knowledgeable than anyone in the Probation Department on budget issues and employment practices. Many in the county viewed her appointment as a coup for the Probation Department. Regardless, the other deputy directors saw her as a threat and treated her as an interloper, a view that was widespread throughout the Probation Department.

During this period, my relationship with Barry changed. We debated the advantages and disadvantages of an outsider versus an insider, often switching roles and challenging the other's logic. We discussed strategies for using the budget process to develop new projects/programs, while demonstrating fiscal responsibility by phasing out traditional, long-standing, and even popular programs. And we shared more of ourselves.

I did not know in advance what the final decision would be, but I did know our commitment to the project and to each other's success was much stronger. For the first time, it truly felt like a partnership.

By May 1988, the appointment had proven invaluable to the Probation Department. The new deputy director had recruited several other highly competent specialists from other county agencies, new fiscal and personnel policies had established greater internal efficiency and accountability, and externally, the department had gone from an image of incompetency to highly competent. Within the executive committee, however, the new deputy director was still an outsider, and it had become increasingly common to offer personal attacks when disagreeing with her suggestions. Privately, several of the deputy directors had stated she had too much influence with Barry.

Recently, another deputy director had retired. Barry appointed a well-respected field manager, who was also a close friend, to the position. Because many members of the organization expected this manager to receive the previous promotion, few were surprised by his selection. He was considered an independent thinker, and some suggested he would align himself more with the new deputy director than with the other three. Throughout the Probation Department, there were rumors of a major power struggle within the executive committee.

As Barry and I ruminated on the executive committee, we reached three conclusions:

1. The executive committee still preferred focusing on operational issues rather than policy development. Although committee members often complained about the lack of time to fully discuss strategic directions, they remained reluctant to delegate operations to subordinates. This attention to operations was reinforced by the successes that had occurred during the last four years.

2. The executive committee members preferred to work alone, interacting only when necessary. In fact, Barry's administrative assistant had to facilitate day-to-day transactions between them. On the other hand, at times of crisis (e.g., detention hall overcrowding, funding difficulties), they worked exceptionally well. An ongoing question was, "How can they be so good at times and so bad at other times?"

3. The executive committee's ability to continue the change effort was questionable. They proclaimed strong commitment and seemed eager to take ownership of the strategic planning process and to plan the next management conference. If they were sincere, they were capable.

As Barry and I completed our discussion, we both realized it was time for me to exit and time for the department to manage the next stages. We both felt good about the previous events and agreed to chat every few months.

> My opinion was that the change process would continue but at a slower rate. This reflected my confidence in Barry, not the executive committee. He was an excellent leader, never losing sight of his vision. If he was committed to unleashing people, it would happen.
>
> I was also glad the end of the contract did not end my involvement in the organization. I would continue working with two task groups, and I would conduct a few management development sessions. The project had been intense, and I felt the need to disengage slowly.

QUESTIONS FOR DISCUSSION

1. In the Los Angeles County Probation Department, multiple interventions were used, including survey feedback, management development, strategic planning, teambuilding, interbureau problem solving, and process consultation. The thread throughout the four years was the managerial development sessions and conferences. What rationale exists for using management development to drive the change project? What are the advantages and disadvantages of this approach?

2. The inability to fully implement and/or sustain a strategic planning process and to gain acceptance for needed structural changes is not unusual. How do you explain these difficulties?

3. The organization development project followed a traditional top-down approach (i.e., chief probation officer, executive committee, managers, supervisors). Given the lack of support within the executive committee, do you believe the changes can be maintained? What recommendations would you offer Barry?

LOS ANGELES COUNTY PROBATION (D)

In early January 1989, Barry, the chief probation officer for the Los Angeles County Probation Department and I met at a local restaurant to discuss my reentry into the department. In a previous telephone conversation, Barry had outlined the current situation:

1. The Probation Department's external credibility and reputation for innovation remained high. The newly developed projects/programs continued to receive favorable publicity (e.g., an expanded work furlough program with the Sheriff's Department to help reduce jail overcrowding) and the county's chief administrative officer had again rated the department outstanding.

Despite these accolades, Barry was concerned. The service delivery processes were not very efficient; standards for performance were outdated or did not exist; and establishing individual accountability was resisted. He also noted new questions had emerged about the quality and timeliness of court reports, the maintenance of facilities, and the management of caseloads. While Barry did not expect any immediate consequences, he was fearful that within two or three years the department could crumble from inside. He stated, "For all our success, I believe we are sitting on a house of cards."

2. Barry was spending increasingly more time away from the department. During the past six months, he had added several additional national and state activities and responsibilities to an already busy schedule. He considered these external opportunities vital adjuncts to the leadership role his department was again assuming in the probation field. Equally important, however, was his admission that he found this aspect of his role to be the most "stimulating and fun."

As a result of Barry's external time commitments, there was increasing discussion within the department about the need to appoint a chief deputy to oversee day-to-day matters. Barry, however, remained opposed to the idea, raising questions about individual abilities and organizational disruptions; he was not convinced the potential benefits outweighed the potential negatives.

3. The executive committee had not changed. The members continued to focus on operational issues, rather than policy development, and to engage in combative interactions with each other. Barry had become frustrated over his inability to develop a team concept, except during crises.

In November 1988, after considerable planning, the executive committee conducted a two-day management conference. Barry stated that while the conference emphasized the "right" topics (e.g., progress reports on the strategic plan, interbureau coordination), it generated little excitement; many managers concluded that the era of change was over and a period of consolidation was beginning.

A second conference for managers and supervisors was scheduled for May 1989. Barry was concerned that any slowdown in the change effort would endanger the institutionalization of the strategic planning process and the building of more constructive managerial-supervisory relationships.

After revisiting these topics, Barry forcefully restated his old vision of unleashing people. He was still committed to the idea and asserted:

> We have many talented, underutilized people who need to be empowered. I'm certain this can be linked to improving the infrastructure of the department. I want you to reenter the department. What do you suggest?

It was time for a new contract.

QUESTION FOR DISCUSSION

What would you formally propose to Barry? What additional expectations need to be discussed (i.e., the psychological contract)?

Author Index

Internal

Driving

- young educated
- Tom Rice — non traditional charismatic leader
- easily motivated (exceed profit goal)
- worked good as team
-

Restraining

- tough production attitude
- Alpha takes all profits
- low interaction
- no teamwork
- low moral

External

Driving

- constant demand
- (Alpha Power)

Restraining

- mature industry
- fierce competition

Author Index